THE YOUNG GIFTED CHILD:
POTENTIAL AND PROMISE
AN ANTHOLOGY

Perspectives on Creativity
Mark A. Runco (ed.)

THE YOUNG GIFTED CHILD:
POTENTIAL AND PROMISE
AN ANTHOLOGY

Edited by

Joan Franklin Smutny

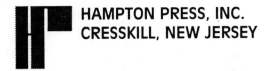

HAMPTON PRESS, INC.
CRESSKILL, NEW JERSEY

Printed in the United States of America

Library of Congress Cataloging-in-Publication Data

The young gifted child : potential and promise, an anthology /
   edited by Joan Franklin Smutny.
      p.   cm. -- (Perspectives on creativity)
   Includes indexes.
   ISBN 1-57273-108-7. -- ISBN 1-57273-109-5
      1. Gifted children--Education (Early childhood)--United States.
   2. Gifted children--United States--Identification.   3. Early
   childhood education--Parent participation--United States.
   4. Gifted children--United States--Social conditions. 5. Gifted
   children--Education (Early childhood)--Social aspects--United
   States.
   I. Smutny, Joan F.   II. Series.
   LC3993.9. Y68   1997
   371.95--dc21   97-39589
                                                                CIP

Hampton Press Inc.
23 Broadway
Cresskill, NJ

To all the talented, gifted young children, often unrecognized, who can and do contribute richly to the lives of all of us who work with them. This book can amplify their voices and we are able to listen. Through this book, we hope to enable others to hear them as well.

I am grateful to Maria Freeman and Cheryl Siewers, who excelled at listening during the development of this text.

Contents

I

Perspectives

Joan Franklin Smutny

"Where there is no vision, the people perish" is an adage applicable to working in the world of the bright and talented young child. The potentially gifted express aptitude with joy and immediacy. We—teachers, parents, college instructors, and health care professionals—are increasingly sensitive to the talents and intelligences of these young children and to our own individual desire to do something for them.

We feel the urgency of early intervention. We believe in communicating early with these bright young children who wait for us to understand their readiness for challenge and opportunity. We want to encourage and support them.

If more than 500,000 bright children are born each year, then every setting where learning and interacting take place must become astute in perceiving the marvelous talents of these young children and their diversified expression. Clearly, a rescue is in order. The intent of *The Young Gifted Child: Potential and Promise, An Anthology* is to offer a framework of understanding for the many adults who cherish these children as students, patients, friends, sons, and daughters.

In speaking, teaching, consulting, and working with adults, I have found that knowledge of these young children—their nature, abilities, and varied states of thought and experience—is essential to advancing and encouraging the expression of their identity. These children are hungry for understanding. Adults are hungry for the knowledge that enables them to advance and enhance each child's individuality.

This book offers, through its 41 chapters, a framework to fulfill these needs. Its 48 authors represent some of the finest thinking in the field of gifted and early childhood education. Each contributor draws on his or her own experience and expertise to enlighten readers about a different dimension that supports the cause of the gifted young child. The result is a framework of theory and application.

The volume is divided into six parts that include an introduction to the subject area and a summary of each chapter within that section. It is designed to serve as a catalyst for discussion on many levels with many kinds of target populations: teachers, parents, counselors, graduate and undergraduate students, researchers, nursery school directors, day-care administrators, health care practitioners. The reader will naturally choose those chapters most applicable to his or her involvement with gifted young children. The anthology offers diversified ideas and applications to many settings.

Part II, *Identification*, begins with sensitivity to early learning, even the gifted infant, his or her characteristics, and the expression of them. The authors dispel the notion that talents begin with third grade, predicted on a test given at the end of second grade. Parents are often apprehensive about acknowledging that their infant and toddler can evidence talent, even though they see it at home each day. Early identification makes it possible to discern the bright child and optimize his or her readiness for larger challenges. To identify the advanced and advancing potential of these children, parents and teachers can draw on identification processes that reach beyond an academic focus. Instead, adults are encouraged to identify multifaceted talents through diversified assessment methods.

Part III addresses the needs of *Special Populations*. Such recognition is a continuous priority among all of us who work with young children in diverse communities. We need insight into how to identify these target populations and what to do for them. These children should not be conveniently ignored or neglected. It is our responsibility as adults to become knowledgeable enough to identify these young children and meet their needs. In this section, the reader will find a rich text of ideas focusing on the talents of the disadvantaged, the low income, the culturally and linguistically diverse, the rural poor, the beginning brilliant, the underachiever, the learning disabled, and the young gifted girl.

Each day I receive many phone calls from parents of gifted children, most ranging in age from infancy to 7 or 8 years. We know that the parent is the most accurate judge of a child's abilities from day 1 to age 7. We also are aware that more learning occurs from birth to age 4-1/2 than during the rest of our lifetime. With justification, parents are concerned about their bright young children and what to do for them.

Parenting is more than an intuitive process. Effective parenting requires an understanding of early identification and intervention. For so many parents of advanced potential children, the early years can be frustrating. The six authors in Part IV, *Parenting the Gifted Child*, provide ideas that will help parents looking for assistance. Each author has worked with hundreds and even thousands of parents and regards their questions with respect.

Meeting Social and Emotional Needs to Effect Growth, the subject of Part V, is important in home and school settings. Many frustrations can be alleviated if adults discern more clearly the diversified social and emotional qualities of the child. Too often these areas are overlooked by adults who tend to emphasize academic excellence and forget the need to minister to the whole child. The bright and talented are still children. Like all children, they are looking for a sense of conscious worth.

Ways to help the young gifted affirm and claim their strength is a basic theme of this section. There is no one theory serving all of these children, one approach that will meet all of their needs. Rather, we offer ideas varied in nature and expression. The authors of Part V's chapters have worked in counseling roles with children, parents, and teachers.

Part VI, the largest of all the sections, concludes the anthology by offering 14 chapters on *Creating Effective Educational Experiences for Gifted Young Children*. This is a marvelous challenge for all of us who work in different learning environments at home and in school. Educationally dynamic environments offering creative ideas and activities for young gifted children are essential in supporting the growth of their talents.

Few universities and colleges or departments of teacher education provide courses in identification and intervention for the gifted young child. Many school districts do not offer specific activities, programs, or curriculum practices appropriate for gifted students under grade three. This is why Part VI can be so useful to the reader, who can examine the models in this section and select what best fits his or her day-care, nursery, kindergarten, or primary classroom most effectively.

The authors, experts in this area, furnish the latest models, theories, program designs, curricula, and specific guidelines for all educators interacting with these children. The writers examine the multiple intelligences of these children and the need to challenge them. It is fitting that the section concludes with a forward-looking chapter on technology-based instruction for young children.

We, the contributors to and readers of this book, are advocates for talented young children. Their voices are heard increasingly by all of us who work with them. Our response must necessarily involve an ongoing process of research and support. We must become increasingly open to new discoveries of who they are and what we can do for them. This ongoing process becomes more fluid and flexible as we expand our framework for identification and our creative strategies for enhancing their talents. We can develop answers to long-standing questions in this field as we participate more thoughtfully and thoroughly. The importance of each adult's role in this process should never be minimized.

Our goal is to maximize the potential of gifted young children. Knowing the multifaceted talents of young children from diversified backgrounds, we realize the urgency of knowing how to support each one. This book provides a sensitive, comprehensive foundation toward the realization of that vision.

II

Identification: Creative Strategies and Techniques

Joan Franklin Smutny

Early identification of gifted children is essential to serving them—to perceiving and meeting their needs. Acknowledging that young children should be identified early is inherent in a total kaleidoscope of understanding gifted children, whether they be several months or 7 years old. The authors in this section offer effective insights into identifying the basic talents, abilities, and characteristics of the young gifted child. The framework offered to teachers and parents is both viable and practical. Readers will appreciate the diversity of criteria utilized to distinguish these gifts in the bright, talented young child, whether he or she be a toddler or a second grader. Readers may wish to choose a specific model to use for identification or elect to gain a more eclectic point of view. Each chapter reflects the expertise of the writer, based on his or her involvement with research and practical experience.

In Chapter 1, Barbara Clark, well known for her seminal work, *Growing Up Gifted*, reaffirms that the potential for giftedness begins very early and that this development is dependent on an interaction between the genetic endowment of the child and the environment in which he or she grows. Clark believes that giftedness has its root in biological origins resulting in accelerated brain development. She feels that the best way to develop giftedness is to allow the child to play in a rich and responsive setting. Appropriate stimulation and supportive, challenging activities result in high levels of function. Clark maintains that even the newborn child is competent and able to learn. Every child's ability can be optimized when teachers at home and at school offer creative opportunities that support this potential.

Judith Gelbrich explores the question of whether infant behaviors have predictive values as a measure of intelligence in Chapter 2. She reviews much of the literature that has touched on this significant issue. Gelbrich seeks clues in infant behaviors, such as crying, visual attention, and visual recognition memory. Given that environmental conditions may have a significant influence on maximizing human development, Gelbrich considers that element as well.

Acknowledging the challenges of identifying bright young children, Bertie Kingore offers alternate methods of assessment, including classroom observation and portfolio development, in Chapter 3. Such methods, says Kingore, are valuable in identifying and nurturing talents in the young. Acknowledging that all children have more potential than educators and parents have recognized in the past, she argues that children need an environment which is nurturing and rich in expectation if high potentials are to be reached. The Kingore Observation Inventory (KOI), an instrument used increasingly to assess characteristics that indicate giftedness, draws on the judgments of teachers. With its help, teachers can more accurately assess children's behaviors for signs of giftedness. Kingore's chapter also focuses on the use of the portfolio as a creative strategy for increasing awareness of multiple kinds of abilities. In this way, they are more likely to recognize a variety of high-level responses.

In Chapter 4, publisher and editor Maurice Fisher acknowledges that many gifted young children have been denied admission to gifted programs because the instruments used to assess their abilities are inadequate. He believes that a dramatic change in thinking and attitudes about appraising young children will be needed to effect more accurate identification procedures. He proposes that gifted education include research programs on the development of *Sensibility* in young children. To Gardner's Multiple Intelligences he adds this unique characteristic of giftedness. Fisher advocates training teachers to recognize and measure the Sensibility level of each student—to assess its maximum potential and expression.

In Chapter 5, Hazel and John Feldhusen draw on many anecdotes about precocious young children and offer varied strategies for identifying talents such as early admission and grade advancement. Ten recommendations are given to assist schools in composing guidelines for making decisions on early admissions and grade advancement. The authors concur that gifted children can be identified and nurtured in homes and schools that accept their diversity from the norm and facilitate its expression.

In the final chapter of this section, Dorothy Sisk includes a recognition of the importance of parents in identifying talents *early.* She also focuses on gifted children from economically disadvantaged homes, who may not demonstrate their giftedness as do peers from economically advantaged homes. Her own program, entitled Project Step-Up, pointed to an eclectic approach in using creative strategies to identify and develop programs for the young. Project Step-Up addressed Mary Frasier's four barriers to identifying gifted disadvantaged students: attitude, access, accommodation, and adaptation. Alternative procedures produced effective screening for the program. Sisk's concluding statement speaks for all of the authors in this section: "The loss of even one gifted child as a potential contributing member to society is one child too many."

1

The Beginnings of Giftedness: Optimizing Early Learning

Barbara Clark

The little girl and her grandmother sat together in the cozy, overstuffed chair reading a book. Grandpa came into the room with two big logs for the fireplace, one in each hand. The child looked up and asked, "What is in your hand, Grandpa?"

"A log for the fireplace, Em."

"What is in the other hand?"

"Another log for the fireplace."

As grandpa placed both logs into the grate and lighted the fire under them, Emily turned to her grandma, "Oh my. We're very proud of Grandpa, aren't we Grandma."

The grandparents exchanged looks and soft smiles as Emily snuggled down for more of the story to be read. This exchange would provide months of retelling for the grandparents as Emily was not quite 2-years-old and they were very proud of her.

The potential for giftedness, or high levels of intellectual development, begins very early in a child's life. Such development relies on a rich and appropriate interaction between the child's genetic endowment and the environment in which the child grows. No child is born gifted; only with the potential for giftedness. Although all children have amazing potential, only those who are fortunate enough to have opportunities to develop their uniqueness in an environment that responds to their particular patterns and needs will be able to actualize abilities to high levels. For those who are vitally involved in the growth of children, their teachers at home and at school, the information from research in psychology, neurosciences, linguistics, and early learning can be most helpful in understanding just how to create responsive environments that allow children to bring out the most of their potential; that is, to create giftedness.

GIFTEDNESS AND INTELLIGENCE, CHANGING CONCEPTS

Giftedness, as discussed in this chapter, is a biologically rooted concept that serves as a label for a high level of intelligence and indicates an advanced and accelerated development of functions within the brain, allowing its use to be more efficient and effective. Intelligence includes all of the areas of brain function, physical/sensing, emotions, cognition, and intuition, and is far more than the outdated restriction to only linear, rational, and analytic thinking. This broader concept of intelligence may be expressed through problem solving, creative behavior, academic aptitude, leadership, performance in the visual and performing arts, invention, or a myriad of other human abilities. Gifted individuals are those who perform, or who show promise of performing at high levels in any such areas and who, because of such advanced and accelerated development, require services or activities not ordinarily provided by the schools in order to develop their capability more fully. Without such opportunities for appropriate challenge, talent and ability can be lost (Clark, 1992).

For decades it was believed that intelligence was complete at birth and that it did not change throughout life. Indeed, it was supposed that intelligence diminished after middle age because after the age of 45 the brain was assumed to slowly die. It is now known that the brain changes in a dynamic and interactive way all through life and responds to the enhancement or inhibition of stimulation allowing intelligence unlimited ability to develop far into later life (Diamond, 1988). High intelligence, regardless of how it is expressed, results from this interaction between inherited and acquired characteristics supported by a rich, stimulating environment. This interaction encompasses all of the physical, mental, and emotional characteristics of the person and all of the people, events, and objects entering the person's awareness. As researchers (Berg & Singer, 1992; Diamond, 1988; Dobzansky, 1964;

Lewontin, 1982; Thompson, Berger, & Berry, 1980) now state, our genes are not a limit, but provide a rough outline of the possibilities of our life. The endless interaction of the environment with this genetic framework creates our intelligence, even our perception of reality. This process begins very early, as soon as the fertilized egg attaches to the wall of the uterus. As the cells divide and the fetus begins to grow, the environment exerts influence, what biologists call *developmental noise*. One could not from this interactive point of view say which is more important, the inherited abilities or the environmental opportunities to develop them. Restriction on either nature or nurture would inhibit high levels of actualized intellectual ability or giftedness.

Even our beliefs about the absolute stability of genes must be reexamined. Slavkin (1987) showed that we can rearrange all the genetic material in the course of expression. The genes are not stable and the transcription of genes from DNA to RNA can actually be rearranged. Whereas genes provide us with our own unique menu, the environment makes the actual selection within that range of choice. Any reference to high-IQ genes must be seen as a misnomer because the discernible characteristics of an organism always depend on its particular environmental history. Environmental interaction with the genetic program of the individual occurs whether planned or left to chance. Teachers at home or at school must be aware that how we structure the environment for children changes their neurological and biological structure.

CHARACTERISTICS OF GIFTEDNESS

When the brain becomes more accelerated and advanced in its function through this interaction, the individual shows characteristics that can be identified with high intelligence. Some of those characteristics can be seen to be the direct result of changes in the brain structures. For example, appropriate stimulation creates an increase in the amount of dendritic branching in the neurons, heightening the child's ability for complex thought and for seeing interconnections. With increased stimulation, the number and size of the synaptic contacts increase, allowing faster thinking and more complex communication within the system. In highly intelligent children, more use is made of the activity of the prefrontal cortex of the brain, allowing more creative behavior, future planning, insightful thinking, and intuitive experiences (MacLean, 1978; Restak, 1979). These changes continue to occur as long as appropriate stimulation is available. Brain research consistently points to the dynamic nature of the brain's growth and the need to challenge the individual at that individual's level of development for growth to continue; unchallenged, the individual will lose power.

It is now possible to see a biological base for the characteristics of giftedness. Although all children have the potential for these biological changes, only some children can be seen to have developed such advanced and accelerated function. Characteristics that result from these changes can be used to identify the gifted learner. Although each child will express giftedness in his or her unique way, behaviors that often can be observed among these children include the following:

> *Cognitive*: intense curiosity; frequent and sophisticated questions; an accelerated pace of thought and learning; complex thinking, often connecting seemingly disparate ideas; persistence in pursuing interests, early development of language and mathematical skills.
>
> *Affective*: heightened awareness of "being different"; unusual sensitivity to people's expressed feelings and problems; early concern for global and abstract issues; idealism and concern for fairness and justice; high expectations for self and others.
>
> *Physical*: unusual discrepancy between physical and intellectual development; low tolerance for a lag between personal vision and physical abilities; preference for games testing personal skill rather than team cooperation; interest in complex games.
>
> *Intuitive*: early awareness and expression of extrasensory perceptions; preference for creative solutions and actions over predictable ones; early use of hunches and best guesses; early ability to relate past, present, and future.

The best way to identify high levels of intellectual development; that is, giftedness, is to observe the child at play in a rich, responsive environment. During the early learning periods of a child's life the most appropriate focus for concerned adults is on allowing the child to continuously interact with materials and people that the child finds interesting. Infants and young children constantly seek novel and unusual experiences that allow them to stretch just beyond their current ability. Although many of the materials and experiences they have previously explored are retained as familiar and favored being sought out over and over again, adding new favorites is a constant occupation. The most important challenge for teachers at home and at school is to stay just ahead of the child in presenting materials and experiences; not too far ahead and yet not presenting too much repetition.

Creating an environment and experiences that respond to the child with an appropriate balance of the familiar and new is the best way to provide for optimal development. Uzgiris (1989), who has spent more than a decade testing infants, urges that all children be given a chance to develop the full range of their abilities because the competencies required for the future are unknown and intelligence is dynamically influenced by opportunities and learning, especially during the childhood years. The identification of experiences needed is the goal of observing the child, not the identification of giftedness. All children must have experiences provided at their level of development because it is during this period and through such appropriate stimulation that intelligence is nurtured and giftedness is developed. Formal testing for identification of giftedness is not only inappropriate and of limited use in the early years, it is much less accurate and productive than is observation for the purpose of providing appropriate experiences from which the child can continue to grow.

BECOMING GIFTED

From this discussion it is easy to see why appropriate and continuous stimulation of infants and children is important. How and when that stimulation is presented is equally important. From the early 1970s, the view of infants as learners has been changing. It is now known that infants are complex, discriminating, socially engaged, curious, and surprisingly sophisticated in their emotional responses and intellectual skills (Chamberlain, 1993; Fantz, 1961; Goode & Burke, 1990; Grunwald, 1993; Meltzoff & Moore, 1977; Verny, 1981). While only a fetus, the senses of taste, hearing, and smell are developed and memory begins. Newborns show depth perception, eye-hand coordination, and sensory processing. They show preferences for certain sounds, patterns, shapes, odors, and tastes. They can almost immediately recognize and mimic expressions and gestures. Evidence indicates that infants can learn, remember, and, as some researchers suggest, even understand basic math concepts. At 4 months babies are found to be "universal linguists," able to distinguish all 150 sounds that make up human speech and show rudimentary knowledge of the way the world should work. They develop schema and theories and show displeasure when events do not match these expectations. Their visual focus is developed to adult levels at 6 months of age. All of this incredible ability is accompanied by a memory that has been shown to be so effective that events experienced at 6 months can be recalled 2 years later.

To continue this amazingly competent beginning, parents will need to provide a rich, responsive environment and guidance based on the unique needs and interests of their children to optimize further growth. Parents are their child's first teachers and are most effective when they help create the appropriate emotional and social climate and tune their behaviors sensitively to their infant's level of development, catching it at the peak of organized engagement and interest rather than simply responding reliably or because research shows it is

Diamond, M. (1988). *Enriching heredity: The impact of the environment on the anatomy of the brain.* New York: The Free Press.

Dobzansky, T. (1964). *Heredity and the nature of man.* New York: New American Library.

Fantz, R. (1961). The origin of form perception. *Scientific American, 204,* 66-72.

Ginsburg, H. (1982). The development of addition in the contexts of culture, social class, and race. In T. P. Carpenter, J. M. Moser, & T. A. Romberg (Eds.), *Addition and subtraction: A cognitive perspective* (pp. 191-210). Hillsdale, NJ: Erlbaum.

Goode, E., & Burke, S. (1990). How infants see the world. *U.S. News and World Report, 109*(8), 51-52.

Grunwald, L. (1993, July). The amazing minds of infants. *Life,* 47-60.

Lewontin, R. (1982). *Human diversity.* New York: Scientific American Books.

MacLean, P. (1978). A mind of three minds: Educating the triune brain. In J. Chall & A. Mirsky (Eds.), *Education and the brain: The seventy-seventh yearbook of the National Society for the Study of Education, Part II* (pp. 308-342). Chicago: University of Chicago Press.

Meltzoff, A., & Moore, M. (1977). Imitation of facial and manual gestures by human neonates. *Science, 198,* 75-78.

Powell, D. (1991). *Strengthening parental contributions to school readiness.* Washington, DC: U.S. Department of Education, Office of Educational Research and Improvement.

Restak, R. (1979). *The brain: The last frontier.* New York: Doubleday.

Rogoff, B. (1990). *Apprenticeship in thinking.* New York: Oxford University Press.

Slavkin, H. (1987, February). *Science in the 21st century.* Speech presented at the 25th Annual Conference of the California Association for the Gifted, Los Angeles.

Thompson, R., Berger, T., & Berry, S. (1980). An introduction to the anatomy, physiology, and chemistry of the brain. In M. Wittrock (Ed.), *The brain and psychology* (pp. 3-32). New York: Academic Press.

Uzgiris, I. (1989). Issue: Infant intelligence arouses controversy. *ASCD Update, 31*(5), 4-5.

Verny, T. (1981). *The secret life of the unborn child.* New York: Summit.

Wilson, R. (1986). Risk and resilience in early mental development. In S. Chess & A. Thomas (Eds.), *Annual progress in child psychiatry and child development* (pp. 69-85). New York: Brunner/Mazel.

2

Identifying the Gifted Infant

Judith A. Gelbrich

In all probability, giftedness is a result of a combination of biological or genetic factors and environmental factors. Sadly, most of the current literature does not attempt to integrate these factors. In fact, most studies seeking to identify cognitive abilities are primarily concerned with identifying predictors of intelligence, not giftedness, and many focus more on the handicapped or at-risk child. This chapter has three purposes: (a) to determine whether the potentially gifted child can be identified during infancy; (b) to review the behaviors and demographic variables that appear to have predictive utility in identifying cognitive abilities during infancy; and (c) to determine which environmental conditions appear to nurture and support development of giftedness.

From a historical perspective, the attempts to characterize and develop a structure for infant intelligence can be divided into two theoretical positions. The first states that intelligence in infancy is a unitary factor, or general capacity for intelligent behavior, known as "*g*." This factor is fairly consistent and is present from birth. The second position states that intelligence is comprised of a set of varied abilities and skills, which are not genetically fixed, but interactive with environmental influences (Dunst, 1978).

McCall (1983) believed that mental development during the first 2 years of life is unaffected by environmental conditions, and that because the human species follows such a similar developmental path up until age 2, predictors of later intelligent behavior are difficult if not impossible to distinguish. Lewis' (1983) research, on the other hand, led him to believe that infant intelligence is multidimensional, consisting of a number of factors that can remain the same, disappear, be transformed, or appear well after birth.

Infant intelligence tests in general appear to have limited value in predicting later IQ scores, particularly giftedness. Most of the research studies using the Bayley Scales of Infant Development (BSID) indicate that there is an insignificant relationship between the scores on these tests administered during the first year of life and later IQ tests (Bee et al., 1982; Lewis, 1973; Lewis & Louis, 1991; Lewis & McGurk, 1972; Willerman & Fiedler, 1974, 1977). Infant intelligence tests do appear to have predictive utility when used to assess the development of a child at-risk for later developmental abnormalities (Fagan & Detterman, 1992; McCall, 1983; Rose, Feldman, & Wallace, 1988; Rubin & Balow, 1979; Siegel, 1981). However, the Fagan Test of Infant Intelligence (FTII) has demonstrated moderate correlations with later tests of IQ.

Thompson, Fagan, and Fulker (1991) used the FTII to test 113 full-term infants at 5 and 7 months. At 12 and 24 months the children were given the Bayley and at 36 months the Stanford-Binet. The FTII simultaneously presents new and previously viewed stimuli to an infant. Viewers record and analyze the amount of time spent looking at both stimuli; the longer the amount of time spent looking at the novel stimuli the higher the score on the measure (Fagan & Detterman, 1992). The correlation with the 12-month Bayley was relatively weak ($r = .21$). However, the correlation between the score on the FTII and the Stanford-Binet was $r = .58$ (Thompson et al., 1991).

A STUDY TO DETERMINE IF GIFTEDNESS CAN BE PREDICTED DURING INFANCY

Using 200 children who were followed at regular intervals from birth through 7.5 years, Shapiro et al. (1989) tried to determine if giftedness could be identified during infancy using the BSID. The subjects were from predominantly white and upper-middle-class homes, lived within the same geographical area, and had similar educational experiences. As a group the children later identified as gifted (IQ score on performance, verbal, or full-scale WISC-R of greater than 135) demonstrated a statistically significant advantage for the following areas: the BSID, age of walking, age of saying two-word sentences, Expressive Language Gradient, and the Stanford-Binet.

Using intervals based on the BSID at age 1, Shapiro et al. (1989) computed the percentage of children later identified as gifted. No children with BSID IQ scores below 85 were later identified as gifted. For the 85-100 range, there was a 14% likelihood of identification of gifted-ness at 7.5, increasing to 22% for the 101-117 BSID range, and decreasing to 16% for the 118-134 range. Only four infants had scores above 134 on the BSID and just two were later identified as gifted using the WISC-R at age 7.5.

The average Bayley score for the group later identified as gifted was 109.8, and the nongifted averaged 104.4. The difference was statistically significant, but for practical purposes the difference between someone with an IQ of 109.8 and 104.4 is not discernible to most people. The correlation between the Bayley and the full-scale WISC-R at age 7.5 was moderate ($r = .35$). However, the Stanford-Binet measure at age 3 and the WISC-R at 7.5 had a higher correlation of $r = .52$. Shapiro at al. (1989) stated that as a group the gifted performed better on tests of infant intellectual development, but that was an "aggregate effect and not applicable to the individual child" (p. 208).

Although this study did not identify any definitive tests for determining giftedness in infancy, it did find significant differences between the gifted and the nongifted, particularly in the area of language expression. It also focused on identifying the gifted child as opposed to the at-risk child and observed and tested children on a prospective basis rather than obtaining retrospective information from caregivers. Shapiro et al. (1989) concluded that intelligence "is not a unitary concept and intelligence tests do not measure the same things at all ages" (p. 209). Tests that focus on information processing or other neuropsychological functions may prove to have greater predictive validity than the Bayley Scales of Infant Development used in this study.

USING FACTOR ANALYSIS TO ANALYZE AN INFANT DEVELOPMENT SCALE

The use of factor analysis to analyze infant development scales appears to have some utility in identifying predictors of intelligent behavior. Lewis, Jaskir, and Enright (1986) computed a factor analysis and rotational method to isolate specific abilities that characterized performance at ages 3 months, 12 months, and 24 months on the Bayley scales. Lewis et al. theorized that some of these related sets of skills change over development, such as social attention at 3 months being related to lexical abilities at 24 months. The authors were able to distinguish verbal, social, and nonverbal paths of mental development and document changes in the nature and composition of skills in the developing infant. However, they cautioned against placing too much emphasis on these related sets of skills as predictors because the item pool for the Bayley is somewhat limited and the correlations between skills over the various ages were not impressive nor markedly different from correlations with full-scale scores and later IQ scores.

Generally, the low correlations of scores on infant scales during the first year of life seem to support McCall's (1983) belief that the developmental path of the human infant is so rigidly defined that the attempt to identify precursors of intelligent behaviors is practically impossible. However, the low correlational scores may be due to the fact that the infant scales do not measure intelligent infant behavior, but only a sensorimotor type of development which is a consistent development in the human species (Shapiro et al., 1989).

THE CASE STUDY APPROACH IN IDENTIFYING COGNITIVE ABILITIES

Although the Bayley infant scale has limited value in predicting intelligent behaviors, and the FTII still needs to be examined from a different perspective to determine if it can identify superior intellect, an ongoing analysis of individual case studies may be useful in helping to identify precursors of giftedness. Brown (1970) summarized the data she collected on Felicia, a gifted and creative child, from the neonate stage to age 8. From the beginning of the study, Felicia showed an unusual ability to control and interact with her environment. She was generally awake more than the other infants in the study and more responsive to external stimuli. She also exhibited a strong desire to control even as a neonate, as she resisted being pulled to a sitting position and did not enjoy cuddling. Felicia also showed early fine motor control, being able to bring hands and mouth together before the end of the first week.

Felicia continued to show advanced development from her peers through age 8 in part because her parents provided an optimal environment for her growth. Her WISC score at age 7 years and 10 months was 141. One of the other children, who shared similar characteristics with Felicia except for a lower level of independence, also developed into a highly intelligent and sensitive child; however, he did not develop creativity to any marked degree. These two examples seem to indicate that infants do not follow a rigid developmental path, but that there are qualitative differences in individual development apparent almost from birth.

Brown's (1970) thorough analysis of Felicia's behaviors from a very early age pinpointed some characteristics in combination with an optimal environment that may indicate the development of giftedness. More longitudinal research that follows infants from the neonate stage through childhood and beyond is needed before any substantial conclusions can be reached. This method of study shows promise as being useful in identifying characteristics, both innate and environmental, that may be precursors of giftedness.

INFANT BEHAVIORS AS PREDICTORS OF GIFTEDNESS

Although current measures of infant intelligence cannot predict individual giftedness, there is a growing body of research that has been able to correlate specific infant behaviors with later measures of intelligence. In a review of the research, Abroms (1982) identified three such behaviors: Auditory perception, crying activity, and visual attention. Lewis and Michaelson (1985) also indicated that visual attention might have some value as a predictor of giftedness. Rose et al. (1988) and Rose and Wallace (1985) found that visual recognition memory is positively correlated with later IQ. Fagan and colleagues (Benson, Cherny, Haith, & Fulker, 1993; DiLalla et al., 1990; Fagan, 1984a, 1984b; Fagan and McGrath, 1981; Thompson et al., 1991) used a novelty problem or preference as a means of determining infant intelligence.

Auditory Perception

The research in the area of auditory perception appears to be more speculative in nature than hard data that actually correlate with the ability to distinguish speech sounds with later measures of intelligence. Infants may be able to discriminate between certain sounds as early as one month (Eilers & Minifie, 1975; Eimas, Siqueland, Jusczyk, & Vigorito, 1971), but whether this ability correlates with later measures of intelligence needs to be determined.

Crying Activity

In a study to determine the relationship between crying activity during early infancy to intellectual and speech development at age 3, Karelitz et al. (1964) found a significant correlation between the number of cry counts (defined as being more interactive and more numerous) and later IQ (.70). Although this finding is tantalizing, Abroms (1982) cautioned against using this study to infer that cry counts and crying activity can be used to predict future giftedness. She pointed out that the study had several methodological flaws such as the lack of a representative sample that included infants from lower socioeconomic status families and whether the stimulus used to elicit the cry counts was controlled in its intensity. However, Abroms did state that this area needs further research and could be promising in helping to develop an understanding of giftedness.

Visual Attention

Measures of Habituation. The area of visual attention or habituation also appears to be promising in identifying a predictor of giftedness. Habituation measures present an infant with a stimulus or pair of stimuli. Viewers and cameras record the infants' reactions. As a stimulus is repeated, the amount of attention the infant gives to the familiar stimulus decreases. This decrement is referred to as *habituation*, which reflects the infant's increasing acquaintance with the stimuli (Bornstein, 1989). Lewis and Brooks-Gunn (1981) found that habituation to redundant and recovering to novel stimuli at 3 months were better predictors of intelligence scores at 24 months on the Bayley than 3-month global intelligence scores. Infants who habituated to a redundant stimulus and recovered to a novel one had higher scores on the Bayley at 2 years. Ruddy and Bornstein (1982) also found that infants who had habituated faster and more often at 4 months had higher Bayley scores at the age of 12 months.

Rose, Slater, and Perry (1986) also investigated whether measures of dishabituation and habituation could predict later performance on an IQ test. In this study 17 infants were tests on habituation over three separate trials and later tested on the WWPSI. Habituation measures such as total fixation time negatively correlated with the WWPSI verbal scores, as did the duration of the first fixation, the length of the average fixation and the average trial duration. These findings are similar to other studies and support the position that measures of habituation have some value as predictors of intelligent behavior.

Visual Recognition Memory. Fagan and McGrath (1981) tested infant visual recognition memory at 7 months, 5 months, and 4 months, measuring the amount of time each child fixated on a novel stimulus. The children were later tested on the Peabody Picture Vocabulary Test at ages ranging from 3.8 years to 7.5 years. Early recognition memory significantly correlated with the later vocabulary scores at 7 months and 3.8 years, also at 5 months and 4.3 years, and even increased with the 4 months and 7.5 years sample (.66 and .46). Continuing to investigate visual recognition memory and intelligence, Fagan (1984b) found an even stronger correlation of ($r = .70$, $p < .0001$) between infant recognition memory performance and IQ scores at age 5. This research led to the development of the Fagan Test of Infant Intelligence (FTII).

Abroms (1982) stated that the "infant who shows relatively advanced visual preferences has a head start in the acquisition of cognitive competence. This facility allows the infant to participate in a more enriched and variegated environment with greater opportunities for learning" (p. 6). She also theorized that this ability might be indicative of "rapid cognitive processing, advanced memory capacity and the preexistence of mental structures" (p. 6). Further research of a longitudinal nature is needed in order to confirm or deny the validity of these findings, but the current research does appear to be promising.

ROLE OF THE ENVIRONMENT IN THE DEVELOPMENT OF GIFTEDNESS

The role of the environment surrounding the child must also be examined in order to identify precursors of giftedness in infancy. In all probability, environmental influences cannot be separated from infant behaviors because both influence and control the development of the other (Scarr & McCarthy, 1983). However, some environmental conditions appear to facilitate and support the development of giftedness more than others.

Quality of Maternal Care

A number of research studies have examined the quality of maternal care and its effect on the intellectual development of the child. Ruddy and Bornstein found that mothers who offered more frequent reinforcement to their babies attention to stimuli at 4 months had babies who could speak more words at age 1. Bee et al. (1982) determined that assessments of mother and child interaction and general environmental quality were among the best predictors of the child's level of functioning at any age. Dunn (1976) found the most important factor related to IQ was the style of maternal talking to the infant at age 14 months and concluded that maternal and infant behaviors were interactive, which made a cause-effect relationship difficult if not impossible to discern. Other research also supports these findings (Moss & Strayer, 1990).

Elardo, Bradley, and Caldwell (1975) used the inventory of Home Stimulation Rating Scale to assess the effects of specific environmental influences on cognitive development and found that a positive correlation existed between it and Stanford-Binet scores at 36 months. The authors hypothesized that a stimulating environment helped to produce a bright child and that the bright child in turn caused the environment to react and become more stimulating.

Infant Stimulation

The home environment appears to play an important role in developing human intelligence, but whether the parent can actually control the environment to such an extent that the child develops high intelligence or giftedness remains to be determined. A growing body of literature points to the notion that early intervention programs, which focus on the caregiver reading, talking, providing tactile stimulation, and the like to the infant may actually raise the measured intelligence due to poor living conditions (Heber & Garber, 1975; Ramey & Haskins, 1981). However, there is a real lack of information on how to affect the intellectual development of an average, healthy child (Watson & Ervy, 1983).

Storfer (1990) suggested that the following mother-infant interactive behaviors have a positive effect on developing IQ: (a) the amount of stimulation specifically directed toward the child is of more importance than the total amount of environmental stimulation; (b) maternal gaze patterns that provide pleasure both for caregiver and child; (c) imitating the infant's sounds of vocalizations; (d) encouragement of child's attention to objects and events within the environment; (e) naming objects; (f) assisting the development of the stage described as quiet alertness in which the baby is awake, but not crying; and (g) creating situations in which infants learn that they can affect a situation by their behavior. Storfer's suggestions are logical and practical, but still need to be validated through empirical research and prospective data.

White's Infant Education Program

White (1988) developed an infant education program in which new parents are trained so they learn how to react to and recognize their infant's needs. Parents are first encouraged to make the environment safe for the child, to encourage exploratory behavior. Next the parents are directed to react to the child's needs by providing comfort, sharing discoveries, and helping the child overcome obstacles. In comparing the results of this type of parenting style, children whose parents had received the training achieved significantly higher scores at age 3 (mean IQ for control group = 103.8, mean IQ for experimental group = 109.6) on the Kaufmann ABC Scales and the Zimmerman Preschool Language Scales than a control group. White also attempted to control for the effects of a self-selected sample by attempting to enroll all parents of newborns within a target area. White also claimed that his sample represents all economic groups.

The results of White's research are impressive and he appears to have succeeded in raising the intelligence level of his subjects, who are average, healthy children. However, White did not have any data on intellectual functioning beyond age 3 and whether the children in his sample will continue to show advanced development remains to be determined.

Doman's Work on Developing Intellectual Giftedness

Whereas White worked with children of normal ability and managed to raise their intellectual functioning from normal to slightly above normal, Doman, Doman, and Aisen (1985) claimed that their system of infant education can raise a child's IQ to near genius level. Doman et al. believe that all intelligence is learned and by systematically teaching or exposing infants to little bits of knowledge such as pictures or great paintings or Japanese writing, the child can assimilate this information and become proficient at using it. However, Doman's claims have not been validated through established research procedures. Doman has never allowed any professional group to examine or evaluate his procedures, his earlier work with brain-damaged children has never been replicated, and the validity of Doman's findings are suspect (White, 1988).

Role of the Father

Generally, the role of the father has not been the focus of determining the variables in infancy that can predict superior intellectual development. However, Karnes and Schwedel (1987) used an interview protocol consisting of 119 items to determine the kinds of behaviors exhibited by the fathers of young gifted children (IQ > 124) in regard to child rearing practices and to compare these behaviors to those exhibited by the fathers of nongifted children. The number of subjects for each group was fairly small (gifted, n = 9; nongifted, n = 10); nevertheless, the fathers of the gifted engaged in several distinct and significantly different practices than the fathers of the nongifted.

Fathers of the gifted reported longer and more frequent instances of reading to their children and showed an overall pattern of greater involvement with their children. Attitudes of the fathers of the gifted differed significantly in regard to the importance of encouraging oral language development with the fathers of the gifted, placing more emphasis on mastering this skill. Fathers of the gifted were also more likely to engage in fine motor activities such as Lego construction, whereas the fathers of the nongifted seemed more concerned with developing overall psychomotor skills. Both groups recognized the importance of developing a positive self-image, but the fathers of the gifted were more likely to report specific strategies that they used to teach their children and more likely to encourage their young children to act independently.

This study provides some interesting information regarding the father's role in developing cognition, yet more empirical research is needed that examines this relationship on a prospective basis from birth through adolescence (Albert & Runco, 1989).

Providing the Optimal Environment During Infancy

Clark (1992) offered several useful suggestions for parents to consider in providing an optimal environment during infancy for the development and support of giftedness. She theorized that the period from birth to 3 months is critical in optimizing cognitive abilities. Her suggestions include providing a responsive environment so that infants and their parents can respond sensitively to each other. She did caution against over stimulation, but believes that parents should not wait for their children to indicate an interest before providing the necessary support activities. Infants should be given many opportunities to experiment and explore so they can begin to develop their intellectual abilities even before they can communicate specific wants and needs.

Clark's theories on nurturing infant cognitive abilities have not yet been tested through established research procedures, but her suggestions for optimizing intelligence are similar to those of Moss and Strayer (1990), and White (1988), and the conclusions of Elardo et al. (1975). Unlike Doman, Clark did not advocate teaching infants in a structured systematic manner, but rather anticipating children's interests and providing ample opportunities to develop them.

INFANT TEMPERAMENT AND ITS EFFECT ON DEVELOPING COGNITIVE ABILITIES

Research in the area of infant temperament and its relationship to cognition is inconclusive, but Lerner and Lerner (1983) believed that cognition is enhanced when the quality of infant care is responsive to the child's temperament. For example, if an infant is rated as having a difficult temperament, the caregiver is less apt to be patient and understanding, which in turn affects the child, causing him to become more demanding and difficult. Temperament appears to impact developing cognition because it affects the perceptions of others and it causes the infant to receive a different type of feedback based on these perceptions and he is changed as a result. Lerner and Lerner's definition of temperament is based on work done by Thomas and Chess (1977), whose model is based on the premise that temperament and the quality of care are interactive. When the infant's environment matches his care (i.e., a baby who enjoys stimulation is given stimulation), a goodness of fit is achieved and the infant's adaptation is enhanced. The inverse relationship is also true, whereby a poor fit means a less than optimal adaptation.

Temperament also appears to affect the acquisition of knowledge as the characteristics of high attention, low distractibility, moderate threshold, and intensity appear to facilitate this process (Lerner & Lerner, 1983). The inverse characteristics appear to have an opposite effect, although children do adapt and change. In fact, the adaptation process appears to be characteristic of higher intelligence. Whether temperament studies have any predictive value in the identification of giftedness still needs to be determined and more longitudinal research is needed before this determination can be made.

Birth Order

The literature also seems to indicate that birth order might have some value as a predictor of giftedness. There seems to be a higher incidence of gifted children among the firstborn (Freeman, 1979), but the actual differential is more probably the quality of parental care, not the child's family position (Lewis & Michaelson, 1985). Also, Storfer (1990) stated that the perceived effects of birth order are reduced when maternal age is factored out.

CONCLUSION

The present research on identifying giftedness in infancy is both incomplete and inconclusive. With the exception of Shapiro et al. (1989), most of the studies that identify infant behaviors which are correlated with intelligence test scores at a later age do not deal directly with the issue of giftedness, and Shapiro et al.'s study used the BSID, which has proven to be of limited usefulness in predicting intelligent behavior. In fact, the Fagan Test of Infant Intelligence may have a better predictive ability for identifying giftedness than the BSID. The moderate correlations achieved by the FTII to Stanford-Binet scores in the DiLalla et al. (1990) and Thompson et al. (1991) studies support the notion that the FTII may be more capable of identifying children who have the potential for giftedness than the BSID. Nevertheless, whether this potential for giftedness can be identified during infancy remains to be determined and more empirical research is needed that focuses prospectively on it.

Research is also needed that focuses on the infant's ability to adapt and control environmental conditions. For example, the infant who at 3 days decides she wants her head in a certain position and cries until she achieves her goal is displaying an ability to control her environment that may be indicative of future giftedness. At the same time, the baby that displays an intense curiosity about the world by continually looking around, lifting his head up at five days, and even resisting being placed in a front carrier, where his vision was obstructed, may also be indicating that he has unusual cognitive abilities. In fact, both of the children described in these examples were later identified as gifted.

Another behavior that may indicate future giftedness is the ability to anticipate an action or event based on a previous experience, such as the baby who looked up and made a blowing motion when he saw a person who had earlier played a blowing object game with him. Perhaps this type of behavior is indicative of an excellent memory, a characteristic often associated with giftedness (Storfer, 1990).

Although measures of habituation indicate that the more intelligent infants tend to habituate faster to novel stimuli, a few infants are able to focus on intricately patterned objects or unusual shapes for fairly long periods of time. Of two children later identified as gifted, one mother mentioned that the first characteristic that she thought was unusual about her daughter was the ability at a very early age to look at and study objects for up to 1 hour at a time. Another mother mentioned that at the age of 6 weeks, her son spent 45 minutes staring at a set of brightly patterned, blue elephants. This ability to pay attention and study objects and events may in fact be a precursor of the ability to concentrate and focus on a specific subject or interest, another characteristic often associated with giftedness.

Although the infant behaviors noted earlier as being possible predictors of future giftedness have yet to be tested through established research procedures, the data from the case study of Felicia (Brown, 1970) tend to reinforce the importance of examining these factors and their relationship to future giftedness. Using infant behaviors, environmental conditions, and demographic variables by themselves do not yet allow the researcher to predict giftedness with an acceptable degree of accuracy. However, using these variables in combination may allow the future investigator to predict giftedness during infancy. The case study approach appears to have the greatest potential for research because it does not attempt to isolate infant behavior from the environment. At any rate, more research studies are certainly needed that examine this phenomenon that are both longitudinal and ongoing. Finally, Tannenbaum (1992) stated that, "giftedness in young children is a treasure waiting to be fully uncovered . . . [and] the prizes which still lie hidden may well prove to be priceless" (p. 129). Hopefully, someone someday will be able to take on the task of deciphering the complexities associated with the beginnings of giftedness and receive their due rewards.

REFERENCES

Abroms, K. (1982). The gifted infant: Tantalizing behaviors and provocative correlates. *Journal of the Division for Early Childhood, 5,* 3-18.

Albert, R.S., & Runco, M.A. (1989). Independence and the creative potential of gifted and exceptionally gifted boys. *Journal of Youth and Adolescence, 18*(3), 221-230.

Bee, H. L., Barnard, K. E., Eyres, S. J., Gray, C. A., Hammond, M. A., Spietz, A. L., Snyder, C., & Clark, B. (1982). Prediction of IQ and language skill from perinatal status, child performance, family characteristics, and mother-infant interaction. *Child Development, 53,* 1134-1156.

Benson, J. B., Cherny, S. S., Haith, M. M., & Fulker, D. W. (1993). Rapid assessment of infant predictors of adult IQ: Midtwin-midparent analyses. *Developmental Psychology, 29,* 434-447.

Bornstein, M. H. (1989). Stability in early mental development: From attention and information processing in infancy to language and cognition in childhood. In M. H. Bornstein & N. A. Krasnegor (Eds.), *Stability and continuity in mental development: Behavioral and biological perspectives* (pp. 147-169). Hillsdale, NJ: Erlbaum.

Brown, J. L. (1970). Precursors of intelligence and creativity: A longitudinal study of one child's development. *Merrill-Palmer Quarterly, 16,* 117-137.

Clark, B. (1992). *Growing up gifted* (4th ed.). Columbus, OH: Merrill/Macmillan.

DiLalla, L. F., Thompson, L. A., Plomin, R., Phillips, K., Fagan, J. F., Haith, M. M., Cyphers, L. H., & Fulker, D. W. (1990). Infant predictors of preschool and adult IQ: A study of infant twins and their parents. *Developmental Psychology, 26,* 759-769.

Doman, G., Doman, J., & Aisen, S. (1985). *How to give your baby encyclopedic knowledge.* Garden City, NJ: Doubleday.

Dunn, J. R. (1976). Mother infant relations, continuities, and discontinuities over the first 4 months. *Journal of Psychosomatic Research, 20,* 273-277.

Dunst, C. J. (1978). The structure of infant intelligence: An historical overview. *Intelligence, 2,* 381-391.

Eilers, R., & Minifie, F. (1975). Fricative discrimination in early infancy. *Journal of Speech and Hearing Research, 18,* 158-167.

Eimas, P., Siqueland, E., Jusczyk, P., & Vigorito, J. (1971). Speech perception in infants. *Science, 171,* 303-306.

Elardo, R., Bradley, R., & Caldwell, B. (1975). The relation of infants' home environment to mental test performance from 6 to 36 months: A longitudinal analysis. *Child Development, 46,* 71-76.

Fagan, J. F. (1984a). Recognition memory and intelligence. *Intelligence, 8,* 31-36.

Fagan, J. F. (1984b). The relationship of novelty preferences during infancy to later intelligence and later recognition memory. *Intelligence, 8,* 339-346.

Fagan, J.F., & Detterman, D.K. (1992). The Fagan test of infant intelligence: A technical summary. *Journal of Applied Developmental Psychology, 13,* 173-193.

Fagan, J. F., & McGrath, S. K. (1981). Infant recognition memory and later intelligence. *Intelligence, 5,* 121-130.

Freeman, J. (1979). *Gifted children.* Baltimore: University Park Press.

Heber, R., & Garber, H. (1975). The Milwaukee Project: A study in the use of family intervention to prevent cultural-familial mental retardation. In B. Z. Friedlander, G. M. Sterritt, & G. E. Kirk (Eds.), *Exceptional infant* (Vol. 3, pp. 399-433). New York: Brunner/Mazel.

Karelitz, S., Fisichelli, V., Costa, J., Karelitz, R., & Rosenfeld, L. (1964). Relation of crying activity in early infancy to speech and intellectual development at age three years. *Child Development, 35,* 769-777.

Karnes, M. B., & Schwedel, A. (1987). Differences in attitudes and practices between fathers of young gifted and fathers of non-gifted children: A pilot study. *Gifted Child Quarterly, 31,* 79-82.

Lerner, R. M., & Lerner, J. V. (1983). Temperament-intelligence reciprocities in early childhood. In M. Lewis (Ed.), *Origins of intelligence* (pp. 399-421). New York: Plenum.

Lewis, M. (1973). Intelligence tests: Their use and misuse. *Human Development, 16,* 108-118.

Lewis, M. (1983). On the nature of intelligence—science or bias? In M. Lewis (Ed.), *Origins of intelligence* (pp. 1-24). New York: Plenum.

Lewis, M., & Brooks-Gunn, J. (1981). Visual attention at three months as a predictor of cognitive functioning at two years of age. *Intelligence, 5,* 131-140.

Lewis, M., Jaskir, J., & Enright, M. K. (1986). The development of mental abilities in infancy. *Intelligence, 10,* 331-354.

Lewis, M., & McGurk, H. (1972). The evaluation of infant intelligence: Infant intelligence scores—true or false? *Science, 178,* 1174-1177.

Lewis, M., & Louis, B. (1991). Young gifted children. In N. Colangelo & G. Davis (Eds.), *Handbook of gifted education* (pp. 365-381). Needham Heights, MA: Allyn & Bacon.

Lewis, M., & Michaelson, L. (1985). The gifted infant. In J. Freeman (Ed.), *The psychology of gifted children* (pp. 35-57). New York: Wiley.

McCall, R. (1983). A conceptual approach to early mental development. In M.Lewis (Ed.), *Origins of intelligence* (pp. 107-133). New York: Plenum.

Moss, E., & Strayer, F. F. (1990). Problem solving of gifted and non-gifted preschoolers with their mothers. *International Journal of Behavioral Development, 13,* 177-197.

Ramey, C. T., & Haskins, R. (1981). Early education, intellectual develop-
    ment, and school performance: A reply to Arthur Jensen and J.
    McV. Hunt. *Intelligence, 5,* 41-48.
Rose, S. A., Feldman, J. F., & Wallace, I. F. (1988). Individual differences
    in infants' information processing: Reliability, stability, and predic-
    tion. *Child Development, 59,* 560-576.
Rose, D. H., Slater, A., & Perry, H. (1986). Prediction of childhood intelli-
    gence from habituation in early infancy. *Intelligence, 10,* 251-263.
Rose, S. A., & Wallace, I. F. (1985). Cross-modal and intra-modal transfer
    as predictors of mental development in full-term and pre-term
    infants. *Developmental Psychology, 21,* 949-962.
Rubin, R., & Balow, B. (1979). Measures of infant development and
    socioeconomic status as predictors of later intelligence and
    school achievement. *Developmental Psychology, 15,* 225-227.
Ruddy, M., & Bornstein, M. (1982). Cognitive correlates of infant atten-
    tion and maternal stimulation over the first year of life. *Child
    Development, 53,* 183-188.
Scarr, S., & McCartney, K. (1983). How people make their own environ-
    ments: A theory of genotype (leading to) environment effects.
    Child Development, 54, 424-435.
Shapiro, B. K., Palmer, F. B., Antell, S. E., Bilker, S., Ross, A., & Capute, A.
    J., (1989). Giftedness: Can it be predicted in infancy? *Clinical
    Pediatrics, 28,* 205-209.
Siegel, L. (1981). Infant tests as predictors of cognitive and language
    development at two years. *Child Development, 52,* 545-557.
Storfer, M. D. (1990). *Intelligence and giftedness: The contributions of
    heredity and early environment.* San Francisco: Jossey-Bass.
Tannenbaum, A. (1992). Early signs of giftedness: Research and com-
    mentary. *Journal for the Education of the Gifted, 15,* 104-133.
Thompson, L. A., Fagan, J. F., & Fulker, D. W. (1991). Longitudinal predic-
    tion of specific cognitive abilities from infant novelty preference.
    Child Development, 62, 530-538.
Watson, J. S., & Ervy, R. D. (1983). Early learning and intelligence. In M.
    Lewis (Ed.), *Origins of intelligence* (pp. 225-254). New York:
    Plenum.
White, B. L. (1988). *Educating the infant and toddler.* Lexington, MA:
    Heath.
Willerman, L., & Fiedler, M. (1974). Infant performance and intelligence
    precocity. *Child Development, 45,* 483-486.
Willerman, L., & Fiedler, M. (1977). Intellectually precocious preschool
    children: Early development and later intellectual accomplish-
    ments. *The Journal of Genetic Psychology, 131,* 13-20.

3

Seeking Advanced Potentials: Developmentally Appropriate Procedures for Identification

Bertie Kingore

Identifying gifted children is always difficult, but it is particularly so with primary children where it is easy to confuse high ability with advantaged backgrounds and a lack of enriched background with low ability. Some children come to school with large vocabularies, rich experiences with books, and social skills developed through high quality preschool experiences. These students are frequently "easier to find" because they are school-ready. Able children from disadvantaged backgrounds are often "difficult to find" because they have had few opportunities to develop the skills and aptitudes that school values.

Researchers currently disagree on the specifics, but there is general agreement that even very bright children vary in the kinds of potential they have, in the areas in which they may excel, and in their rate of development (Gardner, 1993; Sternberg, 1985). Thus our search for advanced potentials needs to be a multifaceted, multidimensional process which includes a wide range of procedures and criteria for discovering talents. As Greenlaw and McIntosh (1988) advised,

"Giftedness must be probed for in as many ways as it is manifested" (p. 88). Standardized tests have long been a mainstay in the identification of special populations; however, standardized tests present too narrow a view of some students' abilities and may be inappropriate for many populations. They also reward procedures where simple correct answers and memorization are more highly prized than high-level thinking (Worthen & Spandel, 1991).

Alternative assessments of gifted potentials need to be incorporated with primary children to overcome the limitations of the identification procedures in the past. As *National Excellence: A Case for Developing America's Talent* cautioned: "Educators must identify outstanding talent by observing students in settings that enable them to display their abilities, rather than relying solely on test scores" (Ross, 1993, p. 3). Classroom observation and portfolio development are two kinds of alternative assessments that have particular value for identifying and nurturing the talents of young children. These alternative procedures are not an added burden to teachers and young children when they are appropriately embedded in regular instruction. They become integrated and a part of everything occurring in learning situations rather than something such as a standardized test where teachers stop teaching and just do assessment.

If we truly wish to develop talents in all children as we seek advanced potentials, the following premises are significant (Kingore, 1995):

- All children probably have more potential than we have known how to maximize in the past.
- Giftedness must not be confused with the value or worth of a child. All children are equally valuable and important. By nature of being a person, every child has the same high value. Children do differ in their needs, interests and abilities. But these differences do not make one child more or less important than another.
- All children are not gifted—not in keeping with the spirit of national and state definitions of giftedness. However, all children are a gift. All children can learn and benefit from high expectations realistically established by caring adults.
- Children learn at different rates. In general, the higher the ability, the faster the rate of learning when the needs of the child are being met. Therefore, children with gifted potential are frequently able to learn with less repetition and develop ideas further than many of their age-mates.
- Children with gifted potential need differentiated curricula. Their learning experiences need to differ in depth, complexity and pacing from experiences needed by other learners.

- Children need an environment which is nurturing in tone and rich in challenges and expectations if high potentials are to be reached.
- A teacher is a powerful influencer and encourager. Each teacher has the power to decide whether to facilitate or dictate the learning of each child.
- The goal is not to push children faster and harder, but rather to establish an encouraging and stimulating environment with a professional educator who is able to respond to children's leads and needs. (p. 1)

DEFINITION OF CHILDREN WITH HIGH POTENTIALS

Educators and administrators of programs for primary children need to enforce the belief that all children can learn when we create quality resources and services for the development of their potentials. However, achieving success for every child is not equated with achieving the same results for all. The content of our curricula and the assessment practices we employ must challenge all students, including those who have advanced potentials. The following definition from *National Excellence: A Case for Developing America's Talent* (Ross, 1993) reflects this search for talent and challenge:

> Children and youth with outstanding talent perform or show the potential for performing at remarkably high levels of accomplishment when compared with others of their age, experience, or environment.
>
> These children and youth exhibit high performance capability in intellectual, creative, and/or artistic areas, possess an unusual leadership capacity, or excel in specific academic fields. They require services or activities not ordinarily provided by the schools.
>
> Outstanding talents are present in children and youth from all cultural groups, across all economic strata, and in all areas of human endeavor. (p. 26)

To put this definition into practice, schools must employ more developmentally appropriate identification systems which enrich and challenge primary children. Analytical observation and portfolio assessment are appropriate choices for identifying and nurturing the talents of young children.

ANALYTICAL OBSERVATION: SEEKING ADVANCED
POTENTIALS THROUGH AN
ANALYSIS OF CHILDREN'S BEHAVIORS

One conclusion in the U.S. Department of Education's report *National Excellence: A Case for Developing America's Talent* states: "Providing opportunities and observing performance give the best information on children's strengths" (Ross, 1993, p. 26). The Kingore Observation Inventory (KOI) is a system that structures classroom observations of the strengths of children through analyzing categories of gifted behaviors (Kingore, 1990). Just as a store manager uses a single set of papers to take an inventory of her stock, teachers use one KOI for each class to note patterns of children's talents and strengths. The intent is to observe all children over 6 weeks or more as they engage in challenging and meaningful learning opportunities in their regular classroom. Figure 3.1 is a example of one KOI after 8 weeks observation in a kindergarten classroom of 24 children. Figure 3.2 provides some description of what each of the categories look like or sound like as children engage in many levels and types of learning opportunities.

Procedures for Using the KOI

Figure 3.1 is a reduced version of the KOI to serve as an example here. The full-sized KOI would be glued inside a brightly colored folder because the folder can more easily be seen when needed for data collection. The folder also makes the inventory more sturdy for marking.

One KOI is used for an entire class. All the incidences of gifted behavior in that classroom are recorded on the same KOI over a 6-week or longer period of observation. When a behavior is observed, the teacher determines the characteristic category for the behavior and writes the observed child's name in the category box. It is not necessary to write the child's name beside a specific behavior indicator. The behavior indicators in each category are there to help teachers understand more specifically what the category involves.

Sometimes an observed behavior will fit into more than one category. That is to be expected, as all of these characteristics are integrated within the whole child. The characteristics are arranged into categories to guide understanding of what is observed. When an observed behavior seems to fit in multiple categories, a teacher tallies it in only one category according to the first or strongest impression. Over time, patterns of the students' strengths and potentials become clear as we analyze the results.

The first time a gifted behavior is observed for a specific child, write the child's name in the appropriate category box. Then a tally mark is added by that name each time additional behaviors are

KINGORE OBSERVATION INVENTORY   (KOI)

Advanced Language

Unassumingly uses multi-syllable words.   JASON
Uses similes, metaphors or analogies.
Modifies language for less mature children.
Uses language to teach other children.   DEBORAH
Uses verbal skills to handle conflicts or influence behavior of others.
Expresses similarities and differences between unrelated objects.
Uses time concepts.

Analytical Thinking

Analyzes classroom tasks.   LENA II   DEREK   DIANA
Is unusually attentive to details in environment.
Sees cause and effect relationships.
Takes apart and reassembles things and/or ideas with unusual skill.
Expresses relationships between past/present experiences.
Makes up or expands songs, stories and riddles about learning experiences.
Organizes collections of things.   MARTIN I   JASON III

Meaning Motivated

Keeps at an issue until it makes sense.   JENNIFER I
Asks penetrating questions.
Is curious; asks how, why, and what if.   DEREK II
Displays unexpected depth of knowledge in one or more areas.
Asks questions about words (in print or oral language).
Remembers!
Has accelerated task commitment and energy when learning.
Wants to do things on own; independent.   DEBORAH

Perspective

See's another's point of view.   LENA
Unexpectedly demonstrates dimension, angle or perspective in art.   JENNIFER III
Creates interesting shapes or patterns.
Spontaneously applies left and right.   JASON I

Sense of Humor

Says or does something indicating a finely developed sense of humor.   DEREK
Catches an adult's subtle humor.   JASON
Uses figurative language for humorous effect.
Understands and uses puns and riddles.
"Plays" with language.   JENNIFER I

Sensitivity

Spontaneously takes action to help someone in need.
Shows non-verbal awareness of other's needs.   DEBORAH I
Uses empathic statements.   MARTIN   DEREK I
Has a strong sense of justice.   LENA
Has high expectations of self and others.

Accelerated Learning

Rapidly accelerates learning after onset.   JENNIFER
Categorizes by more than one attribute.   JASON III
Has unusual ability to comprehend symbols (musical, numeral, alphabet, maps)
Reads consecutive passages at an advanced reading level and explains meaning of what is read.   DEREK III
Has unexpected mastery of numbers.
Has unexpected understanding of addition, subtraction, multiplication or division.
Makes change, understands relationship of coin denominations.

Figure 3.1. Kingore Observation Inventory (KOI)

Advanced Language
The child unassumingly and appropriately displays an advanced vocabulary and an ability to use more complex language effectively in a variety of situations; naturally uses similes, metaphors, and analogies to express relationships.

Analytical Thinking
The child demonstrates an ability to discern components of a whole; strives to determine relationships and patterns in procedures, experiences, ideas, and/or objects. The student may not be "organized," yet enjoys organizing and planning events and procedures.

Meaning Motivated
The child shows curiosity and an inner drive for thorough, independent understanding; typically asks penetrating, intellectual questions and demonstrates an extensive memory.

Perspective
The child displays an ability to understand and incorporate unexpected or unusual points of view through oral language, writing, manipulatives, and/or art.

Sense of Humor
The child demonstrates understanding of higher levels of humor and application of a finely developed sense of humor, either through production of original jokes, riddles, puns, or other humorous effects or through understanding the subtle humor of others.

Sensitivity
The child is intensely sensitive to the needs and motivations of others, demonstrates a strong sense of justice, and sets high standards for self and others.

Accelerated Learning
The child demonstrates mastery and an ability to learn and understand material and concepts beyond the facts and knowledge typical and expected for that age group.

Figure 3. 2. Categories of Gifted Characteristics

observed for that child in that category. Because the KOI helps teachers focus on gifted characteristics, it is probable that the name of every child in a class will not show up on the Inventory. Furthermore, because children show their talents in different ways, most children with gifted potential receive tallies in three or four of the categories rather than an equal distribution in all seven categories. Occasionally, a child will have several tallies in only one category. The professional who knows that child best must determine if that indicates a single talent area in which to focus enrichment, or if he or she views the child as having gifted potential requiring multiple aspects of differentiation.

As Figure 3.1 shows, a relatively few tallies can reveal patterns that increase our insight about children's talents and instructional needs. In this class of 24 kindergarteners, 7 children were observed exhibiting behaviors typical of children with gifted potential. The children who received 1-3 tallies are demonstrating some advanced behaviors and signal the teacher to continue to prompt high responses and observe their reactions. The children who had 4-6 tallies alert the teacher to potential areas of strength for each child and signal that these learners especially need challenge and faster pacing in some areas as further information is collected about their abilities. In this class, the children who most frequently demonstrated gifted potential had 7-12 tallies. While additional information was collected about these children's potential, the teacher began compacting with these children in their areas of strengths, incorporated small group interactions, and used some replacement activities with advanced content as appropriate to each child's readiness. In addition, the teacher challenged herself to integrate more high level opportunities in language areas. She felt her class should have demonstrated more advanced behaviors in that category and determined that she needed to insure that she was offering sufficient enriched content in language. Thus, as this brief analysis illustrates, analytical observation has value for helping teachers respond to children's talents and receive feedback about the effectiveness of the learning opportunities they establish in a variety of settings.

The KOI appropriately applies the professional judgment of teachers and other educators in assessing children's behaviors for evidence of potential giftedness. Although a national distribution of scores is available from the first 2 years of field testing of the KOI (Kingore, 1990), it is recommended that each school develop its own norms as a more valid reflection of the specific student population and professional judgment of the educators in that district. Developing norms allows standards for interpretation of results across that school or district and translates the data into a more meaningful form than raw numbers.

The KOI is intended to be one component in an identification system that accents authentic assessment. The behaviors of children provide *clues, not conclusions*. Only by analyzing patterns of behaviors and then supporting that analysis with data from additional sources may sound educational decisions be made regarding the instructional needs of children.

Developmentally, children's abilities emerge at varying times. Thus, ongoing observation will prove to be in the best interest of primary children. Even after any formal identification period has ended, teachers should continue to observe and tally behaviors. In so doing, teachers increase the likelihood that they remain sensitive to children whose abilities begin to emerge later in the year.

Values of Analytical Observation and the KOI

An Observation Inventory Encourages Teachers to Be "Kid Watchers" and Respond to What Children May Be Trying to Do. Primary teachers who want to understand young children and meet their needs do not just mindlessly observe children in their classrooms. Rather, these teachers are analytical observers who seek to make sense of what they see occurring in learning situations. As teachers analyze behaviors, they frequently talk with the children because kids have significant information to share if we only know to ask. Talking with children about what they are doing may provide a window to their thinking. Hence, teachers attempt to interpret and respond to what a child is trying to do by frequently questioning and probing for clarity. A classic example occurs when a young child scribbles on a piece of paper. That scribble may look like nothing we recognize, yet teachers know they must not say to the child, "What is that?" Rather, teachers respond to the child by saying, "Tell me about your picture." That response suggests to the child that we are interested in what he or she is doing and firmly establishes the child as the expert we need to ask for information.

There are many other statements primary teachers ongoingly use to prompt students' thinking. For example, when a student responds to a question or problem with a correct answer, a teacher might ask: "How did you figure that out?" What often happens, however, is that the child then responds by changing the answer just given: "Oh, I meant 12. Yah, 12 is the answer!" The change in answer suggests that children are typically questioned only when they are wrong. The key point, of course, is that we should question children when they are right to bring to the students' conscious level what strategies work well. Figure 3.3 includes several examples of questions teachers might use to prompt students' thinking and help teachers analyze behaviors for indications of gifted potential.

An Observation Inventory Increases Teachers' Insights About Children and Giftedness as Students Respond at Many Different Levels to the Same Learning Experiences. Observation helps a teacher define and refine understanding of the children's levels of development and needs. The KOI specifically structures what to watch for so teachers become more aware of what gifted behaviors are. Analytical observation has proven to be a strong learning experience in clarifying teacher understanding of and appreciation for the differences among all wonderful children, high achievers, and students with gifted potentials. "This just gives me wonderful information about all of my kids. I'm noticing their strengths for a change instead of their deficits" (Idaho primary teacher).

Tell me about your picture.

Tell me about your work.

What are you thinking?

Tell me some more to help me understand your thinking.

What did you do to figure that out?

What is another way you (I, we) could do that?

Explain what you mean.

Why do you think that is so?

Tell me how you did that.

Tell me how you made that.

How could you (I, we) do that?

What do we need?

What should we do first? Next?

Figure 3.3. Prompting Thinking and Metacognitive Reflection

An Observation Inventory Allows Teachers to Assess the Process Involved in Children's Learning as Teachers Observe Learning Behaviors as Well as Collect the Products Which Result From Appropriate Learning Experiences. For young children, the process is frequently as significant as the product. Tests and paper and pencil tasks customarily reveal what children get right or wrong. What may be equally important, or even more important, is information about how or why they go about developing those answers.

In a second-grade classroom, the desks were arranged in a U-shape. As the teacher was moving around the inside of the U to work with individual children, she noticed that one of her boys had written his name upside-down. When she asked him about it, he replied: "I thought it would be easier for you to read as you come by." His product, instead of being a directionality problem, indicated an awareness of viewing work from the teacher's perspective. Thus, his "error" was really one clue to advanced perspective typical of children with gifted potentials (Colorado classroom).

An Observation Inventory Increases Opportunities for Minority, Disadvantaged, Handicapped, and Other Special Population Students to Exhibit Potential as Teachers Provide Challenging, High-Level Learning Opportunities for all Students. As the definition used in the federal Javits Gifted and Talented Education Act states, outstanding talents are present in children and youth from all cultural groups, across all economic strata, and in all areas of human endeavor (Ross, 1993). In

the spirit of inclusive instead of exclusive, it is helpful to think of the identification process as an ongoing series of opportunities given to all students to prompt potential. This attitude is much more developmentally
appropriate and productive than interpreting screening as a series of
hurdles that students must successfully overcome. The intent is to
include all students by providing multiple opportunities designed to
elicit advanced potential and then observe how students respond.
Some children will not immediately be in a position to demonstrate
their future promise. We must ongoingly provide opportunities and
observe performance while collecting information on children's
strengths or potentials. Our challenge is to develop the talents of all
children as we find and extend the potential of the difficult-to-find primary gifted child.

> Our star is a first-grade girl who was in a Chapter One classroom
> and spoke limited English. Through the KOI, a teacher picked up on
> her high potential despite her current lack of school-related back-
> ground and skills. She was placed in our gifted program and within
> 2 years was one of our school's highest achieving students. We feel
> we could have missed her without the KOI. (Texas Administrator)

*An Observation Inventory Increases the Possibility That the
Identification Process Is Useful for the Entire Class as Teachers Observe
Students at Work in Rich and Varied Educational Settings.* Identification
should not be just a process to end in a score or a decision regarding
acceptance into a gifted program. Rather, it should be a process to
provide information helpful in making instructional decisions for all students. To identify gifted potentials, teachers do not wait to see if
behaviors spontaneously occur. Instead, they set up high-level activities
to engage the entire class. They choose learning experiences and
strategies that are designed to be developmentally appropriate yet
open-ended so children may successfully respond at different levels.
These opportunities possibly enrich all students as they provide the
opportunity for students to bubble up and demonstrate gifted potentials. One example of enriched opportunities is a set of open-ended
questions and statements organized according to the seven categories of the KOI (see Figure 3.4). With minimal preparation time, teachers can use these ideas to generate and lift children's high-level thinking related to any topic of study. One example is provided in Figure 3.5
to illustrate an application for a unit on tools and simple machines.

*An Observation Inventory Ongoingly Assesses Potential as
Teachers Continue Their Analytical Observation Over an Extended
Period of Time.* All children do not emerge at the same time. There truly
are late bloomers who need teachers' ongoing sensitivity to their
emerging abilities. Thus, the screening and identification process must

Open-ended Questions and Statements to Uplift Thinking

Advanced Language

What are other words you can use instead of _____?
This _____ is like _____.
How many different meanings can you think of for _____?
What is another way to say _____?
What could you say to _____ when there is a problem?
Explain _____ to someone who does not understand.

Analytical Thinking

What might happen if _____?
Name all the attributes you can think of for _____.
Get ideas from _____ to improve _____.
How is _____ different from _____? How are they similar?
What could be done to make _____ more effective?
How could we organize _____?
What makes _____?
Look at this _____ and tell me all the things we would need to make one like it.

Meaning Motivated

The answer is _____. Think of as many questions as you can which have that answer.
Let's list all the facts you can think of about _____.
(List on the chalkboard or on a chart the ideas the children share.)
What/Why/How is _____ when _____?
Why does _____?
What might happen if _____?

Perspective

If you were _____, what would you see/hear/taste/feel/smell?
How would _____ be viewed by _____?
What would _____ look like if you were _____ (different places or sizes)?
What would _____ mean to a _____?
What might _____ think about that idea?
Explain, to someone who has never been to your house, how to find where you live.

Sense of Humor

What might happen if _____ had (some humorous attribute) instead of _____?
The funniest thing about _____ is _____.
If you put _____ and _____ together, you could call it a (a new word) and it could _____.
Instead of _____, it would be funnier if _____.
Explain what "you drive me up the wall" means. (Substitute other appropriate examples of figurative language.)

Sensitivity

If you were a _____, you'd be a _____ because _____.
How would _____ feel if _____?
What do you feel about _____?
How does _____ apply to others?
The fair thing to do is/was _____.
What do you think is the best thing to do the help _____?

Accelerated Learning

What symbols could be used for _____?
What sources might be used to find out more about _____?
How many things can you thing of that have both _____ and _____? (two attributes)
List all the things you can think of that are _____ and _____. (three attributes)
Make up a code to _____.

Figure 3.4. Open-ended Questions and Statements to Uplift Thinking

Advanced Language

- This pulley is like _____ .
- What is another way to say tools?
- Explain levers to someone who does not understand.

Analytical Thinker

- Name all the attributes you can think of for a carpenter.
- How is a saw different from an ax? How are they similar?
- Look at this house (barn, doghouse, birdhouse) and tell me all the things we would need to make one like it.

Meaning Motivated

- The answer is wedge. Think of as many questions as you can which have that answer.
- Let's list all the facts you can think of about tool safety. (List on the chalkboard or on a chart the ideas the children share.)

Perspective

- If you were building a treehouse, what would you see/hear/taste/feel/smell?
- What would your home look like if you were to build it so a giraffe could live with you?
- What might a tree think about a saw or a hammer or nails?
- Explain, to someone who has never been to your house, how to find where you live.

Sense of Humor

- What might happen if tools could talk?
- The funniest thing about a wedge is _____ .
- Explain what "you drive me up the wall" means. (Substitute other appropriate examples of figurative language.)

Sensitivity

- If you were a simple machine, you'd want to be a _____ because _____ .
- What is the fair thing to do when two kids both need to use a hammer to build something and there is only one hammer?

Accelerated Learning

- What symbols could be used for the different types of tools?
- How many things can you think of that have both a wheel and an axle?
- List all the things you can think of that are small, hard, and have a lever.

Figure 3.5. Topic: Tools and Simple Machines

late bloomers who need teachers' ongoing sensitivity to their emerging abilities. Thus, the screening and identification process must be considered over a significant period of time. The gifted potentials of some students will become known to us only when enriched environments and nurturing professionals help them to bloom, develop a more positive self-concept, and reach their heretofore hidden potential. The KOI specifically considers the frequency and consistency of gifted behaviors over a period of time, rather than on a one-time checklist response. Through analytical observation, the KOI allows teachers to determine the patterns of children's responses. Differences in students' strengths and the multiple ways they exhibit potential become clear as teachers analyze their tallies on the KOI:

> I think the KOI is very reliable and useful in determining giftedness in students. After using it for less than 4 weeks, I certainly understand why longer observation is recommended. Kids do not always show high potentials in a few days. I am going to tally my kids all year. (Oregon multilevel teacher)

An Observation Inventory Simplifies the Teacher's Paperwork and Increases Accuracy in the Process of Identifying Students Who Exhibit Outstanding Talent or Promise. In the past, the most frequent procedure for collecting information about gifted children in a classroom required that teachers complete a checklist of characteristics. If we truly believe in developing talents in all children, teachers would need to complete these checklists for every child. Filling out scaled checklists typically calls for extensive memory as well as analysis, evaluation, and decision making on the part of the teacher. Past experiences suggest that the completion of these checklists is typically hurried and attempted in one intensive burst of activity. Even the most dedicated teacher can be overwhelmed by the task of remembering and evaluating if and how much an individual child has exhibited each of the multiple characteristics on a checklist. Thus, the process of completing an observation inventory is a sounder practice. Ongoing observation and tallying children's behaviors over a period of time improves a teacher's accuracy in recognizing and serving children with high potential. "Watching kids by completing the KOI has really improved my observation skills and my understanding of my children's abilities" (Georgia kindergarten teacher).

An Observation Inventory Integrates Well With Other Alternative Assessment Processes. Observation complements the development and systematic selection of portfolio data and products useful in child and parent conferencing, as well as in talent development.

PORTFOLIOS: SEEKING ADVANCED POTENTIALS THROUGH THE PRODUCTS CHILDREN PRODUCE

Portfolios can also function as one criterion in the search for advanced potentials. Although not frequently applied in this capacity, portfolios offer a concrete record of the development of students' talents and the identification of gifted potentials. In classrooms where all students develop portfolios, the portfolio process allows each student to be noticed for the level of products he or she produces. Minority, handicapped and economically disadvantaged students are not overlooked because every student assembles a portfolio to reflect their growth and achievement. Thus, through portfolios, educators have an opportunity to increase their awareness of multiple kinds of students' abilities and of the gifted potential of students from special populations. In this manner, then, portfolios increase inclusion instead of exclusion by providing multiple opportunities for every child to demonstrate talents and gifted potential.

Portfolios also offer classroom teachers the opportunity to be directly involved in the search for high potentials through (a) planning and directing learning experiences that elicit high-level products, and (b) assessing the products resulting from those experiences. Teachers involvement in planning learning activities for their children further increases the likelihood that the identification process provides information that is instructionally useful instead of just a means to an end. Sylvia Rimm (1984) noted that identification should provide information which is useful for planning instruction and/or counseling gifted students. Students' portfolios most certainly prove useful in both instructional planning and in conferencing and interacting with individual children. Teachers involvement in assessing the students' products and portfolios also provides information vital to ongoing talent development. Assessment is intended here as the gathering of data to understand needs and strengths rather then the evaluation of products. As Grant Wiggins (1993) explained, the etymology of the word assess is "sit with." In assessment, therefore, primary teachers sit with students to determine what students know and can do. Teachers discuss a student's products with the student to ensure that the student's strengths have been found and acknowledged. This recognition of abilities motivates children and encourages them to have high expectations for themselves.

Definition

A portfolio is a systematic collection of student work selected largely by that student to provide information about the student's attitudes and motivation, level of development and growth over time.

Key Points of Portfolio Development

There are four key points to keep in mind if portfolios are to be an effective tool for developing the talents of all children:

1. **Portfolios must be student-driven, not teacher driven.** Teachers don't need more paperwork to manage and children do need to be the organizers and managers of their own work. Intrinsic motivation and self-esteem increases when primary students have the right and responsibility of selecting most of the products that go into the portfolio. At first, teachers wonder if young children really can learn to file and be responsible for a portfolio, but indeed they can. Children learn to file their selected work in the back of their portfolio so it always approximates chronological order.

2. **Portfolios must involve collection, selection, and reflection.** Portfolios are more than just some stuff put in a file. After collecting several products, students need to analyze what they have accomplished using established criteria such as "a product that shows how much I've learned," or "a hard problem I figured out," or "something I've done very well." Based on that analysis, children then select a product to add to their portfolio and attach a reflective statement to the product telling why it was included. Very young children can write their own reflections using their temporary spelling or an older classroom of students can work with young children as their Big Buddies and complete reflective statements for them. Over time, the portfolio becomes a concrete indication of how much each child has learned and how far each as grown. Portfolios allow schools to honor the diversity in students and discover the strengths of each learner. Increased emphasis on self-reflection and making judgments is one of the values of portfolios for all children.

3. **The process needs to be simple enough that it will work without overworking teachers.** Sometimes primary teachers feel they have to do so much for young children. Of course, children learn by doing; so adopt the rule "Never do for students what they should be doing for themselves!" The ongoing goal is to figure out more and more ways that children can increase their ownership in the process. Primary teachers have increased expectations and are learning that children can do more than we may have expected in the past.

4. **The process requires collaboration and careful planning for action and success.** Portfolio development and assessment is a change in most classrooms. Be prepared to work with colleagues to carefully plan goals, desired outcomes, and management needs before implementation. It is certainly appropriate to pilot the process for the first year with the intention to learn and build on what you have learned about creating the best procedures for authentically assessing children's strengths. Many teachers would do well to give themselves permission

to begin small and to develop the process over time. As the adage notes, "Be not afraid of moving slowly. Be only afraid of standing still."

Plan to involve colleagues in your search. Professional collaboration and conversations are exciting and promote growth and positive change. Share successes, suggestions, valued articles and resources among each other for the benefit of all.

Plan how to involve parents. Communication between schools and homes is vital if parents are to understand and embrace change for children. Very few parents are familiar with the values or purposes of portfolios. Through meetings, letters of information, and shared articles parents can become more informed (Kingore, 1995). Knowledgeable parents will support portfolios as a most worthy tool for maximizing the potential of children.

Portfolio Products

Portfolios will not provide clues to high potentials, however, if they are limited to a collection of grade-level tests, skill sheets, and simple paper-and-pencil tasks. Only to the degree that portfolios include the highest levels of performance on a wide range of student-selected contents and materials can the portfolio process support the search for multiple talents and multiple types of giftedness.

Portfolio products that incorporate complex, in-depth content can provide every student opportunities to demonstrate abilities to think, to solve problems, to create and to excel in selected works. The key point, of course, is that such products can only exist in portfolios if teachers have provided a wide array of challenging tasks for students to do in their classes. *To reach high potentials, learning experiences are not chosen because "they will be fun" or "the kids will like them." Rather, effective learning opportunities integrate the following criteria and result in experiences which are so engaging and satisfying that the children do indeed enjoy learning and have fun. The point is that enjoyment is the result of well-planned learning experiences, not the rationale for the choices* (Kingore, 1995, p. 14).

CRITERIA FOR EFFECTIVE LEARNING EXPERIENCES FOR ADVANCED TALENT DEVELOPMENT

- The activities are more open-ended and less single-answer directed. Open-ended does not mean that all answers are equally correct. Rather, it suggests that more than one right answer is possible and allows children to bring their individuality to each learning situation. Open-ended learning experiences encourage children to risk trying another idea or solution and even build on each others' ideas.

- Persistent high-level thinking is promoted. All children should have time and ongoing opportunities to solve meaningful and challenging problems and complete tasks that involve high-level thinking every day.

- The tasks incorporate appropriate complexity and challenge. Children want to learn. Even very young able learners often have in-depth knowledge in one or more areas that are of interest to them. They must be allowed to expand their learning in those areas rather than just repeat simple concepts: "I don't like to read at school. You never read anything you don't already know" (First grade child).

- A nonthreatening environment is maintained. Each learning experience should allow children to succeed; we dare not risk frustrating students. The goal is an appropriate balance between just enough versus too much challenge.

- Integration of learning is promoted. Effective learning experiences connect prior knowledge and new information rather than stress isolated details. Learning experiences that help children reach high potentials encourage the application of skills across the curriculum and in many different topics.

- Children are actively involved. Young students especially need to be actively involved in the learning process. That ancient Chinese Proverb is still valid:

> Tell me, I forget.
> Show me, I remember.
> Involve me, I understand.

Primary children learn best when their heads, hearts and bodies are all simultaneously involved. They benefit from important content to think about, to react to with their senses and feelings, and to manipulate with small and large motor responses.

- Discussions are stimulated among children and between teacher and child. The most effective learning experiences are designed to inspire children to articulate their ideas as well as to listen and respond to the ideas of others. Oral communication is a mainstay of learning for young children.

- Time for metacognition is provided. Metacognition refers to a child's awareness of the processes and thinking used in learning situations or product development. Metacognitive prompts such as "Tell me what you are thinking" and "Tell me some more so I understand what you mean" increase teachers' insights and learners' self-awareness (see Figure 3.3). Metacognitive prompts such as "What were you trying to do?", "What did you do well?", and "What would you like to change?" increase children's ability to self-evaluate and assess the worth of their own work.

- Teacher preparation is minimized. Most talented teachers are dedicated to helping children reach high potentials but are not looking for more to do! Many teachers already feel overwhelmed by the task of conscientiously trying to meet the individual needs represented by the wonderful but very different children in each classroom. Therefore, teachers must select experiences that can maximize learning opportunities for children without overworking teachers. Incorporate questioning strategies that allow productive thinking and different levels of responses to the same content (see Figures 3.4 and 3.5). Concentrate on experiences in which the children become producers instead of just consumers. For young children, more high-level thinking probably begins with blank paper than with fill-in-the-blank paper.

Planned Experiences

Planned experiences are a special component in the portfolio process to aid in assessing advanced potentials. Planned experiences are sets of high-level, open-ended activities designed specifically to elicit gifted behaviors in schools where teachers do not consistently provide a high degree of day-to-day stimulation and challenge. Gifted potentials can not bubble up if opportunities for high-level production do not occur on a regular basis in classroom curricula. Planned experiences may then be employed to result in products that can validate children's talents and many different kinds of potentials. Several school districts specifically want some activities that all grade-level teachers complete with every student to ensure equal opportunities for advanced behaviors to emerge and to serve as common denominators for assessment.

Planned experiences are not needed when a district's continuous staff development has ensured that all faculty are prepared to develop talent to high levels of performance. Planned experiences are not needed where a district's curriculum is differentiated and designed to ensure that high-level behaviors can emerge in every classroom. However, if differentiation in all classrooms is not complete, a district can ensure that opportunities for gifted behaviors to emerge are being provided in every classroom by selecting several planned experiences to include in its curriculum.

Multiple examples of planned experiences for primary students are included in the book *Portfolios: Enriching and Assessing All Students,*

Identifying the Gifted (Kingore, 1993). Although multiple curricula areas are included, several planned experiences are based on literature for children because quality literature has so many higher level applications and most primary teachers and students love good literature activities. Furthermore, each planned experience incorporates several different gifted characteristics to ensure multiple opportunities for different kinds of potentials to emerge. These activities may also serve to guide schools toward designing their own planned experiences. Developing its own planned experiences allows a school or a district to design planned experiences that thoroughly incorporate district and curricula goals, teacher preferences, and specific population needs. When developing and field testing planned experiences, keep in mind that planned experiences need to be developmentally appropriate to specific grade levels, clearly relate to curricula content, and use simple and readily available materials. The procedures for using and assessing the planned experiences must also be clearly delineated and taught to the entire faculty to ensure equity and reliability.

Recommendations

Alternative assessments such as observation and portfolio development have tremendous promise for finding and enriching talents of primary children. However, implementation depends on the expertise and attitude of the professionals in each school. These procedures will only be successful if accompanied with extensive and ongoing staff development. Alternative identification philosophy and procedures can identify gifted potentials when knowledgeable teachers have training and experience in analyzing the process and products of children. Professional development is needed in alternative assessment practices such as observation and portfolios before teachers can be expected to proceed successfully and positively. They need extensive experiences in rubric development and holistic interpretation to establish interrater reliability. Teachers also need better training in curriculum differentiation and high-level instructional strategies if they are to challenge all students sufficiently.

The search for advanced potentials should model the same high levels of thinking that we expect of students. We must :

- Analyze what students are trying to do;
- Synthesize data from products and observations about each student to determine significant patterns of strengths;
- Evaluate the instructional needs of each student based on our analysis and synthesis over time.

The search for advanced potentials is dependent on administrators and teachers who believe in its value and are well prepared to develop the expertise of children. Someone once told Piaget, "I only know what I see." "No," Piaget replied, "You only see what you know. Before you got the car you now drive, you probably noticed none like it. But, amazingly, after you got your car, there are ones like it everywhere! Of course, these similar cars were always there. Indeed, we only see what we know."

Gifted potentials exist in many children, but we can only see what we know. Primary children with gifted potentials are waiting for us to nurture them. We must learn to successfully use analytical observation and portfolios with these young children so we can clearly see and substantiate to other educators and parents what we know about children's strengths and high potentials.

Professionals need to believe they can influence high potentials:

- You have children with undiscovered talents in your room this year.
- Set up opportunities to find them and nurture them.

In the past, identification of primary gifted children frequently measured where children had been—the result of experiences and learning opportunities they had had. A more helpful attitude in developing talents is to focus on where children can go—to establish high expectations and prompt high responses. As the *National Excellence* (Ross, 1993) report concluded: "Our challenge is to raise expectations for all students in America, including those with outstanding talent" (p. 3).

REFERENCES

Gardner, H. (1993). *Multiple intelligences: The theory in practice.* New York: Basic Books.

Greenlaw, J., & McIntosh, M. (1988). *Educating the gifted: A sourcebook.* Chicago: American Library Association.

Kingore, B. (1990). *The Kingore observation inventory.* Des Moines, IA: Leadership Publishers.

Kingore, B. (1993). *Portfolios: Enriching and assessing all students, identifying the gifted grades K-6.* Des Moines, IA: Leadership Publishers.

Kingore, B. (1995). *Reaching high potentials.* Columbus, OH: DLM Professional Library, Macmillan/McGraw-Hill.

Kingore, B. (1995). Introducing parents to portfolio assessment. *Gifted Child Today, 18*(4), 12-13, 40.

Rimm, S. (1984). The characteristics approach: Identification and beyond. *Gifted Child Quarterly, 28*(4), 181-187.

Ross, P. (1993). *National excellence: A case for developing America's talent.* Washington, DC: Office of Educational Research and Improvement, U.S. Department of Education.

Sternberg, R. J. (1985). *Beyond IQ: A triarchic theory of human intelligence.* Cambridge, England: Cambridge University Press.

Wiggins, G. P. (1993). *Assessing student performance: Exploring the purpose and limits of testing.* San Francisco: Jossey-Bass.

Worthen, B. R., & Spandel, V. (1991). Putting the standardized test debate in perspective. *Educational Leadership, 48*(2), 65-69.

4

A Sensibility Approach to Identifying and Assessing Young Gifted Children

Maurice D. Fisher

When observing young children individually or in groups, we see many behaviors and responses indicative of giftedness. For example, the young child who correctly assembles complex puzzles in an organized sequence of steps, or who tells interesting and imaginative stories for the entertainment of parents and friends is showing advanced reasoning and sequencing processes. Clearly, there is an almost infinite number of behaviors and characteristics that teachers and parents can use to determine a child's giftedness. This abundance of indicators of high ability, however, will lead to chaos if they are not organized into a meaningful system that: (a) provides a systematic description of how gifted children develop; (b) identifies the landmark stages of development and specific cognitive and social behaviors (developmental milestones) shown at each stage; (c) describes a curriculum for educating young gifted children based on these developmental stages; and (d) leads to an assessment procedure that is clearly associated with this curriculum. Giftedness involves unique behaviors, characteristics, and ways of perceiving the world that are extremely different from the norm or average individual, so different that a gifted child cannot validly be assessed with traditional instruments. I call this underlying characteristic Sensibility and have devised an assessment scale which includes that component.

For practical reasons, we must use current theories and systems of child development to assess young gifted children until more knowledgeable approaches are developed. However, these theories and systems need to be modified and adapted to the unique characteristics and behaviors underlying giftedness, including sensibility. This chapter explores some currently available procedures that can be used to identify and measure the abilities of these children with an open-minded vision of the future. We should expect that some of these methods and procedures will be obsolete 5 to 10 years from now, and they will be replaced by more finely tuned to the unique characteristics and abilities of gifted children.

Howard Gardner's (1993b) work on Multiple Intelligences has produced considerable interest during the last 10 years among early childhood educators. Unfortunately, his approach has met some resistance from educators of the gifted because it does not produce a set of standardized test scores for comparative purposes. This assessment problem must be addressed by first considering what is best for measuring the abilities of gifted children. Are intelligence and achievement test scores more for the convenience of psychologists and educators than for the educational welfare of gifted children? Should we concentrate more on measuring cognitive and social processes rather than final results such as test scores? Should we be concerned with determining just one type of intelligence or several different types of intelligence? These and other similar questions will probably take another 10 to 15 years before they are resolved to the satisfaction of school administrators, teachers, parents, and psychologists.

Gardner's work goes against the grain of traditional theories by emphasizing seven unique types of intelligence rather than the single "*g*" factor espoused by a pioneer in this field, Charles Spearman (1904, 1927). I want to emphasize that Gardner (1983) has based his theory on many research and clinical studies that he described in *Frames of Mind*. His concepts are not just the intellectual ruminations of an "armchair psychologist," but are instead based on hard facts about the human brain and human abilities.

The mainstream psychometric community has long been opposed to multiple factor theories of intelligence such as Gardner's theory. The only major success story prior to Gardner was achieved by David Wechsler (1939, 1958) when he propounded the concepts of Verbal and Performance IQ, and developed tests for measuring these two abilities. Today, the Wechsler Scales of Intelligence are widely used in school systems throughout the United States. The popularity of these scales has forced the bastion of the unitary *g* factor, the Stanford-Binet Intelligence Scale (1986), to be modified to suit current needs in American society. It now reflects and measures distinct verbal and nonverbal abilities.

Educators find Gardner's Multiple Intelligences theory useful because it fulfills practical needs not currently being met by single and two-factor theories of intelligence. His theory provides specific categories of ability that make sense because: (a) they reflect current values of our society concerning different areas of achievement; (b) the seven categories can be used to detect giftedness among children who are not usually identified as being gifted such as poor children, ethnic minorities, and handicapped children; and (c) they can help to assess children's abilities (Lazear, 1994) and develop an appropriate curriculum (Lazear, 1991a, 1991b). Gardner's seven categories, including some behavior landmarks associated with young gifted children, are as follows:

- *Linguistic*—Early speech and early reading; the use of advanced sentence structures and language patterns; accelerated literary skills in poetry, drama and writing; ability to express imaginative ideas through writing and speaking.
- *Logical-Mathematical*—Highly original reasoning; asks series of logically organized questions related to solving problems; ability to apply mathematical reasoning to solving everyday and abstract problems; use of advanced arithmetic skills; facility at using practical and hands-on tools such as Cuisenaire Rods, puzzles, and weights and measures to solve logical-mathematical problems (such as Piaget's conservation tasks); understanding and application of computer concepts in playing games, and working on school-related tasks.
- *Musical*—Demonstration of high abilities in basic musical areas such as reading music and maintaining correct pitch and rhythm; skill in singing complex songs or playing difficult passages; excellent memory for melodies and musical scores; high motivation to practice and perform music; creative interest in composing original works.
- *Spatial*—Advanced drawing, sculpting and painting; dedication to expressing ideas through these and other artistic endeavors; highly skilled in drawing forms and structures such as animals, houses, buildings, and vehicles.
- *Bodily-Kinesthetic*—Skill in assembling toys and models, and in constructing objects from basic materials; skillful in dance, mime, and other movement activities; adept at using body movements to express ideas and emotions through acting.
- *Interpersonal*—Strong leadership abilities; motivated to organize peers into problem solving groups; exceptional ability to

understand the needs and problems of adults, classmates, friends and siblings; skill in helping peers to solve personal problems.

- *Intrapersonal*—Insight into one's own needs and problems as demonstrated through discussion and writing; talent in expressing one's perceptions and understandings through speaking and writing; ability to place oneself in the role of other individuals (empathize) to better understand their points of view and problems.

Gardner (1993b) and his colleagues have developed an early education curriculum called Project Spectrum that includes 15 Domains of Knowledge. Teachers assess these domains to determine a child's progress in language, numbers, movement, visual arts, music, social, and science areas. The most relevant point of these assessment methods for gifted children is that they are based on observing their problem-solving behavior and productive activities. They do not rely on using impersonal test scores.

THE STUDY OF THE MOST IMPORTANT CHARACTERISTIC OF GIFTEDNESS—SENSIBILITY

What makes gifted children remarkable in the eyes of their parents and teachers? What makes them unique in comparison to their peers and children of average and even above average ability? Although verbal and mathematical giftedness can be justified because of high intelligence and achievement test scores, there is something more fundamental that serves as the basis for all of the different types of giftedness related to Multiple Intelligences. Based on my work (Fisher, 1988, 1992, 1994a, 1994b) and that of my colleague, Michael Walters (1990, 1992, 1993a, 1993b, 1993c, 1994a, 1994b, 1994c, 1994d, 1994e, 1994f), we have called this underlying characteristic, *Sensibility*. Although the research on human abilities and skills helps us to understand various characteristics of gifted children, the research literature on Sensibility needs to be developed and expanded to gain a better understanding of this characteristic. Six years ago, I published a giftedness assessment scale that focused on Sensibility. My primary interest in developing this scale was to stir educators' interest in this concept, and to improve their understanding of how to measure Sensibility in gifted children and adolescents. Recently, I published a revised edition of this scale (Fisher, 1994b).

This instrument is particularly suitable for assessing young gifted children because it provides a framework for observing them in real-life settings such as the classroom, the home, and play. More important, it can be combined with Multiple Intelligences theory to produce a comprehensive method for determining giftedness across several domains of intelligence. *The Fisher Comprehensive Assessment of Giftedness Scale* (1994b) is based on the idea that children exhibit various behaviors and characteristics indicative of giftedness in *many different settings*. Standardized tests include a limited number of areas for identifying gifted children. The child's behavior and home provide even greater opportunities for demonstrating and measuring giftedness. Standardized tests have a role in identifying gifted children. However, I want psychologists and educators to achieve a balance between using these tests and more nontraditional measures of ability such as observation scales and portfolios. To produce a more comprehensive picture of gifted children's strengths and weaknesses, I recommend that a Sensibility instrument be used together with standardized tests.

The *Fisher Comprehensive Assessment of Giftedness Scale* (1994b) emphasizes the study of children's Sensibility levels. These levels are directly related to the unique behaviors and characteristics of giftedness. Some examples of high Sensibility levels are: (a) a young child who works enthusiastically and successfully on art projects for long periods of time; (b) a kindergartner's excitement about visiting a local museum; (c) a first-grade minority child's "explosions" of creativity in music, drama, and poetry; and (d) a preschool child's strong and continuing interest in classifying and learning about pets, insects, cars, and words.

Sensibility should not be viewed as just high motivation and interest. Walters has provided excellent descriptions of Sensibility in his essays on literature in the *Gifted Education Press Quarterly* and *Gifted Education News-Page*. Some examples of these articles that help to define Sensibility are:

- Walters' movie reviews of *The Lion King, The Secret Garden,* and *The Three Musketeers* (1993a, 1994d, 1994f).
- His discussions of the sensibility of great writers such as George Eliot (1992), Sir Arthur Conan Doyle (1994e) and Ray Bradbury (1994c).
- His detailed essays on Agatha Christie (1993b), Willa Cather (1993c), Mary Shelley (1994b), and C.S. Lewis (1994a).

Walters (1990) has also written a book on one of the greatest exemplars of high Sensibility levels in the history of Western civilization, William Shakespeare. The title of this book, *Teaching Shakespeare to Gifted Students, Grades Six Through Twelve: An Examination of the Sensibility of Genius* shows Walters' concern for studying this domain of giftedness. In his chapter entitled "Shakespeare and the Sensibility of Gifted Students," he said:

Sensibility represents a heightened awareness of the environment, of people and of the products of human thought (e.g., a work of art or literature, a scientific research study). It involves a unique way of perceiving the world as demonstrated by the works of great authors, musicians, and scientists. Some examples of great writers with high levels of Sensibility are Shakespeare, Dickens, Jane Austen, Mark Twain, Willa Cather, and modern authors such as Saul Bellow, Annie Dillard, and John Updike. Since the attributes of Sensibility are closely related to personal productivity, it is a less ambiguous and elitist concept than IQ, ability and achievement. The Sensibility of a great writer, scientist, inventor, politician or statesman is rigorously expressed in his work and accomplishments. In like manner, the sensibility of a gifted child is shown in his or her behavior and accomplishments in the school and home. (pp. 32-33).

Walters demonstrates that Sensibility goes far beyond high motivation and interest to the crux of identifying gifted children—their observable behavior while solving problems in the classroom and home.

My scale for assessing the Sensibility of gifted children is a holistic (Gestalt) concept determined by studying the child in four primary areas—*applied motivation, interest, behavior,* and *creative output.* The term creative output refers to actual products such as stories, poems, musical performance and creation, artistic designs, and dramatic performance. To be identified as gifted on this assessment scale, the child must demonstrate high levels of applied motivation and interest, display exceptional behaviors, and show creative work in such areas as the humanities, art, and science. The instrument includes items that assess these four areas of Sensibility.

- *Accelerated-Precocious Early Development*—Ratings of motor, language, reading, thinking, and artistic/musical abilities are included in this section. To obtain this information it may be necessary to interview parents or to send them a list of questions related to these assessment items.
- *Applied Motivation, Interest, Behavior, and Creative Output in the School and Home*—Includes classroom and outside-of-school behaviors that indicate giftedness. Different areas such as independent learning, self-motivation, inventiveness, task involvement, and reasoning-logical thinking are assessed in this section. This information should be reported by teachers who have known the student for at least one semester. Preferably, at least two teachers who are familiar with the student should complete this part of the instrument.
- *Aesthetic Perceptions and Interests*—The items in this section cover such areas as specific indicators of Sensibility, affinity for discussing ideas, and interest in higher level thinking. They represent the core of the gifted student's mind, particularly

the characteristic of Sensibility. It is possible that the gifted student may not clearly show many of these characteristics until adolescence. However, certain highly gifted youngsters may demonstrate them in elementary school.

Table 4.1 shows the specific behaviors and characteristics assessed in each section of the assessment scale.

USING THE GIFTEDNESS ASSESSMENT SCALE TOGETHER WITH MULTIPLE INTELLIGENCES THEORY

By combining these procedures for assessing young children's Sensibility with Multiple Intelligences, early childhood educators will have a comprehensive tool for identifying young gifted children. Each domain of intelligence should be carefully searched with my Sensibility scale to determine a child's potential giftedness. By perceiving human abilities along two dimensions—Multiple Intelligences and Sensibility—educators will become more aware of the different facets of giftedness, like the facets of a diamond of rare quality. Both teachers and parents will be better able to identify flashes of excellence and outstanding ability as indicating giftedness by using this combined approach.

In the domains of Linguistic and Logical-Mathematical Intelligence, we should determine Sensibility by observing children's speech/language development, early reading, and their ability to express ideas and events in logical sequences. We should also determine whether they engage in the following behaviors and show the following characteristics: independent learning, self-motivation, high levels of concentration, rapid learning rates, questioning attitude toward learning, and creative/imaginative responses. In addition, about 20 other areas of behavior should be studied to identify children with high Linguistic and Logical-Mathematical Abilities.

The third domain of Multiple Intelligences, Musical abilities, involves applying the above categories in relation to musical interests, performance, and composition. The domains of Spatial and Bodily-Kinesthetic intelligence also have strong Sensibility components that should be assessed by studying the production of outstanding creative products, curiosity about analyzing new ideas and products, the ability to solve difficult puzzles, mechanical skills, craftsmanship, and perceptual-motor organization.

The two remaining domains of Multiple Intelligences, the Interpersonal and Intrapersonal domains, have strong Sensibility components concerned with the "Aesthetic Perceptions and Interests" section of the *Fisher Comprehensive Assessment of Giftedness Scale* (1994b). These domains need to be based on observations of the

Table 4.1. Fisher Comprehensive Assessment of Giftedness Scale© (1994)—Areas of Assessment.

Accelerated-Precocious Development	Applied Motivation, Interest, Behavior, & Creative Output	Aesthetic Perception and Interests
Walking/Motor	Independent Learning	Sensibility
Speaking/Language	Self-Motivation/Dedicated	Interdisciplinary Attitude
Follows Detailed Directions	Time-On-Task/Concentration	Personal-Emotional Learning
Early Reading	Rapid Rate of Learning	Self-Understanding
Clear Thinking/Reasoning	Questioning Attitude	Ethical Awareness & Analysis
Artistic/Musical Abilities	Creativity/Imagination/Inventiveness	Learns Both Content & Process
	Outstanding Creative Products	Likes to Discuss Ideas & Issues
	Logical Thinking/Reasoning	Prefers Higher Level Thinking
	Memory for Detailed Ideas & Events	Seeks Stimulating Lessons,
	Actively Plans Future Activities	Experiences & Interactions
	Leadership Skills	Literary Interests
	High Academic Achievement	Science/Mathematical Interests
	Grade Acceleration	Artistic/Musical Interests
	Advanced Verbal Abilities	Identifies Uniqueness of Literary,
	Curiosity/Inquisitiveness	Artistic, & Musical Works
	Solver of Puzzles and Games	Literary Applications
	High Mechanical/Technical Skills	Science/Math. Applications
	Craftsmanship	Artistic/Musical Applications
	Perceptual-Motor Organization	
	Accumulator of Objects & Information	
	Organizer of Information	
	High Energy Level	
	Easily "Shifts Gears" Between Tasks	
	Works Effectively in Ambiguous Situations	

child's personal-emotional involvement in learning, self-understanding, and ethical awareness.

CONCLUSIONS

Many preschool, kindergarten, and primary-level children have, unfortunately, been denied admission to gifted programs not because they lack high abilities, but because the instruments used to assess these abilities are inadequate. Nothing short of a major revolution in attitudes and thinking about the assessment of young children will produce more effective identification procedures and stronger gifted programs in our nation's schools. To expedite this revolution, the gifted field needs to: (a) have systematic research programs on the development and application of Sensibility in young children; (b) train teachers in how to recognize and measure the Sensibility levels of these children; and (c) thoroughly explore the relationship between Sensibility and Multiple Intelligences.

REFERENCES

Fisher, M.D. (1988). *Fisher Comprehensive Assessment of Giftedness Scale.* Manassas,VA: Gifted Education Press.

Fisher, M.D. (1989, March/April). The future of the gifted in the year 2000. *Gifted Child Today,* 10-11.

Fisher, M.D. (1992). Early childhood education for the gifted: The need for intense study and observation. *Illinois Council for the Gifted Journal, 11,* 6-9.

Fisher, M.D. (Ed.). (1994a). *Book and curriculum reviews from Gifted Education News-Page: An information resource for teachers, parents and gifted students.* Manassas, VA: Gifted Education Press.

Fisher, M.D. (1994b) *Fisher comprehensive assessment of giftedness scale: What to look for when identifying gifted students.* Manassas, VA: Gifted Education Press.

Gardner, H. (1983). *Frames of mind: The theory of multiple intelligences.* New York: Basic Books.

Gardner, H. (1993a). *Creating minds: An anatomy of creativity seen through the lives of Freud, Einstein, Picasso, Stravinsky, Ailed, Graham, and Gandhi.* New York: Basic Books.

Gardner, H. (1993b). *Multiple intelligences: The theory in practice.* New York: Basic Books.

Lazear, D. (1991a). *Seven ways of knowing: teaching for multiple intelligences.* Palatine, IL: IRI/Skylight Publishing.

Lazear, D. (1991b). *Seven ways of teaching: The artistry of teaching with multiple intelligences.* Palatine, IL: IRI/Skylight Publishing.

Lazear, D. (1994). *Multiple intelligences approach to assessment: Solving the assessment conundrum.* Tucson, AZ: Zephyr Press.

Spearman, C. (1904). "General intelligence" objectively determined and measured. *American Journal of Psychology, 15,* 201-293.

Spearman, C. (1927). *The abilities of man.* New York: Macmillan.

Stanford-Binet Intelligence Scale. (1986). Chicago: The Riverside Publishing Co.

Walters, M.E. (1990). *Teaching Shakespeare to gifted students, grades six through twelve: An examination of the sensibility of genius.* Manassas, VA: Gifted Education Press.

Walters, M.E. (1992). A study in the humanities: Tribute to George Eliot. *Gifted Education News-Page, 1*(5), 2.

Walters, M.E. (1993a). The Secret Garden: The secret for giftedness. *Gifted Education News-Page, 3*(1), 2.

Walters, M.E. (1993b). The work of Agatha Christie: An excursion into giftedness and mystery writing. *Gifted Education Press Quarterly, 7*(2), 12.

Walters, M.E. (1993c). Willa Cather (1873-1947): The "doer" and gifted women. *Gifted Education Press Quarterly, 7*(4), 11.

Walters, M.E. (1994a). C.S. Lewis (1898-1963): A study in gifted sensibility. *Gifted Education Press Quarterly, 8*(3), 11-12.

Walters, M.E. (1994b). Mary Shelley (1797-1851): The joys of encountering a great woman novelist. *Gifted Education Press Quarterly, 8*(2), 11-12.

Walters, M.E. (1994c). Ray Bradbury (1920-): Mentoring and sensibility. *Gifted Education News-Page, 3*(5), 2.

Walters, M.E. (1994d). Synergy and the gifted: The Lion King (Walt Disney Pictures, 1994). *Gifted Education News-Page, 3*(6), 2.

Walters, M.E. (1994e). The eternal appeal of Sherlock Holmes to the gifted sensibility. *Gifted Education News-Page, 3*(4), 2.

Walters, M.E. (1994f). The Three Musketeers (1993): Movie review. *Gifted Education News-Page, 3*(3), 2.

Wechsler, D. (1939). *The measurement of adult intelligence.* Baltimore: Williams & Wilkins.

Wechsler, D. (1958). *The measurement and appraisal of adult intelligence* (4th ed.). Baltimore: Williams & Wilkins.

Wechsler Intelligence Scale for Children. (1991). San Antonio, TX: The Psychological Corporation.

Wechsler Preschool and Primary Scale of Intelligence. (1989). San Antonio, TX: The Psychological Corporation.

5

Identification and Nurturing of Precocious Children in Early Childhood

John F. Feldhusen
Hazel J. Feldhusen

Sally began to recognize words on billboards and in newspaper ads around age 3. She was also an avid viewer of *Sesame Street* and would come running to the TV set when she heard its familiar theme. She verbalized frequently during the show when questions were asked and laughed loudly at its humor. By age 4 she could count to 20 and even seemed to understand simple addition of the smaller one-digit numbers.

Robert loved to have his mother or father read to him. From age 2 he would sit entranced while his father read stories about animals to him. He loved to hear the same stories over and over and to be quizzed about what would happen next in the story before it was read to him. When his mother improvised changes in stories while she was reading to him, he would react immediately by pointing out her errors. At age 3-1/2 he began to point to words while his parents were reading and say the words as his parents read them.

Jim loves to build and to explore. At age 4 he spent hours building sand structures at the beach. He loved all kinds of assembly toys and would ask questions after question about mechanical things like clocks, VCRs, and microwaves. He also showed advanced ability to draw and color.

Annie loves music and dancing, shows great enthusiasm for classic art when her parents take her to an art museum, and is greatly interested in picture books. She has enjoyed listening to stories on tape and following in a book since age 3-1/2. She is also remarkably empathic, able to relate socially to adults and children very effectively, and loves to draw. Her vocabulary is advanced, and her speech patterns are articulate. She loves to talk with adults who show an interest in her.

These are all precocious children who are exhibiting signs of gifted potential at or just before the time of entering school. All four of the cases described have parents who are responding adaptively to their children's precocity. But once in school, many of these gifted children will be pressured to normalcy or averageness. They will be discouraged from pursuing their bookish or number interests and often will have little time for reflective exploration of devices, pictures, or other phenomena in the classroom. Some of their parents will be counseled to "let them be children" and to avoid any academic activities at home such as reading and discussing books or exploring numbers and science topics. A not-very-subtle message may emerge: reading, exploration, questioning, examining, and number activity are not desirable activities for a young child. Many potentially talented children and their parents will succumb to the pressures from school personnel, counselors, and friends to be normal, to be like everybody else; and the talents will be lost.

The term and concept *gifted* has been used for many years to refer to and label children of high general intellectual ability. However, problems with the conception and labeling of children as gifted have been pointed out by Feldhusen, Asher, and Hoover (1984), and others. Recently, a committee was appointed by the U.S. Office of Education (1993) to study the field of gifted education and establish direction for the future. The committee report calls for an end to use of the term and concept "gifted": "The term 'gifted' connotes a mature power rather than a developing ability and, therefore, is antithetic to recent research findings about children." It goes on to delineate the terms and concepts *talent* and *talent development* as:

Children and youth with outstanding talent perform or show the potential for performing at remarkably high levels of accomplishment when compared with others of their age, experience, or environment.

These children and youth exhibit high performance capability in intellectual, creative, and/or artistic areas, possess an unusual leadership capacity, or excel in specific academic fields. They require services or activities not ordinarily provided by the schools.

Outstanding talents are present in children and youth from all cultural groups, across all economic strata, and in all areas of human endeavor. (p. 26)

Clearly the report calls for a new conception of giftedness and a focus on specific talent recognition as well as talent development.

Talent is not an inexorable phenomenon. It must be nurtured. Gifted children must be allowed to "fly" when they are ready, not forced to crawl along at a snail's pace. Intellectual, creative, and artistic abilities emerge through the experience of challenge, trying to understand and learn how to manipulate things in the world around one. The talented child creates meaning or understanding of clocks, and chairs, and dolls, and books, and people through active interaction with them. Denied those opportunities to experience words, numbers, and people, the child gets a message that says other things like watching TV, taking turns at the swing, always following teacher directions, or walking quietly through the halls are the highest values in our lives.

Elkind (1987) stated the case well when he said:

What intellectually gifted children need most, then, is not early formal instruction but rather a prolongation of opportunities to explore and investigate on their own. The task of the teacher of such children is not to instruct in the conventional sense but to do what the early-childhood educator does, only at a higher level. Much more critical than direct instruction for the realization of their intellectual potential is the providing of the right science material, the right literature, the right math materials, along with thoughtful guidance on what directions to take. (p. 154)

Early admission of precocious children and grade advancement of talented children in school are two of the most successful methods currently available to help them experience academic and social challenges which are more appropriate to their advanced levels of maturity (Feldhusen, 1992). Neither method really involves pushing the child forward; rather, they are methods of placement to fit a child's needs. Reviews of several decades of research on early school admission and grade advancement (Feldhusen, Proctor, & Black, 1986; Proctor, Black & Feldhusen, 1986; Proctor, Feldhusen, & Black, 1988) clearly support these methods. These same authors have also developed guidelines for schools to use in making decisions about early admission and grade advancement—nomination of a child for grade advancement might come from a teacher or parent. A proper response to the nomination would be to consider the following steps or recommendations:

1. There should be a psychological assessment of the child's intelligence, basic skills levels, and personal-social adjustment by a counselor or school psychologist.

2. The IQ should be at least 130, the basic skills two years or more beyond grade placement or beyond the first grade level, and the child should be free of serious personal-social adjustment problems.

3. There should be a conference with the parents and child, preferably conducted by the counselor or psychologist, to determine that the child does not feel unduly pressured by the parents to enter early or be grade advanced.

4. There should be a meeting of the parents and the current teacher (for a child already in school) with the teacher who would receive the accelerated child to determine if the receiving teacher has positive attitudes toward the acceleration and the child, and will endeavor to help the child adjust to the new situation. If the receiving teacher is hostile or pessimistic another receiving teacher should be located or the move should *not* be made.

5. It is desirable to carry out grade advancement midyear. The receiving teacher and the teacher the child is leaving can then easily confer about how best to help the child make a smooth transition. They should especially review the child's basic skills to make sure that the receiving teacher will be aware of any special needs and weaknesses.

6. Public school teachers are often unduly pessimistic about children's social maturity. For a gifted child, they might often confuse the child's dissatisfaction with inappropriate instruction and related misbehavior with immaturity. Judgments about a gifted child's maturity should therefore include input from parents and the counselor or psychologist.

7. In making the decision to admit a child early or grade advance a child there should be as much consideration of the dangers of *not* accelerating the child as there is of advancing him or her. Leaving the child to be admitted later or failure to grade advance him or her may indeed result in more serious problems of demotivation, apathy and maladjustment than accelerating.

8. All cases of early admission and grade advancement should be arranged on a trial basis. Tell the child that the placement will be tried, and that if it does not go well he or she can return to the original grade or dropout from kindergarten or first grade if the case is early admission.

9. Do not build up excessive expectations from the early admission or grade advancement. Some children are so precocious or advanced in their basic and thinking skills that 1 year

of advancement may still leave them bored in school. For a very few gifted children a second advancement should be considered.

10. Some children's basic skills levels vary considerably. That is, they may be very far advanced in mathematics abilities but just moderately above average in language arts or reading. For such children it may be best to keep them in grade but allow them to work with a higher grade for the subject in which they are extremely precocious.

Parents and teachers often express concern about possible social problems if precocious children are admitted early or grade advanced. The research indicates that there should be equal concern with the dangers in not admitting a child early or not advancing him or her in grade.

IDENTIFICATION

Identification of talented children in early childhood is crucial. Stanley (1988) argues that "one cannot stress enough the extreme importance of early identification of intellectually talented boys and girls and the *academic* facilitation of those children from the point of identification all the way through their education to the highest degree attained" (p. ix-x). Feldhusen and Kolloff (1979a) and Koopmans-Dayton and Feldhusen (1987) discussed the problems of early identification of talented children and offered some additional guidelines for parents and school personnel. Shwedel and Stoneburner (1983) also offered good guidelines and reviews of major instruments for the assessment of giftedness and talent in early childhood. Generally, our own experience favors individual assessment of intelligence with the Stanford-Binet Intelligence Scale, Form L-M and the use of checklists and rating scales completed by parents and teachers. Alternatively, the Slossen Intelligence Test can be used for individual assessment. Achievement in basic skill areas can best be assessed with the *Peabody Individual Achievement Test* or the *Wide Range Achievement Test*. Because all assessment in early childhood is less reliable than later assessments, somewhat greater generosity error in interpreting scores is desirable.

Thinking skills can be measured with tests such as the *Wallach and Kogan Creativity Battery*, Torrance's *Thinking Creatively in Action and Movement*, or the *Circus* battery of tests developed by Ward. Again, individual or very small group testing is desirable.

Another good approach to identification of talents at the preschool level and in early childhood is with rating scales and observation of children's behavior. A number of quite specific behavior patterns appear early in the lives of talented children (Karnes & Taylor, 1978; Renzulli, Reis, & Smith, 1981). These scales are useful in alerting parents and teachers to the signs of potential talent, but they are of limited value in making definitive diagnoses for placement, early admission, or admission to a special program. Rarely are there good data on the reliability and validity of the instruments.

PROGRAM SERVICES

Ehrlich (1982), Feldhusen and Kolloff (1979a), Roedell, Jackson, and Robinson (1980), Karnes (1983), and Koopmans-Dayton and Feldhusen (1987) offered abundant suggestions for developing programs, teaching methods, and curriculum resources for young talented children. These suggestions include:

1. Relate teaching methods and curriculum to the characteristics of talented children. If they are verbally talented stress verbal activities such as discussion of stories and authors, telling about books, or writing stories; if they are mathematically talented offer experiences with numbers.
2. Involve the children in many thinking activities, especially creative thinking.
3. Help the children plan and carry out individual and small group projects and investigations.
4. Provide a wide variety of materials and things to explore, examine, or investigate.
5. Encourage the children to verbalize, to ask questions, to discuss activities, to be actively involved in the learning process.
6. Help children pursue their own interests and talents.
7. Listen carefully to the children and teach them to be attentive to one another.
8. Provide a wide variety of experiences and exposure to people in diverse higher level occupations.

Services for talented children in the primary grades can best be provided in special pullout classes of at least 1 day per week or in full-time classes in which a group of academically talented children is organized to meet 5 days a week (Feldhusen & Treffinger, 1985). In both arrangements a specially trained teacher is needed to develop and deliver an appropriate curriculum and to use suitable teaching methods. Feldhusen (1985) delineated the characteristics and competencies of teachers of talented youth and Feldhusen and Hansen (1987) described a special program for training teachers to work with gifted children. They also presented results of an evaluation of the program. Generally, teachers of these children must be project or activity oriented; very flexible in adapting instruction to fit individual children's characteristics; able to deal well with the world of ideas while interacting with the children; able to engage them in more complex and advanced levels of thinking; and full of enthusiasm for thinking, exploring, investigating, questioning, and learning.

INSTRUCTIONAL MATERIALS

Teaching talented children at the preschool and early childhood levels can be facilitated with good instructional materials. Although there is much pessimism on the part of parents and good teachers about ditto sheets and drill-practice activities of a repetitive nature, there can be a valuable role for good materials in helping teachers structure and individualize projects and problem-solving activities. Ideally they can learn new skills and subject matter while being engaged in generative learning activities that require planning, organizing, classifying, analyzing, conceptualizing, judging, and the whole range of thinking skills.

One excellent set of material is Science Research Associates' *Junior Thinklab* (Churchill, Golick, & Golick, 1979). Although designed for children in grades one, two, and three, talented children at the preschool and kindergarten levels can use this program. It is designed to develop children's thinking skills through activities involving five cognitive strategies: ordering, classifying, perception and space relations, reasoning and deducing, and divergent thinking. *Thinklab* is a set of graded problems that are presented on cards. All of the activities require some precocity in reading or mathematics for preschool children.

Another excellent resource is *Resources for Creative Teaching in Early Childhood Education* by Flemming and Hamilton (1977). This is a large compilation of project activities focusing on self-concept development, family activities, seasons, animals, transportation, and the world we live in, as well as on science, mathematics, language, and reading readiness. The authors stress careful curriculum planning for a balanced set of activities, extensive use of learning centers in the classroom, frequent group activities, learning games, outdoor activities, field trips and classroom visitor, and dramatic activities.

The National/State Leadership Training Institute on the Gifted and Talented published another another excellent resource, *Educating The Preschool/Primary Gifted and Talented* (1980). It is a collection of chapters by a variety of specialists in preschool gifted education. Four of the chapters focus on program and curriculum development, four on parents' roles, and six present descriptions of exemplary program models. Notable among the models is the highly academic program at the University of Washington, the Astor program in New York City, and the rural preschool gifted program at Coeur d'Alene, Idaho. These program models range from a strong enrichment and creativity orientation to essential academic emphases.

The Preschool Packrat by Snowball and Armstrong (1982) is a collection of excellent enrichment activities focusing on (a) discovering science, (b) creative art, (c) dramatic play, (d) enjoying music, (e) movement, (f) carpentry, and (g) cooking. The activities are all open-ended and thus adaptable to children's differing levels of precocity or giftedness. Teachers are urged to stress processes rather than products and to get the children to reflect on their experiences while doing the activities.

Karnes (1983) edited another excellent collection of articles on young talented children under the title *The Underserved: Our Young Gifted Children*. There are nine rich chapters, several of which focus on programs and curriculum development. Especially useful to teachers are the chapters on differentiating the curriculum, affective development, creativity and play, and the teacher's role.

Karnes (1986) has long been a pioneer in the area of teaching preschool gifted children and has published *Primary Thinking Skills*, a series of four books of teaching materials designed to promote critical thinking and creativity. The activities stress investigations, brainstorming, creative problem solving, and hypothesis formulation. There is also a great deal of stress on verbalizing cognitive activities and sharing ideas.

Excellent materials for early childhood talent education are also available from a number of other companies, notably Good Apple, Learning Works, and Sunburst. Teachers of preschool gifted children now have a wide variety of instructional resources to facilitate curriculum development and teaching.

Material resources for teaching young talented children should be organized carefully through good curricular design. This entails long-range planning of scope and sequence, stating goals and objectives, designing units of instruction, and developing daily lesson plans. Parke and Ness (1988) also suggested that there are four basic levels which should guide curriculum development for early childhood education of talented children:

1. They have special needs which must be addressed—for example, their precocity in reading;
2. Their childish interests should also guide curriculum development;
3. The curriculum should offer opportunities for play and exploration; and
4. They should be involved in the curriculum decision-making process.

All of these levels grow out of the precocity of talented youth in early childhood. They master earlier and faster and are ready for learning in greater depth.

CONCLUSIONS

Young talented children are easy to identify because they exhibit their precocity more openly than children do when they are older. Later we must depend very much on tests and rating scales. In contrast, in early childhood, talent shows in the form of overt behavior: uses words like "fatigued" or "antagonism" when other children do not yet know their meaning; remembers huge amounts of information; spends a lot of time drawing; loves to listen to stories; knows numbers and the alphabet way ahead of schedule; asks many questions; plays well with somewhat older children; or loves to explore or examine things. When these behaviors are observed by parent or teacher, the child can be referred for further testing.

Program services, including early admission, grade advancement, pullout classes, or full-time placement in a special class, can also be thought of as alternatives to meet the child's needs. Above all these children need specially trained teachers who can adapt teaching methods and curricula to fit their special characteristics.

Major tasks for school and home are to help sustain and augment talented children's motivation, desire to learn, and enthusiasm to learn about the world around them. Another major task that begins in early childhood is providing experiences which help these children understand their own talents and abilities and focus on educational and occupational goals at levels appropriate to their giftedness (Feldhusen & Kolloff, 1979b). Deciding on a career is a process that begins early and culminates typically in adolescence for gifted children.

Talented children are a true joy in the early childhood period for parents and teachers who are flexible and appreciative of their abilities. Ideally, these children are nurtured in homes and schools that accept their diversity from the norm and which encourage them to develop their own individual talents and interests to the fullest extent possible.

REFERENCES

Churchill, J., Golick, J., & Golick, M. (1979). *Junior thinklab*. Chicago: Science Research Associates.

Elkind, D. (1987). *Miseducation, preschoolers at risk*. New York: Knopf.

Ehrlich, V. (1982). *Gifted children: A guide for parents and teachers*. Englewood Cliffs, NJ: Prentice-Hall.

Feldhusen, J.F. (1985). The teacher of gifted students. *Gifted Education International, 3,* 87-93.

Feldhusen, J.F. (1992). Early admission and grade advancement. *Gifted Child Today, 15*(2), 45-49.

Feldhusen, J.F., Asher, J.W., Hoover, S.M. (1984). Problems in the identification of giftedness, talent or ability. *Gifted Child Quarterly, 28*(4), 149-151.

Feldhusen, J.F., & Hansen, J.B. (1987). Teachers of the gifted: Preparation and supervision. *Gifted International, 4*(1), 82-94.

Feldhusen, J.F., & Kolloff, M.B. (1979a). Giftedness: A mixed blessing for the preschool child. In S. Long & B. Batchelor (Eds.), *Helping children cope with change* (pp. 2-9). Terre Haute: Indiana Association for The Education of Young Children.

Feldhusen, J.F., & Kolloff, M.B. (1979b). An approach to career education for the gifted. *Roeper Review, 2,* 13-17.

Feldhusen, J.F., Proctor, T.B., & Black, N.N. (1986). Guidelines for grade advancement of precocious children. *Roeper Review, 9,* 25-27.

Feldhusen, J.F., & Treffinger, D.J. (1985). *Creative thinking and problem solving in gifted education.* Dubuque: Kendall-Hunt.

Flemming, B.M., & Hamilton, D.S. (1977). *Resources for creative teaching in early childhood education.* New York: Harcourt Brace Jovanovich.

Karnes, M.B. (Ed.). (1983). *The underserved: Our young gifted children.* Washington, DC: Council for Exceptional Children.

Karnes, M.B. (1986). *Primary thinking skills-A1.* Pacific Grove, CA: Midwest Publications.

Koopmans-Dayton, J.D., & Feldhusen, J.F. (1987). Gifted preschoolers. *Gifted Child Today, 10*(6), 2-7.

National/State Leadership Training Institute on the Gifted and Talented (1980). *Educating the preschool/primary gifted and talented.* Ventura, CA: Ventura County Superintendent of Schools.

Parke, B.N., & Ness, P.S. (1988). Curricular decision making, the education of young gifted children. *Gifted Child Quarterly, 32*(1), 196-199.

Proctor, T.B., Black, K.N., & Feldhusen, J.F. (1986). Early admission of selected children to elementary school: A review of the literature. *Journal of Educational Research, 80*(2), 70-76.

Proctor, T.B., Feldhusen, J.F., & Black, K.N. (1988). Guidelines for early admission to elementary school. *Psychology in the Schools, 25,* 41-43.

Roedell, W.C., Jackson, N.E., Robinson, H.B. (1980). *Gifted young children.* New York: Teacher's College Press.

Shwedel, A.M., & Stoneburner, R. (1983). Identification. In M.B. Karnes (Ed.), *The underserved: Our young gifted children* (pp. 17-39). Washington, DC: Council for Exceptional Children.

Snowball, M., & Armstrong, B. (1982). *Preschool packrat.* Santa Barbara, CA: Learning Works.

Stanley, J.C. (1988). Foreword. In D.M. Fetterman (Ed.), *Excellence and equality* (p. ix-xi). Albany: State University of New York Press.

U.S. Office of Education. (1993). *National excellence: A case for developing America's talent.* Washington, DC: U.S. Government Printing Office.

6

The Importance of Early Identification of Gifted Children and Appropriate Educational Intervention

Dorothy A. Sisk

A mind is a terrible thing to waste.
—Langston Hughes

Professionals, parents, and the general public need to be convinced that early programming for gifted children is high priority. Too often schools do not identify gifted children early, and, consequently many gifted children do not realize their potential. Sadly, many of these lost gifted children come from economically disadvantaged families. Head Start and Chapter I funds provide low-income children with opportunities to catch up with their peers from more economically favored homes; however, these programs have not placed a premium on identifying and supporting young, gifted, low-income children. This chapter examines the issues involved in identifying young gifted children and providing appropriate educational services to economically disadvantaged gifted children. It offers suggestions for ways that parents can cope with their young gifted children and considers seven specific socializing goals.

IDENTIFICATION OF YOUNG GIFTED CHILDREN

In discussing early identification of young gifted children, one aspect to consider is the importance of the on going nature of the identification process. Talents in young children may not manifest themselves if they are not continually nurtured. We know that all children need encouragement for their talents to emerge (Caplan & Caplan, 1983). In economically disadvantaged homes, young gifted children may receive few opportunities from their parents or caregivers to develop their talents, in comparison to young gifted children from middle or upper socioeconomic levels who are provided ample opportunities to develop their talents through parental interaction, toys, and outings. As a result, gifted children from economically disadvantaged homes may not demonstrate their giftedness as well as peers from more economically advantaged homes. Consequently, performance on standardized tests should be less important in the identification process of gifts than the professional opinions of veteran teachers and parents of young, potentially gifted, economically disadvantaged children.

The normative characteristics of young gifted children documented in the literature usually represent the traditional positive characteristics of giftedness that parents and teachers note in middle-class youngsters. They learn more quickly, are healthy and large for their age, are emotionally better adjusted and socially more mature, have longer attention spans, persist in tasks longer, are happier, and have a keen sense of humor. However, parents and educators know that some characteristics of gifted children are not always positive: They enjoy independence and resist rigid rules and requirements that force them to conform (Munger, 1990; Schetky, 1981). Also, many young gifted children have high social values and can be quite competitive.

IMPORTANCE OF PARENTS IN DEVELOPING AND NURTURING TALENTS

An early study documenting the impact of family support on a child's development is reported by Schaefer (1975). She found that parents have the greatest influence on a child's use of individual potential. Moss and Kagan (1958), Caplan and Caplan (1983), and Sisk (1994) reported that when parents let their children know they value achievement and verbal expression, the children develop into high achievers and are more verbally fluent. Children act out the scripts that parents provide.

The influence of high standards of excellence has been studied by many researchers (Hess, Block, Colstello, Knowls, & Largen, 1971; Rau, Mlodnosky, & Anastasiow, 1964; Rosen & D'Androde, 1959) who indicated as a general rule that children follow the expectations set by their parents. Maternal warmth, high emotional involvement, and high parental interest were found to have a positive relationship with achievement. Early encouragement of independent thought and action was found to be highly related to success in school. Parents' ability to establish limits for behavior has also been identified as an essential factor in school achievement (Samalin, 1987). Karnes, Shwedel, Linnemeyer, and Koenig (1982) reported that parents who explain their requests, consult with their children, and give reasons for discipline have higher achievers.

In general, parents' attitudes, values, and expectations of their young children do influence the child's behavior and aspirations. Parental acceptance of children appears to have a definite positive effect on their self-concept. When young children perceive that their parents have high positive regard for them, they are more likely to feel good about themselves and do better in school.

GUIDING PRINCIPLES FOR PROGRAM DEVELOPMENT FOR EARLY INTERVENTION

1. *The uniqueness of each gifted child is to be recognized and acknowledged.* In any given group of young gifted children, the individual talents will vary considerably. One child may demonstrate advanced reading skills and a well developed vocabulary, while another child may possess advanced motor skills or well-developed social skills. Still another child may have unusual talent in music, or be particularly adept at observing and asking questions. Some young gifted children demonstrate well-developed computational skills, whereas others may have advanced fine motor skills. Each individual gifted child's strengths and weaknesses need to be recognized and appropriate educational interventions need to be planned and developed to address the child's needs.

2. *The gifted child's self concept is to be developed for it is a major determinant of success in school.* Gifted children may be very critical of themselves as learners and sometimes they reflect a poor self-concept. To help young gifted children develop positive self-concepts, feedback from parents and teachers needs to demonstrate unconditional acceptance and regard. Young gifted children may be aware of the discrepancy between their intellectual functioning and motor development. When gifted children attempt to accomplish motor tasks, such as walking a balance beam, they may become quite frustrated. This frustration can lead to a poor perception of self. Another example of the developmental discrepancies which a young gifted child may experience is that the child may be quite capable of verbal-

izing a story with great detail and accuracy and yet be totally unable to write the same story because of inadequate small motor development. When gifted children can't capture their ideas on paper, they need assurance that it is acceptable to have an older child or an adult help write the story. Programs for young gifted children need to take into consideration "the whole child" and to plan specific ways to address the young gifted child's self-critical nature.

3. *Emphasis on the whole child is to be stressed.* Provision of opportunities for progress in all facets of the young gifted child's development ensures that the gifted child will not receive exclusive programming in any one area, such as cognitive development, and have another area, such as motor, social, or emotional development, be neglected.

4. *Gifted children have multiple interests and an educational program needs to provide a wide range of materials.* The instructional materials for the typical 4-, 5-, or 6-year-old child may not adequately meet the needs of young gifted children. With their many interests and advanced skills, young gifted children may require a wide age range of advanced materials including manipulatives, as well as the traditional instructional materials normally provided for young children.

5. *Parents of gifted children need to play a central role in their young child's development.* Cox, Daniel, and Boston (1985) reported that the parents of gifted children play an important role in the child's early development and recommended that programs for the gifted assist parents in learning to nurture the needs of the young gifted child. Through cooperative efforts between parents and educators, young gifted children can make progress toward the total development that they are capable of achieving.

Telford and Sawyer (1981) suggested several specific methods to foster achievement and creativity in programs for the gifted. They include:

> *Perpetuate curiosity.* When young children are rewarded for their curiosity, they continue to experiment. On the other hand, if children are punished when they investigate new experiences, they learn to limit their explorations. Children's curiosity, self-esteem, and creativity are positively related and these aspects of the gifted child grow and develop together.
> *Free people from fear of error.* Young gifted children need to learn that people can learn from their mistakes and that adverturesomeness and exploration are important aspects of the learning process.
> *Encourage fantasy as well as reality-oriented cognition.* Young gifted children enjoy relaxed, make-believe explo-

ration followed by critical exploration. As children experience free movement from fantasy to reality, this type of flexible exploration can help to reinforce the difference between the two for young children.

Encourage contact with creative people. Contact with creative people can provide role models for young gifted children to inspire them to develop the traits that they naturally come to admire in these creative adults.

Encourage diversity and individuality. Young gifted children can learn to appreciate differences in others, as their own individual differences are recognized and valued by the significant adults and caregivers in their lives.

Encourage individual initiative. Young gifted children need many opportunities to build individual awareness of their own strengths and weaknesses. They also need encouragement to experiment with the use of these strategies in carrying out simple daily tasks.

EXEMPLARY PROGRAMMING FOR YOUNG GIFTED CHILDREN

Pioneer efforts in program offerings for young gifted children have been reported in the literature. These programs can provide models for other school districts that may want to develop exemplary programs for young gifted children. Notable among these program offerings are the pioneer efforts of Ehrlich, who worked with gifted children aged 4, 5, and 6 in New York City. Ehrlich demonstrated that young gifted children can be identified and grouped together for accelerated learning. Another exemplary program was developed by Harrison in Coeur D'Alene, ID. This program was based on Bloom's Taxonomy, Guilford's (1976) Structure of Intellect (SOI), and Renzulli's Enrichment Model. Karnes et al. (1982) used the open classroom as a model. Karnes' preschoolers from all socioeconomic areas included gifted handicapped and nonhandicapped youngsters. In her project, there was an emphasis on designing independent study and on encouraging the gifted children to move at their own pace. Karnes compared the open classroom and the Guilford SOI model to educate potentially gifted children, aged 3, 4, and 5 from low socioeconomic homes. Karnes et al.'s (1982) research revealed no significant differences between the two approaches on measures of intelligence, creativity, language development, problem solving, or parent reactions. She concluded that both approaches were equally effective (Karnes et al., 1982).

Another example of exemplary programming for young economically disadvantaged gifted children was a project initiated in Palm Beach County, FL. High-potential children from low socioeconomic areas were selected at age 7 to participate in a program designed to develop unique talents. The children were selected primarily by teacher recommendation and the belief that the children possessed untapped talent. The children demonstrated many of the characteristics of gifted children, such as learning quickly, emotional adjustment, social maturity, having longer attention spans, curiosity, and the ability to persist in tasks. In 1982, 14 children were selected as high-potential and two measures were used as pretest performance—the Cognitive Abilities Test (CAT), and the Otis Lennon School Test (OLSAT). The range of CAT scores for the children was 91-122. None of the scores would have qualified the young children for Florida's intellectually gifted program, requiring a score of 130 plus on individually administered intellectual measures. On the OLSAT, the range of scores were 96-127. At the end of the school year, the children were tested by school psychologists using the Wechsler Intelligence Scale for Children (WISC-R). Forty percent of the children qualified for the state of Florida intellectually gifted program.

The Palm Beach project used an eclectic approach focusing on the SOI and an individually developed program based on each child's academic functioning level. Emphasis was placed on language acquisition and building positive self-concepts and independent learners.

The Palm Beach program provided an active classroom environment in which the high potential children were able to pursue many different projects and to use a variety of teacher-constructed manipulative games and activities. Whenever possible, these activities were based on factors of intellectual functioning as identified by Guilford's SOI.

Building on the positive experience of the Palm Beach Project, Sisk (1994) demonstrated that 50.8% of the economically disadvantaged minority children who were identified as having high potential and provided with accelerated enriched educational experiences qualified for their local school district's gifted program. The program, called Project Step-Up (Systematic Training for Educational Programs for Underserved Pupils), included 216 minority economically disadvantaged children, their parents, and teachers in four states: Arizona, Arkansas, Florida, and Texas.

Project Step-Up addressed Frasier's (1989) four barriers to identifying gifted minority students: (a) attitude, (b) access, (c) accommodation, and (d) adaptation. According to Frasier, there is often a negative attitude toward giftedness in minority groups. To change this attitude, Project Step-Up staff met with central administrators, building principals, teachers, and parents to discuss and to clarify the objectives of the project.

Teachers in the 12 original sites of the project were provided a behavioral checklist developed by Sisk (1991) based on research of minority economically disadvantaged children (Barkan & Bernal, 1991; Bernal, 1990; Cummins, 1984; Machado, 1987; Richert, Alvino, &

McDonnel, 1982; Tonemah, 1985; Zappia, 1989). This checklist included selected characteristics from the four ethnic groups of children participating in Project Step-Up: African-American, Hispanic, Asian, and Native American. Children who demonstrated a majority of the characteristics on the checklist were placed in a schoolwide talent pool. The checklist is included in Figure 6.1. Teachers prepared a portfolio of student products and compiled available achievement and ability test scores. Figure 6.2 represents the Child Find Assessment and Selection Process and Procedures used in Project Step-Up.

Traditional tests were supplemented by alternative tests that included the Raven Progressive Matrices, the SOI battery, and selected problem-solving tasks developed by June Maker based on Howard Gardner's Multiple Intelligences (MI) model. All of this information was considered by teachers, principals, gifted and talented supervisors, and Project Step-Up staff. These data became the baseline information for the 18 children selected to participate in the Project Step-Up class.

None of the children selected for Project Step-Up would have been considered for screening or identification for their local school gifted program. The standard achievement scores of the participating students were, for the most part, well below average. However, all of the students who were administered the SOI battery did achieve a level of giftedness in one or more of the processing and diagnostic abilities. According to Meeker (1969), this performance would qualify the students for consideration as potentially gifted students.

PROGRAM VARIABLES

Program variables that were planned and developed for Project Step-Up included:

1. Direct instruction of thinking skills
2. Language arts integrated with arts
3. Emphasis on content and process
4. Visual reinforcement
5. Positive classroom climate
6. Use of positive language
7. Teacher flexibility and creativity
8. Parental involvement
9. Use of recommended Step-Up teacher materials

The curriculum for Project Step-Up concentrated on more complex tasks, on more sophisticated products and performances, and on higher order thinking. The children were exposed to multiple perspectives through a variety of speakers, visitors, and field trips. There was an

Teacher _____ Date _____
School Name _____ Grade _____

PROBLEM SOLVING

Prefers inferential reasoning (Hilliard 1976)

Prefers practical problem solving and interested in cause and effect (Meeker, 1978; Locke, 1979)

Ability to meaningfully manipulate a symbol system held valuable in their culture (Gallagher & Kinney, 1974)

Uses memory as cognitive strength (Meeker, 1978)

Streetwise (Bernal, 1976)

Approximates space, number, and time (Hilliard, 1976)

Enjoyment of and skill in small group cooperative learning and problem solving (Torrance, 1977)

Problem centeredness (Torrance, 1977)

Ability to use stored knowledge to solve problems (Gallagher & Kinney, 1974)

Ability to think logically, given appropriate information (Gallagher & Kinney, 1974)

SOCIAL SENSITIVITY

Wisdom of life experience (Montgomery, 1989)

Keen sense of justice, quickly perceives injustice (Hilliard, 1976)

Awareness and appreciation of people, interpersonal skills (Bernal, 1976; Renzulli, 1973)

Manipulative behavior (Torrance, 1977; Cronbach, 1977)

Willing to help others, enjoys being helpful. (Bernal, 1976)

Sense of the future (Wong & Wong, 1989)

Impatient (Locke, 1979)

Large social orientation (Montgomery, 1989)

Responds to external motivation, wants to please (Baldwin, 1985; Frasier, 1979)

Community-based entrepreneurship (Cronbach, 1977)

COMMUNICATION SKILLS

Articulateness in role playing and storytelling (Torrance, 1977; Darnell, 1979)

Recalls old legends (Maker & Schiever, 1989)

Attitudes unfavorable to participation in discussion groups (Clark, 1989)

Proficient in nonverbal communication (Hilliard, 1976)

Frequently interrupts others when they are talking (Locke, 1979)

Formulates pertinent questions (Chen & Goon, 1978)

Multilingual (Montgomery, 1989)

Rapidly acquires language when given opportunity (Bernal, 1976)

Enthusiasm in class discussions (Chen & Goon, 1978)

Engages adults in lively conversations (Bernal, 1976)

CREATIVE SKILLS

Enjoys creating interesting games, music, art, stories (Shade & New, 1993)

Theatrical, speaks animatedly (Kochman, 1983)

Original ideas in problem solving (Torrance, 1977)

Articulate in roleplaying and storytelling (Torrance, 1977; Darnell, 1979)

Uses language in personal colorful ways (Torrance, 1977)

Ability to reason by analogy (Gallagher & Kinney, 1974)

Intentional and descriptive language (Shade & New, 1993)

Enjoys and needs strong sensory stimulation (Schmeck & Lockhart, 1983)

Expects and appreciates a variety of environmental interactions with constant change of focus and interest (Boykin, 1982)

Prefers graphs, pictures, and videos and enjoys expressing creativity in these media (Shade, 1990)

Figure 6.1. Teacher Awareness Minority Checklist

Teacher _____ Date _____
School Name _____ Grade _____

SENSE OF HUMOR

Likes to be a clown (Sisk, 1987)

Humor rich with symbolism (Horowitz & O'Brien, 1985)

Loud, laughs uproariously, impetuous (Shade & New, 1993)

Makes up own words, plays with language (Torrance, 1977)

Wants and seeks center of attention (Sisk, 1987)

Memorizes long stories and raps with humorous word play (Meeker, 1978)

Enjoys jokes and funny stories (Darnell, 1979)

Picks up on adult humor (Bernal, 1976)

Puts a new twist on humorous stories (Torrance, 1977)

PSYCHOMOTOR

Hand-eye coordination well developed, physical stamina (Horowitz & O'Brien, 1985)

Excels in physical activities, best runner, likes physical competition (Renzulli, 1973; Torrance, 1977)

Enjoyment of and ability in music and rhythm (Torrance, 1977)

Impetuous, jumps out of seat, bumps others (Shade & New, 1993)

Skilled body movements (Horowitz & O'Brien, 1985)

Demonstrates spatial strength, skilled placement of objects in art (balance) (Meeker, 1978)

Reproduces traditional designs or symbols (Maker & Schiever, 1989)

Sensitivity and alertness to movement (Horowitz & O'Brien, 1985)

Responsive to the kinesthetic (Torrance, 1977)

RESPONSIBILITY

Likes being classroom monitor and exhibits leadership (Bernal, 1976)

Willing to set goals and follow through (Chen, 1989)

Accepts responsibility of younger siblings at home (Bernal, 1976; DeLeon, 1983)

Individualistic, likes to work by self (Locke, 1979)

Responds well to doing things on own (Chen, 1989)

Willing to mentor younger children (Bernal, 1976)

Responsibility to the family unity, enjoys being needed (DeLeon, 1983)

Obedience to the head of household (DeLeon, 1983)

Tends to dominate peers or situations (Locke, 1979)

Willing to help others, enjoys responsibility (Bernal, 1976)

Figure 6.1. Teacher Awareness Minority Checklist (cont.)

emphasis on understanding knowledge, retaining knowledge, and, especially, using knowledge. This focus helped to personalize the children's learning as well as provide them with a specific purpose for their learning.

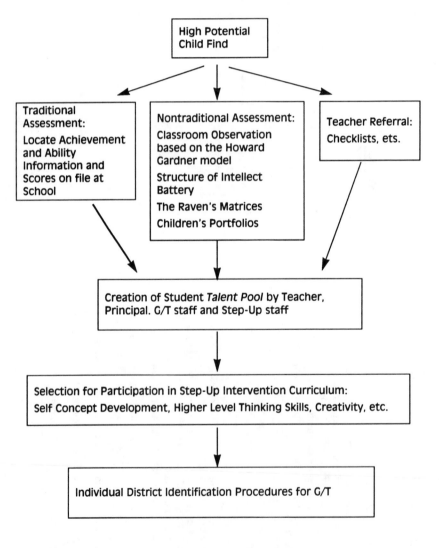

Figure 6.2. Project Step-Up "Child-Find": Assessment and Selection Process and Procedures

CHARACTERISTICS OF TEACHERS

Teachers in the model school program for gifted young children shared two major characteristics: enthusiasm and enjoyment in working with young children, and a commitment to develop each child's individual talents. The teachers also possessed high energy, good interpersonal skills, and a sense of humor. In-service teacher training focused on the needs of young preschool children. One important characteristic of the teachers was that they all were well educated in child development. This factor was reflected in positive interactions with the young children.

PARENT INVOLVEMENT

Parents were involved in the program in two major ways: (a) they were required to agree that their young child could participate in the program, and (b) they were required to attend parent workshops in which important questions and issues were addressed such as the nature of intelligence, how intelligence is measured, and an understanding of what is true and false about the importance of parent involvement in the education of young children. Whenever possible, parent meetings were held in the children's neighborhood and in community settings after school hours. Consideration was given to the fact that most of the parents were working during the day and that school often represented a negative experience for them. Churches and community centers were viewed as more neutral sites.

Glover (1979) stated that there are limits placed on genetic endowment, but that within general and broad bounds, experience makes a difference between a person of average intelligence and a person of above-average intelligence. When this information was shared with parents, the statement helped to emphasize the importance of parents being involved in their child's development. When the parents were provided with a simple definition of intelligence such as the possession of problem-solving abilities in verbal, concrete, and abstract situations, and learned that these skills can be encouraged or discouraged by a child's total environment of people, places, and experiences, the parents became more curious about intelligence and intelligence testing. Topics developed for a national training project for parents by Sisk (1991) were found to be most helpful: Intelligence Testing of Preschool Children, Limitations and Criticism of the IQ Test, and Characteristics of Gifted.

INTELLIGENCE TESTING OF PRESCHOOL CHILDREN

In discussing intelligence testing of preschool children, it is helpful if parents understand that standardized intelligence tests provide a score or IQ that is commonly referred to as an index of intellectual capability or potential cognitive development. A rough estimate is that in North American schools, more than 250 million IQ tests are annually given (Caplan & Caplan, 1983).

We know that a young child's intellectual growth is not static and cannot be predetermined. IQ varies throughout the individual's life depending on the interaction between inherited characteristics and environment. If the environment continues to reward learning, the individual's IQ will continue to grow and to develop. This continual growth was demonstrated by the majority of the original participants in the Terman (1925) study conducted in California. Terman identified 1400 9-year-old students as gifted children. He and his associates conducted follow up interviews throughout their lives (the subjects are in their 80th year), and they certainly have maintained or increased their giftedness throughout their lives.

It is important that parents understand that many factors affect the child's cognitive growth, including the emotional climate of the home and the encouragement that the child receives from parents and caregivers. Children's drive or motivation also affects their use of learning opportunities, especially because motivation often mirrors how the children perceive themselves as learners.

LIMITATIONS AND CRITICISMS OF THE IQ TEST

Educators seldom talk about IQ being static. Many factors affect the scores. Sparkman and Carmichael (1973) pointed out that IQ scores of educationally disadvantaged and poor children are often substantially improved when language development is intensified. They reported that an increase of 15 to 20 points in 1 year is not uncommon. Parents need to be reminded that an IQ is not an innate capacity score, but a measure of the functioning level currently exhibited by the child.

Mussen, Conger, and Kagan (as given in Caplan & Caplan, 1983) reported that favorable or unfavorable changes in environment produce shifts in intellectual performance. It is safe to say that IQ alone cannot ensure success; however, the IQ does help predict what a child may achieve in school, if specific factors such as personality, drive, social behavior, and health are taken into consideration.[1]

---

[1] A useful pamphlet for parents has been prepared by the Psychological Corporation, 757 Third Avenue, New York, NY 10017, entitled "Some Things Parents Should Know About Testing."

CHARACTERISTICS OF GIFTED

Glover (1979) listed 11 characteristics occurring frequently in gifted and talented people. These characteristics can function as a useful yard-stick in understanding gifted children:

- strong sense of curiosity
- highly developed problem-solving skills
- an ability for self-amusement
- a strong fantasy life
- stick-to-it-iveness (task commitment)
- a strong tolerance of ambiguity
- an ability to see complex relationships
- an ability to redefine and elaborate on problems
- inventiveness

Parents profit from discussion groups in which a trained parent leader can encourage them to identify specific examples of ways that their child has demonstrated gifted characteristics. In this type of activity, the list does not remain abstract, but it becomes a useful guideline for parents. One parent shared how her 5-year-old went strawberry picking and set out to fill five baskets. The child stayed with it until he was so weary that he fell asleep right in the patch; however, he did finish filling his five baskets and demonstrated "stick-to-it-iveness."

Parents need to set high expectations for their children, but they need to refrain from applying undue pressure. Parents also need to ask questions about their child's education and to continue asking questions until they feel satisfied (Johnsen, 1994).

Elkind (1987) stated that the price of healthy education is eternal vigilance. He said that whenever we become inattentive to the fact that children are people in their own right, with their own needs, their own special abilities, and their own learning priorities, we are likely to engage in miseducation. Eternal vigilance may sound like quite an order for parents and educators, but the end result is healthy, happy, responsible, and productive people. We need to develop our gifted and talented children from among all children. The loss of even one gifted child as a potential contributing member to society is one child too many.

REFERENCES

Baldwin, A.Y. (1985). Issues concerning minorities. In F.D. Horowitz & M. O'Brien (Eds.), *The gifted and talented in developmental perspectives.* Washington, DC: American Psychological Association.

Barkan, J. H., & Bernal, E. M. (1991). Gifted education for bilingual and limited English proficiency students. *Gifted Child Quarterly, 35*(3), 144-147.

Bernal, E.M. (1976). Gifted programs for the culturally different. *National Association of Secondary School Principals Bulletin, 60*, 67-76.

Bernal, E. M. (1990). The identification blues and how to cure them. *CAG Communicator, 20*(3), 1, 27

Boykin, A.W. (1982). Task variability and the performance of black and white children: Veriestic exploration. *Journal of Black Studies, 12*, 469-485.

Caplan, T., & Caplan, F. (1983). *The early childhood years; The two to six year old.* New York: Bantam Books.

Chen, J. (1989). Identification of gifted Asian-American students, In J. Maker & S. Schiever (Eds.), *Critical issues in gifted education.* Austin, TX: Pro-Ed.

Chen, J., & Goon, S. (1978). Recognition of the gifted from among disadvantaged Asian children. *Gifted Child Quarterly, 20*, 157-164.

Clark, B. (1989). A critique of curriculum for gifted Hispanic students. In J. Maker & S. Schiever (Eds.), *Critical issues in gifted education.* Austin, TX: Pro-Ed.

Cox, J., Daniel, N., & Boston, B.O. (1985). *Educating able learners: Programs and promising practices.* Austin: University of Texas Press.

Cronbach, L.J. (1977). *Educational psychology* (3rd ed.). New York: Harcourt Brace Jovanovich.

Cummins, J. (1984). *Bilingualism and special education issues in assessment and pedagogy.* San Diego, CA: College Hill Press.

Darnell, R. (1979). *Reflections on Cree interactional etiquette: Educational implications* (Sociolinguistic working paper #57). Austin, TX: Southwest Education Development Laboratory.

DeLeon, J. (1983). Cognitive style differences and the underrepresentation of Mexican Americans in programs for the gifted. *Journal for the Education of the Gifted, 6*, 140-153.

Elkind, D. (1987). *Miseducation: Preschoolers at risk.* New York: Knopf.

Frasier, M. (1979). Counseling the culturally diverse gifted. In N. Colangelo & R.T. Zaffran (Eds.), *New voices in counseling the gifted* (pp. 304-311). Dubuque, IA: Kendall/Hunt.

Frasier, M. (1989). The identification of gifted black students. Developing new perspectives. In J. Maker (Ed.), *Critical issues in gifted education: Defensible programs for cultural and ethnic minorities* (pp. 213-225). Austin, TX: Pro-Ed.

Gallagher, J., & Kinney, L. (Eds.). (1974). *Talent delayed-talent denied: A conference report.* Reston, VA: Foundation for Exceptional Children.

Gardner, H. (1983). *Frames of mind: The theory of multiple intelligences.* New York: Basic Books.

Glover, J. (1979). *A parent's guide to intelligence testing: How to help your children's intellectual development.* Chicago: Nelson Hall.

Guilford, J. P. (1976). *The nature of human intelligence.* New York: McGraw-Hill.

Hess, R. D., Block, N., Costello, D., Knowls, R. T., & Largen, D. (1971). Parent involvement in early education. In E. H. Grothman (Ed.), *Daycare: Resource for decisions.* Washington, DC: Office of Economic Opportunity.

Hilliard, P. (1976). *Identifying gifted minority children through the use of non-verbal tests.* Unpublished doctoral dissertation, Yeshiva University, New York.

Horowitz, F.D., & O'Brien, M. (1985). Perspectives on research and development. In F.D. Horowitz & M. O'Brien (Eds.), *The gifted and talented: Developmental perspectives.* Washington, DC: American Psychological Association.

Johnsen, S. (1994, January/February). Understanding what is true and false about intelligence and ability tests. *Gifted Child Today, 17.*

Karnes, M., Shwedel, A., Linnemeyer, S., & Koening. (1982). *The SMART project: A program for parents of promising infants.* Champaign: University of Illinois.

Kochman, T. (1983). Black and white. In J. Hanna (Ed.), *Descriptive school behavior, class, race and culture.* New York: Ganes and Mair.

Locke, P. (1979, March). *Needs of American Indian gifted children.* Presentation to the joint meeting of the U.S. Office of Gifted and Talented and Office of Indian Education, Red Lake, MN.

Machado, M. (1987, February 16). Gifted Hispanics underidentified in classrooms. *Hispanic Link Weekly Report, 5*(7), 1.

Maker, C. J. (1992). *Creativity, intelligence problem solving: A definition and design for cross-cultural research and measurement related to giftedness.* Manuscript submitted for publication.

Maker, J., & Schiever, S. (1989). *Critical issues in gifted education.* Austin, TX: Pro-Ed.

Meeker, M. (1969). *The structure of intellect: Its interpretation and uses.* Columbus, OH: Merrill.

Meeker, M. (1978). Nondiscriminatory testing procedures to assess giftedness in black, chicano, navajo, and anglo children. In A.Y. Baldwin, G.H. Gear, & L.J. Luciyo (Eds.), *Educational planning for the gifted: Overcoming cultural, geographical, and socioeconomic barriers.* Reston, VA: The Council for Exceptional Children.

Montgomery, D. (1989). Identification of giftedness among American Indian people. In J. Maker & S. Schiever (Eds.), *Critical issues in gifted education.* Austin, TX: Pro-Ed.

Moss, H. A., & Kagan. J. (1958, December). Material influences on early IQ scores. *Psychological Reports, 4.*

Munger, A. (1990). The parent's role in counseling the gifted. The balance between home and school. In J. Van Tassel-Baska (Ed.), *A practical guide to counseling the gifted in a school setting.* Reston, VA: Council for Exceptional Children.

Rau, L., Mlodnosky, L. B., & Anastasiow, N. (1964). *Child rearing: Antecedents of achievement behaviors in second grade boys.* (Cooperative Research Project #1939). Stanford, CA: Stanford University Press.

Renzulli, J.S. (1973). Talent potential in minority group students. *Exceptional Children, 39,* 437-444.

Richert, E. S., Alvino, J. J., & McDonnel, R. C. (1982). *National report on identification: Assessment and recommendations for comprehensive identification of gifted and talented youth.* Sewell, NJ: Educational Information and Resource Center

Rosen, B. C., & D'Androde, S. (1959, February). Race ethnicity and the achievement syndrome. *American Sociological Review, 24.*

Samalin, N. (1987). *Loving your child is not enough.* New York: Penguin.

Schaefer, E. (1975). *Family relationships in the application of child development research to exceptional children.* Reston, VA: Council for Exceptional Children.

Schetky, D. H. (1981). A psychiatrical look at giftedness. The emotional and social development of the gifted child. *Gifted Child Today, 18,* 2-4.

Schmeck, R., & Lockhart, D. (1983). Introverts and extroverts require different learning environments. *Educational Leadership, 43,* 54-55.

Shade, B. (1990, August). *Cultural ways of knowing: An Afrocentive perspective.* Paper presented at the Summer Institute of the Council of Chief State Officers.

Shade, B., & New, C. (1993). *Multicultural education.* Boston: Allyn & Bacon.

Sisk, D. (1987). *Creative teaching of the gifted.* New York: McGraw-Hill.

Sisk, D. (1991). *Systematic training for educational programs for the underserved pupils.* (Final report). Washington, DC: Department of Education.

Sisk, D. (1994, Spring). New directions for educating minority, economically disadvantaged children. *Tempo (Journal for the Texas Association for Gifted and Talented),* 7-10.

Sparkman, B., & Carmichael, A. (1973). *Blueprint for a brighter child.* New York: McGraw-Hill.

Telford, C., & Sawyer, J. (1981). *The exceptional child.* Englewood Cliffs, NJ: Prentice-Hall.

Terman, L. (1925). Mental and physical traits of a thousand gifted children. In L. Terman (Ed.), *Genetic studies of genius* (Vol. F). Palo Alto, CA: Stanford University Press.

Tonemah, S. A. (1985). *Tribal cultural perspective of gifted and talentedness.* Unpublished manuscript. (Available from D. Montgomery, Elhnhurst School, Oklahoma City, OK)

Torrance, E.P. (1977). *Discovery and nurturance of giftedness in the culturally different.* Reston, VA: The Council for Exceptional Children.

Wong, S., & Wong, P. (1989). Teaching strategies and practices in the education of gifted Cantonese students. In J. Maker & S. Schiever (Eds.), *Critical issues in gifted education.* Austin, TX: Pro-Ed.

Zappia, I. (1989). Identification of gifted Hispanic students: A multidimensional view. In C. J. Maker & S. W. Schiever (Eds.), *Critical issues in gifted education: Vol. 2, Defensible programs for cultural and ethnic minorities* (pp. 19-26). Austin, TX: ProEd.

Special Populations: Challenges and Opportunities

Joan Franklin Smutny

Gifted children have been and continue to be underserved and ineffectively served. Within the general classification of gifted children, however, there are a number of special populations whose needs have been all but ignored. One sign that gifted preprimary and primary education is finally coming of age is the increased sensitivity to the requirements of such groups. This section includes chapters on children from low-income, culturally and linguistically diverse backgrounds, the rural poor, the highly gifted, the underachiever, the learning disabled, and gifted girls.

    In Chapter 7, E. Paul Torrance offers two major suggestions for identifying hidden talent among the disadvantaged and culturally different children: (a) offering tests of creativity that enable disadvantaged children to respond in terms of their own experience and (b) using creativity workshops to motivate the child to display his or her potential and to feel safe doing so. He identifies a set of 17 characteristics called *creative positives* that can guide the search for talent and that reflect a combination of tests, observations of behavior, performances, and other activities. These creative positives include: ability to express feelings and emotions; ability to improvise with commonplace materials and objects; articulateness in role playing, sociodrama, and story telling; enjoyment of and ability in visual arts, such as drawing, painting, and sculpture; enjoyment of and ability in creative movement, dance, and dramatics; enjoyment of and ability in group activities and problem solving; humor; and originality of ideas in problem solving.

In Chapter 8, Margie Kitano and Rosa Perez seek to encourage the implementation of preschool and primary programs focusing on the needs and talents of young children from low-income, culturally and linguistically diverse backgrounds. Few programs are available for these young children because of major misconceptions about their needs: remedial education is required to prepare them for schooling; children need to master the English language before facing larger challenges; standardized testing is a reliable measure of their talents; and enriched curriculum at the preschool/primary level is developmentally unsound for them. All four of these misconceptions can be replaced by an innovative framework for program development that recognizes and capitalizes on unique strengths of diverse students. Collaborative models (i.e., San Diego's Project Excel and Project First Step) facilitate talent development by encouraging teacher development, promoting program continuity and parent participation, and utilizing site resources efficiently. Early intervention through effective programs can have a successful impact on these children, their parents, and teachers. Suggestions for evaluating early childhood programs for low-income, culturally and linguistically diverse children are included in the chapter.

Patricia Brooks, in Chapter 9, addresses the concern that minority children are grossly underrepresented in gifted programs. This is due to traditional identification methods that rely heavily on IQ and achievement tests. These standardized tests are severely limited in their ability to identify any group outside of mainstream culture. Project STEP (Strategies for Targeting Early Potential) was implemented in Maryland by Brooks as a means of identifying gifted minority students. The program focuses on teachers rather than tests as the prime identifiers. Teachers over the course of a school year are asked to identify those children who demonstrate special abilities in five areas: learning, motivation, leadership, creativity, and adaptability. At the heart of the program is a checklist made up of 40 behavioral characteristics observable in the classroom. Project STEP, which is supported through extensive teacher training, has proven to be highly successful for identification.

Howard Spicker and Thomas Southern (Chapter 10) have found that the identification problems associated with low-income, culturally diverse children are also applicable to children who hail from rural areas. The lack of appropriate role models is particularly disadvantageous for these children. Without appropriate models, children cannot acquire an advanced vocabulary—a key item in intelligence tests.

Poverty and geographic remoteness limit access to cultural opportunities and exposure to the world beyond their own community. Lack of varied career models lowers career expectations and enforces the status quo. Not only do these children need special means of identification, but special programming for these children and their parents is also required. For example, in a parent-student survey instrument developed for Project SPRING, parents were asked questions about their child's ability or interest in fixing, making, and collecting things, as well as writing and reading. Parent information can provide immense insight about the accomplishment of the child outside of school—information that is valuable for identification. Disadvantaged rural children must be judged on a wide range of tasks, not just those that are school related.

In Chapter 11, Stephanie Tolan examines the highly gifted child who embodies an astonishing capacity. The child has both great promise and great risk, according to the author. Early identification is essential to offering learning experiences that can support the development of his or her extraordinary abilities. Indifference to the needs of these children can lead to many insurmountable challenges. Because they are young children, they lack the internal resources and life experiences that enable them to cope. Unusually bright children often suffer in school from problems of boredom, lack of challenge, scarcity of materials, and the inability of the adults to understand the fullness of the child's capacity. Acceleration is suggested even though it has several drawbacks. Home schooling is another alternative. Supporting the capacities of highly gifted children is central to their well-being. "Failing to nourish them distorts their whole being," says Tolan.

Patterns of underachievement can begin as early as the preschool years. Early identification is key to providing appropriate parenting and educational strategies for avoiding underachievement. In Chapter 12, Sylvia Rimm discusses PRIDE (a preschool and kindergarten interest descriptor) as one means of identifying creative characteristics in young children; it also heightens parent awareness about characteristics of creativity. She advises parents on how to avoid inadvertently encouraging perfectionism in a child, which often leads to self-doubt and lowered self-esteem. She cautions parents about the detrimental effects of both understimulation (too much television, for instance) and overstimulation (too much attention from friends and parents). Underachievement can be prevented by offering an environment for healthy psychological development.

Nancy Wingenbach explores the dilemma of the gifted learning-disabled child in Chapter 13: the disparity between potential and performance; the above-average abilities displayed at home compared with the failure to meet school standards; the child's frustration with his or her own inability to turn marvelous visions into equally impressive products. She notes that, by definition, gifted and learning disabled are not contradictory terms. One describes advanced information processing, whereas the other focuses on a specific skill deficit. Wingenbach describes how the school environment in preprimary and primary grades impacts on children who are gifted learning-disabled and suggests means of intervention, including instructional strategies.

In Chapter 14, Jessie Sanders provides an overview of the challenges faced by gifted children who have also been identified as handicapped, learning disabled, or behavior disordered. She advises parents on how best to provide for a smooth transition into the school environment and how to be an able advocate for their special child, both educationally and emotionally. Through parent modeling and an emphasis on gifts rather than hindrances, this young child can grow in self-worth and self-confidence.

Gifted women still persistently underachieve. In Chapter 15, Kathleen and Stephen Veenker point out that these patterns of underachievement can be traced back to the differential treatment given females from babyhood on. Despite the fact that focusing on a girl's interests and gifts is a better way to develop a child, girls are provided with playing materials and peers that develop their "femaleness" and not their intellectual capacity. Gifted girls are treated differently than gifted boys by teachers, and continue to be steered out of male-dominated curricular areas such as math and science, despite abilities in these areas. The chapter offers suggestions for counteracting some of the negative role models and communications that besiege gifted girls.

7

Talent Among Children Who are Economically Disadvantaged or Culturally Different

E. Paul Torrance

How realistic is our dream of educating to the extent of their potential children who live in poverty or in a culture that is different from the "mainstream"?

It is not possible to estimate accurately the amount of unrecognized and unawakened potential lost each year. I offer here two suggestions for finding hidden talent among disadvantaged and culturally different children. It seems to me that part of the difficulty lies in the nature of the talent tests. Most of them require that the child respond in terms of the experiences common in our dominant, advantaged culture. The disadvantaged child is not permitted to respond in terms of his own experiences, common in his culture or unique to himself. In contrast, most tests of creativity—and Torrance Tests of Creative Thinking (Torrance, 1966, 1990; Torrance, Ball, & Safter, 1992) in particular—permit disadvantaged children to respond in terms of their own experiences. This increases the chances of obtaining responses and makes it possible to evaluate the responses in terms of the child's experiences.

Another problem of talent identification lies almost completely outside the nature of the instruments used in the process. In order to obtain an indication of potentiality from a child, it is necessary to motivate him or her to display that potentiality and to feel psychologically safe in doing so. In my own work with disadvantaged Black and White children, I have used the creativity workshop as a vehicle for accomplishing this goal. In this format, I have found that tests of creative thinking ability take on more power than in typical situations (Torrance, 1968). In the creativity workshops, three procedures were used to elicit the hidden verbal abilities for which we were searching. No tests were given until there had been time for the creative processes of the children to become awakened. No time limits were imposed. The examiners offered to record the children's ideas. These procedures were generally quite effective. No one observing these activities or the resulting products could have said that these children were nonverbal.

On the basis of both published and unpublished (Torrance, 1964, 1967) studies of economically disadvantaged and culturally different children, I believe I have identified a set of creative positives that occur to a high degree among these groups and on which I believe we can build successful educational and recreational programs.

The remainder of this chapter is devoted to the identification, importance, and evidence of these creative positives. Because I consider the economically disadvantaged a different culture, for the remainder of this chapter, I include them in the term *culturally different*.

THE CREATIVE POSITIVES

On the basis of studies involving the Torrance Tests of Creative Thinking, a series of summer workshops, and several years of experience working in a day-care center enrolling only poor and culturally different children, I believe I have identified a set of characteristics that can guide the search for talent among these groups. I have called these characteristics *creative positives*.

I must first caution the reader that not all members of economically disadvantaged and culturally different groups are gifted in all of these positives. Many children manifest a high level of ability in these characteristics at these ages, but it disappears by the time they complete the third grade. The creative positives may be found by a combination of tests, observations of behavior, performances, role playing, and other activities. These abilities can be observed with a rather high degree of frequency among these groups.

I have given the following labels to these creative positives:

1. Ability to express feelings and emotions
2. Ability to improvise with commonplace materials and objects
3. Articulateness in role playing, sociodrama, and story telling
4. Enjoyment of and ability in visual arts, such as drawing, painting, and sculpture
5. Enjoyment of and ability in creative movement, dance, dramatics, and so forth
6. Enjoyment of and ability in music, rhythm, and so forth
7. Use of expressive speech
8. Fluency and flexibility in figural media
9. Enjoyment of and skills in group activities, problem solving, and so forth
10. Responsiveness to the concrete
11. Responsiveness to the kinesthetic
12. Expressiveness of gestures, body language, and so forth, and ability to interpret body language
13. Humor
14. Richness of imagery in informal language
15. Originality of ideas in problem solving
16. Problem centeredness or persistence in problem solving
17. Emotional responsiveness

In the remainder of this chapter, I offer some suggestions for identifying strengths in each of the aforementioned 17 areas and for using these strengths to motivate learning. Obviously, much work remains to be done to implement this idea fully. If it is to be implemented, however, this work must be done by those who are concerned with giving an equal chance to gifted youngsters from culturally different groups.

ABILITY TO EXPRESS FEELINGS AND EMOTIONS

I suggest that giftedness in expressing feelings and emotions may be discovered by:

- Observations of facial expression and body gestures
- Analysis of samples of creative writing, especially poetry
- Observations of behavior in discussions, classroom meetings, role playing, sociodrama, creative dramatics, dance, creative movement, music, and rhythm
- Study of visual art products and the processes used in their production
- Observations of response in creative reading

Unless students are provided learning experiences in which they can manifest their giftedness in expressing feelings and emotions, this type of giftedness is not likely to be discovered.

Middle-class society in the United States has tended to derogate emotional expression, and education has stressed objectivity and suppression of emotional experiencing. However, many theories of creative achievement maintain that in creative thinking, especially when this thinking leads to really new ideas and concepts, the emotional and suprarational are important. All admit, of course, that once the breakthrough ideas are produced, they must be subjected to tests of logic. However, the breakthrough ideas themselves cannot be produced by logic.

Because there is a general lack of objective indicators of emotional expression, one is not likely to find much evidence in scientific research for this talent as a strength of culturally different groups. I can only say that this is one of the most frequently observed of the creative positives when my students record their observations of culturally different and poor children in our summer workshops, and that emotional expression has characterized and continues to characterize the artistic performances of the culturally different.

ABILITY TO IMPROVISE WITH COMMONPLACE MATERIALS

The following observation checklist is suggested for identifying giftedness for improvisation with common materials:

- Makes toys from commonplace materials
- Uses common materials to modify toys
- Makes games from common materials
- Uses common materials for unintended uses at home
- Uses common materials for unintended uses in school
- Uses common materials in inventions
- Uses common materials in creative dramatics, art, and so forth

The unusual uses tests in both the Torrance and Guilford batteries appear to be fairly effective pencil-and-paper measures of this kind of talent. It should be noted, however, that culturally different children must be made comfortable and must be permitted to use their usual language or dialect in responding in order for this test to yield a reliable measure. With young children, an adult must record the responses, or spelling and writing skills may interfere with performance.

Rather consistently, we have found that members of culturally different groups score high on the unusual uses tasks of the Torrance

Tests of Creative Thinking. Students in our summer workshops also report a high frequency of this kind of behavior among culturally different children. Middle-class teachers also seem to be more aware of this strength among the culturally different than of any of the other creative positives. Among inservice teachers in a middle Georgia county, 47% checked this as a strength of Black, disadvantaged children, whereas most of the strengths were recognized and accepted by only about 10% of these teachers. After an extensive workshop on the psychology of disadvantaged children, 92% of them checked this strength. Among undergraduates in teacher education programs, 82% recognized this strength as characteristic of Black, disadvantaged children.

The literature concerning almost all of the culturally different groups in the United States is filled with examples of improvisation with common materials. For example, Yoors (1967) described many examples of such improvisation among the Gypsies with whom he lived for 10 years, beginning at about age 12. One of his first startling observations was that Gypsy children had no toys. They improvised, however, all kinds of games and sports. The same is true of other economically disadvantaged groups. If there are no toys, children will improvise with what they have; if items for living are unavailable, children will improvise with what they have.

ARTICULATENESS IN ROLE PLAYING AND STORY TELLING

Giftedness in role playing and story telling becomes evident when the role playing becomes very absorbing and lifelike or when the story being told arouses and sustains the interest of the group. Role playing and improvisation tests have been devised by Moreno (1946), Moreno and Moreno (1969), and others, but a sensitive and alert teacher, school psychologist, or sociodramatic director can discover this kind of talent through observation. It requires a bit more alertness to become aware of the real-life role playing used by many culturally different students as a survival or adaptation technique. However, this may be the "real test."

Scholars in education, sociology, and psychology have often noted the high frequency of outstanding talent in role playing and story telling among culturally different students. For example, Riessman (1962) and Deutsch (1967) pointed out that disadvantaged children who seem to be nonverbal will become quite verbally articulate in role playing. The Black folk tales brought from Africa and adapted to the slave life experience illustrate the cultivation of both role-playing and story-telling skills. Halpern (1973) commented on the lifelong process by which Black children are taught to play roles (pretending to feel and think differently from the way they actually do) as one of their many survival techniques in the "White world." Perhaps to a lesser extent, this has been true of other culturally different groups such as Chicanos, American Indians, and Gypsies.

ENJOYMENT OF AND ABILITY IN VISUAL ARTS

Although there are tests to discover giftedness in the visual arts, research literature does not reveal much of great value. Visual art products are so easy to obtain that most searchers for talent in the visual arts have been willing to rely on judgments of products such as drawings, painting, and sculptures. As an observational screening device for surveying talent in the visual arts, the following checklist is suggested:

- Experiences real joy in drawing, painting, and sculpture
- Becomes deeply absorbed in drawing, painting, sculpture, or other visual art activity
- Understands subject matter by "drawing it" (e.g., illustrates stories, illustrates history, draws biological objects, makes maps)
- Communicates skillfully through drawings, paintings, sculptures, and other visual arts
- Captures the essence of whatever is photographed
- Makes photographs tell a story

Many scholars in the field of creative achievement believe that visual artists have been and always will be the forerunners of human advancement. They point out that the visual artists must show the possibilities of the future before anyone can pioneer breakthroughs in almost any field. Certainly, the visual mode of finding out and communicating is powerful, and most people depend heavily on it.

Evidence Among the Culturally Different

Again, one of the creative positives most frequently reported by my students when they observed disadvantaged Black and White children in our summer workshops is the high level of enjoyment and ability that these children show for the visual arts. A disproportionately large number of children gifted in this area have always been found. Similarly, workers in our creativity test scoring service are almost always amazed at the outstanding talent demonstrated by the Chicano students whose figural creativity booklets they score.

ENJOYMENT OF AND ABILITY IN CREATIVE MOVEMENT AND DANCE

Although some excellent work has been done on the development of tests to assess creativity in movement (Alston, 1971; Glover, 1974; Wyrick, 1966), these tests have not yet been fully standardized and made widely available. Although these tests would doubtless be useful, most workers will probably depend on observations and judgments of performance. For this purpose, the following checklist is suggested:

- Experiences deep enjoyment in creative movement/dance
- Becomes intensely absorbed in creative movement/dance
- Can interpret songs, poems, stories, and so forth through creative movement/dance
- Choreographs dance performance
- Can elaborate ideas through creative movement/dance
- Movement facilitates learning and understanding of events, ideas, concepts, and reading/literary materials
- Spends unusual amount of time in perfecting creative movement/ dance

In my experience in conducting creativity workshops involving both mainstream and culturally different children, the latter clearly excel. Although there are individual differences, there have been times when it has seemed that all of the culturally different children outperformed almost all of the mainstream culture children. Many people even maintain that this ability is inherent in culturally different groups (e.g., Blacks, Chicanos, American Indians, Gypsies, and Appalachian Whites). This does not seem likely, however. A more reasonable interpretation is one based on the differences in the way the cultures encourage and provide opportunity for practice and performance in creative movement and dance (DuBois, 1970; Lowie, 1963; Steiner, 1970). It is a culturally approved type of giftedness in most culturally different groups. Further evidence is that a large share of the greatest dancers and "creative movers" have come from culturally different groups.

ENJOYMENT OF AND ABILITY IN MUSIC AND RHYTHM

Although there are a number of useful tests of musical ability such as the Seashore Measures of Musical Talents (Seashore, 1960), Musical Aptitude Tests (Drake, 1957), and the Musical Aptitude Profile (Gordon, 1965), and although there are measures such as Sounds and Images (Torrance, Khatena, & Cunnington, 1974) and Vaughan's (1971) Test of Musical Creativity that seem to predict certain kinds of creative behavior in the realm of music, actual performance in musical activities will probably continue to be the best route for discovering giftedness in music and rhythm. For this purpose, the following checklist is suggested:

- Writes, draws, works, walks, moves with rhythm
- Rhythm facilitates learning of skills
- Rhythm facilitates learning and understanding of ideas, events, concepts, and so forth
- Creates songs
- Creates music
- Interprets ideas, events, concepts, feelings, and so forth through rhythm
- Interprets ideas, events, feelings, and so forth through music
- Becomes highly absorbed in music and rhythmic activities
- Works perseveringly at music and rhythmic activities
- Is exceptionally responsive to sound stimuli

Giftedness in music and rhythm is so common among culturally different groups that some people believe that such talent comes "naturally" to them. An examination of these cultures, however, usually shows that music and rhythm are approved, encouraged, practiced, and rewarded. Most American innovations in music have come from culturally different groups, especially African Americans. They have made such contributions as spirituals, ragtime, jazz, blues, and rock and roll. Although many children from culturally different groups are resistant to learning the music of mainstream America and some people even believe that they are incapable of excelling in such "higher" forms of music expression as opera and symphony, there are many examples of Blacks and American Indians who have achieved fame in these areas. Among the eminent black artists are such greats as Marian Anderson (opera), Leontyne Price (opera), Roland Hayes (concert artist), Dean Dixon (symphony conductor), William Grant Still (composer), and Quincy Jones (composer and performer). Whenever I have had teachers observe culturally different groups for the creative positives, they have always reported a high incidence of giftedness in music and rhythm.

USE OF EXPRESSIVE SPEECH

Because the social situation is a powerful determinant of speech (Labov, 1972, 1973), the discovery of giftedness in expressive speech among the culturally different requires that the would-be discoverer enter into the right social relationship with the young child. Many teachers, school psychologists, and counselors are unable to do this.

Whether one is searching for giftedness in expressive speech through standardized test situations or in nontest situations, it is important that the culturally different student feel free to use the expressive system that is most comfortable. The following checklist is suggested for young children who might be gifted in expressive speech:

- Speech is colorful
- Speech is picturesque (e.g., suggests a picture)
- Speech includes powerful analogies, metaphors, and so forth
- Speech is vivid (e.g., lively, intense, penetrating, exciting)
- Invents words to express concepts and feelings for which existing words are inadequate
- Combines speech with movement and sound

Evidence Among the Culturally Different

Expressiveness of speech has been a part of the stereotype of Blacks, American Indians, Chicanos, Gypsies, mountaineers, and country people. In fact, it is just this expressiveness that is objectionable to mainstream American society—many believe that it is *too* expressive. Culturally different groups, however, have also been inventive in their language to create words that express meaning to their own group and, at the same time, conceal their meaning from others (DeStephano, 1973; Foster, 1974).

Abrahams (1973) insisted that Black English is not just a linguistic system; it is also an expressive system. Speech as a part of an expressive system is a performance involving interaction with listeners and combining movement with sound. Labov (1973) reported that working-class speakers are more effective narrators, reasoners, and debaters than middle-class speakers who temporize, qualify, and lose their argument in a mass of irrelevant detail.

FIGURAL FLUENCY AND FLEXIBILITY

Both the Guilford (1967) and Torrance (1966, 1990; Torrance et al., 1992) batteries of creativity tests contain measures of figural fluency and flexibility that seem capable of identifying giftedness in this area among culturally different groups. Little or no language ability is required by this type of test, and language handicaps seem not to interfere with performance. One need not be dependent on tests for discovering this kind of giftedness, however. The following checklist is suggested:

- Produces many different ideas through drawings
- Produces many ideas with common objects

- Arranges blocks and other play materials in many combinations
- Assembles and reassembles complex machines with ease
- Produces images in response to music, sounds, or movement
- Sketches maps from memory with ease
- Organizes objects and materials in space

Evidence Among the Culturally Different

Several of the studies cited in connection with the lack of racial and socioeconomic bias in the Torrance Tests of Creative Thinking have indicated that children from socially different groups excel their mainstream counterparts in figural fluency and flexibility (Gezi, 1969; Kaltsounis, 1974; McNamara, 1964; Smith, 1965; Tibbetts, 1968; Torrance, 1967). None of the studies cited gave evidence of deficits among culturally different groups. Both Meeker and Bruch (Fitzgerald, 1975) found strengths in figural and spatial relations for culturally different groups (i.e., Blacks and Chicanos). Counselors and guidance workers have long recognized the strengths of disadvantaged students in the spatial and figural areas and have responded by urging them into shop and industrial arts courses. This has been resented and resisted by both Chicanos and Blacks in protest movements. In my opinion, this alleged practice on the part of counselors represents a limited view of the potentialities based on this strength, because they do not view spatial and figural abilities as capacities for formulating imagery and for productive thinking. Many of the important relationships that must be dealt with in modern society involve figural relationships and new syntheses of them. When this enlarged view of figural abilities is adopted, the implications for culturally different, gifted youngsters become more exciting.

ENJOYMENT OF AND SKILL IN GROUP PROBLEM SOLVING

Although there has been considerable work by social psychologists and educators (Lake, Miles, & Earle, 1973) in the development of tests of group performance, such tests have not been widely used either to discover talent or to evaluate the effectiveness of educational programs. Few such tests have been standardized and made available commercially. Perhaps the best methods for discovering such talent are those that provide students with opportunities for solving problems in groups and for getting important tasks done. The following checklist is suggested as a guide for discovering this kind of talent:

- Influences other students to engage in projects he or she initiates
- Organizes and structures the group and the group task with skill
- Work in small groups facilitates learning and problem solving
- Tries harder in small groups than otherwise
- Produces original and useful ideas in small groups
- Becomes more alive in small groups
- Is highly aware of feelings and skills of others in small groups
- Supports other members of group, displays high group loyalty and involvement
- Initiates activities in small groups
- Is effective in teaching others in small groups

Evidence Among the Culturally Different

There are many indications that culturally different groups have continued to encourage in their members interdependent, cooperative behavior to a far greater extent than has the mainstream culture.

In the case of Blacks and American Indians, tribal living had always necessitated group skills. With the coming of the White man and continued alienation from mainstream society, the Indian has continued to depend on skills of group organization and cooperation for survival. Although slave owners usually separated members of the same tribe from one another to prevent their communicating and organizing, Blacks in slavery times used their skill in social organization and interdependence to survive. Following emancipation, the demands of survival in a segregated society continued to call for these skills. Therefore, a variety of recent studies yield findings that are surprising to many educators—findings that Blacks have a greater willingness and ability to engage in cooperative group behavior than Whites (Richmond & Vance, 1975; Richmond & Weiner, 1973). Reissman (1962), Houston (1973), and others have commented upon the tendency of members of culturally different groups to support and encourage one another in learning tasks.

RESPONSIVENESS TO THE CONCRETE

Frequently, educators derogate concrete thinking as being inferior to abstract thinking. However, responsiveness to the concrete as a creative positive goes beyond what is implied by concrete thinking or concrete operations. The person gifted in responsiveness to the concrete is stimulated by the concrete; thinking and problem solving are facilitated if the problem can be conceptualized in physical terms. This person obtains enjoyment from doing things with his or her hands, from manipulating objects physically, and from using hand tools. Perhaps the best way of discovering this kind of giftedness is through involving culturally different students in meaningful tasks and problems permitting physical manipulation. There are also a number of tests, games, and puzzles that involve this kind of physical manipulation of objects. The following checklist is suggested for discovering this type of giftedness:

- Produces a flow of ideas and alternative solutions when concrete objects and materials are involved
- Tries to conceptualize problems in terms of concrete objects and systems
- Uses concrete objects and systems to generate ideas and solutions
- Works in an absorbed manner for lengthy periods of time on concrete puzzles, mechanical problems, and so forth

In my experience with disadvantaged African American children I have been impressed by their wide practical knowledge, which frequently comes out in group brainstorming sessions. In a contest between disadvantaged teams and advantaged gifted teams (Torrance, 1974), this characteristic was illustrated in their responses to the problem of thinking of unusual uses of junk automobiles. The affluent gifted teams limited their responses almost entirely to the external aspects of junk automobiles—tires, hub caps, wheels, seats, steering wheel. The disadvantaged children thought of unusual uses for spark plugs, carburetors, springs, and the like.

Riessman (1962) identified this practical orientation to learning as one of the characteristics of culturally different children. According to Riessman, they have a physical style of learning and frequently are unable to think through a problem unless they can work with it with their hands. Unless they can manipulate objects physically, they cannot perform adequately. Riessman also coined the term *slow gifted child* to characterize the child who may be a brilliant thinker and excellent problem solver but who takes a long time to think through and solve a problem. Riessman stated that this may be caused at least partially by an emphasis on the concrete and physical. He believed that such physical learners may achieve a different kind of understanding of problems than symbolic learners and approach the abstract from the concrete rather than the other way around.

RESPONSIVENESS TO THE KINESTHETIC

Discovery

There is a danger that responsiveness to the kinesthetic among the culturally different may be equated with a physical or motoric learning style. Responsiveness to the kinesthetic, as I have conceptualized this creative positive, goes far beyond the old concept of a physical style of learning, which is usually thought of as a deficit among the culturally different. It includes not only manipulative movements but also kinesthetic discrimination, psychomotor coordination, endurance, strength, flexibility, adaptive motor skills, expressive movement, and interpretive movement. The following checklist is suggested to guide teachers in screening for responsiveness to the kinesthetic:

- Skillfully communicates ideas through movement
- Skillfully interprets meaning of movement
- Movement is effective as warm-up for creative thinking
- Displays skillful manipulative movement in crayon work, typing, piano playing, and so forth
- Makes quick, precise movements in mime, creative dramatics, role playing, and so forth
- Shows movement in drawings and other visual art products
- Makes fine discriminations of kinesthetic phenomena
- Has excellent memory for kinesthetic information
- Works at movement activities for extended periods of time
- Displays total bodily involvement in interpreting a poem, story, or song, and in creative reading, dramatics, and so forth

As indicated in the preceding section on responsiveness to the concrete, a part of the stereotype of the culturally different is a physical, motoric style of learning. Riessman (1966) pointed out that when compared with children from the mainstream culture, culturally different children are more motoric in their learning, express their emotions physically, and admire strength, endurance, and motor skills. It is also apparent that many of those who achieve outstanding success in kinesthetic areas such as athletics and dance come from culturally different backgrounds.

EXPRESSIVENESS OF GESTURES AND BODY LANGUAGE

Discovery

Expressiveness of gestures and body language as a creative positive of the culturally different overlaps somewhat with the creative positives dealing with creative movement and responsiveness to the kinesthetic. However, in view of the present state of knowledge concerning these types of giftedness, it seems desirable to treat expressiveness of gestures and body language as a separate set of abilities. Its focus is on communicating through gestures and body language and interpreting this kind of communication.

I suggest the following checklist of behaviors:

- Expresses ideas powerfully and accurately through gestures and body language
- Combines speech with gestures and body language to communicate nuances that cannot be expressed by word
- Is skilled in recognizing the needs of other children from their gestures and body language
- Is skilled in recognizing faces
- Is skilled in mimicry, imitations, and impressions
- Is accurate in "reading" the body language of the teacher
- Uses gestures and body language to tell a story
- Is skilled in charades that rely on the use of gestures and body language

Expressiveness of gestures and body language has been one common characteristic of the stereotype of the culturally different person in the United States. Given that anthropologists generally agree that gestures are culture linked both in shape and in meaning, there may be some basis for this stereotype. The folklore, stories, songs, and dances of Blacks, American Indians, Chicanos, Gypsies, and other culturally different groups also suggest that members of such groups are highly alert to a great variety of nonverbal communication and act on such communications.

HUMOR

Discovery

There have been many attempts to develop tests of humor, but at the present time I am unable to identify any well-developed, standardized tests of humor that could be used in discovering giftedness in humor.

There are a great variety of theories of humor (Goldstein & McGhee, 1972), and in each, one may find clues for identifying humor in everyday life and in various creative products such as writing, drawing, and acting. I have tried to find clues to discover giftedness in humor in the creative writings and drawings of children. Some workers might find the following checklist helpful:

- Portrays the comical, funny, amusing in role playing
- Portrays the comical, funny, amusing in drawings
- Makes humorous, original comic strips
- Portrays the comical, funny, amusing in dramatics
- Makes people laugh a lot in games
- Makes up humorous jokes or stories
- Makes people laugh (not "makes fun of") in discussion
- Describes personal experiences with humor
- Plays jokes on others

The problem in using these observations is finding appropriate criteria of what makes something humorous, funny, comical, or amusing. Other than "it makes me laugh," the best criteria I have found include:

- Superior or clever adaptation in triumph or victory
- Joining together of incongruous disjointed elements
- Element of surprise, breaking up a routine course of thought or action
- Experience of two or more incompatible emotions or feelings
- Experience of release from tension or relief from strain
- Joining together of incongruous elements that fall into place
- Making something important unimportant and something unimportant important

A large proportion of famous humorists have come from culturally different groups. The most commonly advanced theory to support this phenomenon is that both the ability to produce humor and the ability to see the humorous in everyday events are survival techniques for the culturally different, especially among those who are disadvantaged.

Although one who discovers giftedness in humor among the culturally different must have some understanding of what is funny in the cultures concerned, my limited experience indicates that it is possible to train the members of one culture to see humor in the productions of members of another culture.

RICHNESS OF IMAGERY

Discovery

Richness of imagery has generally been viewed as a characteristic of creative products (such as poems, essays, and stories) rather than as an aspect of giftedness. Because images may be visual, auditory, or kinesthetic, indications of the ability to produce rich imagery may be sought in all three of these modalities as well as in the processes through which images are produced. The following checklist is suggested as one approach to discovering this type of giftedness among the culturally different using criteria of clarity, intensity, vividness, and liveliness for various types of imagery:

Clear, intense, vivid, and lively

- Imagery in writings
- Imagery in dance, movement, and other kinetic activity
- Imagery in singing or instrumental music performance
- Imagery used in relating personal experiences
- Imagery that emerges from oral reading
- Imagery in role playing and dramatics
- Imagery in drawings and other art work

Importance

A long line of scholars in the field of creativity research (Koestler, 1964; Patrick, 1955; Ribot, 1973) have assigned roles of major importance to imagery in creative thinking. The synectics approach to invention and creative problem solving relies quite heavily on richness of imagery and attempts to increase the richness of imagery of problem-solving teams by combining people from diverse fields (Gordon, 1961). Using measures derived from both Sounds and Images and Onomatopoeia and Images (Torrance et al., 1974), considerable validity evidence has been found to show a connection between richness of imagery and creative behavior in everyday life and in achievements such as musical composition.

ORIGINALITY AND INVENTIVENESS

Discovery

There are a variety of tests that can be used in discovering giftedness in originality and inventiveness among the culturally different. One of the oldest such tests is the Rorschach Ink Blot Test (Klopfer & Davidson,

1962), which uses uncommon responses of good form and human movement as the primary indicators. Several tests that provide measures of originality include the Barron-Welsh Art Scale (Barron, 1969), the Structure of Intellect tests (Guilford, 1967), the Torrance Tests of Creative Thinking (Torrance, 1966, 1990; Torrance et al., 1992), Sounds and Images, and Onomatopoeia and Images (Torrance et al., 1974), and Welsh's Origence measure based on the Welsh Figure Preference Test (Welsh, 1959, 1975).

The following checklist is suggested for purposes of crude screening:

- Produces solutions that others do not think of
- Produces solutions when no one else can
- Solutions are unusual, unconventional
- Stories have unusual, surprising endings
- Stories have unusual, surprising plots
- Comes up with inventions to solve problems
- Innovates with common materials to produce new solutions
- Comes up with solutions to problems that others say cannot be solved

Almost all the breakthroughs in science, medicine, art, literature, and education have come as a result of originality and inventiveness. In my long range studies of creative behavior (Torrance, 1972a, 1972b), measures of originality and inventiveness have yielded the best predictions of adult creative achievement. In many ways, originality is the essence of that type of creativity that changes the world.

Many of the studies of racial and socioeconomic differences in creative thinking using the Torrance Tests of Creative Thinking (Torrance, 1971) have shown originality to be one of the strengths of culturally different groups. There are, of course, difficulties in differentiating between unusual solutions that are common to the culture of an individual and unusual solutions that are unique in all cultures. Some of my students have been working on this problem from a cross-cultural perspective, and at the present time this does not seem to be a really serious problem of measurement. However, it is a factor that does have to be reckoned with. Several years ago, one first-grade teacher who was a student of mine thought that her Black pupils were making up original rhymes. We discovered, however, that although these particular rhymes are almost unknown in the White community, they are quite popular in the Black community. It still seems to be true that society has had to depend on culturally different individuals to produce many original solutions. Culturally different individuals seem to bring a "different" perspective, which provides a new frame of reference and goes beyond solutions of the "more and better of the same" variety.

PROBLEM CENTEREDNESS

Problem centeredness is such a behaviorally oriented phenomenon that it would be difficult to devise a well-balanced test to assess this type of giftedness. However, psychometric procedures have been devised to assess certain aspects of it. Most such attempts have involved the length of time a person is willing or able to continue working on a puzzle or difficult problem. Frequently, teachers and parents are annoyed by the problem centeredness of young children and tend not to recognize this type of behavior as a potential strength to be used in facilitating learning. The following checklist of problem centered behaviors is suggested as a guide in discovering this kind of giftedness:

- Does not give up easily; keeps trying to solve a problem
- Persists in asking questions about a problem or topic
- Shows concern and tries to solve or help solve problems of others
- Is stimulated by difficult problems
- Is hard to distract when concerned about a problem
- Keeps seeing relevance of new information to problems of the group
- Comes back to a problem or unfinished task time after time
- Follows up outside of class with problems generated in reading or class discussion by reading, interviewing, experimenting, and so forth

One of the major differences between creative problem solving that leads to genuine breakthroughs in thinking and ordinary problem solving is that the thinking involved in creative problem solving requires high motivation and persistence, taking place either over a considerable span of time or at high intensity (Newell, Shaw, & Simon, 1962).

The problem centeredness of many culturally different persons is frequently interpreted as a sign of a "one-track mind." Most culturally different groups, however, regard this characteristic in a positive light, as reflected in the Chicano proverb, "A Dios rogando y con el mazo dando" (Pray to God, but keep hammering away at your problem). One reason for this difference is that in most culturally different families, especially poor ones, it is convenient for children to work for long periods at a problem. Such behavior keeps them occupied and out of the way of adults who have to be busy at other affairs. However, such behavior could be annoying in a middle-class, mainstream society family. A child who becomes absorbed in a problem might be forced to leave it for another activity or scheduled event.

In working with disadvantaged Black children in a day-care center, one of my students involved a group of 3- and 4-year-olds in a game of seeing how many ways they could think of for putting an

object in a wastebasket. For a few minutes, all of the children participated. Soon a few of them wandered away to play at something else.
I noted, however, that some of them kept coming back as they
thought of new ways for putting the object in the wastebasket. I have
never observed this kind of behavior among middle-class children.

The following are examples of problem-centered behavior
observed by my students in a day-care center populated almost
entirely by culturally different children, mostly Blacks (Torrance, 1977):

> The children as a group frequently worked together to help solve a
> behavior or coping problem of a group member. They openly dis-
> played awareness of others' problems and would spend an hour or
> more discussing or analyzing the situation. Frequently, they were
> very insistent about reaching a solution before returning to their
> other activities.
>
> Many times I observed children start a project or activity and then
> not want to stop or to go on to another activity. The teacher has a
> hard time with such children when activities are changed. (p. 58)

One assignment of my students working in this day-care center was to
teach problem-solving skills such as brainstorming, evaluating alternatives, and the like. They discovered immediately that they could not
involve the children in a new problem or activity. They found, however,
that they could teach the creative problem skills and the process if they
used the problem or activity in which the child was already involved.

EMOTIONAL RESPONSIVENESS

Because emotional responsiveness is not associated with level of intelligence, this characteristic is not usually thought of as an aspect of giftedness. Although there are tests of empathy and emotionality (Lake et
al., 1973), little or no work has been done to apply such measures to
problems of discovering giftedness among the culturally different. The
following checklist may be useful in discovering this type of giftedness in
the culturally different:

- Listens intently and understandingly
- Feels strong empathy with others and is highly aware of the
  feelings, distresses, and needs of others
- Actively responds to meet the needs of others
- Responds emotionally to stories, events, needs of group
  members
- Is responsive to sincere interest and concern of others
- Seems almost psychic in ability to interpret and anticipate
  the actions of others

Riessman (1962) and many others have identified emotional responsiveness as a strength of the culturally different. Houston (1973) reported that the disadvantaged children in her studies tried to help and support one another when they were reciting, in the games, and other research tasks that she used. Affluent children under similar circumstances laughed at and ridiculed one another. Members of culturally different groups, especially those who are poor, are more responsive to one another's needs than are the affluent.

IMPORTANCE OF EARLY INTERVENTION

In dealing with the problem of talented children among the economically disadvantaged and culturally different, it is important to be aware of the importance of early intervention. By the time these children reach the end of the third grade, they may have surrendered their creativity and their particular creative positive. Please take the warning of the case of Tammy Debbins, who had entered the first grade in 1958, the first year of my 22-year longitudinal study (Torrance, 1980). This tells the story of too many economically disadvantaged children:

> The creativity of Tammy Debbins was still alive when she entered first grade. In 1958, she was the most creative child in the first grade and her estimated IQ was 177. Her teacher and parents, however, were quite concerned that she still had imaginary playmates and they were working to rid her of this behavior. She was one of the children who lived in the "Project" (low-income housing), and the social worker was called upon to help regarding the imaginary playmate. By the third grade, Tammy's creativity and IQ had become "normal"—average.
> From our records we cannot know just what happened to Tammy to diminish her. In her follow-up questionnaire, she tells us that she dropped out of school in the 10th grade to help with the younger members of her family. She was married at age 19 and became the mother of three boys. She reported no high school or post-high school creative achievements. Concerning the primary frustrations of her life, she wrote: "I don't think I'm very smart." (p. 152)

There were a number of attacks on Tammy Debbins' creativity at a rather early age, including the "war" against her imaginary playmate by the school and social worker. I am sure it did not help her self-concept nor her creative development.

This problem is quite frequent among economically disadvantaged girls. Boys who live in poverty fared somewhat better than the girls in this study. Some of the creative ones went into the military service. When they came out of the military service, they could go to college with the help of the "GI Bill." I too had this help. I would probably not have completed my doctorate without it.

WHAT IS NEXT?

There seems to be a little interest in the plight of gifted culturally different children, but very little. The National Association for Gifted Children has just issued a policy statement (NAGC Board of Directors, 1994). It mentioned "cultural diversity" but ignores problems of children who live in poverty. Federal and state governments have recently announced scholarships that may include some disadvantaged older students, but nothing for young children.

There are almost daily threats to creative teaching and the use of imagination and creativity in learning. Out of fear, many teachers are revising their methods of teaching. It is no wonder that teachers are not buying and using books like *The Incubation Model of Teaching* (Torrance & Safter, 1990) and *Save Tomorrow for the Children* (Torrance, Weiner, Presbury, & Henderson, 1987). This is why *Creative Problem Solving Through Role Playing* (Torrance, Murdock, & Fletcher, 1996) is being published in South Africa and not in the United States. That is why great teachers always live with the threat of "crucification."

I admire publishers like Zephyr and Free Spirit Publishing for their attention to imagination, kinesthetic abilities, and other creative positives. I also admire researchers and curriculum workers. Mark Runco (1993) has written a research report entitled *Creativity as an Educational Objective for Disadvantaged Students*. He made significant recommendations, which I hope will be considered.

In another 1993 publication entitled *Students of Promise*, Joseph P. Hester clearly recognized many of the creative positives of disadvantaged and culturally different children. He is developing and using many of the creative positives. We need information such as Runco and Hester are developing to overcome the negative forces that are becoming stronger.

REFERENCES

Abrahams, R. D. (1973). The advantages of Black English. In J. S. De Stephano (Ed.), *Language, society, and education: A profile of Black English* (pp. 97-106). Worthington, OH: Charles A. Jones.

Alston, D. J. (1971). *A comparison of motor creativity with verbal creativity and figural creativity of black culturally deprived children.* Doctoral dissertation, University of North Carolina at Greensboro, NC. (University Microfilms Order No. 71-26,932)

Barron, F. (1969). *Creative person and creative process.* New York: Holt, Rinehart & Winston.

DeStephano, J. S. (Ed.). (1973). *Language, society, and education: A profile of Black English.* Worthington, OH: Charles A. Jones.

Deutsch, M. (1967). *The disadvantaged child: Studies of the social environment and the learning process.* New York: Basic Books.

Drake, R. M. (1957). *Drake musical aptitude tests, grades 3 through college.* Chicago: Science Research Associates.

DuBois, W. E. B. (1970). *The gift of black folk.* New York: Washington Square Press.

Fitzgerald, E. J. (Ed.). (1975). *The first national conference on the disadvantaged gifted.* Ventura, CA: Ventura County Superintendent of Schools.

Foster, H. L. (1974). *Ribbin,' jivin,' and playin' the dozens.* Cambridge, MA: Ballinger.

Gezi, K. I. (1969, March). *Analyses of certain measures of creativity and self-concept and their relationships to social class.* Paper presented at the annual meeting of the California Educational Research Association, Los Angeles, CA.

Glover, E. G. (1974). *A motor creativity test for college women.* Doctoral dissertation, University of North Carolina at Greensboro. (University Microfilms Order No. 74-22,014)

Goldstein, J. H., & McGhee, P. E. (1972). *The psychology of humor.* New York: Academic Press.

Gordon, E. (1965). *Musical aptitude profile, grades 4-12.* Boston: Houghton Mifflin.

Gordon, W. J. J. (1961). *Synectics.* New York: Harper & Row.

Guilford, J. P. (1967). *The nature of human intelligence.* New York: McGraw-Hill.

Halpern, F. (1973). *Survival: Black/White.* New York: Pergamon.

Hester, J. P. (1993). *Students of promise.* Newton, NC: Catawba County Schools.

Houston, S. H. (1973). Black English. *Psychology Today, 6*(10), 45- 48.

Kaltsounis, B. (1974). Race, socioeconomic status and creativity. *Psychological Reports, 35,* 164-166.

Klopfer, B., & Davidson, H. H. (1962). *The Rorschach technique: An introductory manual.* New York: Harcourt Brace Jovanovich.

Koestler, A. (1964). *The act of creation.* London: Hutchinson.

Labov, W. (1972). *Language in the inner city: Studies in the Black English vernacular.* Philadelphia: University of Pennsylvania Press.

Labov, W. (1973). The logic of nonstandard English. In J. S. DeStefano (Ed.), *Language, society, and education: A profile of Black English* (pp. 10-44). Worthington, OH: Charles A. Jones.

Lake, D. G., Miles, M. B., & Earle, R. B., Jr. (1973). *Measuring human behavior.* New York: Teachers College Press.

Lowie, R. H. (1963). *Indians of the plains.* Garden City, NY: American Museum Science Books.

McNamara, B. R. (1964). *Creativity in disadvantaged children of a particular rural area.* Master's research paper, Wayne State University, Detroit, MI.

Moreno, J. L. (1946). *Psychodrama* (Vol. 1). New York: Beacon House.

Moreno, J. L., & Moreno, Z. T. (1969). *Psychodrama* (Vol. 3). New York: Beacon House.

NAGC Board of Directors. (1994). *NAGC issues new position papers.* Communique, 7(1), 1, 6.

Newell, A., Shaw, J. C., & Simon, H. A. (1962). The process of creative thinking. In H. E. Gruber, G. Terrell, & M. Wertheimer (Eds.), *Contemporary approaches to creative thinking* (pp. 63-119). New York: Atherton Press.

Patrick, C. (1955). *What is creative thinking?* New York: Philosophical Library.

Ribot, T. (1973). *Essay on the creative imagination.* New York: Arno Press. (Original work published 1906)

Richmond, B. O., & Vance, J. J. (1975). Cooperative-competitive game strategy and personality characteristics of Black and White children. *Interpersonal Development, 5,* 78-85.

Richmond, B. O., & Weiner, G. P. (1973). Cooperation and competition among young children as a function of ethnic grouping, grade, sex, and reward condition. *Journal of Educational Psychology, 64,* 329-334.

Riessman, F. (1962). *The culturally deprived child.* New York: Harper & Row.

Runco, M. A. (1993). *Creativity as an educational objective for disadvantaged students.* Storrs: University of Connecticut, National Research Center on the Gifted and Talented.

Seashore, C. E. (1960). *Seashore measures of musical talent.* New York: Psychological Corporation.

Smith, R. M. (1965). *The relationship of creativity to social class* (Final report on Cooperative Research Project 2250, U.S. Office of Education). Pittsburgh, PA: University of Pittsburgh.

Steiner, S. (1970). *La raza: The Mexican Americans.* New York: Hatper & Row.

Tibbetts, J. W. (1968). *Relationships of creativity to socioeconomic status, race, sex, and grade-point average in an adolescent population.* Doctoral dissertation, University of Southern California, CA. (University Microfilms Order No. 68-13,589)

Torrance, E. P. (1964). Identifying the creatively gifted among economically and culturally disadvantaged children. *Gifted Child Quarterly, 8,* 171-176.

Torrance, E. P. (1966). *Torrance Tests of Creative Thinking: Norms-technical manual.* Lexington, MA: Personnel Press.

Torrance, E. P. (1967). *Understanding the fourth grade slump in creative thinking* (Final report on CRP Project No. 994, U.S. Office of Education). Athens: The University of Georgia, Georgia Studies of Creative Behavior. (ERIC Document Reproduction Service No. ED 018 273)

Torrance, E. P. (1968). Examples and rationales of test tasks for assessing creative abilities. *Journal of Creative Behavior, 2*(3), 165-178.

Torrance, E. P. (1971). Are the Torrance Tests of Creative Thinking biased against or in favor of disadvantaged groups? *Gifted Child Quarterly, 15,* 75-80.

Torrance, E. P. (1972a). Predictive validity of the Torrance Tests of Creative Thinking. *Journal of Creative Behavior, 6,* 236-252.

Torrance, E. P. (1972b). Career patterns and peak creative achievements of creative high school students twelve years later. *Gifted Child Quarterly, 16,* 75-88.

Torrance, E. P. (1974). Interscholastic brainstorming and creative problem solving competition for the creatively gifted. *Gifted Child Quarterly, 18,* 3-7.

Torrance, E.P. (1977). *Discovery and nurturance of giftedness in the culturally different.* Reston, VA: Council for Exceptional Children.

Torrance, E. P. (1980). Growing up creatively gifted: A 22-year longitudinal study. *Creative Child and Adult Quarterly, 5*(3), 148-158, 170.

Torrance, E.P. (1990). *Manual for scoring and interpreting results: Torrance Tests of Creative Thinking, Verbal, forms A and B.* Bensenville, IL: Scholastic Testing Service.

Torrance, E.P., Ball, O.E., & Safter, H.T. (1992). *Torrance Tests of Creative Thinking: Streamlined Scoring Guide, figural A and B.* Bensenville, IL: Scholastic Testing Service.

Torrance, E. P., Khatena, J., & Cunnington, B. F. (1974). *Thinking creatively with sounds and words.* Lexington, MA: Personnel Press.

Torrance, E. P., Murdock, M. C., & Fletcher, D. (1996). *Creative problem solving through role playing.* Clubview, South Africa: Benedic Books.

Torrance, E. P., & Safter, H. T. (1990). *The incubation model of teaching: Getting beyond the aha!* Buffalo, NY: Bearly Limited.

Torrance, E. P., Weiner, D., Presbury, J. H., & Henderson, M. (1987). *Save tomorrow for the children.* Buffalo, NY: Bearly Limited.

Vaughan, M. M. (1971). *Music as model and metaphor in the cultivation and measurement of creative behavior in children.* Doctoral dissertation, The University of Georgia, Athens, GA. (University Microfilms Order No. 72-11,056)

Welsh, G. S. (1959). *Preliminary manual: The Welsh figure preference test.* Palo Alto, CA: Consulting Psychologists Press.

Welsh, G. S. (1975). *Creativity and intelligence: A personality approach.* Chapel Hill: University of North Carolina, Institute for Research in Social Science.

Wyrick, W. (1966). *Comparison of motor creativity with verbal creativity, motor ability, and intelligence.* Doctoral dissertation, University of Texas at Austin, TX. (University Microfilms Order No. 66-14,343)

Yoors, J. (1967). *The gypsies.* New York: Simon & Schuster.

8

Developing the Potential of Young Gifted Children from Low-income and Culturally and Linguistically Diverse Backgrounds

Margie K. Kitano
Rosa Isela Perez

The historic underrepresentation of children from some cultural and linguistic groups in programs for the gifted has been well documented. Recent reports emphasize in addition the continued and significant underserving of children from low-income homes. One national study found that only 9% of students in gifted and talented programs came from families in the bottom income quartile. In contrast, nearly half (47%) of the students in such programs represented the top income quartile (Ross, 1993). Clearly, potentially gifted children from economically disadvantaged backgrounds who are also culturally or linguistically diverse have reduced opportunities for receiving appropriate services to support their talents.

Research on successful strategies for improving educational opportunities for this population consistently identifies early intervention and parental involvement as critical components. However, systematic preschool education for potentially gifted low-income, diverse students is underutilized by school districts nationally (VanTassel-Baska, Patton, &

Prillaman, 1989). The recent federal report on the status of education for the gifted and talented (Ross, 1993) recommended that we "ensure that all children, especially economically disadvantaged and minority children, have access to an early childhood education that develops their potential" (p. 27). In addition, programs for young children should include preparing both teachers and parents for nurturing talent development and building strong linkages with elementary programs to ensure continuous services.

This chapter seeks to encourage implementation of preschool and primary programs that focus on the needs and talents of low-income and culturally and linguistically diverse children. Essential program elements are described, including a clear sense of purpose; a coherent framework for enriched curriculum and instruction; collaboration among educational units; sustained teacher development; continuous parent involvement; and systematic evaluation. We integrate into the discussion the extant literature as well as our own experiences in directing and evaluating preschool and primary programs designed to develop young children's potential.

CLARITY OF PURPOSE

Given consistent evidence of the need for early intervention programs for young gifted children from economically disadvantaged backgrounds, why are so few programs available? One reason stems from misconceptions about these children's needs.

Misconception 1: All children from economically disadvantaged backgrounds require remedial education, such as drill and practice, in order to be prepared for schooling. In fact, although poverty and racism can produce educational disadvantages, the potential for giftedness exists in equal proportions in all groups (Borland & Wright, 1994). It is essential that teachers working with children from economically disadvantaged backgrounds banish stereotypes and recognize that all children in their classroom possess strengths and that some of these children have the potential for exceptional achievement. Teachers who have such expectations will be more likely to provide enriched rather than remedial curricula and instruction that will encourage children to express their talents.

Misconception 2: Children need to master the English language before being intellectually challenged. Rather, children can be gifted in any language. Current research on bilingual education demonstrates the importance of educating children in their first language during the primary years (Kitano & Espinosa, 1995). Instructional strategies for developing potential can be implemented in any language and by incorporating modalities (e.g., visual/spatial, tactile/kinesthetic) that are less reliant on language.

Misconception 3: Giftedness cannot be identified during the preschool/ primary years because standardized testing is less reliable for young children. To the contrary, current practice demonstrates that we can identify gifted potential at an early age among children from economically disadvantaged backgrounds (Karnes & Johnson, 1991). However, identification methods appropriate for these children de-emphasize standardized measures in favor of trained observation and more authentic forms of assessment within the natural setting (Borland & Wright, 1994; Ramos-Ford & Gardner, 1991).

Misconception 4: An enriched curriculum at the preschool/primary level is developmentally unsound, can "push" children, or rob them of their childhood. This misconception stems from the national debate over early schooling for young children in general (Kagan & Zigler, 1987). However, recent research on cognitive processing of gifted children demonstrates that even young gifted children possess superior ability to generalize knowledge, understand tasks, and learn more efficiently than their average peers (Kanevsky, 1990). Therefore, what constitutes developmentally appropriate practice for gifted children may differ from the typical curriculum. David Elkind (1988), whose work sparked concern for the "hurried" child, admitted that acceleration for a gifted child may be considered matching of curriculum to abilities and hence developmentally appropriate practice.

These misconceptions have contributed to a lack of understanding regarding the purpose of special programs for gifted children from low-income and culturally and linguistically diverse backgrounds. Educators and parents involved in programs for these children need to be clear that the intent of these programs is not to apply a label. Rather, the purposes are to:

1. Offer enriched curricula and instructional strategies for all children that will nurture their strengths and create an environment that stimulates the creative and higher level thinking of all.
2. Provide such opportunities and then informally identify a talent pool of potentially gifted children. The informal identification of potentially talented children encourages teachers to look for all children's strengths and to provide enrichment for all children as they support the special needs of those with superior abilities.

COHERENT FRAMEWORK

In addition to a clear sense of purpose, programs for developing the potential of young gifted children from low-income, diverse backgrounds require a consistently applied framework for program development. For example, several recent projects have developed effective instructional and assessment strategies for this population based on Gardner's theory of multiple intelligences (e.g., Maker, Nielson, & Rogers, 1994; Ramos-Ford & Gardner, 1991). The framework must also include culturally consistent practices and materials, including bilingual education methods as appropriate. Finally, the framework should recognize and capitalize on the unique strengths of diverse students. For example, recent investigations, some with low-income students, suggest that bilingualism may have cognitive advantages as demonstrated by scores on measures of mental flexibility and creativity (García, 1994).

The San Diego Unified School District's preschool and primary developing potential projects, described throughout this chapter, use a "best practices" framework that applies a repertoire of instructional and curricular strategies supported in the literature as effective for talent development. Project Excel, supported by Title VII (bilingual education) funds, applies this framework in bilingual classrooms at the primary grades, thus bridging programs for the gifted and programs for bilingual students. Project First Step, a Javits-funded (gifted and talented) project, extends this effort downward to state preschools that serve low-income culturally diverse and bilingual children, integrating preschool and regular education with bilingual and gifted. Briefly stated, teachers (a) incorporate brainstorming and other divergent thinking strategies, Hilda Taba's inductive thinking strategies, and Parnes' creative problem-solving model (Maker, 1982); and (b) integrate these strategies into thematic interdisciplinary curricula (San Diego City Schools, 1994). The enriched program provides opportunities for children to practice creative, inductive, and higher level thinking applied to meaningful content. In this way, all children have opportunities to enhance their strengths and demonstrate their potential. Teachers then use observations and portfolio reviews to informally identify a talent pool of potentially gifted children. Teacher development, parent involvement, and student readiness constitute the projects' three major components. Together, the two developing potential projects serve preschool through second grade. Formal identification and programming for gifted and talented begins at third grade.

COLLABORATION

Collaboration is an essential component of effective programs designed for gifted young children from low-income and culturally and linguistically diverse backgrounds. In large, urban school districts with high numbers of diverse children, services are provided, usually in isolation, by a number of distinct units: early childhood, regular primary, bilingual, gifted and talented, and special education. Federal, state, and district regulations, funding requirements, political concerns, and resource limitations can present formidable barriers to collaboration among these separate units at the district level. Another source of leadership for collaboration on programs for diverse gifted learners can be found at the school sites that already integrate services from several programs.

San Diego's Excel and First Step projects were implemented at school sites where the leadership of the teachers and principals created a supportive environment for collaboration. Such settings permit easy identification of common ground, overlap in objectives and strategies, and best targets for building linkages between current and new program elements. For example, the state preschools had adopted the High Scope curriculum with bilingual education as appropriate to the children served. These sites already supported collaboration among preschool, bilingual, and primary education. Within this climate, the preschool teachers enthusiastically accepted the challenge of analyzing commonalities between the objectives and strategies of High Scope and the developing potential projects, and of finding creative ways to integrate into the existing program new instructional strategies and higher level concepts.

Collaborative models facilitate talent development in a number of important ways. Collaboration:

- Encourages dialogue about students who demonstrate gifted potential
- Promotes continuity of program and transition from one grade level to the next
- Extends teacher development through a broader knowledge base and encourages peer coaching to implement innovations
- Fosters efficient utilization of site resources
- Promotes parent participation through acquired knowledge and skill in facilitating their children's development
- Contributes to a mutual reinforcing of promising practices that lead to talent development
- Fosters positive attitudes toward the gifted and contributes to the maturity of the site's program for the gifted

TEACHER DEVELOPMENT

Teachers make successful programs. We have found several factors critical to effective teacher inservice:

1. *Sensitivity to the teachers' backgrounds and experiences.*
Early childhood educators typically represent a broader range of educational levels and types of experience than do educators who serve
older children. Some states, for example, do not require the baccalau-
reate degree for preschool teaching. Teachers who work primarily with
culturally and linguistically diverse children may have been selected to
represent the diversity they serve and bring a wealth of cultural and
language backgrounds. Some will bring extensive formal training and
experience in specific early childhood and bilingual curriculum models.
Inservice workshops should consider teachers' current knowledge base
as well as learning needs. A needs assessment conducted prior to training can enable trainers to begin at appropriate levels, recognize and
utilize teachers' current competence, attach new concepts and
strategies to what the teachers already know and do, and engage
them in problem solving around issues of integrating new strategies into
their current programs.

2. *Contact over time.* In our experience, multiple articulated
workshops spread over time provide more effective preparation than
one or two isolated sessions. A series of workshops supports group formation and a sense of trust among presenters and participants. More
frequent contact also permits debriefing after teachers have time
between sessions to implement what they learn. Each workshop should
be of sufficient length to include a discussion of the strategy or topic, a
demonstration, and practice with feedback.

Teachers especially appreciate the opportunity to observe
experienced peers provide demonstrations within the workshop or on site
through a visitation/observation schedule. One Project Excel teacher, for
example, presented to First Step teachers a demonstration of a lesson
combining brainstorming and Taba's developing concepts strategy for
use with Spanish-speaking children who are not yet reading. The demonstration provided an excellent example of capturing children's ideas and
helping them categorize by recording their brainstorming on audiotape,
drawing or cutting out pictures to represent their ideas, and manipulating the drawings to create and recreate categories.

Topics rated highly by teachers include strategies for recognizing gifted potential in culturally and linguistically diverse young children; discovering linkages between the regular (High Scope) and
developing potential models; instructional methods for developing
potential; designing an integrated curriculum; implementing portfolios;
and working with parents. Again, building on the current curriculum,
workshops encourage teachers to appropriately raise their expectations for children's achievement by incorporating higher level or more
complex concepts. For example, one current unit integrated communication, literature, art, and free-play activities around Thanksgiving as a
concept. Teachers can apply similar integration to a more complex
generalization as the unit theme, such as "all cultures celebrate impor-

tant events." A unit on butterflies can be redesigned to support the concept of change and the generalization that living things change and mature. Project staff also include in the workshops the rationale and procedures for program evaluation, given the integral nature of evaluation to be discussed later.

3. *In-classroom assistance.* Conducting planned, on-site visits to observe teachers encourages implementation of new strategies and curriculum components. Structuring observations as peer coaching (Kagan, 1989) rather than evaluation supports a sense of collaborative experimentation and problem solving between teacher and trainer. Peer coaching has three distinct phases: planning, observing, and processing or debriefing. Teachers provide a written lesson plan describing the developing potential strategy they will be implementing, the objectives, and the activity. They indicate what they would like the coaches to observe and how they would like the coaches to participate in the lesson (if at all). During the observation, the coaches record the positive aspects of the lesson, the children's responses to the lesson, and the behaviors targeted by the teacher during the planning phase. Following the observation, the teacher describes her or his feelings about the lesson and outcomes. The coaches share their positive observations, and the team of teacher and coaches problem solve about possible modifications and extensions.

We recently observed a project preschool teacher try Taba's Developing Concepts strategy with her group of 22 children, who represented four different language groups: Spanish, Hmong, Somalian, and English. The teacher presented the children with various food items such as canned and boxed fruits and cereals, natural fruits and vegetables, and canned beverages. She then asked the children to select items that belonged together, to provide a reason for their selection, and to name the group. The teacher expected children to classify the foods according to how they are ingested (things we eat, chew, drink, etc.). One child selected a can of pineapple juice and a box of cereal because "we eat them together." Debriefing with the coaches helped the teacher recognize that the child's response was a relational rather than an analytic one, represented a culturally related style of categorizing, and constituted a valid approach to problem solving.

PARENTAL INVOLVEMENT

Research on effective schooling as well as literature on parents of gifted students from low-income and diverse backgrounds identify parent involvement in their children's education as critical (Strom, Johnson, Strom, & Strom, 1992). Parents can contribute significantly to their young children's growth by observing their behavior, nurturing potential at home, holding high expectations, and becoming advocates for appropriate educational services. Parent training programs can support these goals.

In the San Diego City Schools Gifted Program, the Excel and First Step projects designed parent training as an extension of the teacher development and student readiness activities. The parent component seeks to build a strong knowledge base among parents and to encourage their involvement by providing opportunities for active participation. At each project school, project staff conduct a series of three to five parent workshops for all project parents. As in the teacher development component, sustained training over a period of time is critical.

The parent workshops provide orientations to the district's Gifted and Talented program and to Project Excel and First Step as well as information about definitions and characteristics, early childhood development, multiple intelligences, the project's instructional strategies, and ideas for developing creativity at home through mathematics, science, and language arts activities. Project staff model the instructional strategies to enable parents to experience the processes of higher order thinking and demonstrate how parents might apply these strategies at home with their children. Parents are encouraged to volunteer in their child's classroom and in field trips so they experience the importance of utilizing community resources that have relevance to the growth and development of their child. The acquisition of a sound knowledge base and an understanding of the special challenges of parenting a potentially gifted child support the parent advocacy goals. A site principal commented that parents knock on her door to inquire, if not demand, that their children continue to be placed in a project classroom.

EVALUATION

The importance of designing and implementing a systematic evaluation plan cannot be overemphasized. As cogently observed by Fetterman (1993): "At risk in an unexamined program are no less than the health and well-being of gifted and talented children and the future of the nation" (p. vii). Evaluation data are essential to advance our knowledge about what constitutes effective practices with bright low-income and culturally and linguistically diverse children and to promote replication of effective practices to serve additional numbers. The growth of early childhood programs is hampered by the absence of evaluation studies specific to this population. VanTassel-Baska et al. (1989) found that as a field, we rely too heavily on attitudinal perceptions about program effectiveness rather than evidence of impact on students. However, recent resources assist practitioners in designing and implementing sound evaluation strategies for both program improvement and valida-tion of effectiveness (e.g., Fetterman, 1993; House & Lapan, 1994; Tomlinson, Bland, & Moon, 1993). This section synthesizes problems and suggestions and applies them to evaluating programs for young gifted children from low-income and diverse backgrounds.

Problems

Two critical types of evaluation questions concern (a) process evalua-tion, which asks if the curriculum and methods are consistent with the framework and goals; and (b) product, outcome, or impact evalua-tion, which addresses whether the program leads to changes in the children, such as improved social development, creativity, or knowl-edge, again depending on the program's goals. Outcome or impact evaluation has been of most concern to educators, parents, policy-makers, and taxpayers. The traditional model for outcome evaluation requires random assignment to the special program and comparison of children who complete the program with similar children who did not participate. Lacking such a comparison, gains made by program com-pleters may be attributable to normal maturation. However, administra-tive, legal, and ethical constraints often mitigate against implementa-tion of this "experimental model" for many educational programs. As a result, many programs resort to simply examining pretest-posttest gains of the children who attended the special program.

There are several problems specific to assessing gain scores of preschool-age children. First, the normative sample for some standard-ized measures may not include children from the target income, cultur-al, and language groups. Further, some standardized measures may not have norms for young children. Some with appropriate age norms have too few items at the preschool age level. Second, because of these children's high ability, there may be a ceiling effect that hinders the interpretation of scores. For example, if a child enters and exits the pro-gram with scores at the 99th percentile, have no gains occurred? Third, few instruments are available that assess growth in specific content areas addressed by the curriculum, and many young gifted children cannot express their knowledge in written form or in oral form on demand. Fourth, appropriate goals for young gifted children often are individualized, long-range, or operationally indefinable (e.g., preventing later underachievement; developing risk taking). Finally, even when gains can be determined reliably, no agreed-on criteria exist for the magnitude of gain that defines program success for young gifted chil-dren from low-income and diverse backgrounds. For example, should a 4-year-old gifted child who attends a special program for 1 year gain 1 year's growth, 2 year's growth, or more? In all areas (motor, language, communication, social/emotional, cognitive) or just one?

Alternatives to Experimental Designs

The literature suggests two general evaluation approaches as alternatives to the experimental approach: nonexperimental quantitative approaches and qualitative procedures. Carter (1986) described several evaluation designs for programs for gifted children that permit analyses of quantitative data in the absence of randomly selected control subjects. These include designs which use intact comparison groups, such as (a) equally talented children from districts that do not have programs for the gifted and (b) similar children who receive the same curriculum components as the experimental group but in a different order (counter-balanced designs). In addition, time-series designs permit use of subjects as their own controls. Although such designs strengthen the validity of evaluation results, they frequently require scores or gains derived from standardized or program-developed measures, with the inherent problems described earlier.

Dissatisfaction with quantitative designs has led to the application of more naturalistic or qualitative approaches to evaluation of programs for the gifted. Briefly, qualitative research documents natural events in the classroom and uses these events to describe and interpret program effects (Barnette, 1984). In addition to use of the natural setting as the source of data, characteristics of qualitative evaluation include collection of descriptive (observation, interview, document) as well as numerical data; concern for process as well as product; inductive analysis; and focus on participants' perceptions (Lundsteen, 1987). Although quantitative approaches provide objective evaluations of particular program aspects, qualitative approaches to evaluation capture the real life nature of a program in a holistic way.

Suggestions for Evaluating Early Childhood Programs Targeting Low-Income, Diverse Children

Based on the literature and our experience, we have found the following guidelines helpful in evaluating programs for the target population:

1. *Plan and implement the evaluation component as part of program development and implementation.* As the program's framework, purpose, and goals are shaped, identify the types of data—quantitative and qualitative—that will indicate the extent to which the framework is implemented, the program meets its purpose, and the goals are accomplished. Determine also the criteria to be used to determine success.

More specifically, we have found the following questions, criteria, and indicators to be useful in evaluating programs for the target population:

a. To what extent do the teachers implement the framework and strategies? Do the teachers present challenging concepts and content? Criteria and indicators: in-class observations indicate that 90% of the teachers are applying appropriately the program-supported curriculum and instructional strategies.

b. Do the children respond to the strategies as anticipated? Criteria and indicators: Teacher and trainer observations, parent comments, and child products or portfolios indicate an increase in creative and higher level thinking compared to baseline for all children.

c. What are the children like who are identified for the talent pool? Criteria and indicators: Case studies of a small sample of randomly selected children identified by teachers as potentially gifted demonstrate qualitative and quantitative differences as compared to case studies of children not so identified. Case studies summarize data from teacher and parent interviews, child portfolios, and any concurrent and follow-up assessments. Interestingly, Project Excel's case studies suggest that young bilingual children from low-income backgrounds identified for the talent pool exhibit similar characteristics to mainstream gifted children as described in the literature.

d. Does the program accomplish its purpose of developing potential? Criteria and indicators: The proportion of children from project classrooms who formally qualify for gifted programs is significantly greater than the proportion from similar classrooms that are not participating in the program. For example, during the fourth year of Project Excel, 49 students identified by their teachers for the talent pool received gifted certification compared to only 4 students in the comparison classrooms (nonproject schools).

2. *Incorporate both quantitative and qualitative methods as appropriate to the specific evaluation questions.* Note that the indicators in the examples in #1 include observational, interview, and case study data (qualitative) as well as numbers of children who qualify for special programs and scores from formal assessments (quantitative). For Project Excel, project and comparison children were administered *Aprenda*, a standardized achievement test in Spanish, matching one of the project's objectives concerning reading achievement. Project students generally outperformed the comparison group in all test areas (reading comprehension, reading vocabulary, and total reading).

3. *Use a variety of data gathering methods designed or selected to match the program's framework and goals*—for example, portfolios, products, and other forms of assessment with demonstrated interrater reliability; case studies; test scores, and systematic observation.

Scores on standardized and project-developed measures have meaning in evaluation only to the extent that they provide data that match the program's objectives. Gain or comparison scores on standardized measures of language development in English for example, have meaning only to the extent that the program focused on English language development as an objective.

4. *Collect data from multiple sources in order to assess a broad array of perspectives.* Agreement among the various sources provides a more comprehensive and reliable evaluation than can be achieved through one viewpoint. Useful sources include external evaluators, parents, teachers, and children. Projects serving low-income and culturally and linguistically diverse children require evaluators knowledgeable about this population as well as about evaluation and education of the gifted. Interpretation of data from classroom observations, parent interviews, and tests conducted in the children's home language(s) require evaluators familiar with the language and knowledgeable about bilingual education. Project Excel's evaluation design included use of external evaluators as well as parent and teacher interviews and surveys and student surveys, test scores, and portfolios.

5. *Conduct both formative and summative evaluation to support ongoing program improvement and to assess program impact.* For example, in-class observations to determine level of program implementation can signal a need for modifications in the teacher inservice component early in the project's implementation (formative). Periodic assessment of children's creative expression, if a project goal, can provide data for both program improvement and impact (summative).

6. *Follow the children over time.* Longitudinal followup of children is especially critical for programs serving young gifted children from diverse backgrounds, a population for whom few impact data are available. Important objectives for developing potential programs serving these children are their continued superior achievement and qualification for services, objectives requiring follow-up. The evaluation data for Project Excel, currently in its fifth year, indicate that the longer the students remain in project classrooms, the more likely they are to outperform their nonproject peers on the standardized achievement test. Moreover, students identified for the talent pool outperform those not so identified in project and nonproject classrooms. Further, teacher surveys reveal that teachers of the gifted rate former Excel students similarly to non-Excel gifted students, a remarkable finding considering the nontraditional backgrounds (low-income; culturally and linguistically diverse) of Excel students (Bernal, forthcoming; Millett, 1993).

FINAL COMMENTS

Our experience suggests that if the priority of preschool and primary gifted and talented programs is to provide the best possible education for *all* learners, then no barriers exist to identifying and serving potentially gifted children from low-income and culturally and linguistically diverse backgrounds. Making the needs of these children a priority requires committed and thoughtful collaboration at the site level. In a true collaboration, the need for external resources declines as each site finds and contributes the necessary funding. Collaboration at the site level also supports institutionalization of effective programs because the new program has been built on and extends the best of current practices. Effective programs for diverse, young, potentially gifted children have positive impact on the children themselves, their parents, and teachers. Moreover, successful early intervention supports transformation of the larger gifted and talented program by appropriately diversifying the students served and stimulating curricular and instructional change at all levels.

REFERENCES

Barnette, J. (1984). Naturalistic approaches to gifted and talented program evaluation. *Journal for the Education of the Gifted, 7*(1), 26-37.

Bernal, E. (forthcoming). *Evaluation of Project Excel.* Unpublished manuscript.

Borland, J. H., & Wright, L. (1994). Identifying young, potentially gifted, economically disadvantaged students. *Gifted Child Quarterly, 38*(4), 164-171.

Carter, K. R. (1986). Evaluation design: Issues confronting evaluators of gifted programs. *Gifted Child Quarterly, 30*(2), 88-92.

Elkind, D. (1988). Mental acceleration. *Journal for the Education of the Gifted, 11*(4), 19-31.

Fetterman, D. M. (1993). *Evaluate yourself.* Executive Summary. (Research-based Decision Making Series No. 9303). Storrs: The National Research Center on the Gifted and Talented, University of Connecticut.

García, E. (1994). *Understanding and meeting the challenge of student cultural diversity.* Boston: Houghton Mifflin.

House, E. R., & Lapan, S. (1994). Evaluation of programs for disadvantaged gifted students. *Journal for the Education of the Gifted, 17*(4), 441-466.

Kagan, S. (1989). *Cooperative learning: Resources for teachers.* San Juan Capistrano, CA: Spencer Kagan.

Kagan, S. L., & Zigler, E. (1987). *Early schooling: The national debate.* New Haven, CT: Yale University Press.

Kanevsky, L. (1990). Pursuing qualitative differences in the flexible use of problem-solving strategy by young children. *Journal for the Education of the Gifted, 13*(2), 115-140.

Karnes, M. B., & Johnson, L. J. (1991). The preschool/primary gifted child. *Journal for the Education of the Gifted, 14*(3), 267-283.

Kitano, M. K., & Espinosa, R. (1995). Language diversity and giftedness: Working with gifted English language learners. *Journal for the Education of the Gifted, 18*(3), 234-254.

Lundsteen, S. W. (1987). Qualitative assessment of gifted education. *Gifted Child Quarterly, 31*(1), 25-29.

Maker, C. J. (1982). *Teaching models in education of the gifted.* Rockville, MD: Aspen Systems.

Maker, C. J., Nielson, A. B., & Rogers, J. A. (1994). Giftedness, diversity, and problem solving. *Teaching Exceptional Children, 27*(1), 4-19.

Millett, S. (1993). *Fourth year evaluation of Project Excel: A Title VII federal assistance grant.* San Diego, CA: San Diego City Schools Planning, Assessment and Accountability Division.

Ramos-Ford, V., & Gardner, H. (1991). Giftedness from a multiple intelligences perspective. In N. Colangelo & G. A. Davis (Eds.), *Handbook of gifted education* (pp. 55-64). Boston: Allyn & Bacon.

Ross, P. O. (1993). *National excellence: A case for developing America's talent.* Washington, DC: Office of Educational Research and Improvement, U.S. Department of Education.

San Diego City Schools. (1994). *Thematic interdisciplinary demonstration project.* San Diego, CA: San Diego City Schools School Services Division, Exceptional Programs Department.

Strom, R., Johnson, A., Strom, S., & Strom, P. (1992). Designing curriculum for parents of gifted children. *Journal for the Education of the Gifted, 15*(2), 182-200.

Tomlinson, C., Bland, L., & Moon, T. (1993). Evaluation utilization: A review of the literature with implications for gifted education. *Journal for the Education of the Gifted, 16*(2), 171-189.

VanTassel-Baska, J., Patton, J. & Prillaman, D. (1989). Disadvantaged gifted learners at risk for educational attention. *Focus on Exceptional Children, 22*(3), 1-15.

9

Targeting Potentially Talented and Gifted Minority Students for Academic Achievement

Patricia Reid Brooks

Once upon a time,
    there might have been a time:
    when the sun didn't"t shine,
    when the sea didn't roll,
    when the earth didn't spin,
    and the wind didn't blow.

And once upon a time,
    there must have been a time:
    when nature came alive,
    when things began to grow,
    when creatures stood erect,
    and they began to know.

And through all time
    from then 'till now,
    these creatures humankind,
    have painted life,
    they've run and danced,

composed their works and songs.
They've measured and invented things
and pondered rights and wrongs.
They've laughed and cried,
lived and died,
loved and hated too.

But once upon a time is now
tomorrow's yesterday,
with countless schemes
and life designs
to shape reality.
More will run and dance and sing
compose, invent, and paint
and chart new paths and destinies
where space and time combine.

Who are they,
who will they be,
who line by line
composed the rhyme
of once upon a time?

Once Upon a Time—Clinton Bunke and Patricia Dearborn (1981)

There have always been among us talented and gifted individuals who achieved great things despite significant obstacles placed in their paths. No doubt, for many others, the obstacles were sufficient to delay or deny the fullest expression of their endeavors. Sadly, for some the most significant factor contributing to lack of achievement and personal fulfillment was an educational experience that did not recognize or ignored the individual's potential giftedness. The question posed by Bunke and Dearborn is so critical for future generations that every segment of the school population must be viewed as a potential repository for the talented and gifted. Specifically, we must focus increased attention on those groups who have historically been omitted from programs designed for the talented student.

More than 20 years ago, when discussing the need to increase the number of potentially gifted and talented students, Renzulli (1975) noted that perhaps the largest untapped source of talented and gifted could be found among black Americans and individuals holding membership in the ranks of the economically disadvantaged. In a similar vein, Verma and Bagley (1975) stated that students holding membership in a minority group and differing significantly from the stereotypical middle class faced insurmountable barriers that effectively limited their collective performance on pencil-and-paper tests. As a result, large numbers of students were stigmatized as being unintelligent and disadvantaged and systematically and routinely excluded from participation in Talented and Gifted (TAG) programs.

Historically, a myriad of circumstances too numerous to mention here, but well know to those involved in the educational process, contributed to the lack of attention given to the identification of talented minority students. Unquestionably, the meager search for talent among minority groups was sustained by perceptions and attitudes relative to the capabilities of minority students. It was also affected by the limited definition of gifted and talented and by the use of an identification measure that, seemingly, supports an undying myth conceived years ago which sustains the notion that ability tests measure intelligence. Gould (1981) stated, "Much of the elaborate statistical work performed by testers during the past fifty years provides no independent confirmation for the proposition that tests measure intelligence, but merely establishes correlation with a preconceived and unquestioned standard." This standard is reflected in the values and judgments of the majority middle-class culture.

Further, there is evidence that despite a wealth of information that suggests that traditional pencil-and-paper standardized tests identify a narrow potential—largely the capacity to manipulate verbal and mathematical symbols and abstractions—they continue to be the major consideration influencing decisions concerning the giftedness of the student. The belief that traditional paper-and-pencil tests are the only valid and reliable measure of intelligence has been most detrimental for all students, but especially minority students.

Few would deny that educational opportunities for talented and gifted children have greatly improved over the past two decades. However, much remains to be done, not only in the area of identification for minority, disadvantaged, or linguistically different students, but programming for all students. *National Excellence: The Case for Developing America's Talent* (U.S. Department of Education, 1993), a report prepared under the direction of the U.S. Department of Education Javits Gifted and Talented Program, cites recent studies which show that:

- Gifted and talented elementary school students have mastered from 35% to 50% of the curriculum to be offered in five basic subjects before they begin the school year.
- Most regular classroom teachers make few, if any, provisions for talented students.
- Most of the highest achieving students in the nation included in *Who's Who Among American High School Students* reported that they studied less than one hour a day. This suggests that they get top grades without having to work hard.
- In the one national study available, only 2 cents out of every $100 spent on K-12 education in 1990 supported special opportunities for talented and gifted students.

- The talents of disadvantaged and minority children have been especially neglected. Almost one in four American children lives in poverty, representing an enormous pool of untapped talent. Yet most programs for these children focus on solving problems they bring to school, rather than on challenging them to develop their strengths. It is sometimes assumed that children from unpromising backgrounds are not capable of outstanding accomplishment.

These findings do not bode well for our future national prosperity and advancement. As we face the challenge of preparing students to become successful adults in a increasingly information-based, technology oriented, multinational global society, it is imperative that American education be in the vanguard to design, implement, and evaluate improved programs and processes that assure the earliest possible identification and nurturing of those who have the potential to soothe and excite the senses, challenge and stimulate our thinking, and inspire awe and confidence in the limitless capacity of the individual to make dreams reality. In this effort, if we choose to exclude any segment of the population we do so at our own peril.

The remainder of this chapter presents one school district's program to identify the potentially talented and gifted minority students in kindergarten and first grade and one of the district's elementary school's program to assure that once identified these students are provided opportunities to participate in activities and experiences that foster the fullest expression of the students' talents and gifts.

Prince George's County, MD, boasts the 17th largest school district in the nation with an enrollment of 115,000 pupils. In 1981, Project STEP (Strategies for Targeting Early Potential) was implemented in 9 of the district's 122 elementary schools. By 1985, the success of the project was such that it was part of the curriculum of all of the elementary schools.

Conceived as an aggressive strategy to promote teacher identification of potentially gifted minority students in kindergarten and first grade and to nurture hidden talents, Project STEP activities are appropriate for all student populations. However, to assure inclusion of students who were historically underrepresented in the county's TAG programs, Project STEP (Brooks, 1984) adopted the following definition of the minority student.

Minority children are those children regardless of race or ethnic group, who may have language patterns and experiences, cultural backgrounds, economic disadvantages or differences, which make it difficult for them to demonstrate their potential on traditional identification measures of talented and gifted. Those who met this definition included, but were not limited to students who were:

- African American
- culturally different
- economically disadvantaged
- native American
- non-English speaking as a first language; and/or
- rural white

Because numerous studies have demonstrated that able minority students who hold membership in one or more of the above groups often lack the experiences and language patterns necessary to decode test items or even to understand instructions for completing the test, Project STEP does not rely on the results of a single pencil-and-paper test to identify the potentially talented and gifted minority student. Instead, Project STEP seeks to isolate, identify, and nurture those behaviors which are indicative of the potentially gifted. These become evident and are readily observable as the child participates in classroom or school activities. Ann P. Issacs (1966) developed an inventory of characteristics of gifted children. She reported that gifted children:

- are curious
- have a large vocabulary
- have long memories
- sometimes learn to read alone
- have a keen sense of humor
- are persistent
- like to collect things
- are independent
- are creative and imaginative
- may be bigger and stronger than average
- initiate their own activities
- develop earlier and learn earlier
- enjoy complicated games
- are interested and concerned about world problems
- are original thinkers
- like older children when very young
- set high goals and ideals

Issacs's inventory is consistent with the following definition of gifted and talented used in the federal Javits Gifted and Talented Education Act (U.S. Department of Education, 1993):

Children and youth with outstanding talent perform or show the potential for performing at remarkably high levels of accomplishment when compared with others of their age, experience, or environment.

These children and youth exhibit high performance capability in intellectual, creative, and/or artistic areas, possess an unusual leadership capacity, or excel in specific academic fields. They require services or activities not ordinarily provided by the schools.

Outstanding talents are present in children and youth from all cultural groups, across all economic strata, and in all areas of human endeavor.

Using Issacs's inventory and the definition of giftedness as a conceptual framework, Project STEP focuses on five specific areas with attendant behaviors that are indicative of outstanding talent. The areas and behaviors which may be evidenced are defined below:

Learning. Conversation reveals richness of expression, imagery, elaboration, and fluency; keenly observes and/or listens; demonstrates ability to join smaller ideas into larger concepts or generalizations.

Motivation. Evidences power ability to concentrate; prefers to work independently with minimal direction from the teacher; is self critical and strives for perfection.

Leadership. Accepts or volunteers for responsibility and follows through; evidences self-confidence with adults and classmates; demonstrates flexibility in thought and actions and readily adapts to changes in classroom routine.

Creativity. Displays intellectual playfulness; readily assumes high risks; exhibits curiosity about many things; frequently improvises with common place materials to create original and unusual products.

Adaptability. Displays maturity of judgment; transfers learning from one situation to another; learns through experience and demonstrates unusual resourcefulness.

Because teacher observations and behavior-focused classroom activities are crucial for the identification of the potentially gifted and talented minority student, Project Step includes a comprehensive in-service education program. Attended by kindergarten, first grade teachers, and the principal, the goals of the educational program are twofold. One is to enable the participants to become familiar with Project STEP and the manner in which it is operationalized in the classroom through activities, observations, and documentation. The other is to provide a forum that increases the participants' awareness and understanding of cultural differences that may influence the manner in which potential talents and giftedness is expressed vis-à-vis those commonly evident in potentially gifted and talented students holding membership in the majority culture.

During the training period the teacher is introduced to key Project STEP materials that are integrated into the daily curriculum including the checklist, task and activity records, task cards, and manipulatives. A brief description of each follows.

The checklist is perhaps the most essential document in the Project. Designed to facilitate evaluation of the pupil's demonstrated ability in the five identified areas over a 2-year period, it contains over 40 observable behaviors characteristic of potentially gifted minority children. The checklist weighs heavily in the placement decision made by the TAG Advisory Committee in the Spring of the second year of the student's participation in the Project.

The task and activity record is used to document the teacher's assessment of the extent to which the child has been successful in completing a specified Project STEP activity. For example, the Project STEP teachers may observe and subsequently document the student's success in organizing a complex game on the playground or being accepted into an established work or play group. The degree of success is rated using a scale of 1 to 5. A score of 5 indicates a high degree of success; a score of 1 indicates a low degree of success. At the end of two years, these documented observations provide data which is used to develop a profile of the student's strengths in one or more of the five areas.

The task cards are adapted for use with the lessons plans and curriculum and texts used in the classroom. They offer suggestions for enrichment which provide additional opportunities for the minority student to demonstrate potential giftedness. The cards also provide "cues" that direct the teacher's observation to specific behaviors which may be evidenced as the child completes assignments. These observations are then documented on the Project STEP Activity Record.

Project STEP manipulatives include: people pieces, tangrams, geoboards, balance scales, and puzzles. These "hands-on" instructional tools are incorporated into lesson plans and used when the teacher intends to observe behavior involving sorting, categorizing, predicting, task commitment, independent actions, logical thinking, oral expression, small motor coordination, awareness of spatial relationships, and so on. When manipulatives are needed to perform a task, the specific manipulative required is cited in the procedure section of the task card. As the teacher becomes familiar with the use of manipulatives, learning centers may be created to encourage the student to use the manipulatives to solve problems not addressed during regular classroom instruction. The teacher monitors the student's independent use of the manipulatives to assure each is being used correctly.

As part of the in-service training program, the participants receive a Teacher's Manual which serves as a resource guide and also promotes standardization in Project implementation. Throughout the year the manual is updated as warranted with additional literature and examples to assure that Project activities are relevant for classroom activities. Additional in-service programs are also offered to supplement the initial training. Teachers who are cognizant of cultural differences and similarities are better able to identify and nurture the targeted students and address the needs of all students. Project STEP's success is highly dependent on the teacher's understanding, acceptance, and appreciation of different ethnic/cultural systems and the ability to convey this attitude during interaction with the student. "In the final analysis, only the teacher committed to Project STEP can help us answer the question, 'Who are the gifted children among us?'" (Brooks, 1984).

At the end of the kindergarten year, the completed checklists are passed on to the first grade teacher for the second year of observation. At the conclusion of the second year, a comprehensive review and evaluation of the student's performance is conducted by the TAG committee, which is composed of the TAG coordinator, school principal, selected faculty members, and Project STEP teachers. The committee reviews and evaluates data reported on the checklist, standardized ability tests, and county and state criterion-referenced tests, as well as parent reports and recommendations and teacher recommendations. The consensus of this committee is the basis for a recommendation regarding trial placement in the TAG program, which commences in grade two. Students identified for the TAG program have two options; they may participate in a weekly two hour "pull-out" program at the local school or participate in the "full day" at a designated magnet school.

Heather Hills Elementary School is a kindergarten-grade 6 Talented and Gifted (TAG) magnet school with an enrollment of 500 students. Located in Bowie, MD, the school has a heterogeneous population with students of various ethic and socioeconomic backgrounds. As a magnet school Heather Hills offers a TAG program for students in grades 2-6 as well as a Comprehensive program for the all others in kindergarten-grade 6. Heather Hills's TAG population is notable in that it is one of the district's mirror magnet programs that draws only black students into the predominately white school community. Many of the school's Talented and Gifted magnet students have been identified using the Project STEP procedure. Providing enriched opportunities and developing talents for a population with such a wide spectrum of academic performance presented challenges for the staff.

In 1986, when the incumbent assumed the position of principal, the first order of business was to organize the staff to see the challenge as an opportunity to provide what William Durden (Durden & Tangherlini, 1994), Director of the Johns Hopkins University Center for Talented Youth, called the "Optimal Match" approach in education. This is based on the fundamental principle that learning is a basic human phenomenon that unfolds both developmentally and contextually. This match can be achieved when the teaching context and the level of subject matter are responsive to the child's readiness to proceed. Designing the optimal match is beneficial for all students, but it is required for the Project Step-identified students whose language patterns, economic standing, and/or experiential or cultural background violate the performance expectations for traditional talented and gifted programs.

The second step was to focus directly and explicitly on the achievement and quality of school life for the minority student in general and the Project STEP-identified student, specifically. A careful review of the archival and disaggregated data revealed a disturbing trend. Despite the school's relatively high overall academic standing in the county (23rd out of 122), minority students were lagging far behind their white classmates in both the TAG and COMP programs. Additionally, African American males as a group were the lowest performing students. These same students, many of whom were the academic stars in their previous schools or, at the very least, promising academic stars identified as potentially gifted through Project STEP, suddenly seemed to have lost their momentum and motivation and most assuredly their direction. The staff launched into action.

The third step entailed providing the specialized academic accommodations needed to accomplish the challenge of providing the optimum match. The school organized into three teams. These teams consisted of a primary k-3 team, an intermediate 4-6 team, and a special team comprised of the music, physical education, and reading teachers, and the counselor and TAG Coordinator. These teams have done much to eliminate the sense of isolation the classroom teacher feels. Additionally, teams foster a multidisciplinary view of the child and provide increased opportunities for feedback about successful classroom strategies for a student or a group of students which may then be implemented by a colleague.

The intermediate team is departmentalized. All team members teach both TAG and COMP classes. Although the primary team is not departmentalized, through creative scheduling and innovative programming, they are provided with a common period for team planning. The primary teachers find many opportunities for their students to work with the intermediate students or visit intermediate classes in which exhibitions, demonstrations, or projects are being featured or presented. The Intermediate teachers, in turn, make an effort to know and work with the primary students in order to nurture and develop some hidden or latent talent. Special programs such as Designers, Inc., a watercolors class instructed by a primary teacher. develops the talents of the highly able artists in grades 2- 6. Project GROW, an agronomy class taught by a primary teacher. delivers science, mathematics, and writing instruction in a way that compliments the learning style of students who need concrete hands-on opportunities in grades 4 and 5. KIDS Club (Kids Into Doing Service), designed to enhance leadership and mediation skills in selected students from grades 3-6, is sponsored by a primary teacher, an intermediate teacher and the school counselor. Again, creative scheduling allows for a common period for sponsors to implement the program. This "one big family" atmosphere has produced amazing results for all of the students, but especially the minority students identified through Project STEP.

The fourth step, the introduction of school-based management by the superintendent, John Murphy, was precisely the vehicle needed for the staff to transform not only the instructional delivery system and the academic performance of all students, but specifically the gifted minority student. School-based management supported the principal's effort to have the instructional teams engage in collaborative decision making. To the greatest extent possible, the instructional teams are responsible for organizing instruction and resources to facilitate the academic success of all students. Simply stated, the teachers are involved in shared decisions relative to the curriculum, purchasing, and allocating resources. Most notable, teachers are free to research their practice and design and implement innovative programs that enhance and foster increased student achievement for all students, with special focus on poorly achieving minority students. As will be noted later, all students have benefited from the empowerment of the instructional staff.

Three years after the successful implementation of school-based management, the state of Maryland, under the leadership of state superintendent Nancy Grasmick, launched the fifth step: an ambitious reform effort. This effort revolutionized the teaching and learning process by not only setting the standards of academic excellence and authenticating the achievement assessments but also by mandating a reinvestment and improvement of educational services for talented and gifted students.

Finally, the sixth step was to institutionalize a program that nurtured those students who were identified as potentially talented and gifted through Project STEP, as well as enhanced learning opportunities for all students, with a special emphasis on the lowest performing students. In order to accomplish this the staff developed "Potentially Yours," an unique program based on Howard Gardner's (1983) theory of multiple intelligences. His work with brain-damaged patients persuaded him that rather than being a single entity, intelligence exists as a variety of aptitudes. Although Gardner identified seven intelligences or distinctive aptitudes, "Potentially Yours" is designed to provide instruction and authentic learning opportunities that strengthen intelligences or aptitudes that are traditionally ignored in the classroom. "Potentially Yours" addresses five of the intelligences Gardner identified: *spatial intelligence*, the consequence of visual perception and imagination that allows the individual to internally visualize shapes and spaces from a variety of dimensions; *bodily-kinesthetic intelligence*, skill in using the body for complex movements and in manipulating objects; *interpersonal intelligence*, an aptitude for communication, leadership, organization, and awareness of the motivation of others; *intrapersonal*, an unusual ability to correctly recognize personal strengths and weakness and to make choices based on this recognition; and *musical intelligence*, facility with melodies, rhythms, timing and pitch.

Thus conceived, it follows that the student may demonstrate talent in a variety of ways. Unlike many TAG curricula, which are programmatically oriented toward linguistic and logical-mathematical intelligences, Heather Hills offers a variety of avenues to foster the expression of one or more of all of the seven intelligences. The incorporation of activities to encourage demonstration of abilities relative to the five intelligences has been especially beneficial for the minority student, who formerly, though identified as a potentially talented and gifted student, became a low achieving student as he or she progressed through grades 2-6 without nurturing and accommodations in learning styles.

Each "Potentially Yours" activity is designed with one or more of the seven intelligences in mind. It should be noted that student participation in these activities is aggressively promoted to assure participation by those students who otherwise would continue to remain "passive observers." Indeed, nearly 100% of the lower achieving students participate in one or more extra curricula activities. Further, the student is targeted for participation in a particular activity based on information gained from learning inventories administered in the fourth, fifth, and sixth grades to determine the student's preferred learning style. In addition to the three activities previously described—Designer's, Inc., Project GROW, and KIDS Club—"Potentially Yours" includes the following activities described next:

Project Snap (photography) and Project News (photo-journalism) are clubs designed to foster expression of visual-kinesthetic intelligence. Bodily kinesthetic intelligence is expressed through participation in pop, line, modern, and square dancing, intramural sports competitions, and a daily before-school basketball game for those in the High Hoopster club. The school counselor works with the students to nurture intrapersonal intelligence by conducting sessions that offer personal journal writing, learning inventories, role playing, and games to build self-esteem and self-understanding. To nurture musical intelligence, the student may participate in instrumental music lessons; students with exceptional ability are encouraged to join the Jazz Combo. The Heather Hills Chorus, which requires an audition before the vocal music director, offers the student an opportunity to strengthen acting as well as singing skills. Some of the activities designed to nurture spatial intelligence include robotics, designing, and programming robots with motorized Lego blocks; classes in crafts, calligraphy, clay sculpture, strategy-focused board games, computer programming, and logical problem-solving exercises. Students involved in these activities are frequently the school representatives for the Odyssey of the Mind, a national problem solving competition.

The activities complement other activities offered by the school including *Write a Book*, a program that requires students to write and bind a personal work of fiction or nonfiction, and a student run supply store with students responsible for purchasing, pricing, marketing, and selling the products.

Several of these programs were designed specifically to increase the achievement of black male students, thereby providing Project STEP-identified students the nurturing and support required for successful participation in a rigorous talented and gifted magnet program. These programs have been supported financially by the Prince George's County School District's Black Male Achievement and Mentoring Programs.

The confluence of performance-based learning and assessment, teaming, and school-based management, with an overarching shared vision of teaching for learning for all and a desire "to inject vitality and real-world purpose into the curriculum" (Greenleaf, 1994), created the conditions for dynamic change and innovation at Heather Hills. That the school has been successful in this Herculean task is evident from internal measures of performance as well as the awards and honors which have been bestowed. In 1987, when the incumbent assumed the position of principal, two-thirds of the students in the TAG program were white and middle class. As expected, these students scored well on the California Achievement Test (CAT). In comparison, the minority students in the TAG program lagged far behind their classmates. The disparity was particularly noticeable with the African American male students, who performed in the bottom quartile in both the TAG and COMP program. Disaggregated data revealed that overall (TAG and COMP), this cohort ranked at the 16th percentile on the CAT. Although the school ranked fifth in the county on the Otis Cognitive Abilities test, the school ranked 23rd in the county on the standardized achievement tests. Of equal concern was the inverse relationship found for African American male students between length of attendance at Heather Hills and school performance. In general, the longer the African American male student remained at the school the lower his academic performance. Frequently this was accompanied by nonparticipation in school activities.

By 1990, change was evident as Heather Hills became the number one ranked school in Prince George's county. Heather Hills was designated a Blue Ribbon School of Excellence. The school moved from its previous standing of 23rd to first. Enrollment in pre-algebra class moved from a total of 7 with no African American students, to 13, three of whom were African American, to the current enrollment of 38, with 11 African American males. By 1991, scores on the California Test of Basis Skills, the county and state criterion-referenced tests, revealed that black male students had significantly narrowed the gap between their scores and those of their white classmates. In the subtests of mathematics and science there was enjoyable difference between the performance of African American male students and their white classmates. By 1994, minority students as a cohort attained a rating of satisfactory in their performance on the rigorous Maryland School Performance Assessment Program, a state mandated criterion performance test.

By 1994, 17 of the school's teachers had received awards for excellence. The principal was selected for the Harvard Graduate School of Education's Principal's Center Summer Institute Staff and was chosen the 1994 National Distinguished Principal for Maryland by the U.S. Department of Education and the National Association of Elementary School Principals (NAESP). Additionally in 1994, the principal was recipient of a $25,000 award from the Milken Family Foundation. Awarded to only 150 educators nationwide, the award recognizes outstanding performance in public education. Finally, Heather Hills was featured in the premier publication of NAESP's *Middle Matters*. This article detailed the innovative "Potentially Yours" program and its impact on student achievement generally, and minority student achievement, specifically.

In conclusion, Heather Hills exemplifies the school as a powerful and the most appropriate environment for identifying and nurturing gifts and talents, albeit hidden or marginally evident, in the minority student. The Heather Hills experience aptly demonstrates that these gifts and talents burgeon when a committed principal and instructional staff hold a shared vision of promoting the highest standards of academic achievement for all students in a carefully crafted environment that demonstrates the belief that that which makes the student different from the "norm" is not to be denigrated or devalued but rather recognized, cultivated, appreciated, and celebrated. That this can be done successfully for the minority student portends a future in which the intellectual and creative boundaries of all students will be extended and enriched.

REFERENCES

Brooks, P. R. (1984) STEP: *Strategies for targeting early potential: A teacher's guide*. Prince George's County Public School System, Prince George's County, MD.

Bunke, C., & Dearborn, P. (1981). Thinking responsibly about giftedness. *Early Years, II*(8), 22, 81-84.

Durden, W.G., & Tangherlini, A. E. (1993). *Smart kids—How academic talents are developed and nurtured in America*. Toronto: Hogrefe & Huber Publishing.

Gardner, H. (1983). *Frames of mind: The theory of multiple intelligences*. New York: Basic Books.

Gould, S.J. (1981). *The mismeasure of man*. New York: Norton.

Greenleaf, T. (1994, Fall). Middle matters. *National Association of Elementary School Principals, 3*(1), pp. 1-6.

Isaacs, A. F. (1966) A survey of suggested preparation for teachers of the gifted. *The Gifted Child Quarterly, 10,* 72-77.

Renzulli, J. S. (1975) *Psychology and education of the gifted.* New York: Irvington Publishers.

Verma, G., & Bagley, C. (1975). *Race and education across cultures.* London: Heineman Educational Books.

U.S. Department of Education, (1993). *National excellence: A case for developing America's talent.* Washington, DC: Office of Educational Research and Improvement.

10

Early Childhood Giftedness Among the Rural Poor

Howard H. Spicker
W. Thomas Southern

Despite a long-standing trend toward urbanization and school consolidation in the United States, there exists a large portion of the population who reside in rural areas. Although rurality is often described in terms of population, this condition cannot be characterized simply in terms of population density. The traditional rural community tends to be characterized by conservative attitudes, adherence to traditional values, traditional patterns of expression, and self-reliance.

The conditions of poverty and rurality make the difficult task of preschool identification even more arduous, and impose serious problems in designing programs for young gifted children. The economically disadvantaged and the rural child each possess inherent abilities equal to more traditional populations. The problems arise when they confront traditional school-type settings and practices. In interactions with formal instruments, with teachers, even with peers, they suffer from a perceived deficit. Therefore, the emphasis for these children must shift away from intensive, separate identification and programming to the

147

use of activities that serve *both* programming and identification purposes. Every effort must be made to develop the ability of teachers to
recognize talent in expression and content that is different from that
which they have learned to expect. Programming must take into
account the lack of human and material resources and the isolation
inherent in the most impoverished and rural areas.

IDENTIFICATION WITH FORMAL INSTRUMENTS

Perhaps the most often employed instruments for identifying very
young gifted children are intelligence tests. There are, however, drawbacks associated with their use. Predictive validity measured against
grades, teacher ratings, or later school achievement is not as impressive with preschool populations as it is with older populations (Anastasi,
1976; Cronbach, 1977; Ehrlich, 1986; Kitano & Kirby, 1986). Three possible explanations exist for this: The tests themselves may be measuring
something other than cognitive ability, they may not be measuring
abilities required for school performance, or they may be failing on
both counts.

In describing the development of his cognitive aptitude test,
the K-ABC, Kauffman (1984) said that the tasks used for very young children (2 yrs. 6 mos. to 4 yrs. 11 mos.) differ significantly in kind from those
administered later. Similarly, the Wechsler Battery employs an entirely
different test to assess preschool children (WIPPSI) than it does to
gauge the ability of school-age children (WISC-III). The difference
seems to reside in the kind of tasks assessed. Preschool batteries
emphasize visual and auditory perception, recognition vocabulary,
gross motor, and school-related fine motor development. Later
demands include the linguistic manipulation of verbal items, the acquisition of knowledge through experience, and school-related logical
thinking and reasoning tasks (Kauffman, 1984).

Suppose for a moment that the tasks used to assess ability in
later childhood were actually only measures of the requirements of
scholastic achievement, and that school achievement were more or
less independent of "real" ability. In such an instance early childhood
abilities might be more closely related to actual ability than the criteria
currently employed to validate the tests. This is not a far-fetched suppo-
sition. Estimates of predictive validity for these instruments often include
teacher-derived estimates and achievement test score criteria
(Anastasi, 1976). We currently accept the notion that teacher developed tests and grades may not accurately reflect all kinds of abilities.
Teachers do not seem to recognize the creatively gifted child, and as
we see later are not proficient without training in finding the culturally
different student (Borland, 1978; Gear, 1978). Some researchers have

found teacher ratings to be poor predictors of high IQs in their pupils (Gridley & Treloar, 1984; Pegnato & Birch, 1959). Furthermore, predictive validity resides in the later IQ estimates, and achievement test results.

Even if the results of testing were accepted for standard populations of gifted children, there would be enormous negative implications for the rural or the economically disadvantaged child. McKenzie (1986) and Rost and Albrecht (1985) noted strong negative correlations between the identification of gifted students and variables such as eligibility for free or reduced school lunch, and a strong positive correlation to the median price of homes in the school district. It would seem that a large number of the measures commonly used in identification may reflect the effects of economic disadvantage, at least to some extent.

Poverty and social disadvantage can exercise deleterious effects on at least three elements necessary for superior performance on a standardized test: a rich verbal background, accumulation of experiences related to the expectations of the test constructor, and the attentional and fine motor skills demanded by the test. We often characterize the handicapping conditions of disadvantaged students as a deficiency in language opportunities and language development. For most populations this is a somewhat oversimplified characterization. In fact, the socioeconomically disadvantaged child is often beset by stimuli. In urban settings, the problem becomes one of screening out a cacophony of language and noise. Urban youth have been shown to have extraordinary and colorful verbal skills, and many researchers have pointed out that poor children actually perform better on verbal batteries in intelligence and aptitude tests than they do on non verbal ones (Sattler, 1982).

All human beings develop rich language skills because we are genetically programmed to learn language. However, children from impoverished environments are exposed to a more limited vocabulary and to different lexical items with a different set of subtleties and ambiguities. The range and qualities of vocabulary tapped by IQ and achievement tests, will predict increasingly less success at school as the child advances through the grades. Middle-class children are generally exposed to a wealth of models who use language in a wide variety of contexts. For these children, testing is a process that measures assimilation and learning in an environment that provided ample exemplars. For poor children this is not the case. Renzulli (1973) asserted that the major characteristic of the disadvantaged is a failure to master the linguistic and grammatical structures of the dominant culture.

Parents in poverty may not be able to provide the experiences requisite to developing the natural abilities of the child. The demands of subsistence may preclude extensive interaction by either parent. In addition, poverty is increasingly represented by the single-parent household, in which there is a sole provider of adult-child interaction, and adult language modeling. At the end of the day, where parent and child are separated by the demands of work and day care, and in a system where day care is inadequate at best, the opportunities for expansion of learning experiences are limited. In addition, the high cost of transportation, and admission to various cultural opportunities screen out the poor from participation in community enrichment activities. Again, the formal instruments generally employed in identification reward children who have had the opportunity to participate in these activities.

The tests assume that there has been some experience with the paraphernalia of testing, such as, scissors, crayons, beads, and so on; and that the child will respond positively to the play value of the test items. For children from poverty backgrounds, some or all of these assumptions may be faulty. The kinds of toys used in the testing to establish rapport may not have appeared in the home. Moreover in such an environment, children may not have been exposed to the kinds of verbal reinforcements that are typically used by examiners to reward good performance on a test. In consequence, the testing experience is not the same for economically disadvantaged children as it is for middle-class ones.

With the advent of modern transportation, rapid communication, and instantaneous audio-visual information sources, it would appear that the underreferral of rural students using standardized instruments is a problem of the past. Whereas, in the 1937 revision of the Stanford-Binet (Terman and Oden, 1947) rural children scored more than 10 points lower than urban children; on the most recent version of the Binet, (Thorndike, Hagen, and Sattler, 1986), a reversal of that differential can be observed. However, some of the apparent reversal must be explained in the changing nature of the definition of rural. It is no longer sufficient to merely characterize rurality by population as was done in the Binet validation report. Gjelten (1982) classified five different rural populations. These included a new rural population of middle-class urbanites in flight from the problems of the city, as well as, rural settings developed as recreational retreats for the urban wealthy (i.e., ski resorts and beach-front communities). The overall population living in areas classified as rural under the federal definition is more numerous now than in 1960, but it is also richer, and more cosmopolitan.

However, in at least three of the settings described by Gjelten (1982), these factors may result in depressed scores for rural children. In rural areas defined by geographic isolation, among rural populations described as "stable, and in those characterized as depressed, there is a lack of the kind of language modeling required to perform well on aptitude and IQ measures (Spicker, Southern, & Davis, 1987). Sparse populations reduce the contact outside the home, and interaction with others may be extremely limited. In the latter setting, language patterns, dialects, and a deemphasis on verbal ability may also reduce the language models available. Again, this does not mean that these children are not verbal, or that they have inadequate vocabularies.

Given the right context, a child may be able to provide a large number of lexical items related to the environment he experiences daily. These items are rarely asked on tests.

Experiences are also limited. Geographical isolation and attitudes of satisfaction and self-sufficiency within the community help limit the access children have to the experiences that would benefit them in the testing situation.

For both economically disadvantaged, and rural children the conditions that limit their performance on tests also conspire to lower the expectation of the families and communities in which they live. The child from poverty is less likely to be encouraged by his parents to change his or her economic status through education (Sisk, 1975). In rural areas, parents emphasize traditional values that promote acceptance of the status quo, and a limitation on career goals (Carmichael, 1982). In many rural communities, teachers may be the only persons who have elected to go to college. Indeed, the school may be the largest employer of college graduates. Students who are not interested in a career in education may have few other college graduates to view as role models.

ALTERNATE SOURCES OF IDENTIFICATION

Professional educators and persons who provide day care for children tend to develop negative expectations about children who exhibit the behaviors that are often learned in impoverished environments. Rural and economically disadvantaged children are not as likely as middle-class children to be reading, may not know numbers and colors, and may not meet the teacher's expectation in terms of fine motor skills and attention. In addition, they may not speak a standard English dialect, or have familiarity with school-related vocabulary. Sisk (1975) also pointed out that economically disadvantaged children may not have positive attitudes toward school, may have an inability to focus on long-term goals, and may resort to violence to solve problems.

Because these characteristics violate behaviors one tends to associate with giftedness, teachers often do not identify gifted students among the poor or rural settings. In fact, over time, a teacher's expectations begin to be associated with other factors that are even less related to ability. Rist (1970) noted that teachers may divide a class early in the school year apparently using traits that have more to do with social class than with academic performance. One group of kindergarten children placed together for instruction wore older clothes, showed considerable discomfort in interaction with the teacher and fellow students and spoke with a marked nonstandard dialect. All were from families receiving welfare assistance. This was in contrast to another instructional group who wore newer clothes, appeared more confident in teacher and peer interactions, and spoke with a more traditional dialect. None of these students were from families receiving welfare assistance. All the students and the teacher were Black, and there was no difference in IQ between the two groups. However, because the teacher expected little from the disadvantaged group, she expended little effort on them and provided significantly better instruction to those who were economically advantaged. The situation resulted in a self-fulfilling prophecy that saw the disadvantaged group fall academically behind the advantaged group through the next two school years. Teachers tend to expect poorer performance from economically disadvantaged children, teach them less well and, therefore, attain performance results that validate their initial poor performance expectations.

Children from rural or economically disadvantaged classrooms often have strengths that are not highly visible or valued in the preschool or kindergarten. For example, early mathematical or spatial abilities, fluency in nonverbal communication, responding well to and with visual media, entrepreneurial ability, leadership in the peer group, may not be evoked in many preschool and school settings. Even if the child is given a chance to perform in an area of strength, the performance may be undervalued in settings where a premium is put on verbal production. Teachers must learn that some abilities often ignored or discounted are highly consonant with giftedness.

Table 10.1 illustrates the problems rural teachers face when asked to recommend children for their district's gifted program. Most teachers expect gifted children to exhibit the behaviors shown for advantaged students. However, on the basis of a 3-year study of rural disadvantaged Anglo gifted children, Spicker (1993) found that the characteristics of disadvantaged rural gifted children shown in Table 10.1 often differed significantly from those of advantaged rural gifted children. If one wishes to identify and nurture the abilities of bright disadvantaged rural children, teachers must be trained to recognize their unique characteristics.

Parents have been cited in the literature as potentially valid identifiers if they are requested to provide information about their child's *present* behaviors (Silverman, Chitwood, & Waters, 1986). One of the most reliable report inventories is Rimm's (1985) Preschool Interest Description (PRIDE). The instrument provides information about the child's interests, independence-perseverance, imagination, and originality.

A somewhat different approach to eliciting child information from rural parents was the Parent-Student Survey Instrument developed for Project SPRING (Spicker & Poling, 1993). Parents were asked questions about their child's ability or interest in fixing things, making things, collecting things, writing things, and reading things. In response to "fixing things," a parent reported that her son is very good at figuring out how things are put together. "Eli was 4 when his dad brought home a wheel barrel [sic]. My husband left instructions but was having trouble trying to figure them out. He left the room. When he returned, Eli had assembled it and my husband tightened the bolts down" (p. 43).

Table 10.1. Characteristics of Rural Gifted Students.

Advantaged Rural Gifted Students Middle-class children whose behaviors reflect the traditional values of the dominant culture	Disadvantaged Rural Gifted Students Economically disadvantaged and/or geographically isolated children whose behaviors reflect traditional Anglo-Appalachian cultural values
1. Speak standard English	1. Speak a nonstandard regional dialect
2. Are verbal and have good communication skills	2. Are less verbal in oral communication skills
3. Are active participants in classroom activities	3. Tend to be passive participants in classroom activities
4. Perform tasks within time limitations	4. Are relatively unaffected by time pressures; work slowly but meticulously
5. Complete classroom assignments and homework	5. Are likely to be lax in completing assignments and homework
6. Perform well on standardized tests	6. Are not likely to perform well on standardized tests
7. Perform well in all subjects	7. May show exceptional ability in one subject and average to below average in others
8. Produce written work in proper grammatical form with good spelling and legible handwriting	8. Have written products that may be of high quality in content but of poor quality in grammatical form, spelling, and handwriting
9. Demonstrate their strengths within the academic classroom	9. More likely to demonstrate their strengths outside their classroom, i.e., auto and tractor repair, knowledge specific to their rural environment, creativity related to 4-H projects, talent in music and the performing arts
10. Usual perform equally well on verbal and nonverbal tests	10. Are likely to perform better on nonverbal than verbal test.

Parent information provides rich information about a child's out-of-school accomplishments. Such information should receive serious consideration when searching for gifted children in rural communities.

Unfortunately, parents of rural or economically disadvantaged children are less likely to provide the same level of information that a middle-class parent might. They have less time to fill out lengthy information forms and their writing skills may be such that they are unable or unwilling to provide extended and elaborate information. They may be suspicious toward schools and view with distrust requests for information.

An incidental point needs to be raised concerning the participation of disadvantaged and rural students. McBeath, Smart, and Blackshear (1981) noted that once the student is identified, there is no guarantee that he or she will stay in the program. In their study these researchers examined a number of variables associated with groups of successful and unsuccessful participants including those who refused to attend, or who dropped out before the end of the year. The one variable that significantly predicted entering and staying in the program was socioeconomic status. It seems that poverty may also add burdens to the participation of students beyond the demands of cognitive ability because all of the students selected for participation in this study had similar test scores. The lack of transportation and the potential differences occasioned by dialect or dress may cause economically disadvantaged or rural children to opt out of a special program. Even preschool and primary children are not immune from this problem. If a parent can't get the child to the program, or if the participants appear to be different from their normal peers, the child will not attend.

IMPLICATIONS

The aforementioned concerns indicate a serious difficulty in identifying potentially gifted children among the poor and the traditional rural populations. How effective will any identification system be for very young children, given the nature of formalized testing with preschool children, and the overwhelming influence of extensive preschool learning experiences on formal and informal assessment? It seems likely that a number of students we identify at preschool ages will later on decline in relative performance, while an equal number will be overlooked who are capable of high achievement. If a way is found to have the children themselves demonstrate their need, then an identification system that is justifiable and fair can be devised.

It is necessary to restructure the conception of identification for preschool children, especially among disadvantaged and rural populations. We must judge children on a wide range of tasks, not just those that are school related. We must provide for them opportunities to develop potential abilities in a variety of contexts, and we must with-hold judgements based primarily on their language and appearance. This entails in-service training for teachers designed to make them aware that children from these populations have abilities comparable to those exhibited by middle-class students. Identification must include instruction on how to look for the positive characteristics of these popu-lations. One of the most comprehensive guides for identifying gifted behavior in preschool children by means of teacher observation is the Preschool Talent Assessment Guide developed by Karnes and Taylor (1978) and recently modified by Karnes (1993a) for use with disadvan-taged children. The guide includes talent checklists for observing the intellectual, academic, creative leadership, visual and performing arts, and psychomotor characteristics of preschool children.

We must also emphasize the search for potential ability over demonstrated ability. This is roughly analogous to looking primarily for ores rather than refined metal when seeking natural resources. We must learn to look for ability in forms and settings that may look no more like the finished product than bauxite looks like aluminum. We have to widen our view of what shows evidence of superior ability. The opera-tional definitions of ability applied in school settings are closely tied to school type performances. Reading, fine motor skills, and traditional ver-bal behavior may be a desired outcome of schooling, but in examining disadvantaged and rural populations we should be looking for perfor-mances that are nonverbal, visual, kinesthetic, and imaginative. We should also categorize potential in a manner suggested by Feuerstein (1979) for estimating ability. We should seek out evidence of how stu-dents respond to the learning task and document superior responses to instruction. Such an approach was implemented by Karnes (1993b). The program, known as Curriculum Aimed Toward Amplifying Learning in Young Students (CATALYST), begins with the presentation of a learning task or novel problem to students and then observing the quality of responses and the rapidity with which they were solved. Observations in natural instructional settings help provide estimates of ability that can then be used to determine if students required differential curriculum responses. For rural children it is important to use instructional opportuni-ties that are closely related to the environment and experiences of the students being taught. In this way instruction can focus on the experi-ences to which rural students have been exposed and use the actual resources the community possesses to make the process relevant.

Except in cases of highly precocious development, early and intensive differentiation of gifted children runs a high risk of errors. For this reason, preschool programs should include children of varying abili-ties and should provide a rich variety of activities that will afford oppor-tunities to observe children's performances across a wide array of cog-nitive, motoric, social, and effective activities. It is our contention that many gifted children can benefit from an enriched preschool program.

Given exposure to such enriched programs and opportunities for developing social maturity, rural disadvantaged children are likely to produce the kinds of performances that will eventually identify them for inclusion in programs for the gifted when they enter the primary grades.

Student Profiles

These practices also reveal an alternative way of viewing student performance. Unlike static, one-time, one-dimensional assessments, student profiles provide dynamic views of student progress. As implied in Karnes' (1993a) Preschool Talent Checklist, student performance should be tracked across a number of different skill areas and contents including creativity and the arts. In traditional identification, a common practice is to reduce this relatively rich information down to a single criterion (Richert, Alvino, & McDonnell, 1982). However, it is much more helpful to retain all the information in a format that allows examination of comparative strengths and weaknesses. In addition, comments and scores on a variety of measures can be included to provide supporting or focusing evidence concerning each of the performances. The resulting student profile is a much richer source of assessment and programming data than any number can be. Figure 10.1 is illustrative of such a profile.

SUSAN

The composite profile in Figure 10.1 exemplifies the characteristics of a typical potentially gifted, economically disadvantaged, third grade, 8-year-old child identified by Project SPRING.

In Section A—*Formal Measures*—this student's standardized achievement test scores are in the low-to-average range, with the exception of Reading, which at the 87th percentile is remarkable in view of her intellectual and other achievement test scores in this section. In Section B—*Informal Measures*—the Classroom Teacher placed this student at the 79th percentile, and the Special G/T Teacher at the 83rd percentile. Although no ranking was assigned to the Parent Survey, information provided under *Other Informal or Anecdotes* shows that the parent responded with the following:

> Susan makes games; word searches, mazes, and word games. She has done this since she was 4 years of age. She has collected stamps for the past 2 years, and rocks and fossils for 5 years. Before she could write she told stories to her older brother and sister, and continues to write humorous short stories. She reads for information, and is especially interested in history. Susan is interested in making

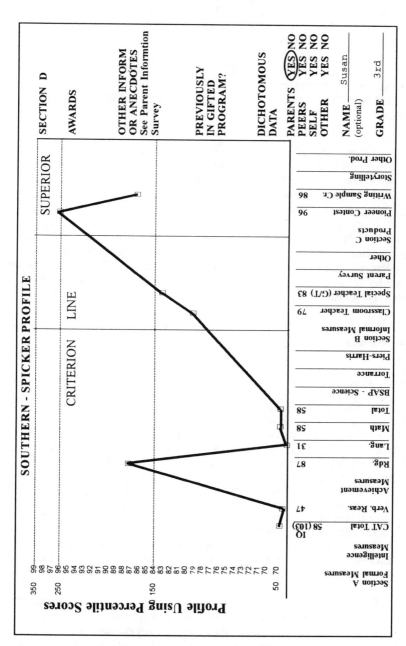

Figure 10.1. Profile Using Percentile Scores

things; anything to do with building, creating something out of scraps of paper, material, or anything that happens to be around the house. Also, she has been able to do perspective drawings since she was 6 (parent included sample artwork).

Continuing with Section C—*Products*—Susan received a score of 29 out of a possible 30 (96th percentile) for her creation of a New Plant, entitled "The Thorney Thing." Susan wrote the following about her product:

> The Thorney Thing is a very feathery plant. It has very bright colors and is half poisonous and half-not. I found it in the woods of Little Africa. And it has a little bug always by it. Sometimes when it is happy it send orange things down to earth. Don't touch them they have thorns on them.

The New Plant was three-dimensional and used feathers, clay, and pipe cleaners. She also completed a Creative Writing Sample which was evaluated on the basis of creative content only. Out of a possible score of 15, this student received a score of 13, which placed her at the 86th percentile.

The following is a story Susan wrote in response to the prompt "The Flying Monkey." Grammar, spelling, and punctuation have been edited for readability purposes.

> Once upon a time there was a monkey named Robby and he always dreamed of flying. Every night he would wish upon a star to be able to fly the next day. So he kept on wishing and kept on. Then one day it was his birthday and his owner gave him a big birthday party. He got ready to blow out his candles and Bobby, which was his owner, said wait make a wish. So he did and everybody was wondering what his wish was except Bobby he knew his wish was to be able to fly. He always wanted to be able to fly over the cities and rescue babies and rolling strollers for Mommys. Then that night he make that same wish and when he did he saw a bright light behind him. Then he turned and looked and there laid a suit that said Super Monkey. Then he tried it on and he started flying around the room. The next day he set out for a rescue mission. He saved 10 babies that day. Everybody called him Super Monkey just as he wanted.

For an 8-year-old, Susan's story is exceptional. She develops the events of her story in a logical sequence; uses numerous verbal elaborations to describe each aspect of her story; and demonstrates a great deal of creativity in developing her plot. Had Susan's story been evaluated on the basis of handwriting, spelling, and grammatical form, it is unlikely that Susan's story would have compared favorably with that written by a traditionally identified gifted child. In fact, if Susan had been evaluated for her school's gifted and talented program *only* on the basis of her standardized achievement test scores, it is unlikely that she would have qualified for the talent pool. However, by considering her out-of-school interests, creative writing, and the product Susan created for the Pioneer Contest, she should be regarded as a viable candidate for a gifted program.

Student Portfolios

As desirable as profiles can be, they nevertheless provide only the beginnings for directing meaningful enrichment. It is also important to view student performance across time. Student portfolios allow assessment of the curve of student learning after exposure to instruction. This allows the viewer of the portfolio to mitigate the effects of experience outside the classroom because the products being examined resulted from an instructional process. The second view allows the reviewer to see whether intra-individual differences remain constant over time. Apparent patterns of strengths and weaknesses may not appear salient after viewing the full range of information across extended periods of time. The third view possible in portfolio assessment provides a profile of inter-individual performance within the same context on similar tasks. The reviewer can compare different student performance on single tasks or on related tasks across time, thus comparing absolute performances and comparing relative learning curves. For example, the portfolio reviewer can look at specific creative writing samples in every student's portfolio and at writing samples across time in all the portfolios to assess how well individual students compare to other students at any one time and how rapidly their skills are improving in relation to other students.

Portfolios can include samples of common assignments as well as examples of superior individual performance. It is important in sampling student performance to sample widely to provide information about a variety of performances, and to sample frequently. This requires that preschool and primary teachers be trained in the characteristics of gifted children at these ages and that they become aware of the kind of examples of performance one might see among rural and disadvantaged students. Teachers must be trained to record both classroom products and anecdotal information that provide evidence of ability across many domains.

EDUCATIONAL PROGRAMMING

If educational programs are to deal with the special needs of bright rural and economically disadvantaged children, the curriculum must provide the student access to those resources, models, and interactions they have not had in their environment.

Programs must emphasize vocabulary acquisition and richness. Story telling by teachers and students, interactive puppetry, creative dramatics, and extensive reading are important activities.

The content of the program needs to also contain opportunities to address novel problems and develop creative problem solving skills. An extremely innovative program for developing the creative and critical thinking abilities of gifted Head Start children was designed by Karnes and her associates (Karnes & Johnson, 1987) at the University of Illinois. The program, known as BOHST (Bringing Out Head Start Talents), is based on Guilford's (1967) Structure of the Intellect model. Innovative lessons were designed to develop the convergent, divergent, and evaluative thinking skills of 4- and 5-year old Head Start children. The thinking skills were introduced by three animal mascots, Delores Detective (convergent), Ivan the Inventor (divergent), and Julius the Judge (evaluative). Pictures of the mascots provided children with cues to the kind of thinking they were expected to use in each lesson. The pre-post child change data after one academic year of intervention were based on Torrance's (1980) Thinking Creatively in Action and Movement (TCAM), four subtests of the K-ABC (Kaufman & Kaufman, 1982), and the Self-Concept and Motivation Inventory (SCAMIN; Milchus, Farrah, & Reitz, 1987). On all three measures the intervention group of 234 Head Start children, made significantly greater gains than a comparison group of 212 children. The 24 children identified as potentially gifted who received the higher level thinking skills intervention did better than all other groups. This study has special significance to the field of education, in that it demonstrates that lessons designed to increase higher level thinking skills are of benefit to all children and not just those who are identified as gifted.

OTHER PROGRAM ELEMENTS FOR ECONOMICALLY DISADVANTAGED AND RURAL CHILDREN

As mentioned earlier, programs should fully use the resources available within the community. The students should be exposed to a wide range of adults in various settings in school and out. Interventions with parents to raise their awareness of the potential ability of the children and to assist them in building on the resources available at home are needed to extend what is really a very limited school experience. In the 1970s Head Start attempted to intervene early with children to break the cycle of poverty. The programs that were most successful included those where a home-intervention component was part of the educational efforts. It is essential to convince family members that education is the means for their children to achieve a better life. In rural areas particularly, it is necessary to emphasize that the development of talent can also preserve the best of what is in the local community. Efforts in rural areas to use local resources to develop the program have a greater chance of success if the effort is grounded in the concerns and strengths of the community.

THE ELECTRONIC INFORMATION REVOLUTION

In areas of geographical isolation and intense poverty, educational resources may appear to be out of reach. In these instances, it is necessary to program ways to link students (and their teachers) to the resources in other ways. Thirty years ago, it was assumed that television would break down the barriers of education and culture. Unfortunately, these predictions have not been realized. What has changed is the availability of electronic information resources to the most isolated and rural of areas. The computer is a tool that bodes major significance for the geographically isolated (Harlow, 1984). With the addition of a fairly inexpensive modem and a modest subscription fee, the machine puts anyone in touch with information systems that are sophisticated and wide-ranging. CD-ROM programs allow students to tour the San Diego Zoo, visit the Louvre and the Uffizi galleries, stage a Shakespearean play, and travel with Marco Polo.

Southern and Spicker (1989) described a program linking gifted students from seven rural communities via a computer bulletin board and working thematic educational units on ethnic heritage and environmental problems. Although this project was conducted with older students (ages 9-14), the possibility of such linkages for younger rural children offers access to a vast array of new resources as well as opportunities for interacting with bright children like themselves.

Unfortunately, computer technology appears to be exacerbating the differences between traditional and nontraditional gifted students. Middle-class students have access to these machines at home. Parents have invested in hardware and software to tutor and interact with their children in addition to the experiences they already provide. For the disadvantaged, or for students from backgrounds where such elements are not considered to be important, no such opportunities exist. Programs that deal with these populations must also take into account the increasing gap between the haves and the have-nots in computer literacy. They must also take into account the apparent discrepancy that has been noticed between male and female students in computer usage. Females tend to be less frequent users of technology, and computer-related activities are less attractive to females. Females, in general, are less apt to see curricular implications of computer presented technology. In contrast, males spend more of their leisure time computing, and have many more gender role models in computing than do female peers. Inherent motivation is higher for males with computer applications, and the result is that females opt out of such programs in much higher numbers than males. Among rural populations, the slower evolution of female roles may make this trend even more salient.

Like reading, computer skills will be a prerequisite for adequate attainment in schools in the near future. Computers should be part of programming for young children, in the same way that reading readiness and socialization are currently. Among rural and economically disadvantaged populations, the onus is even stronger to provide experiences that can help compensate for the lack of electronic resources in the home environment.

CONCLUSION

Shaw (1986) asserted that if no attempt is made to take into account nontraditional populations of gifted students, the last bastion of segregation in the classroom may be gifted education. With preschool and primary populations there is also a danger that the student tracked into programs will represent not only a predominantly White population, but also a wealthy and suburban one. It is essential that we take cognizance of the differences between very young children and those later in their school career when designing educational programs. Attempts to implement programs that are exclusive, or those that do not recognize the unique strengths and abilities of children who are economically disadvantaged and geographically isolated will leave a major source of talent untapped.

REFERENCES

Anastasi, A. (1976). *Psychological testing* (4th ed.). New York: Macmillan.

Borland, J. (1978). Teacher identification of the gifted. A new look. *Journal for the Education of the Gifted, 2,* 22-32.

Carmichael, D. (1982). The challenge of rural education. *The Rural Educator, 4*(1), 5-10.

Cronbach, L. J. (1977). *Educational psychology*. New York: Harcourt Brace & Jovanovich.

Ehrlich, V. Z. (1986). Recognizing superior cognitive abilities in disadvantaged and other diverse populations. *Journal of Children in Contemporary Society, 18,* 55-70.

Feuerstein, R. (1979). *The dynamic assessment of retarded performers.* Baltimore: University Park Press.

Gear, G. H. (1978). Effects of training on teachers' accuracy in the identification of gifted children. *Gifted Child Quarterly, 22,* 90-97.

Gjelten, T. (1982, May). *A typology of rural school settings.* Summary of presentation prepared for the rural education seminar. Washington, DC: U.S. Department of Education. (ERIC Document Reproduction Service No. ED 215 858)

Gridley, B. E., & Treloar, J. H. (1984). The validity of the scales for rating the behavioral characteristics of superior students for the identification of gifted students. *Journal of Psychoeducational Assessment, 2,* 63-71.

Guilford, J. P. (1967). *The nature of human intelligence.* New York: McGraw-Hill.

Harlow, S. (1984). The computer: Humanistic considerations. *Computers in the Schools, 1*(1), 43-51.

Karnes, M.B. (1993a). *Talent Identification and Child Data Forms manual.* Urbana: University of Illinois.

Karnes, M.B. (1993b). *CATALYST: Trainers guide.* Urbana: University of Illinois.

Karnes, M. B., & Johnson, L. J. (1987). Bringing out Head Start talents: Findings from the field. *Gifted Child Quarterly, 31,* 174-179.

Karnes, M. B., & Taylor, J. (1978). *Preschool Talent Checklist: Manual.* (ERIC Document Reproduction Service No. ED 160-226)

Kaufman, A. S. (1984, November). K-ABC and giftedness. *Roeper Review,* 83-88.

Kaufman, A. S., & Kaufman, N. L. (1982). *Kaufman Assessment Battery for Children.* Circle Pines, MN: American Guidance Service.

Kitano, M. K., & Kirby, D. F. (1986). *Gifted education.* Boston: Little, Brown.

McBeath, M., Smart, L., & Blackshear, P. B. (1981, August). *Identifying low-income, minority, gifted and talented youngsters.* Paper presented at the Annual Meeting of the American Psychological Association, Los Angeles, CA. (ERIC Document Reproduction Service No. ED 214 328).

McKenzie, J. A. (1986). The influence of identification practices, race and SES on the identification of gifted students. *Gifted Child Quarterly, 30,* 93-95.

Milchus, M. J., Farrah, G. A., & Reitz, W. (1987) *SCAMIN self-concept and motivation inventory.* Dearborn Heights, MI: Person-O-Metrics, Inc.

Pegnato, C. W., & Birch, J. W. (1959). Locating gifted children in junior high schools: A comparison of methods. *Exceptional Children, 25,* 300-304.

Renzulli, J. S. (1973). Talent potential in minority group students. *Exceptional Children, 39*(6), 438.

Richert, E.S., Alvino, J.J., & McDonnel, R.C. (1982). *National report on identification: Assessment and recommendations for comprehensive identification of gifted and talented youth.* Sewell, NJ: Educational Improvement Center-South.

Rimm, S. (1984). The characteristic approach: Identification and beyond. *Gifted Child Quarterly, 28*, 181-187.

Rist, R. C. (1970). Student social class and teacher expectations: The self-fulfilling prophecy in ghetto education. *Harvard Educational Review, 40*, 73-88.

Rost, D. H., & Albrecht, H. T. (1985). Expensive homes; clever children? On the relationship between giftedness and housing quality. *School Psychology International, 6*, 5-12.

Sattler, J. E. (1982). *Assessment of children's intelligence and special abilities.* Boston: Allyn & Bacon.

Shaw, F. W. (1986). Identification of the gifted: Design defects and the law. *Urban Education, 21*, 42-61.

Silverman, L.K., Chitwood, D.G., & Waters, J.L. (1986). Young gifted children: Can parents identify giftedness? *Topics in Early Childhood Education, 6*, 23-28.

Sisk, D. (1975). Communications skills for the gifted. *The Gifted Child Quarterly, 19*, 66-68.

Southern, W. T., & Spicker, H. H. (1989). The rural gifted child on line: Bulletin boards and electronic curriculum. *Roeper Review, 11*, 199-202.

Spicker, H.H. (1993). Indiana Site. *Final Report of Project SPRING.* Bloomington: Indiana University. (ERIC Document Reproduction Service No. 365 067)

Spicker, H. H., Southern, W. T., & Davis, B. I. (1987). The rural gifted child. *Gifted Child Quarterly, 31*, 155-157.

Spicker, H.H., & Poling, S.N. (1993). *Identifying rural disadvantaged gifted students.* Bloomington: Indiana University. (ERIC Document Reproduction Service No. 365 065)

Terman, L.M., & Oden, M.H. (1947). *The gifted child grows up: Twenty-five years' follow-up of a superior group. Genetic studies of genius: Vol. 4.* Stanford, CA: Stanford University Press.

Thorndike, R. L., Hagen, E. P., & Sattler, J. M. (1986). *The Stanford-Binet intelligence scale: Technical manual* (4th ed.). Chicago: Riverside.

Torrance, E. P. (1980). *Thinking creatively in action and movement.* Bensenville, IL: Scholastic Testing Service.

11

Beginning Brilliance

Stephanie S. Tolan

In order to meet the needs of our brightest children, it is necessary first to identify them. This can be done in various ways, such as giving standardized intelligence tests or observing precocious developmental patterns and behaviors. It is not always easy, however, to learn exactly where on the broad span of the human intellectual continuum an individual child's cognitive capacity may fall.

Many people do not believe it is important to have this information. They assume it is enough to know that the child is above normal, intelligent, "smart," *gifted*. Within the gifted range, however, there is a far larger span of cognitive difference than there is between normal and gifted. In order to address a child's intellectual needs appropriately, it is important to have a reasonably solid idea of just how different those needs are. The terms *highly*, *exceptionally*, or *unusually* gifted are not exact, and the degree of giftedness they indicate is not precisely defined, even when derived from IQ scores. They refer to a range, and a rather broad one. The baseline score for exceptional giftedness has been put anywhere from 145 to 160. However, a score over 150 is commonly used to identify a child as highly or exceptionally gifted. Children with scores over 180 (extrapolated scores on the Stanford-Binet Form L-M can go well above 200) are sometimes called *profoundly* gifted. These are children so far from the norms that they are likely to have difficulty finding a comfortable place for themselves in the world. They sometimes seem stranded between worlds, not quite children, not quite adults.

OTHER METHODS OF IDENTIFYING

Although a high score on an IQ test is an almost certain indication of extreme intelligence (it is unlikely that a child will "test high" by accident), tests are not as reliable for this population today as they have been in the past. Recent revisions of the Stanford-Binet and Wechsler tests have virtually eliminated the high scores that act as identifiers (Silverman & Kearney, 1992a, 1992b). It is critical to remember that when the scores that allowed us to identify the upper range of the population are no longer obtainable, the upper range does not disappear. These children will merely be harder to find and identify accurately. If a thermometer with no markings higher than 102 is used to determine the temperature of a sick child, the child's temperature will appear to be 102°, whether it is 102° or 104° or an immediately life-threatening 106°. The new tests, like such a thermometer, leave us without a solid quantitative measurement.

With tests no longer accurate at the highest ranges, we are forced to rely on more qualitative (and more subjective) means of recognizing extreme intellectual capacities. We can observe that a child accomplishes a particular cognitive task earlier than others, or with greater depth or complexity, but we are forced to rely on our limited experience of normal performance for comparison, rather than on the vast pool of children who have taken IQ tests over the years.

If no IQ scores are available, or if the child's scores have been achieved on the newer tests and are below traditional cutoff points, we can look for many of the same traits and characteristics that identify more moderately gifted children. The differences we can expect in the higher ranges will be in intensity and degree of precocity. A gifted child may enjoy math and function 1 or 2 years ahead of age peers in the subject, for instance, whereas a highly gifted child may be virtually obsessed by math, functioning 4 or more years ahead. Although most unusually bright children show preferences for one or more general cognitive areas, they typically excel to one degree or another in many. Unusual intensity and precocity usually show up in all of them.

Children given the "highly gifted" label may be prodigies in one or more culturally recognized fields (chess, music, art, math, or writing for instance) or they may show extreme capabilities in unusual domains, such as creating complex and fully developed imaginary worlds; developing, displaying, and cross-referencing arcane collections that are unlikely to interest other children; or researching a particular narrow subject, developing a range of knowledge that approaches that of an adult expert. On the other hand, they may develop a rich internal life and keep their unusual mental processing to themselves, seldom displaying it in public.

COMMON CHARACTERISTICS

- Very early language development, large and precise vocabulary, complex sentence structure
  (children have been reported speaking in three or four word sentences as early as 4 months; whenever spoken language begins there is a high rate of vocabulary acquisition, accompanied by a concern with precise terminology)
- Very early manipulation of numbers
  (a passion for counting, numbers, and measurement; self-taught math concepts—addition, subtraction, and beyond)
- High levels of energy
  (some highly gifted infants and toddlers seem to need less sleep than their parents; even those with normal sleep patterns are able to bring intense energy over long periods to projects that engage them; sitting still can be difficult; mental activity seems to generate physical energy)
- Extreme levels of curiosity and highly connective mental processing
  (every answer to one question brings a flurry of further, elaborative questions, a process that often goes on until the answerer, rather than the questioner, tires)
- Capacious and clear memory, observable early
  (spontaneous memorization of songs, jingles, commercials, and whole picture books; memory may be "photographic"; the memory process is often associative and accompanied by a refusal or apparent inability to memorize by rote)
- Early reading or early comprehension and use of other written symbol systems, such as numbers and musical notation
  (some begin reading soon after their first birthdays; they are likely to grasp not only words, but also the uses of punctuation; some children take note of spellings, while others perceive sounds and meanings and virtually ignore the arrangement of letters)

- Precocious sense of humor
(recognition and enjoyment of puns, witticisms, and the surprise endings of complex "shaggy dog stories"; many children are able to compose jokes, riddles, and puns that make adults laugh; some have a taste for the bizarre)
- Powerful imagination
(daydreaming, pretending, inventing complex stories that may be built serially for days, weeks, and longer; imagining new uses for old objects or inventing and constructing new objects)
- Unusual levels of empathy and connectedness to other children and other life forms
(an exaggerated focus on "fairness"; a tendency to be traumatized or depressed by cruelty and random violence; an insistence on precise honesty; concern that behavior fit expressed principles)
- Precocious interest in spiritual/religious, moral/ethical, metaphysical, and philosophical issues
(early questions about life and death, time, God, the boundaries of the universe, and so on, often accompanied by high levels of emotion; fears and stress levels on these topics may seem exaggerated)
- Desire for close friendships, often a preference for a few deep relationships rather than many short or shallow ones
(in lieu of such friendships a child may invent several imaginary friends—even whole cities or countries of them—or form intense attachments to pets, dolls, or stuffed animals; many highly gifted children prefer the company of adults or older children to that of their age peers)

Not every highly gifted child, of course, will exhibit all of these characteristics; however, if a child shows more than one or two on a consistent basis, it is safe to assume a very high-level of intelligence.

NATURE OR NURTURE

The debate over nature or nurture continues to rage in academic circles, fueled by our egalitarian social and political beliefs ("all men are created equal") and what has been called the "Standard Social Science Model" (Pinker, 1994), which asserts that the human psyche is molded by the surrounding culture. Books and clinics offer advice to parents on the best way to raise a more intelligent child. In addition, parents of many obviously brilliant children (with little or no experience of children other than their own) take credit for making them brilliant, telling other parents that they need only "do what we did" to "have what we have."

The mother of a child known as an "antiques prodigy" explained on a Phil Donahue show in 1993 that he was a perfectly normal child, but she had talked to him as if he were an adult rather than as if he were a child and that accounted for his unusual abilities. A family in Ohio claims to have "created" four intellectual and musical prodigies by an intensive coaching effort that began before the girls were born. When unusual parent-child interactions or intense coaching has taken place, it is difficult to disentangle the strands of nature and nurture in the child's later intellectual achievements.

However, there are many other parents whose unusually capable offspring came as something of a shock. "My son began speaking three and four word sentences at 6 months," the mother of a child who graduated from high school at age 10 says. "People asked me what I had done to make him do that. What do most mothers do with a new baby? I changed him and bathed him and fed him and put him to bed—and suddenly he was talking to me!" The mother of a boy who achieved a score of 750 on the Math portion of the SAT at the age of 8 says that when he was still in the womb she could tap on her belly and he would kick back, matching the number of her taps with the number of his kicks. These parents do not take credit for their children's differences because their experience of child rearing has been not an effort to teach and lead, but a constant struggle simply to keep up!

In other cases extreme intelligence has been found in children whose early environment was anything but intellectually nourishing. Torey L. Hayden's (1980) book *One Child* is the story of "Sheila," a girl whose Stanford-Binet IQ score of 182 was attained at age 6 after a life of extreme abuse and neglect and after the child had been diagnosed as emotionally disturbed.

It is clear that biology plays a crucial, probably the crucial role in the creation of unusual intelligence. "They absolutely came this way," is how the harried mother of three highly gifted children put it:

> My first born sat for two hours the day we brought her home from the hospital, looking at the kitchen with great interest and intensity. Her eyes moved carefully from one side of the room to the other taking in one detail at a time. This was no passive, unfocused, unseeing lump of protoplasm! Strapped into that infant seat, she was systematically investigating her world the only way she could.

In studies of twins reared apart, intelligence has been found to be among the most heritable of individual characteristics (Bouchard, Lykken, McGue, Segal, & Tellgen, 1990). The heritability of intelligence may be one reason it is hard for parents (and observers) to determine how great a role their parenting plays in their children's unusual intellectual functioning. The gifted parent is likely to respond naturally to an infant's intensity and curiosity, recognizing it and supporting it. These are the parents who are most likely to read to a nursing infant, to use a large and precise vocabulary both in speaking to their children and in dealing with the world, to fill the household with stimulating sounds, sights, and activities. In sharing with their children what they love themselves, they enrich the learning environment even without specifically intending to do so. Dylan Thomas attributed his poetic gift in part to the fact that his father sat by his crib every night and read Shakespeare aloud to him.

We may never be able to draw a clear line between nature and nurture. Sheila's case shows that even a hostile and severely deprived environment may not destroy innate intelligence; Dylan Thomas's case shows that providing a bright infant with a rich and nourishing intellectual diet can encourage the full development of innate gifts. What we do know is that not all parents who (by following the prescriptions of books or clinics) attempt to make what one clinic calls "better babies" actually succeed in creating unusually bright children and not all unusually bright children come from specially enriched environments.

NURTURE VERSUS PUSHING

It may be important to point out here that there is a big difference between following a child's lead, providing the information, materials, and resources a fast-growing intelligence demands, and pushing the child to constantly prove that intelligence. Even the most cautious parents may find themselves overinvesting in their child's gifts and abilities. Even the best coach or teacher may find it difficult to allow a brilliant and capable child to sometimes relax into childhood, whatever childhood may mean for an individual precocious child. A restless, searching intelligence may drive a child to attempt to do and learn everything; adults may need to help him set a few limits and learn to take an occasional break from his normal, frenetic pace. An obvious potential for major achievement can be a trap, leading everyone to focus on achievement to the exclusion of every other aspect of life. Cognitive ability is not everything; it may not even be all that goes into unusual intelligence.

DABROWSKI'S CONTRIBUTIONS

The Polish psychiatrist and psychologist Kasimierz Dabrowski, studying gifted and creative clients, including children and adolescents as well as adults, recognized five dimensions in which they showed greater than normal psychic intensity. He called these intensities *overexcitabili-*

ties (OEs; Piechowski, 1979, 1986). They are not negative characteristics, but constitute a heightened awareness of and sensitivity to various stimuli. The OEs are thought to be innate and can be found so consistently in gifted children that they may one day serve as one means of identification.

OVEREXCITABILITIES

Psychomotor. An unusual need for physical activity and movement. Energy may be converted into rapid talk, pacing the use of hand gestures.

Sensual. Greater than normal perceptiveness of sensory experiences; unusual awareness and enjoyment of sensation. Aesthetic awareness.

Imaginational. Inventiveness, the ability to visualize clearly, metaphorical speech, dreaming, daydreaming, fantasy and magical thinking.

Intellectual. The desire to question, to analyze; the ability to delight in the abstract and theoretical, in logical thinking and puzzles and problem solving.

Emotional. An intensity of feeling and of relationships; preference for few close friends rather than many acquaintances; natural empathy and compassion. Susceptibility to depression, anxiety, loneliness.

The first two of these OEs, although constantly observed in highly gifted children, have not been shown to differentiate between this population and others, but Imaginational, Intellectual, and Emotional do. Gifted children tend to exhibit most or all of them in different degrees. An individual child's profile depends on which overexcitabilities are the strongest.

Children who lead with intellectual OE are more likely to be identified as gifted in school; those who lead with imaginational may be less recognizable in an academic environment. These are the "space cadets"—the dreamy, creative, fantasy builders, the poets and artists and visionary scientists. If these children *are* recognized as gifted, they are likely to be labeled underachievers.

Although it would be a surprise to many who think of giftedness purely in terms of cognitive ability, Dabrowski considered Emotional OE to be central. It accounts for the extreme sensitivity often seen in highly gifted individuals, both children and adults. It can leave many of them feeling (and appearing to others) "crazy" or neurotic.

Many highly gifted children experience both internal and external pressure to keep this OE hidden, something they may be able to do by focusing their energies on the products their Imaginational and Intellectual OEs make possible. It is Emotional OE, the ability to relate deeply to others, to experience a full range of human feeling, however, that Dabrowski believed was critical to the unusual levels of moral/spiritual development he saw that gifted individuals could achieve.

It is Emotional OE that accounts for the 2-year-old child who, in tears, brings her piggy bank to her mother and begs her to send all the money to the victims of an earthquake half a world away. Or the second grade boy who refuses to go to recess with the other children because he can't bear to watch the bullying that regularly takes place on the playground. As with other aspects of unusual intelligence, it is important that this one be recognized as a normal feature of the child's development rather than an anomaly that needs correcting.

ASYNCHRONOUS DEVELOPMENT

Recently, a group of parents, psychologists, and educators known as the Columbus Group (1991) suggested a new definition of giftedness:

> Giftedness is asynchronous development in which advanced cognitive abilities and heightened intensity combine to create inner experiences and awareness that are qualitatively different from the norm. This asynchrony increases with higher intellectual capacity. The uniqueness of the gifted renders them particularly vulnerable and requires modifications in parenting, teaching, and counseling in order for them to develop optimally.

Highly gifted children begin and live their lives on a developmental trajectory that is outside the norms. This trajectory assures that they won't fit the expectations of a culture based on norms. They will be out of sync with family, school, and society in a variety of ways, from when they begin speaking to what they notice and care about, to what games they like to play. However, asynchrony is not only external; it is internal as well. Their cognitive development proceeds at a different rate from their physical, their social, their emotional, or their spiritual development.

In an article entitled "Giftedness, A View from Within," Morelock (1992) told the story of Jennie, a 4-year-old whose grandfather has recently died. In addition to her grief over the loss, Jennie is now imagining her mother's death and her own. Her mother has tried to assure her that Grandpa was old and that she and her mother are not, so she promises they will not die soon. Jennie is not comforted. Tearfully, she tells her mother that she can't make such a promise; mothers do die, even children die:

In order to feel secure, to trust in the world and to begin to develop her own identity, Jennie requires a certain comfortable predictability in her daily existence. She also needs to have a simple, solid trust in the strength and reliability of her parents. However, the fulfillment of those 4-year-old emotional needs is complicated by Jennie's extraordinary capacity for abstract thought. Her internally imposed demand for logical consistency leaves her emotionally unable to accept anything contradicting it. . . . For Jennie—and for other gifted children like her—the world can threaten to dissolve into unpredictable and frightening chaos. (pp. 11-12)

Many parents and school programs expose very bright children to the news of the world, assuming that the cognitive capacities that lead the children to an early interest in world affairs will enable them to handle what they learn. Unaware of the problems inherent in asynchronous development (coupled with Emotional Overexcitability), most adults fail to offer sensitive and appropriate support for the emotional consequences of the information to which the children are exposed.

The concept of "mental age" is useful in grasping cognitive differences in children at the highest ranges. We understand that a 6-year-old with an IQ of 200 (a mental age of 12) is likely to be desperately out of place in a first grade classroom. However, mental age is too narrow a concept to help us cope with asynchronous development. There are many ages within any highly gifted child, and the interaction of those ages is complicated. Parents usually have at least some sense of the age variation. One mother explained that her 8-year-old son Tad is "8 on the soccer field, 14 in algebra class, 20 when pleading the case for more challenging school work, and 3 when he can't find his teddy bear at bedtime." The fact that all of these developmental levels are present in one small boy trying to find a place in a world that thinks it knows about 8-year-olds makes his task even harder than his mother may grasp.

Teachers aren't likely to be as aware as parents of the complexities of asynchronous development. Even a teacher who sees and adapts to Tad's extraordinary cognitive needs may expect him to be normal in all other ways, failing to understand the social and emotional pressures he faces. It is important to recognize that when he is in class with age mates, he is attempting to relate to children who are in many ways far younger than he, and when he is in class with his intellectual peers, he must relate to children in many ways much older. Nothing about the process will be ordinary and in neither of these settings will he find a fully comfortable fit.

Michael Grost's first day in kindergarten is an example of the difficulty. Seeing another child coloring an apple blue, Mike compared her choice of color to Picasso's. She asked where Picasso was sitting. Mike attempted to explain Picasso's blue period. She pointed out that she didn't know which crayon was the red one. He showed her where the color name was printed. She said they wouldn't learn to read until first grade (Grost, 1970). Although Michael's case is the extreme case of a child above 200 IQ, children less dramatically different neverthe-less face the complex task of trying to understand the behaviors and conversations of age mates. Their own minds are the only minds they know, so they naturally expect other children to think, act, and speak as they do. When they discover this is not the case, they must come up with some sort of explanation, and then attempt to establish relation-ships across the gulf that divides them from others. This is virtually impos-sible for a very young child without adult help.

In the movie, *Little Man Tate*, we see the discrepancy from the other side, as a child tries to build a friendship with a college student classmate. Humans have always had difficulty establishing and main-taining friendly contact with people perceived as "other." For highly gifted children, it can seem that everyone in the world is "other." Like E.T. they may feel a desperate longing to "phone home." Unlike E.T., they know this is the only home they have.

THE ACHIEVEMENT FOCUS IN EDUCATION

The Columbus Group's (1991) emphasis on the internal reality of the gifted provides an important balance for the growing emphasis in the academic world on performance and achievement. The definition pro-posed in the 1993 Report of the Office of Education Research and Improvement makes this emphasis clear:

> Children and youth with outstanding talent perform or show the potential for performing at remarkably high levels of accomplish-ment when compared with others of their age, experience, or envi-ronment.
> These children and youth exhibit high performance capability in intellectual, creative, and/or artistic areas, possess an unusual lead-ership capacity, or excel in specific academic fields. (p. 3)

Before dealing with the issue of achievement raised in this fed-eral definition, we should take note of the absence of the term *gifted*. Because that word carries considerable negative baggage, the current educational fashion is to substitute the word talented. Unfortunately, *tal-ent* has its own long-established meaning; it refers to *an* aptitude or abil-ity. One may be very talented in one or more ways and yet not show the integrative intelligence that has been referred to throughout this century as giftedness. Whether the change in terminology will bring a change in concept or approach, effectively eliminating attention to the phenomenon of extreme intelligence, it is too soon to tell.

Schools, themselves evaluated on the achievement and performance of their students, must continually measure achievement and performance. Because unusually bright children have a *potential* for unusual performance, many educators have come to equate that performance with giftedness, assuming that children who perform unusually well in the classroom are gifted and children who do not are not. Children who do not get good grades may be refused admittance to special programs. In some cases where test scores consistently show potential well beyond academic performance, children are said to have "overachieved" on the tests, suggesting the incredible idea that they have achieved beyond their capacities.

In other cases in which test scores outdo school performance, children are labeled underachievers and a search may be started to find emotional problems or learning disabilities to account for the discrepancy between aptitude and achievement. Although it is true that there *could* be learning disabilities or emotional problems involved, the discrepancy between highly gifted children's cognitive capacities and the tasks they are asked to perform in the classroom is a far more common culprit in underachievement.

Consider the plight of Nicole, a 6-year-old girl with an IQ score over 150, who reads and comprehends at the eighth grade level but is put into the first grade with her age mates. In her school the recent emphasis on "inclusion" has dictated that all first graders use the same reading text. It is impossible for Nicole to exhibit an eighth grade reading level on the primer she is given (she can't read the words "I see the dog" eight levels better than any of the others). Further, she is likely to find the tasks in the accompanying workbook to be boring at best (how can she help but compare "I see the dog" to the rich language and complex stories of *Wind in the Willows* that she is reading at home), incomprehensible at worst. She may either refuse to do them at all, or do them so carelessly that her performance is actually poorer than that of children far less able. Her handwriting, far too slow to keep up with her agile mind, is ponderous and messy; for this reason she often writes short, simple sentences rather than the complex ones she is thinking. Even in open-ended writing assignments she is unable to show her level of verbal reasoning.

Matt, a first grader with an IQ over 170, is not a math prodigy, but does have an intuitive grasp of the conceptual connections between adding and subtracting, multiplying and dividing. He understands simple fractions and is able to do complex mental arithmetic problems using his fingers to keep track of the process. Week after week he is given timed tests on "addition facts under 10" with the rest of his class. Occasionally his score is a perfect 100 (which never earns him a reprieve from the inevitable Friday tests), but far more often it is 60 or 40 or even 10. His mother asks him for an explanation of the erratic scores that have occasioned a note from the teacher. "I get to playing in my mind," he says, "and all of a sudden, the time's up." Knowing that there is nothing to be gained by doing perfectly on any given test, Matt cannot keep his mind focused enough to complete them. There are too many more interesting things to think about.

Teachers who equate good classroom performance with intelligence may evaluate children who get top scores on normal first grade tasks (children who may have only slightly above normal cognitive capacities) as far more gifted than Matt or Nicole.

The word *potential* can create confusion. It is not the capacity that is potential; the capacity is actual and (unless affected by physiological damage or emotional trauma) constant. The highly gifted child processes and draws meaning from experience in ways unusual for his or her age all the time, whether the expression of that unusual processing is obvious or not. It is only achievement that is potential.

A highly gifted child can fail to achieve for an almost infinite variety of reasons—from a wish not to appear different from the children around him or her, to an inability to relate to the tasks at hand, to a sense that her internal reality is so aberrant that it must be denied. Decades ago Hollingworth (1942) observed that children above 170 IQ could learn all that was available in the regular classroom in less than a quarter of the time provided. Highly gifted children, when not given curriculum and materials suited to their cognitive abilities, waste most of their time in school, doing their best to find ways to occupy their active minds. How they do that determines how they will be evaluated, and how successfully they will survive their early school years.

LEARNING

From their earliest months, highly gifted children absorb information from the world around them at an astonishing rate. Outside the school environment their learning and development may proceed naturally, encountering few obstacles. Although parents may not always be prepared to provide optimum learning experiences and materials, they aren't likely to actively work against the child's development. It would be a rare mother who would tell her 9-month-old to stop speaking in full sentences and start babbling like other children his age.

Once unusually bright children begin formal schooling, however, this open-ended learning environment almost always disappears. For the first time they are expected to conform to a learning curve that bears no relationship to their own. They are expected to stop learning and wait for the other children to "catch up." (Given the differences in developmental trajectories, this can no more happen than a younger sibling can catch up in age to an older one.)

In school the problems of boredom, lack of challenge, dearth of materials, and adult failure to recognize the extent of the children's capabilities combine to short-circuit learning. Teachers who have been taught that skipping stages can adversely affect a child's development frequently insist that every child proceed through the prescribed steps in order and on time. They may not understand that the highly gifted children has already taken those steps, both far earlier and far faster than other children.

Parents often rush to the schools to ask for (or demand) special attention for children who are exhibiting boredom, frustration, listlessness, disinterest, or hostility to school. "I can hardly believe the change in Amy since school started," a father tells his daughter's first grade teacher:

> She used to run on high from dawn till dark, doing, doing, doing. She was always in the middle of a project. Sometimes three or four. Now she comes home and flops on the floor in front of the television. And when it's time to leave for school in morning she complains of headaches or stomach aches. Sometimes she gets nosebleeds.

Taking their case to teachers, principals, even superintendents, parents may encounter a brick wall—there is no flexibility in the school's basic program and no special program for the gifted. They may be told that a gifted program begins in the fourth grade, so their daughter should just hang on until then. Sometimes they are told they're lucky; the school has a wonderful program beginning in first grade and their daughter is eligible. Only after she has been in that gifted program for a few weeks do the parents discover the painful truth. Few gifted programs anywhere are designed to meet the needs of exceptionally gifted children.

ACCELERATION

There are ways to keep highly gifted children learning, even in a school that has no special programs, provided there is a willingness to address the child as an individual and be flexible. There is no way to fully meet the educational needs of the highly gifted solely by providing "enrichment" of the regular curriculum, however. Acceleration becomes part of any individual program simply because of the speed with which these children learn and because they are already accelerated before school begins.

Moving a child either in grade level or in subject matter does not "push" the child; it merely acknowledges the actual level of knowledge and capability and the child's rapid learning rate. Off-level testing can provide an estimate of even the brightest child's highest level of achievement and placement in all subjects can be determined from that information (according to the available opportunities and resources). Sometimes it is scheduling and transportation rather than programming rigidity that create problems, particularly when appropriate placement requires that a child travel from an elementary school to a middle or high school for a single subject or a part of the academic day.

Both parents and teachers often worry that moving a child ahead will leave gaps in his knowledge. This is *not* a concern that justifies keeping that child in a class that is not appropriately challenging. It is essential to remember that these children learn very quickly, even more quickly when they perceive a genuine need for the information. Gaps can be filled with very little effort when they become apparent.

The other worry about acceleration is social. How will the young child get along with older students? This is the time to consider the child's own preferences. If she is eager to move ahead and get out of a boring class, she will be far more likely to take social complications in stride. Furthermore, when considering acceleration too many parents and teachers forget that staying with age mates is *not* the ideal situation for an asynchronous child. Age mates are not true peers. There are social difficulties for the child in their company that can be made worse by the complications of boredom or an effort to hold back intellectually in order to "fit" better.

If a school adamantly refuses to consider acceleration of any kind, there are other options. Some parents have found mentors for their children in subjects covered by the school curriculum or in subjects far afield. Adults with a passionate interest are often delighted to share it with a bright, interested child. Parents may let their children stay out of school one or more afternoons a week to spend time with their mentor. Although it seems unreasonable to force a child to sit in a classroom that isn't providing real learning all day every day, some school situations give families no way out; mentorships can occur on weekends or during the evening.

Some colleges, museums, art studios, and learning centers offer evening or weekend classes for adults and will allow a child to attend either as an auditor or with an enrolled parent. Some may even accept a child as a student on the basis of an interview.

From time to time a child follows in the footsteps of the fictional "Doogie Howser" and becomes a full-fledged college student when other children of the same age are still in the primary grades. Whether to take such a radical step depends on the child. Michael Kearney, who graduated from college in 1994 at the age of 10 simply could not find the intellectual challenge he wanted in any other way. He had consumed the K-12 curriculum by the time he was 6 years old, and did not want to be held back. College was the challenge he wanted; his mother attended classes with him, but he did the work himself. On the day of his graduation (an event covered by most of the major media) he had no regrets. He was full of ideas and eager to get on with the next phase of his life. He has since appeared on many television news magazine programs and worked as a roving reporter on a syndicated talk show.

HOMESCHOOLING/UNSCHOOLING

More and more parents are choosing either not to send their exceptionally bright children to school at all or to take them out of school environments that are unsatisfactory and educate them at home. Usually called homeschooling, this process varies from family to family. Some parents create a school-like environment and schedule, designating one room or area as the school and providing "lessons" for as much as half of every day. Curriculum is planned by adults (or purchased) or created or revised in collaboration with the children. Few families devote as many hours to formal learning as schools seem to (although school schedules can be deceiving, with much learning time lost to a variety of nonacademic activities) because these children learn so quickly.

Other parents maintain the same sort of environment they provided for their children when they were toddlers. One mother of two 180+ IQ children prefers to call her family's program "unschooling." She wants nothing in her children's lives that smacks of school, which she associates with being forced to do things of little or no interest for little or no reason. "Shelley learned incredibly well when she was 18 months old and I wasn't trying to teach her anything. Why should I start teaching her now? Her brother likes different subjects and does different things, but he learns quite well on his own, too."

These two children make out their own schedules and devise their own learning plans, checking them with her and getting her help to find the resources and materials they need. They seem willing to take adult advice, but resist efforts to get them to add a subject they aren't interested in pursuing at the moment. When they take standardized achievement tests, their scores surprise even their mother—they are well beyond their age mates even in subjects they have made no apparent effort to study. In subjects of current interest they are routinely off the scales:

> No matter how haphazard our system might appear, I don't think it can be educationally any worse than school. And both of my children are more comfortable with themselves than they would be if they had had to endure the incessant teasing of other children about their differences. They are independent learners, independent thinkers, and happy kids. I doubt if they would be any of these if they went to school.

The decision to educate children at home, whether formally or informally, can be a difficult one. All 50 states currently allow homeschooling, but regulations vary from state to state. Some districts are friendly and accommodating, allowing homeschooled children to use school facilities for nonacademic subjects for instance, while others purposely set up roadblocks to discourage parents from taking children (and state money) out of the system.

Homeschooling is not for everyone. There are families that have tried homeschooling and found it too demanding. Other families need two incomes and can't arrange to have one parent at home all day every day. Many parents fear that they don't "know enough" to homeschool. Some families have chosen homeschooling for a year or two in order to get past a particular problem in their local school and then allowed their children to return.

For some the obstacle to homeschooling is social. Many highly gifted children are introverts and don't seem to need the constant companionship of other children, but others are extroverts. The mother of one such admitted to being disappointed when her son chose to stay in a seriously unchallenging school environment instead of staying at home. "I need the kids, Mom," he told her. "I can learn stuff after school and on weekends and during the summer, but I can't have friends with me at home all day." She comforted herself with the understanding that bright as her son was, intellectual challenge was not his only need.

A SENSE OF SELF

Some people may wonder whether it is really important to focus so strongly on highly gifted children's differences. They're just children after all. Can't they be left to find their own way?

The answer to that question is a resounding *no*. They are children whose differences affect every aspect of their lives, both internal and external. Leaving them in a world designed for other children is like leaving Hansel and Gretel alone in the deep woods. *Because* they are only children, they have few internal resources and little life experience to help them cope.

The capacities these children bring with them are fully integrated with who they are. Failing to nourish them thwarts and distorts their whole being. Psychiatrist Theodore Isaac Rubin (1990) believes that much psychic pain and disorder in adults is caused by deprivation of the resources and support necessary to fully develop their abilities: "The stunting and crippling effect of deprivation is directly proportional to the innate capabilities and potential of the person in question" (p. 18). Highly gifted children bring into the world with them astonishing capacities. They are children of great promise, and children at great risk. Whether they will be able to develop a firm and realistic sense of self and fulfill their promise largely depends on the adults in their world.

REFERENCES

Bouchard, T. J., Jr., Lykken, D. T., McGue, M., Segal, N. L., & Tellegen, A. (1990). Sources of human psychological differences: The Minnesota study of twins reared apart. *Science, 250,* 223-228.

The Columbus Group (1991). Unpublished minutes.

Grost, A. (1970). *Genius in residence.* Englewood Cliffs, NJ: Prentice-Hall.

Hayden, T. L. (1980). *One child.* New York: Putnam.

Hollingworth, L. (1942). *Children above 180 IQ.* Yonkers, NY: World Book.

Morelock, M. (1992). Giftedness: A view from within. *Understanding Our Gifted, 4*(3), 11-12.

Office of Educational Research and Improvement. (1993). *National excellence: A case for developing America's talent.* Washington, DC: U.S. Government Printing Office.

Piechowski, M. M. (1979). Developmental potential. In N. Colangelo & R. T. Zaffran (Eds.), *New voices in counseling the gifted* (pp. 25-57). Dubuque, IA: Kendall/Hunt.

Piechowski, M. M. (1986). The concept of developmental potential. *Roeper Review, 8,* 190-197.

Pinker, S. (1994). *The language instinct.* New York: Morrow.

Rubin, T. I. (1990). *Child potential, fulfilling your child's intellectual, emotional, and creative promise.* New York: Continuum.

Silverman, L., & Kearney, K. (1992a). Don't throw away the old Binet. *Understanding Our Gifted, 4*(4), 1, 8-10.

Silverman, L., & Kearney, K. (1992b). The case for the Stanford-Binet L-M as a supplemental test. *Roeper Review, 15,* 34-37.

12

Creativity and Underachievement

Sylvia B. Rimm

The nurturance of creativity and the prevention of underachievement begin in early childhood, before children enter school. Creative achievement is fostered when the psychological defenses that cause children to underachieve or not to perform productively (Rimm, 1995) are prevented. These defenses are often caused by pressures children feel that lead them to unconsciously manipulate adults in dependent or dominant ways. They want to protect themselves because they fear that they may not be "smart" or creative enough. Parents of gifted preschool children should read about underachievement before their children even enter school because the seeds of underachievement are often planted during those preschool years. Statistics from The National Commission on Excellence in Education (1984) indicate that 50% of gifted children underachieve.

EARLY ENRICHMENT AND ATTENTION

Biographies of gifted and eminent achievers as well as family histories of underachievers reflect early enrichment and positive attention (Rimm & Lowe, 1988). However, clinical experiences provide some real concerns about the degree of positive attention. For example, did you ever hear parents repeatedly say to their children the following words: "You are the most perfect of all beautiful children"?

Those words of love conferred onto the beautiful first-born girl used to call up the positive image of a loving, caring, and delighted parent. My impressions would probably still be the same if I were not a psychologist. Instead, those words only evoke the image of a perfectionistic little girl, a preadolescent obsessed with concerns about designer clothes and makeup, or an eating disorder or depressed adolescent—the "daddy's little girls" of a child and adolescent psychological practice.

The sad and frustrated parents explain to me that Dr. Spock said you couldn't love babies too much. They add that the behavioral psychologists say that positive reinforcement and praise help children learn. The parents explain that they were positive, loving parents and that they tried to build self-confidence in their children: lots of encouragement, lots of attention, lots of praise for creativity, intelligence, and beauty.

With all that self-concept building, why do these children not feel smart and creative and beautiful? The IQ tests say they are gifted, the creativity tests list high scores, and your eyes tell you that they are attractive young people. Why the terrible feelings of inadequacy? Why the self-doubt and poor self-image?

The world of encouragement and love and support is surely the ideal environment in which children should be raised. However, for some children there is so much praise, so many comments about beauty and perfection and brilliance, so much enthroning as prince or princess that when new siblings come into the family, or when they must share attention in school, they feel "dethroned" (Rimm & Lowe, 1988). By comparison to their former feelings of perfection, they feel less loved, less beautiful, less creative, and less intelligent. No words or accomplishment seem to satisfy their never-satiated need for praise. Therefore, in some ways, too much praise becomes too much of a good thing. Adjusting to the less "special" environment of schools can cause children to feel pressures that they do not understand (Rimm, 1987, 1990, 1996).

Parents of preschoolers do well to enrich, encourage, and praise. If they could moderate that praise just a little bit, children might become less dependent on that praise and might be more likely to develop their own personal intrinsic motivation.

Stay positive, but avoid the superlatives like *brilliant, gorgeous, perfect,* and *genius.* Instead, you could replace those with *good thinker, hard worker, bright, clever, imaginative, kind, sensitive,* and *attractive.* Those words are more realistic and enable children to live up to reasonable standards of performance and appearance. Even these positive statements should not accompany the child's every word or performance or they come to depend on that extrinsic reinforcement for their motivation.

Here are some additional precautions for preschool children (Davis & Rimm, 1994):

1. Television watching, which is basically a passive-receptive activity, should be monitored and limited (Morrow, 1983). High-interest kindergarten readers come from homes in which there were rules regarding television and in which mothers watched less television than mothers in the homes of low-interest readers. However, educational programs could be exceptions to this policy. Creativity is an active process, and television may inhibit that.

2. Overstimulation, such as from too many peers or too much adult talk, can confuse children and detract from active involvement, concentration, and learning. Although parent communication to the child is desirable, continuous talk and long abstract lectures may seem meaningless and boring and exceed children's limited attention span. For some children, endless chatter will cause them to become restless and "hyperactive"; they know they should pay attention, but they cannot. For other children, overwhelming talking by a parent has the opposite effect, preventing the child's contributions and encouraging him or her to slow down and become very quiet. They give up trying to communicate with this parent.

3. If your child is spontaneously reading, teach the child some basic writing skills. A simple workbook that can be purchased from a local department store can be used for teaching the child to copy printing. Encourage coloring, drawing, cutting, and pasting as well. Exercising that fine motor coordination will help a gifted child feel more evenly skilled in the classroom. Teachers usually suggest leaving the learning of printing until school, but this unevenness in abilities often causes children anxiety related to their writing skills. Be sure not to pressure the child. Five minutes a day will provide your child sufficient practice and will make them feel more comfortable with pencils. Hopefully that practice will prevent the "pencil anxiety" which so many verbally gifted children feel.

4. Some daily "alone time" for a preschool child also is helpful. Interaction with peers and siblings is important to preschoolers, but some small amount of time each day for a child to play alone will encourage independent behavior and imagination. Creative persons of all ages seem to thrive on some amount of time alone.

All four of these precautions can help children very early to take initiative and to be active participants in their environments, rather than to receive stimulation only passively.

EARLY ASSESSMENT

There is good evidence that supports parents' abilities to recognize their children's giftedness early. Identification results of a national survey of 1,039 parents of gifted children indicated that 70% of these children were identified accurately by parents by age three (Gogul, McCumsey, & Hewett, 1985). Of the characteristics that caused parents to suspect giftedness, "early verbal expression" was mentioned most frequently. Other observed characteristics included an unusually long attention span, a good memory, high level of curiosity, and an early demonstration of original and creative behavior.

The reliability of parents' recognition of preschool giftedness was also supported by a program at Towson State University in Baltimore, MD (Hanson, 1984). Parents were encouraged to enroll their children in a program for 4-, 5-, and 6-year-old gifted children based on their own perceptions of the children's verbal giftedness. After enrollment, these children were given a battery of tests. Ninety percent of the children tested at least 1 year above grade level in reading, and all of the 5- and 6-year olds had high scores in the Fund of Knowledge subtests. Mathematics scores were not as consistently high, but parents had not been asked to consider math skill in their decision making.

Research certainly does confirm parents' ability to recognize giftedness in their children. Although we have no way of knowing the percentage of children who are missed by the parent identification procedure, at least we can substantiate that parents do not overidentify to the extent that teachers have often believed. In fact, studies indicate that parents usually underestimate, rather than overestimate, their children's giftedness (Chitwood, 1986).

If parents believe their preschool children are gifted, they might ask when and why it would be good to have them tested. Tests of preschool children are appropriate with the caution that such early tests may be somewhat unreliable. Scores can be adversely affected by many factors, including fatigue, stress, and diet (Perino & Perino, 1981). The scores should not be taken as an absolute measure of the child's ability and certainly not viewed as a limit to that ability. Tests of young children are likely to be conservative estimates of their ability since "test construction makes it virtually impossible to perform at a level higher than their potential" (Chitwood, 1986); but they can perform at a lower level.

If parents are considering early entrance to school or entrance to a particular school, preschool testing can help them to make a more informed decision. Although research (Davis & Rimm, 1994; Rimm, 1992) supports the success of early entrance to kindergarten for gifted children, that decision should not be made lightly. In addition to IQ test scores above 135, children should have good emotional adjustment. Girls accelerate more easily than boys and tall boys a little better than short boys. Height is not an important factor for girls (Lueck, 1989). Observation in a nursery school environment may be helpful to guiding the decision, provided that the nursery school teacher is not biased against early entrance to kindergarten and knows about the characteristics of gifted children.

If parents have doubts about early entrance, typical age entrance is recommended together with subject acceleration in the child's area of greatest strength. Observation by the teacher over time in the accelerated subject will provide the required evidence for the next decision. Teachers will be good observers provided they too have knowledge about gifted children and acceleration research.

CREATIVITY TESTING

Assessing children's actual creativity is certainly difficult in the preschool years. It may, however, be useful to know whether you are encouraging creative attitudes and behaviors in your child. PRIDE, a Preschool and Kindergarten Interest Descriptor (Rimm, 1983), was developed to identify creative characteristics in young children. It is a good measuring instrument for identifying highly creative children as well as an appropriate approach to heightening parent awareness about characteristics of creativity.

PRIDE is an easy-to-administer, reliable, and valid instrument for use in screening preschool and kindergarten children for programs for the creatively gifted. It was preceded in development by The Group Inventory for Finding Creative Talent (GIFT; Rimm, 1976), a K-6 creativity inventory; The Group Inventory For Finding Interests (GIFFI I; Rimm & Davis, 1979), a creativity inventory for grades 6-9; and GIFFI II (Davis & Rimm, 1980), a creativity inventory for grades 9-12. Because a student self-report inventory tends to be unreliable of children who are aged 3-5, PRIDE was created for use by parents based on their observation of their children. (See Table 12.1 for sample items.)

The purpose of PRIDE is to identify children with attitudes and interests usually associated with preschool and kindergarten creativity. Those attitudes include many interests, curiosity, independence, perseverance, imagination, playfulness, humor, and originality.

These test scores must be used with caution. That is, creativity inventory scores, like achievement test or IQ scores should be utilized to

Table 12.1. Sample Items From PRIDE.

#	Item	Characteristic
1	My child gets interested in things for a long time.	Wide interests, task commitment
9	My child has a make-believe friend.	Imagination
12	My child likes to make up jokes.	Sense of humor
17*	My child gets bored easily.	Independence
18	My child likes to take things apart to see how they work.	Curiosity
19	I enjoy make-believe play with my child.	Biographical
20	My child has many interests.	Wide interests
22	My child is quite reflective, rather than impulsive.	Reflectiveness
26*	My child usually does whatever other children do.	Independence
27	My child often does two things at the same time that aren't usually done together.	Unusual interest, attraction to complexity
29	My child seems to do things differently than other children.	Independence
32	My child can do some things that seem very difficult.	Attraction to complexity
37*	When things get hard, my child gives up and does something else.	Independence
38	My child likes to take walks alone.	Independence

*Negatively related to creativity.

screen children "into" gifted programs and not "out." For example, a child with a high PRIDE scores should be included in a program even though the child may not have been selected by a teacher. However, a child who is selected by a teacher as being highly creative should not be eliminated from the program because of a low or average PRIDE score. Creativity is a subtle characteristic that is difficult to identify. PRIDE can help schools in that identification process, and PRIDE can help parents be sensitive to their children's creativity.

PRIDE results in a total score and four dimension scores. Descriptions of dimensions follow:

1. Many Interests. High scorers are curious and ask questions. They show high interest in learning, stories, books, and things around them. Low scorers show less curiosity and have fewer interests.
2. Independence, Perseverance. High scorers play alone and do things independently. They do not give up easily and persevere even with difficult tasks. Low scorers tend to prefer easier tasks and are more likely to follow the lead of other children.
3. Imagination, Playfulness. High scorers enjoy make-believe, humor, and playfulness. Low scorers are more serious and realistic.
4. Originality. High scorers tend to have unusual ideas and ask unusual questions. They are inventive in their art and play and tend to think differently than other children. Low scorers' ideas and artwork appear to be more typical of children of similar age.

Preschool and kindergarten teachers and parents of creatively gifted children will benefit from the use of PRIDE as long as they recognize its limitations. PRIDE may help to identify highly creative children. It may also help to identify children who are too dependent and need encouragement toward independence and creativity. Finally, it heightens everyone's awareness about the characteristics of creative young children.

ENCOURAGING CREATIVITY THROUGH BUILDING CONFIDENCE AND INTERESTS

Creativity and underachievement are tied together in this chapter to provide suggestions to parents and teachers about ways in which children can be encouraged to develop the confidence to create and achieve while preventing the problems of dependencies and the pressures that inhibit creative productivity. Therefore, underachievement is prevented by providing an environment for healthy psychological development. The assessment component of this chapter permits parents and teachers to have a better understanding of where their children are in terms of intellectual growth and creative characteristics. Therefore, assessment, if interpreted and used carefully, can help adults guide preschool children to intellectual confidence.

REFERENCES

Chitwood, D. G. (1986). Guiding parents seeking testing. *Roeper Review, 8*(3), 177-179.

Davis, G. A., & Rimm, S. B. (1980). *GIFFI II: Group inventory for finding interests.* Watertown, WI: Educational Assessment Service.

Davis, G. A., & Rimm, S. B. (1994). *Education of the gifted and talented* (3rd ed.). Needham Heights, MA: Allyn & Bacon.

Gogul, E. M., McCumsey, J., & Hewett, G. (1985, November/ December). What parents are saying. *Gifted Child Today,* 7-9.

Hanson, I. (1984). A comparison between parent identification of young bright children and subsequent testing. *Roeper Review, 7*(1), 44-45.

Lueck, R. (1989). Psychosocial factors in the acceleration of gifted elementary school children. In S.B. Rimm, M. Cornale, R. Manos, & J. Behrend (Eds.), *Guidebook—Underachievement syndrome: Causes and cures* (pp. 360-370). Watertown, WI: Apple Publishing.

Morrow, L. (1983, April). *Home and school correlates of early interest in literature.* Paper presented at the American Educational Research Association, Montreal, Canada.

National Commission on Excellence in Education (1984). *A nation at risk: The imperative for educational reform.* Washington, DC: U.S. Government Printing Office.

Perino, S. C., & Perino, J. (1981). *Parenting the gifted—Developing the promise.* New York: Bowker.

Rimm, S. B. (1976). *GIFT: Group inventory for finding creative talent.* Watertown, WI: Educational Assessment Service.

Rimm, S. B. (1983). *PRIDE: Preschool and kindergarten descriptor.* Watertown, WI: Educational Assessment Service.

Rimm, S. B. (1987, November/December). Why do bright children underachieve? The pressures they feel. *Gifted Child Today,* 30-36.

Rimm, S. B. (1990, May/June). Parenting and teaching gifted—A theory of relativity. *Gifted Child Today,* 32-36.

Rimm, S. B. (1992, March/April). How acceleration may prevent underachievement syndrome. *Gifted Child Today,* 9-14.

Rimm, S. B. (1995). *Why bright kids get poor grades and what you can do about it.* New York: Crown.

Rimm, S. B. (1996). *Dr. Sylvia Rimm's smart parenting: How to raise a happy, achieving child.* New York: Crown.

Rimm, S. B., & Davis, G. A. (1979). *GIFFI I: Group inventory for finding interests.* Watertown, WI: Educational Assessment Service.

Rimm, S. B., & Lowe, B. (1988, Fall). Family environments of underachieving gifted students. *Gifted Child Quarterly, 4,* 353-359.

13

The Gifted-Learning-Disabled Child: In Need of an Integrative Education

Nancy Wingenbach

As parents and educators, we are constantly striving to meet the needs of gifted children. There exists, however, a subpopulation of gifted children in desperate need of our services. The gifted-learning-disabled child does exist, most often immersed in frustration: the child's, the parents', and the teacher's. The core of the frustration varies. The child, as is characteristic of giftedness, is sensitive to the discrepancy between potential and performance but does not know what to do about the inability to read or the inability to organize thoughts or the inability to remember on a short-term basis the symbols used in the classroom. The parent is aware of the child's frustration, sometimes the specific disability, the strengths in learning displayed at home, and the gap between the child's general ability to learn and the efforts to meet the school's requirements. The teacher is cognizant of the variation in the child's performance within the context of the classroom; recognizes the insightfulness, the conceptualization, the knowledge retained; and contrasts these behaviors with the apparent deficit in specific skill areas. In order to understand and then serve these gifted-learning-disabled students, attention must be focused on the interactive effects of giftedness and learning disabilities and on the educational concerns and strategies for meeting their needs.

PROFILE OF THE GIFTED-LEARNING-DISABLED CHILD

Definitions abound for *gifted* and *learning disabled*, but to keep them in proper perspective for this discussion, consider the definition of gifted (Whitmore & Maker, 1985):

> The mind of the gifted person processes and produces information with distinctive facility and qualitative results. Cognitive characteristics that reliably discriminate gifted from nongifted cluster around four key abilities:
> 1. communication of ideas
> 2. problem-solving skills
> 3. creative production or thought
> 4. retention and use of knowledge (p. 7)

The emphasis in this definition is on the processing of information for a variety of purposes, from communicating it to simply building up or retaining knowledge.

Sternberg (1985) presented a conception of giftedness that is especially appropriate. Intelligence is described as two-fold: reflecting a knowledge of the world and possessing a general set of cognitive information processing skills. The essence of intelligence is metacognitive: knowing how to assemble, control, and execute the cognitive processes needed to use available information. In other words, a gifted individual is aware of the knowledge possessed and how to process the knowledge most effectively.

These definitions of giftedness are particularly appropriate if we look at the gifted-learning-disabled person who can process and produce information rapidly and qualitatively but who has a "short circuit" in one or more of the four abilities included in the above definition of giftedness. As an example, Marcia, the case study presented in *Intellectual Giftedness in Disabled Persons* (Whitmore & Maker, 1985), was dyslexic but managed to compensate in a number of ways during her educational experience. Her dyslexia was not specifically identified until she was in medical school and heard a lecture that clarified for her the learning disability she was experiencing. Marcia compensated for her inability to read by using her exceptional skills in auditory processing of information. Marcia expressed her sense of feeling dumb and inadequate, yet her ability to successfully compensate to the point of completing medical school speaks of her giftedness.

RD is basically a nonreader (Mindell, 1982). However, at 26, he is an accomplished, successful metalsmith, earns a living by designing and crafting jewelry, and has been the recipient of numerous awards at all levels of competition from local to national. The combination of giftedness and learning disability created extreme frustration with his educational experience, which continually focused on remediation of reading skills. RD also felt deep frustration for society's views in general, as reflected in his statement:

> I have experienced firsthand the anguish, despair, and utter frustration of the inarticulate child who cannot tell the literate person that literacy is not the only level on which he exists; that he is a whole person with many ways of giving and receiving information other than reading and writing, and that the social environment demand for functional literacy tends to overshadow all the other potentials that an individual may possess. . . . The essence of my message is that functional literacy is not the only measure of an individual and never was. (p. 23)

A definition or description for the gifted-learning-disabled child is derived from those examples:

> A learning disability is a disorder in psychological processes involved in understanding or using the spoken or written language. For the gifted-learning-disabled, the disorder focus is reflected in either communication of ideas (reading or writing development) or in retention of knowledge (short-term memory) or use of knowledge (organizational skills) or a combination of the above. The disability results in a discrepancy between potential and performance. (Whitmore & Maker, 1985, p. 184)

The specific learning disability results in the discrepancy between the potential of the child to succeed on school tasks and his or her performance on those tasks. The discrepancy is noted and the school may or may not determine to remediate depending on the child's performance in relation to grade level functioning. Many gifted students performing on grade level may in reality be either underachieving or inhibited in performance by a learning disability. Note, however, the emphasis on remediation as opposed to recognition of strengths and weaknesses.

An important component which separates the gifted-learning-disabled child from the nongifted-disabled child is the interactive effect of the giftedness and the disability. The gifted-learning-disabled child may use strengths to overcome the limitations imposed by disabilities (e.g., Marcia and RD). Whitmore and Maker (1985) described the positive and negative consequences of specific attributes associated with giftedness interacting with aspects of disabling conditions:

> The positive effects can be regarded as strengths that allow such individuals to overcome their disabilities and achieve goals of success not attained by nongifted persons similarly disabled. Apparently, a strong desire to be independent, tendencies toward perfectionism and high aspirations for contributing to society, and intense drives to attain knowledge, to gain understanding, and to master skills and problems all nourish an exceptional capacity for perseverance and unrelenting motivation to attain goals. (p. 11)

Another interactive effect which is negative, however, is frustration experienced by the gifted-learning-disabled child who is sensitive to the disability, experiences the feelings of inadequacy, and acknowledges the deficit between potential and performance. This child's self-concept rapidly deteriorates. At times, the learning disability has been disabling in performing in class and, as a result, the child experiences feelings of inadequacy, embarrassment, and frustration. The feeling of being inadequate then complicates the effort of managing or mastering the instructional task and the process becomes a "vicious cycle" from which there seems no escape.

As a summary of characteristics of the gifted-learning-disabled child, certain specifics surface:

1. A learning disability in one or more areas.
2. Low self-esteem—sets high goals and finds self wanting, yet does not know how to compensate.
3. Low tolerance for frustration—born out of the inability to compensate in an acceptable way.
4. Preference for projects, concrete learning experiences, may operate well on an abstract, creative level.
5. Dislike for basic skill remediation completed in isolation from global learning.

EDUCATIONAL CONCERNS AND STRATEGIES

Too often in our classrooms, the educational emphasis is on specific skill development or fragmented learning. However, in order to meet the needs of the gifted-learning-disabled child as profiled earlier, the emphasis must shift to integrative learning. In *Growing Up Gifted* (1992) and in *Optimizing Learning* (1986), Clark explained intelligence as no longer confined to intellective/cognitive functioning but as the result of total and integrative brain functioning. If a child is learning disabled in a specific information processing mode such as reading, that disability is not reflective of the whole child or that child's potential. For years, we have classified as below average, average, or above average in terms of performance on school tasks. The educational process should change focus and view the child in terms of strengths and weaknesses as opposed to overall classification. From the new perspective, the gifted-learning disabled-child can be identified as strong in some information processing modes and weak in others.

As we focus on the "whole child," we also need to focus on "whole learning." The educational goal is to teach the child to process information in such a manner enabling him to cope well and interact successfully with the world in which he lives. As an example, if a gifted child can not read because of learning disability but is capable of processing information, conceptualizing, problem solving, and applying knowledge, then perhaps, while still working with reading development, a larger concentration should be placed on the modes of information processing the child uses successfully (e.g., Marcia's use of her auditory information processing strength). No matter the mode of information input/output, the important concern is the internalization of knowledge in combination with the conceptualization and application or use of that knowledge within the context of the child's daily life.

Within the classroom we have options for meeting the needs of the gifted-learning-disabled child. The one exercised most frequently is remediation of the skill deficit. Perhaps a more effective option related to the integrative education concept is to assist the child in compensating for the disability by altering the mode of processing information to fit with the strengths of the child. The gifted-learning-disabled child may have been altering the processing for years and researchers are just catching on to what the student already knows. The gifted-learning-disabled student identifies and recognizes the weakness and compensates with the strength. Marcia, for example, was dyslexic but used auditory strength to remember class lectures, discussions, key words, and concepts and thus did not "read" texts. These students have exhibited the metacognitive control to which Sternberg (1985) referred.

For those gifted-learning-disabled students who have not identified their strengths and weaknesses, one of the school's strategies might be to develop awareness of their capabilities: bring to consciousness the strengths and weaknesses of the individual, and then teach the child consciously to compensate and to be aware of compensation already occurring. Remediation should not be ignored but should be a reliable part of the program. However, if the gifted-learning-disabled student is aware of the specific information processing disability, aware of strengths in other modes of information processing, and can become functional within the school setting using those stronger information processing modes, chances are greater that remediation can take place. No longer does the child face the confounding dilemma of "not performing up to his or her ability." Instead, only one circuit is down but the whole system is still functioning and sometimes most effectively to the end that education exists: to learn to process information such that the individual functions effectively within the context of daily life.

As we consider the educational context, there are at least four gifted-learning-disabled concerns that need to be addressed:

1. The need to remediate deficits becomes a greater concern than the need to nurture special talents in children. Diagnostic results focus on deficits rather than a profile of strengths and weaknesses (Fox, Brody, & Tobin, 1983). Too often, the child's identified weakness becomes the hub around which all lesson plans and teaching strategies revolve. The child's particular strengths are not reinforced and the compensatory practice of using alternate modes to process information is not encouraged.

2. The gifted-learning-disabled student is generally referred not because of performance (skill) deficit but because of psychological manifestations of stress (Fox et al., 1983). The gap between the child's perception of what he can do and the reality of what he is doing becomes a pressure point for all involved. As the disability affects one or more of the standard modes of processing information within the regular classroom, the child, without support, reacts in frustration. The frustration and inability to cope within the area of disability combine and are manifested in a variety of ways from behavioral to emotional.

3. The gifted-learning-disabled student is frequently identified as learning disabled but rarely identified as gifted. The manifestations of the psychological stress result in attempts on the part of the school system and the family to remediate. Again, the strengths in the other modes of information processing seem to disappear in the emphasis on the disability.

4. The gifted-learning-disabled child possesses two sets of exceptional characteristics: giftedness and disability. The interactive effects of the giftedness and learning disability, as well as the characteristics themselves, must be the basis for educational programming (Whitmore & Maker, 1985). In order for the gifted-learning-disabled child to receive the full benefits of the educational experience, all needs must be met. The educational programming should either specifically through an IEP or generally through classroom instructional planning attend to both strengths and weaknesses.

In addition to the previously recommended option for schools to implement and encourage metacognitive strategies as a means for gifted-learning-disabled students to recognize and control the processing of information, several other recommendations are available for use in the instructional setting:

1. Facilitate the gifted-learning-disabled student in the use of strengths.
   • if student has strong visual ability and weak auditory, encourage information processing through visual practice (e.g., reading, writing).

- if student has strong auditory skills, weak visual, encourage use of listening skills to compensate for reading or writing disability.
- if student is disabled in a subject area (e.g., math), strong in creative thought production, encourage creative development of high-interest projects that may incorporate math as a part of the whole.
- if student is not a writer, utilize tape recorder or dictation to record thoughts, or use computer/word-processing systems like Bank Street Writer.
- if student has difficulty in sequential development of ideas, begin with broad ideas and model breaking down into parts, demonstrating sequence.

2. Too often, remedial techniques focus on isolated basic skills such as vocabulary development. There is a need to concentrate on strengths in integrated learning situations. Renzulli's (1977) Triad Model has proven effective:

I. Students are exposed to a variety of interesting topics.

II. Students select a topic of special interest for the application of critical and creative thinking skills to gather research data. Using modalities of strength, students may interview, do creative problem solving, develop drama, and survey. All activities involve acquiring knowledge and a variety of skills but in an integrative process.

III. Individual or small group investigate a research problem (the high interest area identified in I and II) with tentative solutions as the end product.

3. Break down assignments, projects, even ideas into steps leading to the final result. Guide through each step with deadlines for each. Refer to the "Guided Listening Activity" (see Table 13.1).

4. Most important, teachers need to model skills, processes, and procedures for the gifted-learning-disabled student. Too often, assumptions of student's ability are incorrect and result in frustration. The teacher should analyze the assignment and demonstrate an approach to meeting the requirement. Refer to "What I Know Sheet" (see Table 13.1).

As an educational community, we are becoming more aware of special needs of gifted students. The gifted-learning-disabled child does exist in our classrooms and does have special needs. Perhaps the most important of those needs is to have the significant others in his or her life recognize the gift, the disability, and the special interactive effects of each. Recognition and awareness should lead us to assist the gifted-learning-disabled child with compensating for the disability in an information processing mode by using other strong information processing modes to handle, internalize, and conceptualize the knowledge needed to cope successfully with everyday life and enjoy the chal-

Table 13.1. Simple Strategies.

ACTIVITY	LD	OBJECTIVES
Guided Listening Procedure (Cunningham, 1975)	Reading	•lifts reading burden
1. All students listen to and discuss selection	Writing	•provides 3 opportunities for
2. Recall recorded on board	Organization	auditory input
3. Listen again for verification	Short-term memory	•provides input and structure
4. Short-term memory test		from peers
5. Feedback		•experience group modeling of
6. Long-term memory test		organizing material
What I Know Sheet (Heller, 1986)	Organizational skills	•triggers prior knowledge
1. Discuss reading topic	Reading	•gives control over reading
and identify purpose for reading		
2. Group discussion of what already know, list		•identifies known information
3. Read individually		•assists in determining
		what is to be learned
4. Discuss what know now after reading, list		•provides for auditory input
5. Identify confusing ideas, terms		
6. Reread to clarify		
7. Discuss confusions		
Sample		
Reading Topic:		
Purpose for Reading:		
3 columns across page:		
What I know,		
What I now know,		
What I don't know		
answer to "purpose" question		

lenge of learning and producing. While working with the strengths and fostering a more realistic and positive self-concept, we must also attend to the disability and develop with the child the most appropriate methods for either remediating the skill or compensating for the disabled information processing mode. The educational program must be based on both the child's giftedness and disability. As parents, teachers, and coordinators involved in gifted education, we must identify the gifted-learning-disabled student for service. Otherwise, this child will continue to experience the debilitating frustration of being both gifted and learning disabled.

REFERENCES

Clark, B. (1983). *Optimizing learning: The integrative education model in the classroom.* Columbus, OH: Merrill.

Clark, B. (1992). *Growing up gifted.* (4th ed.). New York: Macmillan.

Cunningham, P.M. (1975, November). Transferring comprehension from listening to reading. *The Reading Teacher, 29*(2), 169-172.

Fox, L., Brody, L., & Tobin, D. (1983). *Learning disabled/gifted children: Identification and programming.* Baltimore: University Park Press.

Heller, M.F. (1986, February). How do you know what you know? Metacognitive modeling in the content areas. *The Journal of Reading, 29*(5), 415-422.

Mindell, P. (1982, February). The gifted dyslexic: A case study with theoretical and educational implications. *Roeper Review, 4*(3), 22-23.

Renzulli, J.S. (1977). *The enrichment triad model.* Mansfield Center, CT: Creative Learning Press.

Sternberg, R. J. (1985). *Beyond IQ.* New York: Cambridge University Press.

Whitmore, J., & Maker, J. (1985). *Intellectual giftedness in disabled persons.* Rockville, MD: Aspen Systems.

14

Gifted Special Populations: Overcoming Hindrances, Developing Gifts

Jessie Hugh Butler Sanders

For many people, gifted children represent a disembodied stereotype of intellectual, behavioral, and social perfection; prodigies who, immune to the problems faced by others, seem destined for greatness, achievement, and good fortune. However, this stereotype is both misleading and dangerous, as it can blind parents and educators alike to both the uniqueness of each gifted child and the problems each must face. One needs only to read any number of biographies to see the great number and diversity of obstacles faced by gifted and talented people throughout history.

When one examines these barriers to achievement, several distinct categories begin to emerge: physical hindrances, such as vision or hearing impaired gifted learners; intellectual/social handicaps, including the learning-disabled and the behavior-disordered gifted; and environmental handicaps, such as being born into an inner-city ghetto, living far from others in a rural setting, or having to learn a second language to communicate with peers. When their gifts are overlooked, these children are in danger of "slipping through the cracks" of a standard educational setting.

The key to developing the potential of special education populations is early identification of both the gift and the hindrance by parents. Once this is accomplished, parents have opportunities to intervene and help children to overcome handicaps by capitalizing on their talents. Each of the aforementioned special populations demands a unique approach with unique goals for parents and children. This chapter examines each population and suggests ideas and guidelines for helping gifted children become more self-assured, socially well-adjusted, and better prepared to meet the challenges of both the school and work environments.

PHYSICAL HINDRANCES: SUCCEEDING IN STEPS

For children born gifted but physically handicapped, realizing potential can be an arduous process. All too often, parents concentrate their attention of children's handicaps rather than on their strengths, de-emphasizing them or ignoring them altogether. Children with a physical handicap of vision impairment, for example, might have superior musical talent that is being overlooked, or perhaps a strength in mathematics that could be utilized in a computer-related field. Parents should seek the advice and help of professionals to determine the extent of the impairment, possibilities for correction or improvement, and the long-range outlook for the child. The emphasis should be on correcting handicaps as completely as possible while developing children's strengths.

The development process for physically handicapped children is twofold. The first goal, removing the physical barriers that the handicap presents, takes place in a number of steps. Some physical handicaps can be removed completely with therapy, corrective equipment, or medical intervention. In these cases, the children are then wholly free to pursue their areas of strength. For other handicaps, a marginal amount of improvement is the best that can be expected. In those cases the second goal becomes especially important, that is, to concentrate on children's areas of strength, give constant support and reinforcement, and help them to adapt to the handicap and develop a positive self-image centered on their gifts.

Children's families should work regularly with them to encourage their interests, foster thinking skills, and help them feel a strong sense of self-worth. In doing this, the families guard against overemphasizing the handicaps and give the children motivation to overcome the obstacles in the way to success. Without such encouragement, physically handicapped gifted children often begin to feel inferior, a sentiment that, if left unchallenged, can lead to depression, problems relating to their peer group, and underachievement. These gifted children should be reminded of the numerous leaders, great thinkers, artists, and other role models who succeeded in life despite physical handicaps. Vision-impaired children can be reminded of Louis Braille and Ray Charles. Hearing-impaired children can make Thomas Edison and Ludwig van Beethoven their role models. Those stricken with degenerative motor diseases can look up to President Franklin D. Roosevelt and scientist Stephen Hawking. In all of these cases, the person's gifts came through despite some physical handicap. In modeling after these people, gifted children learn not only positive values but something about science, history, music, and other fields of endeavor.

INTELLECTUAL/SOCIAL HINDRANCES: FINDING THE GIFT

The special category of gifted that includes those with learning disabilities and behavior disorders is an especially difficult one to deal with. The first problem is perhaps the most daunting—that of identifying these children as gifted. The difficulty arises from the fact that their gifts are often hidden beneath processing difficulties, developmental delays, social maladjustments, hyperactivity, attention deficit disorder, conduct or personality disorders, or any of a long list of other hindrances of varying degrees. These outward appearances make early identification by parents unfamiliar with characteristics of the aforementioned problems next to impossible. Whereas a physician, psychologist, or early childhood teacher might be able to make this identification based on previous case experience, the majority of parents have no frame of reference in which to put such a child. Parents who suspect that their child might have such a hindrance should immediately seek a professional evaluation. Often it is a day-care worker, friend of the family who is familiar with the behavior of children, or even a baby-sitter with considerable experience who may mention the child's different behavior or learning patterns to the parents. Any of these opinions should be seriously considered and acted on by the family. A follow-up evaluation by a professional from the school is available in most states and is often helpful in determining the nature of the child's problem.

Gifted children who are learning disabled are in a frustrating situation, as they do have high cognitive ability, but may have difficulties integrating into a particular learning style. They may feel less intelligent, generally inferior, and even retarded when around their peers. Parents sometimes draw the same conclusions, setting lower expectations for their child or even denying the problem for fear it is insurmountable. These factors create a stressful situation for the entire family, and especially for the child, who is in danger of developing behavioral problems as a side effect of this treatment. By seeking professional help at early hints of such a situation, families avoid both needless frustration and shame for the child and tension within the family unit. Such children can often learn to compensate for their learning disability, excelling in school, social settings, and other interests.

Behavior-disordered children present a separate set of challenges. Their potential may not be so deeply buried, nor their behavior quite so difficult to recognize, but intervention and treatment is often a painstaking procedure, taking place slowly over a long period. These children must be evaluated to determine if the hindrance is being created by a conduct disorder, a medical problem, or an emotional problem. Each of these possibilities requires a somewhat different plan for remediation. All involve active participation by all family members, much patience, and the realization that it is those with the most disturbing behavior who are in the greatest need of love and understanding, as well as firmness and fairness from authority figures. Those who suffer from a serious medical problem or a severe emotional problem may require the attention of a specialist over a long-term period, special medication, or individual therapy to bring about a normalized behavioral state. Again, as with learning-disabled children, behavior-disordered children and their families must not lose sight of their giftedness or the special potential they offer.

HINDRANCES: OVERCOMING AGAINST THE ODDS

If someone had said to young Abraham Lincoln that he would someday grow up to become President, chances are he would have chuckled politely and dismissed the thought as absurd. President he was, however, and he became so in spite of his rural background, few early educational opportunities, and many other obstacles. History is full of these success stories, and the gifted children who come from such situations must use their creativity and perseverance to achieve their goals. Unfortunately, the problems that environmentally hindered children must face are many and varied. These can range from growing up as a minority in a prejudiced community, to living in a ghetto, to growing up in an isolated rural area. All of these circumstances are unfortunate and hindering to children, but the main emphasis for both the concerned parents and gifted learners should be the gifts possessed. None of these environmental problems are insurmountable, and rarely is professional help necessary to create a better learning environment.

Early identification of the situation is, as always, extremely helpful in ensuring the best outcome for these children. Parents who feel their child is at a disadvantage because of some environmental factor should do their best to remedy the problem, starting in the home. Although the environment outside the home can sometimes be controlled directly by concerned parents, the home itself can definitely be made conducive to learning, even if the family cannot provide the latest technological advances or luxurious furnishings. Reorienting the family to a more positive, enriching environment will give children a higher level of self-esteem, an asset they may need in the world outside the front door. Allowing them to pursue collections, hobbies, and other interests to a reasonable and affordable extent also increases the children's development of their gift. Any travel families can do as a unit is doubly helpful, as it both allows gifted learners to experience more of the world around them and gives families time to grow closer emotionally. These and many other activities can be invaluable in the environmentally hindered gifted children's preschool development.

The key to providing the best possible surroundings is imagination—both on the part of parents and children. Most gifted preschoolers become interested in highly fantastic or unusual subjects at one time or another, and parents need only follow up on children's innate desire to learn to provide them with hours of enrichment. The only difficulty with this system is that once gifted youths have devoured every available shred of information on a given subject, they usually move on to something completely different and delve into it with equal fervor. This type of motivation, when properly fed with a supply of materials (not necessarily huge) and some creativity, is usually enough to get children started on a track that will lead them to overcome their surrounding hindrances.

The aforementioned plan succeeds well if the environmental hindrance is merely a lack of resources or opportunity—children simply seek out their own enrichment under the guidance of parents. However, if the hindrance is of a social type, several other related problems can arise.

If children are of a minority background, there exist areas of the country in which they are at a considerable disadvantage. Unfortunately, the diversity that makes our nation unique is nothing more than a premise for prejudice in the eyes of some, and for gifted minority children this prejudice is both confusing and undeserved. These children may feel it necessary to justify their every action to the neighborhood bully, leader of the local clique, or other of their peers. These behaviors may lead to a loss of self-esteem that hinders their development in an already demanding situation. Further, this situation can even prevent children's access to certain materials. Of course, in extreme cases legal recourse is available and usually quite successful; however, as far as children are concerned, there are several simpler ways of maintaining pride in both themselves and their heritage. First, children should be encouraged to study their heritage. Knowing how their ancestors were, where they came from, what they did, and how they overcame their difficulties can be the beginnings of a lifelong interest in history, cultures of various groups, or other culturally related fields. In dealing with their peer group, children should be instructed that their own self-worth is more valuable than others' opinions. Also, children must learn to ignore the often insulting remarks that come from other children. Parents may run out of patience in this respect just as quickly as their children; however, they too must realize that the other children are being taught from the ingrained beliefs of parents who are prejudiced. Eventually, these children will form their own opinions based on their experience with each racial and ethnic group; minority gifted children are then in an unparalleled position to be a positive influence on the lives of these other children.

Another challenge is that of gifted children who must learn English as a second language before they can even begin to communicate with their prospective peer group. Many gifted children are from families who immigrate to the United States, move from a neighborhood that speaks a foreign language predominantly, or are adopted from a non-English-speaking background. For some, learning English encompasses not only a different set of names, rules, and idioms, but even a new alphabet. Young children may be frightened by the strange, indecipherable signs surrounding them, especially if they have already begun to read in their native language. The ideal approach to this situation is to turn it to as great an advantage as possible through learning both languages. The younger children are, the more easily they can learn languages, and, if children have suitable opportunities, it is quite conceivable that they could be comfortable in either language—a significant ability in the ever-shrinking modern world. Joining children in this effort should be their parents, although it may be considerably more difficult for them to adapt, whether they speak English and are learning another tongue, or vice versa. An example of this effort is a family who found a camp in a neighboring state that provided education and cultural activities for the entire family, all presented by bilingual instructors. Their two adopted children were thus able to learn English more effectively, and the family as a whole became much closer more quickly for the investment of a little money and 2 weeks in the summer. However, acculturation need not be even this elaborate. The family unit can become cohesive simply by sharing experiences from both cultures and comparing them. Children who come from a Latin American culture, for example, could relate the contents of their latest book on farm animals to their Spanish-speaking parents, who might then tell them (in English or Spanish) about the farms they knew in their original homes. The possibilities in these cases are, again, numerous.

GETTING MORE HELP: OVERCOMING HINDRANCES FOR THE ENTIRE FAMILY

All gifted children, just like all other people, have problems from time to time. The term *special population* applies to those gifted who fall within the parameters of another previously defined, uniformly measurable group: learning-disabled children, for example, are defined with a specific set of standards that varies little from state to state. Several organizations exist at different levels to serve these youth and others in similar situations. These provide various services, such as professional periodicals; conferences and workshops; newsletters containing information about gifted programming, both during the school year and during the summer; state advocacy to improve gifted educational programming and to increase funding for such programs; information about obtaining gifted literature; and references to family counseling centers and other public support services. School district personnel can usually provide names and addresses of these organizations, as well as valuable personal insights concerning the most effective methods of enrichment for specific situations. These resources are generally aimed at working with the entire family, especially with preschool gifted, to achieve a better overall environment for overcoming the children's hindrances. Often these services are free or inexpensive.

THE ONGOING PROCESS: CONTINUING DEVELOPMENT INTO THE PRIMARY SCHOOL YEARS

All too often, the advent of grade school brings about an end to the close contact families have with their children. Students are on their own to succeed in this new environment, and may feel alone and frightened by the new faces and names they must remember and befriend. For the special gifted population, this is an even more critical time developmentally, as they are putting to the most severe test in their lives the beliefs, attitudes, and ideas they have been taught.

In preparing gifted special population children for their first school experience, it is important for family members to attempt to allay children's fears and anxiety about beginning school. Parents should arrange a meeting with school officials to discuss the special nature of their child's giftedness as well as his or her hindrances in order to arrive at a satisfactory educational plan. Through advocacy groups, readings done individually, formal information gathering, or other methods, parents should know what to expect in terms of a plan for their gifted child. Often parents who have not prepared in this manner feel intimidated or inadequate in the face of the body of knowledge possessed by the special services coordinator of their school system. This feeling tends to alienate the parents further from the formalized educational process. The end result of this can be that there is no coordination between the school and the family, and the child suffers the detrimental effects.

One method of gaining knowledge of the school process and the support system for parents of these special population gifted is through joining or forming a parent organization whose purpose is to serve families of gifted children who suffer from some kind of hindrance. Such a group can often coordinate more directly with the policy-making branch of the school system, providing parents significant input into the decisions the school makes regarding programs concerning their children. Parents can also learn more about the special services offered by the school system, thus preparing them for their own children's entry into school. The key elements in this preparation are interest and active participation—children must understand what they are getting into and parents must be ready to answer both their children's questions and their own. Only with a clear understanding of the educational program, confidence in knowing the goals and policies of the school system, and parents' active participation in the education of gifted children can the beginning years of gifted special population students' education meet the great potential they possess.

EPILOGUE: HEALTHY, HAPPY, CREATIVE DEVELOPMENT

When Albert Einstein enrolled in grade school, he was looked on as different, unusual, and completely hopeless as a student, yet he overcame these stereotypes to become one of the greatest physicists in history. Through his determination, brilliance, and creativity, he caused his gift to be seen by the entire world. This spirit must be shared by each participant in the educational process. First of all, parents of gifted but hindered children must be the best possible role models, teachers, motivators, and molders of their children's values and outlooks. Through their efforts, children must become assured that they can and will overcome the obstacles ahead of them and lead happy lives, with high self-esteem and positive outlook. Parents of all gifted children have been blessed with tremendous responsibility, but those of special-population gifted children have the additional responsibility of never letting their children forget the wonderful gifts they possess despite any and all hindrances in their way. These parents must become mentors, teachers, reference books, referees, arbitrators, and counselors by turn, learning as much as they can to help their children understand the blessings that have been given. The job is a tough one, and sometimes the only reward is a satisfied look on the face of a child who has just accomplished something he or she once thought impossible, but in the end, that is enough.

Educators of gifted have the responsibility of being counselors not only for the children in the classroom, but for the entire family in many situations. In the case of gifted special-population children, teachers hope to see children who recognize the fact that they have both a gift and a hindrance. Both factors play a part in these children's educational process and only with an awareness of these two facets of the child's persona can real education live up to its potential. Educators rely on the family to ingrain within these children the motivation to excel despite obstacles, the persistence to keep trying even though the way is often difficult, and the maturity to relish their last success only long enough to set their course for the next goal.

The greatest task lies with the gifted special-population children themselves. With these children lies the responsibility to spend the long hours in physical therapy, adapt to a new way of learning or a new language, or whatever else is necessary to fulfill the gifts they possess. As much as parents may coax, teachers may inspire, and friends may encourage, it is up to each person, gifted included, to do those things that are necessary to succeed. Children who have been well taught and in whom has been instilled a high sense of self-worth have an advantage, but in the end it is up to them to decide what they will do. Perhaps the most important sentiment for gifted special-population children to be aware of is that the love and support they are receiving from others is not for the hindrances they have nor for the gifts they possess, but for who they are.

15

Gifted Girls

Stephen Veenker
Kathleen Veenker

The feminist movement of the 1970s focused considerable attention on the differences in treatment of boys and girls in society as a whole and in our educational system. Clark's (1992) *Growing Up Gifted* cited numerous studies published in the 1970s and 1980s that document these differences. "From the beginning," Clark declared, "girls are taught to be passive, accepting, nurturing. They are expected to enjoy quieter games and activities and not to take risks. They receive these messages from many places and many people in our society" (p. 456). The results are especially debilitating to young gifted girls, noted Clark, as "risktaking, self-trust, and independence are necessary to the development of high levels of intelligence. Studies show that bright girls consistently underestimate their own ability" (p. 457). Kerr's (1985) *Smart Girls, Gifted Women* discussed in detail the barriers to achievement experienced by gifted girls and presented a number of strategies for overcoming these barriers.

Where are we a decade or two after all this attention? To be sure, there's been progress. However, two important recent works published (AAUW, 1992; Sadker & Sadker, 1994) show that much, much more needs to be done. Gender equity may be getting closer, but not close enough or quickly enough.

THE PROBLEM

Let us begin by offering the position that there are behavioral differences between boys and girls. In large part these are culturally acquired and perpetuated. That's not inherently evil, just a description. However, when these differences get in the way of equal opportunity for a public school education that is intended to be delivered equally to all students, then the system needs some fine tuning.

First, let us look at the passive and accepting role Clark (1992) described. It is a throwback to the "sugar-and-spice" notion that seems old-fashioned today. Parents used to teach kids that girls are like soft boys: not as strong, not always as smart, and prettier, weaker beings who deserved and needed accommodation and protection from chivalrous boys. If they no longer needed dragons slain on their behalf, boys were still taught to open doors for them. Just because most of us look on this kind of treatment as silly doesn't mean the treatment will go away overnight—and it hasn't.

If we felt by the 1980s that we were on the threshold of the age of enlightenment, we were a bit hasty. In 1992 the American Association of University Women prepared and released a sizeable summary of the status of women in American Schools. Its findings were widely reported. Consider first the workplace:

Women make up 45 percent of the nation's work force, and this percentage is increasing. But women are heavily concentrated in a narrow range of occupations traditionally considered appropriate for them. Sixty percent of all women working outside the home are working in clerical, service or professional positions, and more than sixty percent of these professional women are in female-intensive areas such as school teaching and nursing. Occupational segregation among women of color is even more extreme.

Women with eight or fewer years of education earn only 66 percent of the wages of similarly educated men; even women with five or more years of college make only 69 cents for every dollar earned by their male colleagues with an equal number of years of education. . . . Women earn less than men even when they hold identical jobs.

But the subjects that women study in school make a difference. Wage differentials favoring men are considerably less—or disappear altogether—for women in their early thirties who have earned eight or more mathematics credits in college. (pp. 4-5)

Small wonder that girls find little incentive to be ambitious about careers. The AAUW report found:

High school girls, even those with exceptional academic preparation in math and science, are choosing math/science careers in disproportionately low numbers. A study of Rhode Island seniors found that 64 percent of the male students who had taken physics and calculus were planning to major in science or engineering in college, compared to only 19.6 percent of the female students who had taken these courses. (p. 27)

However, the different treatment of girls begins long before it is time to pick a career track. For some it begins on the first day of preschool. The AAUW report cited research by Selma Greenberg of Hofstra University documenting that:

Rather than being better for girls, it would appear that many schools engage girls in activities in which they are already more proficient than are young boys. The traditional working assumption at the preschool level is that children need impulse-control training, small-muscle development, and language enhancement to be successful in their early years in school. Since many girls tend to achieve competency in these areas before they arrive in group settings, teachers turn their attention toward boys, whose development in these areas lags behind that of girls.

Many activities chosen by young boys, such as large-motor activities and investigatory and experimental activities, are considered "free play" and are not part of the regular, structured curriculum. If young girls are not specifically encouraged to participate in these "boy" activities, they do not receive a full and balanced set of educational experiences. (p. 18)

And that's just the beginning, in a number of ways. Carefully documented classroom observations show that teachers react differently to girls and boys. They tend to praise and identify boys' effort and intellectual processes, while praising girls' neatness or appearance; not their word choice, but their penmanship (or is it penpersonship?). However boys don't lose points if their writing is sloppy or messy. If classroom seating is random and boys tend to clump together, most teachers will end up speaking from a position nearer the boys' part of the room. Boys are found to be more likely to volunteer questions and answers in general discussion without waiting to be called on.

Teachers tend to wait longer for boys' answers than for girls'. It's a kind of encouragement—as though to say "you're worth the wait, we know you've got it in you."

Waiting longer for a student to answer is one of the most powerful and positive things a teacher can do. It is a vote of confidence, a way of saying, "I have high expectations for you, so I will wait a little longer. I know you can get it if I give you a chance." The boys try harder to achieve. As girls struggle to answer under the pressure of time, they may founder and fail. (Sadker & Sadker, 1994, pp. 57-58)

Less assertive in class and more likely to think about their answers and how to respond, girls may need more time to think. In the real world of the classroom, they receive less.

One test of a certain aspect of mental acuity has to do with comparing views of irregularly shaped objects. Boys seem to score consistently higher than girls. The researchers feel their advantage may come from greater experience with spatial exercises, like sports, and games like tangrams and jigsaw puzzles. When the tests are timed, the boys are at an advantage. They suggest practicing timed exams like this one, and more sports or activities that require visual processing. The difference might be diminished if the test were not timed (Gallagher & Johnson, 1992).

Our culture still appears to lag when it comes to getting children off to equal footing. For example:

1. Boys are more likely to be encouraged to climb trees, roll around, explore.
2. Boys get credit for pushing limits, trying new things, taking chances, whereas girls are praised more often for their appearance or neatness.
3. Our literature still overwhelmingly portrays boys as doers, professionals, producers; and girls as watchers, helpers, and consumers.

Are these really still issues, you ask, a full generation after we were first enlightened about gender equity?

Ask Myra Sadker, who has monitored and reported classroom progress in this area for a quarter century. With collaborator Nancy Frazier she authored *Sexism in School and Society* (1973). She and her husband David, both on the faculty at American University in Washington, DC, summarized three years of research of gender bias in elementary and secondary classrooms for the National Institute of Education in 1984 and published a benchmark book in 1994, *Failing at Fairness: How America's Schools Cheat Girls.*

In classroom visits they record that cooperative learning groups appropriately mix ages and ethnicity, but are rarely integrated by gender. At recess, they observe that boys systematically take all the equipment and nearly all the space devoted to play and that girls routinely take what is left.

Curriculum seems to be institutionalized as well. The Sadkers point out that new history textbooks devote as little as 2% of their space to women. A 600+ page text for sixth-graders had only seven pages devoted to females; none of the 11 it named were adult Americans.

The impact of this kind of inequity is dramatically demonstrated in the Sadkers' classroom presentations, which they have made in several states. They ask students to name 10 famous men and 10 famous women from history. The only restriction is no athletes or entertainers. Lists of men are compiled with fluency in moments. But thinking of 10 women from all of world history is tough. Many students run out of names after three or four. The chore is so difficult for some students they they name Mrs. Fields, Betty Crocker, Sarah Lee, and Aunt Jemima. Others listed American presidents and put "Mrs." in front (Sadker & Sadker, 1994, pp. 60-72).

Why do we devote so much time and space to these issues if they are common and predictable? Because your children are unlikely to be immune to these kinds of discomfort and inequity. There are, however, some steps and some factors that may alleviate some of the discomfort and possibly even the score where we see inequities today.

SOME SOLUTIONS

Like charity, remediation begins at home. From the earliest age, gifted girls need a foundation of confidence and self-worth that will carry them through times when friends and community may not be supportive.

Silverman (1989) published a concise list of guidelines for parents of younger gifted children:

- Identify them early (best done between ages 4 and 7);
- Find them gifted peers;
- Place them in special programs;
- Consider early entrance to school;
- Don't let them drop out of math;
- Introduce them to role models;
- Involve Dad in their lives;
- Hold high expectations;
- Avoid sex-role stereotyping;
- Encourage independence and risk taking. (pp. 7-9)

From early childhood our daughters perceive our expectations, even when we don't consciously. The mood and atmosphere we create in our homes, the way we speak of the future, the surroundings we provide set the stage.

Consider play things. It isn't enough to hand them a toy or game or book and leave them to self-direct a lifestyle. Rather, we bring and share and show what it means to be young at an exciting time in history. The Sadkers (1994) quoted a father who bought and brought home an elaborate physics kit, presenting it with a flourish to his daughters. Then he forgot about it, until some time later. He asked the girls what they produced from the kit. Their reply was unexpected: He never showed them what it was supposed to do, they said, so they traded it for Barbie dolls!

We would also endorse the AAUW's conclusion to encourage young girls to participate in large-motor activities. In the preschool classroom this may mean restructuring the curriculum to include so-called "free-play" activities.

Please take time to choose gifts carefully. Many people still buy pink things for baby girls and blue things for boys . . . and still give girls dress-up or makeup kits, saving the exploratory things for boys.

Introduce some nontraditional stuff: the National Women's History Project has a wealth of materials, including classroom graphics—coloring books of important women, none of whom wears four-inch heels or even remotely resembles a Barbie Doll.[1]

Some magazines provide sensitive materials for children.

- Cricket magazine is a consistent source of imaginative fiction with bright, involving original illustration. It is unsophisticated and refreshingly unhip.[2]
- A fledgling publication that deserves to fly is New Moon, a magazine edited by girls aged 8 to 14 and published with the help of some caring adults. A review in the Chicago Tribune described it: "Designed to help girls discover what they can be, instead of what society tells them they should be." The six bimonthly issues include profiles, "herstories," and slices of life contributed by girls in various parts of the world.[3]

Quite properly, publishers of children's literature are producing biographies and nonsexist fiction. The collection grows each month. The Sadkers (1994) offer a 10-page bibliography of works they find appropriate, from picture books for younger children to young-adult biographies of appropriate role models. Find the many books primarily for young people, including those by Madeleine L'Engle. For a good time, read them aloud.

---

[1]They send their catalog of 300 items from 7738 Bell Road, Windsor, CA 95492, or (707) 838-6000.

[2]Cricket is available from Box 387, Mt. Morris, IL 61054.

[3]From PO Box 6255, Duluth, MN, 55806. A parents' guide enables caregivers.

We continue to believe that outside activities and interests contribute measurably to girls' continuing feelings of self-worth. One doesn't need to be good at everything, but it's valuable to try a variety of things:

- A sport, music, or active hobby introduces new places and faces, giving fresh perspective. In activities like skating, soccer, and swimming, brawn doesn't outweigh brain; they help teach task commitment, goal setting, strategizing. Team sports also expose shy girls to agemates from other schools, promote stature in an area separate from academics, and encourage interaction and team cooperation that build confidence and bolster self-image.
- Girl Scouting, with dedicated and effective leadership, can forge friendships that last through stormy years, providing long-term scaffolding of acceptance. Activities like overnight tent camping teach girls to be self-reliant. Girl Scouts have done an admirable job of modernizing programming and badge work with fulfilling activities that build competence and confidence.

For children approaching the age where many girls dig in and hide their abilities, Eby and Smutny (1990) offered a formula for equalizing math expectations, recomputing the theory that math and science are mostly for boys. First, restructure math classes so that flexible groups work on many possibilities. Second, make sure girls see women working in science and math. Third, encourage creativity, not just technical proficiency. We need visionaries who can take on the theoretical: "The cutting edge of math and science fields requires boldness in creative thinking and the ability to pierce through technological training to the perception of new strategies for solving persistent problems" (p. 136).

Use any of these suggestions to nourish and nurture your younger girls and you may all have a smoother ride on that roller coaster we call adolescence. Your daughters might get more out of school without a tax increase, and some day their daughters might even wonder what all the fuss was about when their mothers were young.

REFERENCES

American Association of University Women, AAUW Educational Foundation. (1992). *The AAUW Report: How schools shortchange girls: A study of major findings on girls and education.* Washington, DC: Author.

Clark, B. (1992). *Growing up gifted* (4th ed.). New York: Merrill/Macmillan.

Eby, J., & Smutny, J.F. (1989). *A thoughtful overview of gifted education.* New York: Longman.

Gallagher, S., & Johnson, E. (1992). The effect of time limits on performance of mental rotations by gifted adolescents. *Gifted Child Quarterly, 36*(1), 19-22.

Kerr, B. 91985). *Smart girls, gifted women.* Columbus: Ohio Psychology Press.

Sadker, M, & Frazier, N. (1973). *Sexism in school and society.* New York: Harper & Row.

Sadker, M, & Sadker, D. (1994). *Failing at fairness: How America's schools cheat girls.* New York: Scribner's.

Silverman, L.K. (1989). Reclaiming lost giftedness in girls. *Understanding Our Gifted, 2*(2), 7-9.

IV

Parenting the Gifted Child: Enabling and Encouraging Parents

Joan Franklin Smutny

The principles that generally apply to good parenting are certainly just as appropriate for gifted children. However, good parenting is more problematic with gifted children because issues of independence and control can be larger problems with youngsters of advanced language skills, reasoning skills, and creative problem-solving abilities. This section examines ways for parents to communicate effectively and develop relationships with the young gifted child from infancy through the primary grades. These authors bring diverse backgrounds and expertise in communicating with bright children in a variety of settings.

In Chapter 16, Phyllis Perry highlights the vital responsibility of parents to support the growth of the gifted child from toddler to school age. For the very young child, Perry gives the following advice: promote growing independence; set clear limits and guidelines; listen; provide a variety of materials; help develop special skills; promote creativity; and model desired behaviors. Once the child begins school, Perry advises parents to take on new responsibilities: join parent support groups; become acquainted with school curriculum, gifted programming and other enrichment offerings; volunteer to help with special classroom projects or go along on field trips. Most importantly, we should not underestimate parent power as a means of supporting and eliciting positive change.

Sally Walker recognizes the challenges of parenting gifted young children in Chapter 17. Because they see the world differently and are unaware that others do not view things the way they do, they may suffer from feelings of isolation. Coping with perfectionism may be very difficult. Walker believes that gifted children need to be taught that learning requires taking risks. Parents need to understand their child's desire to do well and help them cope with the fear of failure. The obvious result will be a home climate far safer for exploring new concepts and activities. The author admonishes parents to set realistic goals, to listen, and to value their bright child. She counsels parents to know their child's school and teacher, and to communicate with both about the development of the child's gifts. The result for the child will be less stress and negative feelings.

In Chapter 18, Tom Potter urges parents to participate in parent education programs that will help them support the development of social skills and healthy emotions in their child. He outlines, beginning with babyhood, the path for well-adjusted infants, toddlers, and preschoolers, discussing such varied issues as intelligence, social development, and small and large muscle development. An area of special interest to education researchers and psychologists are the qualities of curiosity, spontaneity, and creativity. Parents are encouraged to find suitable programs that will support their growing knowledge of their young child. Utilizing tips for parenting infants and toddlers applied to all ability levels, parents will have a sound basis for understanding the gifted young child.

Parents have a primary responsibility as role models to support the educational efforts of their children. If parents can communicate that learning is important for themselves, that they are not afraid of taking risks, and that understanding something new may be difficult but rewarding, then they can help avoid underachievement in their children. In Chapter 19, Judith Wynn Halsted advocates preparing gifted children to be independent caretakers of their own talents. She chooses "Steven," a composite figure of several gifted children, to illustrate how bright children can recognize and make constructive use of their own interest in learning, and understand how to protect their need to learn. Parents can teach their sons and daughters to pursue their interests in diversified settings, not just in the classroom, thereby enabling them to become self-motivated learners. Children, Halsted advocates, must not be made to feel powerless regarding the direction of their schooling.

In Chapter 20, Pamela Hildebrand focuses on the importance of reading as a framework to encourage bright children to grow. She recognizes that parents may be afraid to participate in their children's reading development. Instead, she says, they should see themselves as natural teachers in a learning process that happens in the home with regularity and consistency. The home can be a learning resource when parents know how to respond to the reading needs of their children. Early reading memories must be positive. As early language and reading development promotes intellectual and academic achievement, it also enhances children's relationships with their parents. Literature can become the vehicle for parents to help shape the sense of self. Parents are urged to read to their children early and often, and to see this activity as a catalyst for growth in self-esteem.

In the section's last chapter, Gina Riggs encourages open communication between parents and teachers, readily acknowledging that a child's education often depends on the parents' ability to work with the people who teach the child. Riggs speaks of the parent as a learner, a helper, a resource person, and an advocate. She offers a "fool-proof" plan for school-parent partnerships, which can result in schools welcoming supportive parents as partners in the education of their gifted children.

16

Enjoying and Encouraging the Young Gifted Child

Phyllis J. Perry

Research strongly suggests that the family and the home climate have more to do with the kind of person a child will eventually become than any other factors. For parents, that is challenging and a little scary.

Many parents think that educating gifted, creative, and talented youth is primarily the function of the schools. They believe that parental responsibility for gifted education lies in finding and supporting first the right preschool and then the appropriate public or private school setting for the child. Although it is true that a parental partnership with the schools is certainly to be encouraged, much can and should be done at home before schooling begins, and the promotion by parents of the child's talents continues throughout all the school years.

Fox (1993), in his article "The Wrong Whipping Boy," went so far as to suggest that although schools are not perfect, many of the faults ascribed to them are flaws in parenting, rather than in schooling. He strongly suggested that all parents, not just parents of gifted youth, must take a hand in the education of their children.

The preschool years are critically important for all children and especially for the gifted child. This is true not only because this is a time for the acquisition of knowledge, but also because of the self-concept formed by relationships in the family. The way a child perceives him- or herself and views the world plays a major role in the extent to which that child can benefit from educational opportunities.

UNDERSTANDING, SUCCESS, AND A MINIMUM OF CRITICISM

The young gifted child needs a cheerleader more than a critic. The gifted child, like all children, learns through play in the early years. Toys, books, games, and interaction with playmates and family members contribute to growth—and such growth may come unevenly, in delightful spurts and with dismaying plateaus.

Parents of gifted youth sometimes need to be especially understanding of the slow development of social skills, which doesn't always keep pace with intellectual growth. A gifted child may become very impatient with others who are not as quick to understand and may even spurn playmates of his or her own age and seek out older children and adults. Older children may resent the young tagalong, and as a result, the gifted child may become isolated from peers.

Parents sometimes idealize a child's gifts and expect success in all undertakings. This is unrealistic. It is important to know and to help the child recognize areas of lesser strength in himself or herself and to accept and realize that a greater effort may be required in such areas. This is also an opportunity for the gifted child to learn to appreciate the strengths of others.

Pressey (1955), an American psychologist, explained the emergence of exceptional abilities and performance in any category as the result of a process of cumulative success. He suggested that genius is produced by giving a capable young person encouragement, intensive instruction in special areas, and continuing opportunity for creative work. Parents are in a prime position to assure cumulative success in a child.

PROMOTE GROWING INDEPENDENCE

Parents must be open to letting the child try. They don't need to fret if the T-shirt is put on backwards. When a child is asked a question by another adult, parents must resist the urge to quickly supply the answer. The child needs to have some think time. The youth who never gets the opportunity to try something new, or to question or respond may become shy and remain on the fringes of every group.

Flowers, Horsman, and Schwartz (1982) pointed out that:

> Parents of gifted children will want to support their interest binges.
> Try to do anything and everything possible to help the child's explo-
> ration of any area of interest; help find the books and the material.
> Be willing to discuss the subject past the point of boredom; whenev-
> er possible, coordinate outings with interests such as a visit to the
> museum, planetarium, aquarium, zoo, historical sights, etc.; and
> when possible, purchase that chemistry set, telescope, or coin-col-
> lecting magazine. (p. 20)

The gifted child learns from parents both to accept responsibility and to live with choices. This can begin by simply letting a child
choose whether to buy the new blue sweater or the gray sweater. If
parents ask for the child's ideas or opinions, they should of course use
them. When a gifted child does make choices, he or she is certain to
make some mistakes. Creating a home environment where it is safe to
fail is significant to the growth of gifted youth. Learning from a mistake
and moving on is a skill vital to all children.

SET CLEAR LIMITS AND GUIDELINES

As children grow, parents have the joy of guiding them to the most
appropriate challenges. A 6-year-old who announces that she is going to
build a TV set might be encouraged to begin working first with some
bulbs, batteries, and wires. Then she might move on to a simple radio set.
The boy who wants to dig up the whole back yard and farm might be
successful with a small plot of land in which to raise flowers or vegetables.
A curious child may want to take everything apart. Parents
need to feel comfortable in setting reasonable limits on time, activities,
and materials and in supplying necessary guidance. Flexibility helps. If a
child's room isn't neat because he or she got so involved in a science
project that time was forgotten, the parent may need to make some
reasonable compromises.

COMMUNICATION

When parents talk with their gifted child and share enthusiasms, they
open up lines of communication. If parents really both talk with and listen to the young preschool child, they may avoid some of the problems that arise during adolescence with an uncommunicative teen. It
takes some patience and modeling for children to learn to listen to others, to question, and to take turns talking.

In families where there are several children, parents may need to work out a schedule when they are assured a few minutes of private time with each child. This may not seem as natural and spontaneous as many would like, but unless time is built in, a quiet time for talking and listening may simply not occur.

PROVIDE A VARIETY OF MATERIALS

Parents don't need to buy every fancy new toy that comes on the market, but some basic materials and space are essential for the gifted child. Sometimes what is needed is simply discarded newspapers, magazines, margarine tubs, and egg cartons at a cleared kitchen table. Here's another opportunity for a child to learn responsibility and resourcefulness, how to make do with simple objects, how to care for supplies, and how to clean up messes.

Not every child will have his or her own room. Often, space will need to be shared with others, but the gifted child does need a place where a project in process can be left in safety. It may be a desk or shelf or corner in a bedroom or basement or garage. Whatever the arrangement, it is worth taking the time to work it out.

The young child who begins scribbling needs some paper and a writing instrument. Depending on the child, and the child's age, there will be a need for books, access to a computer, scissors, glue, containers for collections, display space for art work, and a wide assortment of valuable junk. Giftedness and creativity are not always neat. Marconi's mother found space in the attic for her son to work with wires and equipment after his father wrote him off as a failure because the boy didn't want a military life. Developing a tolerance for constructive messiness is difficult for some parents.

HELP DEVELOP SPECIAL SKILLS

Parents need to be alert to a child's special interests and be willing to further them. When a parent notices that a child became fascinated in trying to connect up wires, bulbs, and batteries, the parent can promote that interest by making more time and materials available. A child who shows an interest in music may enjoy listening to records or attending a tiny tot's concert.

Sometimes the child's interest may be subtle. Einstein's uncle is credited with making the time to play math games and work puzzles with a shy and quiet boy who didn't easily enter into conversations.

Remember that every area of endeavor has a specialized vocabulary and tools of the trade. Bright children, for whom much information comes easily, often hate to admit a lack of understanding. Parents need to do frequent informal checks when a new skill has been introduced. They may find that a child's unfamiliarity with specialized vocabulary underlies the lack of immediate understanding. In Beverly Cleary's children's story *Ramona the Pest* a kindergarten child is terribly disappointed when she is asked to "wait here for the present" and then doesn't get a gift. After learning to sing a patriotic song, Ramona is puzzled that her family laughs at her when she asks if they have a "donzer lee light."

As a result of many factors, the storybook character, Ramona, briefly becomes a kindergarten dropout. In a less humorous vein, many older gifted youth really do drop out, sometimes because their intense specialized interests are not promoted or appreciated in either the home or school setting.

PROMOTE CREATIVITY

Too often the term *creative* is applied only to an end product. For example, we tend to say, "This is a fine piece of creative writing." However, there is far more to creativity than end products. Adults can help children find opportunities to sense problems, gather information, and create and test solutions. In order to do this, parents first need to become familiar with the signals of creativity so that they can recognize and encourage creative behavior. Torrance (1962) suggested that there are many indicators of creativity. Among these are intense absorption in listening, observing or doing, and intense animation and physical involvement. The creative child may use analogies in speech, challenge authority, check many sources, look very closely at things, demonstrate an eagerness and excitement to tell about discoveries, want to continue after the scheduled time ends, manifest curiosity, guess and test outcomes, honestly and intently search for truth, state bold ideas, not be easily distracted, manipulate things into new combinations, ask penetrating questions, self-initiate learning, and display a willingness to toy with "what if."

When parents are confronted with these behaviors, they need to be alert to appreciate the creative thinking that is involved and to prize the individuality that a child brings to a process.

It is also important to realize that thinking does not always mean doing. A child needs time for quiet meditation and for daydreaming. Parents who become too concerned with music lessons, dancing lessons, trips, language study, religious study, soccer, scouts, and so on, can get their gifted children caught in a tyranny of over-scheduling. Every moment is programmed. This can result in denying the child any incubating think time. There is no magic formula for promoting creativity or helping a gifted child become more creative, but modeling approaches to problem solving can be tremendously valuable (Osborn, 1967; Parnes, Noller & Biondi, 1977; Williams, 1970).

PARENT AS MODEL

There's an old saying: "The fruit does not fall far from the tree." All children pick up on the habits and beliefs of their parents and teachers. Significant adults in a child's life become models whether they want to or not.

Parents also want their gifted children to gain in confidence, which is bred by success. One way to support a positive self-concept is to encourage, appreciate, and compliment sincerely. For example, when a young child succeeds in writing his or her name on a birthday card to send to Grandfather, you can compliment the child on the fact that all the letters are there instead of pointing out that the "s" is backwards and the spacing uneven. As parents model genuine appreciation for efforts of all family members, and build on strengths, the gifted child gains an appreciation for the worth of all members in the family unit.

Parents can also model being risk takers, even if there are some failures involved. Perhaps the new cake recipe turns out to be a flop, or putting tab A in slot A-1 results in a part of the doll house being built backwards. The child nonetheless learns that the adults in the family consult recipes and blueprints, are willing to try new things, and sometimes meet with success and other times with failure.

A common parental complaint is that children spend too much time watching television. Remember that parents also model TV viewing. Reports indicate that in most homes where children watch TV excessively, their parents do, too. Much time may also be spent in computer games. Many skills can be developed in an interactive mode, but this time also can be monitored.

Parents also model responses to social relations. If over the dinner table parents constantly ridicule co-workers, complain about slow-witted postal clerks, or criticize the school's teachers or principal, the children pick up on this. The result may be that gifted youth ridicule teachers, siblings, and others.

WORKING WITH THE SCHOOL

When a gifted child enters school, the parents quickly learn that the outside world is a formidable rival to the influences and values of the

home. Graue (1982), in writing about beginning a child's formal education, suggested, "Parents must sometimes be persistent in finding the
right program for their gifted child. It is important enough to your child
and to your investment in his education to take the time to look over
the situation carefully" (p. 159). Being concerned about matching a
child's needs with a school program that fits is an important parental
responsibility. Parents need to visit the school and take advantage of
the options that they have. They need to listen to what their child tells
them about how he or she is getting along with the teacher and with
the other students.

There may be a parent support group in the community for gifted education as well as a school parent-teacher organization. Parents
of gifted youth need to get involved and learn as much as they can.
They will probably learn that the school system provides a number of
options that are open to gifted primary children. These might include
enrichment, acceleration, grouping, and pull-out programs. Different
districts use different terms to mean quite different things.

Perhaps through a newsletter parents can be informed of
Saturday arts and crafts classes, of science field trips for young natural-
ists, of shows at a planetarium, or tiny-tots concerts. Some enrichment
opportunities will be available in the classroom or as after school clubs.
Parents may be called on to provide an extra pair of hands for a crafts
project, to coach an Odyssey of the Mind problem-solving team, to go
on a field trip with a group of Young Astronauts, or to help conduct a
chess tournament.

Although no one expects any parent to be Super Mom or
Super Dad, it also isn't fair to refuse all requests for help from the school
with the excuse that "We both work." Increasingly that statement is true
of most families, but parental participation in the life of the school is still
needed. Parents need to be proactive in prompting companies and
businesses where they are employed to be flexible about allowing
some time to occasionally be involved in the schools. Some corpora-
tions are now encouraging employees to take leadership roles in some
community project.

If the school personnel discuss acceleration for a gifted child,
parents need to learn all the details. Will the child be accelerated for
part of the day in just one subject area to a different grade or classroom, or will the curriculum be compacted in the home room so that
he or she may move more quickly through it and progress more rapidly
in a subject area? In this school system, does acceleration mean grade
skipping? In making decisions about acceleration, the parent needs to
reflect on whether his or her child normally chooses older students to
play with anyway so that grouping with older children makes sense, or
whether the child in question is shy or small and may feel uncomfortable with older youth.

If a pull-out program is in use in the school, parents must seek information about what is involved. Will the child go to a different classroom or travel to another building? Are the activities tailored for individual gifts or talents or are all gifted youth brought to one place to study one topic? Does the regular classroom teacher follow-up on activities introduced in the gifted pull-out program or will the child be gifted only on Tuesday and Thursday mornings? Is the child expected to make up work that went on in the regular classroom while he or she was in the "gifted classroom?"

Education has may exciting and promising practices that influence teaching, the curriculum, and the education of the gifted. Currently we hear a lot about cooperative learning, discipline-based arts education, critical thinking, global education, cross-curricular units of study, and personal technology, to mention only a few. One development that made a tremendous impact on elementary education was the endorsement of the "whole language philosophy" or "literature based language instruction" promulgated by such educators as Graves (1983) and Calkins (1986). Although in the mid 1990's, some districts question this approach and blame declining tests scores on it, others are highly supportive. This philosophy has lead to quite a different language arts education for young gifted children from that which parents themselves experienced in school.

Beginning in kindergarten, children are taught to write in a way similar to that in which they learned to speak, by adults applauding approximation. Just as a young child learns to say "da-da" for father and is rewarded with responsive smiles and shouts of joy by surrounding adults, so a kindergarten child may label a zoo picture "elfnt" for "elephant" and is delighted that teachers and others can read his writing. This invented or temporary spelling begins with scribbles, single letters, initial consonants, and finally the addition of vowels and spacing between "words."

With the application of the whole language philosophy in the primary grades, there is much more literature instruction and a movement away from the extensive use of work sheets, basal readers, and traditional reading groups. Parents need to become knowledgeable about major new philosophic approaches to effective teaching and learning. With this knowledge base, they can both appreciate the progress of their young gifted child and also support the efforts of the school to empower all young children to become effective writers and readers.

This same understanding and acceptance of change is also needed in the area of educational technology. Even the youngest students are becoming computer literate with a whole new curriculum that embraces Writing to Read Labs, Primary Editors, Bank Street Writer, Logo, The Voyage of the Mimi, use of interactive CDs, and a myriad collection of computer software.

Disciplines are developing standards such as those produced by the National Council of Teachers of Mathematics in 1989. These standards stress many aspects of math literacy in addition to whole number computation and familiarity with fractions and decimals. Students learn about mathematics as communication, are encouraged to use calculators when appropriate, to estimate, and to understand such topics as statistics and probability.

Although no parent can be expected to keep up with all that is happening in the field of education, having an open mind to new methods and materials locally and nationally is important. The National Education Goals Panel (1995) makes available each year data on progress toward achieving national education goals in the various disciplines.

In addition to coming to an Open House, or volunteering in the classroom, parents may also be asked to come to school to meet with a building committee on gifted education or to take part in a staffing for their identified gifted child. It can be a little intimidating to be the only person around a conference table who is not a trained educator, but parents should not be afraid to ask clarifying questions and to seek information. They need only remember that parents know their child better than anyone else. Parents have valuable information to share in making decisions about the best education for their children.

Parents also need to realize that there is more screening than evaluation that typically goes on in a school's gifted education staffing. They should not mistake a single number on an IQ test or standardized achievement test for a thorough evaluation.

Parents may be asked to complete a form or to examine a check list that the child's teacher has completed. On it the parent will typically find such items as: persistence and power of concentration, a wide range of interests, use of exceptional language, remarkable memory, independence, likes to organize and bring structure, grasps the abstract and cause-and-effect relationships, shows leadership, is an alert and keen observer, is a creative problem solver, and is sensitive. Not all of these may apply to every gifted child. Not all are easily observable in a structured school setting. Parents need to give the data thoughtful consideration and add to it their observations from the home.

Parents need to realize that even if a child has very high intelligence, it does guarantee that he or she will meet with outstanding success. When Terman and Oden (1947) in their follow-up studies on genius tried to explain the success of some gifted adults and the lesser achievements of others equally gifted according to test scores, they identified four traits on which the two groups significantly differed. These traits involved persistence in the accomplishment of ends, integration toward goals, self-esteem, and freedom from inferiority feelings. It is clear that parents can make a significant contribution to each of the aforementioned areas in the life of a young child.

THE UNDERACHIEVER

Too often words get in the way of action. School personnel may categorize a child as an underachiever. Parents learn that a child gets good test scores, sometimes asks good questions, and participates in discussions, but most of the time daydreams, does careless work, loses assignments and books, and appears to be uninterested in school. Having shared that information with the parent, school personnel may then feel they have done their duty.

Parents who are confronted with an underachieving gifted child must take action. First they should check out the obvious physical causes. They should check sight, hearing, possible infection or disease, amount of rest, and nutrition. Parents also need to consider the emotional scene of the child. Has there been frequent moving, is there a severely strained sibling relationship, do parents bicker continuously, has there been a separation or divorce?

Careful consideration must also be given to the school. What are the teacher expectations? Are they realistic? Are individual differences respected? After gathering all available information, the parent can provide a one-on-one expression of interest in the child that may turn the tide. The underachieving gifted need affection, recognition of achievement, and help in building realistic aspirations.

Eby and Smutny (1990) discussed underachievement in their book *A Thoughtful Overview of Gifted Education*, and pointed out research that indicates some of the causes may be related to an environment in which parents allow the child to be too dominant or too dependent. They also suggested that inappropriate interventions may exacerbate the problem.

PARENT POWER

Parents should never underestimate their power. There is much that parents can do to improve opportunities for gifted youth. A single step taken by a concerned parent may be small, perhaps the writing of a letter to the editor of a local paper praising a piece of successful gifted child programming. Parents may form or join existing advisory groups. They can attend school board meetings and speak out on instructional issues affecting gifted youth. Parents need to exchange views with others, share ideas, read, and keep up to date on educational issues.

There is a subtle peril in being the parent of a gifted child. The world is sympathetic to children who face learning and physical challenges and to their families but is not as eager to talk about the problems associated with being gifted. Gifted education parent groups are often unfairly characterized as being elitist. Accept the fact that gifted child education is a special interest group—an essential one. Then recognize the need for as many parents as possible to become committed, outspoken advocates for our gifted youth.

REFERENCES

Calkins, L. M. (1986). *The art of teaching writing.* Portsmouth, NH: Heinemann.

Eby, J. W., & Smutny, J. F. (1990). *A thoughtful overview of gifted education.* New York: Longman.

Flowers, J.V., Horsman, J., & Schwartz, B. (1982). *Raising your gifted child.* Englewood Cliffs, NJ: Prentice-Hall.

Fox, J. (1993). The wrong whipping boy. *Phi Delta Kappan, 75,* 118-119.

Graves, D. H. (1983). *Teachers and children at work.* Portsmouth, NH: Heinemann.

Graue, E. B. (1982). *Is your child gifted?* San Diego, CA: Oak Tree.

National Education Goals Panel. (1995). *Data volume for the national education goals report.* Washington, DC: U.S. Government Printing Office.

Osborn, A. F. (1967). *Applied imagination.* New York: Scribner's.

Parnes, S. J., Noller, R. B. and Biondi, A.M. (Eds.). (1977). *Guide to creative action.* New York: Scribner's.

Pressey, S. L. (1955). Concerning the nature and nurture of genius. *Scientific Monthly, 81,* 123-129.

Terman, L., & Oden, M. (1947). *The genetic studies of genius: The gifted child grows up.* Stanford, CA: Stanford University Press.

Torrance, E. P. (1962). *Guiding creative talent.* Englewood Cliffs, NJ: Prentice-Hall.

Williams, F. E. (1970). *Classroom ideas for encouraging thinking and feeling.* Buffalo, NY: D.O.K.

17

Successful Parenting

Sally Walker

No matter what one may do for a living, the difficulty of that job pales in comparison to the difficulty of *being a parent*. Parents are responsible for their child's moral as well as physical, social, emotional, and intellectual growth. It is *overwhelming* to say the least. Put into this glorious and painful job of raising a gifted child and parenting takes on other dimensions. Parenting the young gifted child is not necessarily harder, but it is different.

Society is ambivalent about the gifted. We want our problems solved, new conveniences, easier lives, and peace without the inconvenience of dealing with gifted kids. Our society is so interested in making everyone equal that often gifted kids are discriminated against or never recognized, which adds to the difficulty in parenting them. Our society values sports and entertainment and tends to reward mediocrity and conformity in academics more than creativity and innovation. No wonder kids want learning to be fast, entertaining, and easy. Gifted children fall into the trap of expecting everything to come easily. Their parents feel frustrated by seeing their child's ability often go unrecognized or untapped.

Parenting gifted children is a challenge because gifted kids do things *differently*. These children may go against the grain and make others uncomfortable. Gifted children need to recognize that a price tag is attached to nonconformity. Because the interests of young gifted children may differ from age peers, the gifted child may be regarded as a "nerd" or socially maladjusted. This can lead to feelings of isolation or depression, even at a young age. At age 4 one gifted child told me he thought that he was stupid. When I replied, "Oh, no! You certainly are not," he responded, "But, I think so differently." It is difficult being young and gifted because the young child does not have the perspective in which to view being different.

Many gifted children feel that they can't ever let themselves be wrong. They feel that to compliment someone else, or to acknowledge that a classmate had a good idea, somehow diminishes them. So they tend to be stingy about complimenting others. They have trouble sharing the limelight. This doesn't make for much popularity among the playground set.

Gifted children tend toward perfectionism. What's so bad about perfectionism? To begin with, perfectionists don't like to try new experiences. Trying means maybe failing—judged by their own impossibly high standards—so these kids never achieve a fraction of what they might (Walker, 1991). Some do not give themselves permission to fail in anything. Their options become more and more restricted and severely defined.

Perfectionism even explains some cases of underachieving. When there's a huge gap between the ideal and what the child sees him- or herself as being capable of, sometimes she simply gives up. Too often gifted children think that everything should come easily. Because much of what school requires takes minimum effort, these children gain the mistaken idea that if risk or hard work is involved they must give up, lest they fall short. It is easier to save face by saying, "I didn't try" than to admit, "I tried my hardest and fell short of someone's expectations." It becomes especially difficult for the child if he feels that his parents value only academic achievement, not him as an individual.

Gifted children need to be taught that learning, by its very nature, means taking risks. Parents can model this by demonstrating their own willingness to attempt difficult projects. The hardest idea to get across is that missing a goal doesn't equal failure; instead, it can be an opportunity to grow. That's why it's so important to allow these kids to experience failure within a safe environment. Parents should never set their child up for failure, but provide experiences in which he or she will have to stretch him- or herself in a nurturing, encouraging way, not a stress-filled, ego-damaging way.

A pattern of nonstop reaching for more and higher and better may be fostered by parents who are in awe of their gifted child and praise every milestone. We have been told and believe that praise is positive. This is not necessarily the case, for it can bring about an unhealthy response. For example, if I praise my child for every accomplishment, does the absence of my praise mean that I don't appreciate the accomplishment? Not necessarily, although the gifted child might misconstrue it to be just that. This does not mean that an accomplishment should *not* be praised, but rather praise should be concentrated on the child's *efforts*. "I can tell that you've spent a lot of time on that project." "It looks like you're really excited about that topic."

Perfectionism can be aggravated by unclear rules and/or focusing on the negative. Constant referral to the importance of making the grade, growing up, getting ahead, and getting better may place subtle pressure on the gifted child. Dawdling on easy tasks to avoid harder ones may be the result. Some perfectionistic gifted youngsters work so slowly that it drives teachers and parents to distraction. At other times the child may procrastinate by postponing work. In doing so they hope to avoid failure. Parents need to understand their child's desire to do well, along with their fear of failure. The result will be a home safer for exploration of uncharted topics and ideas.

Parents can model acceptance of their own mistakes, showing that they are not crippled for life by a dumb error. They need to resist the temptation to say "I told you so" or "You should know better." How much better to say, "What can be learned from this?" Strive to make the problem work *for* rather than *against* her. Instead of being proud of the task completed or the race that was run, the gifted child may only notice that she did not win any prizes or set any records. Realistic goals need to be set for parents and children alike.

Adults need to learn to relax. Help children to distinguish times when it is important to give your all—and times when it is more important just to let go. Some school tasks are simply done to document that the child can do it, that he has the knowledge. They don't require perfection. In the whole scheme of things other matters take priority. Setting priorities helps eliminate unwarranted perfectionism.

Parents need to *listen*! Offer a calm comment in the face of frustration like "you'd like that to be finished perfectly" or "you're really struggling. I appreciate your effort." Remind your gifted child kindly that goofs and mistakes happen to everyone, and that they are not costly. Those who have achieved eminence have all had to deal with failure.

By listening, parents also let the child know that they *value* him or her. Listening builds trust; it shows you care. How can children learn to listen if they are never listened to? TV is one of the biggest handicaps to listening. Most children watch over 40 hours of TV a week. According to National PTA research, by the time children graduate from high school, they may have spent 20,000 hours watching TV compared to

13,000 hours in the classroom. More American households have TVs than have indoor plumbing. This is not all bad. TV can open doors by exposing kids to new information. Programs can be educational, thought provoking, or relaxing. It is when TV becomes a barrier, an avoidance mechanism to tasks that need doing, an escape, or a built-in babysitter that its use should be questioned.

Sometimes it is particularly difficult to find a time and place where there are no interruptions. The phone rings, the dog barks. I have found the car, without the radio on, to be the biggest listening device. Going for an ice cream cone, alone with one child, gives the opportunity for one on one listening. Don't express your advice and experiences unless asked. Make your child the one who expresses ideas and questions, and challenges and explores the possibilities and consequences. Allow the child to express and explore his or her feelings. This does not mean that you agree with, or even like his or her point of view. It does mean that you are allowing the child to own and express his or her feelings, a valuable gift. At bedtime or at the evening meal share the best thing, or the worst thing, that happened that day. By starting at an early age children can become accustomed to sharing their feelings.

Gifted children don't develop equally in all areas at the same time. Intellectual, physical, and social/emotional ability may all develop at different rates. Judgment and intellect are not related and may not correspond. A child may be very bright and still use poor judgment. Parents need to teach tact and proper timing. Leta Hollingworth (1975) noted that these children "do not suffer fools gladly." It is important that the gifted children learn that there are times when being right is not important. Manners and rules of politeness may mean holding your tongue and keeping quiet. For example, when Grandma uses incorrect grammar, as she has her entire life, it is better to accept the words in loving fashion, rather than critically. Gifted children may be excluded by peers and do not seem well trained in using their intelligence to solve that problem. Tact, manners, and social amenities need to be taught. If your gifted child seems to have an especially large, critical "*mouth*" it may mean that he or she does not feel particularly good about him- or herself. By cutting others down, by finding their faults he or she may be trying to elevate his or her abilities. The child may be saying to you, "Look at me and notice how good I am".

To assume that because a child is gifted he or she will be maladjusted socially is a misconception. Terman, in his studies of the gifted in the 1920-1930s, found that they tended to be well liked, highly regarded, and socially adept. On the other hand, gifted does not necessarily mean happier. In terms of social and emotional characteristics, gifted may indicate a common collection of concerns that the gifted have, although these do vary in degree. If the gifted child feels like a failure socially, he or she may focus on his or her cognitive ability. This is not good if the student's only success is academic and social interaction is totally avoided. I do *not* mean that gifted children should be pushed into social situations which are not comfortable. I am suggesting that their life have a degree of *balance*, both in academic and social activities. The true measure of "social adjustment" really is how the child feels about him- or herself. Some parents have reported that being in a gifted program helps. Appropriate placement, where the child can exchange ideas with intellectual peers who are also chronological peers, is invaluable.

Their heightened awareness and sensitivity to small changes can make them especially vulnerable. Sometimes they misconstrue the information, thus causing their own problems. Being young and bright, the gifted child may pick up on information that other children disregard. They may not have the knowledge and wisdom to put the information into its proper perspective. One 5-year-old boy came to class and told me that he could not concentrate on reading that day. I asked, "Why?" He responded that he was afraid that his grandmother's house was going to be bombed. He explained that he was at her home the night before and she was working on her income tax. I assured him that this was something every working American did and was not cause for worry. His fears continued. I probed further asking what led him to believe that income tax and bombing were related. He then told me that he was watching the evening news and saw that the IRA was involved with bombing and his grandmother had an IRA with her income tax. I then explained that indeed the letters were the same, but an Individual Retirement Account and the Irish Republican Army were in no way related.

Gifted children's supersensitivity makes them aware of hypocrisy, social injustices, falseness, and image making. Gifted children often turn away from self-concern earlier than their age peers. They are idealistic and insist on answers to uncomfortable questions. They see atrocities on the news and they read about unfairness and unethical practices in the paper. Parents may not even be aware that a child has heard information, let alone that the child is anxious or afraid because of it. The children fail to understand how we, their parents, can allow some practices to go on. Why do people have to go hungry? How come industries pollute and nothing is done? How can politicians say one thing, get elected, and then do something else? The gifted child may see the world as a scary, ugly place, becoming afraid to grow up, and for this reason act particularly immature at times. Being babyish is safe. To act adult-like and think adult-like may be too much of a burden for the gifted child. The goal is to encourage the gifted child to develop his or her capabilities, to be constructive and to help solve problems. Be comforted in their idealism—it's the hope of the future.

From the time gifted children first associate with other children, they begin to realize that they are different. The gifted child may need help to accept these differences, not to deny them. Schools tend to reward conformity rather than divergence. Their extraordinary minds and abilities are both their biggest assets and largest liabilities. That mind can quickly accelerate the gifted child into stressful situations, and at the same time be used to address and correct the stress. Bringing the problem into awareness may be half the battle. Some strategies for helping gifted children cope with problems involve problem-solving strategies, the use of humor, questioning whose problem it actually is, ignoring the problem, or compartmentalizing their thinking so that the gifted child sees that just one area of their lives is affected, not all areas (Webb, Meckstroth, & Tolan, 1982).

Parents can find that stress arises from working with the school because the gifted child may have discipline problems arising from boredom or challenging the system. Parents need to be open to school personnel. They need to be ready to hear both positive and negative things about their child without trying to rationalize or defend the child's behavior. Parent denial of problems, according to many school officials, is one of the biggest stumbling blocks.

Zaffrann and Colangelo (1979) summarized several studies and found that gifted children need more than the usually expected amount of guidance in order to be mentally healthy enough to be creative. However, very seldom are counselors found at the elementary level, let alone the primary or preprimary level.

Too often counseling is reserved for crisis situations. "Preventive" counseling is necessary in order to head off the crisis situation. It takes much less time and energy to resolve a problem before it gets out of hand.

When schools that provide counseling services are so limited that help is minimal, parents may need outside help. Looking for a counselor is no easy task. Be sure to check your insurance policies beforehand to establish coverage. Before seeing the counselor on a professional basis it is a good idea to check out how she feels about issues that are important to the adults. The counselor also needs to understand gifted children and how they behave. Surprisingly enough, not all counselors do. Parents also need to be sure that the counselor's values are the same as their own; parents need someone with whom they can communicate in a relaxed fashion. It is often helpful to go in as a family so that the child feels comfortable, and the therapist gets to know the family. Trust is an equally important issue. Parents must find someone who understands the problem and with whom they and their child feel safe.

Unfortunately, some people still feel that there is a stigma attached to seeing a counselor, a "shrink." If a child had a reading problem parents generally would not hesitate to see a reading specialist. Counselors are for interpersonal help, to expand our minds rather than to "shrink" them. Too often, in a family situation all are emotionally involved and can't see the forest for the trees. The objective help of a trained outsider can provide needed perspective.

Tips for parenting the gifted child include:

- Expect achievement.
- Relationships are most important motivators. Test score results may vary drastically in school with the rapport of your child and the test giver. Children do much better on tests when they feel good about the test giver.
- Avoid sarcasm and ridicule. It never results in improvement, it only worsens the situation.
- Recognize accomplishments in varied ways. Written praise is the most powerful.
- Teach self-sufficiency, goal setting and value clarification. Don't reward garbage. Support with the left hand, push with the right. In goal setting, set short-term, immediate goals. Write them down (and the steps along the way). Adopt an action plan. Take action. Reward attempts.
- Try to maintain a healthy balance between the two extremes of overstructuring and abandoning the gifted child. Allow enough independence and privacy for children to pursue their own activities and profit from their own mistakes, but be there when they need help to lend support, understanding, guidance, or simply (and perhaps most importantly) a sympathetic ear. One gifted third grader told me that he never wanted to take another lesson. When I asked why, he responded that when his parents found that he was capable of doing so many things they scheduled him with lessons every waking moment. He explained that he never had time to just play. Gifted children are children. They need time to play, to contemplate, to daydream—luxuries we don't seem to have as adults. If overscheduled, the child may become dependent on adults for "what to do" and be incapable of managing his or her own time. Remember that there's a fine line between pressure and challenge. A child needs lots of intellectual stimulation and plenty of opportunities to stretch to fulfill her potential, but he or she also needs time off for having ordinary kinds of fun, unstructured time to play, to act his or her age, to be a kid.
- Avoid comparing children in an evaluative sense to peers (brothers, sisters, classmates, neighbors' children, other gifted children). Strive to understand and accept the strengths and weaknesses of each child and to value the uniqueness of each. Respect for individuality is contagious.
- Remember that *all* children need to share in responsibilities (at home, in school, within the community) and to be held accountable for age-appropriate standards of behavior. Giftedness is not moral superiority, not an excuse for misbehav-

ior, not an excuse to get out of work. Gifted children, because of their verbal adeptness, may try to argue with you and to push their limits. They are aware of your weak spots and which buttons to push. Some issues are nonnegotiable. Parents are older, have lived longer and are therefore wiser. They have wisdom that only comes with experience. Their job is to parent, not to run a popularity contest. Some issues are not debatable.

- Genuine praise and encouragement are essential to all children and need not be feared as causes for self-consciousness or elitism. Avoid comparisons—they can be deadly. Appreciate and respond to the special joys, needs, and problems that separate your gifted child from other children, and do the same with the joys, needs, and problems that he or she has in common with other children.

- A child's teacher, as well as the school administration, parent groups, and legislators, need information and support so that *appropriate* education for *all* children will take place. Teachers and administrators sometimes fear or dread parents of gifted children, thinking that they will demand more than can possibly be provided or try to promote and show off their child. Teachers are becoming more aware of the gifted child and his or her needs, but may not be able to do as much as they wish because they are held by the constraints of the system.

- Parents need to know their child's school and teacher. Teachers deserve professional respect, even though parents may disagree on an issue. Find things that children like about the class or the teacher and relay positive feedback to the teacher. Teachers need support. Never attack a teacher's ability or character. Offer time to help the teacher when possible. Teachers and parents are both in the position of helping kids and should therefore strive to make experiences the best possible for all children.

- Be sure to inform teachers about the child's special interests and abilities. Examples of special things the child does at home or on vacation should be shared with his or her teacher. Pictures of special projects or constructions that cannot be kept can be taken and filed. A portfolio to show evidence of the child's growth is an excellent vehicle to relay information of this type. Educating is not the sole responsibility of the school—continue the child's education by going places: museums, libraries, summer or weekend camps, special classes, parks, and so on.

Being a parent is *never* easy; however, parents of gifted children tend to feel an even greater responsibility. They ask, "Am I doing ok?", "Is nothing ever enough?", "Is my child really gifted?" Just as burnout exists in other occupations, it also exists in parenting—it is simply not popular to admit it. Adult social and emotional needs are also important and should not be ignored. Steps are needed to assure that parents are healthy people:

- Have a life of your own.
- Develop your hobbies and interests.
- Take pride in your job.
- Be careful not to overinvest in the gifted child. Living their life for them is not beneficial to anyone. Parents need to have dreams and goals of their own. Problems are created when parents try to live through their child.
- Adults need to take time for their creative self. Find a medium by which feelings and thoughts can be expressed. Discover things that energize, that renew, and do them.
- Stressful thoughts should be replaced with calming ones. Concentrate on the positive. Appreciate the good things going on around and the people that are valued. It's all too easy to be caught up in the negative "ain't it awfuls" or "if onlys."
- Have adult friends. This may sound silly, but with the time commitments that gifted children require, some parents don't allow themselves time to be with their own friends. Find friends that inspire and give energy, rather than those who consume energy.
- Find and accept help when needed. There are times when all of us face problems that are overwhelming. The help of a trained professional can put things into proper perspective.
- Laugh, Love, Lighten up! Let the kid inside out.

In 100 years it will not matter what my bank account was, or the kind of car I drove, but the world may be different because I was important in the life of a child.
    —Anonymous

REFERENCES

Hollingworth, L. S. (1975). *Children above 180 IQ*. New York: Arno.

Walker, S. Y. (1991). *The survival guide for parents of gifted kids*. Minneapolis, MN: Free Spirit.

Webb, J., Meckstroth, E., and Tolan, S. S. (1982). *Guiding the gifted child: A practical source for parents and teachers*. Columbus: Ohio Psychology Publishing.

Zaffrann, R. T., & Colangelo, N. (Eds.). (1979). *New voices in counseling the gifted*. Dubuque, IA: Kendall/Hunt.

18

Tips for Parents of Infants and Toddlers

Tom Potter

> You get more information with your new car than you do with your
> new baby . . . we need to treat parents as teachers and give them
> tools to do the job.
> —B. L. White (1983)

This statement is used to summarize the situation regarding how much informational help parents traditionally need on entering parenthood. In recent decades, however, parent education programs have become much more available for parents who wish to utilize them.

In addition, thousands of public and private programs have been created for families at all income levels, and for good reason. Parents are interested. In a Gallup poll of public school parents, 78% thought it would be beneficial to have parent education courses (Schaefer, 1983).

WHAT DOES PARENT EDUCATION HAVE TO DO WITH CHILDREN WHO ARE GIFTED AND TALENTED?

My approach has been to seek to help all parents provide a sound basis for parenting their children in the first 3 or 4 years to bring out the gifts and talents inherent in all children. Hopefully, you will agree that although you want to provide the best for your child, almost all parents want the best for their children, too. By utilizing some of the following tips for parenting infants and toddlers gleaned from the field of parent education, you, too, can provide a sound basis for your child's emerging gifts and talents.

INFANTS

As far as the first 8 months are concerned, child development is fairly automatic. An infant's vision, hearing, muscles, and coordination will improve with little parental assistance. The most important developmental concern in the early months is the building of attachment between the parents and the child. It begins by treating the child with care and love. For most parents, this comes quite naturally. Responding promptly and consistently to a baby's cries is very important. An infant senses loving care instinctively, and a positive, two-way relationship between the parents and child soon develops.

One school of thinking regarding child development refers to infants who develop a sense of trust as "securely attached children" (Ainsworth, 1982). This does not mean attached in the sense of "clinging to mommy's apron strings." It describes a child who feels secure in his or her relationship with parents. To go a bit farther, the child enjoys the relationship. Sroufe (1979) determined that securely attached children become better problem solvers and are more socially adjusted as they grow older. They also appear to develop more quickly intellectually, and use more of their potential than insecurely attached children. Therefore, it appears that infants who are loved and well cared for stand a better chance of sound emotional, social, and intellectual development.

FROM INFANCY TO CHILDHOOD

At approximately 8 months an infant has undergone enough sensory and muscle development to begin acquiring some new capabilities. At this point, in addition to developing attachment, direct parental involvement becomes more important. Developing specialized skills and attitudes demands more than love and caring for the basic physical needs of the child. Without parental involvement, the child is "at risk" of slowed, or even retarded, development in five major areas. These at-risk areas are:

1. language
2. curiosity, spontaneity and creativity
3. intelligence
4. social
5. small and large muscle development

LANGUAGE

Many parents note progress leading up to the first "Mama" or "Dada," but because they may not have enough language background, they may worry too much about baby's progress. One of the subtle areas of speech development relates to *receptive language*. Imagine a 14-month-old child sitting on the living room floor with three or four toys scattered in front of her. One of them is a ball. The child is able to say "Mama" and "Dada." The mother says to her baby, "Say 'ball.'" After several tries, the only response is "Mama." The child looks at the ball, but the word is not spoken. The mother says, "Go get the ball." The baby shows, by looking at the ball or getting the ball, that she knows what a ball is. She is "receptive" to language—she just isn't ready to hold a press conference on the matter yet. In time, mother won't be able to keep her quiet.

CURIOSITY, SPONTANEITY, AND CREATIVITY

This is an area that is of special interest to creative education researchers and psychologists. It is also often misunderstood. Many people think that curiosity is something you either have or you don't. For babies who are just learning to crawl, and have spent most of their life in a crib, the entire world is full of new stimuli. Of course, this means that a baby must have access to this world, and be able to examine what he or she wants to examine, not just what mommy or daddy dictates.

To nurture curiosity, spontaneity, and creativity it is a good idea to let a baby out of the playpen as often as possible. A playpen stifles curiosity by limiting the size of the child's explorable world. Allow your child play with objects, self, and you. Show a positive interest in your child's play (Bredekamp, 1987). However, it is *extremely* important to "childproof" your home before allowing baby to explore.

INTELLIGENCE

Intelligence is somewhat dependent on curiosity. People can be taught, but the most intelligent people are usually curious people who go beyond what they are taught and learn on their own initiative. As with walking and talking, guidance from parents may not make a child learn faster, but will probably help him or her develop at a rate closer to their highest potential.

One way that parents can help children develop intellectually is to provide a great deal of small object play. It's a good idea to have many small toys (at least 1-1/2 inches minimum diameter to prevent swallowing and/or choking) scattered around the house. Don't keep toys only in the playpen—let the entire house be a playpen. This helps capitalize on the child's curiosity, spontaneity, creativity and need to explore. Select a diverse range of toys for your child, from blocks to rubber duckies to cars and spaceships. This helps infants explore a wide range of interests and develop a larger vocabulary at an earlier age. Dozens of inexpensive toys ($1-$2 each), as well as pots and pans, plastic cups, and many other household items, are much better than a single talking teddy bear that might cost $100 (Potter & Parnes, 1995).

SOCIAL DEVELOPMENT

This area of development often causes the most frustration for parents when things don't go well. Children who have social adjustment problems can often be more difficult to live with than children who have physical or intellectual development problems. This is particularly true when the problem involves discipline. However, discipline is not the only important social adjustment factor. Indeed, how well or poorly a child behaves is often related to several internal and external influences.

The internal influences involve the child's emotional makeup (personality). Even infants have distinct personalities. In the early months, we usually judge a child's personality by how little or how much a child cries, smiles, and how he or she reacts to people other than the parents. Some children are slow to warm up, other children easy to be with, and still others may be the active, energetic type. There is a wonderful video entitled *Fearful, Flexible, and Feisty* that does an excellent job of portraying these three major personality types and how best to respond to differences in children (Lally, 1992). By the time a child is 2 years old and is more mobile and physically and verbally expressive, personality traits manifest themselves in many more complex patterns of behavior. Even child psychologists often disagree on the causes of difficult behavior, and parents with little training on the subject can be overwhelmed. Many just roll their eyes and say, "Oh, he's just going through the terrible 2s." However, the "terrible 2s" need not be so terrible if some external influences are brought into the picture.

These external influences involve how the world treats the child. This includes *everything* the child experiences; both people *and* the environment. For example, many children, whether they be infants or 3 years old, are sensitive to, or afraid of, sudden loud noises. We can't turn down the volume on a thunderstorm, and we shouldn't try to, but we can comfort a distressed child by holding him or her. We can prepare for the next thunderclap by saying, "Do you think there will be another big noise? If you smile and talk about the experience, and show you aren't afraid, you may prevent the establishment of a lifelong fear. At the very least, you may help your child learn to cope with unpleasant situations. Coping with fear is important for good social development. There are other ways to help your child grow socially and many ways you can act as a positive external influence.

Give your child plenty of opportunity to find and follow his or her own interests. Most adults don't like being told what we should do. When this happens we often become disinterested and even irritable (filing our income taxes might be a good example). The same is true for young children, especially when they begin to crawl around and explore. Let them investigate what they're interested in, as long as they don't try to pry the back off of the TV set. Allowing children the freedom to find and develop their own interests involves many of the same procedures that are used to cultivate curiosity and intelligence.

Remember that your child has certain possessions that are just as valuable to him or her as your most prized possession is to you. Put yourself in your child's place and you may come to realize that she doesn't just *like*, she *loves* that teddy bear. Children may not know what the word "appreciate" means, but somehow they know the feeling. If you show your child that you appreciate their sphere of existence, he or she will be more likely to appreciate yours. This "reciprocal appreciation" is an important trait to nurture as we help our children become pleasant to be around most of the time.

If there is any single element that is crucial to good social development, it is probably discipline. The obvious reason why we discipline children is to curtail behaviors or actions that are socially undesirable or unsafe. On a more positive note, we hope to instill a sense of self-discipline in children. We want children who will practice appropriate behavior on their own initiative and not misbehave in the first place.

The most important guideline to discipline is "Speak once—then intervene." Don't get into the habit of speaking three, four, five, six, or seven times. This puts the child in charge of the situation. It also gives the parent more opportunity to lose patience and regret it later. It's best to speak firmly, not to shout. If a child ignores the first command, intervene immediately. Disciplining may involve taking something away from the child or moving the child to another part of the room. Be sure you show the child acceptable alternatives to his or her actions or words. Naturally, if the child's action puts him or her in immediate danger of injury, intervention should be immediate. As you intervene, explain why you are doing so in a serious, firm tone of voice. Even if the child doesn't understand your words, he or she will probably understand their context. They will eventually begin to realize that there are limits to behavior, and that you are serious about enforcing them.

SMALL AND LARGE MUSCLE DEVELOPMENT

Much of what is necessary for good muscle development during the early years comes naturally with practice. For example, small muscles in the hands and fingers are strengthened through play with small objects. Equally important is the child's ability to use these muscles in a deliberate fashion (manual dexterity). Plenty of play helps both strength and dexterity. The earlier suggestions about childproofing a home so that baby is free to roam give a child plenty of opportunity to crawl and develop the strength and coordination needed for the demands of learning to walk.

YOU AND YOUR CHILD

By following many of this chapter's suggestions, you, too, may find parenting a more pleasurable experience at the same time that you are laying the groundwork for the emerging gifts and talents of your child. The majority of the information in this chapter came from a parent education program entitled Parents As Teachers (PAT), whose original consultant was Burton White. As of August 1996, 1,907 PAT programs exist in 47 states as well as in New Zealand, Australia, Great Britain, the West Indies, and Canada. Many other parent education programs offer similar information as well.

FINDING A PROGRAM IN YOUR AREA

At the "Investing in the Beginning" conference Weissbourd (1987b) stated:

> There are thousands of programs around the country . . . that include parent involvement in a variety of forms. The programs are located in hospitals, mental health centers, public schools, universities, community centers, voluntary service agencies, and on military bases. The services include many different kinds of programs: drop-in cen-

ters, warm lines, hot lines, parent discussion groups, parent education classes, home visitors, peer support groups, health care and education groups, and self help groups with a particular focus. (p. 45)

The best way for a parent, or expectant parent, to find a suitable program is to consult a local social service agency, or consult with a pediatrician.

WHAT TO LOOK FOR IN A PARENT EDUCATION PROGRAM

Although content such as that contained in this chapter coming out of a parent education program may be very beneficial to you, there are some criteria to keep in mind about which parent education programs would be of greatest value to you. In essence, the finding that very different programs can positively affect parent-child interaction and children's development suggests that the key to success lies less in specific curricula or structure than in the quality of the programs and the relationships they foster (Wandersman, 1987).

In a nutshell, the characteristics of quality and relationship to look for are differentiated between the now outdated deficit model of intervention and today's more productive strength's approach to primary prevention as a basis and intervention when necessary.

Historically, parent education has served as one of the roots of and now important elements of the modern family support programs (Weissbourd, 1987a). The definable characteristics to look for in a quality parent education program (which may be part of a larger family support program) are based on some basic assumptions:

- All families need support, regardless of economic status or specific concerns. Most parents want to be good parents no matter what their resources are. The varying kinds of support provided by family resource programs are determined by the needs of the parents and are responsive to the cultural and social characteristics of the communities in which the families live.
- The availability of social networks, mutual aid, and peer groups is essential to the family's ability to enhance the child's development.
- Information on child development, obtained both formally and informally, assists families in their child-rearing role.
- Support programs increase the family's ability to cope rather than provide a system on which families become dependent. Support should build on the strengths that whole families and individual family members already have. The confi-

dence that family support helps parents build enables families to manage their own lives and participate in shaping the environment in which they live.

- Providing support during the first years of a child's life serves a preventive function. Early and continuing support is aimed at strengthening the family unit and preventing family dysfunction.
- Because families are part of a community, their needs cannot be met in isolation from it. Support is provided in the context of community life and through links with community resources (Family Resource Coalition, Fall 1981).

If the parent education or family support program in your area is based on these principles, then you and your children may be greatly benefited in preparing for their emerging gifts and talents. You may benefit in many ways as well.

CONCLUSION

Today we stand on the verge of more systematically providing the essential information parents need to raise well-adjusted children. This would certainly help all the children involved to reach their own, highest level of achievement. Perhaps in years to come we can revise the quote with which we began this chapter to read:

> You now can get more information with your new baby than you do with your new car. We are treating parents as teachers and giving them the tools to do the job.

REFERENCES

Ainsworth, M.D.S. (1982). Early caregiving and later patterns of attachment. In M.H. Klaus & M.O. Robertson (Eds.), *Birth interaction and attachment* (pp. 35-43). Skillman, NJ: Johnson & Johnson.

Bredekamp, S. (1987). *Developmentally appropriate practice in early childhood programs serving children from birth through age 8*. Washington, DC: National Association for the Education of Young Children.

Family Resource Coalition. (1981). *Statement of philosophy, goals, and structure*. Chicago: Author.

Lally, J. (1992). *Fearful, flexible, and feisty*. [Video]. Far West Laboratory. Available from Bureau of Publications, Sales Unit, California Department of Education, PO Box 271, Sacramento, CA.

Potter, T., & Parnes, B. (1995). *Parenting playfully: Dancing the develop-mental ladder, Birth to three.* Olean, NY: Parent Education Program Press.

Schaefer, E.S. (1983). Parent-professional interaction: Research, parental, professional, and policy perspectives. In R. Haskins & D. Adams (Eds.), *Parent education and public policy* (pp. 283-303). Norwood, NJ: Ablex.

Sroufe, L.A. (1979). The coherence of individual development: Early care, attachment, and subsequent developmental issues. *American Psychologist, 34,* 834-841.

Wandersman, L.P. (1987). New directions for parent education. In S. Kagan, D. Powell, B. Weissbourd, & E. Zigler (Eds.), *America's family support programs* (p. 213) New Haven, CT: Yale University Press.

Weissbourd, B. (1987a). A brief history of family support programs. In S. Kagan, D. Powell, B. Weissbourd, & E. Zigler (Eds.), *America's family support programs* (p. 53). New Haven, CT: Yale University Press.

Weissbourd, B. (1987b, October). New directions in public policy for young children and their families. In *Investing in the beginning* (p. 45). [Conference Report].

White, B.L. (1983, November). *Parenting for the first three years of life.* Seminar, Newton, MA.

19

Keeping Curiosity Alive

Judith Wynn Halsted

Although gifted children are eager learners in the preschool and early elementary years, for some of them, disturbing changes occur during the school years. At first they may show reluctance to attend school, even developing physical symptoms of stress. By the mid-elementary years, some are quietly hiding their ability, answering fewer questions and curbing their efforts on assigned work to avoid being too different from the norm. In the middle school years, they may turn their backs entirely on academic achievement as they pursue social or athletic interests.

During these years, other gifted youngsters retain their eagerness to learn. They continue to invest a great deal of energy in exploring an astonishing variety of interests. Apparently knowing that learning, for its own sake, is important to them, they are willing to forego popularity in favor of developing their intellectual or artistic abilities. Some inner drive helps them set priorities and protect the time and space they need to pursue their interests against the incursions of family and friends.

As young adults, they learn to wear their giftedness comfortably, modestly, but affirmatively. They take deep, quiet pleasure in their abilities. They live with a sense of purpose, although they may not yet be able to articulate what it is. However out of place they may have been in a fourth grade classroom, they are increasingly suited to the world of achieving adults as they grow older.

How can parents and teachers help all gifted children continue to be as invested in their own learning process as they were when they were preschoolers? Adults who work with preprimary and primary gifted youngsters—before negative changes occur—will wish to consider what steps they might take not merely to teach these children, but also to ensure that each child will retain his or her natural curiosity.

Adults who work with gifted children must provide enrichment activities for them, but they must go beyond that. Whatever *action* is taken to satisfy curiosity and to enrich the child's experience, it is the underlying adult *attitude* that says that learning is important—for its own sake and to the child—that is critical. These children must learn that they enjoy learning, and they must be encouraged to integrate that knowledge into their developing self-concepts.

All the while, parents and teachers of preprimary and primary gifted children should realize that they are preparing the children for the time when they will be responsible for meeting their own need to continue learning. As they learn to become independent in recognizing and meeting their needs to stay warm, dry, fed, and out of physical danger, they must also recognize and respond to their natural need to learn. For gifted children, this recognition of their need to learn and the development of a sense of responsibility for it are necessary survival techniques, as important to the healthy growth and development of the organism as being warm and dry, fed and safe.

The process of preparing gifted children to be independent caretakers of their own talents—helping them recognize and make constructive use of one of their basic resources, their own intense interest in learning—has four components:

- providing information and enrichment
- letting children see adults learn
- advocating learning as a source of pleasure
- teaching children to protect their need to learn

The remainder of this chapter presents some childhood experiences of "Steven," a composite of several gifted children, arranged according to these four components.

PROVIDE INFORMATION AND ENRICHMENT

It sounds simple: Adults should nurture the natural curiosity of young gifted children by providing information and enrichment. They should answer questions, arrange for exposure to a variety of experiences, take them to lessons and concerts and plays. Why do some children who are privileged and have all of these advantages nevertheless enter junior high school with a bored, blasé attitude toward school, whereas others, not so privileged, are avid readers, creative artists, dedicated musicians, thoughtful young scientists? The answer lies not only in *what* parents do to provide information and enrichment, but also in *why* they do it; more elusively, it lies in the attitudes behind what they do and in the child's perception of those attitudes.

Steven came home from first grade for lunch one day with a new idea buzzing in his head. A visitor from the Arts in the Schools program had brought a print of Georges Seurat's *Sunday Afternoon on the Island of La Grand Jatte* and had talked to the class about pointillism, how dots of paint that seem meaningless when viewed from close up blend into a picture if we stand far enough away. His mother knew very little about art or about this painting, but she caught his enthusiasm clearly enough, and while he ate his soup and sandwich she looked Seurat up in the encyclopedia. Sitting at the kitchen table with Steven, she read the article aloud, stopping to listen when he had more to add from the class visitor's talk. References at the end of the Seurat article led them on to other articles about French painters and painting. Steven was so busy learning more over his lunch that he was nearly late getting back to school that afternoon.

Steven's mother seized a moment that presented itself serendipitously, and used it to offer enrichment to Steven. By providing additional information, she *satisfied* Steven's curiosity. But she went beyond increasing his knowledge. By indicating to Steven how much more there is to learn about this painter and his art, she also *whetted* his curiosity for further learning. Further, her willingness to stop everything in order to learn more conveyed the message that information is exciting and important—an underlying attitude that Steven adopted for his own as he grew, from this experience and others like it.

Planning for Enrichment

Valuable as spontaneous learning opportunities are, parents cannot always wait for them to occur and cannot always use them when they do occur. Therefore, parents of young gifted children may put considerable time and effort into planning enrichment opportunities for them. Usually they simply take advantage of classes or other activities offered in the community—swimming, tennis, art, library story hour, dance, or music. The result can be a haphazard collection of experiences that may turn out to be entirely appropriate. However, enrichment can be more deliberately planned, with goals determined through careful thought.

One goal might be to give children exposure to a wide variety of activities so that they may learn of talents and interests that would otherwise go undiscovered. Enrichment activities would incorporate experiences parents want their children to have over the years of childhood: music, art, literature, nature, math, astronomy, athletics, and so on. Even if interests are pursued for only a short time in childhood, they may lodge in children's minds for recovery later, when as adults they cast around for leisure activities that will complement their professional life, enrich their family life, or control stress. Choral singing, painting, or tennis may be ignored for decades and then picked up again, an interest sparked by a memory of childhood pleasure.

Developing an enrichment program that addresses intellectual, emotional, social, physical, artistic, and spiritual development does not have to be a daunting task if parents plan time for each *over the span of the school years*. Children whose parents discuss this approach as decisions are made will gradually learn the value of making room in their lives for all of these dimensions of a complete person.

Parental Motivation

To promote children's inner direction and motivation, parents should begin by examining their reasons for promoting each enrichment opportunity. Are they taking their cues from the individual child, basing decisions on his or her present and potential interests and needs, or are they indulging their own desire to see their child excel in tennis? If the parents' underlying purpose—which children can clearly read—tells them that they are offering enrichment to help them to learn more about their interests and abilities, their natural motivation to learn will be called into play, and their awareness that learning is important *to them* will be strengthened.

LET CHILDREN SEE ADULTS LEARN

Parents of gifted children sometimes fear that the child is smarter than they are and that this will undermine their authority. In fact, adults who freely acknowledge that they still have much to learn retain the respect of their gifted children far more surely than those who rely on superior knowledge for their authority.

If Steven's mother had been intimidated by her young son's acquisition of information she did not have, she could simply have failed to respond to his enthusiasm. The conversation at lunch that day would have proceeded as it did on any other, and she would have maintained for a little longer the role of all-knowing adult, basing her authority and control over Steven on an ever-shakier foundation. How often do adults not respond to children's questions because they are "too busy," when in fact they are turning quickly away from a confrontation with the limitations of their own knowledge—afraid to let children see them learn?

Planning for Children to See Adults Learn

Normal family life provides opportunities for children to watch adults learn, and parents can increase these learning events if they choose. Instead, some parents may actually minimize such opportunities because of their reluctance to admit ignorance—not allowing children to help assemble a new bicycle, for instance, or failing to ask directions when traveling.

Circumstances that parents can easily arrange for letting young children see them learn include:

- Taking children to the library, and checking out books for both parent and child
- Reading newspapers and books for pleasure, and commenting to the child about what the parent learns
- Watching television news, concerts, and educational programming, inviting the child to join in the viewing, and commenting on what the parent learns and enjoys
- Taking up a new hobby, such as fly-fishing, photography, or gardening, and discussing with the child the reasons for the parent's interest, and the research necessary to begin
- Taking the child to the hardware store while the parent gathers both information and supplies for a home repair job
- Asking for the child's comments and opinions about books, television shows, and movies; listening attentively and responding to the answer

Many more examples could be listed. The important thing for the child's future development as a continuing learner is the parent's underlying attitude, which optimally includes a cheerful willingness to admit ignorance of the topic at hand, a readiness to learn from anyone (including from the child), and an openness to risk.

Admitting Ignorance

Steven's mother knew so little about Seurat that she had to ask Steven how to spell the name to look it up in the encyclopedia. However, she did not need to know art in order to validate and build on Steven's excitement over what he had learned at school that morning. Her very lack of information was useful. She was learning with Steven, and in letting him see her learn, she was passing on to him something more important than information: her recognition that learning continues into adult life to be a source of satisfaction and pleasure. Her comfort with admitting her ignorance turned her lack of information from a negative to a positive attribute.

Learning from Children

Steven learned that he could bring information home from school and teach his mother. His mother already knew that she could learn from her gifted son. Because parental authority rests on far more complex variables, such as mutual respect, fairness, reliability, and consistency, rather than on superior knowledge, this did not damage her authority in Steven's eyes. Steven's mother was not threatened by the fact that he knew something she did not know, and Steven added to his growing self-esteem an instance in which he was able to contribute something of value to the life of someone he loved.

Risk Taking

Steven grew up in a small town. When he was 8, his parents decided it was time to visit a city. Steven watched from the back seat while his parents drove into the center of Chicago for the first time. Tension built as mother read the map and father drove through crowded, narrow streets to their hotel, whose tower they could see but could only circle in frustration until they understood the one-way street system.

What did Steven gain from watching his parents learn in this situation? He saw that to them, learning something new was worth the required risk. He realized that people from small towns can find their way in cities—this was a challenge his family (he) could meet. The capacity to take such risks to reach a valued goal became part of the foundation of Steven's growth as an independent learner.

ADVOCATE LEARNING AS A SOURCE OF PLEASURE

Providing enrichment and modeling learning is not enough. Parents and teachers must help children see that learning is a source of pleasure, despite possibly conflicting messages from the culture. In addition, each child must be helped to internalize the knowledge that he or she enjoys learning.

To understand the negative attitude toward learning that permeates our society, it is helpful to compare the connotations of *learning* and *working*. From television, jokes, and comments tossed off by adults, children learn at a very early age that a common goal in our society is to avoid work. The message is clear that the aim of workers at any level is to be able to retire as soon as possible. The ideal vacation is on a beach in Florida, and the more time one is able to spend there, the better off one is.

The same attitude exists in school. Learning is the work of children, and our attitude toward work translates into their attitude toward learning, often to their detriment. Therefore, a high grade is more acceptable if one has not worked for it. Industrious students get along better if they manage to hide their industry. The easiest grade, socially as well as academically, is "the gentleman's C."

The popular attitude toward work and learning, however, is usually not the real attitude of gifted people—adults or children. Many gifted adults, holding jobs they enjoy, are quickly bored on what is supposed to be a relaxing vacation. They may prefer to take some work or work-related reading along, and to balance a vacation day between work and play. To "relax," that is, not to work, for a whole week can be more stressful for them than being at home and working at a meaningful task.

Parents and teachers should realize that a positive attitude toward work is characteristic for gifted people, and actively encourage it in young children. Work and learning are not to be avoided; rather, they are sustaining and refreshing sources of pleasure.

Recognizing Joy In Learning

The first step is to help children know that they enjoy learning, and that they can find activities which create that enjoyment.

Parents can develop responses to help children toward this goal. When a child is learning something new, parents can identify and verbalize what the child is feeling: "Looking at the constellations makes you happy and excited, doesn't it?" Parents can then go on to mention when they experience the same feeling: "I feel the same way when I get a new idea at work that helps everyone work together better," or "That's how I feel when I learn to play a piece really well on the violin."

Children gradually learn that when they are out of sorts it may be because they are hungry or tired, and they can act to improve the situation by finding something to eat or taking a nap. In the same way, they can learn that when they feel restless, ill at ease, or purposeless, the remedy may be to turn to something that they know interests them—rather than to turn on the television set. Parents can identify children's interests for them at first: "You're enjoying this fingerpainting so much, why don't we remember it the next time you are bored and ask what you can do?" "You know you like to learn about dinosaurs; shall we see if the library has any new books about them?"

Internalizing Joy in Learning

The second step is to help children include their pleasure in learning in developing self-concept.

One way in which parents help build children's self-concept is by labeling feelings, thereby guiding them to recognize and express emotions. For example, children who experience anger and express it inappropriately can learn to recognize the feeling and name it.

In the same way, parents can help young children identify and express their enthusiasms and interests: "I'm interested in the constellations," "I enjoy fingerpainting," "I like to learn about dinosaurs." And more generally: "I like to read," "I like to learn about practically anything." As children vocalize these facts they internalize them, and their self-concept expands to include love of learning.

Parents may help children integrate the joy of learning into their self-concept quite spontaneously, without realizing they are doing it. When Steven was 3 and 4, he and his mother would sit at the piano after lunch while she played folk songs. After they had sung for a while he would go to his room for quiet time, while she continued playing some of the songs they had just sung as well as other, slightly more complex music. Steven would listen from his room, remembering the words and absorbing the tunes. From this gentle beginning Steven has grown into an adult who uses music—piano, guitar, recorder—as a source of quiet relaxation. Without conscious teaching, he learned at an early age that he loves to make music. It is part of who he is.

TEACH CHILDREN TO PROTECT THEIR NEED TO LEARN

Gifted children may be said to have not only an interest in learning but a *need* to learn, in order to be content. Young gifted children show a strong natural awareness of this need, absorbing new information eagerly, persistently, and constantly. As they grow older and respond to messages from the culture, this natural curiosity may fade until they actually lose touch with it and no longer recognize it as part of themselves. For this reason, their early natural motivation to learn must be brought to the level of conscious awareness, so that gradually they know intellectually that they need to learn.

Children whose environment has included the components discussed earlier—information and enrichment provided with their own interests and potential in mind, opportunities to observe adults who are enthusiastic about learning, and the message that learning is a source of personal pleasure—should be aware by the end of the primary years that they are happier when they are learning. In the years to come, they must strengthen this knowledge and then move beyond it, developing the ability to protect their need to learn. What can be done in the preprimary and primary years to prepare them for this?

How Parents Protect the Need to Learn

Steven entered a new school for second grade. He waited patiently and quietly for what he knew would have happened in his old school. As soon as he demonstrated to the teacher his comprehension of the math assignments, she would move him to a more challenging book. In the new school, however, this did not happen. During the winter of his third grade year, he finally mentioned the problem to his parents. Although test results indicated that Steven indeed was capable of moving ahead faster, the principal explained to his parents that this was not possible in the present situation. Steven's parents found a school where he could advance at his own pace. Here, in a better learning environment, he moved ahead in all areas.

Furthermore, he had learned that he had some control over his own education—a first step in taking responsibility for it. As a third grader he had little power, but his parents listened to his request and pursued it. Their willingness to take action for him at this age set the stage for the determination required of him later on, when he found his interest in learning at variance with that of his high school classmates.

The need to learn can be protected in more subtle ways. It is manifested in children whose powers of concentration prevent them from hearing the maternal voice when they are reading—a screen of privacy they erect to protect their reading time. One of Steven's traits as he grew older was a stubbornness about being interrupted when reading. In various ways he learned to protect the time he needed to learn, until those around him came to respect it too.

Although preprimary and primary children do not yet need to counteract many other demands on their time, parents can encourage them to protect their learning time by permitting them to have time alone. As they assure their children that learning time is important and commands respect from other family members, they prepare them to protect their need to learn.

At 24, Steven has focused the wide-ranging curiosity he exhibited as a preschooler. The way has not been easy for him: he has experienced his share of the difficulties of growing up in a society that does not value his intense intellectual curiosity and drive to learn. Unlike many gifted children who as preschoolers had similar interests and intensity, however, Steven never lost his early enthusiasm for learning, never tried to mask it in order to fit in with his peers. The eagerness of the young gifted child has developed and matured until, as an adult, he is able to use it as a vital resource in his pursuit of a fulfilled life.

There can be many more Stevens if parents and teachers provide experiences in the preprimary and primary years that permit and encourage gifted children to learn in many settings, not just the classroom. These children must see that learning is for them a life-enhancing pursuit over which they can exercise increasing autonomy and control as they grow older. That vital bit of self-knowledge—"I like to learn"—can carry them through the discomforts of dyssynchrony, when intellectual development outstrips social growth; it can diminish their interest in experimenting with drugs; it can guide them through the challenge of a career decision; and it can keep them young into old age. If at an early age they become self-motivated learners, the benefits will enrich their entire lives.

20

From the Beginning:
Parents as Teachers and Home
as a Reading Resource

Pamela M. Hildebrand

Learning requires patience, effort, self-discipline, concentration, practice, and a sense of value and worth in what we are doing. It involves making choices or difficult decisions. Above all, it involves timing and our use of time. The way parents use time with their children becomes one measure, not only of the worth of the relationship, but of all that is to follow in their children's lives.

Early learning (that is, from birth) was once considered by some educationalists to be a *waste of time*. It was thought that gifted children who learned early would "burn out" or that average children who learned later would "catch up." It was thought that reading developed before school entry was often the result of overanxious parents pressuring their children to do "formal work" before they were ready, in their zeal to push their children ahead. We now know, of course, that although some parents have unrealistic expectations of their children and reading, not only do gifted children learn to read spontaneously at home, but early reading in gifted children plays a crucial role in their academic success, and may even be one of the keys to expanding their potential.

Early reading and a love of reading in young gifted children is not just a *matter of chance*, but is the result of a *sensitive and dynamic reading partnership* between parent and child beginning from the moment of birth.

HOW BEING READ TO HELPS CHILDREN READ

Gifted children who grow up reading naturally are read to by parents. These readers do not accomplish their feat alone; they are nurtured through the reading experience. They learn about reading, before they can read themselves, by copying the reading behavior of parents. Specifically, the listening language they build up when read to provides the rich basis for the reading language they need when they begin to read books alone.

By listening to parents read, children also gain experience with the mechanics of reading and the structure of stories. They notice how the parent attends to the black marks and how the reading is interrupted if the pages are turned too soon. They notice that a book has a beginning, middle, and end, that it should be held the right way up, and that reading is an activity done from left to right. Print becomes so familiar that they can consciously find landmarks, note regular features such as letters, spaces, commas, and full stops, and predict common language patterns, such as "once upon a time" and "they lived happily ever after." They learn about characters and settings by memorizing how fairies and witches and clowns behave in the world they inhabit in books. This enables children to predict character development and to plot patterns when new stories are read to them. Their familiarity with stories and their predicting ability about what comes next becomes so proficient that even very young children are aware if parents omit anything when reading aloud from their favorite story books. A whole storehouse of learning is developed from constant exposure to stories—this is the basis on which children learn to read. The knowledge and experience with beginning reading is what they use or bring to bear to help them work out new and harder reading material.

Therefore, a lifelong, ever-expanding, reading cycle is set in motion; experience and knowledge of reading lead to further knowledge and further experiences. The reading cycle accelerates as children become more proficient readers. Gifted children who have *rich early experiences* with reading have a head start that can never be eclipsed.

Parents who read often to their children take them on a reading journey they cannot go on by themselves. Being read to also nurtures a love of reading in children which is initially fostered through the feelings of comfort and security engendered within a child while sitting on an adult's lap, listening to a story and looking at the pages. The earliest memories of love and language and story not only stimulate and expand the thinking and imagination of gifted children, but help form their emotional attachment to books. Therefore, children who have been read to lovingly will not only be *able* to read, but will *want* to read and to read *often*. A lifelong love of reading has begun.

PARENTS AS TEACHERS

The majority of parents want to do the best they can for their young gifted children, and yet, despite all the evidence that it is vital to do so, many still fail to be active participants in the reading development of their children. Why is this so?

- First, it seems that many parents are afraid of participating in their children's reading development because they underestimate or do not even realize their potential as teachers. As Kohl (1975) wrote, "Many of us underrate what we know or forget how we learned ourselves and therefore do not believe in our capacity to teach" (p. 6).
- Second, many parents are afraid to involve themselves with their children's reading because they see this as the role of the professional teacher. They have been conditioned to believe that real reading only takes place when children begin school.

It does not matter that parents are not professional teachers. What matters is that parents love reading, love sharing literature, respond positively to their children's joyous reaction to stories, and are willing to spend the time and energy to do so.

Parents are not teachers in the formal systematic sense, but are natural teachers who act as guides for their children in more informal and incidental ways. The fact that their teaching and the learning of their children takes place in a less structured environment than occurs in a school should not lead parents to believe that the learning that is happening in the home is either *not important* or *not real* or *not good enough*. In relation to reading, nothing could be further from the truth.

THE HOME AS A READING RESOURCE

Family homes, with their informality and opportunity for incidental teaching and learning, can provide intimate settings within which rich reading experiences can and should take place. This is true for several reasons. Let us look at the following examples:

- In the home, children can be surrounded on a continual basis by a rich tapestry of conversation, listening and questioning, vocabulary and printed matter of all kinds, thus providing an environment in which the reading behavior of others can be copied in a natural way.
- Within the home, competition from the outside world is minimal—there is no pressure from other students or teachers, no set timetables or formal tests, and learning has no rigid limits, conditions, or restrictions.
- The home is an ideal setting for providing one of the key requirements for reading development—practice.

At home, parents can provide the vital opportunity for practice by reading independently alongside their children who are also reading. In this situation, children are likely to follow the model of their parents' reading behavior. Parents are also more likely to be available for help when needed. Practice such as this is not seen as a lesson but as a pleasurable activity that connects emotional security with reading. Children who have been given the opportunity to practice at home in this way usually develop into readers who spend considerable parts of their lives reading widely by themselves for their own pleasure. As adults, they will probably read to other children (perhaps their own), and thus continue the positive reading cycle.

PARENTS KNOW THEIR CHILDREN BEST

Parents know their children more intimately than anyone else. They are aware of their strengths and weaknesses, their passions and interests. They see what situations their children find frustrating or stimulating. They have a wealth of knowledge and insight into how, when, and why their children learn to their maximum capacity. Parents understand what situations or experiences induce confidence or disappointment, apprehension or determination, fear or exhilaration in their children. For these reasons, parents are in a unique position to respond in an immediate and spontaneous way to the reading needs of their children.

Immediate response to natural curiosity about words, stories, and books is vital because it allows children to be dynamic participants in the reading process. Reading developed in such a spontaneous ways teaches children that reading is a joy rather than a duty.

EARLY READING MEMORIES MUST BE POSITIVE

Parents who love to read clearly convey by their expressions, tone of voice, interest, and excitement the magic that reading can bring. As Kagan (1991) wrote, they convey "how miraculous it is that a human being, long after death could reach across the years and conjure images in a reader's head, images, tears, and laughter" (p. 83).

Parents who share reading in a relaxed, patient, and encouraging way are in a real sense shaping the attitudes of their children toward reading. It is those first positive memories of reading that give their children their first image of themselves as readers. If children have received loving feedback and recognition of their successes from their parents about reading, then the memories of those past successes will give them confidence to take the risks necessary for broader and more challenging reading experiences. Conversely, if the first experiences of reading with a parent include bad memories of harsh criticism, impatience, and indifference, even the brightest of children can come to believe they are poor readers. It is significant that many eminent people who reached the top of their profession have reported that their first experiences with their area of giftedness were spontaneous and informal, and that early lessons were remembered for the positive feelings they engendered (Bloom, 1985).

Make no mistake: a love of reading can be lost at a very early age. Without confidence in their reading ability, even the most talented of children may give up, simply because they are convinced they will not succeed.

The apparent ease with which gifted children naturally learn to speak and read at home sometimes conceals in the eyes of parents and of the world the magnitude and importance of the hard work and accomplishment of both parties. This is a parent-child reading partnership, not an accidental happening, yet its importance and results are often minimized, trivialized, or ignored.

PARENTS IN THE RIGHT PLACE AT THE RIGHT TIME

The development of reading in young children involves the element of timing. We know that approximately one half of a person's ultimate intelligence is developed by the age of 4. We also know that the optimum time for learning language and language-related activities such as reading occurs between approximately 18 months and 4 years of age. The learning potential for language and reading may occur at a faster rate during this period than may ever again be possible. Therefore, parents who are with their children during this time of rapid language growth are in the *right place at the right time to capitalize* on what is veritably a language and reading explosion.

LANGUAGE IS VITAL

Parents need purposefully to provide their children with language and reading experiences of the highest quality from the *moment of birth*. However, they will only do this if they fully understand how significant language and reading development are to learning and life.

Language with all its richness and complexity sets human beings apart from the plant and animal kingdoms. Language becomes the vehicle for thought and gives us the ability to think in the abstract and to speak of things we cannot see. It is a tool we can use to retain, recall, and transmit information, or to help control our environment. In fact, language influences to a large degree how we think and behave.

Through reading, language helps us to learn more about ourselves and others. It deepens our understanding of who and what we are, or could possibly become, and so helps us to be aware of our common humanity.

Time spent by parents developing language and reading in their gifted children in those crucial, early years can not only lay the foundation for children's future learning but may make the difference between average and gifted performance (Clark, 1992).

DEVELOPING RELATIONSHIPS THROUGH READING

The value of early language and reading development in young gifted children is not only evident in their intellectual development or academic achievement. Butler (1980) suggested in *Babies Need Books* that books are the best parents' aid for establishing and maintaining a relationship with their child. Reading can become a bridge to connect the inner worlds of parent and child, as readers share experiences through reading together, even if their interpretations differ. In fact, parents and children who share books often come to share the same frame of reference. Both bring to the story their own thoughts, ideas, emotions, and past experiences. This engagement with a story, this dynamic partnership between listener and reader, brings about the opportunity for mutual growth and change.

Listening to stories in books is only one way that relationships can be fostered through language and reading. Parents who are storytellers in their own right can take their children on exciting journeys of their own making. Kagan (1991) recalled her first story created by her mother about an elf-man who lived in a grand piano and emerged to perform small feats of magic. She said that "the performer of magic was, of course, my mother." From these wonderful creations she learned "how to be still: to see, to hear and to feel the magic animus in every living thing" (pp. 82-83).

Parents who tell stories to children about themselves and their childhood help their children learn about themselves and about life through their family heritage. Stories of both positive and negative experiences, which either enhanced a parent's life or made it difficult, can be a source of insight, delight, and comfort to children. It can enable them to see that parents have grappled with the same problems, fears, and needs that they are experiencing, so they know that parents are in a position to understand and empathize with whatever is currently happening in their own lives. This mutual understanding and support through story telling strengthens the parent/child bond.

Parents are better able to understand the learning needs of their children, if they ask themselves questions about what was and was not helpful in their own childhood learning experiences—questions such as:

- How did I feel when I started school?
- Was my childhood reading experience happy and productive?
- What motivated me to read?
- How did I feel when I read aloud to others?
- How did I feel towards my teachers?
- Which reading experiences made me feel successful and confident?

By discussing their own reading experiences and by admitting difficulties (if they had any), parents will show that they understand that learning to read is complex and involves hard work. From these personal stories about reading, children will learn that, as Simon, a young gifted reader commented, "Reading takes time. You have to start when you are young" and "Life needs reading."

TIME AND TELEVISION

Time, along with love and good health, is one of the most precious gifts human beings are given. Everything we do in life takes up our time, and in this regard television is no exception.

Debate rages about the negative effects of television on our children, yet one thing is certain—the number of children in our society who are watching an excessive amount of television is growing at an alarming rate. Children who are watching television for 30 hours or more per week, as statistics indicate, are being cheated. Cheated, because time spent watching an endless diet of undesirable behavior is not only damaging in itself, but is time spent away from other vital things that enable children to develop into loving, healthy, happy, productive adults. It is not only "what" many children are watching on television that is so horrifying: it is that they watch so much television that there is little time in their lives for communication with family and friends, for imaginative play, or involvement with creative pursuits such as painting, drawing, music, writing, or reading. Time lost in the early formative years is time never to be regained again!

Young gifted children, with their huge capacity for imaginative thought, are often the ones traumatized by the barrage of cruel, aggressive behavior that is commonly seen on our television sets. They often experience intense fear and sadness when bombarded with violent images because their heightened ability to empathize deeply with the feelings of others and to feel compassion for those who are hurt or are being hurt induces in them much pain and suffering. At the same time, many gifted children also experience a sense of powerlessness and bewilderment that the adults in their lives often trivialize or are indifferent to their troubled reactions. This compounds their suffering even further and can lead them to doubt their own true perceptions. It is sobering to realize that even the most compassionate of gifted children can gradually become desensitized to the suffering of others. This happens if they are subjected to a television diet of never-ending violence early enough, for long enough, and if they are deprived of other creative experiences, such as reading, that encourage empathy and emotional development.

Television limits critical thinking because it seldom shows characters thinking through a problem; further, television frequently encourages "deceptive" thinking—simplistic solutions and easy answers—particularly through advertisements (Trelease, 1989).

Parents should not be deluded into thinking that the number of hours their children spend watching television or that the quality of the programs watched has no effect on their children or their children's behavior. Everything we do and experience, especially early in life, affects us either positively or negatively. If we do or experience something often and for long periods of time, then the effects will be multiplied. As custodians of their gifted children, important decisions during the early years reside almost entirely with parents. In fact, at various times, children need their parents to make the hard decisions for them (Peck, 1994). This is certainly true of television watching—parents need to minimize and monitor the television viewing of their children, thus giving them more time for better things.

Parents should not make the mistake of thinking that because children are gifted, they need less time for love and relationships, for learning and creativity, or less opportunities for achievement. In fact, the opposite is true—the greater the gift, the more time needed for development. Having the potential for excellence is, on its own, not enough. Gifts have to be nurtured, and the nurturing of gifts takes love, time, training, and involvement. When parents read with their children, they are giving them one of their most precious possessions: *their own time.* Through this time together, children come to know not only that reading has value but that they have value too. By learning how important they are to their parents, they may also develop a sense of their own value in the wider community.

LITERATURE AS A VEHICLE

Throughout childhood, gifted children show many remarkable traits: They have a multipotentiality that not only needs to be encouraged and developed, but also needs to be protected.

The many indicators of their giftedness, such as their superior intelligence, heightened emotional development, unusual compassion and selflessness, and concern with ethical and moral issues, are sometimes the very things that lead them to self-doubt because they often cannot share their awareness with peers or teachers and remain *at the same time* accepted and liked for who they are. To understand and accept who they truly are is vital because often young gifted children receive misinformation or inaccurate feedback about their abilities from others who are threatened by their capacity. This can result in either an attempt to repress or hide their true talents, or in a devastating loss of self-esteem.

As parents help shape the sense of self in their children and as self-esteem and performance go hand in hand, parents need to use every means at their disposal actively to support and nourish the inner resources of their children. Actively to protect and affirm the perceptions of children while they are in the early, crucial, and fragile stages of developing a sense of self, is important not only for their later achievements but also for their whole lives.

Parents have, at their disposal, the wonderful resource of fine literature to use as a vehicle. They can purposefully choose to share with their children books that confront and explore some of the special qualities, joys, and difficulties associated with giftedness—thus bringing to gifted children an awareness that *they are different, but not alone.* Good books not only express, through their characters and situations, that it is all right for gifted children to be themselves, that is it all right for gifted children to express their gifts to the highest standard and in whatever form they may take, but that *it is imperative that they do so.* Such books, when shared in the security of a home and in the intimacy of a parent-child relationship, can give gifted children a sense of "yes we are" and "we could become," rather than a sense of "perhaps we're not" and "we do not dare." To help with the identification, affirmation, and encouragement of their true worth is not a small or trivial thing; it may be, along with love, one of the greatest gifts parents can give their children.

WHAT CAN GOOD BOOKS OFFER GIFTED CHILDREN?

Let's look more closely now at three aspects of giftedness, and what it is that gifted children who have these attributes need to find in books, if books are to be of value to their special needs.

First, gifted children have a huge capacity to think (and to think creatively). Therefore, above all else, gifted children need books that will stimulate thought. These books should include language that is rich, precise, and varied. They should have a complexity of plot and character that allows the reader to imagine, to evaluate, interpret, and weigh pros and cons.

Books that display a particular genre of thought, such a poetry, myths, biographies, or fiction, give a new insight into a particular way of thinking, thus challenging gifted children into a new awareness and enabling them to look at things from new and differing perspectives. Such books provoke, question, probe, engage, and disturb. They deal with complexities, dilemmas, paradoxes, and mysteries. Therefore, they often pose more questions than they provide answers, and they are often open-ended in order to encourage the gifts of contemplation and reflection often present in gifted children. Polette and Hamlin (1980) said, "Our gifted children need deeper, more beautiful, more heart-stretching and mind-stretching ideas to confront. They need to be offered books with a variety of levels of meaning to free their minds for the gymnastics of which they are capable" (p. 16). Sadly, many parents mistakenly believe that young gifted children should not be exposed to such literature as it is too hard or beyond the understanding of small children. In the case of gifted children, the opposite is, in fact, true. To wrestle or struggle with new and difficult thoughts and concepts, to attempt to push back the barriers of their understanding, are the very things on which gifted children thrive. New and complex thoughts are, for them, stepping stones to further awareness and further challenges.

Second, a key characteristic of gifted children is a tendency towards perfectionism; they need to excel at everything. This characteristic in itself is neither good nor bad, yet young gifted children often feel guilt or confusion because this desire that they have to do things as perfectly as they can is often not valued by peers, parents, or teachers. In fact, they find themselves in a society that not only sees this trait as undesirable and best eliminated, but one in which the opposite tendencies are lauded and promoted; a society in which "second best," "second rate," or even "shoddy" work is taken for granted and in which to do one's best is seen as "elitist" or "obsessive." Gifted children who wish to pursue their interests to a high standard by spending many hours honing their skills alone are further maligned, as this need to work alone is seen by our society as "odd," "antisocial," or even "maladjusted."

Perfectionism should be looked on as a passion; an invaluable and emotive force that propels gifted children towards higher achievement. The way this passionate drive is viewed and dealt with by parents, teachers, and gifted children themselves can decide whether it becomes a positive or negative force in the lives of gifted children. Books, and the discussion of books that explores perfectionism in all its dimensions, are of immense value in this regard. This is where the reading of biographies of outstanding achievers is so appropriate. Biographies of famous musicians, artists, writers, scholars, researchers, scientists, and doctors, to name a few, invariably are about people who possess, among other things, a "burning desire" to excel. The characters themselves and the situations with which they have to grapple, provide a framework through which gifted children can come to understand this characteristic more fully.

By seeing that perfectionism plays a positive and powerful role in enabling many great people to be highly creative and productive, gifted children have an opportunity to connect this with their own lives. They can see that this trait is a driving force for success and not a recipe for failure.

By learning more about the coping mechanisms of others in dealing with the problems perfectionism can bring, and by modeling on them, gifted children can develop coping strategies of their own. By understanding where perfectionism is appropriate to be used and where it is not, they can learn to become more selective in its application to their own lives. By identifying with the inner conflicts and doubts of others, gifted children can see that such feelings and thoughts are normal for some people and that outstanding achievements and personal growth can come from the depth of despair, or in the confusion and pain of wanting and needing to succeed while living or working in environments that are not conducive to success.

Third, gifted children have advanced moral and spiritual development, often based on their exceptional ability to feel compassion. Gifted children need books, therefore, that deal directly with questions of origin and destiny, and that delve into those themes which are aspects of both; issues such as birth, death, love, hope, and forgiveness.

Books in which moral issues and values are explored inevitably provide a framework through which gifted children can also view the never-ending struggle between good and evil. Good fantasy, of which fairy tales are an example, makes use of moral writing. Even simple stories, such as The Three Billy Goats Gruff, Snow White, or Cinderella, can present good triumphing over evil. In these books, the emphasis is placed on the development and maturing of heroes and heroines and on the gaining of personal skills and strengths to overcome problems (Hildebrand, 1991). Identification and "feeling" with such characters and, in a sense, momentarily "becoming them," helps gifted children relate the character's situation to their own lives, thus helping them develop tolerance and respect and expanding their ability to empathize with others even further.

I've often been asked, "Doesn't the portrayal of serious issues in books, such as good and evil, threaten children and make them anxious?" My answer is that these things are part of life and, in fact, are part of the lives of many of the children who would read about them. American psychoanalyst Bruno Bettelheim, (1981) said, "You cannot deal with anything serious without creating some ambivalent feelings or even some anxiety. Children have to learn that a certain amount of anxiety is manageable. They need to know, 'I can get into difficult situations, but I can manage them'" (p. 32). By seeing that life is complex and difficult and that it is necessary to work at problems, relationships, and skills, good books help gifted children relate reading to real life.

Imagination conjured in fairytales and other fantasy is important—a world without imagination is shocking to contemplate. We need imagination to feel compassion, to think beyond the known facts. We need imagination to explore other human dimensions such as greed, envy, humility, trust, heroism, and commitment. Imaginative thought evoked from stories often forms the basis of imaginative thought in real creations in real life. We could not have conceived of flying, for example, without imagining the possibility first—conceived perhaps in the images of flying horses or witches on broomsticks. Perhaps that is why when Albert Einstein was asked what children should read that would best help them to become scientists, his response was "fairytales." Perhaps that is why so many eminent leaders and thinkers of our time also remember a childhood enriched by parents reading fairytales and fantasy to them.

If, as it seems, many gifted children will become the eminent thinkers and leaders of the 21st century, then in a very real sense, the impact that parents have on their early years will, to a large degree, dictate the kind of thinkers and leaders they will become. The world needs thinkers and leaders who can help form a moral society. This means we need people of outstanding intellect and strong character; people whose ethics are not rooted in the quest for money or power, but who have vision, goodwill, and integrity. Parents have a pivotal and unequalled role in the fashioning of that society, for it is they who have the power and the responsibility to shape and guide the thoughts and emotions and values of their children from the moment of their birth. If gifted children can be inspired from the beginning through fine literature to emulate the lives of other great people who have trodden unknown paths and who had the courage to stand out against the crowd, then reading for those children becomes a connection; a connection with themselves and others, with the past and with the future; a connection so deep that it can not be broken with age and experience, but rather strengthened by them.

I urge the parents of young gifted children to:

- choose to read to your children
- choose to do it from the beginning
- choose to do it often
- choose to select literature of quality and
- choose to read joyfully and willingly

Therefore, reading will become for your children not just a "skill," not a "pastime," or even just a "pleasure." Rather, reading will become an essential part of life, as basic as breathing or sleeping. Reading will become, as Robertson Davies wrote in his wonderful fiction, *The Cornish Trilogy*, "something that is *bred in the bone*."

REFERENCES

Bettelheim, B. (1981). Our children are treated like idiots. *Psychology Today, 15*(7), 24-44.

Bloom, B. (Ed.). (1985). *Developing talent in young people*. New York: Ballantine.

Butler, D. (1980). *Babies need books*. London: Bodley Head.

Clark, B. (1992). *Growing up gifted* (4th ed.). New York: Macmillan.

Hildebrand, P. M. (1991). *The reading connection—Secrets of better reading for parents, teachers & students*. Melbourne: Australian Scholarly Publishing.

Kagan, D. M. (1991). Gifts my mother gave me. *Educational Leadership, 49*(3), 82-83.

Kohl, H. (1975). *Reading, how to*. Middlesex: Penguin.

Peck, S. (1994). *A world waiting to be born*. New York: Bantam.

Polette, N., & Hamlin, M. (1980). *Exploring books with gifted children*. Littleton, CO: Libraries Unlimited.

Trelease, J. (1989). *The new read-aloud handbook*. New York: Penguin.

21

Parents of Gifted Children: Sheep in Wolves' Clothing?

Gina Ginsberg Riggs

The parents of your gifted students are like your relatives or in-laws: They come with the arrangement. Unlike your relatives, however, you do not have them for life—but you are stuck with each other for one year, no exchange or refund. Therefore, for one year, you might as well be friends and take advantage of the last free labor in today's money-conscious lifestyle. Read on and cash in.

Have you stopped to think that parents are the largest group of people anywhere? That they outnumber educators by far? The same is true in education of the gifted. If parents of gifted children, and let us not forget their increasingly youthful and vigorous grandparents, would really get it together, there are certainly more than enough of them to push for that precious opportunity for their children to learn all they are able to learn.

To learn all they are able to learn: Is that not what education is all about? And is that not what all parents of gifted children want for their kids' education? Yes, that is really all—*to learn all they are able to learn like all other students*—no more but certainly no less.

Teachers often think that most parents believe that their children are all geniuses. When it comes right down to it, however, that is not true. With a clear and precise definition of giftedness, parents have proven themselves to be fairly accurate identifiers of gifted children—especially young gifted children.

When you do find a pushy or bragging parent, please consider that maybe all that bravado only hides doubts and concerns that this child may not be as smart or quick or creative as the one next door or in the next seat. Next time you have to listen to all the miracles your students perform at home, please give parents the benefit of second thoughts and wonder why such claims have to be made.

Talking about pushy parents, perhaps it is best right up front to talk honestly and openly about those parents of gifted children who can and sometimes do make your professional lives miserable. Let us count their ways:

- First, there are ignorant parents. They may have pretty bright kids but they do not know the first think about how a school works. Parents who know that school policies are set by the board of education will not blame the teacher if they do not like them. Parents who know how many hours teachers really put into their work will stop believing that teaching is a cushy job. *Educate the parents of your students because an informed parent is a friend of the school.*

- Beware the angry parent! They are often angry because their gifted children already know the curriculum—or because they believe that the school's goals are set too high. They are angry because they wanted a different teacher at the beginning of the year, and that is surely not your fault. They are angry because too much science is taught—or not enough, and they don't even know that somebody else makes curriculum decisions. Some parents blame teachers for everything that is not perfect in this imperfect world. The teacher may not even be to blame but the teacher is visible and on the frontline for potshots.

- "Concerned" parents self-identify themselves. They go into shock over any grade less than "A," they panic over projects, and they send medical bulletins to school with the first sneeze. Not all parents learn at the same time that gifted children are a lot of fun.

- Resign yourself to complainers; there is no pleasing them. You may teach yourself into retirement but you will never teach yourself out of new and different complaints. The fact remains that some parents need to complain lest the school think that they are pushovers.

- Look out for horror story parents. They are part of a carefully organized underground network that disseminates, nurtures, alters, exaggerates, and rearranges misinformation simply because negative information keeps them going.
- Make your peace with deaf parents who cannot hear a word of what you are trying to tell them because their ears are so full of timidity, confusion, anger, fears, and misinformation that they are unable to hear even if the information is welcome.
- Then there is the parent who unfailingly shows up at 3:00 to discuss her (it is usually a "her") child when you want to go home and take off your shoes. A pain in the neck? No, a treasure! Here is a parent who has too much of what you don't have enough: time and energy. Put that parent to work on a legitimate and time-consuming project that you always wanted to do and never had the time. Add praise and appreciation and get that parent out of your hair and busy to make her feel good about herself and less concerned about the youngster who will benefit from the opportunity to grow up by standing on his own little feet.
- Sometimes you are stuck with a parent who is truly a challenge and your best efforts have made no difference. First give silent thanks that you are only stuck with each other for one year and then sit yourself down and write that parent a thank-you note. A thank-you note? Yes, indeed, a thank-you note for sending a child to school in a pretty new outfit, for the red curls you always wanted, for sharing a birthday, a ball, a book . . . for anything at all. Chances are that this particular parent does not get thank-you letters and yours will be remembered. Things will go better afterwards.

WHY DO WE HAVE PARENTS WITH NEGATIVE FEELINGS?

In my opinion, these feelings stem from lack of basic information about what goes on in the school: how children are chosen for gifted programs, which decisions go into the makeup of reading groups, what educational goals govern the new social studies curriculum, who decides to discontinue the foreign language program, and why, when, and how decisions are made about next year's placement.

We can blame parents for not making it their business to find these things out, but it would be better if the school assumed some responsibility for making sure that parents are better informed about what happens to their kids in school and why.

Educators may not realize that parents often do not feel part of the school, and parents of gifted children may feel particularly isolated.

They feel like outsiders and tend to react defensively. The more information a parent has about the school, the more that parent is going to feel involved in the whole educational process and become part of the school bureaucracy. Involved parents invest their time and energies to help the school help the children.

A CHILD'S EDUCATION OFTEN DEPENDS ON THE PARENT'S ABILITY TO WORK WITH THE PEOPLE WHO WORK WITH THE CHILD

Parents without information, or with wrong information, perceive themselves to be second-class citizens. Nobody likes to feel like that—and nobody should. Parents who feel isolated, be this isolation self-imposed or laid on by the school, are a dissatisfied lot—dissatisfied and unhappy. Unhappy parents do nothing for the mental health of their children. Parents who are dissatisfied with the school usually have children who are less than enthusiastic learners. It is a vicious cycle in which the kids stand to lose the most.

At the start of the school year, parents would really appreciate receiving some basic information from the teacher about what is to be learned, what is expected from students, and how parents can help. Even simple information about labeling yellow slickers and on which day gym clothes have to come to school are so welcome! I will never forget the breakfast announcement, with the school bus at the corner, "We have to come dressed as pilgrims today."

It is to educators' benefit to educate parents about the school and how it works.

The good thing is that parents usually support education. Parents of gifted students particularly often move heaven and earth to help the school. On the other hand, they can also be a pain in the neck, and in my opinion, teachers get to choose which it shall be.

HINTS FOR TEACHERS

Here are some hints for teachers toward parental support and practical help in terms of time and energy:

- Examine your own attitudes first to make sure that last year's difficult parent has not soured your expectations of all future ones.
- Know your students' parents and what they do for a living, what their hobbies and passions are that can enrich your

classroom. Find those parents who have time to spend during the day, and then use that time for those chores that take time away from your important teaching.

- Use your experience with gifted students to help parents of gifted children cope at home. Help parents understand the fine difference between encouraging and pushing. Explain about peer pressure and form a teacher-parent team to remediate underachievement.
- Include negative parents in your planning. You need to know how they are thinking.
- Let parent-teacher conferences be honesty time as your opportunity to give parents *all* information about his or her child in the classroom—and always finish on a positive note because there surely is not a child anywhere about whom you cannot say something nice.
- Communicate, communicate, communicate. Inform parents about what you are teaching and how their children are responding. Ask for help and suggestions—and then be prepared to accept both, but with your good judgment. There is probably a volunteer behind every suggestion.
- There are still parents at home during school hours who can perform valuable services for the school—and their kids. Let us itemize their different roles:

The parent as a learner must become comfortable with the school bureaucracy before being able to provide meaningful services to the school. They must understand, for the sake of their gifted children, what is possible now, what may be possible later, and what will never be educationally defensible—now or later. Just like their children, parents have to start their involvement with the school by learning, and educators can help parents learn how a school works.

The parent as a helper has always helped the school in many ways. Parents help run sports events, organize book fairs, sew costumes for school plays, and count milk cartons in the classroom. They help by filling in forms, finding single galoshes, and matching a lost owner with a found yellow slicker. They come early and stay late—and they work cheap. There is no union for parents. Parent helpers save teacher time—time to get back to the precious job of teaching.

The parent as a source of information can provide three kinds of information to the school:

1. Information about the student. The child at home may be a different person than the one in school. If a second grader reads the New York Times at breakfast but does not complete reading assignments, teacher and parent need to get together.

2. Information about the parents themselves. Parents of gifted children live, work, and play everywhere. They may be at home during the day, or they may be almost never available to the child. Knowing about the parents helps the teacher understand the child.
3. Information about the student's family. Changes at home may help the teacher understand changes in student behavior in school.

The parent as a resource person can donate his or her many-splendored training and experience to contribute talents and know-how. They can enrich the classroom by giving information about their careers and by sharing their experiences, collections, travels, and hobbies. They can become consultants by using their knowledge to plan a more efficient lunchline or better scheduling. Just about everything a school does can probably be done more efficiently and economically with the help of expert parents.

The parent as an advocate can be well informed and supportive to speak up on school matters when school people have to remain silent to keep peace in the educational family or to protect their jobs. Parents can spread positive feelings toward school and education among friends and neighbors. They can demonstrate to their children through their attitudes, words, and deeds that there is joy in learning, that teachers are to be respected, that homework is student responsibility, and that the school is a good place.

For advocacy purposes, the writer would like to offer her definition of *giftedness*. Everyone can relate to the fact that some children run faster. Others tie their shoes earlier—and gifted children think *earlier, better, faster, and often differently* from most others. This is an unthreatening definition, without educational jargon, to which most people can comfortably relate.

The following fool-proof plan for school-parent partnership may be helpful for those projects for which there never seems to be enough time and energy:

1. The old-fashioned needs assessment; or, which project, carried out with the help of parent power, would benefit your gifted students and the school?
2. Test the waters. Make sure that the finished project will be accepted and appreciated by students, educators, and parents.
3. Communicate with everyone every step of the way.
4. Assess your parent resources. There is virtually no limit to what a teacher can do who knows what his or her students' parents do for fun and profit.
5. Set up a working committee: 50% educators, 50% parents.

6. Agree on goals and objectives, complete with timeline.
7. Adopt an organizational pattern. Write down who is going to do what by when to complete the agreed project.
8. Agree on job descriptions for everyone involved.
9. Design evaluation for success.
10. Get board of education approval. If you don't need it, advise the board anyway and get its blessings.
11. Keep records such as scrapbooks, progress reports, newsletters, kids' letters, etc.
12. Get free advertising; inform the media every step of the way.
13. Present a scrapbook at the conclusion of project to the appropriate person.
14. Say "Thank you. That was great. What shall we do next?"

This kind of cooperation will open school doors wide to welcome supportive parents as partners in the education of their gifted children.

Surely among us—educators and parents alike—we have the dedication, expertise, determination, time, worldly goods, and leadership to help gifted children learn all they are able to learn!

> We must dream of an aristocracy of achievement arising out of a democracy of opportunity.
> —Thomas Jefferson

V

Meeting Social and Emotional Needs to Effect Growth

Joan Franklin Smutny

In this section, seven educators and counselors describe the social and emotional development of young gifted children, acknowledging that they are often at variance with each other. All stress the need for parents, educators, and counselors to become more cognizant of the needs of these young children, the unique challenges they face, and how adults can be helpful to their growth and development in a variety of settings. All individuals interacting with these bright young children can support their capacity to cope and to enhance their strengths.

The affective characteristics of gifted children, such as hypersensitivity, perfectionism, and nonconformity, may bring them into conflict with their environment. Distrust of themselves may result in self-denial and under-utilization of their talents, say Elaine LeVine and Margie Kitano in Chapter 22. They suggest existential therapy as a means to help gifted children reclaim their strengths and their giftedness. They outline this therapy in six stages: reduction of nihilism; recognition of problems and feelings; development of realistic alternatives for solving problems; acceptance of alienation; acceptance of autonomy and its consequences; and positive action and generalization of control. Through this process the child sees better how to apply new learning to everyday life and learns how to choose growth-oriented decision making in which he or she can take control.

In Chapter 23, Elizabeth Meckstroth advocates Dabrowski's theory as a means of understanding and nurturing gifted children. His theory of emotional development offers a framework for self-actualization and for adults to perceive their part in supporting a child's potential. Intensity, a characteristic of gifted children, is explained in terms of *overexcitabilities*, or heightened responses to stimuli and catalysts. The theory includes psychomotor, sensual, intellectual, imaginational, and emotional characteristics. Adults can enable young children to perceive which behaviors will work for and against them, so that they are less vulnerable and can become "their best selves." The author believes that a teacher's implementation of Dabrowski's theory would encourage and develop a more fulfilling curriculum for each child.

Philip Perrone distinguishes between social and psychological development in Chapter 24. Problems occur for gifted children when social achievement and psychological growth are incompatible. In other words, a gifted child's unusual need for self-actualization leads to behaviors that alienate him from the group. Perrone identifies four types of gifted students. Each personality type evidences unique patterns of behavior, requiring different responses from parents and teachers. Teachers and parents face the challenge of making learning not only a socializing but an actualizing experience.

In Chapter 25, LeoNora Cohen considers the significance of long-term interests in bright young children. Cohen asserts that these interests are often clustered around a few recurring motifs. Cohen has identified six major themes: control; nature-nurture; putting it all together; people-relationships; aesthetic-expressive; and symbols and symbol systems. She proposes suggestions for educators and parents who wish to facilitate the young child's interests. These are clustered around Six Simple Rules taken from *Educating Gifted Children* and applicable to all children: focus on the strengths and interests of each child; group by interest or ability at least part of the time; move as fast and as far in basic skills as possible; enrich individual interests; provide the tools for lifelong learning; and offer mediation and counseling from caring adults to optimize potential.

Focusing on the affective domain, Dorothy Knopper discusses characteristics that pose particular challenges for the bright young child in Chapter 26. She avers that psychological adjustment problems are not separate from giftedness. Parents live with stressful social and emotional aspects of giftedness every day. Sharing their insights with teachers can be more effective than reactive solutions to classroom crises.

As Patricia Hoelscher discusses in Chapter 27, the pediatrician also has a responsibility to the gifted population. Too often, pediatricians are not familiar enough with the characteristics and challenges of a gifted child to provide adequate counseling and make referrals. The child who has complained of chronic stomach problems ever since he started first grade but has no physiological disorder should be questioned regarding stress associated with giftedness. Unfortunately, this rarely happens. Reasons for this void in professional capacity may include the fact that courses in gifted are not required in medical school, as well as the prevailing myth that gifted children will make it on their own.

22

Helping Young Gifted Children Reclaim Their Strengths

Elaine S. LeVine
Margie K. Kitano

The growing literature on giftedness suggests that many gifted children possess unique social and emotional characteristics and needs. Many young gifted children are characterized by heightened social awareness, personal sensitivity, advanced moral reasoning, and perfectionistic tendencies (Tucker & LeVine, 1986). Some experience emotional problems associated with these traits. For example, their perfectionism and sensitivity can lead to low self-esteem. The heightened awareness may promote them to put others' needs and judgments before their own (Miller, 1979). Consequently, traits associated with their giftedness can be liabilities rather than strengths.

Although a number of authorities recommend supportive therapy for gifted children (e.g., Colangelo & Davis, 1991; Colangelo & Zaffrann, 1979; Delisle, 1985), little guidance has been offered in the way of specific therapeutic approaches. The present authors' work with gifted children (Kitano, 1986; LeVine, 1984) and the work of others in the field (Piechowski, 1979, 1991; Silverman, 1983) indicate that gifted children struggle with issues that can be considered largely existential in nature. Our approach for conducting therapy with the gifted is built on their previous work, which amplified existential approaches to child therapy (Kitano & LeVine, 1987).

The purpose of this chapter is to explore ways of assisting young, emotionally distressed gifted children reclaim their personal strengths, their giftedness, for their own and others' benefits. Toward this goal, personality traits associated with giftedness are reviewed. Emotional problems most characteristic of this population are also discussed. Finally, an existential framework for assisting these children is presented.

PERSONALITY CHARACTERISTICS OF THE GIFTED

Historically, gifted individuals have been considered especially vulnerable to mental illness (Andreasen, 1977; Lombroso, 1895). However, Terman's (1947) longitudinal study of intellectually gifted children dispelled the myth of mental instability by demonstrating that such children tend to be better adjusted than unselected peers and to maintain their superior adjustment over time. However, recent authors (e.g., Kaiser & Berndt, 1985; Whitmore, 1980) have challenged the view of the well-adjusted gifted individual as the "Terman myth," noting that although many gifted children tend to possess high self-concepts, some have serious self-doubts or high self-concepts only with respect to academic achievement.

Tucker and LeVine's (1986) review of literature on the affective traits of gifted children identified several commonly cited characteristics: hypersensitivity, heightened social awareness, perfectionism, and nonconformity.

HYPERSENSITIVITY AND HEIGHTENED SOCIAL AWARENESS

Gifted children appear to possess a heightened awareness of environmental phenomena, as observed in their ability to draw information from their surroundings. Cruickshank (cited in Whitmore, 1980) posited a neurological explanation, suggesting that supersensitivity of the nervous system creates intellectual giftedness by allowing assimilation of extraordinary amounts of sensory input. Dabrowski's (1964; Dabrowski & Piechowski, 1977) theory of positive disintegration also suggests that gifted individuals possess *overexcitabilities*, or extreme sensitivities in psychomotor, sensory, cognitive, imaginative, and emotional areas. These overexcitabilities render them susceptible to emotional disequilibrium. Possession of overexcitabilities is positive in that they permit intense experiencing of life events and can ultimately lead to high levels of emotional development. However, conflicts produced as a result of heightened sensitivity may generate extreme discomfort in children.

Whitmore (1980) noted that one effect of the gifted child's hypersensitivity is a keen perception of interpersonal relationships and group dynamics. Related to these traits may be a tendency for idealism and concern over social issues (Delisle, 1985). Gifted children tend to be more concerned about their role in the universe than average children (Rimm, 1993), are more likely to make altruistic wishes (Karnes & Wherry, 1981) and to worry about nuclear war (Clark & Hankins, 1985).

Perfectionism

Despite generally high scores on standardized self-concept measures (Kitano & Kirby, 1986), many gifted children manifest perfectionistic attitudes and related feelings of inadequacy and fear of failure (Strang, 1951; Whitmore, 1980). Kitano (1985) found that gifted preschool-age children often express desires to be "the best" as well as dissatisfaction with their personal performance. Gifted children's high expectations for themselves may be accompanied by high standards for others that affect their view of the world, how others perceive them, and interpersonal relationships.

Nonconformity

Creatively gifted individuals in particular tend to experience adjustment difficulties stemming from nonconforming attitudes. Reviews of literature (Getzels & Dillon, 1973; Lovecky, 1992) indicated that creative individuals can be characterized as holding high theoretical and aesthetic values and demonstrating self-sufficiency, stronger interest in ideas than people, disinterest in social activities, independence, lack of inhibition, low extraversion, resistance to group pressure, and high risk taking. Nonconformity may be manifested in independent thought and action. For example, Tucker and LeVine (1986) found that creative children are more willing than their other peers to stand up against those they can reason are unfair.

EMOTIONAL PROBLEMS OF GIFTED CHILDREN: AN EXISTENTIAL VIEW

Adjustment difficulties of gifted children can be perceived as stemming from an interaction between their affective traits of heightened sensitivity, perfectionism, and nonconformity and the surrounding environment. These adjustment problems include school-related concerns, such as lack of intellectual challenge; interpersonal conflicts with peers, parents, and siblings; and intrapersonal issues, such as self-esteem, identity, and personal contentment. Moustakas (1959) described existential sickness in children as rooted in rejection by others, leading to self-rejection and self-denial. The child gives up "the essence of his being and the unique patterns that distinguish him from every other person" (p. 3). In contrast, healthy behavior is authentic—spontaneous and expressive of the child's true feelings. Gifted children may be particularly prone to existential sickness. Their heightened sensitivity, perfectionism, and nonconformity often lead to conflict with the typical school environment, which presses to maintain the status quo. Frequent conflict with others leads to rejection, and, following Moustakas' thinking, self-rejection and self-denial.

Elsewhere we described the tenants of existential psychology and their application to child therapy (Kitano & LeVine, 1987). Briefly, existential psychology views the primary task of human beings as the creation of meaning in life through decision making. Within certain limits, individuals have broad powers of self-determination. All decisions essentially constitute a choice between the acceptance of the unfamiliar and challenging on the one hand and continuing the familiar and comfortable on the other. In short, decisions involve a commitment to growth or stagnation. Existential psychology attributes to individuals an awesome freedom and responsibility for self-determination while recognizing the pain entailed in consciously relinquishing security for growth.

The relatively limited attention to existential psychology in child therapy appears to rest on the assumption that children's freedom and responsibility are inhibited by their parents and powerful others. However, current understanding of child development reveals that basic assumptions for the application of existential theory are met. Current research on systems theory well emphasizes that when any member of a family, even a very young child, changes his or her behavior, the roles and behaviors of all other members change to establish a new homeostasis within the system (see Keeny & Ross, 1985).

A gifted child's presence alters normal family roles, for example, when the gifted child's adult-like ways are not congruent with parents' assumed style of discipline or when the parents feel added responsibility to provide the appropriate stimulation for the gifted child (Hackney, 1981). Within the limits imposed by significant others, children possess the freedom to make decisions, and hence can accept responsibility for much of their current circumstances.

CONDUCTING EXISTENTIAL THERAPY WITH CHILDREN

Kitano and LeVine (1987) identified six stages through which existential child therapy progresses. On referral, the child is living in an inauthentic way of relating. Early therapy focuses on reducing feelings of nihilism (meaninglessness) and on recognizing feelings and problems. Gradually, the child begins to learn more about authentic ways of being and develops more realistic alternatives to problems. Then the child is able to understand and to accept a certain degree of aloneness that is part of the human condition. Understanding these existential truths enables children to feel more autonomous within their environmental limits so that they will feel free and powerful enough to select positive actions and increase their control over their lives.

In the following sections, the guidelines for conducting existential child therapy are applied specifically to young gifted children. By reference to cases of gifted children, it is demonstrated that existential child therapy is particularly applicable to the gifted population because the goals of existential therapy and the stages of existential child therapy as identified by Kitano and LeVine (1987) are especially relevant to this population. More specifically, as mentioned earlier, gifted children are especially troubled by the need to do well and to combat feelings of meaninglessness, are searching for ways to feel good about their uniqueness or aloneness, and are highly motivated to be autonomous and impact their environments. To explicate the application of existential thought to therapy with gifted children, the six stages of existential child therapy are elaborated in more detail with particular reference to cases, goals, and techniques employed with gifted children.

Phase 1: Reduction of Nihilism

Nihilism is a term in existential thought that refers to a sense of meaninglessness catalyzed by denying what is important to oneself and defaulting on setting goals for personal growth. Inauthentic children enter therapy with a denial of their feelings and perceptions of reality, with the effect of their refusing to recognize the "problem."

Gifted children often receive criticism or even rejection from others who do not understand the nature of their giftedness, their unusual perceptions or creative thoughts. As a consequence, gifted children may internalize unrealistic or negative self-attributes about their thoughts and abilities. They may evidence nihilism, a denial of their own ideas and feelings, because of the lack of consensual validation by peers.

The goal of existential child therapy for gifted children at the primary stage is to reduce nihilism, to help gifted children identify and appreciate their uniqueness and to trust their own feelings and perceptions. Therapy at this initial stage requires establishment of an authentic relationship with the child. Communicating genuine acceptance, empathy, and respect creates a permissive atmosphere in which the child feels free to reclaim his or her perceptions and feelings. The therapist, through acceptance, encouragement, and direct communication, affirms the child's unique talents.

For example, 6-year-old Brian was referred by his teachers because they viewed him as immature, overly active, and often behaving and responding in ways that seemed irrelevant to the activities of his first-grade class. In the first existential child therapy session, Brian picked up a plastic object that was "supposed to be" a saddle for a horse and generated four alternative uses for it. "What is this?" he asked. Then he quickly answered, "It could be a boat; or if you turn it this way it might be a swing for the King; it looks like you would use it for a sling shot; I wonder if it's strong enough to be a lift?" The therapist queried, "What do you suppose others think it is, Brian?" "Just a saddle for a horse." A number of times in early sessions, the therapist helped Brian understand that his views were often different from others, but were valid views of reality. Through her interest and her words, she communicated, "You're a person with many good and unusual ideas."

The therapist also encouraged Brian's parents to validate Brian's views. They helped him to understand that many of his thoughts were unusual but contributed a new and meaningful way of analysis. One day in therapy Brian announced, "Nobody else thinks like me, but that's okay. I try not to bother them with my ways and I think I do a pretty good job of that." Brian became increasingly more accepting of his ways. Secure in himself, he had less need to make others notice him, although his products continued to be quite unique.

Phase 2: Recognition of Problems and Feelings

Within the supportive therapy environment, the child begins to acknowledge his or her problems and feelings associated with these problems. It has been mentioned that gifted children are often hypervigilant to the environmental stimuli and empathic with others. They have a tendency to feel responsible for solving others' problems and relieving emotional distress. In addition, gifted children are often the object of other children's ridicule or rejection. In each of these cases, gifted children need to recognize and discriminate their problems and feelings from those of others. In phase 2 of existential child therapy, gifted children begin to understand that although their attributes and behaviors may engender certain feelings in others, they should not feel bad about their giftedness. One daycare worker for Marshall, a gifted 3-year-old, recommended therapy because the child often commented that no one liked him. The daycare worker had observed that he was increasingly isolating himself from others. For example, Marshall was upset about an intense verbal conflict with his peer, Steve. While playing dinosaurs, Marshall commented to his friend that dinosaurs had once existed and were now extinct. His friend disagreed because he could accept only the alternatives that dinosaurs were fantasy creatures or that they presently existed; but he could not simultaneously comprehend that they had been real and did not now exist. At one point in the altercation the daycare worker reported that Steve left to play with another more "reasonable" peer. Marshall was visibly upset and retreated to a corner of the room. When the mother brought Marshall to the therapist, she added that her son had stated that he felt something must be wrong with him because the other children got mad at him a lot.

In therapy, Marshall was first helped to feel proud of his deeper understanding. Then he was helped to see that he was not responsible for others' frustrations. These understandings were directly discussed with Marshall and also expressed through play material. For example, in a puppet show created by Marshall and his therapist, a fox and a field mouse become good friends. In this show, the fox was always getting frustrated because he could not outsmart his friend, the field mouse. One time the two of them got locked in a shed. The fox had a good idea, but one that only the mouse could implement. He showed the mouse how he could crawl through a little hole and unlock the door from the other side. Gradually Marshall learned to recognize that he should be proud of his understandings and that his friend's frustrations did not mean that he, Marshall, had done something wrong.

In phase 2, the child further begins to learn about his or her own "throwness," that is, existential limits. Through frank discussions, the therapist helps the gifted child learn that he or she can care about others but cannot live for or resolve their difficulties. For example, 7-year-old Johna was brought to therapy by her parents because of chronic insomnia. Johna explained that she could not sleep at night because she was so worried—worried if her sister would be happy at camp, and why her mother looked so tired, and if her parents' friends were all right since their daughter's illness was diagnosed. In each case Johna felt responsible for aiding the other. Gradually Johna was helped to identify her own feelings about others; to express her feelings, concerns, and suggestions directly to others; and to learn to have confidence that others could and wanted to master their own lives just as she could gain control over hers.

Phase 3: Development of Realistic Alternatives for Problem Solution

In phase 3 the child is assisted in perceiving his or her role in the problem situation. The therapist emphasizes the positive aspects of accepting personal responsibility. If gifted children learn to focus on implementing their own deep thinking, they can change their own lives and perhaps have a constructive impact on the world.

As the child learns to express authentic feelings, he or she may experience emotions ranging from relief and hope to guilt and despair. Initially, the child's ideas for problem solution may be unrealistic and ineffective. For example, gifted children may consider hiding their abilities to gain acceptance or criticizing their peers as a way of gaining control over the rejector-rejectee relationship. In addition, gifted children often hold self-blaming attributes about their unique views and products and may become passive, refusing to produce anything and thereby defaulting on their abilities.

Having established a firm, trusting relationship, the therapist may use confrontation to help the child face reality. The therapist counteracts unrealistic or nonadaptive tendencies by encouraging gifted children to view their capacities as gifts that should not be wasted. The therapist emphasizes that they have a responsibility to share their gifts with those who are less endowed. In phase 3 of development of realistic alternatives, the therapist encourages gifted clients to identify socially valuable and constructive ways to use their talents. The precise avenue for implementation will depend on the child's particular talent and previous ways of defaulting on that talent.

For example, Jenny was a bright youngster who began reading at age 4. Her mother reported that when she took her as a preschooler to the library Jenny would stroll away from the children's books and glance through the science section for books on outer space. She reported being bored in kindergarten and by first grade refused to participate in class activities. By second grade she not only was refusing to participate, but was reading science fiction books all day by hiding them in her desk. In therapy, it was suggested to Jenny that she was defaulting on her gift by not sharing her scientific wisdom and instead succumbing to passive self-absorption. Jenny was pressed to give some science lessons to the class. After several presentations, she expressed some satisfaction. "I didn't want to do that, but it was fun to help." Soon she became an active member of the class again.

Therefore, in phase 3 the therapist continues to be accepting and empathic of the gifted child's feelings, but guides the child toward recognition of his or her ability to change the situation. In Jenny's case, options include finding more compatible associates and learning to appreciate her gifts and to accept the limits of her peers. An unaccepting alternative is hiding her intellectual acumen. This option is incompatible with the phase 1 goal of self-acceptance.

Phase 4: Acceptance of Alienation

The child's growing recognition of responsibility leads to feelings of vulnerability and isolation—the realization that significant others are separate from the self and cannot by totally responsible for the child's circumstances. Rather than rescuing the child by denying his or her sense of alienation, the therapist seeks to help the child accept aloneness as a natural condition of life. While empathically reflecting the child's feelings, the therapist also helps the child view isolation as a challenge that can be managed. Existential therapy thus emphasizes rather than minimizes an individual's ultimate separation from others.

For gifted children, existential alienation has two facets. Like all their peers, gifted children must confront issues of their existential aloneness in the sense of being separate from all others. In addition, their high intelligence, creativity, and concomitant affective characteristics render them alone in the sense of being misunderstood. Acceptance of alienation for the gifted can be defined in terms of a constant dilemma. They must select between two imperfect alternatives: (a) to gain acceptance through conformity and hence to deny their own beliefs; or (b) to preserve their principles and face rejection by their peers. The therapist helps gifted children recognize and accept that a cost of their gift is a degree of social marginality. Society pressures them to conform, whereas their own sensitivity, perfectionism, and differing views push against the status quo.

By way of illustration, 8-year-old Antonio was brought to therapy by his mother for recent academic failure and increasing social isolation. Early in therapy, Antonio revealed that he found great enjoyment in artistic pursuits but was nearly incapacitated by feelings of guilt and inadequacy over his failure to please his father. Antonio had joined a Little League baseball team under pressure from his father, who openly communicated concern about his son's masculinity. Antonio was also trying to participate in the activities of the neighborhood boys but abhorred his peers' interest in forming rival "clubs" and finding reasons to test each others' physical prowess. Antonio's father berated him for his lack of courage, with statements such as, "Boys aren't supposed to be sensitive."

As a result, Antonio began to see himself as different from other boys and to internalize doubts about himself, especially about his interest in visual arts and concern for fair treatment of other human beings. Antonio was torn between his desire and duty to please his father and his personal values and interests. He admitted that his failing grades served to give him some control over his own life. When Antonio learned to accept a degree of difference from his father, he no longer had to be autonomous in inauthentic ways (for example, failing grades). With recognition of his difference from his father and his father's expectations, Antonio became more spontaneous, happy, and productive. However, he did suffer a feeling of loss in being different from what his father wanted.

Phase 5: Acceptance of Autonomy and Its Consequences

In phase 5 the child recognizes his or her responsibility for making choices to solve the immediate problem but vacillates between comfortable (stagnating) and unfamiliar (growth) alternatives. The child may try out new, positive ways of behaving but revert back to original modes. The therapist guides the child toward growth-oriented choices and helps the child accept anxiety as a natural corollary of growth. The therapist works toward understanding of the logical consequences of each choice and the advantages of growth-oriented decisions. The therapist does not choose for the child, but accepts the child's decisions and the child's responsibility for the consequences. Therefore, existential therapists do not claim to be value-free, but guide the child toward the difficult, challenging alternatives. The child must make the final decisions regarding his or her behavior and accept the consequences.

Selection and implementation of growth alternatives cause anxiety about the unfamiliar and unknown, even as they lead to growth. For the gifted, the consequences of social marginality and nonconformity may be so extreme, so punitive, that many situations may require a decision to compromise. In language the child can understand, the therapist should help the child recognize that a certain degree of social marginality is adaptive and probably a necessary concomitant of one's intelligence and creativity. However, extreme inner-directedness and consequent loneliness can be debilitating. For example, in the case with Marshall discussed previously, when he complained about his friend not understanding him the therapist made the following comment: "You sure do know a lot about dinosaurs, but does Johnny have to understand to be your friend? Maybe you could use your good thinking to figure out what you both know about and would like to do."

Gifted children must learn to recognize the point at which loneliness and anxiety become so overwhelming that overall functioning is impeded. At that point, the child must compromise and sufficiently adapt to the social matrix. In such cases, the therapist helps the gifted child to trust his or her own perceptions about when compromise is the best alternative: when alienation becomes overpowering and a need exists to set aside personal values and choose relatedness.

For example, the present therapists have noted that a number of gifted child clients tend to dress quite unusually. Their garb may have an artistic flair, be representative of their favorite era (when Dickens wrote or when airplanes were invented), or simply be a way of expressing their unconventionality. One gifted Hispanic 7-year-old, Reymundo, was basically quiet and unassuming. However, he liked to dress like mythological superheroes, especially Aramis, one of the "Three Musketeers." The children repeatedly ripped his cloak off of him and stomped on it. Some of his Hispanic peers seemed particularly uncomfortable with his dress, as they seemed to view his behavior as a disavowal of the present ways of demonstrating ethnic identification. One child commented, "Why don't you act like you're supposed to, like your brothers?" Reymundo and his therapist discussed whether his unusual dress was worthy of the harassment he received. Reymundo was proud of being Hispanic, so he decided to modify his dress somewhat so that others would know his deeper feelings and so that he would have the energy and confidence to express his unique and important ideas in other realms.

Phase 6: Positive Action and Generalization of Control

This last phase is characterized by simultaneous change in several aspects of the child's life. The goal is for the child to take control over his or her life by making growth-oriented decisions, implementing these decisions, and generalizing these behaviors to a variety of situations. The therapist continues to emphasize the connection between the child's decisions and behaviors and others' responses, applying the connection to different areas of the child's life: with peers, parents, siblings. The therapist also encourages the child to recognize limits outside the child's control. For gifted children, positive action and generalization of control necessarily imply responsibility to assume a leadership role in improving social welfare.

Jenny, the science prodigy who became isolated in second grade, continued to experience more success in her classes through third and fourth grade by leading her peers in scientific projects. However, new problems emerged in fifth grade when many of her girlfriends became extremely interested in their physical appearance and in boys. "Boys think you're too egghead," explained one friend. Another friend's comments were extremely painful to Jenny. "I'd like to spend more time with you, Jenny, but the guys might think I'm smart like you and they think that's `dorky.'" Jenny requested sessions with the therapist again. Due to her giftedness, she was able to remember much of what she had learned in her previous therapy but did have some difficulty applying those understandings to her new dilemma. With the therapist's support, she decided that the best way to handle this problem was to be a leader in her school in a different way; she organized a club of boys and girls who were high achievers in school. With the support of the principal and teachers, her group developed a school newspaper that was very clever and became quite popular among all fifth graders. Soon Jenny and her newspaper coeditors were viewed as more desirable. Taking action with her giftedness reduced her feelings of marginality and increased her feelings of control of her life.

As with other therapeutic approaches, a major goal of existential therapy concerns application of new learning to everyday life. "If the environment is partially negative, then a strong developmental potential can overcome it, although not totally" (Piechowski, 1991, p. 298). Existential therapy can enhance the developmental potential. The focus of existential therapy is on choosing growth-engendering alternatives and in recognizing both possibilities and limits in effecting change.

REFERENCES

Andreasen, N. C. (1977). Creativity and psychiatric illness. *Psychiatric Annals, 8*(3), 23-45.

Clark, W. H., and Hankins, N.E. (1985). Giftedness and conflict. *Roeper Review, 8*(1), 50-53.

Colangelo, N., & Davis, G. A. (Eds.). (1991). *Handbook of gifted education.* Boston: Allyn & Bacon.

Colangelo, N., & Zaffrann, R. T. (1979). *New voices in counseling the gifted.* Dubuque, IA: Kendall/Hunt.

Dabrowski, K. (1964). *Positive disintegration.* Boston: Little, Brown.

Dabrowski, K., & Piechowski, M. M. (1977). *Theory of levels of emotional development* (Vols. I and II). Oceanside, NY: Dabor Science.

Delisle, J. R. (1985). Counseling gifted persons: A lifelong concern. *Roeper Review, 8*(1), Special issue.

Getzels, J. W., & Dillon, J. T. (1973). The nature of giftedness and the education of the gifted. In R. M. W. Travers (Ed.), *Second handbook of research on teaching* (pp. 689-731). Chicago: Rand McNally.

Hackney, H. (1981). The gifted child, the family, and the school. *Gifted Child Quarterly, 25*, 51-54.

Kaiser, C., & Berndt, D. (1985). Predictors of loneliness in the gifted adolescent. *Gifted Child Quarterly, 29*(2), 74-77.

Karnes, F., & Wherry, J. (1981). Wishes of fourth- through seventh-grade gifted students. *Psychology in the Schools, 18*, 235-239.

Keeny, B. P., & Ross, J. M. (1985). *Constructing systematic family therapies.* New York: Basic Books.

Kitano, M. K. (1986). Counseling gifted preschoolers. *Gifted Child Today, 9*(4), 20-25.

Kitano, M. K. (1985). Ethnography of a preschool for the gifted: What gifted children actually do. *Gifted Child Quarterly, 29*, 67-71.

Kitano, M. K., & Kirby, D. F. (1986). *Gifted education: A comprehensive view.* Boston: Little, Brown.

Kitano, M. K., & LeVine, E. (1987). Existential theory: Guidelines for practice in child therapy. *Psychotherapy: Theory, Research and Practice, 24*, 404-413.

LeVine, E. (1984). The challenge of creative children: Implementing their divergency in the service of therapy. *Psychotherapy: Theory, Research and Practice, 21*, 31-38.

Lombroso, C. (1895). *The man of genius.* London: Scribner's.

Lovecky, D. V. (1992). Exploring social and emotional aspects of giftedness in children. *Roeper Review, 15*, 18-25.

Miller, A. (1979). *Prisoners of childhood: The drama of the gifted and search for the true self.* New York: Basic Books.

Moustakas, C. E. (1959). *Psychotherapy with children.* New York: Harper & Row.

Piechowski, M. M. (1979). Developmental potential. In N. Colangelo & R. T. Zaffrann (Eds.), *New voices in counseling the gifted* (pp. 25-57). Dubuque, IA: Kendall/Hunt.

Piechowski, M. M. (1991). Emotional development and emotional giftedness. In N. Colangelo & G. A. Davis (Eds.), *Handbook of gifted education.* Needham Heights, MA: Allyn & Bacon.

Rimm, S. (1993). Gifted kids have feelings too. *Gifted Child Today, 16*, 20-24.

Silverman, L. K. (1983). Issues in affective development of the gifted. In J. Van Tassel-Baska (Ed.), *A practical guide to counseling the gifted in a school setting* (pp. 6-21). Reston, VA: Council for Exceptional Children

Strang, R. (1951). Mental hygiene of gifted children. In P. A. Witty (Ed.), *The gifted child.* Boston: D. C. Heath.

Terman, L. M., & Oden, M. H. (1947). *The gifted child grows up. Genetic studies of genius* (Vol. IV). Stanford, CA: Stanford University Press.

Tucker, S., & LeVine, E. (1986). Emotional needs of the gifted: A preliminary, phenomenological view. *Creative Child and Adult Quarterly, 11*, 156-165.

Whitmore, J. R. (1980). *Giftedness, conflict, and underachievement.* Boston: Allyn & Bacon.

23

Complexities of Giftedness: Dabrowski's Theory

Elizabeth A. Meckstroth

Some of us say that gifted children are like other children, but more so. They overreact, they're too sensitive, hyperactive, in their own world, perfectionistic, weird, idealistic, and just make too much out of things.

Diversity defines gifted children. They differ from each other more than they resemble each other. Any quality we might choose to describe one gifted child, the opposite will define another. Children with the same IQ will have different interests, personalities, abilities, and temperaments. Gifted children are intricate, contradicting, complex; and the brain that drives them intensifies everything they do. Intensity gives energy to intelligence and abilities.

Dabrowski's theory of development is gaining recognition and appreciation among people who want to understand and nurture gifted children (see Dabrowski & Piechowski, 1977; Piechowski, 1979). Kazimierz Dabrowski (1902-1980) was a Polish psychiatrist/psychologist who studied the lives of highly self-actualized people to learn more about their development. He examined the lives of the world's great moral leaders. artists, and scientists. Dabrowski searched for insights into how the development of accomplished, highly moral people differed from most others. He found that these unusual people had intense experiences of their life encounters that led them to create their own ways of coping and living (Grant, 1992). This chapter focuses on the part of Dabrowski's developmental theory that describes *overexcitabilities*. Dabrowski's theory explains why some people cannot see or feel things the way others do. This model, known as Dabrowski's Theory of Emotional Development, and his concept of overexcitabilities is a framework for self-efficacy and actualizing a child's potential.

Gifted children can be exhausting, demanding, perplexing enigmas. They are not normal in many ways and very few mental health professionals have any training in meeting their particular emotional needs.

Intensity is a characteristic of gifted children. Dabrowski explained this intensity in terms of overexcitabilities and a greater capacity to respond to stimuli. A person's overexcitability permeates their existence. An overexcitability orients and focuses us. Like a plant turns toward light, our overexcitability draws out our thoughts and behaviors. An overexcitability is a temperamental disposition toward a class of stimuli—what we notice and how we respond. An overexcitability is a lens that opens and widens and deepens our perspective.

An analogy may be drawn between people's overexcitabilities and television hook ups. Most of us are wired to receive five channels. Others come equipped with cable. Some have a satellite dish. They receive and respond to signals of whose existence people are not aware.

PSYCHOMOTOR

The *psychomotor* overexcitability has been found to be the one of Dabrowski's classifications that is the most significantly correlated with high intelligence (Ackerman, 1993). There appears to be a consensus that gifted children characteristically exhibit a high energy level. In the "Preschool Years" chapter of *Your Gifted Child*, "has a high energy level, needing less sleep than age mates" is listed as a characteristic behavior (Smutny, Veenker, & Veenker, 1990, p. 37). In *Gifted Children, A Guide for Parents and Teachers*, Virginia Ehrlich (1985) characterized the gifted child: "Is energetic and active; occasionally may be mislabeled 'hyperactive,' especially during early years; enjoys athletic games and excels in athletic activities" (p. 27).

What are some of the behaviors that characteristically exhibit psychomotor overexcitability? These children can appear very busy and restless. As infants, they require less sleep than normal for babies

(Munger, 1990; Schetky; 198). In young gifted children we hear rapid, seemingly excessive, almost compulsive speech. They can explain things until you beg them to stop! They may gesture with their entire body, much beyond punctuating hand gestures. Some gifted children have a voracious appetite for activity; they're always moving— "antsy."

This concept of psychomotor overexcitability has extensive implications for parents and teachers. When McCallister (personal communication, October 11, 1991) was conducting a gifted program for 3- to 5-year-old children, part of the 3-hour sessions was scheduled during the other children's rest period!

It is essential that parents and school personnel aim to integrate gifted children's often intense, highly active physical needs. We might think that gifted children are too precious to waste their time with sports and other "dumb jock" activities. They may even be persuaded to avoid physical activities, especially when the child's intellectual peers are older and more physically developed. In these situations, brighter children may feel physically inadequate and avoid playground games that demonstrate their relatively inferior psychomotor development. This is particularly devastating to children with psychomotor overexcitability: every cell in their body wants to participate, their bright mind imagines a high standard of performance, but their fragile pride may restrict their experience.

Often, preschool and other early childhood school experiences focus on "socializing" beginning students. "Rugtime" or circle time can become excruciatingly constricting to small bodies urging to move about. Sometimes, with gifted students who have a great deal of psychomotor overexcitability, rugtime compliance becomes an educational goal. Paradoxically, encouraging these children to move about— as long as others are not disrupted— can facilitate their learning.

We almost need to use a martial arts approach to work *with* the high energy of these young children. It is likely that these high energy children are not deliberately trying to irritate us; they were born in overdrive! Although we might like to be in control of their energy expression, the wish is futile. Rather than resisting and fighting it, we can plan for their need to be more on the move than most other children and attempt to harness it in constructive ways. They don't have to sit down to read; let them stand up. They can quietly twiddle with some plaything to release energy while they are listening in a group. Many young, "wired" children have found that martial arts lessons offer an attractive merge of focused mental concentration, body control training, and energy release. If children with psychomotor overexcitability are not expected and encouraged to move, they may be on a collision course.

Another helpful strategy to allow these children to appropriately participate in daily routines and requirements is to teach them relaxation techniques. Some parents have found audiotaped music and messages particularly calming. If impulsiveness interferes with performance, halting or quieting techniques (take a deep breath; count to 10; smile) can gently intercede and promote self-monitoring and control. It is sometimes difficult for children with abundant physical energy to shut down at the end of the day. To ease into bedtime, it may be helpful to do more calming activities in the evening.

One caution about the psychomotor overexcitability in girls: There is a long, strong social history that boys will be boys, and that girls will be compliant. It is damaging to expect that girls should be more sedate than boys. Adults should not deceive girls to betray their strengths, but allow them to be as dynamic as boys.

Parents of young gifted children will often admit that it is exhausting to keep pace with them. I've heard, "I know what David needs, he needs a new family; there just isn't enough of me to go around." "My husband and I have decided that we will just have to cancel our lives for the next 6 years to have enough energy just to keep up with our kids." Parents need to give themselves permission to "put their own oxygen mask on first" so that they can be satisfied with their own lives and model for their children that it is good to grow up. If parents do not demonstrate that they have needs and voice how they are meeting their own needs, they miss modeling personal integrity.

SENSUAL

Sensual overexcitability gives children a heightened experience of seeing, smelling, tasting, touching, and hearing. They seek pleasures of sensing and can attribute huge reactions to sensory experiences. Smells, sounds, and tastes are more pungent to them. They have an avid aesthetic appreciation. Some children simply experience their body differently. They are more aware of how elements in the environment impact how they feel. Deidre Lovecky's (1986) article about gifted adults, "Can You Hear the Flowers Singing?" portrays such heightened experiences of people with sensual overexcitability.

It is as if these children see through a different set of glasses than most of their age peers. Some of these exceptional children view the world through a microscope as compared with normal vision. They sometimes see what others cannot even imagine (Webb, Meckstroth, & Tolan, 1982). They catch details, are drawn to the beauty of a glistening drop of fat floating across a cup of bullion; love color as an entity that they can hear, feel, smell. They also may read other's almost imperceptible body messages that can be incongruent with what they hear. This can create stressful confusion about how to respond.

These children can have intense reactions to certain odors: They just love to smell tar or refuse to go into a bathroom for an hour after someone else has used it. The fragrance of fire burning can completely captivate them so that they have mentally separated from the surrounding group and entered another realm.

Some hunger for certain music and can listen to *Scheherazade* until they are exhausted. Others can gain real comfort from hearing gravel crunch under foot. Some sounds become excruciatingly invasive to these children. They may have extreme reactions to the smack of gum chewing or the general din in the cafeteria. Children may have trouble filtering out background sounds and are equally aware of distant traffic sounds as the voice on the radio.

My clinical and general experience with families of gifted children suggests that many are "picky eaters." Some eat no "mushy" vegetables, others only pizza, bread, and peanut butter. Perhaps their intense sense of taste inhibits savoring a large range of flavors.

Maybe a low threshold of sensing touch is most apparent in families with sensual overexcitability. Whenever I address an audience of parents of gifted children and mention that some of these children insist that tags be cut from the back neck of shirts, or that seams at the toe of socks almost paralyze them, parents gasp, groan, and laugh in recognition! Elastic at wrists and ankles can become a tortuous bind. Almost any clothing may irritate their skin so that they prefer to be bare.

There is an informal consensus that often gifted children feel warmer than conscientious mothers suspect that they could be. They leave for school with jackets unbuttoned, won't wear sweaters during the winter, and insist on short sleeves during cold weather.

In addition, these same children may choose sensual expression of emotional tension. They just can't function until their socks are changed or turned inside out. If they are sad, they may try to comfort themselves with food. Some choose sensory pleasures such as comforting themselves by stroking the cat.

It may be soothing to adults to let go of the notion that these overexcitable children are just being ornery, manipulative, and know how to control our life by their exaggerated complaints. In many ways, they are more tender and permeable than we may be. Although it is not in our realm of reality to have such outrageous reactions, for them, these perceptions are real.

We can help these children develop a range of options to cope with whatever annoys them, and we can encourage them to seek what gives them pleasure. Let them be responsible for adjusting their responses and environment as much as is appropriate. Our goal as parents and teachers is to work ourselves out of a job, to promote self-efficacy. Rather than rescuing these children, we can become ingenious in encouraging them to be effective managers of their selves.

INTELLECTUAL

Exploring intellectual overexcitability is essential in understanding Dabrowski's (Piechowski, 1979) developmental theory and in supporting young gifted children. Children with intellectual overexcitability have a voracious appetite and capacity for intellectual effort and stimulation. Identification of intellectual overexcitability can almost be done by asking, "Does she go to bed with a flashlight under the covers?"

Their mental activity is intensified and accelerated. This urges them to relentlessly probe the unknown. They are riveted with curiosity and persist at problem solving. The "why" questions sometime become annoying to parents and teachers and even may be interpreted as offensive and manipulative, rather than as sincere inquiry. They often are avid readers, are intrigued in introspection, and their thinking may be theoretical.

If they seem to daydream, they may be filling a void with their own intellectual work. The complex mental projects that these children construct for themselves can become actual projects to which they are devoted. They may be constructing elaborate exercise techniques for their gerbil, calculating the number of steps they need to walk to the bus or ranking the values of gems that they will someday own.

Our intellectually overexcitable gifted children are already aware of what is unknown to most of their classmates. The U.S. Department of Education's (1993) report, *National Excellence: The Case for Developing America's Talent*, acknowledged, "Gifted and talented elementary school students have mastered from 35 to 50 percent of the curriculum to be offered in the five basic subjects before they begin the school year" (p. 2). Acknowledging these children's intellectual capabilities has enormous implications for these children, their families and society.

It is evident that intellectually overexcitable, gifted children require intellectually substantial fuel to maintain optimum cognitive and emotional running order. What happens if you fill a Lamborghini with cheap gas or allot 1,000 calories per day at the training table? These nourishments may be more than enough for some people, although they would leave others starving.

In a classroom, intellectually overexcitable children can be exhausting and challenging to a teacher who may have trouble keeping up with them. Such cognitive complexity can enable these children to claim alternative viewpoints. Original thought can ensue from so much intellectual practice. This may often be received as criticism by those whose life experience does not include the range of knowledge that these highly intellectual children soon acquire. These children's divergent thinking abilities may lead them to hold concurrently a range of opinions about a single idea. For this reason, true-false and multiple-choice test items can be a perplexing dilemma for them.

Some of this avid intellectual activity may lead to acquiring stringent standards for monitoring their own performance. In their minds they have conceptualized how something should be. Sometimes teachers and parents then assign a somewhat pathological diagnoses on these children who attempt to work out the intricacies of their inner ideal—*perfectionist* or *picky*. These children may be continually striving to know and to actualize their evolving truths. For them, it just makes sense to synthesize their inner knowledge and their physical world.

The field of gifted education is replete with means to accommodate children's intellectual needs. A child's intellectual overexcitability signals a need for more supportive response from parents and teachers: Some direction comes from recognizing that, for these children, their intellect can become their comfort zone. In their little lives they have been recognized and rewarded for displaying how much they *know*. Highly intelligent children are particularly vulnerable to serving some of their parents' ego needs by vicariously accomplishing what reflects pride for these well-meaning parents (Miller, 1981).

Perhaps readers will recognize someone who reverts to their thinking, cognitive functioning when experiencing intense emotional entanglements or has an opportunity for aesthetic pleasure. Adults need to help these children integrate their intellectual function with the other aspects of their lives, not allow their intellect to run them. For this, Clark's (1986, 1992) books offer excellent suggestions.

IMAGINATIONAL

Implications for parents and teachers are based in recognizing that these children assume that other people also share their reality—because it is the only reality that they have ever known. Children with heightened imagination expect that other children and adults are as intensely concerned about the same thoughts that fill their own consciousness, and would be surprised to learn that other children and adults see and know some things differently. Parents and teachers can help young children discern between what they imagine and what actually happens.

If you suspect that a child is describing some event from his imaginings as if it were actual experience, you might help him discern the difference. This can usually be accomplished with gentle questions. Whatever the imaginary events might be, the accompanying feelings are real. Accepting the child's feelings, whatever the source, can keep trust in place between the two of you. This child might feel safe enough to reveal some of her elaborate thoughts to you again. Perhaps some readers remember how painful it was to be chastised for expressing something you cared about by being told, "Oh! it's all in your head!"

Parents and teachers can enjoy and encourage children to use their imaginations as a best friend. Imagination is a safe place to self-rehearse and to mentally try out new experiences and anticipate consequences. One of the strategies to help children tame their brain is to help them to consider their mind and behavior as instruments they can regulate. They can evaluate if their thoughts are working for them or against them. It might be helpful if children with heightened imaginations would, again, compare their minds to television sets. First, they need to become aware that they always have pictures and a voice in their head. Then, they can consider if the words and pictures are helpful or not. Here, they can use their consciousness to "switch channels" if they want to direct another program to come into view! Some simple biofeedback techniques might empower children to use their thoughts to help themselves.

These children can imagine so many tantalizing possibilities and then impose infinite tasks on themselves in an attempt to actualize what they suppose. Problem-solving techniques are especially helpful. Maybe the most potent way to teach this is to verbally explain your own thinking process as you proceed to prioritize and problem solve. Helping children prioritize activities and become aware of time management is essential. It takes only moments to think of what they want to do. They may need help translating these actions into chronological time.

All time with our children is quality time. Indulge in enjoying and appreciating the privilege of being with children who think, see, and feel differently from the way we do. These children lavish more life on us. We can let them expand—even explode—our reality. They invite us to share their awesome, wondrous world. Probably, only if they feel that we appreciate and admire them, will they trust us and reveal some of their extraordinary visions and sensitivities.

EMOTIONAL

In the early history of gifted education, few leaders recognized the special emotional attributes and ensuing counseling needs of gifted children. Generally, mental health professionals were not considered an integral part of gifted education (Colangelo, 1991). More recently, however, the emotional intensity of gifted children has been widely acknowledged.

Among Dabrowski's categories, the expressions of emotional overexcitability are the most extensive (Piechowski, 1979). Intense feelings manifest themselves in extreme, complex, positive, and negative ways. These children seem to have extra emotional antennae, to be permeable by feelings and impacted by emotions. It is as if everything gets inside of them and they feel it. They are much more emotionally endowed.

Such endowment is often regarded as maladjustment and an interference with productive, rational life. However, emotional overexcitability can be recognized as a form of giftedness, a finely tuned awareness. For Dabrowski, emotional overexcitability is the most important aspect of human development. It is a significant, logical component of developing a person's potential. Emotions can keep people in touch with themselves and their own needs for change. Conversely, low emotional excitability seriously curtails people from developing their potential (Piechowski, 1979).

Emotional overexcitability exists in a myriad of ways: To define emotional overexcitability in language is like depicting the Grand Canyon with a set of Tinker Toys. Emotional overexcitability is depth and breadth of feeling, an intense emotional response to the most minute nuance of meaning. It becomes an apology to the fallen leaves that remain ungathered for the first grader's leaf collection to be ironed between wax paper.

These intensely emotional children may be bearing enormous loads of feelings that accumulate from fears, concern about death, anxieties, love, loneliness, deep caring for others, and excruciating self-scrutiny. They are exhilarated in joy and affection, and also know compassion encompassing ecstasy and despair. When they are joyous, their radiance lights up the whole house! When they are disappointed, the weight of the world is on their shoulders.

Their feelings can be complex, ambivalent. They can simultaneously experience an entire range of contradictive reactions. They may be riveted in an approach-avoidance dilemma. Sometimes emotional overexcitability inhibits children. They feel so much that they are almost paralyzed to act for fear that they might act wrongly or get a negative reaction from someone.

Relationships are extremely important to these children, although their most significant emotional attachments may not be with their age peers. Adults may be concerned that the emotionally sensitive child has no friends. Perhaps he has reverted to find emotional connections among younger children.

Emotionally overexcitable children tend to absorb and respond to the feelings of others. Sara came home from second grade and told her mother that she hated math. Her mom reminded her that she was doing very well in math. Sara explained that the other kids were having trouble learning it. Much of the time, emotionally sensitive children are protective and considerate of their peers' feelings. Sometimes they cannot conceive the idea that other children just do not feel what they feel. Shirley, age 5, explained to her mother, "I understand other children better than they understand me." These emotionally astute children are perplexed about wondering how other children can be so inconsiderate.

These children tend to personalize their world and attribute other people's behaviors to intentional meanness towards them. They may wonder why they are disliked. If Sean doesn't like the way his eggs are cooked in the morning, he'll complain: "You people treat me like trash."

Emotional overexcitability extends to somatic expressions. Often children cannot find the words they need to describe what they are feeling. Perhaps they have not yet learned how their deep feelings represent responses to what they are experiencing. Their little bodies can take over and quiver, or beg for comforting through headaches, stomachaches, and rashes.

Adults who care about these children can be the safe haven where young ones can express their deep feelings. *Listen to them with your entire body, mind, and spirit as if nothing else at that moment matters as much as this child's thoughts and feelings.* Listening conveys that what they have to say is important, and thus you build the self-esteem and respect required for them to actualize some of the intricate wonders they feel and know. Careful listening can be a lifeline in a world where others do not take them seriously, which can lead to not trusting themselves. Careful listening can convince children that there is someone who thinks that they are valuable and worth understanding. Your listening creates courage, understanding and trust for children to eventually be their own source of power, possibility, and safety.

Respond to their feelings; affirm their feelings. Help them label their feelings. If a child can identify their feelings, they then can doing something about what their feelings are telling them. Proactive listening with critical care is especially worthwhile with gifted children because most of them are essentially introverts (Silverman, 1988). That is, they tend to protect their very vulnerable feelings inside themselves. What they reveal may not nearly be as significant as what they guard within. Adults also can help children distinguish between their feelings and their behaviors: Thinking and feeling does not mean doing.

It is unfair to allow children to perpetuate socially inappropriate behaviors. They are harmed if they do not learn what behaviors will work for them and against them. What good is it to be highly skilled and talented if other people want to close you out?

Being emotionally overexcitable can be particularly devastating for boys. At an early age, they may wonder about their masculinity. These boys, as well as girls, can benefit if they are reminded that their being so sensitive is a precious, rare quality that may not always be appreciated by many others.

EPILOGUE

Overexcitable children live intensely. They "overreact." They "make too much" out of things. Many gifted children have keen memories and may respond to the huge amount of past learning and experience that is presently conscious. Therefore, what may be obscure to others may have significant meaning to them.

Because of gifted children's uneven development, their cognitive and emotional intensity and complexity renders them discrepant in some ways from their chronological peers. Thus they have less available emotional support from these age mates. Their behaviors can become increasingly apparent and set them apart from the rest of the classroom. The class group can also be cruel to the child who does not fit in. The young child who is in a chronic state of overexcitability begins to question, "What's wrong with me?" Therefore, teachers, parents, and counselors need to become even more protective and supportive of these more emotionally vulnerable, precocious children. Sometimes, well-meaning educators and other professionals search for applicable psychological labels in order to better understand these "deviant" children.

In a self-contained classroom for children with IQs of 140 and above, all but one boy was referred for attention deficit disorder (ADD) evaluation by the teacher! Sometimes gifted children, especially those with psychomotor overexcitability, can be confused with the pathological diagnosis of ADD or hyperactivity (Lind, 1993).

There are conditions that exacerbate overexcitabilities and interfere with enlisting a child's abilities to facilitate their lives such as high incidence of allergies among the gifted population. Lovecky (personal communication, November 3, 1994), who specializes in assessment and treatment of gifted children with learning and behavior difficulties, has found high incidence of allergies among children diagnosed as ADD. Allergies to dust mites and milk are especially prevalent. She reported that behaviors and focus improve when allergens are eliminated.

What are some of the ways that parents and teachers can help children manage their overexcitabilities and harness some of the intensity and vigor to serve them? A valuable, practical popular resource for parents of children who exhibit overexcitabilities is Kurcinka's (1991) *Raising Your Spirited Child: A Guide for Parents Whose Child is More Intense, Sensitive, Perceptive, Persistent, Energetic*. The book has hundreds of specific suggestions for helping overexcitable children self-monitor and develop control of themselves. Some suggestions presented in *Raising Your Spirited Child* call attention to overload and mobilize overexcitabilities to serve children, rather than restrict them. More excellent help to bring out and honor children's exceptional sensitivities and abilities is found in *Self-Esteem: A Family Affair* (Clarke, 1978). The author continually coaches adults how to encourage children to be their best selves.

Overexcitabilities guide a child's life, shape his or her focus and values and create his or her unique inner life. Overexcitabilities arouse inner conflict and some variance with common society. They help evolve an individual's value structures. It is the strength of these overexcitabilities combined with special abilities that compose a child's developmental potential for self-actualization (Silverman, 1993).

REFERENCES

Ackerman, C. (1993). *Investigating alternative methods of identifying gifted children.* Unpublished master's thesis, Department of Educational Psychology, University of Calgary, Alberta, Canada.

Clark, B. (1986). *Optimizing learning: The integrative education model in the classroom.* Columbus, OH: Merrill.

Clark, B. (1992). *Growing up gifted* (4th ed.). New York: Macmillan.

Clarke, J.I. (1978). *Self-esteem: A family affair.* New York: Harper & Row.

Colangelo, N. (1991). Counseling gifted students. In N. Colangelo & G.A. Davis (Eds.), *Handbook of gifted education* (pp. 273-284). Needam Heights, MA: Allyn & Bacon.

Dabrowski, K., & Piechowski, M.M. (1977). *Theories of levels of emotional development: Vol. 1. Multilevelness and positive disintegration.* Oceanside, NY: Dabor Science.

Grant, B. (1992, Spring). Is giftedness just high intelligence? *Talent Development, 17.*

Kurcinka, M.S. (1991). *Raising your spirited child: A guide for parents whose child is more intense, sensitive, perceptive, persistent, energetic.* New York: Harper Perennial.

Lind, S. (1993). Are we mislabeling overexcitable children? *Understanding our Gifted, 5*(5A), 1-10.

Lovecky, D. (1986). Can you hear the flowers singing? *Journal of Counseling and Development, 64,* 572-575.

Miller, A. (1981). *The drama of the gifted child: The search for the true self.* New York: Basic Books.

Munger, A. (1990). The parent's role in counseling the gifted: The balance between home and school. In J. VanTassel-Baska (Ed.), *A practical guide to counseling the gifted in a school setting* (2nd ed., pp. 57-66). Reston, VA: The Council for Exceptional Children.

Piechowski, M.M. (1979). Developmental potential. In N. Colangelo & R.T. Zaffrann (Eds.), *New voices in counseling the gifted* (pp. 25-57). Dubuque, IA: Kendall/Hunt.

Schetky, D.H. (1981). A psychiatrist looks at giftedness: The emotional and social development of the gifted child. *Gifted Child Today, 18,* 2-4.

Silverman, L.K. (1988). On introversion. *Understanding our Gifted, 1*(2), 11.

Silverman, L.K. (1993). The gifted individual & A developmental model for counseling the gifted. In L.K. Silverman (Ed.), *Counseling the gifted & talented* (pp. 3-28, 51-78). Denver, CO: Love.

Smutny, J, F., Veenker, K. & Veenker, S. (1989). *Your gifted child.* New York: Ballantine Books.

U.S. Department of Education, Office of Educational Research and Improvement. (1993). *National excellence: The case for developing America's talent.* Washington, DC: Author.

Webb, J.T., Meckstroth, E.A., & Tolan, S.S. (1982). *Guiding the gifted child.* Dayton: Ohio Psychology Press.

24

Psychosocial Development of Gifted Children

Philip A. Perrone

Differentiating between social and psychological development is essential. Social development proves difficult for gifted persons primarily because of being out of sync with the standards defining normal behavior. In North American society almost every human endeavor and human characteristic is "normed." Deviating as little as a few weeks from the norm in taking one's first steps can be cause for celebration by parents. The greater the deviation from the norm, the greater the abnormality, and the greater joy when the abnormality is viewed positively by society in general. However, specific age-grade social norms applied to children become a source of early conflict, much of it internalized, for gifted children. Deviating from the norm becomes painful when viewed negatively by society.

Some deviations, such as physical dexterity, early reading, and musical talent, may be well received and well regarded by nearly everyone, although eventually even deviations in these areas may place stress on a family or school system, which need to extend themselves to accommodate large discrepancies from the highly valued age-grade norm.

Other abnormal age-grade behaviors are not well received, such as assertiveness, extreme social awareness, and sensitivity, asking questions and creating issues that adults are neither accustomed to hearing nor prepared to answer or cope with. This leads to my first hypothesis; namely, the greater the deviation from the age-grade norm, and the less valued or understood the particular attitude or behavior, the greater the degree of social pressure experienced by the child to conform.

Psychological development, on the other hand, arises more from internal imbalances that I attribute both to pressures to conform and differential rates of physical, psychological, and emotional development. Uneven development in gifted children was probably first noted by Hollingworth (1926) and has been the subject of more recent discussions by Delisle (1990) and Kerr (1991). Morelock (1992) used the term *asynchrony* to describe different rates of cognitive, emotional, and physical development experienced by gifted children.

Not all gifted pupils respond alike to the external pressure to conform and to their internal dissonance. In a study conducted several years ago (Perrone, Pribyl, & Chan, 1985), four "types" of gifted elementary school pupils were identified. Some types experience more internal or external stress than others. Three types contributed equally to 90% of the gifted pupil population and the fourth type included the remaining 10%. We profiled the four types as follows:

> Type I —Generally high achieving but not outstanding; somewhat sensitive to one's own needs; limited curiosity, slightly focused, unassertive, unemotional, a little timid, passive, and conforming.

Many would label this group as well-adjusted. They could also be described as field-dependent (Witkin, Moore, Goodenough, & Cox, 1977). These pupils tended to be quite dependent on adults for direction and recognition. Their standardized test scores were high average.

> Type II —High achievers in math and reading, highly assertive in their quest for knowledge, and energetic. Limited creativity and curiosity, conforming. Neither adaptive nor introspective.

This group of pupils were more field-independent (Witkin et al., 1977) and assertive relative to learning math and reading but not assertive socially. They achieved well in the two most valued elementary school subjects—reading and arithmetic—so they received much positive feedback and behaved in accord with the norms of the gifted elementary school program. These pupils might have experienced social problems if they were in a regular classroom, however.

Type III—High achievers, particularly in language arts. Very curious, adaptive, determined, venturesome, introspective, and creative. A little assertive, playful, energetic, and not very emotional.

This group tended to be field sensitive and verbally assertive in their relationships with other pupils. They were leaders in different ways. This group of students probably would have been well received in the regular classroom because they exercised self-control and directed their energies appropriately.

Type IV—These pupils were beginning to show signs of under-achievement and teachers were concerned because of their disruptive classroom behavior. They were highly emotional, energetic, playful, and nonconforming. They were somewhat creative, venturesome, and curious. They evidenced little self-understanding or self-control.

In some respects, this last group of pupils were close to running wild. The information available regarding their families suggested these pupils experienced very little in the way of consistent behavioral limits or consistent discipline at home. They were field independent and assertive. The lack of consistent discipline in the home probably contributed to their behaving as if no limits existed and they behaved without any apparent sense of purpose or direction.

The second hypothesis I would like to offer is that there are at least four, and possibly more, discernable personality types which exist among the gifted child population. Each type will evidence unique patterns of behavior calling for different responses from parents and teachers.

What drives the gifted child? I have suggested (Perrone, 1986) that an attribute common among gifted children is a high level of psychological energy. In effect, their higher energy level, combined with more efficient perceptual and information processing systems, serve as a foundation for their giftedness. At birth this surplus of energy lacks a particular focus or direction. What I have described as high energy differs in one aspect from what Dabrowski (1964) and Piechowski (1975) described as *overexcitabilities* (see Meckstroth, Chapter 23, this volume). These theoreticians discussed overexcitability in terms of a gifted person's intensity, which suggests a combination of high energy and cognitive focus. It may prove helpful to differentiate between unfocused high energy and focused high energy (overexcitability), because to intervene effectively it is necessary first to assist children to be able to focus, then help them design and implement schemes by which they can effectively direct their energy.

It would seem that three parent behaviors are necessary for surplus energy (giftedness) to become focused and for behavior to be sustained. Infants must be provided physical and emotional nourishment or this energy will be dissipated. Infants should experience manageable amounts of stimuli, which becomes more complex as they grow into more effective "data processors." Consistent communication with at least one adult is likely to result in the gifted infant-child becoming emotionally bonded to this adult. This bonding will fuel the infant's high energy level because of concerned and concentrated adult attentiveness.

The idea of an energy surplus is essential in better understanding why the thoughts and behaviors of gifted children are qualitatively different from their peers. Given an energy surplus, gifted children likely seek and test standard limits (norms) rather than simply fit into these norms. Surplus psychological energy is frequently reflected in social, intellectual, or physical assertiveness. Understanding one's personal potency is not easy and unless parents and teachers help gifted pupils better understand the power within them, it is possible social, psychological, and physical harm will result.

Striving for actualization (Maslow, 1970) is evidenced by gifted children in their wanting to make things happen. At an early age, reading is one example where socializing and actualizing are compatible quests. In learning to read, young children are set free from depending on others to read to them and at the same time learning to read allows children to better understand their environment and themselves. Almost everyone is excited when a young child learns to read, and the younger the age when this occurs, the greater the pride and excitement. Freeing oneself from the dependency of having others read to you is an actualizing behavior. Reading itself is a highly valued social behavior, thus socializing and actualizing are mutually attainable.

Unfortunately, reading is one of the very few areas whereby achievement increases personal power in a socially valued way. Viewed from another perspective, as gifted children mature, one of their greatest frustrations is not being able to apply their knowledge, their insights, and their creativity, in personally meaningful and socially valued ways.

The need to actualize may prove particularly frustrating for gifted children who achieve high grades and have no actualizing outlet in the arts, athletics, through leadership roles, or out-of-school activities. The socializing responsibilities of parents and teachers place them in a position to provide or withhold tangible rewards and social recognition, making parents and teachers particularly attractive targets for gifted children who need to test limits and engage in interpersonal power struggles. Adults have to be both knowledgeable and secure to respond in a manner which is unyielding yet growth-enabling.

PARTICULARLY DIFFICULT TRANSITIONS FOR GIFTED
CHILDREN

To the extent that gifted children have been the center of attention at home and are encouraged to pursue their personal interests, entering school requires major, and often difficult, personal and social adjustments. The elementary school curriculum has been designed to meet pupils' general learning needs, pacing, and instruction is at the group norm, both in terms of rate and complexity. Learning in school is no longer an individualized, actualizing experience. In kindergarten, for example, the emphasis is on socializing, probably at the expense of intellectual actualizing. In addition to social "maturation" being separated from psychological development, socialization takes precedence. Also, beginning with kindergarten, learning is teacher-directed instead of child-centered, resulting in gifted children experiencing a further loss of personal potency and control that may lead to a lowering of self-esteem, assertive, or aggressive behavior.

Another major adjustment occurs around age eight or nine (third or fourth grade) when gifted children begin experiencing two stressors unique to their advanced conceptual development. Although nearly all fourth-graders feel the pressure to conform to peer standards, gifted children are torn between their desire to achieve higher level adult standards while experiencing mounting peer pressure to fit in with much lower peer achievement standards. Bowing to either peer or adult pressure, or even trying to reach a compromise between the two, represents a further threat to the gifted child's actualization tendency.

At about the same time, the strong emotional bond with "the" significant adult (parent) may now be perceived by the child more as a constraint to growth than supportive. Gifted children may have difficulty recognizing, let alone articulating, their mixed feelings about this relationship. They typically lack both the skills and resources to create a solution on their own. Misunderstanding and poor communication can contribute to increased conflict, resulting in verbal or even physical power struggles between the previously enabling parent and child. Power struggles may also be apparent in the classroom—but teachers and gifted pupils are usually not as emotionally bonded as parents and children, so the conflict may not be quite as intense.

Another source of confusion and possible stress occurs when gifted fourth-graders enter what I term *psychological adolescence*. In this writer's view, psychological adolescence begins when children become aware of their finiteness (Frankl, 1962), that is, when they recognize that no one, including themselves, lives forever. Once a sense of finiteness is internalized, a series of psychological and behavioral changes are likely to follow. The most significant change for the gifted pupil is acquiring a future time perspective, leading to a clearer understanding of cause and effect relationships—which is the basis for inferential thinking.

An additional consequence of comprehending and accepting one's finiteness is to experience a strong desire to exercise more control over one's behavior. The strong parent and teacher bond may be further tested, and possibly resented, as the child's desire for individuation and actualization is heightened, resulting in parents and teachers being perceived as over-controlling.

Giftedness can occur in discrete areas of learning. In the very young, giftedness is most often defined in terms of verbal-linguistic exceptionality as evidenced by excelling in reading and oral communication. Later, if a gifted child struggles with problem solving, particularly in mathematics, the gifted child, the parents, and teachers may come to question the child's giftedness. Unfortunately, nearly everyone seems to believe that being gifted means learning is easy for these children in all subject areas.

Why do some gifted students have difficulty learning to solve math problems? One reason is that more complex, abstract problem solving requires use of the long-term memory as contrasted to the short-term memory functions used in reading, speaking, and mathematical computation. It may take considerable effort to develop comparable skills solving math problems through the use of long-term memory functions (Gardner, 1983). Because the verbally gifted are not in the habit of working hard to learn, they may either avoid "difficult" learning tasks such as problem solving in mathematics or, just as unfortunately, they may believe they are no longer gifted when they struggle to learn, which translates into a lowering of self-esteem, achievement motivation, and eventually achievement itself.

Because gifted often are more ego-involved in what they do, they quickly become impatient with anyone not sharing their level of involvement and task commitment. Impatience is particularly noticeable when they have a chance to lead or organize the work of others. Learning to accept individual differences and offer constructive suggestions requires both patience and tact, which are not virtues many gifted children have acquired. In the end, their level of intensity and impatience may alienate peers, particularly when gifted children are unable to delegate and end up doing all the work themselves.

Gifted pupils may also need to learn how to better apportion their time and energy given how involved or overinvolved they tend to become. They may even require help in avoiding overinvolvement in particular activities. Pupils who strive to excel in school while participating in several extracurricular activities are liable to experience frustration when they lack the time and energy needed to excel in each. There is a danger of always being "in process" and not having the opportunity to achieve goals and obtain closure. The conflict for many gifted pupils arises from "needing" to be involved and "having" to excel.

There are two additional aspects of giftedness that may go unattended in children. Their cognitive complexity leads them to envision more broadly and experience more of the environment than their peers. Visualizing a *white, plastic, cup* may help explain this phenomenon. If the norm is to perceive the cup concretely, it would be viewed in terms of *color* (white), *material* (plastic), and *function* (cup). More complex and abstract perceptions would include "seeing" *shape* (cylinder), *volume* (8 ounces), state (empty); and even more abstractly, seeing it as (nonbiodegradable) *a future state*. When gifted pupils perceive aspects of their environment in more abstract terms than the concrete dimensions seen by the majority of peers, gifted pupils will need help in resisting the pressures to restrict their thinking to the concrete, to the norm.

Conceptually complex perceiving pupils may also have difficulty validating their highly individualized, multidimensional, abstract perceptions. These perceptions can best be validated through dialoguing with a knowledgeable, sensitive, and responsive adult. However, when curriculum, instructional methodology, and examinations are more oriented toward the concrete, gifted pupils find themselves faced with having to think and respond "normally" or concretely in order to succeed in school. This results in having to repress their more abstract, individual perspectives, which is the essence of both their individuality and their giftedness.

One of the most difficult situations for gifted pupils occurs when solutions to problems are viewed in absolute terms, that is, right and wrong. The absolute world is a world of black and white, yet the world of the gifted consists of all the shades in between. In their relative world it may take longer to make decisions with so many factors to consider. Again, gifted pupils may be accused of being slow, when in fact they are being deliberate. They can be placed in a real quandary, and may end up trying to ignore their own complex and abstract thought processes when there is social pressure to make a decision or to take a stand immediately. Opportunities for gifted pupils to think, ponder, and examine with teachers and others who appreciate more complex, abstract, relative, and hypothetical views of the world are sorely needed.

The relatively slow pace of normal classroom instruction is another source of dissonance for gifted learners. One explanation for this slower pace of instruction is that effective teachers adopt a slower pace in order to bring slower students along, consciously or unconsciously expecting gifted students to adapt to a slower pace without complaint and without loss of learning. Gifted pupils may be found talking to others while the teacher is talking or they may daydream to fill the cognitive void they are experiencing.

Often, independent study is prescribed for gifted pupils. However, independent study may create difficulty for gifted pupils with a predominantly field-sensitive learning style. Perceptual field sensitivity and field independence (Witkin et al., 1977) are learning styles that appear to have a genetic base, although both are influenced by the socialization process. Field-independent pupils will respond more eagerly to opportunities for independent study. In our culture, males are reinforced more for independence, for speaking out, and knowing their minds. It is not surprising that a greater percentage of males evidence field-independence. Students who are field sensitive, a greater proportion of whom are female, are socially reinforced for "understanding and nurturing" behaviors. Field sensitive learners are more comfortable with concrete learning experiences and learn best when receiving support, direction, and immediate feedback. Field independents are more comfortable with long-term activities (e.g., abstract "problem solving" in mathematics and science), whereas field-sensitive learners are more comfortable with short-term memory activities (e.g., social sciences). Pupils can learn to develop strategies that enhance their less natural learning style but it takes time and encouragement. Pupils' dominant learning styles need to be recognized when deciding whether to give long or short-term assignments, whether to expect pupils to work at their own pace, and how much support and direction to provide.

At every age gifted persons are happier, more productive, and develop higher level skills and acquire more knowledge if they have the opportunity to communicate with persons who understand, accept, and challenge them as individuals with a gift. The challenge to teachers and parents is to make learning not only a socializing, but an actualizing experience.

REFERENCES

Dabrowski, K. (1964). *Positive disintegration*. Boston: Little, Brown.

Delisle, J.R. (1990). The gifted adolescent at risk: Strategies and resources for suicide prevention among gifted youth. *Journal for the Education of the Gifted, 13*, 212-228.

Frankl, V. E. (1962). *Man's search for meaning*. Boston: Beacon Press.

Gardner, H. (1983). *Frames of mind: The theory of multiple intelligences*. London: Basic Books.

Hollingworth, L.S. (1926). *Gifted children: Their nature and nurture*. New York: Macmillian.

Kerr, B. (1991). *A handbook for counseling the gifted and talented*. Alexandria, VA: American Counseling Association.

Maslow, A. (1970). *Motivation and personality* (2nd ed.). New York: Harper & Row.

Morelock, M.J. (1992). Giftedness: The view from within. *Understanding Our Gifted, 4*(3), 1, 11-15.

Perrone, P.A. (1986). Guidance needs of the gifted child, adolescent, and adult. *Journal of Counseling and Development, 64*(9), 564-565.

Perrone, P.A., Chan, F., & Pribyl, J. (1985). Differential characteristics of gifted and talented elementary school pupils. *Roeper Review, 7*(3), 190-192.

Piechowski, M.M. (1975). A theoretical and empirical approach to the study of development. *Genetic Psychology Monographs, 92,* 231-297.

Witkin, H.A., Moore, C.A., Goodenough, D.R., & Cox, P.W. (1977). Field-dependent and field-independent cognitive styles and their educational implications. *Review of Educational Research, 47*(1), 1-64.

25

Facilitating the Interest Themes of Young Bright Children

LeoNora M. Cohen

Ross danced around the room, swept up by the Beethoven sonata his father played on the piano. Suddenly he halted his twirling and said, "Stop, Daddy. Please show me that chord you just played. I want to see what it looks like in the score."

This child, aged 5-1/2, spends hours studying scores, both piano and orchestral. He appears to understand the form of the music, the conventions, and the structure. He plays the piano, composing his own melodies and asks his father to write them down. He is also involved in elaborate fantasy play with an imaginary playmate, who serves as a filter for working out concerns and trying out ways to make make sense of the world (when "Yellowy" gets a blood test, it doesn't hurt if the bandage is put on before the needle). He devours books; both those his parents read to him, and what he can read himself. He loves working over math problems and theory, pours over maps to figure out how to get places, and studies house plans. He uses some sophisticated software on the computer to make up imaginary schedules or compare different versions of spreadsheets, as well as writing a guide to nonexistent software, "Windows 8.5." He goes to gymnastics class, but is unhappy when the instructor does not follow his suggestions about rules for "playing the games," as he prefers to be in charge of his own activities.

Ross, a highly gifted child, has considerable competence in music, math, spatial thinking, and language. What marks him as extraordinary, however, is not these abilities but the passion with which he pursues his interests and the depths he plumbs them, marked by intensity, sensitivity, and a desire for control. This type of commitment to interest pursuit is not unusual for gifted children. Terman (1925), Thorndike (1939), and Janos and Robinson (1985) all found that the personality characteristics that most consistently differentiate young gifted children from their average peers are intense, early interests, marked by enthusiasm, perseverance and energy.

However, relatively few studies have been done on the interests of children, gifted or otherwise. Although many experts on educating gifted children suggest that teachers should attend to children's interests (e.g., Clark, 1992; Renzulli, 1977a, 1977b; Shore, Cornell, Robinson, & Ward, 1991; Shore & Kanevsky, 1993), few suggest ways to do so, or offer a theoretical framework that recognizes their importance. This chapter provides a brief overview of the state of research on children's interests, offer a theoretical base for understanding interests, and provide ideas and suggestions for teaching to interests in the classroom or supporting them at home, focusing on the young bright child.

RESEARCH ON INTERESTS OF THE GIFTED

Recent research on interests among gifted children is limited. Cohen and Gelbrich (in press) found that the few studies done focused largely on differences compared to the average population. Although there are some mixed results (Gelbrich, 1992, found no differences in interest preferences on an interest theme inventory), gifted children were generally found to have more mature, wider, and more intense interests; to be more adventurous, have greater interest in nonphysical games, aesthetic activities, and reading; to be less inclined to social and physical activities and sports; to have interests that portended their adult careers; and, as teenagers, to put more time into classwork, studying, reading, thinking, doing art or hobbies, and watching television, compared to average teens (Coy, 1923; Csikszentimihalyi, Rathunde, & Whalen, 1993; Goertzel, Goertzel, & Goertzel, 1978; Rice, 1968; Terman, 1925; Thorndike,1940). There were preferences for specific interests such as dinosaurs, power, fantasy play, and superheroes. Gifted boys preferred chemistry, rocketry, cartooning, working on small engines, chess, and puzzles. Gifted girls preferred not to play house, and enjoyed journalism, mime, and sign language (Cohen, 1988a, 1988b; Harrington, Harrington, & Slatow, 1986; Schowalter, 1979; Terman, 1925; Thorndike, 1940).

Most of these studies, however useful, do not explain why interests are such a salient feature of the young gifted child or why children are so passionate and intense in pursuing them. Let us explore the theoretical base for understanding the importance of interest development in the bright young child.

A THEORETICAL FRAMEWORK FOR UNDERSTANDING INTERESTS

Piaget (1969/1970) stated that interest is the dynamic aspect of assimilation when the "self identifies with ideas or objects, when it finds in them a means of expression and they become a necessary form of fuel for its activity" (pp. 158-159). He said that interests are engaging to a child because they help to restore equilibrium or balance as well as energize activity. Piaget noted that interests control intellectual functioning, helping the child to build structures and wholes. Therefore, interests have a very important adaptive function.

For Piaget (1975/1977), the learner seeks to restore balance to the knowing structures when something conflicts with what is understood, a process he called *equilibration*. We can think of the process to be something like putting information into file folders, but it is not simply additive, as in adding a sheet of paper to the file. It requires restructuring the file, giving it a new label, or perhaps even reorganizing the whole filing system under a new set of organizational principles (as in when a child moves from preoperational to concrete operational thinking). When a child is profoundly interested in something, we need to ask ourselves, "Why is this interest so important to him or her?" "What questions/problems/conflicts is this child trying to work out?"

Types of Interests

Cohen (1988b) distinguished two major types of interests through her longitudinal case studies: those that are extrinsically stimulated (Type I) and those intrinsically stimulated (Type II).

Type I Interests. Type I, extrinsically stimulated interest, is expressed when a child deals with a novel situation—a new kitten, a new way to check addition problems, a new vocabulary game. We know that children seek novelty and thrive in environments where moderate novelties (not too foreign, not too familiar) are presented. Such novelty stimulates brain development.

Type II Interests. A second type of interest, Type II, also found in very young children is intrinsic. Type II interests are operationally defined as:

1. Involvements that endure over a long period (2 months or more) in a child over 24 months. In a younger baby, 1 month is sufficient
2. Characterized by intensity of attention (1 hour or more per day, but not necessarily in a single block of time) and with an unwillingness to leave the activity when engaged (may be less in child under 2 years)
3. Question- or problem-focused (not necessarily expressed orally—these must be inferred, especially in the preverbal child) with a willingness by the child to tackle difficulties
4. Expanding—the interest extends to ever-widening areas and results in the development of infantile expertise
5. Permeable to other areas of life
6. Fantasy life focused on the interest (after about age 2)
7. Characterized by pleasure and excitement in the child

THE STRUCTURING OF INTERESTS

In longitudinal observations of interest development, young children's Type II interests often change (Cohen, 1988b). Some children pursue one area intensely for a while and then move to another, whereas others work on several interests at once. In these changes, there is a pattern or structure, rather than random jumping from one involvement to a different one. We have found that interests are structured around *themes* (Ferrara, 1984), which are the core, the constant and recurring motif that gives coherence and pattern to the evolving passionate pursuits.

A brief description of one child studied from age 8 months through 12 years, 6 months demonstrates this structuring along two major themes, "Power-Control" and "Putting it All Together," evident before his first birthday (See Figure 25.1). A third theme, "People-Relationships" began at about age 8.

Mike is a sturdy, energetic, and highly intelligent boy, a bit short for his age, with exceptional verbal, musical, mathematical, and spatial abilities. His fine and gross motor skills are about average. He is friendly, cooperative, and outgoing, although lazy about doing required tasks if they are not of interest to him. He was identified for his school's gifted program in kindergarten and has attended classes for gifted students since.

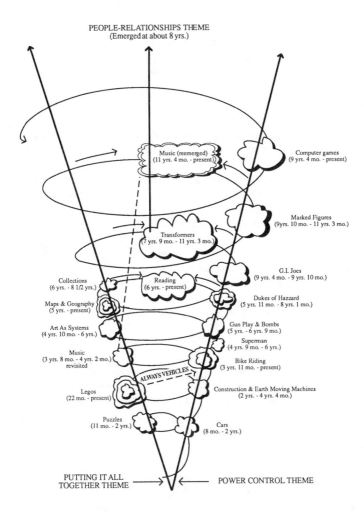

Figure 25.1. Interest and Themes of Mike (age 12-1/2)

P.C.—Power-Control Theme (subthemes: action, power, control). Mike's power-control theme began at 8-1/2 months when he showed a decided preference for moving cars and other vehicles. By age 2, the interests became more focused on earth moving and construction equipment. A month before his fourth birthday, Mike learned to ride a bicycle, the action and power thrilling him. Superman fantasies at age 4 years, 9 months, gunplay at 5 years, and the Dukes of Hazzard TV program (5 years, 11 months) were the next action-power interests.

By matching names and data on baseball stickers to corresponding blanks in his sticker book, Mike taught himself to read the month of his 6th birthday. Reading coordinates both Power and Action and Putting it All Together. From age 7 through 12-1/2, Mike read voraciously, working his way through a set of children's encyclopedias among other fare. In his questions, "Which animal eats the most for its weight?", "Where is the tallest mountain?", or "Can you name all the transformers in this set?" he was not raising questions for information, but was the one who knew the answers and felt power in demonstrating his knowledge. The quest had grown from an action orientation to more of a power orientation, and it no longer had to be physical power.

When we was 9 years old, Mike focused on GI Joes, small war toy figures and vehicles through which he could express power. From 9 years through age 12-1/2, Mike loved to play computer games where he could control the little figures on the screen. He also became very interested in role-playing games where he could control, to a large degree, the character he created and he could have all manner of powers. This interest was combined with his Putting it All Together theme, as role playing requires inventing, retaining, and integrating a great deal of complex information about the different characters and plots. It also involved the later development of the People-Relationships theme, as role playing is done with others.

P.A.T.—Putting It All Together Theme. The second theme in Mike's development was Putting it All Together. This began at 11 months with a car puzzle. Puzzles for children through age 6 were his passion until his second birthday. At 22 months, he became involved with Legos, which soon replaced puzzles as his major interest.

An interest in orchestral music surfaced at about age 3-1/2. His concerns were with classifying the instruments, finding their ranges, listening to their sounds in ensemble. In short, Mike's concern with music was Putting It All Together. His art work also reflected this, beginning at a few months before his fifth birthday. Drawings of the household plumbing system or the inner workings of a whale, raven, and rabbit were typical.

Collections of baseball stickers, football cards, and "Garbage Pail Kids" were important from just before age 6 through age 8-1/2. Mike wanted to put all the members of each team together. He studied the cards and retained every statistic. He saved his allowance to try to get complete sets of cards or stickers and traded with classmates for missing pieces.

An interest that typified both Putting it All Together and Power-Control themes was a passion for transformers. From 7 years, 9 months through 11 years, 3 months, Mike was consumed with these toys, which had great and often magical powers and could be put together in different forms. Mike enjoyed taking them apart with a screwdriver and putting them together with parts of other compatible figures, as well as transforming them in the standard way.

A reemergence of interest in music, beginning at about 11 years typified both themes as well. Mike played in three bands, enjoying "putting sound all together" with other young people. But the control theme was evidenced in wanting to play every brass and woodwind instrument in the band, and he spent much time mastering all 12 scales on his trumpet, as well as working on French horn, baritone, saxaphone, and oboe.

P.R.—People-Relationships. A new theme began to emerge around age 8, a great concern with friendships and relating to other children as well as morality. This may be a theme of the preteen age period, but Mike preferred to play with others rather than to play alone and he frequently organized activities around his interests for his friends. He was also very concerned with what was right and was disturbed by people (particularly other kids) doing the wrong thing.

Sometimes one interest theme would dominate, then another, or he would weave between them. Stretching to conquer a challenge would occupy his efforts, inducing a state of "flow," or at-onement with the interest (Csikszentmihalyi, 1990). When the interest was at the confluence of two or more themes, it was of longest duration and intensity.

Themes: The Vectors for Interest Development

A child can be thought of as having several interacting systems: universal knowledge and nonuniversal knowledge, affect, perception, intuition, purpose, and the physical system. When gaps or lags occur from one to another (for example, the preschooler's perceptions of his or her small size conflict with emotional desires to be big and powerful) the result may be an intense interest in being Superman, Princess of Power, or an angel. Themes are remarkably stable, although interests change. For example, the same child who wants to be a brave, strong policeman at age 5 may become fascinated with superhero comics at age 8 and energetically pursue football at age 11, all aspects of the Power-Control theme. Themes give a pattern to interests and serve as vectors or trajectories for interest development. I have found that by the time the child is about 4 years of age, themes are consistently evident.

Themes and Variations. In case studies of developmentally advanced young children, Cohen (1988b) has identified six major themes and their variations. They are: (a) control, (b) nature-nurture, (c) putting it all together, (d) people-relationships, (e) aesthetic-expressive, and (f) symbols and symbol systems. As is typical with qualitative research, these categories are regarded as provisional, although the pattern appears to be substantiated by teachers and parents who have used the interest themes. Most of the children studied have between two and four strong themes, although all children probably have a little of all of them.

Theme 1 Variations: Control.

1. Control—The child wants to be in charge of the self and the world, seen in such interests as being Superman, or conducting an orchestra.
2. Mastery—The child practices gymnastics, a piece of music, or drawing a horse to perfect them.
3. Action/Movement—Examples are playing ball, running, jumping, dancing, and other gross motor activities.
4. Power—The child is interested in objects of power, external to the child, such as cars, volcanoes, or hero figures.
5. Rules/Order/Limits—The child is fascinated with the parameters, requirements, structure, and organization of things, events, and feelings.
6. Adventure/Exploration—The child seeks opportunities to explore or adventure independently. "Leave me here in the woods; I want to explore" (girl, age 3-1/2).
7. Independence/Do it myself—"I dood it myself!"; The child makes attempts at dressing, feeding, reading.
8. Getting Attention—"Look at me, watch me!" The child constantly calls attention to self.
9. Experimentation—The child sets up experiments and tries to prove her hypothesis. "When I leave these mushrooms in water, they will turn blue."

Theme 2 Variations: Nature-Nurture.

1. Nature—The child expresses a profound interest in plants, animals and other aspects of the natural world.
2. Nurture—Caring for, loving, dressing. The child makes a habitat for the baby fish in the creek, dresses her cat, hugs and cuddles her doll.
3. Belonging—A concern with being part of groups, particularly families, is evident.

Theme 3 Variations: Putting It All Together.

1. Putting it all together—The child expresses a profound interest in puzzles, Legos or blocks, maps and globes.
2. Meaning/function of objects—What is it? What does this do?
3. How things work—The child asks questions about things, or takes them apart to figure out how they work.

4. Relationships—Here, the attention is on cause and effect (not social), such as interest in light switches and computer keys. "What happens if I hit two keys at the same time?"
5. Origins—How things begin is the focus of attention. "What was the very first seed?"
6. Transformations—The child plays with clay, transformer toys, costumes, and dressing up.
7. Understanding world/life—The child expresses interest in people and languages of different lands, life cycles, and so forth.
8. Experimenting with objects—"What happens if I put water in the gas tank?"

Theme 4 Variations: People/Relationships.

1. People puzzles—The child spends considerable time observing people and asking questions about their behavior; "Why is that man shouting at the lady?"
2. People relationships—The child is interested in relating to people and curious about family roles and relationships; "Who is Daddy's brother to me?"
3. Being liked—The child may choose toys she knows a friend will like, or may abdicate her own interests and profess interest in a friend's involvements in order to encourage a relationship.
4. Friends/Companionship—The child wants companionship all the time and prefers activities with other, talking about friends constantly.
5. Communicating—The child is intent on getting his ideas across; "It's my turn to tell a story."
6. Morality—The child is concerned with good/bad; proper behavior; world problems.
7. Feelings—The child asks often about how another feels; "Are you sad, Mommy?"
8. Imitation—The child imitates what mommy or daddy does and enjoys sitting at his desk and working on his papers while mom marks tests.
9. Roles—The child takes on different roles, such as being Cinderella or the Big Bad Wolf.
10. Helping people—Examples are setting the table; offering to help with cooking; washing the car; helping grandpa cross the street.

Theme 5 Variations: Aesthetic/Expressive.

1. Aesthetic—The child expresses sensitivity to and delight in beauty and appreciation of the arts; makes subtle observations; demonstrates openness to the world. A 2-1/2-year-old

says, "Mommy, see how the artist painted the shadow of the birds on the sand? How pretty it is!"

2. Artistic expression—Expression through the visual arts attracts the child's interest.
3. Musical expression—The child plays an instrument, sings, conducts, or listens to music for long periods.
4. Expression (general)—The child combines areas of expression such as art and song; acting; expressive body movement.
5. Sensuality—The child revels in pleasures to the senses, such as rubbing a blanket over her cheek or delighting in tasting something.
6. Expressing feelings—The child lets her feelings be known, as opposed to interest in other's feelings (see theme 4, variation 7).

Theme 6 Variations: Symbols and Symbol Systems.

1. Cognitive skill acquisition—The child works on learning about words, letters, numbers.
2. Meaning/Function (Semantic)—What does P-A-B mean? What does this mark (') do?
3. Representations—The child is interested in how different languages are written and pays attention to images.
4. Symbols—The child inquires what symbols stand for, decodes symbols, or wants to learn different ways to say or write a word or number.
5. Abstractions—The child looks for mathematical or other symbolic or semantic relationships.

Identifying the Theme. The same interest may evidence different themes. For example, many children are interested in animals, but this interest could actually evidence any of the six themes. It is the actions of the child relative to the interest that are important:

Theme 1—Control: Teaching the dog to sit; roll over.
Theme 2—Nature-Nurture: Petting, hugging, cuddling pet; dressing it up; making habitats for it.
Theme 3—Putting it All Together: Learning all about the members of the cat family, whale family.
Theme 4—People-Relationships: Pretending to be a dog, horse, cat; perhaps how people look like/are like animals; humanizing animals by having them take roles in play (Puffy is Cinderella's stepsister).
Theme 5—Aesthetic/Expressive: Drawing horses; pleasure in colors and beauty of birds or butterflies.
Theme 6—Symbols/Symbol Systems: Writing lists of animals; spelling names; reading about animals.

FACILITATING INTEREST THEMES

This section focuses on how parents and teachers can facilitate interest themes. It begins with why interests are so important.

Importance of Interests

Intrinsic interests are important to our understanding of development because they occur naturally and spontaneously. This is not to say that interests develop in a vacuum, but the baby or young child selects from the environment he or she is offered and uses these interests in a free and joyful way to try to make sense of the world. Type II interests most directly reflect the interactions of heredity, the social milieu, and the physical environment (Cohen, 1985, 1987a, 1987b, 1988a).

The Type II interests of a child are very important because they help to resolve inner conflicts, allowing the child to develop a healthy self concept. Interests are a child's way of working out the internal stresses. It is essential that parents and teachers understand their significance and support their development.

Facilitating Interest Development

The teacher or parent may need to become a resource gatherer, finding people, materials, or places that can facilitate the child's evolving abilities and interests. A kindergartner is very excited about how the body works and shares her transparent model of the human body. The teacher invites her friend, a physician, to come to class to share a real skeleton and to discuss the children's questions. This benefits not only the interested child, but opens doors for other children in the class to become interested as well. Loving adults can support the child's direct requests for help: "Would you help me cut out these airplanes?" or "Please help me make a teepee." Too often the parent or teacher is worried about the child naming letters, making numbers, or other recognized school skills in order to insure school success. The very important studies made by the child in explorations of interests are ignored, and the child soon learns to give up these pursuits for adult-approved learning.

Instead, a child's interests can be extended by getting books about a topic of involvement from the library, offering a simple motor for Lego materials, showing a child how to make a wax resist of crayon and watercolors.

Finally, the involvements can be observed and the deep questions figured out, with an offer of a question, a book, or an extension to a new interest at the right moment.

Tuning in to Personal Agendas. We know that children can be exceptional learners when interested in something. In fact, when children can be in control and are allowed to pursue interests, later underachievement may be less of a problem. Whitmore (personal communication, April 1987) believes that interests may be less observable in older underachieving children because they have not been supported, leading to both loss of interests and underachievement. It may be that some children are more vulnerable than others to erosion of interests (Horowitz & O'Brien, 1985), whereas other underachievers persist in pursuing a profound, consuming interest and ignore the other school "stuff" they consider trivial.

Teaching to Themes. Teachers could teach to themes, some with the whole class, perhaps as thematic units, others for individual children. For example, children who have a *Putting-it-All-Together Theme* might especially enjoy geography, music, geometric puzzles, or attribute games. Such children might relish techniques such as mind mapping, webbing, and finding associations or relationships (Cohen, 1994).

For children with a *power variation* on the *Control Theme*, rocketry, aviation, and volcanoes are naturals. Such children (or those with a *Control Theme*) would enjoy fantasizing about the magical power they would most want in a story they write. Those children with a *Getting Attention* subtheme might have a part in a play or put on a class talent show. Children with a *Control/Independence Theme* would particularly need a class climate where they can feel in charge of their learning experiences. In fact, as the *Control Theme* was found to be central to all these bright children, a classroom for the gifted must support autonomous development, the chance to control the self and the environment. Therefore, Betts' (1986) Autonomous Learner Model is especially appropriate, as are open classroom and facilitative teacher models (see Cohen & Jipson, chapter 31, this volume). I would hypothesize, however, that this theme is central to all children and to adults as well, not just to the gifted.

Children with a *Nature-Nurture Theme* could be in charge of plant or pet care. They might make a terrarium, write a story about an animal, help a handicapped child, or be special friend to a new child in the class. Children with *People/Relationships Themes* might also do these last two activities, as well as writing about an interesting person they have known, looking at different ways people (or animals) communicate, or conducting a survey on moral issues or on how to be a friend.

Those youngsters with *Aesthetic/Expressive Themes* would enjoy "sharing time," creative dramatics, art and music activities, or creative writing. The aesthetic and sensual sides of all children should be developed, helping them to observe and appreciate the wonder around us. Going for a magical mystery walk where each child tries to find something wonderful or new to share with the class could appeal here. The 4-year-old who shows her preschool class a bunch of broken glass on the sidewalk and says, "Look, here is a city with all the buildings and busy people. And over here (pointing to a single glass fragment) is a lonely child," clearly has an aesthetic sensibility (and is also an analogical thinker!).

Children with *Symbols and Symbol Systems Themes* surprisingly may not be the teacher's dream, especially if they come to school with abilities far above their classmates. It is critical that such children be allowed to pursue these skill areas at their level of ability and with their own pacing to maintain the interest. Sometimes a mentor or resource person may be needed to help such a child. One boy in my study had extraordinary math skills going into the first grade. He knew all the squares of numbers up to 450, the cubes up to 150, and had figured out all manner of number patterns. This child spent hours each day on mathematics and computing. Placing him in a third or fourth grade class for math would probably not be appropriate, as he would have been far ahead of many students at that level, yet might have some gaps (knowing the algorithms for long division, for example, or inability to write numbers fast enough to keep up with much older students) which could lead to feelings of inadequacy. Clearly, any first grade teacher would need help with such a child.

Integrating interest themes in regular curriculum could make a big difference in motivation. Marcia Rau, one of my graduate students, was required to use basal readers in her fourth grade classroom. She modified the questions at the end of each chapter, offering the children the choice of an interest-theme activity related the story. The result was a change from reluctance and boredom to enthusiasm. Applying the interest-themes to any topic of study or any subject could lead to similar results. How, for example, would you get a child with a strong aesthetic-expressive theme interested in math? What about a child with a people-relationships theme?

Encouraging a Sense of Purpose. The 7-year old girl who loves horses could read about them, draw them, learn about their history, breeds, and training. Instead of basal reading, she could do a research report on horses with help from the teacher or librarian. It is the consuming passion for a subject and the willingness to wrestle with difficulties that marks the creative person. The reading skills develop because there is a purpose for reading.

Young children may be very serious about their involvements. One boy of 4-1/2 spent hours each day working on what he called "aerodynamically sound" paper airplanes, varying the wing widths, paper clip and tape weightings, and folds until the plane did what he wanted. He had considerable grasp of the principles of flight (Cohen, 1989), yet some 5 years later in the school setting he was failing science because his interests in all manner of scientific things were being squashed with requirements to comply with all assignments that he found utterly boring. At the time, he simply could not bring himself to fill in the blanks on the order of planets in the solar system, a topic that had fascinated him and he had mastered at age 4.

Helping Ross and Others Like Him at Home and at School

Ross, the little boy we described at the beginning of this chapter, is almost of school age. His parents have done a superb job supporting his interests to date. At times, they have felt lonely and concerned that they were not able to find other parents or young children who shared his involvements. The little boy dreams of finding friends with whom to share his interests. Ross's mother hoped that her son could find a few compatible peers and a teacher who would take this child in gentle hands, stretch his mind, and allow him to pursue his passions at least some of the time.

What kind of school setting could address the needs of this young child and others like him? One option is home schooling, and for some parents and children, this may be the best or even the only option. Another is private schooling if such schools are available and if they address the needs of bright children. However, public schools can and should be able to accommodate children and their interests, whether or not they are intellectually able. In fact, if schools recognize that motivation is not a problem when interests are addressed, they will pay more attention to them. Following are a few specific suggestions for educators who may have one or more young children like Ross in their classrooms. These are clustered around Six Simple Rules, principles taken from educating gifted children that can be applied to teaching all children (Cohen, 1991/1992):

1. *Focus on the strengths and interests of each child to empower excellence.* Rather than determining what a child cannot do and remedying it (a deficit or medicinal approach), find out what the child is good at and interested in. Approach skill development through those interests and abilities. A beginning reader will be much more likely to want to learn to read if he can choose books about dinosaurs, an area of passionate interest. A figural learner might demonstrate competent understanding if she can connect information in a mind map rather than writing about it as narrative.

Being a resource gatherer becomes necessary—finding people to serve as mentors, materials that challenge, and other children with like interests. Parents of children in the school can be resources and the child can also find resources for himself. For example, because Ross is so interested in musical composition, he could telephone the university music school and make an appointment to meet with a composer (with the teacher's help of course). The danger, with children like Ross, would be to focus on what is less developed in the child and consider it a weakness. For example, following are actual report card comments for kindergarten and first grade about a boy named Tom:

Kindergarten

Tom's interest in, and knowledge of, volcanoes and the universe has led him to become a resource for the class and myself . Tom tends to put pressure on himself to get things "correct," which inhibits his confidence, although throughout the year he seems to have eased this pressure. Tom is a happy and cheerful child who enjoys his peers' company.

Grade 1

Tom enjoys being the center of attention and will disrupt the class to this end. He is rather self-indulgent. He becomes very indignant if someone does to him something he deems unpleasant, yet is thoughtless in his verbal and physical actions to others. He is a high achiever and pretends not to pay attention when a new concept is introduced, preferring to wait until he completely understands it, and will succeed, before participating. He resents help or advice. Tom is popular with his classmates. (Cohen & Frydenberg, 1996, p. 55)

As can be imagined, Tom's school experiences went steadily downhill, as did his confidence, self-esteem, and peer relationships, once the focus was on what was not developed, rather than his strengths and interests. The teacher's belief system determines how he or she views the child, influences how others in the class perceive him, and how the child views himself as well. What a difference it makes when the teacher values the child's interests as a resource and makes room for the complexity of a child's character.

2. *Group by interest or ability at least part of the time for healthy social and emotional development.* To avoid social and emotional difficulties that arise out of feeling different and alienated, group children by interest or ability at least part of the time. If no special programs for gifted students are available, cluster a few bright children in the same class with a teacher who wants to work with them, preferably one who has had some training in gifted education. Because Ross is quite sophisticated on the computer, he would probably enjoy working with others who are likewise interested, perhaps across grade levels. He and his fellow computer buffs might design a computer game for other students or learn to use telecommuncations to find others with common interests on a ListServ. A child who loves to write might create a play or produce a newspaper with other interested classmates. So many skills can develop in this way, around shared concerns, with com-

patible peers, and with a purpose to produce something useful. With an extraordinarily gifted child like Ross, finding true peers becomes more difficult and yet more critical, if the child is to feel good about him or herself in the school setting.

3. *Move as fast and as far in basic skills as possible.* Skill development in such areas as math or reading can be done with individualized programming using computers, or learning packets. It can involve cross-grade grouping, multiage grouping, use of learning centers, grouping within the classroom, pairing of students of similar abilities in class, or moving students to higher grades for some instruction. The age-in-grade lockstep needs to be avoided.

Check for efficiency. A kindergartener may figure out how to solve a math problem using repeated subtraction, but could be much more efficient if division were understood. Teaching the child how to use simple algorithms when needed can be done quickly with a bright child. By allowing children to move at their own pace, novelty keeps things interesting and the child is not bored.

Adults can utilize the principle of moderate novelty to maintain interest in routines or in school work (Type I interests). By varying approaches to dittos or worksheets, or adding a game to what is too often repetitive math work, the novelty is maintained and the interest in the subject is heightened instead of reduced. However, too often, this is the end point in the school setting, and intrinsic Type II interests are not identified or supported.

If teachers offer a range of options from which to select, students can integrate learnings in a product that is intrinsically interesting to them. For example, if the class topic is seeds and plants, rather than having everyone plant the same three lima beans and measure growth with rulers, another option would be to suggest activities on the topic related to the interest themes. For example, for two of the themes:

> *Power/Control*—Superplant: Try to grow the tallest and/or sturdiest bean plant in the class in the next three weeks. What type of soil will you use? What nutrients? Will you plant one bean or several? Will you try different combinations to grow "Superplant?" Before you begin, read about plants in the class science books and from books in the library. Write your hypothesis (an educated guess about what you predict will happen). Measure your plant(s) every day and keep a chart of your measurements. How will you know if your plant is "Superplant?"
>
> *Aesthetic/Expressive*—Plant Patterns: Carefully take the "skin" off a lima bean, open the seed, and draw what you see. After you plant diferent seeds and the sprout emerges, make a drawing of the plant(s) each day for 3 weeks. Is there a pattern in which leaves

come out first? Does the plant lean in a particular direction? Read about plants and see if you can find out why they grow the way they grow. What is the seed pattern or symmetry? Can you find plants or fruits with patterns based on 2, 3, 4, 5, or 6? Are there any other patterns you discover in studying different plants? Does a seed reflect the pattern of the "parent" plant? Plan a presentation to the class about your project or make a display for the hall show case.

Have high expectations. The plant activity suggested here could actually be done by young children, even at kindergarten level, if directions were read aloud and volunteer help were available.

4. *Enrich individual interests: To foster autonomy and creativity, offer the opportunity to explore areas of great interest in depth and to purposefully investigate real problems.* Identify and share children's interests early in the year. For instance, Miriam Winegar, a superb kindergarten teacher in Eugene, OR, gives the children circles of varied sizes. She asks them to think about their favorite interests and draw those in the largest circles, working down to smaller circles for interests less important to the child. These interest pictures are then glued around a small photo of the child in the center of a sheet of paper, and a little is written about each interest. These are displayed around the room so children can quickly find friends with similar interests, especially when time is provided to circulate, study the pictures, and find others with whom to share a common interest (see Figure 25.2).

When a child is intensely interested in something, allow time to pursue the interest in class, integrate it in skills or topics and have children share interests with each other. Often, doors are opened for peers when a child shares an interest. If Ross played his musical composition on the piano, for example, another child might become interested in learning more about music.

Eastside School, an alternative elementary school in Eugene, OR, offers a model that addresses children's interests as well as meeting needs of able learners in the regular school context. Children are family grouped for homeroom across all grades (one to five), where an affective curriculum is delivered. They are ability grouped for Reading/Language Arts in the morning and for Math after lunch, with flexibility to move children as needed. Every 3 weeks or so, students choose two "projects" among three or four offered for each level, which typically span two to three grades. These are scheduled four days per week for one hour each day, one project following the Language Arts and the other, Math classes. Often, the choices involve required curriculum in science, art, social studies, or health, but liberal doses of what teachers love and want to share are also included. The Oregon Trail, Native Americans, printmaking, marine biology, rocketry, stamp collecting, surfing the Internet, and many other topics allow stu-

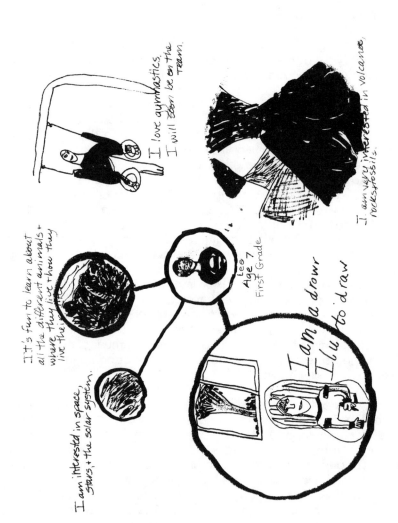

Figure 25.2. Winegar's Interest Profile

dents to make decisions about what they want to learn and when they want to learn it. Projects typically are action-focused and students enthusiastically commit themselves to learning when they can choose projects of interest to them. Finally, one afternoon each week, Wednesday Workshop provides exploratory activities for 1 hour. Students sign up the day before from a feast of choices, some led by parents and children, as well as teachers. One fourth grader taught landscape drawing and another child shared origami, for example.

5. Provide the Tools for Life-long Learning.

- Research Skills—for accessing information
- Higher Level Thinking Skills—for processing information
- Creativity Skills—for adapting, modifying, or transforming information
- Communication Skills—for sharing information
- Study Skills—for organization and use of time and materials
- Metacognitive Skills—for monitoring and control of learning strategies
- Technology Skills—For ease, efficiency, aesthetics, and artistry in all the above

The tools for lifelong learning (Cohen, 1987c) are learned easily when the child is engaged in an area of interest. For example, the second grader (described earlier) who did the project on horses for the hallway display case was motivated to learn research skills so she could find out about the different breeds and other facts she wanted to include. She learned to use library materials and interviewed a stable owner. She used higher level thinking through analyzing and evaluating the information to display, and synthesized what she learned in the book she wrote, *A Horse of Your Own*. Her creativity skills were enhanced in that process as well, as she transformed the material into information of interest to other young children. She developed communication skills by writing her book and choosing material to display for an audience. She learned to use her time wisely, the study skills. Her skills in technology developed through learning basic word processing and keyboarding on the computer in order to "publish" her book and make labels for her displays. She also learned to use a camera to take pictures of different breeds of horses. In addition, with the help of the school librarian, she reflected on the process, monitoring what she knew, determining what she still needed to find out, and selecting strategies for gathering more information—the metacognitive aspect.

Although these tools were developed and infused in the context of the child's interests, pointing them out, giving labels, using the language of thinking, and directly teaching some of these skills ("Here's how to use an index") is necessary. When several children are at a similar point in needing a skill (writing conversation or using a ruler, for example), group instruction can be offered. The context of the interests makes the skill development relevant.

6. *Offer mediation, counseling, mentoring, and facilitation from caring adults to optimize potential.* The caring relationship of an adult with a child is a key ingredient in supporting learning and growth, particularly when the adult is aware of where a child is developmentally and how to lead him or her to higher understandings. Many parents of gifted children apparently do this intuitively (Moss, 1992). These parents help their children to interpret the world of senses ("How does the wind feel in your hair?"), feelings ("You are really, really angry now!"; "You feel so sad when Grandma has to leave."), and relationships ("How would you feel if Jenny took your shovel?"). They lead the child to anticipate and predict ("Which building block should go on next?" "Do you think we need to take an umbrella?"). They also model interest pursuits that may be emulated. Ross is interested in several areas that he shares with his father, particularly music and the computer. However, it may be observing his dad's passion for work that contributes to Ross's own willingness to put forth effort in mastering something.

Parents and teachers are instrumental in mediating and facilitating interest development (see Cohen & Jipson, chapter 31, this volume). They should, at the same time, respect a child's wishes. Lisa, a 4-year-old, wanted to learn to swim, but she wanted to "do it myself." She did not want an adult to help hold her, show her swimming strokes, or to get her a tube, although she asked for feedback on her progress ("Look, Mom, I got my face all the way wet!"). To facilitate interest development, the following have been suggested in this chapter:

1. *Expose the child to possibilities.* Without exposure, an interest cannot develop.
2. *Identify interests.* Observe what the child selects to do in choice or free play activities, tune in to play, or think about what that child is "into."
3. *Facilitate direct requests for help.* ("Dad, please help me tie a really strong knot.")
4. *Extend the interests.* Offer questions, materials, or resources that would help the interest develop or open new avenues.
5. *Figure out the deep questions and interest-themes.* Ask yourself, "Why is this so interesting to this child?"

By determining why an interest is so important to the child and by understanding the child's pattern of interests, parents and teachers can provide the support needed to help the child develop most naturally and fully, answer his or her own profound questions, and regulate the self. High expectations for the child's learning, based on deep understanding of and respect for his or her passions, result in experiences of flow, enthusiasm, and energy, as well as growth in competence. These early interests may be the seeds of a lifetime of productive involvement that you helped to foster!

REFERENCES

Betts, G. (1986). *The autonomous learner model.* Greeley, CO: Autonomous Learner Publications.

Clark, B. (1992). *Growing up gifted* (4th ed.). Columbus, OH: Merrill.

Cohen, L. M. (1985). Towards a theory for gifted education. *Dissertation Abstracts International,* 8509318.

Cohen, L. M. (1987a). Techniques for studying the interests of infants and young children. *Gifted International, 4*(2), 15-32.

Cohen, L. M. (1987a). Maestro Ben. *The Gifted Child Today, 10*(1), 55-57.

Cohen, L. M. (1987b). Indian summer. *The Gifted Child Today, 10*(3), 37-39.

Cohen, L. M. (1987c). 13 tips for teaching gifted children. *Teaching Exceptional Children, 20*(1), 34-38.

Cohen, L. M. (1988a). Infant interests: Seeds of creative development. *Illinois Journal for the Gifted, 7,* 32-36.

Cohen, L. M. (1988b). Developing children's creativity, thinking and interests: Strategies for the district, school, and classroom. *OSSC Bulletin Monograph, 31*(6), 1-10.

Cohen, L. M. (1989). Understanding the interests and themes of the very young gifted child. *Gifted Child Today, 12*(4), 6-9.

Cohen, L. M. ((1991/1992). A gifted education for all children. *Our Gifted Children, 6,* 22-30.

Cohen, L. M. (1994). Mode-switching strategies. In J. Edwards (Ed.), *Thinking: International interdisciplinary perspectives* (pp. 230-240). Melbourne: Hawker-Brownlow.

Cohen, L. M., & Frydenberg, E. (1996). *Coping for capable kids.* Waco, TX: Prufrock.

Cohen, L. M., & Gelbrich, J. (in press). Young chidren's interests: Seeds of adult creativity. In A. S. Fishkin, B. Cramond, & P. Olszewski-Kubilius (Eds.), *Investigating creativity in youth: Research and methods.* Cresskill, NJ: Hampton Press.

Coy, G. L. (1923). *The interests, abilities and achievements of a special class for gifted children.* New York: Teachers College Press.

Csikzentimhalyi, M. (1990). *Flow: The psychology of optimal experience.* New York: Harper Perennial.

Csikszentmihalyi, M., Rathunde K., & Whalen S. (1993) *Talented teenagers.* New York: Cambridge University Press.

Ferrara, N. (1984). *Network of enterprise and the individual's organization of purpose.* Unpublished doctoral dissertation, Rutgers University, Newark, NJ.

Gelbrich, J. A. (1992). *Children's interests and themes: A factor analytic study and a comparison of interest preferences between children identified as gifted and children who have not been identified as gifted.* Unpublished doctoral dissertation, University of Oregon, Eugene, OR.

Goertzel, M. G., Goertzel, V., & Goertzel, T. (1978). *300 eminent personalities.* San Francisco: Jossey-Bass

Harrington, B. , Harrington, J. , & Slatow, D. (1986). What interests bright kids in grades 4-6? *The Creative Child and Adult Quarterly, 11,* 174-176.

Horowitz, F.D., & O'Brien, M. (1985). Epilogue: Perspectives on research and development. In F.D. Horowitz & M. O'Brien (Eds.), *The gifted and talented: Developmental perspectives* (pp. 437-454). Washington, D.C.; American Psychological Association.

Janos, P. N., & Robinson, N. M. (1985). Psychosocial development in intellectually gifted children. In F. D. Horowitz & M. O'Brien (Eds.), *The gifted and talented: Developmental perspectives* (pp. 149-195). Washington, DC: American Psychological Association.

Moss, E. (1992). Early interactions and metacognitive development of gifted preschoolers. In P. S. Klein & A. J. Tannenbaum (Eds.), *To be young and gifted* (pp. 278-318). Norwood, NJ: Ablex.

Piaget, J. (1970). *Science of education and the psychology of the child.* New York: Penguin. (Original work published 1975)

Piaget, J. (1977). *The development of thought: Equilibration of cognitive structures.* New York: Viking. (Original work published 1975)

Renzulli, J. S. (1977a). *The Interest-A-Lyzer.* Mansfield Center, CT: Creative Learning Press.

Renzulli, J.S. (1977b). *The enrichment triad model: A guide for developing defensible programs for the gifted and talented.* Wethersfield, CT: Creative Learning Press.

Rice, J. P. (1968). A comparative study of academic interest patterns among selected groups of exceptional and normal intermediate children. *California Journal of Educational Research, 14*(3), 131-144.

Schowalter, J. E. (1979). When dinosaurs return: Children's fascination with dinosaurs. *Children Today, 8*(3), 2-5.

Shore, B. M., Cornell, D. G., Robinson, A., & Ward, V. S. (1991). *Recommended practices in gifted education: A critical analysis.* New York: Teachers College Press.

Shore, B. M., & Kanevsky, L. S. (1993). Thinking processes: Being and becoming gifted. In K. A. Heller, F. J. Monks, & A. H. Passow (Eds.), *International handbook of research and development of giftedness and talent* (pp. 138-147). New York: Pergamon.

Terman, L. M. (Ed.). (1925). *Genetic studies of genius, Vol. 1: Mental and physical traits of a thousand gifted children.* Palo Alto, CA: Stanford University Press.

Thorndike, R. (1939). Responses of a group of gifted children to the Pressey Interest-Attitudes Test. *Journal of Educational Psychology, 30,* 588-594.

Thorndike, R. L. (1940). Performance of gifted children on tests of developmental age. *The Journal of Psychology, 9,* 337-343.

26

Social/Emotional Considerations in Young Gifted Children

Dorothy Knopper

Defining giftedness in young children is somewhat like trying to pick up mercury. Just when you think you have it all in place, it slides away from you. Priscilla Vail (1979), in *The World of the Gifted Child*, appropriately titled the chapter on identification "Catching Quicksilver." Vail believes that there is no one measurement to determine who the gifted child is; instead, we must use both objective data and subjective observations, and "trust our own ability to recognize giftedness when it crosses our path" (p. 28).

Researchers and practitioners in the multifaceted field of gifted education have developed and refined various instruments to determine intellectual levels and potential for achievement, but it is generally agreed that they should be used in combination with a knowledge of gifted children's social/emotional behavior. Because we are not dealing with a homogeneous group it is helpful to recognize the gifted child in terms of affective characteristics as well as academic levels. Brodsky (1992) suggested that we emphasize diversity and individuality, developing "measures of attitudes and beliefs about the gifted that give them chances to make greater differentiations than past measures often allowed." Therefore, stated Brodsky, we can lessen the "discrepancy between what we know about the heterogeneity among gifted children and what we measure through research" (p. 58).

REFINING THE DEFINITION

Traditionally, giftedness has been defined in terms of achievement or performance, offering a narrow perception of bright children and a limited range of solutions for teachers, parents and counselors who must understand all aspects of children's development in order to meet their needs. Therefore, it is interesting to note Freehill's comments, as early as 1961, that appropriate education for the gifted includes "emotional and character development" and that there is a significant relationship between "intellectual growth and emotional welfare"(p. 396). He concluded that "brightness implies a large empathic or feeling range"(p. 385).

Marland's (1972) landmark definition of gifted and talented children does not include reference to the affective area. The characteristics of *general intellectual ability, specific academic aptitude, creative or productive thinking, leadership ability, visual and performing arts, psychomotor ability* (p. 10) became a model for many achievement-based definitions on which programs for gifted students would be built.

It was not until 1991 that the Columbus Group developed a more comprehensive view with the following affective-based definition:

> Giftedness is asynchronous development in which advanced cognitive abilities and heightened intensity combine to create inner experiences and awareness that are qualitatively different from the norm. This asynchrony increases with higher intellectual capacity. The uniqueness of the gifted renders them particularly vulnerable and requires modifications in parenting, teaching and counseling in order for them to develop optimally. (Morelock, 1992, p. 14)

This definition moves beyond giftedness as merely external behaviors, products, and achievements to an understanding of giftedness as producing "atypical development throughout the lifespan in terms of awareness, perceptions, emotional responses, and life experiences" (p. 14). Morelock described highly gifted children whose rates of cognitive, emotional, and physical development display lack of synchronicity. Although their emotional development is age appropriate, their abstract thinking and cognitive abilities are far ahead.

SOCIAL/EMOTIONAL CHARACTERISTICS

According to Clark (1992), maximum intellectual capacity can only be reached through the development of all aspects of the individual: cognitive, affective, physical, and intuitive. Clark's statement that "a limit to any one function limits all functioning" (p. 117) points out the difficulty of discussing a child's total being in terms of only intellectual potential, social/emotional behavior, or physical development.

We must thus be aware of the importance and uniqueness of the affective area for young gifted children, while considering it in relation to other developmental areas. Lovecky (1992) mentioned several social/emotional traits:

- perfectionism
- sensitivity
- intensity and reactivity
- feeling different
- uneven intellectual and emotional development

Add to the list (Knopper, 1994):

- curiosity
- memory
- abstract thinking
- frustration (with uneven development)
- impatience (with perfectionistic expectations of themselves and others)
- intense interests
- sense of humor

We now have a multifaceted picture of giftedness as it is typically exhibited in children of preschool and early elementary ages.

TRAITS THAT CAUSE TROUBLE

"Act your age!" shouts 5-year-old Amy's exasperated mother. Amy's tearful response is, "I am!" Because her child is well beyond her chronological years in intellectual development, it's easy to forget that socially and emotionally she is only a little girl. Amy's development is uneven or asynchronous; her body and her emotions are age appropriate, but her cognitive abilities are several years ahead. Such youngsters live with the frustration of maxi minds in mini bodies. Adults expect more mature behavior, and the children expect their muscles to perform as easily as their minds.

As a result of uneven development in social, cognitive, and physical skills, gifted youngsters experience unique adjustment problems, often resulting in temper tantrums, depression, and aggressive behavior. Children like Amy need to have the opportunity to interact with mental as well as chronological peers, but finding peers with similar interests and intellectual abilities may be difficult in traditional school settings. Depending on the activity and interest area, Amy may require older, same-age, or younger children—or adults.

Such children may be well advanced intellectually but become frustrated because they lack life experiences and the physical capabilities needed to carry out their complex projects. Imagine an 8-year-old who designs a nonpolluting automobile engine but is too young to obtain a driver's license!

Entry into preschool and kindergarten are often critical periods of adjustment for young gifted children. They enter with enthusiasm, excitement and high expectations, only to return home crying, "I didn't learn anything new!" Kerr (1991) suggested that disappointment and boredom connected with the reality of school may lead to:

- fear and anxiety about attending school
- arguments with playmates
- withdrawing into fantasy and daydreams during school

According to Fiedler (1993), gifted students are "caught in clashes that result from the interaction between the characteristics that make them unique and the traits of typical school environments. Simply being gifted is enough to make them feel like "square pegs in round holes" (p. 1). She mentioned sources of stress:

- functioning at advanced cognitive levels
- contacts with older peers
- early onset of and rapid progress through developmental stages
- awareness of being different

Lovecky (1992) concentrated on the problem areas of:

- divergent thinking
- excitability
- sensitivity
- perceptiveness
- entelechy (high motivation to pursue goals/strong will)

Children with these traits find it difficult to follow typical organizational patterns, preferring their own unique sense of creativity; they feel emotions intensely and are more empathic than most of their peers; they have insight and intuition regarding various aspects of situations; and they are intense in the pursuit of their passions and goals.

Knopper (1994) emphasized the stressful combination of sensitivity, intensity, and perfectionism; the cry for help from gifted youngsters who possess these traits; and the critical need for awareness, empathy, and support from parents and teachers. A strong sense of justice and compassion; intense focus on interests, tasks, and relationships; and compulsive worry about doing everything perfectly lead to fear of failure and reluctance to take risks. The adults in their lives must understand that gifted children often feel "weird" and suppress their talents in order to fit in.

The characteristics discussed in this section may lead to anxiety and depression, even in younger children. The component of giftedness is usually an integral part of the problem and must be understood and dealt with. Psychological adjustment issues should not be considered separately from giftedness (Kerr, 1991).

CLASSROOM INTERVENTION STRATEGIES

As elementary classroom teachers face higher numbers of students, greater ranges of needs, and fewer resources and support staff, they must rely on what works efficiently and easily for gifted students with the special academic and social/emotional needs described in this chapter. The best credo for overworked but caring teachers must be "If it works, do it." In other words, use common sense in balancing the requirements that work for most students, as well as the flexibility gifted children require. If the curriculum calls for completion of five pages of addition problems, and the gifted child has grasped the concept after five problems, go on to something more challenging. Pretest and posttest to determine bright children's levels of functioning in measurable subjects, such as math, reading, spelling. Use tests from higher grades when appropriate. Once you determine that children are functioning above grade level, you'll save your time and theirs—and prevent future problematic situations—by challenging them with advanced work.

Gifted students frequently pursue intense passions outside of school. Find out the nature of those interests and bring them into the classroom. Research on dinosaurs, an original computer program, a model of a space shuttle, or a compilation of baseball statistics can be shared with the entire class.

According to Canfield and Wells (1994), the most important thing teachers can do to help their students both intellectually and emotionally is to establish a classroom atmosphere of mutual support and caring. Children must feel that school is a safe and secure place for them. Canfield and Wells suggested that teachers and students "freely discuss cooperation and competition, trust and fear, openness and deceit" (p. 5). Their book, *100 Ways to Enhance Self-Concept in the Classroom*, contains exciting and practical strategies to use in a classroom.

Delisle (1992) pointed out the critical role of affective education in the curriculum:

> To go to school is to be socialized; to learn content is to be left a more educated person than before; to discuss issues and problems is to learn to respect and value both our individual differences and our collective similarities. (p. 111)

PARENTAL SUPPORT

Tyler informed his parents that first grade was "dumb." "All we read are easy books with pictures," complained the 6-year-old. When asked what he would choose, he ran to the bookshelf and selected *The Hobbit*. His mother wisely contacted his teacher and asked if he could bring a favorite book to read in school. The teacher had not realized that Tyler was reading at such an advanced level, because he spent reading periods staring out the window or bothering other children. She encouraged Tyler to select his own books, and life became easier for all. Common-sense communication between parents and teacher opened an avenue of excitement for a young gifted child.

As their children's best advocates, parents can communicate information about their outside interests and passions. Parents can also share their own hobbies and talents, and they can work with teachers to establish mentorship programs and other supplemental learning projects. Eby and Smutny (1990) described Worlds of Wisdom and Wonder and Summer Wonders, successful weekend and summer programs for able preschool and elementary students, providing stimulation and fun for children, support and flexibility for teachers, and speakers and discussion groups for parents. Eby and Smutny suggested that such a program can be organized by an independent parent-teacher coalition.

Parents live daily with the challenging—and often stressful—social/emotional aspects of giftedness described in this chapter. Proactive sharing of their unique perspectives with teachers before school begins is more effective than reactive solutions to acute classroom situations.

CONCLUSION

It is difficult to separate academic needs from social/emotional concerns in the young gifted child. There is no typical gifted child; nor are there traits that fit every child. We must consider each individual as a whole entity and include the role that giftedness plays in the development of the total child.

According to Saunders (1991):

> Gifted individuals can be successful, but there is a certain amount of pain and suffering that comes along with the package. To be a child of promise is to be interesting, creative, and exciting. It is also to be at risk for certain emotional problems. (p. 22)

REFERENCES

Brodsky, R. (1992). *From the attic*. Roeper Review, *15*(1), 58.

Canfield, J., & Wells, H.C. (1994). *100 ways to enhance self-concept in the classroom: A handbook for teachers, counselors, and group leaders*. Boston: Allyn & Bacon.

Clark, B. (1992). *Growing up gifted* (4th ed.). New York: Merrill/ Macmillan.

Delisle, J.R. (1992). *Guiding the social and emotional development of gifted youth: A practical guide for educators and counselors*. New York: Longman.

Eby, J.W., & Smutny, J.F. (1990). *A thoughtful overview of gifted education*. New York: Longman.

Fiedler, E. (1993). Square pegs in round holes: Gifted kids who don't fit in. *Understanding Our Gifted, 5*(5A), 1, 11-13.

Freehill, M.F. (1961). *Gifted children: Their psychology and education*. New York: Macmillan.

Kerr, B. (1991). *A handbook for counseling the gifted and talented*. Alexandria, VA: American Association for Counseling and Development.

Knopper, D. (1994). *Parent education: Parents as partners*. Boulder, CO: Open Space Communications.

Lovecky, D.V. (1992). Exploring social and emotional aspects of giftedness in children. *Roeper Review, 15*(1), 18-25.

Marland, S.P., Jr. (1972). *Education of the gifted and talented*. Report to the Congress of the United States by the U.S. Commissioner of Education. Washington, DC: U.S. Government Printing Office.

Morelock, M.J. (1992). Giftedness: The view from within. *Understanding Our Gifted, 4*(3), 1, 11-15.

Saunders, J., with Espeland, P. (1991). *Bringing out the best*. Minneapolis: Free Spirit.

Vail, P.L. (1979). *The world of the gifted child*. New York: Walker.

27

The Role of the Pediatrician

Patricia Duggins Hoelscher

Those who interact with children on a regular basis must have general knowledge of the broad range of child development characteristics outside their area of specialization. Pediatricians, who once had the isolated job of attending to the physical well-being of a child, now must broaden their focus and be cognizant of the characteristics of development beyond the physical body. They must be familiar with the characteristics and needs of young gifted children, as well as the professional resources available to assist parents in raising healthy children.

In assessing the rate and extent of development, the whole child must be considered. The relationship between physical health and cognitive and emotional development is well documented (Webb, Meckstroth, & Tolan, 1982). Inattention to the observable characteristics of giftedness can create problems.

To assist in accomplishing accurate cooperation with the health care professional, parents should record data describing their child's growth and development. "Baby Book" records usually include

347

facts such as dates when the child first walked and talked and what was said. Frequently, such records give an indication of abilities developing more rapidly than chronological age norms show.

Anecdotal records are short descriptions of something a child did or said that seemed unusual, perceptive, or advanced when compared with the responses of other children of the same age. Observant parents and preschool teachers or day-care workers should write down events as they occur. Parents can often recount humorous events involving their child that sound unbelievable, yet are true. Parents often "know" their child has advanced abilities before others recognize it.

A characteristic of giftedness that is particularly wearing to new parents is the high energy level of these babies and their baby's need for much less sleep than expected. The constant motion of arms and legs and a strong innate desire to explore the world help him discover how to flip over and scoot. His curiosity and coordination soon allows him to pull himself up and in many cases work his way over the side of the crib and into the open world. Surprised to find her young child in the kitchen when he had been put down for a nap, the mother is sure this is an unusual occurrence.

Other babies might be extremely sensitive to stimuli. Perhaps sounds that are at a normal level are particularly uncomfortable. Clothing, which to adults feels soft and smooth, has tags, seams, ridges, threads, or folds that some children find excessively uncomfortable. Such a child settles down only when the troublesome item of clothing is removed.

Frequently, gifted children will begin speaking well before the age norms suggest. Early, single words move rapidly into three- and four-word sentences. Occasionally, a young child will barely respond to a pediatrician's questions or efforts to build rapport, but once back in the car can recount in detail and in sequence all that was said and done.

Informal assessment does not have to be elaborate or complicated. It does have to be specific and organized. Parents should include the major areas of developmental skills for young children: expressive and receptive language, cognitive, gross motor, self-help such as eating or dressing, social or behavioral, and perceptual.

Parents need continually to observe and respond to their child's behavior. A variety of situations over time need to be observed. Parents should collect samples of the child's work and date it. The pediatrician should gather data regarding the family history. Interviews with parent and child should help support that these characteristics were evident in other family members. The testing of mental ability during the first couple years of life does not reliably predict future advanced ability. By age 2, a definite positive correlation does seem to develop between scores on the Bayley Mental Index and those on the Binet or WISC over the next several years (White, 1987).

Between 18 months and 4 years, virtually all children have available an innate ordering device for language learning, the Language Acquisition Device (Linfors, 1987). Never again will language learning be as easy. Parents need to be encouraged to read to, talk with, and listen to their child. Expression of feelings through words should be promoted. Once verbal skills develop, those skills usually stay ahead of verbal skill norms at the same chronological age. Early bilingual ability is a natural for children at this age when family and environmental factors allow. Adults will determine whether the language acquired is a tool to handle biological and social needs or an instrument of clarity and precision.

The parental perspective of preschoolers shows a carryover of some characteristics from the previous age grouping and the evidence of additional characteristics. They continue to have high energy levels and require less sleep. They often have vivid and elaborate fantasies. In retelling events, their embellishments are not intended as lies, just the intervention of their imagination. Frequently, children have an imaginary friend. The experiences they share are very real and can continue for several years.

Gifted children exhibit a diversity of interests. Their rooms are collages of collections. They have thirst for knowledge, a strong desire to know how people and objects work. They can noticeably learn faster, remember more, and think more deeply than chronological age norms expect. Children might exhibit a marked interest in specific areas. Children, who at age 2 can sing on pitch the correct melody of a wide variety of songs might also have artistic talent above most comparably aged peers. A high percentage of gifted children have taught themselves to read prior to entering kindergarten.

This age span can be a perplexing time for children who have feelings of being different but do not understand why. Frustrated by an uneven rate of development they are experiencing, they cannot print their name or tie their shoes, but they can read. Their quick minds cause them to interrupt as their ideas leap ahead in the conversation. Their attempts at leadership appear bossy. Their unrealistic goals and desire for perfectionism increase existing frustrations. They do not finish their Mother's Day card because they cannot draw the flowers on it the way they want them to look. If parents are aware of advanced abilities, they may place pressure on their child, unknowingly, by demanding higher expectations of achievement or by exploiting abilities to increase their status. Already stress is coming to bear.

Recommendations should include contact with gifted peers. Health care practitioners should be able to provide resources to which parents can turn. Children need peers with like abilities to learn contexts, relationships, and applications of their capabilities. They need to learn it is all right to be different. They need feedback from peers and an opportunity to develop social skills. They need to explore and take responsibility for their learning. Dramatic play is valuable because it encourages language development, problem-solving skills, self-control, sharing, creativity, dealing with abstractions, and acquiring new knowledge.

Parents need to be encouraged to support children's creative behavior to encourage and engage in playfulness and fantasy. Children also need quiet alone time. A quiet body does not mean a quiet mind. Young children need time alone to think.

Pediatricians should be able to guide parents to resources that match the child's interests. As the interests change, so also can the mentors and resources. Diversity and exploration are hallmarks of gifted children.

Some characteristics of giftedness that became evident between the ages of 2 and 5 may become of particular concern when children enter school. For 5 years, they have learned easily. They could absorb an unusual quantity of information with great retentiveness. In kindergarten or first grade, children might frequently awake with stomachaches or headaches and not want to go to school. It could be that they are bored with a slow-paced routine, are impatient waiting for the group, or have poor relations with less able peers.

The verbal ability of gifted children has been encouraged from the time they were newborns. The parents enjoyed the conversations with their preschoolers because they were almost adult-like. In school, these children have been perceived as show-offs for their use of extensive vocabulary and ideas. They usually dominate discussions and are adept at using verbalism to manage others and avoid tasks.

Creative children's ability to use flexible thought patterns and solve problems in diverse ways had been a delight to their parents. Their teachers see their creativity as disruptive and disrespectful to authority. They are frequently penalized for not following directions.

Gifted children stretch the boundaries of the school curriculum. They leap-frog through the curriculum disregarding the hierarchy of skills. They bring a different kind of logic to studies such math. They use unusual but accurate methods to divide or manipulate fractions.

Gifted children know now more than ever that they are different and might still not understand why or if it is all right. The beginnings of underachievement are set in motion as children seek to be average and hopefully acceptable to their peers. The parents have watched their curious 3-year-old turn into a bored third grader.

For other children, the requirements to conform to the group can be overwhelming. Once a pediatrician has confirmed that no apparent physiological reasons exist for recurring headaches and stomachaches, it is time to delve further into sources of stress in the child's life and possible resolutions to the situation. If the pediatrician feels that even limited counseling is beyond his or her capabilities, then referral to other resources is the logical step. Mentors matched children's particular interests continue to provide a positive experience for learning at a challenging and appropriate pace. Parents need a peer group of other parents of gifted children just as children need peers of their ability. Health care practitioners can be alert to parents with children of like abilities so they can provide support for each other.

School age gifted children show unusual sophistication in their understanding of world events. Therefore, they can be more pessimistic about the future than children are expected to be. Discussion with them about their role in the larger problem and how they can be effective helps to give children a feeling of control over situations that otherwise would make them feel helpless. Once in school, characteristics of giftedness such as academic proficiency, memory, linguistic and computational fluency, and analytical ability help children succeed within or surpass the expectations that society holds. However, intellectual nonsequentiality, divergent thinking and high creativity can cause a child to be in conflict with or threaten the expectations of society.

Children are first children. Their differentness must be recognized so they can understand it. They must develop resiliency to the stresses of being different. Gifted children are a widely diverse group around which no definitive pattern can be drawn. They have a wide range of interests and abilities. It is important for all who have contact with them to be aware of the positive characteristics of giftedness as well as the negative ones that catch other's attention. Parents frequently seek help for medical problems but often do not approach a health care practitioner about nonmedical or emotional problems. Pediatricians and family practitioners must create an open and caring attitude, be willing to listen, and encourage the parent to share questions and concerns related to their child. Parents need the support and expertise of a responsive medical professional to help provide adequate and appropriate services.

There are several factors affecting the unresponsiveness typical of many pediatricians toward characteristics of giftedness. Health care workers are usually trained to focus on delays in children rather than advanced abilities. The myth that gifted children make it on their own discourages professionals from pursuing knowledge about the characteristics and needs of the gifted children they serve. For many medical professionals, the characteristics of particular subgroups of children, such as gifted children, are not included in their already full medical training.

Research in the field of giftedness continues to grow. Just as medical professionals keep current with new advances in the field of medicine, so also should they remain aware of research in the field of giftedness. Current brain research suggests biological factors that support various observed characteristics associated with giftedness. Moving the study of giftedness into the medical research of neuroscience would make it more visible to medical professionals. Research on giftedness should appear regularly in a broad range of professional literature. The attention of professionals in a wide variety of fields can be focused on the need for an interdisciplinary approach to the topic. Giftedness is a very important area to be included in the training of pediatricians and family practitioners. As in other fields, until it is required for accreditation or certification, its omission will continue. At present, continuing education programs, workshops, and conference sessions may be the best place to create an awareness of the need for attention to giftedness.

Health care professionals should be sufficiently cognizant of basic characteristics of giftedness and subsequent needs related to those characteristics. They should provide support and guidance for the family, should be aware of available resources that are both local and within a broader area to which they can refer parents, and should encourage their professional peers to develop a greater awareness of and knowledge about gifted children.

Recognition of the existence of characteristics associated with giftedness and referral to appropriate resources can provide important support to families of young children who appear to be gifted. Although it is beyond the scope of health care professionals' role to declare a child gifted or not, or to judge the quality of local options for gifted children, he or she can provide supporting data when necessary to assist a family in negotiating the option they have chosen for their child. Educators frequently do not look for giftedness until the middle of elementary school. Health care professionals in partnership with parents can support the development of the whole child at an early age, encouraging the maximum potential of the child to be realized.

Recognizing and supporting parental observations of giftedness should be a natural extension of the medical professional's role in caring for the whole child. To be effective, the health care professional need only have a working knowledge and understanding of giftedness. Referral to other resources would be a primary role.

When children are young, intervention must occur. Cooperation between the parents and all professionals with whom the child interacts is important to fulfill early indications of giftedness. The pediatrician, the first professional to be involved with the child, has a part of that initial responsibility.

REFERENCES

Linfors, J. W. (1987). *Children's language and learning* (2nd ed.). Engelwood Cliffs, NJ: Prentice-Hall.

Webb, J.T., Meckstroth, E., & Tolan, S. (1982). *Guiding the gifted child.* Columbus: Ohio Publishing.

White, B. (1987). *The first three years of life.* Englewood Cliffs, NJ: Prentice-Hall.

VI

Creating Effective Educational Experiences for Gifted Young Children

Joan Franklin Smutny

Creating and implementing effective learning experiences is inherent in our growing sensitivity for the young child's gifts and talents. To perceive what is developmentally appropriate for a child's growth involves knowledge of all the components that impact his or her involvement in learning: environments, programs, curricula, and activities. Teachers can create opportunities for self-discovery and self-actualization through participation in higher levels of critical and creative thinking. The authors in this section focus on practices and models reflecting integration, interdisciplinary frameworks, project approaches, higher level thinking skills, interactive communication between teacher and students, thematic orientation, connectedness, and ongoing assessment. Such perceptive treatment of different educational experiences will be of inestimable support to all working in diversified learning settings with gifted children.

Beverly Shaklee, acknowledging the special needs of young gifted children, proposes a developmentally appropriate learning environment for bright young children in Chapter 28. Teachers as facilitators and managers of instruction will want to foster independence in learning, problem solving, and choosing the next step. Educational environments that enable children to find their own sources of intellectual stimulation will equip them for lifelong learning. An integrated curriculum and the use of innovative assessment tools are requisite to establish an environment that nurtures young gifted children.

Implementing child-centered settings is a focal point of Chapter 29 by Susan Belgrad. Creating an enabling environment for young gifted children requires teachers to learn how and when to encourage intellectually challenging play. Adults need to engage in modes of interaction that will help the child develop an awareness of his or her own abilities. Real learning takes place when children participate with adults in interactional skills and in the process of thinking and problem solving.

In Chapter 30, Carolyn Cummings and Jane Piirto relate components of school reform to the educational experiences of young children engaged in reading, discussing, sharing personal experiences, and interests. Both authors encourage educators to understand how to take part in constructivist ways that enable bright children to learn best. A constructivist approach to early childhood education naturally includes such activities as involvement in projects, conducting interviews, and researching reports. Young talented children can set personal goals for themselves and assess their fulfillment of them. In this orientation, education is not what is being done to the student, but what the student does with his or her own knowledge.

LeoNora Cohen and Janice Jipson describe and assess those models considered appropriate for young gifted children in Chapter 31. They note that many models used in preschool programs can be downward extensions of models used in elementary school. Of all the models recommended, however, both Cohen and Jipson have found the modified constructivist model most effective, based on the works of Piaget, Feuerstein, Vygotsky, Renzulli, and Gardner. They examine the theoretical aspects of this model, focusing on children's constructions of meaning, levels of student competence and interests, and the effect of these on different learning outcomes. Cohen and Jipson advocate the use of early education models in regular classrooms to help all children maximize their talents.

Starr Cline proposes integrating models of gifted education to meet the needs of gifted children who are not being served well in the regular classroom in Chapter 32. She discusses two major issues that must be addressed if appropriate programming for gifted students is to be actualized: teacher training and dispelling the myth that all programs for gifted are costly. Cline proposes a differentiated curriculum for gifted children that includes increased breadth, depth, and tempo; expansion of basic skills; process modifications; and independent study. Programming alternatives include: in-class resource room, revolving door, acceleration, telecommunications, mentoring, after school classes, computers, provisional augmentation, supported by professionals, and community residents. She avers that the "glass ceiling" which educators have created for the gifted can and must be broken through.

Systems theory enables us to look at major influences on the world of the young gifted child. Hollingsworth utilizes systems theory to describe a world that functions best when all components are working together to develop responsible children in Chapter 33. For the system to work toward talent development and creative productivity, the child must be the energy source. Parents can provide child-appropriate opportunities to make choices, and schools can create open-ended opportunities for feedback. In this way, different parts of the system, Hollingsworth concludes, reinforce each other and enable everyone to work toward the development of each individual's talents.

Designing a preschool program for the gifted/talented child, Gail Hanninen says in Chapter 34, is a process that examines basic beliefs, clarifies expectations, and assures quality experiences for children. The home, school, and community environments must be responsive to the learning strengths and interests of each child. The Coeur d'Alene project is cited as an example of a program that provides each child with the best services possible. Criteria for defining an effective program include student performance standards, parent participation as an integral part of the learning environment, and qualified personnel who understand giftedness and intellectual challenge.

Joan Vydra and Judy Leimbach propose that educators examine the value of compacting, pacing, acceleration, enrichment, independent projects, and higher level cognitive and creative thinking activities to challenge the gifted child. In Chapter 35, the authors elaborate on some of their favorite books, references, and materials, and offer examples of activities they have designed to support the curriculum of the regular classroom. They examine basic subject areas and include a section on integrated curriculum to create a classroom dynamic that is inviting and exciting for the gifted child who is looking for compelling challenges in the regular classroom.

Bob Stanish believes that creative, productive thinking has high value in the classroom learning setting, as shown in Chapter 36. The skills of creative, productive thinking can be utilized with good results when related to subject matter content or taught solely for the purpose of developing creative thinking ability. Importantly, such an orientation can benefit teachers as well as students. Stanish has developed a series of useful thinking exercises to enhance the creative-thinking responses of children. His exercises focus on developing fluency, flexibility, originality, elaboration, and the skills of making transformations (including the visual and analogical or metaphorical thinking). The skills of creative productive thinking can apply to various models of problem solving, applicable to all children.

Linda Meininger emphasizes the importance of programs based on developmentally appropriate practices. Developmentally appropriate is not synonymous with "age appropriate," which can place ceilings on children—especially those who are gifted. She offers a summary of curriculum perspectives which include the traditional classroom, the developmental, and appropriate modifications for gifted. Meininger advocates moving beyond the traditional to a more integrated, responsive learning environment that honors diversity of ability, and provides opportunities for children to learn at their highest level. In such an environment, the gifted teacher can discern and meet the needs of each individual learner. With a developmental perspective, appropriate modifications for gifted can effect a tapestry of learning for all.

In Chapter 38, Corliss McCallister and William Nash focus on a Javits-funded project that identified creatively gifted children from economically disadvantaged backgrounds. Three preschools were developed with effective results. The project's goals represented four ideals or theories used in gifted education programs: congruity, coherence, completeness, and continuity. The success of fulfilling such goals corroborated this project's offering to both the theoretician and the practitioner. Directions in examining and serving this population of creatively gifted children emerged. Although there are many barriers, these are not insurmountable, as the project has proven.

As shown in Chapter 39, Susan Baum believes that educators should examine diversified curriculum possibilities that elicit authentic learning experiences for students and choose those strategies most supportive of their abilities. She speaks of the excellence of designing picture book experiences and chooses *Thunder Cake* to illustrate the possibilities of using literature to develop and enrich curriculum. If a book is rich in complexity, it can provide many multifaceted, creative learning experiences. Exciting long-term projects that enrich the curriculum and integrate learning skills will not only nurture students' talents, but also help teachers recognize their abilities. She includes a comprehensive picture book bibliography, reflecting biology, ecology, geology, botany, mathematics, literature/writing, anthropology, sociology, history, and fine arts.

Janice Jipson urges the importance of interconnections among all aspects of each child's learning and development. In Chapter 40, she proposes an examination of strategies for implementing developmentally appropriate early childhood curriculum, such as incidental teaching and thematic instruction. Units based on conceptual themes have great potential for involving the interests of the gifted young child, as they open the curriculum to a richer variety of experiences. She avers that if curriculum is truly developmentally and culturally appropriate, then the needs of the gifted child will be met.

In Chapter 41, Sandra Berger and Jay McIntire advocate technology as a means to expand the learning experience and to make it a more individualized, interactive process. Technology provides access to more information, more varied content, and more complex and abstract ideas and priorities for highly able learners. Young children respond readily to technology-based instruction. The open-endedness of communication systems permits children to make choices and go beyond the information they already know. They are freed from the barriers of producing traditional products and feel comfortable interacting with high-level content. The authors include an appendix of major Internet links and sources of information, which should prove valuable to all who work with children, especially the bright ones. Berger and McIntire contend, "The future will, in large part, be driven by new and emerging technologies, and young gifted children will be the engineers as well as the users." Parents and educators of these children need to encourage this creative use of technology and its vital impact on the future.

28

Educationally Dynamic Environments for Young Gifted Children*

Beverly D. Shaklee

The topic of research was "Why Do Bubbles Have Rainbows?" The scientist was a 5-year-old girl. After hearing her presentation, an interested observer asked, "Kaylia, do you understand the words on your poster? For example, can you tell me what 'refraction' is?" "Oh! Ms. Hansford, don't you know what refraction is? Refraction is when the light is bent going through the bubble, that's what creates the rainbows!" an enthusiastic Kaylia replied.

How do we create appropriate learning environments for young gifted children? What should we be attentive to when we establish a curriculum and which instructional strategies match our goals and objectives for child development? Is there any "right" way to go? Are there guidelines to follow? How do we encourage and nurture a child like Kaylia?

*The contents of this chapter were developed, in part, from a grant from the Department of Education. However, these contents do not necessarily represent the policy of the Department of Education and one should not assume endorsement by the Federal Government.

Teaching young gifted children is a lot like gourmet cooking. There are certainly a few recipes (or guidelines) to follow, but most of what we should be doing with young gifted children should be particularly adapted to the individual differences of the child. In early childhood education, we call this *developmentally appropriate practice* (Bredekamp, 1987).

DEVELOPMENTALLY APPROPRIATE PRACTICE

Early childhood educators have long acknowledged that children create their own knowledge by processing information gained from experiences (Spodek & Saracho, 1994). They develop an understanding of what the world is like and interpret what they learn and experience through their individual lenses on the world. New information and experiences help children to expand their view of the world. We continue to learn through this process throughout our lifetimes. Researchers such as Piaget, Vygotsky, and Bruner have helped us describe the processes that children use when constructing knowledge. The term *constructivist theory* is used to describe this process of learning.

In addition to describing how children learn, early childhood educators have attempted to describe the environments which foster optimal learning for all young children. Standards to ensure quality include the extent to which knowledge of child development is embedded in program practices and the degree to which the program responds to two dimensions: age appropriateness and individual appropriateness.

Age appropriateness, as defined by the National Association for the Education of Young Children (NAEYC) indicates that there are universal and predictable sequences of growth and change that occur in children. Knowledge of typical development provides a framework from which to plan a program. *Individual appropriateness* recognizes the fact that each child is a unique individual. As a unique person, each child brings a different personality, learning style, and family background as well as variations of growth and development (Bredekamp, 1987).

Early childhood educators use their knowledge of typical development to create a range of experiences and activities to use in the classroom. However, it would be inappropriate to stop at this point. A sound early childhood program couples the knowledge of typical development with the unique and individual needs of each child to create an optimal learning environment. From the perspective of gifted child education, we sometimes see wonderful classrooms that are age appropriate but pay little attention to the individual needs of the gifted child. The balance of attention to both age and individually appropriate experiences and activities classifies an early childhood program as *developmentally appropriate*.

Six guidelines established by NAEYC (Bredekamp, 1987) can be used as benchmarks in our examination of programs for all young children:

1. Developmentally appropriate curriculum provides for all areas of a child's development: physical, emotional, social, and cognitive through an integrated approach.
2. Appropriate curriculum planning is based on teachers' observations and recordings of each child's special interests and developmental progress.
3. Curriculum planning emphasizes learning as an interactive process. Teachers prepare the environment for children to learn through active exploration and interaction with adults, other children, and materials.
4. Learning activities and materials should be concrete, real, and relevant to the lives of young children.
5. Programs provide for a wider range of developmental interests and abilities than the chronological age range of the group would suggest. Adults are prepared to meet the needs of children who exhibit unusual interests and skills outside the normal developmental range.
6. Teachers provide a variety of activities and materials; teachers increase the difficulty, complexity, and challenge of an activity as children are involved with it and as children develop understanding and skills. (pp. 3-5)

Sounds like a good program, doesn't it? Let's look at the NAEYC guidelines in light of young gifted children. What would we see and what would children be doing if our programs for young gifted children were also developmentally appropriate?

YOUNG GIFTED CHILDREN

Some young children are easily recognizable. They clearly distinguish themselves from other students through their performance. Other children, however, are not so easy to find. Their abilities or willingness to perform may be masked by environmental factors that are beyond their control. In our work with young gifted children (Shaklee et al., 1993), we have been using indicators of exceptional potential (see Table 28.1). In the case of either performance or potential, a developmentally appropriate environment which is attuned to the unique individual differences of all children and capitalizes on those strengths can significantly enhance a child's development.

Table 28.1. Primary Identifiers of Exceptional Potential.

Exceptional learner	Exceptional user	Exceptional generator	Exceptional motivation
• exceptional memory	• exceptional use of knowledge	• highly creative	• perfectionism
• learns quickly and easily	• advanced use of symbol systems	• atypical thinking	• initiative
• advanced understanding	• demands a reason • reasons well	• self-expressive • keen sense of humor • curiosity	• reflective • long attention span • leadership • intensity

THE GOURMET CLASSROOM: PUTTING IT ALL TOGETHER

As we consider the environment that prompts learning for young children, we must consider the age appropriate behaviors which influence a child's growth. All young children need a dynamic, active learning space that is both physically and psychologically safe. Because a growing child needs physical movement and interaction to construct knowledge (Spodek & Saracho, 1994), sound early childhood classrooms are sometimes misperceived as too chaotic or too noisy. In fact, it is exactly that productive noise and movement which provides children a means to acquire new information, "test" out ideas and experiences, and create new knowledge. What you wouldn't want to observe is children sitting for prolonged periods doing "seatwork" or a silent classroom. After all, how can a child acquire skill and facility with language, the building blocks of cognitive development, if no one allows them to speak? Three major components form the basis of a sound educational program for young gifted children: interactive teaching, integrated curriculum, and assessment.

INTERACTIVE TEACHING

Teachers of young gifted children should be facilitators and managers of instruction. This is not to say that teachers do not have direct knowledge to transmit to children. However, it is to say that the style of teaching should be reflective of what we know about young gifted children. We know that children construct knowledge through interaction, and it only makes sense that we provide a wide variety of materials, methods, and experiences which help a child explore the world. For young gifted children this sometimes seems like an overwhelming task. Because these children may often be described as "little sponges," teachers (parents included) are constantly searching for more of everything—books, building blocks, paints, pictures, sand, water—in short, resources. Although it is important to help locate resources, it is also important to make this a joint venture with the young gifted child. We want to foster the notion of independence in learning, problem solving, or thinking through to the next logical step. As facilitators we help the child learn to make choices and decisions, and sometimes mistakes, in a safe environment. If we always provide "everything," the child learns quickly not to help him- or herself because we'll do it for them! This is particularly important for young gifted children. Although we would like to think that all educational environments will be appropriate, we recognize the fact that sometimes it will be up to our children to seek out their own sources of intellectual stimulation and pursue their own learning. We begin at a very early age to equip our children with the attitude of a life-long learner by equipping them with the skills and confidence to do so.

The role of teacher as facilitator also means asking a lot of good questions. Much of what a child learns is through direct interaction with adults. It is up to us to ask good questions that help a child problem solve and think through information. Divergent questioning such as, "What made you think of . . .?" or "How could you put that together in a different way?" are the kinds of open-ended questions that help a child develop thinking skills. As teachers look at materials and resources used in the classroom, they should constantly be thinking about the types of questions they could ask to prompt a child's growth. We can also see this with early readers. All too often a child who reads early and is reading advanced material is left to read independently, that is, totally alone. Without adult interaction and questioning, many children will not continue to develop their reading skills. Yes, they will continue to read but their comprehension and understanding of what is being read may suffer because they are not being given the stimulation to "stretch" their thinking. A teaching style that facilitates a child's growth, is sensitive to individual learning strengths, and constantly searches for new questions and new forms of interaction. This is the kind of teaching which fosters intellectual development. Another example can be seen in the use of computers. If the type of software we use is that which "always asks the questions" or is similar to an electronic worksheet, then it is inappropriate software to use with children. In our work with authentic uses of technology, we have found that classrooms that foster inquiry, using computer technology as you or I would, is the kind of process that fosters student development (Peck & Hughes, 1994). The software selected to promote inquiry and reflection should be the kind where the *child* asks the questions, not the computer.

INTEGRATED CURRICULUM

Young gifted children can be those who demonstrate a singular interest over a long period of time (i.e., dinosaurs) or they can demonstrate a wide variety of interests, sampling our world as they grow. A sound early childhood curriculum is one in which the teacher builds an environment to demonstrate relationships between and among areas of the content. For example, in many early childhood programs we see an examination of Me/Myself as a starting point of understanding how "I fit" into the world around me. The teacher may create a series of experiences or activities that expand the child's notion of "me" to include Me/My Family or Me/My Community. For young gifted children it is important to remove the "glass ceiling" of some primary classrooms and also examine Me/The World. Because of the unique learning attributes associated with giftedness, some children can go beyond the bounds of regular curriculum for young children. An early childhood classroom that is developmentally appropriate will be attuned to individual differences and literally expand the integrated curriculum to provide for those children who can go beyond traditional practices. An integrated curriculum will provide children with the opportunity to see relationships between language, reading, mathematics, music, art, science, and social studies.

Embedded within an integrated approach is the teacher's ability to differentiate experiences according to individual needs. To continue our look at the Community, one team of primary classroom teachers differentiated within the regular course of study for individual learning needs. Mrs. Adams and Mrs. Trivelli looked carefully at the children within the primary team and looked at the corresponding curriculum. Knowing that some children would be able to go beyond others in their learning and understanding of community, they began a process of constructing some activities for the whole group, some for smaller groupings, and some for individual students. The unit included demonstrations and discussions with community leaders for all students, a walking tour of the community with all students, specialized "map makers," specialized "interviewers," and specialized "videographers" for other elements of the unit. Although all students participated in some elements and many participated in others, they designed a unique match between skills, abilities, and interests for their identified gifted students. In short, an integrated curricular approach, whether thematic or interdisciplinary, holds great potential for being able to diversify the curriculum to meet the individual learning needs of young gifted children. However, early childhood educators need to be sure that they have removed the "glass ceiling" from primary classrooms and have expanded their vision of what young children could and should do.

ASSESSMENT

The third element from our research that appears to significantly impact early childhood environments is the nature and use of the tools of assessment. Gifted child education has long used standardized testing for admission to gifted education programs. However, we have not always used the information we collect to modify classroom practices or gifted education programs. Numerous researchers have criticized the inappropriate and biased use of standardized tests for admission and service in gifted child education (Frasier, 1987; Shaklee, 1992; Shaklee & Hansford, 1992; Whitmore, 1985). Further, our community members recognize that we spend a great deal of money on standardized testing and that we publish the results in local newspapers. What they don't realize is how little time is spent to use the information in a beneficial fashion for children and for teachers.

Assessment is a broader construct than giving a standardized test and one which holds potential for all early childhood educators. Assessment is a process of observation and evidence collection that documents, over time, the strengths and areas of development for children. The purpose is not to include or exclude a child from services, but to benefit the child. When assessment is congruent with the goals and objectives for the curriculum, it is also used to modify classroom practice, curriculum, and instruction accordingly. Assessment is an ongoing process that includes parents, students, and teachers in designing appropriate curriculum and instructional strategies for each child. There are many ways to approach the issues of appropriate assessment.

The Early Assessment for Exceptional Potential project (Shaklee et al., 1989) designed a portfolio process that includes five kinds of evidence derived from four different sources to be used during the school year to identify and provide services for young gifted children. The types of evidence include: a parent/community survey; anecdotal records; demonstration teaching and observation; pupil products contributed by parents, students, or teachers; and a peer- self-nomination survey. All of the information is related to the primary identifiers of giftedness and results in a profile of student strengths. The teacher uses this information to create an action plan for individuals or groups of students according to their interests, learning needs, and abilities. A teacher might, for example, choose to differentiate instruction, accelerate the curriculum, provide learning centers, or create an independent study based on assessment evidence. As the action plan is implemented, teachers and students continue to assess student responses and progress through anecdotal records, observations, and collection of pupil products. When the current action plan comes to a close, the teacher evaluates the impact of the plan, reviews progress with the student using the portfolio, and creates a new action plan. Not only does the teacher become more observant of student abilities and interests, she also becomes more aware of how curriculum and instruction can be modified to optimize the classroom for each pupil (Shaklee, 1993; Viechnicki, Barbour, Shaklee, Rohrer, & Ambrose, 1993; Viechnicki, Shaklee, Barbour, & Ambrose, 1994). As noted by Hills (1994) and others (McAfee & Leong, 1994), assessment information should be used to provide information for decision making and to answer the following questions:

> What are this child's strengths, needs, and learning processes?
> How is this child doing?
> How will this child's instruction and guidance be planned?
> Does this child have special needs?
> Can this child's needs be met in this program?
> If not, how does this program need to be supplemented?
> Is this program, as now implemented, meeting its goals and objectives? (p. 45).

Certainly, the guidelines on assessment from NAEYC (Bredekamp & Rosegrant, 1994) can be shaped and effectively used to support the growth and development of young gifted children as well.

THINKING AHEAD

As we continue to think about the best possible environment for young gifted children, we must recognize that we are still learning about this group of children. The literature on young children gives us a good starting place. Paying attention to age appropriate and individually appropriate experiences, ensuring that the classroom is interactive and dynamic, using an integrated curriculum, and establishing a sound assessment system can all contribute to establishing the kind of environment which nurtures all children. Looking carefully at young gifted children in this setting can provide further information and insights about their particular growth patterns and educational needs. Finally, sharing what we know among ourselves and from our parents, community members, and children themselves will empower us to make the best decisions to *benefit each child*—and that is what education is all about!

REFERENCES

Bredekamp, S. (Ed.). (1987). *Developmentally appropriate practice in early childhood programs serving children from birth through age 8.* Washington, DC: National Association for the Education of Young Children.

Bredekamp, S., & Rosegrant, T. (Eds.). (1994). *Reaching potentials: Appropriate curriculum and assessment for young children.* Washington, DC: National Association for the Education of Young Children.

Frasier, M. (1987). The identification of gifted black students: Developing new perspectives. *Journal for the Education of the Gifted, 10,* 155-180.

Hills, T. (1994). Reaching potential through appropriate assessment. In S. Bredekamp & T. Rosegrant (Eds.), *Reaching potentials: Appropriate curriculum and assessment for young children* (pp. 43-61). Washington, DC: National Association for the Education of Young Children.

McAfee, O., & Leong, D. (1994). *Assessing and guiding young children's development and learning.* New York: Allyn & Bacon.

Peck, J. K., & Hughes, S. V. (1994, April). *The impact of an inquiry approach to learning in a technology-rich environment.* Paper presented at the Annual Meeting of the American Educational Research Association, New Orleans, LA.

Shaklee, B. (1992). Identification of young gifted children. *Journal for the Education of the Gifted, 15,* 134-144.

Shaklee, B. (1993). Preliminary findings of the Early Assessment for Exceptional Potential Project. *Roeper Review, 16,* 105-109.

Shaklee, B., Barbour, N., Ambrose, R., Rohrer, J., Viechnicki, K., & Whitmore, J. (1993). Early assessment of exceptional potential in young minority and/or economically disadvantaged students. In C. Callahan, C. Tomlinson, & P. Pizzat (Eds.), *Contexts for promise: Noteworthy practices in the identification of gifted students* (pp. 22-43). Charlottesville, VA: National Center for Research on Gifted and Talented, U.S. Department of Education.

Shaklee, B., & Hansford, S. (1992). Identification of underserved populations: Focus on preschool and primary children. In *Challenges in gifted education* (pp. 35-40). Columbus: Ohio Department of Education.

Shaklee, B., Whitmore, J., Barton, L., Barbour, N., Ambrose, R., & Viechnicki, K. (1989). *Early assessment for exceptional potential in young minority and/or economically disadvantaged* (Contract #R206A00160-90A-02). Washington, DC: Office of Educational Research Improvement, U.S. Department of Education.

Spodek, B. & Saracho, O. (1994). *Right from the start: Teaching children ages three to eight.* New York: Allyn & Bacon.

Viechnicki, K., Barbour, N., Shaklee, B., Rohrer, J., & Ambrose, R. (1993). The impact of portfolio assessment on teacher classroom activities. *Journal of Teacher Education, 44*, 371-377.

Viechnicki, K., Shaklee, B., Barbour, N., & Ambrose, R. (1994, April). *The influence of portfolio assessment on teacher attitudes and behaviors.* Paper presented at the Annual Meeting of the American Educational Research Association, New Orleans, LA.

Whitmore, J. R. (1985). New challenges to common identification practices. In J. Freeman (Ed.), *The psychology of gifted children* (pp. 93-113). New York: Wiley.

RESOURCES

Young Gifted Children

Alvino, J. (1989). *Parents' guide to raising a gifted toddler.* New York: Little, Brown.

Alvino, J. (1985). *Parents' guide to raising a gifted child.* New York: Little, Brown.

Eby, J., & Smutny, J. (1990). *A thoughtful overview of gifted education.* New York: Longman.

Roedell, W., Jackson, N., & Robinson, H. (1980). *Gifted young children.* New York: Teachers College Press.

Saunders, J., & Espeland, P. (1986). *Bringing out the best: A resource guide for parents of young gifted children.* Minneapolis, MN: Free Spirit.

Whitmore, J. R. (1986). *Intellectual giftedness and young children.* Binghamton, NY: Haworth.

Young Children: Curriculum and Assessment

Bredekamp, S. (1987). *Developmentally appropriate practice in early childhood programs serving children from birth through age 8.* Washington, DC: National Association for the Education of Young Children.

Bredekamp, S., & Rosegrant, T. (1994). *Reaching potentials: Appropriate curriculum and assessment for young children.* Washington, DC: National Association for the Education of Young Children.

Genishi, C. (Ed.). (1992). *Ways of assessing children and curriculum.* New York: Teachers College Press.

Grace, C., & Shores, E. (Eds.). (1992). *The portfolio and its use: Developmentally appropriate assessment of young children.* Little Rock, AR: Southern Association on Children Under Six.

McAfee, O., & Leong, D. (1994). *Assessing and guiding young children's development and learning.* New York: Allyn & Bacon.

Wiggins, G. (1993). *Assessing student performance.* New York: Jossey-Bass.

29

Creating the Most Enabling Environment for Young Gifted Children

Susan F. Belgrad

As today's parents, teachers, and administrators of programs for young children struggle to make sense of the immense amount of new research on learning and information on positive parenting and effective teaching, it becomes increasingly difficult to know just what is best for children. This predicament is amplified in children who at a very young age demonstrate giftedness in the ways they approach and interact with their world. In this chapter I hope to slice through to the real core of what we now know about how children learn and what they most need in the way of nurturing climates and adult interaction in order to thrive.

At the outset, I must clearly state that the common thread in child development research, studies of learning, and early childhood education reveal that children do best when they are well-nurtured. This suggests that, in addition to being loved and physically cared for, children need to be respected for who they are—for their unique interests and dispositions—and for having the capacity to learn and create by both their parents and their teachers.

Parents are successful in their child-rearing practices when they engage their children in warm, positive home relationships. Here, healthy attitudes toward people and the world are initiated and developed. Within these relationships children are appreciated and encouraged as capable persons. They are recognized for their own power to initiate exploration and discovery, to test predictions, and to construct new knowledge.

Teachers are similarly successful when they focus their instructional efforts on developing the child's positive sense of self. They are also instrumental in helping children develop confident attitudes toward others. Their guidance expands each child's developing capacities and dispositions to discover relationships, meanings, and facts about the world.

In my work as a teacher, educational researcher, and consultant, I often discuss concerns with other teachers about how to meet the intellectual and social needs of children who we find to be gifted in a particular area. For example, one kindergarten teacher pointed Daniel out to me as a child whom she described as "quite advanced in his numerical and verbal thinking ability." Even though she had conscientiously provided a rich classroom setting with many opportunities for exploration, discovery, prediction testing, and problem solving, she felt uncertain that the environment provided enough to challenge and extend the thinking of this 5-year old. As a responsible kindergarten teacher, she felt that the materials and experiences which Daniel encountered in her classroom should respond to the ability level that he demonstrated. Even more, she felt that she should challenge him to move beyond that level.

She was also concerned about Daniel's need to have positive and cooperative play experiences within the social learning environment of the classroom. She was aware that his precocious intellectual ability was emerging far ahead of his social skills. She appreciated his human need to become a valued group member. Her goal was to assure that he develop important tools of social interaction such as sharing, listening, and cooperating as an equally important aspect of his growing intellect.

Following a most enjoyable morning visit in her classroom, I was pleased to share with her that I had seen much evidence that her classroom was meeting each of Daniel's learning needs. For example, I had observed him engaged in active problem solving with many materials, and had listened to some animated and detailed explanations of his discoveries to his eager classmates. When it came to creative and well-designed block structures and railways, Daniel was the sought-after leader!

Together, Daniel's teacher and I brainstormed to identify some ways that she could do more to bridge Daniel's active and concrete learning experiences to his quickly emerging critical thinking capacity.

We also thought about ways to provide him with the tools he needed to remain an active member of the classroom community.

I pointed out to her how, following a *Math Their Way* experience building "skyscrapers," Daniel had orchestrated (through remarkable leadership skills) his own free-play activity. It involved several other children who had spontaneously begun to cooperate to connect all of their unifix cubes. They created a very long snake that covered the entire expanse of the kindergarten classroom. When all the cubes were attached, he announced to the children playing with him, "Now we can count them!" As the children eagerly proceeded to count the long serpent, he kept a mental note of the 10s and then the 100s—all the while keeping the other children mindful of the number to which they had progressed!

Had my colleague enjoyed my visitor's vantage point of the active thinking and learning that occurred in her classroom, she would indeed have seized on this as what the renowned early childhood educator Montessori (1912/1964) called "a teachable moment." As we reflected on Daniel's play, we discussed how similar experiences in the future could be extended to verbal, written, or mathematical thinking. In the example I just described, we thought of how the children could have written about their snake, recorded Daniel's count of the number of cubes, or graphed the number of colors in the entire snake.

Her kindergarten children were well aware of the practical uses of graphing. They had already charted how many children in the class were girls and how many were boys. They also had graphed (by sitting along a large vinyl grid) how many of them liked to eat hot dogs, and how many preferred hamburgers. She saw the relevance of encouraging children to extend their discovery of naturally occurring mathematical experiences into more written or representational accounts, such as when they engaged in recording the counting of 100 items and then seeing how number problems are written to represent events.

Many early childhood teachers, like my colleague, recognize the importance of integrating the use of writing and graphing as thinking tools in the kindergarten classroom. Teachers can give children an opportunity to see evidence of their increasing mental capacity while achieving "voice" and ownership of that process. To classroom teachers like my colleague, the essence of learning in the early years is focused on the child's realization that he or she has actually made a breakthrough in thinking or achieved understanding of something previously believed to be mysterious. To the young gifted child these active learning experiences are the nourishment that sustain and assure the development of his or her social and symbolic thinking and problem-solving abilities. Choosing to introduce higher order thinking and problem solving through the natural play milieu of the child therefore becomes the essence of a most enabling learning environment.

Another important outcome of the visit and discussion my colleague and I shared was the affirmation that within a developmentally appropriate and caring classroom setting, this young gifted child had been enabled to grow new wings through a rather simple play activity. We recognized the importance of the teacher's role in serving as a bridge to both higher order thinking about logical mathematical concepts as well as successful cooperative learning experiences. In the example of Daniel, a child and his peers achieved breakthroughs both within and outside the watchful presence of the teacher. Bringing children together before the daily dismissal to share and reflect on these unexpected yet significant experiences is not only great fun for the children, but serves as an opportunity for the teacher to learn how children are continually growing and emerging as socially and intellectually active people. This is why the early childhood model of education known as High Scope promotes participation in planning, playing, and recalling the experiences that more than often result in something "bigger" than what they originally planned.

This event in the daily play of Daniel and his peers served as an exciting learning experience for both the kindergarten teacher and myself. She was able to affirm her work in developing a child-centered, multidimensional classroom that was woven together with a rich social learning climate which valued both individual and group work and play. I was able to see the importance of creating child-centered learning environments that provide the teacher with many opportunities to respond to and extend the total development of every individual child. Together we recognized that in order to obtain more opportunities to engage in observation and facilitation of higher level thinking and problem solving among children, the setting needs to be rich enough to serve as a stage on which learning by doing occurs on a regular basis.

Young, gifted children need a nurturing, open, and child-centered setting similar to the one I have described. A classroom where they can freely express their ideas in innovative, constructive ways needs to be provided if the early foundations and dispositions toward learning are to be positive. However, a most enabling environment alone is not enough. Whether in the home or in the classroom, children require caring and responsive interactions with adults and peers. To provide this, caring adults need to know how to respect and affirm children's development while encouraging simple, often subtle suggestions that bridge to the next higher levels of problem solving or leaps of thinking to highly complex critical thinking. Similarly, we need to be mindful of acknowledging and extending the social skills and communication tools that children need to become successful and contributing members of their play and work groups.

Teachers like the one I have described often express a desire to be able to teach this way, for it is indeed a high level of teaching. However, as the kindergarten teacher in this example revealed, "If one is not able to observe children while they interact, many teachable moments will be missed!"

Parents and teachers who value their children's attempts to grow can become better at reflecting on their interactions with children and consciously working toward developing more complex and positive modes of interacting. To accomplish this they will require a broader understanding of what I describe as "children's ways of knowing." When carefully observed and respected by the adult, the child's natural way of learning about his or her world can guide us in our interactions and teaching decisions within a most enabling environment for children.

CHILDREN'S WAYS OF KNOWING

Research on child development and cognition continues to provide a rich foundation on which our decisions regarding children's daily growth and learning can be based. We know, for example, that the child's "playful modes of learning" include imitation, exploration, prediction testing (or trial and error), and construction. Imitation, which is the most basic form of learning, occurs when the child observes an event or action in the environment and attempts to repeat or replicate it. As adults, we enjoy the infant and toddler's early attempts to imitate our actions and find it a fascinating expression of intelligence.

As the child grows into toddlerhood, *exploration* becomes the dominant theme as Nature seemingly pushes the child to investigate everything that can be seen, touched, or put in the mouth. With maturation, our child learns to engage in higher level thinking, which is expressed in the toddler's *trial-and-error* behavior. This occurs while learning to throw a ball, jump a rather large mud puddle, or work a simple puzzle. As adults, we marvel at the "stick-to-it-iveness" that children engaged in *prediction testing* display, and how repetition seems to be second nature to many favorite activities of preschoolers.

Even more magical is the way in which preschoolers begin to construct—to transform simple materials in the home and classroom into novel reproductions of their imagination. The ability to construct with materials or ideas, or *constructive behavior*, is, after all, a characteristic that most differentiates the human from the remainder of the animal world. The young child achieves the ability to construct as early as the beginning of the second year when language emerges. He or she soon becomes an active builder of towers, trains, buildings, collages, and all manner of wondrous structures by the age of 3. He or she also is able to create dramatic representations or enactments of the social events he or she observes all around him or her. These four modes of play and learning develop and combine during the preschool years. They are greatly enhanced by what I call adults' modes of interacting. While the child demonstrates the acquisition of imitation, exploration, prediction testing, and construction, the parent and teacher provide him or her with the opportunity to consolidate these learning tools and the support to engage in further interaction with people and materials in the world around him or her. Table 29.1 gives a sample look at the necessary interaction between the child's modes of learning and adult interaction.

THE IMPORTANCE OF ADULT INTERACTION IN CHILDREN'S LEARNING

As Table 29.1 demonstrates, the adult who wishes to encourage the child to engage in imitative behavior demonstrates, or perhaps *tells*, the child what to do. Most of us know this mode of interaction very well, because it has been the prevalent mode of teaching in our schools for many decades. There are still many skills and much knowledge that are appropriate and *necessary* to learn through direct instruction and imitation. We don't, for example, want the child to learn through discovery why we don't chase balls into the street without looking out for approaching cars. We are careful to provide clear, firm direction when we do not wish children to be endangered as they explore the world around them.

When *exploration* is a mode of play and learning that adults value for the child, a home or classroom will be prepared by removing anything which can endanger (or be endangered by) the child engaged in exploration. Instead, materials are provided that lead to increasing knowledge and thinking skills. This is why a variety of blocks,

Table 29.1. Correspondence between Children's Modes of Learning and Adults' Modes of Interacting.

Modes of play/learning	Modes of interacting
imitation	direct instruction (showing, telling)
exploration	inquiry, discovery, questioning
prediction testing (trial and error)	leading to discovery, bridging
construction	responsive interaction, facilitating, providing open, novel settings and experiences

puzzles, and construction materials are of such importance in the child's home and school environments. Even more important, however, is the way in which adults seek to engage the child in responding to and interacting within the setting. If the adult is adept at using questioning techniques in ways that respect and develop the child's thinking, a never-ending process of discovery can occur. Questions like "What else do you see," or "What does it feel like," lead the child to recognize that the drive to explore (which we call curiosity) is an important behavior for one to use and develop.

The next interactional skill shown in Table 29.1, prediction testing, is a highly complex behavior which is difficult for even the most skilled of teachers to promote in the child. This is because it requires that we understand how the child is thinking and see ourselves as a bridge to new ideas rather than a fountain of knowledge that we readily pour into the child's mind. To lead a child to the development of new knowledge we need to become careful observers of the child's acting and thinking and wise managers of our own desire to instruct the child. This careful observation accompanied with thoughtful response such as, "Yes, I see that doesn't fit. What can you do?," enables the child to press on to new discovery and problem solving. As in the case of the kindergarten teacher I described, I have often found that if adults do not have opportunities to actively observe their children, they are limited in their ability to support their efforts to create meaning, solve problems, and discover mathematical and scientific wonders of the world around them.

Within this prediction testing mode, the adult then becomes a *bridge* or *facilitator* of the child's thinking. The ways in which this is done are varied, but they all require complex thinking on the part of the adult. Some of the questions one must ask oneself while observing young children include: "How did she know to do that?" "What could I say that would help him to see that he really knows how to do this himself?" "What is really the problem here?" As adults, it is often very difficult to watch children experiencing feelings of inadequacy and frustration as they struggle to solve problems that we could simply *show* them how to solve. However, we can learn how to demonstrate our respect for children's need to experience optimum or moderate levels of frustration, which not only builds within them the desire to know and to do, but also propels them beyond their confusion to real learning.

I recently viewed a teacher-training videotape that beautifully demonstrated this idea. It portrayed preschool children who were struggling to fit wooden planks over two rows of large hollow blocks that had not been built parallel to each other. One end was wider than the planks, which resulted in a problem that had the children perplexed. They each tried and tried, but had a difficult time figuring out what to do. Because some of the children were "young 4s," the predominance of magical thinking characteristic of their age allowed them to try quick-fix balancing acts as a possible remedy. It wasn't until a 5-year-old stood back and examined the rows carefully that he hit on the right idea of moving the rows closer together. For them, prediction testing resulted in success as the children implemented his solution with cries of triumph, glee, and relief. Had the teacher who observed quietly from a nearby vantage point interacted with direct instruction—showing them where the problem was—she may have denied them the affirmation and confidence of self that occurs when problems are independently solved.

In addition to active observation, however, adults also need to develop skills in "getting inside the child's head." This means that one needs to understand the nature of the young child's thinking as well as develop strategies for ascertaining what the child may be thinking. By asking the child questions like: "How did you think of that?", "How did you get that answer?", or "Can you think of another problem that you solved that could be like this one?" parents and teachers gain the child's viewpoint or "voice" in his or her learning.

This is actually one of the most difficult interactional skills to integrate into our communication with young children. This is because it requires continual critical thinking on our part. We need to know when and how to search for understanding within the child. Nonetheless, it is an important skill to develop, if assuring the child's optimal development is the goal.

Another important reason for parents and teachers to engage in this mode of interaction is to help the child to develop an awareness of his or her own cognitive abilities. Often referred to as *metacognition*, the child who is assisted by the adult in identifying his or her own strategies and "maps of thinking" becomes better able to purposefully use problem-solving as an important ability in many every day situations and events. The added benefit of these types of interactions with children is that they recognize the child's developing thinking capacities while affirming and validating the child's sense of self-esteem. Effective teachers in particular are often able to assist children by recognizing that there is just as much "gold" in an incorrect answer as there often is in a correct response. By focusing on the *process* of the child's critical and creative thinking rather than the *products* or answers themselves, the adult supports and affirms risk taking in thinking and problem solving as an important goal of learning. Just as we are learning in physics and many other branches of science by challenging the rightness of even well-accepted theories and ideas, we can promote tremendous breakthroughs to new and important learning for the child. Therefore, within this interactional mode, it can often be the incorrect answer that leads to the seed of new learning or creativity.

The constructivist mode of playing and learning requires a prepared environment that is continually responding to and facilitating the child's need to create and construct. The adult in this mode of interaction observes and facilitates as needed—perhaps quietly arranges, rearranges, or introduces materials that enhance the child's creative and problem-solving constructivist activity without verbal interaction. *Responsive interaction* describes this mode as one in which the adult acknowledges and supports the child's initiative in creating and transforming the materials before him or her.

A good example of the importance of this type of interaction occurred to me while visiting a prekindergarten classroom in an urban setting. The children in the classroom had recently attended a field trip to the Chicago Art Institute, where they had enjoyed a special visit to the workrooms of the art students. As one of the children was proudly showing me around the classroom, we passed by the art-media center where the products of many easel paintings were gaily displayed while drying on clothesline. "And this is our art museum," the child nonchalantly remarked to me. I was quite impressed that he had been able to transfer one meaningful class trip to a classroom activity which held similar value to him. It was also a charming reflection of this child's creative response. I ventured a suggestion, "What a wonderful idea to call it your art museum! Can I help you make a special sign for your "Art Museum" so every visitor will know this?" The child eagerly brought me to the writing center, where we found all the necessary materials to create a sign bearing his title.

BRINGING IT ALL TOGETHER

My favorite time to visit the preschool classrooms of exceptional teachers is during the latter part of the school year. In the spring, the children have learned a great deal about the social behaviors and routines necessary to maintain order in the active learning classroom. Being older and wiser in May, they are much in control of their classroom setting—or so they believe. For all practical purposes, the teacher seems to have put him- or herself out of a job because he or she is apparently needed only to acknowledge and share the child's joy in appraising a painting or a building like "Sears Tower," which one child has created, or affirming the children's solution to a social dispute. The teacher appears to have become a background player in the life of the classroom while the children engage in a variety of experiences.

The truth is that the teacher is engaging in active observation, bridging, and responsive interaction. She has succeeded in creating a harmonious setting in which she orchestrates the children's daily experiences. Such a classroom encourages children "with a light touch" to internalize social and intellectual learning that they will carry with them into their future years of schooling and beyond.

In setting out to create a most enabling environment for young gifted children, we must therefore, realize that we will be called on to engage in complex critical and creative thinking—so we know how and when to *expand* the child's exploration and to *bridge* the child's many modes of play into the application of abstract and critical thinking in the study of the world around us. Just as we encourage the child to be an information seeker and constructor, we must view ourselves as the information seekers of children's individual capacities and constructors of expanding means to discovery for every child.

Learning how to think and act in these ways is not an easy task, but can be acquired through consciously applying the knowledge we gain from studying, observing, and respecting children's thinking. Because our learning about children begins with observation, we need to develop this skill so that we can truly see how children go about exploration and problem solving. We need to engage in comparing their thinking patterns to ours, to those of their peers, and to those which they have previously experienced. We need to hypothesize how we might create the bridges in thinking which I described earlier. We need to engage in prediction testing behaviors before we interact (e.g., "If I offer these materials to the child now, perhaps she will continue to discover the properties of wet sand versus dry sand"; or "If I wait for just a few seconds, perhaps she will figure out why the hose is stuck"). As we engage in this "If-P-then-Q" thinking we will often find that our hypotheses based on intuition are correct. Even when they do not act within our predicted outcomes, however, we deepen our recognition and respect for the fact that children's thinking and learning patterns are quite complex and therefore really deserve our most creative and reflective thinking.

I have found it to be quite helpful for many teachers whom I have assisted in implementing child-centered settings to record their interactions with children over a short period of time. Following my observation, I categorize or sort their interactions into the four categories that I described earlier (see Table 29.2): direct (telling or showing), inquiry, facilitating and bridging, and responsive interaction. When I have completed this simple analysis, I offer teachers the opportunity to review the record of their interactions as well as the patterns that arose from the sorting. I am often impressed with the ways in which teachers can use this feedback to affirm their work and to set goals and strategies for new ways to improve the quality of interactions in which they engage children.

If our young gifted children are to achieve the rich and important potential with which they were born, they will require an optimal combination of love, nurturing, opportunity to explore and discover, and adult interactions that offer them the keys to unlock the powers of their minds. A "most enabling environment" is not only a home or classroom that adults create and modify with the child's continued growth

Table 29.2. Sample Analysis of Adult Modes of Interactions.

Interaction	Direct	Discovery	Bridging	Responding
(Direct quotes of adult's interaction)	.	.	.	.
"Please sit down here."	✓	.	.	.
"Can you tell me what this is?"	.	✓	.	.
"How did you know that?"	.	.	✓	.
"What made you think of that?"	.	.	✓	.
"Yes, I think that is a good idea!"	.	.	.	✓

and development, but a setting in which the child receives respect as an individual with unique ability to learn, to know, and to express him- or herself. Within such thoughtfully prepared and orchestrated settings, parents and teachers can assure that all our children's gifts for the future will be enjoyed by them and by the world in which they live.

REFERENCES

Montessori, M. (1964). *The Montessori method.* New York: Schocken Books. (Original work published 1912)

30

The Education of Talented Young Children in the Context of School Reform

Carolyn Cummings
Jane Piirto

Young children are being placed into heterogeneous groups as a response to school reform elements and to the call for developmentally appropriate practices and learner-centered classrooms. Intellectually precocious or academically talented youngsters continue to be schooled with other students not as academically advanced. Although proponents of special education for the talented (Piirto, 1994; Smutny, Veenker, & Veenker, 1991) have often called for separate arrangements, or at least part-time pullout classes, for young talented students, the reality is that young precocious students are most often educated in heterogeneous classrooms.

Because of the questionable validity of the result of standardized assessment instruments with this age group (Lewis & Louis, 1991), the uneven nature of development (Terrasier, 1985), and the differences between and among the physical, cognitive, social, and emotional developmental domains within each child, attempts to separate and group children according to talent or readiness or social development have decreased dramatically. *All* children, regardless of chronological age, developmental readiness, and physical or intellectual differences are included. In addition, many state and district plans include planning and implementing multiage classes with the inclusion of all children.

Is this necessarily bad pedagogically for talented youngsters? How are the diverse needs of young children in heterogeneous groups being met? What are the classroom components and practices that can provide for differences in age, interest, and learning styles and in levels of talent and achievement? Certain commonalities exist that are basic to quality early childhood programming. These are discussed here with relationship to components of school reform.

DEVELOPMENTALLY APPROPRIATE PRACTICES

Developmentally appropriate practices as defined by the National Association for the Education of Young Children (NAEYC; Bredekamp, 1987) are age-appropriate and individually appropriate to any group of children. Each child's needs are addressed. In public schools this also means the blurring of the very definite and arbitrary grade level boundaries of the past, as there is a recognition that there is no such thing as a "first grader." Instead, educators acknowledge and accept that any first grade is composed of children of varying chronological and developmental ages as well as different abilities and talents, and therefore all students do not master the same material in the same way in the same length of time. Children quickly comprehend and embrace that they will not be doing the same things as the other children, although adults are often concerned that the children will feel "different" if they are doing different things in class.

In observing such classrooms, we have noticed that the teachers use teaching strategies that allow children the opportunity of working on different activities simultaneously. Learning centers or stations where children work at a variety of activities in a number of subject areas or workshops where children labor in the same subject area (math, writing, reading) but at different ability levels are common. The students can be observed making their own choices about what they are learning. The dangers for talented students are those of underestimating their abilities, and of underchallenging their potentials. Inservice and staff development on the potentialities and abilities of talented children must be conducted by school districts intent on meeting the needs of all children, including the academically talented.

Child choice is often referred to in the literature on giftedness and talent, and in the new primary classrooms students do have choices. The literature on developmentally appropriate practices

(Bredekamp, 1987, 1991; Foreman & Kushner, 1983; Katz & Chard, 1989; Kostelnik et al., 1991; Kostelnik, Soderman, & Whiren, 1993; National Association of Elementary School Principals, 1990) as well as the Presidential Task Force on Psychology in Education and the American Psychological Association in the document *Learner-Centered Psychological Principles: Guidelines for School Redesign and Reform* (1993), defined learning as a "natural process of pursuing personally meaningful goals," adding that learning should be "active, volitional, and internally mediated" (p. 6).

In these classrooms children make choices and are involved in the planning and monitoring of their own learning. They may have some assigned tasks, but they have choices not only among these tasks, but of when, with whom, and how long they will spend in completing them. Contracts and planning sheets provide the record-keeping and assessment bases as the children develop skills of making good choices and good use of their time.

In such classrooms, materials are open-ended; that is, there is no one way to use them nor one correct answer, but rather each child operates on the materials according to ability, level, and phase of learning. Some children may make a few letters and letter-like forms in their first-grade journals; verbally precocious children may write stories or even lengthy poems they have already memorized. In the block corner, spatially precocious children may make detailed symmetrical replicas of pictures of buildings or of those observed and studied locally, whereas other children make haphazard arrangements. Other open-ended materials include art and construction materials, dramatic play materials such as props and puppets, musical instruments, science materials, and other objects that encourage exploration, manipulation, and experimentation.

In today's developmentally appropriate early childhood environment where choice is key, both play and exploration are valued as appropriate ways for young children to learn. Risk taking, learning by trial and error, and other creative approaches are encouraged and respected. Perfect products are not expected. Such open-endedness may produce anxiety in perfectionistic academically talented children. Gardner (1993) described a mathematically precocious child in Project Spectrum who had difficulty in other domains because of his fear of being wrong. When anxiety occurs, bright children who may have experienced such praise at being right that they are afraid of ever being wrong should be encouraged to explore their own domain of strength as well as other domains, in emotionally safe ways.

Within the same classroom, children can work on a *concrete* level—they can build and act out their own worlds. On a *representative* level, they can draw and construct replicas of their experiences. Finally, on an *abstract* level, they can read and write, calculate, compute, and organize information for use in their lives. The teaching strategies that encourage children's choice and planning for their own learning, the use of open-ended materials, and an emphasis on process rather than a demand for products contribute to children operating at their own levels of learning according to their comfort and ability. All children move at their own speed through different phases of learning: (a) exploration, (b) acquisition, (c) practice, (d) generalization, and (e) application (Michigan State Board of Education, 1992).

In the developmentally appropriate classroom, the role of the teacher has changed. Formerly, the teacher was someone who told and imparted all of the knowledge. Now the teacher is one who extends, engages, questions, affirms, and challenges children as they are constructing knowledge. There may be times when the teacher has to use specific instructional strategies to provide information to children if they cannot construct it on their own. However, the majority of the time is spent in assisting and supporting children as they move through the phases of learning. In such a classroom, the teacher can provide a challenging environment for talented children, who need very little time in the practice phase, to proceed without inciting boredom or careless learning habits.

RELATED COMPONENTS FROM THE SCHOOL REFORM MOVEMENT

The emphasis on learning content through the integration of subject matter, on the application of learning, and on the involvement of the learner in planning for, conducting, and assessing his or her learning are components of general school reform (Bechtol & Sorenson, 1993) and are evident in these programs. Each of these components contributes to and increases the ability of teachers to meet the varying needs of a diverse group of learners.

Content

Young children have an internal need to learn about things—how they work, what they do, who is involved, and how they personally can be involved. Children attempt to make sense of the world. Children absorb, experience, and discover new information and work at grouping, sorting, and organizing what they have learned into concepts, constructs, and schemata. In the past we filled their school days with the learning of skills and lists, of assorted facts and information, segregated into subject areas. Science time was from 2:00 to 2:25 p.m. Teachers taught from a science book that was written at a first- or second-grade level of understanding, with many colorful photographs and a few simple statements. Many children already knew what the books attempted to teach. Other children had no prior information or experience and therefore the books had little meaning. None of the science information was connected or related to what was learned during social studies time or during reading, writing, spelling, and mathematics time. Limited content work was done in any of these "subjects." Students learned skills in order to do well on tests rather than to be able to transfer them to use in real life experience.

With school reform, teachers have been urged to develop themes, topics, and issues where the children can learn concepts in context that helps them to see the applications of what they are learning. The old unit method of instruction included the selection of the topic by an adult. Then seemingly related activities were planned in science, reading, art, math, social studies, music. Often little was actually learned about the topic, but instead a sort of connective string made the activities appear related. Writing about bubbles in an exercise that uses the sentence starter "If I were a bubble . . ." teaches nothing about bubbles. Writing is itself valuable, but its value could be increased exponentially if children had prior experiences and some knowledge and were writing to share knowledge about bubbles—how to use bubbles, how to make bubbles, why bubbles form—bubbles as part of a larger concept of science, gas, air, and matter.

In today's developmentally appropriate, open classrooms, thematic content is carefully selected. The day of the dinosaur as theme is gone. Many of the activities in teacher idea books and the gimmicks and games at teacher stores that teachers deem "cute" but that provide for little learning, are gone. There actually is limited information about dinosaurs that is age-appropriate for young children. Size and time are abstract concepts for them. Teachers have children memorize the period in the study of paleontology and draw a time line to see when these prehistoric beasts lived. They further have children put masking tape through the school halls to "experience" the size of these creatures and when these activities are completed, they still have children who ask, "If dinosaurs were so big, why didn't helicopters fly into them?" Children are discovering relationships between the facts. Even talented children with IQs in the 140s have trouble with certain metaphors and time concepts.

Analogy construction in young children has a specific developmental path. Castillo (1994) said that first, talented children (and all children):

> Should be given many opportunities to construct analogies based on themselves. For example, when studying botany, "person:arm:: tree: branch" is relevant; when studying transportation, "person: feet::car:wheels." After they have gained experience with self-analogies, they can branch out to more distant comparisons. (p. 64)

Domain analogies such as "sail:boat::wings:plane" can come next, and then cross domain analogies such as "yolk:egg::filament:lightbulb" can be attempted. Talented children can soon master cross-domain analogies, whereas some children may be limited to self-analogies and others to domain analogies.

Children sometimes make faulty relationships among the facts, and often do not truly comprehend the information in the dinosaur unit, for example. Certainly it is fun for children to learn and say dinosaur names and become aware of the different types of these prehistoric animals, but this can be done very easily through the numbers of children's books written on the topic. Four- to 6-week periods of time in which children eat, count, paint, write about, graph, and read about dinosaurs does not seem to be the best use of their time, nor does it help them to organize and make sense of their worlds.

Other frequently selected unit topics—for example, "phases of the moon" or "the solar system"—are also abstract, and it is more appropriate to introduce these to children through children's literature. Children become aware of these things at a social knowledge level (knowledge from other people), but few young children, even those with high IQs, can conceptualize revolutions, rotations, eclipses, and relationships such as the distance from the sun and the shadow of the moon. Those "highly gifted" children who can comprehend such mathematical relationships need special accelerative opportunities with a grounding in social relationships among age and intellectual peers (Piirto, 1994).

When Cummings (1995) visited learner-centered, developmentally appropriate classrooms around the United States during a Carnegie-funded study, theme topics that worked well became apparent. Kindergarten, first-, and second-grade topics included "ocean life" (in Scarborough, ME), "farms and farm animals" (in Iowa City), "our school woods" in (Franklin County, MS), "cats" (in Midland, MI), "cycles as patterns of change" (in Pacific Grove, CA), "communication" (in Nome, AK), and "families" (in Albuquerque, NM), among others. Some of these topics are inclusive, whereas others are more specific. Depending on the training that the teachers have had, some select themes for the entire year and build and weave, integrating a number of topics within the themes, whereas others have more specific topics that they relate to each other over a school year's time. Whichever method of selection and integration is used, the themes themselves are developmentally suitable for young children of all abilities.

An example of this connectedness of several topics was observed in an Iowa kindergarten where they moved from studying farms to farm animals that are raised for products, to those that are kept as pets, to those that are found wild in the area, including bears. That led to discussions of being afraid of bears and to teddy bears' affect on feelings, to feelings other then fear. The connectedness and progression was a natural one and rather than spending 2 weeks on "the farm," and 2 weeks on "pets," and 2 on "wild animals," and 2 on "teddy bears," each in isolation, the young children could make the connection with the farm, which was home to many of them. Rather than teddy bears being used in a number of cute activities, children were learning that people aren't afraid of all bears, and that teddy bears are lovable bears, helping them to deal with their feelings.

Another example of this attempt to connect topics was in a first-grade classroom in Michigan where teachers at each grade level had a number of topics that were assigned to the district. A large bulletin board had different pictures in the categories of "living" and "nonliving" things. The teachers then moved to a study of animals and began to classify animals into the groups of mammals, birds, reptiles, amphibians, and fish. The students discovered and identified the differences and commonalities among these groups. They next moved beyond the physical characteristics to discovering and researching the homes of each group, their diets, and how many animals lived in groups such as communities. The class finally moved to discussing the shared needs of humans and from studying the community in the classroom to the community in which they lived.

A similar theme in a New York City classroom at the Hunter College Elementary School (D. Freeman, personal communication, August, 1993) brought in a professor of urban history to lead the children on walks through various neighborhoods with various styles of architecture and longer or shorter histories. The deep knowledge of the speaker was tried and challenged by the high-IQ youngsters, who avidly asked questions at a surprisingly abstract level. Not only was connectedness demonstrated in such thematically structured classrooms, but students with different abilities or different interests had opportunities to research and explore. Even among students with high IQs, there are many different needs and competencies. The students had research partners and made projects based on their explorations of home, neighborhood, and community.

Critics of this approach would say that these topics, common in state curricula for early childhood education, are too simple for talented children. They believe that it is necessary for them to be studying more esoteric and even exotic subjects because of their ability. It is true that these children are able to memorize large numbers of facts and that they take delight in learning anything new. The concern, however, is whether or not they are actually making connections with what they know and whether or not the connections are accurate. When learnings are scattered and separate, even intellectually talented students have difficulty in placing the learnings into context. As children create their own meaning and interpretations, based on their prior experiences and knowledge, if there is limited experience or few concepts for them to use as reference there is a chance that misconceptions will occur. Young children learn from the global to the specific and the wealth of general background knowledge that young talented students often bring to school will serve them well as they move from the general thematic context to the more esoteric, exotic, and specific.

Umbrella-like themes offer inclusion and connectedness for many topics that may be found in district curricula. The "cycles as patterns of change" theme, for example, offered the teachers a chance to include the cycles of a frog's life (because a child brought a frog to the classroom early in the school year), the cycles of the monarch butterfly's life (because the town had a local annual celebration of this butterfly), the cycles of an apple tree (growing outside the classroom window), a plant, human life, the moon, the calendar, the seasons, the tides, food, and water. In all cases, the district curricular topics were grounded in the theme.

In discussing thematic content, it is important to note that not all study will relate to the theme, and that natural integration should be emphasized. Adults may attempt to contrive activities that relate to the theme but which are often related in adult minds only. Learning centers can help. The theme is not the only topic being studied and discussed in the developmentally appropriate classroom. Instead, the classrooms are rich and fascinating environments where children are actively engaged in learning about all kinds of things, through exploration with new materials, reading quality children's books, discussing current events, sharing personal experiences, hobbies, and interests.

Application

Projects based on the theme emphasize this constructivist approach to early childhood education. Constructing a replica of their community or a communication center and making simulations, reports, videotapes, interviews, dramatizations, paintings, and models, as well as creating displays and "museums," books, diaries, and presentations are some ways children can share their learning. Whenever possible, the children should apply what they have learned to real-life situations (Piirto, 1989), taking action, writing letters to the editor, and getting others involved in a cause or issue.

Not only does such active involvement in projects help students experience the utility of their learning, but the diverse talents, interests, and ages of the learners can be accommodated. Multiage classrooms are now common, and in the school reform jargon, where "time is the variable," the needs of talented learners can be served if the teachers are trained in characteristics and needs of such children, and willing to differentiate according to these needs. The depth and pace can easily be adjusted by perceptive teachers. Organizing data, conducting interviews, and researching reports are several ways that precocious students can have their educational needs met in the heterogeneous classrooms of today's early childhood movement.

OVERVIEW AND CONCLUSIONS

Learning was defined earlier as a natural process of pursuing personally meaningful goals. In learner-centered classrooms, children not only set personal learning goals for themselves, but they work with teachers on monitoring their own progress and they begin to do self-evaluation of their learning. No longer is the learner expected to sit passively and wait to be told what the teacher has decided is important to be learned. Learning in the thematic classroom arises from the situation, and progresses through connectedness and interrelatedness of topics. Expectations, or learner outcomes, are known. Teachers, parents, and the students know what they are expected to learn, and behavioral indicators of the acquisition of such learning are clearly set forth. These expectations also guide the setting of goals, and progress is monitored according to these expectations. Evaluation also follows the expectations. Children need to know, for example, what they need to do to be good writers, good readers, adept users of mathematics, or cooperative members of a group.

Even very young talented children can set goals for improving their journal entries, and then can use the goals to see whether they have or are doing so. Personal goals can be written down and students can monitor whether they achieve these goals. For example, a talented student may set very difficult or very easy goals. In conference with the parent and the teacher, the student may set out to reach the goals and then decide whether the goal is achievable or too simple. The education is not being done to the student, but *with* the student's knowledge, cooperation, and input.

Including all children in classrooms is both natural and fair. Questionable testing practices and tests, the oversimplification of child development timelines, and the challenges of family and neighborhood-like groups with models and peer interaction have contributed to current practices of early childhood education. The opportunity to educate talented students within the heterogeneous classroom is to understand their potential for fast acquisition of essentials and their need for in-depth learning. Designing suitable projects can be instituted by knowledgeable teachers. The imperative is for educators to promote these possibilities, to make changes, and to provide information to parents and the community. No children should be meeting failure, and no children should go unchallenged, but all should be learning in the constructivist ways in which young children learn best.

REFERENCES

Bechtol, W., & Sorenson, J. (1993). *Restructuring schooling for individual students.* Needham, MA: Allyn & Bacon.

Bredekamp, S. (1987). *Developmentally appropriate practices in early childhood education: Serving children from birth through age eight.* Washington, DC: National Association for the Education of Young Children.

Castillo, L. (1994). *The effect of analogy instruction on young children's metaphor comprehension.* Unpublished doctoral dissertation, City University of New York.

Cummings, C. (1995). *Creating good schools for young children.* Alexandria, VA: National Association of State Boards of Education.

Foreman, G., & Kuschner, D. (1983). *The child's construction of knowledge: Piaget for teaching.* Washington, DC: National Association for the Education of Young Children.

Gardner, H. (1993). *Multiple intelligences: The theory in practice.* New York: Basic Books.

Katz, L., & Chard, S. (1989). *Engaging children's minds: The project approach.* Norwood, NJ: Ablex.

Kostelnik, M., Howe, D., Payne, K., Rohde, B., Spalding, G., Stein, L., & Whitbeck, A. (1991). *Teaching young children using themes.* Glenview, IL: Good Year Books.

Kostelnik, M., Soderman, A., & Whiren, A. (1993). *Developmentally appropriate programs in early childhood education.* New York: Macmillan.

Learner-centered psychological principles: Guidelines for school redesign and reform. (1993). American Psychological Association.

Lewis, M., & Louis, B. (1991). Young gifted children. In N. Colangelo & G. Davis (Eds.), *Handbook of gifted education* (pp. 365-381). Needham Heights, MA: Allyn & Bacon.

Michigan State Board of Education. (1992). *Early childhood standards of quality for prekindergarten through second grade.* Lansing, MI: Author.

National Association of Elementary School Principals. (1990). *Early childhood education and the elementary principal: Standards for quality programs for young children.* Alexandria, VA: Author.

Piirto, J. (1989, July/August). What do you do in a primary gifted program? *Gifted Children Today, 33-34.*

Piirto, J. (1994). *Talented children and adults: Their development and education.* New York: Macmillan.

Smutny, J., Veenker, K., & Veenker, S. (1991). *Your gifted child: How to recognize and develop the special talents in your child from birth to age seven.* New York: Ballantine.

Terrasier, J. C. (1985). Dyssynchrony: Uneven development. In J. Freeman (Ed.), *The psychology of gifted children* (pp. 265-274). Chicester, England: Wiley.

31

Conceptual Models: Their Role in Early Education for the Gifted and Talented Child

LeoNora M. Cohen
Janice A. Jipson

The main purpose of this chapter is to examine the conceptual models that have been described as appropriate for the education of young children with special abilities and talents. We begin with an overview of models used in general early childhood classrooms and then review specific models used in talented and gifted preschool programs. In conclusion, we describe how a constructivist model might be modified to provide a developmentally appropriate program for young gifted children.

HISTORICAL OVERVIEW OF CURRICULAR MODELS USED IN EDUCATION OF THE GIFTED AND TALENTED

Conceptual models are based on theories of learning and consist of principles for guiding instruction that can be applied in a variety of administrative arrangements (Renzulli, 1986). Until quite recently, most conceptual models for delivery of programs, services, and curriculum for the gifted have been based on general education models. In Maker's (1982) book, *Teaching Models in the Education of the Gifted*, the first of its kind in the field, only one model—Renzulli's Enrichment Triad—was specifically designed for the gifted. According to Maker, the others were all developed for regular education, to enhance creativity, to explain human intelligence or moral-ethical development, for classification purposes, or for developing intelligence and creativity in all children.[1]

Some 4 years later, however, Renzulli's (1986) edited book, *Systems and Models for Developing Programs for the Gifted and Talented*, presented 15 models specifically for the gifted, which had been developed or had evolved from general education and administrative models.[2] Other conceptual models not discussed in either book but worthy of consideration are Ward's (1961,1980) Axiomatic Approach, VanTassel-Baska's (1992; VanTassel-Baska et al., 1988) Comprehensive Curriculum; Milgram's (1990) 4 x 4 Model of the Structure of Giftedness; Cox, Daniel, and Boston's (1985) Pyramid Model; and Jellen and Verduin's (1986) Differential Education for the Gifted.

Gifted education is a relatively recent field, with most development occurring in the last 25 years (Karnes & Johnson, 1986). Districts jump on the band wagons of competing new models, some largely untested, particularly if a few easy steps to accomplishing the task of educating gifted children are prescribed (Ward, 1986). Conceptual models are also mixed and matched, bits and pieces from several combined into one program. However, educating gifted children appropriately is not a simple process, nor is it possible to merely stir together a batch of fragments from various models. If a model has been carefully constructed on theoretical grounds, such practice can violate its integrity. On the other hand, conceptual models with common theoretical cores can be combined without this problem, including models not specifically designed for use with gifted children

---

[1]Bloom and Krathwohl's Cognitive and Affective Taxonomies, Bruner's Structure of a Discipline, Guilford's Structure of Intellect, Kohlberg's Moral Dilemmas, Parnes's Creative Problem Solving, Taba's Teaching Strategies, Taylor's Multiple Talent Approach, Treffinger's Self-Directed Learning, and Williams's Teaching Strategies for Thinking and Feeling.

[2]The models applicable to young gifted children include the radical acceleration model of Johns Hopkins University (SMPY), Betts's Autonomous Learner Model, Clark's Integrative Education Model, Feldhusen and Kolloff's Purdue Three-Stage Enrichment Model, Kaplan's Grid Model for Constructing a Differentiated Curriculum, Meeker and Meeker's SOI System, Renzulli and Reis's Enrichment Triad, Taylor's Multiple Talent Model, Schlicter's Talents Unlimited, Tannenbaum's Enrichment Matrix, Treffinger's Independent Learning Model, and Williams' Cognitive-Affective Interaction Model.

(Cohen, 1988, 1992; Cohen & Ambrose, 1993). Reflecting on the follow-ing questions provides the keys to such decisions: (a) Is the model selected cohesive, organized, theory-based, and qualitatively different from the regular program? (b) Does the model recognize differences in the thought processes of the gifted child? (c) Does the model support the individualized needs and strengths of gifted children and extend their interests and possibilities? (d) Does the model meet the needs of the district or school that plans to use it?, and (e) Is the philosophical/theoretical base compatible with others with which it will be combined?

We first look at models for regular education curriculum to identify the sources for development of curriculum for young gifted children.

MODELS USED IN REGULAR EARLY CHILDHOOD CLASSROOMS

Early childhood education and gifted education are indeed compati-ble. Intersections can be found and should be maximized, particularly if developmentally appropriate practices are viewed as underpinnings of both (Barbour, 1992). In looking at early childhood curriculum, sever-al perspectives are important. Spodek (1986) described three dimen-sions as influencing early childhood curriculum: the knowledge, the developmental, and the cultural-context dimensions. The knowledge dimension considers the content of the curriculum, the question of what is worth knowing for young children. The developmental dimen-sion reflects how children mature and develop and relates to early childhood programs as it examines the developmental appropriate-ness of the learning experiences. The cultural-context dimension includes both the social and historical values that characterize a given early childhood program and considers whether the curriculum is worthwhile. It is in the interrelationship of the three dimensions that a particular early childhood curriculum is defined.

Although we agree with Spodek about the importance of all three dimensions, we would like to broaden what he called the devel-opmental dimension to include differing assumptions about teaching and learning. We therefore call this aspect the *psychological dimen-sion*. We would also like to expand his definition of the cultural context to include a more comprehensive consideration of the child's personal history and cultural background in the context of the family, the school, and the community. Finally, we would like to include an additional dimension to these three: the *mediative dimension*, which we discuss in the last sections of this chapter.

CONCEPTIONS OF CURRICULUM

The Knowledge Dimension: What Children Learn

This section focuses primarily on what Eisner (1979) referred to as the *explicit* curriculum—that which is intentionally taught to preschool and primary children. It is important to consider, as Eisner reminded us, whose knowledge it is that has been targeted as the focus of the curriculum. In early childhood education, the explicit curriculum is more frequently described as being what teachers think children should learn rather than what teachers think they should teach. Although a teacher still defines what is worth knowing for the young child, she or he recognizes that much of what is learned by the child may not be the direct result of instruction.

Three major views of early childhood education have characterized the field during the last two centuries: (a) maturation, as seen in *traditional* preschool programs; (b) cultural transmission, as seen in *academically oriented* programs, and (c) cognitive development, as seen in *developmental* programs. The following section discusses each of the three as they relate to early childhood curriculum.

Traditional Curricula: Maturation. The prevailing curriculum model in early childhood education for much of its history has been the traditional, child-centered approach based on play and on social interactions between teacher and child and among the children themselves. This model represents the maturationist approach. Child-selected activities within teacher-planned interest centers such as drama corner, sand table, block corner, housekeeping area, and book corner are intended to encourage the unfolding of the child's natural abilities as well as self-confidence and social skills. The teacher and the environment must be flexible enough to allow the child's abilities to emerge. Therefore, the focus of the formal curriculum within this model is the enhancement of the child's self-esteem, self-confidence, natural abilities, and resourcefulness. The model also encourages making choices, taking initiative, cooperating, and communicating.

Academic Curricula: Cultural Transmission. Academic curricula include *discipline, knowledge,* and *skill-based* approaches. The shared feature of these models is the goal of transmitting a common set of culturally-valued knowledge and skills to the child. The most common form of curriculum for school-aged children has been the subject-oriented or *discipline-based* curriculum. In many early education programs, the response to the question of what to teach has taken the form of organizing the children's day into subject area periods such as music, art, social studies, science, language arts, and mathematics.

The *knowledge-based* approach refers to a curriculum that includes a prescribed set of declarative information to be learned by the child such as the names of objects, letters, numbers, shapes, and colors, whereas the *skill-based* approach usually includes such skills as counting, cutting, pasting, and writing one's name. Therefore, the acquisition of information and the accumulation of skills become the focus of the curriculum. The two are frequently combined or placed within the framework of a subject matter approach. They may also be joined with such behavioral goals as sitting quietly, raising one's hand, and standing in line to constitute what is known as a readiness curriculum.

Developmental Curricula: Cognitive Development. The third major form of curriculum in early education emphasizes the child's natural development through invariant sequential stages with a particular focus on cognitive processes. The development of the child's problem-solving abilities and thinking skills are central to this approach. The curriculum focuses on active involvement and direct experience with real objects in the environment. The curriculum also concerns itself with defining those experiences that are considered to be developmentally appropriate for a child of a particular age. The curriculum experienced by a child might include opportunities to see what happens when cornstarch, water, and food coloring are combined; to compare the rapidity with which various objects roll down inclines of various slopes; and to predict the length of their own shadows under different light conditions.

The Psychological Dimension: How Children Learn

The second perspective on early childhood curriculum comes from the psychological literature on learning. The ways in which children are thought to learn determine how the explicit curriculum is organized and constitute much of the implicit curriculum. Wolfson (1984) and Kohlberg and Mayer (1972) have described three major psychological orientations that direct the delivery of the formal curriculum: *phenomenological, behavioral,* and *developmental.* Although these orientations are rarely clearly observable in particular classrooms, the interactions of teachers and children suggest the orientation and belief systems of the particular teacher. Obviously, the three types of curricula in the knowledge dimension discussed previously are most often linked to one or another of these psychological orientations.

Phenomenological psychology, according to Wolfson (1984), focuses on the discovery of the individual's unique development as an active, feeling, thinking person. Self-actualization and the development of the self-concept are central to this process as is the individual creation of meaning from experience. This orientation suggests an accepting environment where the child can freely explore and within which native abilities can emerge. The child in this classroom can choose to paint any picture, construct a zoo or a boat from blocks, or role play a barber or waitress, depending on his or her fantasies and interests. The child thus experiences the formal curriculum in his or her own personal and unique way. The role of the teacher is to facilitate the child's choice. This orientation is most often linked to the traditional curriculum.

Behavioral psychology emphasizes the role of the external environment in shaping behavior. Knowledge is acquired and skills are learned through explicit instruction, through the imitation of appropriate models, and through the systematic use of reinforcement and feedback. Knowledge is transmitted to the child under the direction of the teacher. The focus is on cause-and-effect relationships, the breaking down of curriculum into small segments, the use of direct instruction and repetition, and the employment of curriculum-based assessment to determine learning. The child may recite the alphabet or name objects at the teacher's request, be asked to reproduce a picture of a flower, or follow explicit steps in completing an activity sheet. The teacher controls not only what the child can do but the standards the child must meet. This orientation is most commonly linked to the academic curriculum.

Developmental psychology describes the process of normal development, primarily in the areas of cognition and language. and is obviously linked to developmental curricula. Kohlberg and Mayer (1972) defined the acquisition of knowledge as active changes in "patterns of thinking brought about by experiential problem solving situations" (p. 454). Children are seen as constructors of knowledge through their interactions with each other and the environment and through their resolution of personally encountered conflicts and problems. A child in this classroom would be free to explore the interest centers and activities designed by the teacher to facilitate cognitive development. The teacher's role is to observe the child's interests and questions and to intentionally plan learning experiences designed to foster cognitive growth.

The Cultural Dimension: The Context In Which Children Learn

The third dimension suggested by Spodek (1986) is the *cultural context* of the teaching-learning environment. The social and cultural context in which a curriculum is situated shares equal importance with the formally selected curriculum and the way it is presented. All are part of the curriculum experienced by the child. Economic, cultural, historical, and political factors involving the community, the school, and the participating families, as well as characteristics of teacher and student— social class, race, ethnicity, native language, religion, and gender—all influence the curriculum as each unique group of teachers and children combine. The relationship between each teacher and child's personal history, and the social environment of the school and classroom, become essential parts of the curriculum whether it is experienced, transmitted, or constructed. Graue (1993) and Lubeck (1994) discussed the multiple interactions among these factors. The curriculum in use, therefore, reflects our notions of what young children should know, how they learn, and what the relations among children, teachers and the environment should be.

In the next part of this chapter, we examine the conceptual models used in various preschool gifted programs. Discussion is restricted to the preschool level because most programs in kindergarten and primary classrooms are part of the regular schoolwide offerings for gifted students and are not necessarily geared to very young children.

It is important to distinguish between programs and models. Programs are arrangements in which children are offered regularly scheduled classes or services that address their educational and other needs within a specific educational setting. Models may be administrative or conceptual. Administrative models are generic arrangements for provision of services such as home schooling, differentiation in the regular classroom, or placement of a child in a higher grade. Conceptual models are generalized philosophical/ theoretical frameworks for organizing the curriculum that transcend the limitations of a specific site or administrative arrangement and are the focus of this chapter. A given program may incorporate one or several conceptual or administrative models. Some of these programs are enumerated next.

PRESCHOOL GIFTED PROGRAMS: FEW AND FAR BETWEEN

Few special programs for gifted preschoolers have been developed, largely because of the lack of state and federal legislation mandating use of public funds for preschool gifted programs (Karnes, Schwedel, & Linnemeyer, 1982). A useful summary of five enduring programs was made by Kitano and Kirby (1986a)—the New Mexico State University Preschool for the Gifted, Seattle Child Development Preschool, University of Illinois Champaign-Urbana Programs, Hunter College Elementary School of New York, and the Astor Program of New York. Some other programs described in the literature are the Hollingsworth Preschool, Teachers College, Columbia University (Wright & Coulianos, 1991); the MISC-G program of Bar Ilan University Israel, (Klein, 1992); the P.I.P.P.I. Project (Goldman & Rosenfield, 1985); and Project Spectrum, based on Gardner's multiple intelligence theory, jointly sponsored by Harvard and Tufts Universities (Buescher, 1985; Krechevsky & Gardner, 1991).

Mandates extending funding for preschool gifted children in Louisiana and Florida have augmented the number of public preschool programs (see Mathews & Burns, 1992), but many states do not require any educational provisions for children under kindergarten age, let alone programs for gifted preschool children. In fact, most states actually prohibit children under age 5 from entering public school programs (Karnes & Johnson, 1991). Some private schools not attached to universities provide for preschool talented and gifted children, but information about their programs for very young children is scant and more often connected to descriptions of the entire school (see *Gifted Child Today, 14*, 5). Robinson (1993) listed a handful of preschool programs for the gifted in the international arena as well.

Although more programs exist at the kindergarten level (Jenkins, 1979, identified 20 at this level), most are tied in to regular elementary programs for the gifted. Still more options exist at the primary level, although the admittance to gifted programs most often begins at about age 9, according to Karnes and Johnson (1986), who posited the following reasons for lack of programming and identification of young children:

1. Children age 9 or above are easier to identify because their performance is more stable and the number of standardized instruments available for testing is greater.
2. Parents of young children are not as assertive about appropriate programming for their gifted children as parents of older children.
3. Specialists who train teachers of the gifted are not usually trained to work with young children and therefore tend to focus on the upper elementary level.
4. The focus on handicapped gifted young children has been on their deficits, rather than their gifts. Special educators working with the handicapped rarely have any training in gifted education and do not recognize or know how to assist gifted children. The same is true for disadvantaged children.

To this list Karnes and Johnson (1991) later added financial constraints, which inhibit development of nonmandated programs, and legal roadblocks, which prohibit public school programming for children below age 5. Such policies and financial problems are particularly detrimental to the disadvantaged, who are at risk for losing their giftedness if it is not identified and nurtured early (Lewis & Louis, 1991). Their potential treasures may remain hidden (Tannenbaum, 1992).

MODELS USED IN PRESCHOOL GIFTED PROGRAMS

According to Robinson (1993), models used in preschool programs are almost always downward extensions of models developed for older gifted students. She suggested that these varied approaches share three commonalties: focus on the social milieu (playmates who share more mature interests and a supportive social climate), emphasis on appropriate content and methods to match the differentiated needs and rapid developmental pace of gifted young children while recognizing their need for physical action and less mature fine-motor skills, and enhancement of thinking strategies and creative imagination.

No one model has been found to be better than another, but having a conceptual model is important. In fact, using more than one model may be beneficial (Karnes, Kemp, & Williams, 1983; Maker, 1982; Roedell, Jackson, & Robinson, 1980). Model selection should be based on a consideration of whether it is consistent with both the program philosophy and goals and the nature of the population served (Cohen, 1992; Kitano & Kirby, 1986b). Any model for gifted education must be qualitatively distinctive to address the different thinking patterns of gifted children (Ward, 1961; 1980). Shore and Kanevsky (1993) suggested seven such ways in which gifted children differ in their thinking—a more extensive and interconnected memory and knowledge base, greater metacognitive skills and self-regulation, rapidity of thought, skill in categorizing and representing problems, procedural knowledge (use of appropriate strategies), flexibility of thought, and a preference for complexity.

To ensure that a program is qualitatively distinctive and linked to these differences in thought processes, Kitano (1982) recommended that whatever the model selected for young gifted children, emphases should be on enhancing creativity, developing higher cognitive processes, developing executive operations, promoting inquiry and problem solving, promoting affective development, and incorporating both process and content objectives into units. Parke and Ness (1988) suggested that the primary focus in making curriculum decisions for gifted young children should be on their particular interests and needs and should emphasize play, exploration, and manipulation.

Table 31.1 provides an overview of the major conceptual models used in preschool gifted classrooms. Models that share psychological orientations are more compatible for combining. For example, Gardner's Multiple Intelligences and Constructivist approaches both have roots in developmental psychology. The scope of the model (what it chooses to illuminate) often is different, so combining can provide greater breadth. For example, Bloom's Taxonomy, Structure of Intellect, Schlicter's Multiple Talents, and Gardner's Multiple Intelligences all focus on thinking as their major concern. Others, such as the Traditional Model or Open Classroom, are more concerned with environment. The Constructivist Model focuses on development of thinking through the interaction of child and environment. The Academic, Units, Thematic, and Renzulli Enrichment Models have as their scope the content or organization of curriculum. Combining a model that focuses on thinking with others that have different

Table 31.1. Conceptual Models Used in Preschool Gifted Programs.

Model/ Developer	Description	Where Used/ Other Considerations	References
Taxonomy of Educational Objectives (Bloom, 1956)	Structures cognitive processes through use of a hierarchy of classes of thinking (knowledge, comprehension, application, analysis, synthesis, and evaluation) to move children's thinking to a higher level.	• Sunburst Program, Coeur D'Alene, ID • Pippi Project, Harlem, NYC • Astor Program, NYC • Gifted/Handicapped Program, U. North Carolina, Chapel Hill • General model for preschool gifted	• Hanninen, 1979; Roedell et al., 1980 • Goldman & Rosenfeld, 1985 • Ehrlich, 1984; Karnes et al., 1983 • Blacher-Dixon & Turnbull, 1978 • Bailey & Leonard, 1977
Structure of Intellect (Guilford, 1967; Meeker, 1969)	A factor-analytic model of cognitive functioning consisting of 120 different thinking abilities, resulting from a combination of operations (cognition, memory, convergent production, divergent production, figural evaluation, contents symbolic, semantic, behavioral), and products (units, classes, relations, systems, transformations, implications). Used for instructional programming and assessment.	• RAPHYT Program for gifted/handicapped, U. of Illinois • A summer program parent curriculum	• Karnes et al., 1983 • Strom, Johnson, Strom, & Strom, 1992

Table 31.1. Conceptual Models Used in Preschool Gifted Programs (cont.).

Model	Description	Program/Application	References
Multiple Talents (Taylor, 1967)	A teaching model to promote thinking development consisting of skill components (productive thinking, planning, forecasting, decision making, aademics, communication), model instructional materials, inservice, and student assessment to help students solve problems, and develop inquiry, organization, and management skills.	• Talents Unlimited (Not specified where used)	• Schlicter, 1985, 1986; Taylor, 1986
Multiple Intelligences (Gardner, 1983)	There are seven biologically-based intelligences (linguistic, logical-mathematical, spatial-visual, musical, bodily-kinesthetic, interpersonal, intrapersonal), each defined as ability to solve problems or make products valued in a particular cultural context.	• Project Spectrum, Harvard & Tufts Universities • A Brazilian preschool program (combined with Bloom's Taxonomy) • Crystallizing experiences	• Buescher, 1985; Krechevsky & Gardner, 1991; Ramos-Ford & Gardner, 1991 • Salgado-Gama, 1991 • Walters & Gardner, 1985, 1986 a & b

Table 31.1. Conceptual Models Used in Preschool Gifted Programs (cont.).

Model	Description	Examples	References
	Young gifted children are considered to be "at promise" in one or more of these intelligences. Involves observational assessment and instructional aspects.		
Open Classroom (origins in Dewey, 1966/1916)	Aim is to nurture whole individuals who are responsible for own growth. Children learn through their activity, when material is interesting and relevant. Teacher arranges environment to facilitate children's development. Curriculum emerges from children. Focus is on how to learn. Flexible approach.	• University of Illinois (with disadvantaged) • Roeper School, Bloomfield, MI	• Karnes et al., 1983 • Roedell et al., 1980
Traditional Models	A child-centered, maturational approach based on play and social interactions within centers such as block and book corners and housekeeping, which allow child's natural	• Evergreen School, Seattle, WA	• Roedell et al., 1980

Table 31.1. Conceptual Models Used in Preschool Gifted Programs (cont.).

abilities, self confidence, and social skills to emerge.

Model	Description	Programs	References
Academic Models	Focus is on cultural transmission through specific disciplines, knowledge or skills. Typically, instruction in reading, mathematics, and writing is provided. Acceleration is often encouraged.	• Pilot project in Illinois • Hunter College, NYC • Seattle Country Day School • Evergreen School, Seattle • Seattle Project • Project L-E-A-P, Dundalk Community College, Baltimore, MD • Creative Learning Center, Dallas, TX • Astor Program, NYC	• VanTassel-Baska, Schuler & Lipshutz, 1982 • Jenkins, 1979; Roedell et al., 1980 and all other locations)
Unit Model (Kitano & Kirby, 1986b)	A seven-step model that is systematic, sequenced, comprehensive, and preplanned, wherein the educator selects the content and encourages higher level thinking. Student interests are included.	• New Mexico State University Preschool for Gifted	• Kitano & Kirby, 1986b

Table 31.1. Conceptual Models Used in Preschool Gifted Programs (cont.).

Model	Description	Site	Reference
Thematic and Integrative Models (Kaplan, 1986)	Involves crossing of subject lines and integrating elements from several subjects, as well as student involvement in planning. Themes are broad and interdisciplinary, such as adventure, changes, or patterns. Children learn in holistic ways over blocks of time.	•Recommended for Oregon early childhood gifted programs •Hollingsworth Preschool, Teachers College, Columbia U. •Giften/handicapped project, Chapel Hill, NC (with Bloom) •Multi-Methods (Site not described)	•Cohen, Burgess, & Busick, 1990 •Wright & Coulianos, 1991 •Blacher-Dixon & Turnbull, 1978 •Hall, 1983
Enrichment Triad (Renzulli, 1977; Renzulli & Reis, 1985)	Based on interaction of three types of enrichment activities: Type I-General Exploratory, Type II-Group Training, and Type III-Individual and Small Group Investigations of Real Problems. Children selected when displaying interacting behaviors: above average intelligence, task commitment, and creativity.	•Colonel Wolf School, U. of Illinois •Sunburst Program, Coeur D'Alene, ID •PIPPI Project, Harlem, NYC	•Karnes et al., 1983 •Roedell et al., 1980 •Goldman, 1980

emphases could provide a broader base. Two models have not been included in Table 31.1 because we expand on them in the next sections. They are the Mediated Learning Model, which focuses on the role of the adult, and a Modified Constructivist Model, based extensively on Piagetian theory.

Mediated Learning Model

Kanevsky (1992), Moss (1992), and Klein (1992) suggested that *mediation* is an important element in both the development of giftedness and in appropriate programming for gifted young children. Mediation is the assistance or scaffolding provided by parents, teachers, or caregivers who understand where the learner is in the learning process, the demands of the task or environment, and how to best help the learner progress and benefit from future learning experiences (Klein, 1992). Although mediation could be classified as an aspect of the cultural context for learning described by Spodek (1986), we believe it is so important that we separate the mediative aspects to focus on the role of significant adults in the child's life. The works of two theorists, Vygotsky and Feuerstein, have been employed in mediation models for the gifted.

Over 60 years ago, Vygotsky (1934/1962), suggested that determining the child's *zone of proximal development*—the discrepancy between the child's actual mental age and what problems she or he can solve with assistance—could indicate potential for success in school. Vygotsky found that instruction "marches ahead of development and leads it" (p.104), assisting in the ripening of structures. Therefore, the adult plays an important role in mediating the learning process by providing hints, guidance, and correction. The child may request assistance or the adult may anticipate the needs of the child in this process. Through interactions with the mediator, the child internalizes the processes for solving problems and gains control over them. As the child becomes more able to generalize and transfer what is learned, the adult becomes less of a guide and more an encourager.

Feuerstein's (1980) Instrumental Enrichment Model was originally developed to assist retarded performers to improve in their intellectual abilities. However, it has also been found useful in identifying and serving the gifted (Klein, 1992). According to Feuerstein, intelligence is dynamic and modifiable, not static. The intelligent person is able to effectively gather needed information and use that information to express solutions to problems, or to generate new information. Direct intervention in an individual's cognitive development through mediation of a caring adult is needed to optimize the effectiveness and efficiency of that development. Through the benefit of such mediation, called the *mediated learning experience* (MLE), the individual becomes more open to experience and more adaptable to new situations. Feuerstein (1979) proposed that several basic skills underlie learning. He specified how these can be mediated, based on dynamic assessment, wherein the mediator determines what children can do with what they learn rather than what they know. This model may have particular applicability for identifying and supporting underserved gifted populations.

Applied as models for educating gifted children, Kanevsky (1992) utilized the work of Vygotsky, suggesting that the Zone of Proximal Development (ZPD) for the gifted child is considerably wider than that of the average child. This means that with appropriate mediation, the gifted child can learn more complex, abstract, and difficult concepts. Kanevsky linked the importance of affect in the learning process to Csikszentimihalyi's (1990) concept of "flow," a state of "at-oneness" with one's tasks where time is forgotten and pleasure in the effort is evident. Moss (1992) used Vygotsky's theory to study the role of mothers as mediators in the development of their preschool children. She found that the mothers of gifted children directed metacognitive development toward the highest levels and used feedback from their children to determine how fast to progress. Klein (1992) used Feuerstein's *mediated learning experiences* to teach low-income parents of gifted young children how to "increase a child's capacity to benefit from new experiences" (p. 257). She found that parents were eager to learn how to help their children and all progressed in the ability to mediate positive, exciting learning experiences. Mediated learning, especially when utilized with other models, appears to be particularly beneficial in teaching young gifted children.

THE MODIFIED CONSTRUCTIVIST MODEL FOR THE YOUNG GIFTED CHILD

We recommend a modified constructivist or developmental model based on the works of Piaget, combined with the mediational aspects of Feuerstein and Vygotsky, and with Gardner's notion of Multiple Intelligences as particularly applicable to the education of preschool gifted children. It might also be possible to incorporate aspects of thematic approaches or Renzulli's Enrichment Triad as well. The core philosophical assumptions of these models are compatible and their scope complementary. Therefore, these models can be combined without violating the integrity of any.

Constructivist preschool and kindergarten programs are in evidence throughout the United States and appear to be the prevailing paradigm at this time (Brooks & Brooks, 1993). The fundamental tenet in this paradigm is that the child constructs his or her own understandings through both physical and mental actions. Children's constructions of meaning are understood to differ, depending on their previous experiences, level of competence, and their interests, so learning outcomes differ in terms of how and what information is integrated. In the Modified Constructivist Model (MCM), the teacher functions to support learning as a caring mediator and to provide opportunities to develop in each of the seven intelligences.

Next we describe the theoretical aspects of the constructivist model, contrast it with other models, look at its recent application from the literature, and describe constructivist preschool and kindergarten classrooms in Eugene, OR, that typify the model. We then describe how the mediational and multiple intelligences aspects fit.

Theoretical Aspects of the Constructivist Model

Piaget's (1977, 1980) constructivist-developmental theory portrays intelligence as an ability to adapt. Intelligence develops through the interaction of the child with the environment as a result of the child's actions (both mental and physical) and reflections on those actions using the mechanism of reflective abstraction. In the process of reflective abstraction, the individual constructs relationships not inherent in the elements being put together together. For example, when a child discovers that whether you add three beans and four beans or two beans and five beans, you get the same total, it is not the beans but the order and relationships the child has imposed on the beans (or any other objects) that has led to the construction.

According to DeVries and Kohlberg (1987), the constructivist model asserts that a basic objective of education is to foster structural change in children's reasoning. It also emphasizes the importance of action by the child for learning. Learning is not merely accumulated facts acquired through external reinforcement. Rather, it is constructed through mental functions that are based on biological processes of adaptation (Forman, 1987). The child uses these functions in interaction with the physical world to construct internal structures such as class inclusion, conservation, or transitivity, that help him or her to understand the world. This process, called *equilibration*, involves assimilating new information and accommodating that information by modifying the knowing structures. For example, if a bright preschool child has constructed the notion that meat is good to eat and then discovers that animals have to be killed for food, the child may become vegetarian to deal with the discordant (and to a very sensitive child, painful) information. Or he or she may partially accommodate to the idea by denying that bacon is meat because it comes in rectangles and meat is irregular in shape, thereby allowing him- or herself to eat it.

An individual's thinking evolves through distinct levels or stages of organization over time. As was demonstrated in the meat example, advances in development are based on conflicts, disturbances, or gaps that are discordant to the child's mental organization and provide the impetus for reorganization. Therefore, the child adapts to the environment by modifying him- or herself. Each equilibration leads toward higher and broader levels of understanding. Related to gifted education, giftedness may involve higher stages beyond formal operational thought, faster or perhaps somewhat different movement through the stages, or a difference in the equilibration process and construction of the mental structures (Cohen, 1985).

Forman (1987) suggested four implications for any classroom:

1. Knowledge can never be reduced to information learned from the senses; rather, it must be structured or organized by the individual to make mentally available what is dealt with physically. The teacher thus supports the child's active involvement with facts, ideas, or objects and mediates through sensitive listening, discussing, encouraging and questioning.
2. Development is marked by learning to think about and reflect on one's mental processes. The teacher helps the child think about reasons for his or her answers or errors.
3. Learning only results when the child, rather than the teacher, asks and answers his or her own questions. Depth of learning results as the child relates what is being learned to what he or she already knows. The teacher respectfully supports such questioning and asks the child to share his or her discoveries.
4. Children are best taught by giving them the opportunity to explore and experiment. The teacher provides a rich problem-solving environment in which this can occur. Traditional subjects such as spelling or math are areas for experimentation. Invented spellings or math rules result. Errors provide a base for the next experiment.

A Comparison of Models

In many ways, the early childhood constructivist classroom resembles other early childhood classrooms, particularly those using open classroom or traditional approaches. Typical materials, equipment, and activities such as art, block building, sand, and water play are often provided. Dramatic play areas, puzzles, and games are also common. Space is organized in such a way as to suggest various areas of interest but is also changeable by both teacher and children because of moveable furniture and dividers.

Time within the early childhood constructivist classroom is also structured similarly to some other early childhood programs. Large blocks of free-choice time permit wide variety in activities. Children can decide when to begin, when to stop, and how long to continue a particular activity. Daily group time and outdoor play time provide opportunities for social interactions between children for large motor activity.

However, there are differences between the Constructivist Model and the Open Classroom Model (the most closely related). In the open classroom, the teacher is the facilitator/supporter who sets up an interesting and intriguing environment in response to the expressed interests of the children. The purpose is to motivate, rather than elicit cognitive change. The child seeks knowledge based on interest and intrinsic motivation. The child has much input into the curriculum and the learning environment and the teacher responds to the concerns of the child.

In the constructivist classroom, the teacher prepares and changes the environment to stimulate and generate student thinking. The child seeks and constructs knowledge from this planned environment. The focus is on psychological change with the teacher as a guide or mediator. There is shared control of the learning environment by child and teacher. As with the open classroom model, the teacher's role in the constructivist classroom is to create an environment conducive to learning and to help the child extend his or her ideas. In addition, the teacher in the constructivist classroom provides materials and suggests activities in response to his or her assessment of each child's thinking and responds to each child in terms of the kind of knowledge involved (DeVries & Kohlberg, 1987).

Another thing that distinguishes the early childhood constructivist model from most other early childhood models is the focus on physical knowledge activities. The forms of interactions between teachers and children both during group time and free choice time may also differ from other early childhood models. Teacher-child interaction is characterized by teacher-posed questions intended to introduce a problem or focus on a puzzle. It may also be used to extend the child's thinking in new directions. Such discussions may be planned to stimulate a particular activity or avenue of play. Child-child interaction is encouraged because it is believed that children also learn from each other as they solve problems and play.

Two Constructivist Programs

On entering the Early Childhood Center or Elga Brown's Kindergarten, the visitor might not be aware of the theoretical orientation of the program. Only after observing the actions of the children and listening to the interactions of children with teachers and with each other would the visitor recognize the significant differences in the programs. Next, we follow two children to school— Erik, age 3, and Adam, age 5-1/2.

Erik: A Constructivist Preschool. Erik is the last child to arrive at the Early Childhood Center. Pancake in hand, he explains that "I got up too late and so I had to bring breakfast along." The head teacher greets him with a smile and invites him to sit at a table while he finishes eating.

A group of children are painting with colored shaving cream on both sides of a Plexiglas sheet, hung vertically. Erik, having finished his pancake, approaches and proceeds to squeeze a large handful of shaving cream into the nearby sand box. When asked, he says he wants to see what would happen when you mix sand and shaving cream. The teacher then asks him to make a "prediction about how the sand will feel."

"Slimy." Erik then tries to paint with sandy shaving cream on the plexiglass. The sand-cream runs off. Erik speculates "It was too heavy." Another child says, "It was too lumpy."

Meanwhile, a teacher has put out a pitcher of juice and a plate of crackers and apple slices. A sign directs the children to take "1⬚, 2⬚⬚,& 2 ◖◗. Jenna wanders over and helps herself to four crackers. Ryan reminds her that if she eats four there won't be enough for everybody. About this time the teacher starts a soft music tape and invites the children to do their "fair share of clean up." The assistant teachers remind individuals to pick up Legos or blocks. The children negotiate who should pick up how many toys. Duncan says, "Erik, you can come to my birthday party."

Erik replies, "Yes, and I won't bring you any war toys." He begins to sing "I know an old lady who swallowed a fly" as he wipes up shaving cream from the floor. The teacher begins a story and the children settle into a circle, waiting for parents to come and take them home.

Adam: A Constructivist Kindergarten. The only rule in the alternative kindergarten class is that everyone should have a good day. It is written on a strip of paper prominently displayed in the front of the room. Adam enters the classroom, turns his name tag over, is greeted with a hug by his teacher, and joins a group of children working on a block representation of their classroom, a project that has been ongoing for the week. "Let's see. Here's the bookshelf next to the door. We need to make it higher, 'cause it's taller than me." A discussion ensues with several other children as to how many blocks high it should be. They decide on four, because, as Anna explains, " The bookshelf has four shelves." Other children are working on representing the post office, the doll corner, the art center, and other areas and objects.

The children are called to circle time on the rug by a signal on the teacher's xylophone. The calendar is done by Jamal, the "child of the week," who also notes on the number line going around the room that they are on the 125th school day. Adam declares, "That's like a dollar and a quarter!" "Oh, yeah," says Marta. That's what five quarters make."

The teacher, noting this interest, asks the children what other combinations of coins would make $1.25. The children get deeply involved in this problem, talking among themselves. One child gets out a box of Cuisinaire rods. Another takes an abacus. They come up with several combinations. The teacher accepts their responses, representing them on a chart on the blackboard. She encourages other alternatives. "Let's see how many different ways we can come up with to make this amount of money by tomorrow."

The children are asked whether anyone is missing. They look around the room and point out that Amanda's name tag is the only one not turned over. The child of the week takes the attendance slip to the office. The teacher introduces new learning centers for the day. A mother who is a physician has brought in a plastic child-sized skeleton to share with those interested. A bin of soap bubbles, straws, and various cans and rings are available. Waxed paper, leaves, paper strips, and crayons are out on the art table and poster paint is available at the easel. Other already familiar centers are also options. The teacher then asks each child which two activities they plan to work on that morning. If they ask for blocks, she asks them how many sets of 10 they want and how many blocks that will be. The children know how many individuals can work on centers where limits are needed. They quickly let the teacher know their choices and go off to work once everyone has made their choices.

Adam has selected the soap bubble activity. He is fascinated by the shapes created by the bubbles when they bunch together. He describes these to the teacher as hexagons. She asks him if they always take that shape. He studies the bubbles further and works on the problem. When she circulates back to the bubble area, he describes the results of his research. The teacher takes a straw and tries to poke a hole in a bubble. "I wonder why this doesn't work," she muses. Another investigation is launched by Adam, who is intensely curious about the structure of things.

A group has gathered around the doctor to learn about bones. She had been invited specifically to help Todd, a child who is unable to talk about his father's recent back surgery. Todd did not choose this center, but was drawn to it, as the teacher knew he would be. He told the parent-physician, "My dad just had an operation on his back." The doctor was able to get him to point out the particular bones that were the problem, and Todd could at last discuss his father's surgery.

Adam chose next to work at the art center. He tried drawing on the leaves through wax paper, then tried painting the leaves directly. Other children were experimenting with using the leaves in their artwork, drawing on them, printing with them, and experimenting with wax paper and crayons. The teacher stated, "I didn't know you could color on leaves. Look at what you discovered today!"

Adam then went back to the block activity he had joined when first entering the room. If children finish with their choice of activities, they are free to move to another. Children had represented the class post office with tiny letters they cut from paper scraps. They had incorporated small plastic figures in the doll corner, and had made "books" by stapling together layers of paper cut into small rectangles. The representation of the room was from their own perspective, and they had extended it to show the relationship of the kindergarten to the rest of the school. A long line of blocks almost to the doorway represented the hallway. Although the project had been ongoing for several days, the children were very respectful of each others' work and carefully avoided wrecking it.

The class members were called to clean up and come back to circle. Good-natured negotiating ensued. Jill, who did not want to clean up the blackboard on which she had been drawing the day before, was given the challenge: "How could you still draw on the board but have very little to clean up?" Today, she made tiny drawings and proudly announced, "I just had to make one wipe with the eraser."

At circle, the teacher described the things she had learned that day. "I didn't know you could draw on leaves, but Amy showed me that. I didn't realize that the soap bubbles form hexagons when all joined together. Adam pointed this out. What did you learn today?" Children shared their discoveries and remarked on discoveries of other children. They were dismissed individually with a hug and "I hope you had a good day."

The Constructivist Model and the Gifted Child

For gifted children, such principles provide for active, self-directed, reflective learning experiences. Because the focus of the model is on the construction of knowledge from exploration and experience by individual children, it lends itself particularly well to the varying abilities and interests of gifted children. In addition, the characteristics of the gifted child—curiosity, long attention span, ability to conceptualize, generalize, and abstract—are favorably facilitated by the constructivist approach. The danger is the inappropriate application of constructivist developmental notions in algorithmic fashion. In the name of developmentally appropriate, for example, a bright 4-year-old might not be allowed to learn to read even when she asks for instruction because children are "not supposed to be developmentally ready" for formal reading instruction until age 6 or 7.

The uniqueness of the constructivist model for gifted education was eloquently shared by Elga Brown, teacher of the Alternative Kindergarten Program: "There is no limit to what can be learned, but also there is no comparative evaluation which makes children feel more or less capable than their peers. Understanding grows naturally as children work with materials and explore their possibilities" (cited in Klauke, 1988, p.19).

Modifying the Constructivist Model

Returning to the two early childhood classrooms just described, we see that both have a rich array of materials that could enhance the Multiple Intelligences. Observing which centers Adam was attracted to (block building, soap bubbles, and art) would indicate that he appears to be at promise in the figural-spatial and logico-mathematical intelligences, although much more observation would be needed to make a definitive assessment. Conscious attention to this aspect would assist in developing multiple modes of thinking in Adam and the other children. It would assist teachers and the children themselves in learning about strengths and interests. In fact, asking children to switch modes might be critical in integrating understandings (Cohen, 1994). For example, if Adam were to draw his hexagonal bubble discovery or try to use his body to make the shapes, he might learn a great deal more.

In these two constructivist examples we also find the role of teacher as mediator of learning in the context of an environment that recognizes the whole child—the social, emotional, physical, intuitive, and perceptual aspects as well as the cognitive. For example, the kindergarten teacher seized the interest in the number 125 and led the children to think about other combinations to make that number. She encouraged reflection on what they had accomplished at the end of the day, mediating the development of metacognition. She focused the children's attention on what they had discovered, reacted with excitement and rewarded their creative thinking. She also set the stage for development of whole, healthy people, through her one simple rule that everyone should have a good day. This mediational aspect is the fourth dimension of the curriculum that we would like to add to Spodek's three: the knowledge, psychological, and contextual dimensions.

However, mediation goes beyond the notion of a caring adult helping a child to grow in thought. We suggest that mediation can be of four types: (Cohen et al., forthcoming):

1. *Metacognitive or self mediation* occurs within the learner through the voice of inner dialogue. Individuals can learn to mediate for themselves, becoming aware of their own thinking, creating, and feeling processes. Metacognition involves monitoring and controlling thinking (Presseisen, 1991). Monitoring means that the learner becomes aware of pacing requirements, task demands, social context, as well as what she or he knows and does not know. Ben, aged 3-1/2

says, "I want to tell you everything I know and don't know about volcanoes." Selection and control involve choosing strategies appropriate to the task. Heather, aged 4, is asked how she remembers her brother's birthday and replies, "I picture it in my head, or I make up a song about it, or I say 'June 21, June 21' over and over." She has begun to control her strategies for memory. Kanevsky (1992) found evidence of this in the preschool gifted children who demonstrated better "gamesmanship." Very young bright children apparently are more metacognitively aware than their less able counterparts and can be supported to reflect on how they think.

2. *Mentor mediation* between the known and unknown through intervention by a loving, caring individual who serves to bridge and interpret between the new and the known. The mediator recognizes where difficulties lie for the learner, senses the potential for growth, and provides materials, tools, questions, or strategies that assist the learner in gaining understanding. The mediator attempts to connect the past with the present by bringing order to feelings, emotions, ways of knowing, and ways of being. This is the classic form of mediation described in the Mediated Learning Model.

3. *Cooperative or diplomatic mediation* between individuals in groups. This kind of mediation can be done by adults or children. For example, Hannah, aged 4, could often get her peers to come to peaceful resolution when there were hard feelings. Helping students understand roles in groups, effective leadership, communicating for understanding, learning to cooperate, and sharing responsibility all are aspects of cooperative or diplomatic mediation. Children need to be helped to be social beings. For gifted children, this may mean helping to make the "rules of the game" explicit—"If you want Justin to be your friend, will telling him his drawing is yucky make him want to spend time with you? How would you feel if he said your drawing was yucky?"

4. *Cultural mediation* between subgroups and their community. The cultural mediator brings meaning to cultural diversity within and among groups while expanding others' points of view in such areas as values, ethics, mores, aesthetics, and interpersonal and intrapersonal understanding. The mediator emphasizes cooperation, not competition, to achieve this end. Through networking and strategic alliances, the mediator organizes ideas and people in constructive ways to build bridges between people with diverse expectations, cultures, and religious heritages. Cultural mediators interest themselves in tasks that do not fragment processes or people. This role is central to the formation of multiple perspectives, so that bias

and prejudice may be replaced with fresh insights and inno-vations. Early childhood is an ideal period to provide cultural mediation, before prejudices are entrenched. The teacher, each child, and his or her family member are invited to tell their stories. Maria tells how she got a new puppy that chewed her shoe. Aki's father describes his disappointment over a torn kite when he was a little boy in Japan. Ryan's grandmother describes helping her mother pick cotton in the heat of an Alabama summer when she was a small child. The teacher tells how she disobeyed her mother and jumped in mud puddles. Such stories help to create a sense of class-room and wider community as well as develop literacy (see Paley, 1995).

By integrating aspects of mediation and Multiple Intelligences, the Modified Constructivist Model could well be applied in regular preschool and early childhood classrooms. Such a model would meet the needs of the gifted child, particularly if other intellectual peers were in the classroom. In fact, we advocate the use of gifted education models in general early childhood classrooms to help bring about a paradigm shift in general education that helps all children and better serves the needs of very bright young children.

REFERENCES

Bailey, D.B., & Leonard, J. (1977). A model for adapting Bloom's Taxonomy to a preschool curriculum for the gifted. *Gifted Child Quarterly, 21,* 97-103.

Barbour, N. B. (1992). Early childhood gifted education: A collaborative perspective. *Journal for the Education of the Gifted, 15,* 145-162.

Blacher-Dixon, J., & Turnbull, A. P. (1978). A preschool program for gift-ed-handicapped children. *Journal for the Education of the Gifted, 1*(2), 15-23.

Bloom, B. S. (1956). *Taxonomy of educational objectives: The classification of educational goals. Handbook I: Cognitive domain.* New York: David McKay.

Brooks, J. G., & Brooks, M. G. (1993). *The case for constructivist class-rooms.* Alexandria, VA: Association for Supervision and Curriculum Development.

Buescher, T. (1985). Seeking the roots of talent: An interview with Howard Gardner. *Journal for the Education of the Gifted, 8,* 179-186.

Cohen, L. M. (1985). *Towards a theory for gifted education.* Dissertation, Temple University, Philadelphia. (University Microfilms No. 8509318).

Cohen, L. M. (1988). "To get ahead, get a theory": Criteria for evaluating theories of giftedness and creativity applied to education. *Roeper Review, 11,* 95-100.

Cohen, L. M. (1992). Ownership to allship: Building a conceptual framework for educating of the gifted and creative. In N. Colangelo, S. G. Assouline, & D. L. Ambroson (Eds.), *Developing talent: Proceedings from the 1991 Henry B. and Jocelyn Wallace National Research Symposium on Talent Development* (pp. 204-222). Unionville, NY: Trillium.

Cohen, L. M. (1994). Mode-switching strategies. In J. Edwards (Ed.), *Thinking: International interdisciplinary perspectives* (pp. 230-240). Melbourne: Hawker-Brownlow.

Cohen, L. & Ambrose, D. (1993) Theories and practices for differentiated education for the gifted and talented. In K. A. Heller, F. J. Monks, and A. H. Passow (Eds.), *International handbook for research on giftedness and talent* (pp. 339-363). Oxford, UK: Pergamon.

Cohen, L. M., with Ambrose, D., Sterling, A., Beranek, D., & Rimington, H. (forthcoming). *Role-based education: Making active learning happen.*

Cohen, L. M., Burgess, A. C., & Busick, T. K. (1990). Teaching gifted kindergarten and primary children in the regular classroom. *OSSC Bulletin, 33*(7 & 8), 1-107.

Cox, J., Daniel, N. & Boston, B. O. (1985). *Educating able learners: Programs and promising practices.* Austin: University of Texas Press.

Csikszentmihalyi, M. (1990). *Flow: The psychology of optimal experience.* New York: Harper & Row.

DeVries, R., & Kohlberg, L. (1987). *Programs of early education: The constructivist view.* New York: Longman.

Dewey, J. (1966/1916). *Democracy in education.* New York: The Free Press.

Ehrlich, V. Z. (1984). *The Astor Program for young gifted children: Ten years later.* New York: Teachers College Press.

Eisner, E. (1979). *The educational imagination.* New York: MacMillan.

Forman, G. (1987). The constructivist perspective. In J. Roopnarine & J. Johnson (Eds.), *Approaches to early childhood education* (pp. 71-84). Columbus, OH: Merrill.

Feuerstein, R. (1979). *The dynamic assessment of retarded performers.* Glenview, IL: Scott, Foresman.

Feuerstein, R. (1980). *Instrumental enrichment.* Glenview, IL: Scott, Foresman.

Gardner, H. (1983). *Frames of mind.* New York: Basic Books.

Goldman. N. T. (1980). *The P.I.P.P.I. Program.* Presentation at the Council for Exceptional Children Convention, Philadelphia, PA. April 20-25.

Goldman, N. T., & Rosenfield, S. (1985). Meeting the needs of preschool gifted children. In R. H. Swassing (Ed.), *Teaching gifted children and adolescents* (pp. 92-133). Columbus, OH: Merrill.

Graue, M. E. (1993). *Ready for what? Constructing meanings of readiness for kindergarten*. Albany: State of New York Press.

Guilford, J. P. (1967). *The nature of human intelligence*. New York: McGraw-Hill.

Hanninen, G. (1979). Developing a preschool gifted/talented program. *G/C/T, 9,* 18-19, 21.

Jellen, H., & Verduin, R. (1986). *Handbook for differential education of the gifted*. Carbondale: Southern Illinois University Press.

Jenkins, R. C. W. (1979). *A resource guide to preschool and primary programs for the gifted and talented*. Mansfield Center, CT: Creative Learning Press.

Kanevsky, L. (1992). The learning game. In P. S. Klein & A. J. Tannenbaum (Eds.), *To be young and gifted* (pp. 204-241). Norwood, NJ: Ablex.

Kaplan, S. (1986). The grid: A model to construct differentiated curriculum for the gifted. In J. S. Renzulli (Ed.), *Systems and models for developing programs for the gifted and talented* (pp. 180-193). Mansfield Center, CT: Creative Learning Press.

Karnes, M., Kemp, P., & Williams, M. (1983). Conceptual models. In M. Karnes (Ed.), *The underserved: Our young gifted children* (pp. 40-60). Reston, VA: The Council for Exceptional Children.

Karnes, M. B., & Johnson, L. J. (1986). Identification and assessment of gifted/talented handicapped and non-handicapped children in early childhood. In J. Whitmore (Ed.), *Intellectual giftedness in young children: Recognition and development* (pp. 35-54). Binghamton, NY: The Haworth Press.

Karnes, M. B., & Johnson, L. J. (1991). The preschool/primary gifted child. *Journal for the Education of the Gifted, 14,* 267-283.

Karnes, M. B., Schwedel, A., & Linnemeyer, S. (1982). The young gifted/talented child: Progress at the University of Illinois. *The Elementary School Journal, 82,* 195-213.

Kitano, M. (1982) Young gifted children: Strategies for preschool teachers. *Young Children, 37*(4), 14-24.

Kitano, M. K., & Kirby, D. F. (1986a). *Gifted education: A comprehensive view*. Boston: Little, Brown, & Company.

Kitano, M. K., & Kirby, D. F. (1986b, March/April). The unit approach to curriculum planning for the gifted. *G/C/T,* 27-31.

Klauke, A. (1988). The developmental approach to kindergarten: Profile of an expert teacher. *OSSC Bulletin Monograph, 31*(8).

Klein, P. S. (1992). Mediating the cognitive, social, and aesthetic development of precocious young children. In P. S. Klein & A. J. Tannenbaum (Eds.), *To be young and gifted* (pp. 245-277). Norwood, NJ: Ablex.

Kohlberg, L. & Mayer, R. (1972). Development as the aim of education. *Harvard Education Review, 42,* 449-496.

Krechevsky, M., & Gardner, H. (1991). The emergence and nurturance of multiple intelligences. In M. J. A. Howe (Ed.), *Encouraging the development of exceptional skills and talents* (pp. 222-245). Leicester, U.K.: British Psychological Society.

Lewis, M. & Louis, B. (1991). Young gifted children. In N. Colangelo & G. A. Davis (Eds.), *Handbook of gifted education* (pp. 365-381). Boston: Allyn & Bacon.

Lubeck, S. (1994). The politics of developmentally appropriate practice: Exploring issues of culture, class and curriculum. In B. Mallory & R. New (Eds.), *Diversity and developmentally appropriate practices: Challenges for early childhood education* (pp. 17-43). New York: Teachers College Press.

Maker, C. J. (1982). *Teaching models in education of the gifted.* Rockville, MD: Aspen Systems.

Meeker, M. N. (1969). *The structure of intellect: Its interpretation and uses.* Columbus, OH: Merrill.

Milgram, R. M. (1990). Creativity: An idea whose time has come and gone? In M. A. Runco & R. S. Albert (Eds.), *Theories of creativity* (pp. 215-233). Newbury Park, CA: Sage.

Moss, E. (1992). Early interactions and metacognitive development of gifted preschoolers. In P. S. Klein & A. J. Tannenbaum (Eds.), *To be young and gifted* (pp. 278-318). Norwood, NJ: Ablex.

Paley, V. G. (1995). *Kwanzaa and me: A teacher's story.* Cambridge, MA: Harvard University Press.

Parke, B. N., & Ness, P. S. (1988). Curricular decision making for the education of young gifted children. *Gifted Child Quarterly, 32,* 196-199.

Piaget, J. (1977). *The development of thought: Equilibration of cognitive structures.* New York: Viking. (Original work published 1975, in French)

Piaget, J. (1980). *Adaptation and intelligence: Organic selection and phenocopy.* Chicago: University of Chicago Press (Original work published 1974, in French)

Presseisen, B. Z. (1991). Thinking skills: Meanings and models revisited. In A. L. Costa (Ed.), *Developing minds* (pp. 56-62). Alexandria, VA: Association for Supervision and Curriculum Development.

Ramos-Ford, V., & Gardner, H. (1991). Giftedness from a multiple intelligences perspective. In N. Colangelo & G. A. Davis (Eds.), *Handbook of gifted education* (pp. 55-64). Boston: Allyn and Bacon.

Renzulli, J. S. (1977). *The enrichment triad model: A guide for defensible programs for the gifted and talented.* Mansfield Center, CT: Creative Learning Press.

Renzulli, J. S. (Ed.), (1986). *Systems and models for developing programs for the gifted and talented.* Mansfield Center, CT: Creative Learning Press.

Renzulli, J., S., & Reis, S. M. (1985). *The schoolwide enrichment model: A comprehensive plan for educational excellence.* Mansfield Center, CT: Creative Learning Press.

Robinson, N. M. (1993). Identifying and nurturing gifted, very young children. In K. A. Heller, F. J. Monks, & A. H. Passow (Eds.), *International handbook of research and development of giftedness and talent* (pp. 507-524). New York: Pergamon.

Roedell, W. C., Jackson, N. E., & Robinson, H. B. (1980). *Gifted young children.* New York: Teachers College Press.

Salgado-Gama, M. C. (1991). *Planning curricula for Brazilian preschoolers with gifts and talents: A model incorporating Bloom's Taxonomy and Gardner's theory of multiple intelligences.* Unpublished doctoral dissertation, Teachers College, Columbia University, New York. (University Microfilms #AAC 9136440)

Schlichter, C. L. (1985). Help students become active thinkers: It's never too early to start. *Early Years, 15*(5), 38-41,44.

Schlichter, C. (1986). Talents unlimited: Applying the multiple talent approach in mainstream gifted programs. In J. S. Renzulli (Ed.), *Systems and models for developing programs for the gifted and talented* (pp. 352-390). Mansfield Center, CT: Creative Learning Press.

Shore, B. M., & Kanevsky, L. S. (1993). Thinking processes: Being and becoming gifted. In K. A. Heller, F. J. Monks, & A. H. Passow (Eds.), *International handbook of research and development of giftedness and talent* (pp. 138-147). New York: Pergamon.

Spodek, B. (1986). *Today's kindergarten.* New York: Teachers College Press.

Strom, R., Johnson, A., Strom, S., & Strom, P. (1992). Designing curriculum for parents of gifted children. *Journal for the Education of the Gifted, 15,* 182-200.

Tannenbaum, A. J. (1992). Early signs of giftedness: Research and commentary. In P. S. Klein & A. J. Tannenbaum (Eds.), *To be young and gifted* (p. 3-32). Norwood, NJ: Ablex.

Taylor, C. (1967). Questioning and creating: A model for curriculum reform. *Journal of Creative Behavior, 1*(1), 22-23.

Taylor, C. W. (1986). Cultivating simultaneous student growth in both multiple creative talents and knowledge. In J. S. Renzulli (Ed.), *Systems and models for developing programs for the gifted and talented.* Mansfield Center, CT: Creative Learning Press.

VanTassel-Baska, J. (1992). *Planning effective curriculum for gifted learners.* Denver, CO: Love Publishing.

VanTassel-Baska, J., Feldhusen, J., Seeley, K.,Wheatly, G., Silverman, L., & Foster, W. (1988). *Comprehensive curriculum for gifted learners.* Boston: Allyn and Bacon.

VanTassel-Baska, J., Schuler, A., & Lipshutz, J. (1982). An experimental program for gifted four year olds. *Journal for the Education of the Gifted, 5*(1), 45-55.

Vygotsky, L. S. (1962). *Thought and language* (E. Hanfmann & G. Vakar, Trans.). Cambridge, MA: MIT Press. (Original work published 1934, in Russian)

Walters, J. M., & Gardner, H. (1985). The development and education of intelligences. In F. R. Link (Ed.), *Essays on the intellect*. Alexandria, VA: Association for Supervision and Curriculum Development.

Walters, J., & Gardner, H. (1986a). The crystallizing experience: Discovering an intellectual gift. In R. J. Sternberg & J. E. Davidson (Eds.), *Conceptions of giftedness* (pp. 306-331). New York: Cambridge University Press.

Walters, J. M., & Gardner, H. (1986b). The theory of multiple intelligences: Some issues and answers. In R. J. Sternberg & R. K. Wagner (Eds.), *Practical intelligence: Nature and origins of competence in the everyday world* (pp. 163-182). New York: Cambridge University Press.

Ward, V. A. (1961). *Educating the gifted: An axiomatic approach*. Columbus, OH: Merrill.

Ward, V. A. (1980). *Differential education for the gifted*. Los Angeles: National/State Leadership Training Institute on the Gifted and Talented.

Ward, V. S. (1986). Criterially referenced curricular design: A critique of "Qualitatively differentiated curricula." In C. J. Maker (Ed.), *Critical issues in gifted education: Defensible programs for the gifted* (pp. 135-145). Rockville, MD: Aspen Systems.

Wolfson, B. (1984). Psychological theory and curricular thinking. In A. Molnar (Ed.), *Current thought on curriculum*. Alexandria, VA: Association for Supervision and Curriculum Development.

Wright, L., & Coulianos, C. (1991). A model for precocious children: Hollingworth Preschool. *The Gifted Child Today, 14*(5) 24-29.

32

The Cline Cube: Integrating Models of Gifted Education

Starr Cline

WHY THE MODEL

Timothy had completed the first half of kindergarten when we met. His parents and his teacher were concerned that he might be regressing academically. During our meeting I saw samples of his work. In the first half of kindergarten Timothy was writing original stories (see Figure 32.1), reading on a high school level, and handling double digit mathematical problems (see Figure 32.2). Figure 32.3 presents a sample of his work in January of the same academic year. With some minor modifications in Timothy's program, which included bringing high level books into the room, accelerating his mathematics, and arranging for him to have time in the computer center to compose stories, he began again to excel.

The following year, at "back-to-school" night, Timothy's parents sat in his first-grade classroom and listened to how the children were being taught to read. When Timothy' s parents asked whether the

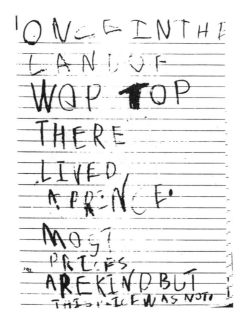

Figure 32.1.

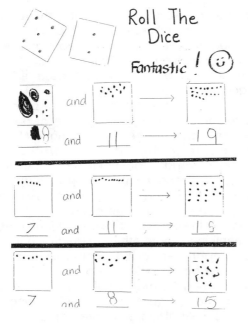

Figure 32.2.

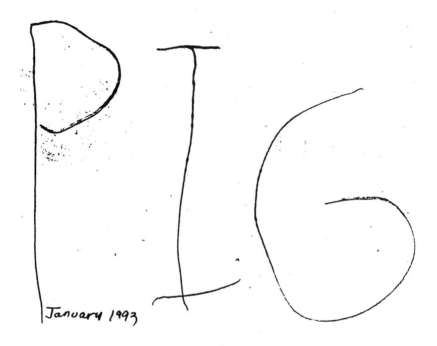

January 1993

Figure 32.3.

teacher had made any provisions for Timothy, she responded that she had to make sure that he had mastered every phoneme and grapheme.

Timothy began exhibiting signs of depression. When gifted children become keenly aware of what they can do compared to age-mates, they feel out of step, and, as in the case of Timothy, begin to hide their gifts and regress (Gross, 1993).

Even though a classroom teacher might be concerned about a student's development,he or she might be at a loss as to how to accommodate highly able children. According to *National Excellence —A Case for Developing America's Talent* (U.S. Department of Education, 1993) gifted children are not being well served in the regular classroom. The report emphasizes the importance of expanding effective programs and introducing advanced materials into the regular school program. There appears to be a movement afoot to subsume gifted education into the general curriculum. When meeting the needs of the gifted is mentioned, more often it is an afterthought.

The U.S. Department of Education work recommends that strategies developed for the gifted be provided for all students. How might this be done when the majority of classroom teachers have had no training and are not aware of the strategies being discussed? Two other questions follow: What strategies are appropriate for all children, and how does one differentiate for the gifted?

The aforementioned work also describes how we are being faced with a "quiet crisis" in gifted education. Much of what has been developed for the gifted might be appropriate for all students, and in some instances might serve to identify those who are gifted. In the present economic climate, however, the expedient avenue might be taken. This involves introducing some of the strategies that have been designed to differentiate the curriculum for the gifted into the regular classroom, and decimating programs that do indeed differentiate. Not only do we not realize the promise these children hold, but we create stress and emotional problems for the child (Gross, 1993).

Two major issues should be addressed if we are to provide appropriate programming for gifted students. First, teacher training is critical. Second, the myth that programs for the gifted are costly must be dispelled. Creative administrative planning can make differentiating the curriculum cost effective.

THEORETICAL BASIS FOR AN INTEGRATED MODEL

There are now many sound philosophies on which we can draw to help guide educational institutions and administrators in the development of programs. To name a few, Tannenbaum (1983) and Passow (1986) have described their views of a differentiated curriculum in terms of topic and organizational plan. Van Tassel-Baska (1988) outlined in detail specific content modifications. Reis, Burns, and Renzulli (1991) have presented ways of enriching the curriculum for all students and suggested strategies such as compacting to accommodate the gifted.

Curriculum planning and development considers who is to be taught, what is to be taught, when it is to be taught, where it is to be taught, and for what purpose (Passow, 1986). A well-designed curriculum can serve as a vehicle for authentic assessment of individual talent and ability in each of the content areas. Students may be gifted in many areas, or their gifts may be domain specific (Gardner, 1983). As students are exposed to content areas at various thinking levels, potential can be determined. As student's talents and abilities are noted, appropriate differentiation can be planned.

INTEGRATING MODELS

The model presented here makes a distinction between content and strategies that differentiate for the gifted as compared to those appropriate for all children. It suggests ways that administrative and organizational planning can take place and recommends additional content areas based on research (see Figure 32.4).

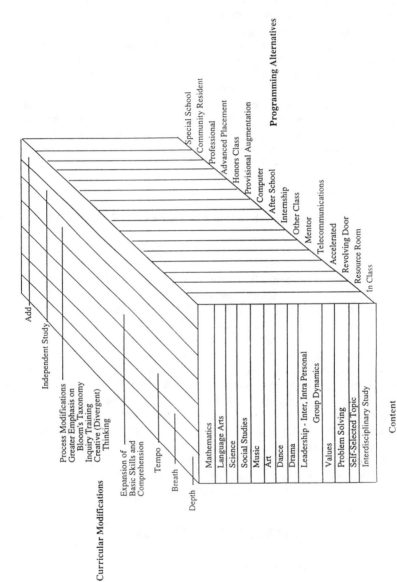

Figure 32.4.

Most teachers have not been trained in gifted education strategies that might benefit all students, nor have most been introduced to methods of curriculum differentiation. The model can serve as a useful tool or guide for curriculum coordinators to determine what staff development is necessary. School districts can use it to note strategies already in place, and which gaps may be filled that require long range planning.

Content Areas

Subject matter that should be taught to every child includes:

- Mathematics
- Science
- Language Arts
- Social Studies
- Music
- Art

Opportunities to study the following domains should be provided for all students early on. They are too often limited to magnet or specialized schools:

- Dance
- Drama
- Leadership (including inter- and intrapersonal skills and group dynamics
- Problem Solving
- Values (the need to establish a code of ethics as a component of what is to be learned; Phenix, 1964)

The following areas should be included to assist in the identification of special abilities and allow for greater complexity in curriculum design:

- Interdisciplinary Units
- Self-Selected Subjects and Independent Study. A self-selected topic will often tap into an individual's talents and abilities and reveal a passion for a topic at an early age (Cline, 1986). Individuals may not reach their potential because of a mismatch between their abilities and their profession (Hyatt & Gottlieb, 1987); an IQ score does not always dictate a particular direction in one's life. A high IQ gifted writer might make a very unhappy physician.

Curricular Modifications

Once areas of strength are noted, a differentiated curriculum can be designed. It may take many forms. Very often, the nature of the content will assist in dictating the type of differentiation that can occur.

- Depth. Social Studies lends itself to both depth and breadth. Students choosing a topic might become interested in one aspect of it (e.g., a student studying the revolutionary war might focus on one battle or one person).
- Breadth. A student who has studied the Indian tribes native to a particular area and who exhibits interest in the topic may expand the breadth of his study and be allowed to pursue a study of all North American Indians.
- Tempo. Acceleration—often referred to as telescoping (Tannenbaum, 1983) or compacting (Reis et al., 1991). This strategy is most suitable for mathematics (Stanley, 1977) and foreign language learning (Van Tassel-Baska, 1988).
- Expansion of Basic Skills and Comprehension. Tannenbaum (1983) described this category of skills as "tool subjects" necessary to master conventional disciplines. Students exhibiting interest in a topic should be exposed to professionals in a field and how they work. A budding writer should be exposed to authors and learn about literary forms not necessarily part of the core curriculum. A potential scientist should learn the skills used in that field, and a precocious history student would be exposed to historiography.
- Process Modifications. Greater emphasis should be placed on the upper levels of Bloom's (1956) Taxonomy. Gifted children are often capable of mastering information quickly. Inasmuch as one of the goals for this population is to assist them in becoming producers of information (Tannenbaum, 1983) the higher levels of the Taxonomy (i.e., application, analysis, synthesis and evaluation, essential components of creating, designing and inventing) become important. In addition, teachers can use levels of the Taxonomy to help determine which students enjoy being challenged and are capable of operating on higher levels. This, too, can serve as an authentic assessment of one's ability and can be used as a "marker" of giftedness. Once students are identified, teachers can continue looking for specific domains of giftedness as they emphasize the higher levels of Bloom's Taxonomy in the student's assignments.

  Inquiry Training and questioning are also important and can be integrated into all aspects of the curriculum for students and can assist in the identification of gifted students.

Creative and divergent thinking and problem solving are important for inventing, designing, and synthesizing information. Students should have the opportunity to be introduced to these strategies to determine ability in these areas and to assist them in thinking creatively in specific domains.

- Self-Selected Topic or Independent Study. Students can be provided with the opportunity to be involved in an independent study in a variety of ways. As a result of telescoping or compacting, students could be allowed to cover a topic required by the district on their own, or they might self-select subjects and be matched with an individual who can guide them (Cline, 1986).
- Adding Subjects and Topics. Able students should be allowed to add subjects to their schedule over and above what is normally allowed. A gifted linguist might be allowed to take additional languages. A gifted musician might be allowed to study more than one instrument. A student might add a topic in another domain altogether.

PROGRAMMING ALTERNATIVES

The programming of alternatives refers to how services will be delivered. They should not be confused with curriculum differentiation. Administrative options should be as flexible as possible to allow for the range of needs and abilities of the students. A list of possibilities follows, but should not be limited to these. When establishing programming alternatives, it is important that gifted students be grouped together for part of their schedule. This will enable them to interact in settings where they will be challenged by peers and assure that they do not feel out of step in terms of social development.

- In class. There is much that can be accomplished by the regular classroom teacher. When teachers note areas of special ability, compacting or telescoping might be used to allow the student to accelerate in that subject or engage in a self-selected topic. Teachers can also decide to extend the breadth or depth of the subject for a student. They can share information about students in their room and arrange for students of like ability or interest to spend time together.
- Resource room. In some school districts, there are personnel who work with talented students on a regular basis. Is there a librarian or a department chairman who would be able to provide services for the children? Once personnel are identified, information about the student collected from the stu-

dent, classroom teacher, and parents can assist administrators as they plan meaningful curriculum for pupils.

- Revolving door or Pullout Program. Some school districts have an administrative design in place where students, as a result of an exposure experience, select a topic on which they wish to work. They are then provided with the time and resources to study that topic.

- Accelerated Learning. Accelerated learning can be a form of differentiation as well as an administrative provision. Inasmuch as some students are capable of learning at a more rapid rate in a particular domain, accelerated classes should be made available for whole groups of students of like ability.

- Telecommunications. As telecommunication equipment becomes available in school districts, students who have talents and abilities in specific areas can communicate with students of similar talent and ability and receive instruction from a teacher at another site. With budgetary cutbacks in school districts, offerings to the gifted at the high school level are often eliminated because the number of students selecting topics becomes too small to support a special class. Telecommunications can allow one teacher to work effectively with students in a wide geographical area.

- Mentor. Mentors can come from any number of places. High school students can mentor elementary students. Faculty with expertise in specific areas can serve as mentors to students not in their class. Parents of students or community residents can serve the students and arrange to meet with them regularly.

- Other class. Teachers within a school district can collaborate and determine if there are teachers with specific areas of expertise. Students from one class can attend another class for a part of the day or week to meet with other students with similar interest or ability for purposes of acceleration or for exposure experiences. One teacher might work with children gifted in the area of language arts while another might work with mathematics.

- After school. Learning is always taking place. Very often individuals are involved in activities after school. Students may take a language, or be involved in the study of the culture of their native country. Students should be given credit for such involvement. In addition, students may chose a self-selected topic that can be completed after school.

- Computer. With the advent of computers, much has become available to students. Students can accelerate in subjects and be exposed to enrichment with appropriate selection of software.

- Provisional augmentation. Curriculum can be covered in specific topics that might not be part of the prescribed scope and sequence offered by a school district. In addition, provisional augmentation can include a topic that is of interest to a particular teacher and is not required content. Provisional augmentation could provide for instruction in an area such as leadership or values. Education in these subjects should be a part of all subjects, but this may not always be the case. They can be provisionally provided for as units of study or woven into a specific part of the social studies curriculum.
- Professionals. Professionals near and far can successfully become a part of educational planning for the more able student. Students can work with professionals in their communities or correspond with those not easily accessible. They need not be available on a regular basis as a mentor might, but might meet with the student once and serve as an inspiration or role model.
- Community resident. Community residents can work with students in the classroom or after school. Senior citizens can be wonderful resources who might willingly volunteer their time. Classroom teachers do not always have the time to work with students individually. With the guidance of a community resident, students might work their way through a required curriculum or be afforded the opportunity to study a topic not usually available (e.g., a primary student interested in science might be able to pursue the topic of chemistry, experiments and all, with an adult present).
- Special schools. If a student exhibits a specific talent or ability and specialized schools are available, parents should be informed. Schools do exist in certain geographical areas in mathematics and science, music and art.

Each principal could examine the opportunities offered in each classroom, resource room, and library. After surveying teachers, administrators could provide for flexible programming for individual students with specific needs. A student might attend a higher grade for a particular subject or be provided with a mentor from the community or from the high school.

Assessment of a student's ability can take a variety of forms. Level of ability can be determined from responses to a higher level or more complex curriculum, or it can be the result of using posttesting as a pretest for purposes of diagnosis. Acceleration has proven to be a worthwhile option in the area of mathematics (Stanley, 1977). A student might move through the mathematical sequence offered in a school district rather rapidly, if allowed so to do. In addition to acceleration, a student might study a mathematical topic in greater depth or explore areas that are not part of the curriculum. If a student has already mastered the prescribed curriculum, instruction can be delivered in a variety of ways, such as other class, computer, telecommunication, or mentor.

If a student appears to be gifted in the area of language arts, teachers would want to expand basic skills and comprehension. Programming might take place in the regular classroom, possibly enriched by a mentor, a professional, a community resident, or another class.

Topics in the social studies domain would lend themselves to breadth and depth modifications along with expansion of basic skills and comprehension and inclusion of process modifications. Any of the sciences allow the student to learn at an early age how professionals work.

Certain content lends itself to provisional augmentation (Tannenbaum, 1983). Leadership, problem solving, and values are examples. These should be woven into all areas of the curriculum, not necessarily in the form of scope and sequence, but as a planned overlay with particular units of study. Some children may reveal exceptional social skills, whereas others may demonstrate deficiencies at an early age (Nowicki & Oxenford,1989). For the gifted, deficits in these areas should be addressed. Gifted individuals do not always possess the social skills necessary to achieve career success (Hyatt & Gottlieb, 1987). Values education is an important element of every career, and assuming that gifted individuals will someday be in decision-making positions, it is even more critical that this be a part of their education.

CONCLUSION

Exposure, support, and challenge (Bloom, 1985; Csikszentmihalyi, 1990) are the keys to success. We have created barriers and boundaries for our "Timothys" that should not exist. The present educational climate dictates that all of our students should achieve at specified levels. What about those students, like Timothy, who can go further? We have created a "glass ceiling" for the gifted through which we must break if our children and our nation are to succeed.

REFERENCES

Bloom, B. (Ed.). (1956). *Taxonomy of educational objectives: Cognitive domain.* New York: David McKay.
Bloom, B. (Ed.). (1985). *Developing talent in young people.* New York: Ballantine.

Cline, S. (1986). *The independent learner*. New York: D.O.K.

Csikszentmihalyi, M. (1990). *Flow: The psychology of optimal experience*. New York: Harper & Row.

Gardner, H. (1983). *Frames of mind: The theory of multiple intelligence*. New York: Basic Books.

Gross, M. (1993). *Exceptionally gifted children*. New York: Routledge.

Hyatt, C., & Gottlieb, L. (1987). *When smart people fail*. New York: Simon & Schuster.

Nowicki, S., & Oxenford, C. (1989). The relation of hostile nonverbal communication styles to popularity in preadolescent children. *Journal of Genetic Psychology, 150*, 39-43.

Passow, A.H. (1986). Curriculum for the gifted and talented at the secondary level. *Gifted Child Quarterly, 30*, 186-191.

Phenix, P. (1964). *Realms of meaning*. New York: McGraw Hill.

Reis, S.M., Burns, D.E., & Renzulli, J.Z. (1991). *Curriculum compacting: The complete guide to modifying the regular curriculum for high ability students*. Mansfield Center, CT: Creative Learning Press.

U.S. Department of Education. (1993). *National excellence—A case for developing America's talent*. Washington, DC: U.S. Government Printing Office.

Stanley, J.C. (1977). Rational of the study of mathematically precocious youth (SMPY) during its first five years of promoting educational acceleration. In. J.C. Stanley, W.C. George, & C.H. Solano (Eds.), *The gifted and the creative: A fifty-year perspective* (pp. 75-112). Baltimore, MD: Johns Hopkins University Press.

Tannenbaum, A. (1983). *Gifted children*. New York: Macmillan.

Van Tassel-Baska, J. (1988). *Comprehensive curriculum for gifted learners*. Boston: Allyn & Bacon.

33

The World of the Young Gifted Child Viewed through Open Systems Concepts

Patricia L. Hollingsworth

One day Mary's father, in exasperation, said, "Mary, stop acting like a 2-year-old," to which she correctly responded, "But Daddy, I am a 2-year-old." When Mary was 3 she tried to get her playmates to pretend they were archaeologists. Mary's playmates looked at her blankly and continued shoveling sand. Then she tried to get them to write numbers to a thousand with her on the sidewalk, to no avail. In preschool, Mary was often angry and clenched her fists as the teachers taught the children number concepts to five. At home, Mary was, at her own request, adding and subtracting double digit numbers. By kindergarten, her parents had found a school that was a good match for her, and she was happily involved in challenging academic pursuits. Not all academically gifted children are so fortunate.

As a democratic nation, we have difficulty with the concept of special services for *gifted children*. Indeed, our national viscera bristles at the term gifted children, which is fraught with overtones of elitism. However, we are ambivalent because deep in our democratic hearts, we believe that all people should have a chance to develop to their fullest potentials. We seem to feel particularly uncomfortable with academic or intellectual giftedness. Our democratic values cause us no angst when the giftedness is musical or athletic.

PROBLEMS FACED BY GIFTED CHILDREN

Many gifted children, extremely aware of the social setting, sense that their intelligence is not valued or appreciated (Dahlberg, 1992). These children, at an early age, begin to feel isolated and lonely because of their advanced academic abilities. They begin to feel that no one shares their interests or concerns. One child said he felt as if he had been dropped here from another planet. Even some teachers view gifted children as strange and bizarre.

The established school curriculum does not always fit the child. For example, one of the main goals of first grade is to teach children to read. When a child comes into school knowing how to read very well, it may pose a problem for the teacher. Some gifted children become behavior problems in the classroom because they already know all that is to be taught that school year (Taylor & Frye, 1988).

Others underachieve because school has been too easy. For many gifted children, the first few years of school bring almost no challenge. These children frequently refuse to do any homework, and prove to themselves that they do not need to by making high scores on tests. These students do not learn to work hard nor do they see the connection between effort and outcome.

There are some bright youngsters whose intellectual abilities cause them intense pressure to be perfect. Some students develop perfectionistic tendencies because they have been called "smart" for so long that they fear making any kind of mistake (Rimm, 1986). They greatly fear that a wrong answer will lower them in the eyes of their teachers and peers. Some perfectionists become afraid to start a task for fear that the idea or the product will not be outstanding.

Parents sometimes feel as if they are in endless debates with their bright children. On the one hand, parents understand that school is not challenging and that classmates and teachers do not always appreciate the child's special qualities, but on the other hand, homework needs to be done. Looking at the system in which all of this is occurring can provide some helpful guidelines.

THEORIES AND RESEARCH

Theories and research sound so far removed from common sense that one might wonder where they could lead. Actually, theory and research can help us look at problems from perspectives and gain insights into possible solutions.

Open Systems

Systems theory (Bertalanffy, 1968; Katz & Kahn, 1966) encourages us to look at major influences of a system. A system is a set of interrelated components operating for a purpose and exists on a continuum from closed to open. An example of a *closed* system would be a *terrarium*, which, when balanced, provides for every need of the plants and animals within. An example of an open, evolving system might be the United Nations, or in the case at hand, the world of a young gifted child:

- Components and Purposes. Although there are other influences, the components with which we will deal, the child, the parents, and the school, are crucial in the world of the young gifted child. An emotionally healthy purpose of this system might be the fullest development of all of its members. Obviously there are many others, and it is important to ask oneself what seems to be the goal of a particular system.
- Systems within Systems. Systems are composed of smaller systems and are part of larger systems, all of which are interactive. Each individual is a system in a larger system, and is composed of smaller systems, such as the nervous and the circulatory systems and include task commitment, motivation, persistence, and personal interests. Internal systems of schools include teachers and curriculum.
- Interrelated Parts. In systems theory elements are related; thus, when one aspect is altered, all others might be altered. A system involving humans is, as Gruber (1988) described, a loosely coupled, evolving system.
- Boundaries. An open system with its set of components has a boundary to filter inputs and outputs. Sometimes this is a physical barrier, such as a fence, but most often it is an invisible wall, such as a set of beliefs or principles. Boundaries of the systems are permeable and interaction with other systems and subsystems occurs constantly.
- Inputs and Outputs. Each system receives input, transforms it, and produces output. For example, a teacher takes a course in gifted education, and, consequently, changes the way she

teaches to include independent investigations. She has taken an idea from the course, adapted it for use to her classroom, and witnesses the response of the students. She probably will receive feedback from parents regarding the innovation.

- Constant Energy Source, Equifinality. Systems need a constant source of energy because they are subject to entropy. Equifinality means that a system has a variety of ways to reach its goals. For example, if optimal development is a goal of the human system, then there are many ways for the individual to reach that goal.

Differentiated Model of Giftedness and Talent

Gagne's (1991) differentiated model of giftedness and talent works well to explain a systems approach to education for the gifted. The model describes giftedness as the demonstration of natural, untrained abilities in at least one ability domain, whereas talent is the expression of systematically developed abilities, skills, and knowledge in a field of endeavor. The model shows giftedness becoming talent through learning, training, and practice, which is influenced by intrapersonal components and environmental components:

- System's Purpose: Talent Development. Viewed through systems theory, the gifted child, the parents, the school, the culture have a stake in the development of giftedness into talent. Therefore, a primary goal of this system is talent development. Whether this talent becomes developed depends on whether learning, training, and practice occur. From the aforementioned underachievement problem, one knows that gifts do not always become talents.
- System's Energy Source: Child's Motivation & Personality Characteristics. In Gagne's model, initiative, interest, and persistence create motivation for the hard work involved in talent development. Autonomy, self-confidence, and self-esteem also influence talent development. From systems theory, we know that all of the components are interactive and influence one another.

CREATIVE PRODUCTIVITY THROUGH IDEAL ACTS OF LEARNING

Another important systems-like theory is Renzulli's (1992) theory of the development of creative productivity through the pursuit of ideal acts of learning. The dynamic interrelationship of the components (the learner, the teacher, and the curriculum), lead to creative productivity.

- System Purpose: Becoming a Creatively Productive Person. The student, guided by an effective teacher, is involved in a differentiated curriculum that leads to the goal of creative productivity. A multiple menu for developing differentiated curriculum is based on a discipline's structure, content, and methodology, as well as an appeal to the imagination. An effective teacher is one who loves a discipline, knows that discipline, uses a range of flexible teaching styles, and understands the goal of creative productivity.
- Energy Source: Child's Personality, Physical Makeup, and Interest in the Subject. Energy is derived from the interaction of personal abilities, personality, and the interest in a subject. This dynamic interplay is intertwined with and helps produce task commitment.

PARENT AND CHILD RELATIONSHIPS

Both Gagne's (1991) model and Renzulli's (1992) theory aim toward optimal development and allude to the need for the child to be the system's energy source. At times, parents unknowingly preempt the child's role. Research provides guidelines for parents who want to facilitate talent development and creative productivity.

- Avoid Giving Too Much Power Too Soon. Parents of gifted children need to beware of giving too much power to young children. Parents must be in charge of the family regardless of how adult-sounding the child is. This part of parenting gifted children is counter-intuitive. It is very difficult for parents who have little experience with children not to adultize a charming, highly verbal, young gifted child. Too much power, at too early an age, creates attention-addicted little dictators. Adult power and status should not be conferred prematurely (Rimm, 1990; Rimm & Lowe, 1988). Instead of giving a child confidence, too much power causes a child to feel insecure and lonely. Intuitively for the child, it is frightening to be running the family. Insecurity and anger occur because the child can find no one who cares enough to be in charge. However, these children do not give up power easily. No child will say, "Mom and Dad please be in charge, I am too young for the job." Adult status gives young children more power than the rest of the world will afford them. When they are dethroned, they will strive mightily to regain that power, usually in negative ways. There are many decisions appropriate for young children to make but they need to be age-appropriate. These are discussed under styles of parenting.

- Set Limits. Most angry children have parents who have not set reasonable limits and consequences. To a child, it is as if no one cares enough to take the responsibility for parenting. Therefore, the immature, inexperienced child rushes in and inappropriately fills the void. For a child to have to be the person in charge, because parents will not fill the role, is enough to keep a child angry for a long time.
- Model Enjoyment of Work. Children need to hear and see that their parents enjoy and find fulfillment in work (Rimm & Lowe, 1988). When the only message a child receives concerning work is that it is drudgery, he or she will have little reason to follow in those footsteps. Parents who share the satisfaction of accomplishment are likely to engender that feeling in their children (Robinson, 1993).
- Teach and Model Responsibility. Parents need to verbalize that each day, each person is choosing how he or she is going to respond to what happens. Much of what happens to us cannot be controlled. Our freedom is in our response. We even have control over how we feel. It is not true to say that someone makes me angry. I have a choice. I am choosing to be angry.
- Chores and Homework. Rimm (1986) found that achieving children carry out home chores and school work. Parents need to expect and require that children do their jobs both at home and school. This needs to be done without extensive reminders, yelling, or nagging. Parents can establish a set of rewards and consequences that are initiated in response to the child's behavior. Children need to complete homework independently in a room away from others. Parents may need to monitor the completed product, but not the doing of the work. Children need to learn to work independently.
- Parenting Togetherness. Rimm and Lowe (1988) concluded that similarity in parenting style is even more important than specific style. Trouble develops for children whose parents have different rules, expectations, and limits. The parent with high expectations gets classified as the "bad" parent, while an alliance between the permissive parent and the child is formed. This is another instance when the child is given adult power in opposition to adult authority. When this child becomes a teenager, the oppositional behavior is most often directed at challenging all adult authority.
- Organizational Skills. Parents need to model reasonably effective organizational skills. Underachieving children are usually disorganized and forgetful, particularly about assignments. Parents can show that being organized leaves more time for personal interests and activities (Rimm & Lowe, 1988).

- Styles of Parenting. Baumrind (1971) stated that an authoritative, not authoritarian, style of parenting is the most effective.
  One of the most easily remembered approaches to authoritative parenting comes from Fay (1988). He vividly described
  three styles of parenting, which are the Helicopter, the Drill
  Sergeant, and the Consultant:
  - Helicopter Parents Rescue. Helicopter parents hover over
    children, make lots of noise, and think of themselves as
    good and kind parents, who understand their children
    when the rest of the world does not. They are superb at
    rescue operations. They can not stand to see their children
    suffer in the slightest or to struggle. "Here, let Daddy or
    Mommy help you." Some will say, "I don't want my child
    to go through what I went through as a child. I want my
    child to have all the things I never had." The Helicopter is
    too kind, too tolerant, and too understanding. Helicopters
    encourage dependence and reliance on others. Children
    of Helicopters learn to give up easily because they know a
    rescue team is on the way. If your child forgets lunch or
    homework, let the child feel the consequences without
    rescuing or nagging. Helicopters steal initiative and prob-
    lem solving from their children.
  - Drill Sergeants Give Orders. Drill Sergeant parents know
    everything that everyone else should do. They are often
    strict authoritarians who use power and punishment to
    keep children in line. They bark instructions that sound like,
    " You'll do it now because I told you to and you'll feel my
    belt if you don't." The power may work, but resentment
    and hatred build in the child, often developing into pas-
    sive resistance. It is hard to establish cooperation when
    both parent and child see each other as the enemy.
    Those who had bitter experiences with Drill Sergeant par-
    ents, who have sworn to be different, sometimes turn out
    to be Helicopters who rescue and overprotective. Fay
    (1988) said if you had to select between the Helicopter
    and the Drill Sergeant, the Drill Sergeant is the better
    choice. Fortunately, there is an alternative: the Consultant.
  - Consultant Parents Give Choices. Consultant parents do
    not spend much energy on any battle that they cannot
    win. They do not try to make a child eat, sleep, talk, think,
    or other things you cannot make people do. They do not
    use endless strings of Drill Sergeant commands. They tell the
    child what they are going to do, and they provide choices.
    "I will take you to your friend's party when your room is
    clean." "You don't seem to like the food we're having for
    breakfast. No problem. Come back at lunch and see if you

like what we have then." If the child is misbehaving, calmly and quietly say, "Do you want to stay here and behave properly, or go to time out." If misbehavior continues, say in a calm and quiet voice, "Oh, I see you have chosen to go to time-out." Then promptly make sure that he or she does.

- Consultant Parents Let the Child Problem Solve. If the child is having a problem, the Consultant says, "That really is a big problem. What are you going to do about it? Don't know? Well, I'll be glad to tell you how other people have solved it if you're interested." Again, the child is given a choice. The Consultant shows full confidence in the child's problem-solving abilities. Let your child know that you are there to give suggestions for solving the problem, but only if the child wants to hear them. You are not trying to solve the problem for the child, only serving as a consultant.
- Consultant Parents Have Dialogue With Their Children. Meaningful dialogue with adults is often missing in the lives of children. It is through dialogue that parents establish that they are interested in and understand their child. It is in dialogue that parents get to know their child. It is not a time for drill or rescue.

THE SCHOOL, PARENT AND CHILD RELATIONSHIP

The world of the young gifted child functions best when all components are working together to develop responsible children. Brilliance is wonderful, but without responsibility, there will be no talent development or creative productivity.

- Overtly Express Respect for Schools. When parents and children align themselves against the school, the most likely outcome is underachievement. If parents want their children to achieve in school, it will be necessary for them to voice respect for schools and teachers. Problems between parents and schools need to be kept strictly among the adults involved. Rimm (1987) stated, "Children will not work or learn in classrooms led by teachers who are not respected by their parents" (p. 36).
- Avoid Oppositional Alliances. If the child is involved in allying against teachers or the school, this is almost identical to a child and parent allying themselves against another parent. The child obtains too much power and may become oppositional to all authority. If there are irreconcilable differences, the adults need to work out the problems among themselves, without the child's advice or knowledge.

- Parents Thinking and Acting As Partners of Schools. Joe had completely shut down. He was not doing classwork or home-work; however, he was still able to score in the 99th per-centile on standardized achievement tests. Joe's concerned parents began following the school's parenting system, which involved teaching Joe to take responsibility. Such par-enting programs help parents realize that even though chil-dren can converse and reason like adults, they are not adults. The programs emphasize the importance of not rescu-ing children from problems, but rather teaching children to solve their own problems.
- Parents and Teachers Learning. When parents and the school work together, such problems as underachievement, lack of motivation, and manipulation can be turned around. Parents and teachers can help children become achievers. Parents and teachers can recognize the value of low-stakes competitions and sports (Dahlberg, 1992), and they can learn to send achievement messages, help their students develop responsibility, be respective of others, and help stu-dents be self-directed (Rimm, 1986, 1990).
- Feedback to the Parents from the School. Joe's parents were given weekly feedback from the school concerning Joe's homework. For younger children, daily feedback may be necessary. It can be a check-off sheet that describes the child's behavior, task commitment, and completed assign-ments, where applicable. These can usually be quantified so the parent has a basis for rewards and consequences. Joe is now developing responsibility and organizational skills and using his academic talent.
- Effort and Outcome Connection. One of the most important things that specific feedback from the school can do is teach the connection between effort and outcome. The most effective parents directly tie rewards and conse-quences to the feedback sheets. Often, bright students get by with little work or effort and consequently they learn noth-ing about the connection between effort and positive out-comes. Without hard work and effort there is little basis for self-esteem, no matter how bright one is. School should be a place where students are academically challenged, work hard, and learn responsibility. Gardner (personal communi-cation, October 7, 1992) has his young son practice piano twice each day for a short time—not particularly to learn piano, but to learn to work hard at something. Joe recently said, "School is a lot of hard work, but it's much easier and more fun if you are responsible."

THE CHILD, THE CURRICULUM, AND THE TEACHER RELATIONSHIP

This section demonstrates the system tenet of equifinality. There are a variety of ways to help young gifted children develop talent and creative productivity:

- Interests and Independent Investigations. Renzulli (1992) emphasized the importance of interests in creative productivity. Many young gifted children have keen interests that they pursue relentlessly. Teachers of young gifted children can learn to capitalize on these interests by providing opportunities for independent investigations (Renzulli & Reis, 1985).
- Open-Ended Tasks. One of the simplest ways to adjust the curriculum to meet student's needs is to provide open-ended tasks. Writing is one of the most creative and productive ways to individualize for students (Breyman, 1991; Johnson, 1987). Students provide the reading, writing, spelling, and grammar material from their own interests and experiences.
- Help for Perfectionism. There are a number of curriculum materials that allow students to achieve mastery and move at their own pace. One of the most effective is Kumon math (Hollingsworth, 1991), which provides a standard completion time, as well as an acceptable number of mistakes. For fear of making a mistake, perfectionistic children are often so careful that they become inordinately slow, particularly in math. Kumon is helpful to children with perfectionistic tendencies because it gives permission to make a reasonable number of mistakes.
- Overt Teaching Plus Modeling. Just as parents need to teach overtly about responsibility, so do teachers. They must say and model: "It does not matter that you make a mistake, as everyone does, what matters is what you do with your mistake. One of the purposes of your good brain is to figure out what to do with your mistakes."
- Developing Student Potential. There is a vast amount of pertinent literature for developing curriculum for gifted children. Some of the most interesting comes from brain research (Caine & Caine, 1991), which basically says that providing many, complex, and concrete experiences optimize learning. The brain can make infinite connections that create meaningful, long-term learning. Experiences such as projects, trips, performances, and stories make learning more enjoyable, meaningful, and long-lasting.
- Active Learning. Gardner's (1983) work on multiple intelligences has encouraged a wide variety of active ways to

stimulate and nurture intelligences (Hollingsworth & Hollingsworth, 1989; Lazear, 1991). All of these sources encourage the use of integrated, experiential learning in which the learner is actively engaged in constructing knowledge. In response to theory and research, a variety of strategies, such as active learning (Harmin, 1994; Marzano, 1992), kinesthetic learning (Herman & Hollingsworth, 1992), and hands-on learning, seek to involve and engage students in a meaningful way. These may include an assortment of physical and mental activities such as drama, storytelling, creative writing, art, dance, computer usage, movement, simulations, discovery activities, developing thinking skills, and independent research (Caine & Caine, 1991; Harmin, 1994; Lazear, 1991; Renzulli & Reis, 1985).

- Thinking and Problem Solving. The Enaction Curriculum (Hollingsworth, 1985, 1988) is designed to meet the special needs of able learners by developing their capacities for thinking and problem solving through the use of active learning and creating knowledge. The Enaction Curriculum is based on Ohlsson's (1983) theory and Glaser's (1984) position on the importance of domain specific knowledge. The Enaction Curriculum embraces an interdisciplinary, active learning approach that asserts that the highly complex activity of thinking and problem solving is facilitated by students' interactive use of such things as models, diagrams, maps, drawings, and simulations (Hollingsworth, 1988; Ohlsson, 1983). Enaction theory postulates that thinking is a matter of running and refining a self-created simulation in one's head. In other words, students are creating their own knowledge based on prior experience. The steps involved are creating a mental model, manipulating that model, and developing a strategy for problem solving. An example of a classroom activity to help students create and manipulate a mental model of the circulatory system involved students physically walking through a huge chalk drawing of the human body.

CONCLUSION

Open systems teach us to look at the major interactions of the system. For the system to work toward talent development and creative productivity, the child needs to be the energy source. Parents can facilitate this by being in charge of the family in an authoritative, not authoritarian, manner, giving the child appropriate responsibility, being consultants, giving messages of parental togetherness, and providing reasonable organization. When parents provide many, child-appropriate opportunities to make choices, solve problems, and make decisions, the child gains both experience and confidence. The school can provide open-ended, active learning, opportunities for independent investigations, and feedback to parents. In these ways the parts of the system reinforce each other, and work toward the development of the potential of each.

REFERENCES

Baumrind, D. (1971). Current patterns of parental authority. *Development Psychology Monographs, 4*(1).

Bertalanffy, L. von (1968). *General systems theory.* New York: Braziller.

Breyman, J. (1991). The teacher of writing at the University of Tulsa School for Gifted Children. *Network News Quarterly, 6*(1), 2-5.

Caine, R., & Caine, G. (1991). *Making connections: Teaching and the human brain.* Alexandra, VA: Association for Supervision and Curriculum Development.

Dahlberg, W. (1992). Brilliance—The childhood dilemma of unusual intellect. *Roeper Review, 15,* 7-10.

Fay, J. (1988). *Helicopters, drill sergeants, and consultants.* Golden, CO: Cline/Fay Institute.

Gagne, F. (1991). Toward a differentiated model of giftedness and talent. In N. Colangelo & G.A. Davis (Eds.), *Handbook of gifted education* (pp. 65-80). Boston: Allyn & Bacon.

Gardner, H. (1983). *Frames of mind: The theory of multiple intelligences.* New York: Basic Books.

Glaser, R. (1984). Education and thinking: The role of knowledge. *American Psychologist, 39,* 93-104.

Gruber, H. E. (1988). The evolving systems approach to creative work. *Creativity Research Journal, 1,* 27-51.

Harmin, M. (1994). *Inspiring active learning.* Alexandria, VA: Association for Supervision and Curriculum Development.

Herman, G. N., & Hollingsworth, P. L. (1992). *Kinetic kaleidoscope.* Tucson, AZ: Zephyr.

Hollingsworth, P. L. (1985). Enaction theory, simulations, and the gifted. *Roeper Review, 8*(2), 93-95.

Hollingsworth, P. L. (1988). Enaction theory: A theoretical validation of the enrichment triad model. *Roeper Review, 10*(4), 222-225.

Hollingsworth, P. L. (1991). A reformer's retrogression: Speaking out for Kumon mathematics. *Education Week, 11*(13), 23.

Hollingsworth, P. L., & Hollingsworth, S. F. (1989). *Smart art.* Tucson, AZ: Zephyr.

Johnson, K. (1987). *Doing words.* Boston: Houghton Mifflin.

Katz, D., & Kahn, R. (1966). *The social psychology of organizations.* New York: Wiley.

Lazear, D. (1991). *Seven ways of teaching.* Palatine, IL: Skylight.

Marzano, R. (1992). *A different kind of classroom: Teaching the dimensions of learning.* Alexandria, VA: Association for Supervision and Curriculum Development.

Ohlsson, S. (1983). The enaction theory of thinking and its educational implications. *Scandinavian Journal of Educational Research, 27*(2), 73-88.

Renzulli, J. S. (1992). A general theory for the development of creative productivity through the pursuit of ideal act of learning. *Gifted Child Quarterly, 35,* 170-182.

Renzulli, J., & Reis, S. (1985). *The schoolwide enrichment model.* Mansfield Center, CT: Creative Learning Press.

Rimm, S. B. (1986). *Underachievement syndrome: Causes and cures.* Watertown, WI: Apple.

Rimm, S. B. (1987). Why do bright children underachieve? *Gifted Child Today, 53*(10,6), 30-36.

Rimm, S. B. (1990). *How to parent so children will learn.* Watertown, WI: Apple.

Rimm, S., & Lowe, B. (1988). Family environments of underachieving gifted students. *Gifted Child Quarterly, 32*(4), 353-359.

Robinson, N. (1993). *Parenting the very young child.* Storrs, CT: National Research Center for the Gifted and Talented.

Taylor, B.M., & Frye, B.J. (1988). Pretesting: Minimize time spent on skill work for intermediate teachers. *Reading Teacher, 42*(2), 100-103.

34

Designing a Preschool Program for the Gifted and Talented

Gail E. Hanninen

Designing a preschool program for youngsters who are gifted and talented requires an examination of basic beliefs and expectations to assure quality experiences for children. The focus of this chapter is to guide the reader through a process for shaping such a program.

WHAT DO WE BELIEVE?

Acting on the need to identify and serve young gifted children requires briefly examining answers to the following questions:

1. How does our society value early childhood education and giftedness?
2. What is the relationship of the "hurried child" concept as presented by Elkind (1981) as compared to the readiness of each gifted child (Pines, 1981)?

3. How can the debate surrounding the identification of gifted-
    ness during the preschool years be answered? Should gifted-
    ness be identified early?
4. What should the relationship of gifted preschool experiences
    be to a continuum of comprehensive gifted program services?

In his book *Excellence: Can We Be Equal and Excellent Too?*,
J.W. Gardner (1961) presented a powerful discussion of the core of the
American value system: egalitarianism versus individualism. Does a
commitment to individualism mean a commitment to individual potential? Does egalitarianism mean that all people have equal opportunity
to achieve?

What kind of paradox do these questions create for educators
and parents? Fetterman (1988), in his discussion of *Excellence and
Equality*, commented that "both goals are good and necessary if we
are to maintain our commitment to quality, our democratic ideals, and
our multicultural traditions. The strength and vitality of our nation and all
nations are dependent on the gifts and talents of individuals" (p. xiii).
Certainly, the development of services for young gifted children can
be either supported or opposed by such a value based system. A U.S.
Department of Education (1993) report on gifted education, *National
Excellence: A Case for Developing American's Talent*, recognized the
need to develop young talent:

> The nation must ensure that all children, especially economically
> disadvantaged and minority children, have access to an early
> childhood education that develops their potential. Young children
> need rich, varied learning opportunities and teachers and care-
> givers who look more for their strengths and potential rather than for
> their perceived weaknesses. (p. 27)

The research and writing of many professionals continues to
remind us of the importance of early childhood education (Bloom,
1985; Pulaski, 1971; Piers, 1972; Smutny, Veenker, & Veenker, 1991).
Some parents may ask, "If my child learns all of these things in
preschool , then what will he or she do when in first grade?" This concern is valid for parents and educators, as the traditional design of
learning has focused more on grade level performance of a group
and not individual student levels of mastery and understanding.
Preliminary studies show that when ability is influenced by early education, the maintenance of such gains is dependent on (a) the home
environment, and (b) the continuation of comparable educational
experiences in the future (Handler, 1972; Slavin, Karweit, & Wasik, 1993;
Whitmore, 1986). Recent studies also discuss the importance of early
childhood education in preventing early school failure and underachievement (Barbour, 1992; Slavin et al., 1993; Whitmore, 1986).

The concept of the "hurried child" as presented by Elkind (1981) reflects a concern for the pressures placed on young children by adults to achieve. It is removing "child" from "childhood." The concern of pushing a youngster beyond his or her level of readiness is valid and should not be ignored. "School readiness represents an optimal match between child and challenge. The under-challenged child has nothing to learn; the over-challenged child is unprepared to learn" (Robinson, 1992). Young children of high ability display a tremendous excitement for learning and an insatiable drive to learn. Not to respond to such thirst for learning is damaging and may result in behavior problems caused by a creative spirit, boredom, and idleness.

Comprehending the complexity of child development is also important. This means considering the intellectual, physical, social, and emotional development of the young child. The early standard bearers for research of normal child development rests with such pioneers as Piaget and Gesell (Gesell et al., 1940; Pulaski, 1971; Robinson, 1993). Of particular help to the educator was the emergence of a sequence of developmental stages and related tasks. These stages placed emphasis on normal behaviors at specific ages. For youngsters with advanced abilities, such normalcy may be defied and areas of growth may be erratic and unpredictable. Of specific interest is the area of cognitive development. The fields of cognitive psychology and brain research provide educators and parents of young children with even more information (Clark, 1986; H. Gardner, 1983; Sternberg & Davidson, 1986).

The question surrounding the identification of giftedness in young children raises the most controversy, even within the field of gifted education. The primary purpose of early identification of abilities is not to exclude children from services, but to include them in appropriately challenging learning experiences. Because of the erratic nature of child development, different dimensions of giftedness may surface at any time (Roedell, 1989).

The essentials of quality programs transcend age groups and may include the following (Kitano, 1986; Office of Superintendent of Public Instruction, 1989; Parke, 1989):

1. Program organization as defined by a vision, purpose, and goals;
2. Assessment activities result in the identification of gifts and talents of students;
3. Provisions for effectively meeting the needs of each gifted learner, including an individualized plan for curriculum and instruction, flexible pacing, and multiple learning options;
4. Teaching staff trained in the nature and needs of youngsters who are gifted, including developmental differences and related learning needs;

5. Provisions for parent and community involvement; and
6. Systematic evaluation of program services to student and families.

WHAT DO WE DO AND WHAT CAN WE DO?

Five criteria define the critical elements of an effective gifted preschool program.

> Criteria #1. Student assessment provides meaningful information and insights about the child which are used in planning learning opportunities.

A preschool child who functions significantly above age level in any number of areas such as language development, cognitive ability, social skills, physical development, creative ability, or leadership may be considered as gifted and talented. Specific criteria for selection varies depending on the preschool program or service provided. Several assessment instruments and activities should be used to determine the degree and areas of giftedness. Such instruments may include an intelligence or cognitive abilities test, a developmental assessment, a language assessment, parent interview, or an expert's referral.

What constitutes giftedness in preschool children? If only test scores are considered, the traditional definition of a gifted child would be one who scored two standard deviations above the mean. A more common practice established among federally funded projects has been to use 1-1/2 standard deviations (Hanninen, 1979; Karnes, 1983).

In addition to testing, observation and documentation of certain behaviors can support the placement of a child in a preschool for the gifted (Hanninen, 1985; Robinson, 1993; Roedell, Jackson, & Robinson, 1980):

1. Appropriately uses vocabulary considered to be advanced for age level;
2. Spontaneously elaborates on new experiences and observations;
3. Constructs interesting or unusual shapes or patterns using blocks, play dough, drawing materials, and similar items in an innovative manner;
4. Demonstrates the ability to assemble new or difficult puzzles;
5. Employs a sense of humor in general conversation;
6. Expresses an understanding of abstract concepts, such as death, fairness;

7. Displays an ability to remember details, experiences, or events after a long period of time;
8. Easily picks up musical themes or songs and embellishes on the theme;
9. Possesses the ability to master a new skill without undue repetition (e.g., new concept, foreign language, song, etc); or
10. Uses an identifiable reasoning process to explain why something is occurring or how it could be used.

With our society's continued emphasis on creating a "superbaby" or a high achieving young child, how does one differentiate the preschool child who is gifted and talented from the child who has been highly stimulated? Should that be a concern? Generally, gifted preschoolers can be recognized by their ability to deal with abstract concepts and to use pieces of information appropriately in a new situation. For example, the 3-year-old who describes the difference between the numbers 9 and 5 is very different than the highly enriched 4-year-old who counts from 5 to 9, but cannot deal with the numbers out of sequence. If the child is highly verbal, listening to his or her reasoning strategies is important. The challenge of identifying giftedness early is more difficult for the less verbally oriented youngster. In such cases, observation of the child working puzzles or mechanical devices helps understand the child's reasoning abilities.

When using standardized tests, the following questions should be asked (Hanninen, 1984):

1. Were young gifted children included in norming population?
2. Will the instrument accurately assess the abilities of the young child?
3. To what degree are the time limits of the subtests actually inhibiting the child's performance.
4. Does the child have other handicapping conditions that may have a negative impact on performance, such as visual or hearing impairment?

A SAMPLE IDENTIFICATION PROCEDURE

The children, aged 3-5 years, selected to participate in the Rural Preschool Gifted and Gifted Handicapped Model Project with Panhandle Child Development Association in Coeur d'Alene, ID were administered the following assessment instruments: the Peabody Picture Vocabulary Test (PPVT), the Columbia Mental Maturity Scale (CMMS), or the Draw-A-Person Test. Based on information collected from a parent interview and results from the testing, the child was admitted to the Project. A standard deviation of 1-1/2 above the mean on any one of the aforementioned tests was used as a guide for program placement. If a discrepancy existed between test results and the response to a Parent Interview form, the child was admitted for a 3- to 6-week observation period. After 2 years, 103 children were screened, with 58 admitted. Six of the seven students considered for further observation were admitted to the program, thus supporting the value of observational data.

The selection of the instruments used was based on the following criteria:

1. Each instrument provided information about a different type of ability; for example, PPVT emphasized language, CMMS measured abstract reasoning with minimal emphasis on language, and the Draw-A-Person used minimal expressive language and cultural dependency while providing information about perception, recall, and basic knowledge.
2. Each instrument could be administered by a teacher.
3. Norms were sensitive to the younger child.

An analysis of the students identified in each of the age groups by the PPVT, CMMS, and Draw-A-Person test indicated that the highest percentage of students were admitted on the basis of PPVT and complimentary Parent Interview form results.

Parents have valid insights into their child's abilities (Robinson, 1993; Roedell, 1989). Table 34.1 provides a sample of the items adapted from the work of Martinson (1975) and used on the Parent Interview form. The parents checked the column that best described their child's level. A child was not expected to be high on all items.

Table 34.1. Parent Interview from Sample Items.

Rate items on a 1 (Little) to 5 (Much) scale:

1. Knowledge and skills (possesses a comfortable knowledge of basic skills and factual information).
2. Concentration (has ability to concentrate, is not easily distracted)
3. Persistence (has ability and desire to follow through on work; concerned with competition, able to see a problem through)
   In own interests . . . .
   In assigned tasks . . . .

Narrative items:

4. Describe any unpredictable behaviors that interfere with play, such as wandering away without apparent purpose.
5. Describe examples of your child's creative thinking.

The assessment activities and the identification procedure should be as efficacious as possible. Teachers trained in administering the specific tests may need to be the professionals conducting the assessment activities. When further test data are needed, contracting for a psychologist to administer such individualized tests as the Stanford Binet Intelligence test or the Wechsler Preschool and Primary Scales of Intelligence-Revised can be most helpful.

Diverse issues have been investigated surrounding the use of standardized tests with young children (Ehrlich, 1986; Hanninen, 1984; Robinson, & Robinson, 1992; Shaklee, 1992; Silverman & Kearney, 1992). One major criticism of standardized tests is that of cultural bias. As Ehrlich (1986) so aptly pointed out:

> often it is not the test that is biased but rather that the examiner has not done his/her homework. It is the responsibility of planners to see that the selection of a test is appropriate for the age level and the population concerned. (p. 60)

With greater value being placed on performance-based assessment, the use of alternative assessment activities with young children has gained momentum. Common criticisms of standardized testing addressed by observation activities are those of time, flexibility, and sensitivity to individual differences. Being able to conduct assessment activities over several days increases the chances of observing young children at their best moments in contrast to trying to capture that best moment in a 2- hour test period.

Observational data may be collected in many ways and, like standardized testing, users must be aware of its vulnerabilities. Examples that may be misleading when identifying giftedness in young children include:

1. Perceiving the quiet, more reserved child as not gifted because our society associates giftedness with being highly verbal;
2. Interpreting a child's ability as gifted when mimicking information used by adults, instead of using the information in a new or unusual context;
3. Thinking a child who has a limited use of English as not being very capable, only to discover that the child is bilingual and English is not his or her native language (Ehrlich, 1986);
4. Interpreting a child's misuse of an object as a deficiency in skill or ability instead of a lack of experience (e.g., use of scissors; Johnson, 1983).

Using alternative forms of assessment means making behavior observations meaningful by establishing a frame of reference for what constitutes age-expected behaviors and what are unusual behaviors for that specific age level. For example, Susan as a 3-1/2-year-old was asked by the teacher "to cut along a line" that had been drawn on a piece of paper. A couple of minutes later, Susan showed the two pieces of paper to the preschool teacher. She said, "I cut along the line the best I could." On one piece of paper the teacher noted the pencil-drawn line beside which the cutting of the paper had been made. Such a precise interpretation of directions by a 3-1/2-year-old is a bit unusual. It is that knowledge of child development that is so important when interpreting behavior as being potentially gifted or not.

Based on Vygotsky's (1978) work, support is given to reconsidering our use of tests to determine a child's mental ability because such tests tell us only what the child has learned, not what he or she is capable of learning. The result is a shift to more dynamic forms of assessment (Kanevsky, 1992). When using dynamic forms of assessment, the child is presented with problems to solve that are beyond his or her current skill level. Training is provided to the child so that the task can be completed independently. The administrator of the tasks records information concerning the amount and type of assistance required by the child in order to solve the problem. The result is an assessment of potential ability to learn and not a measure of what has been learned (Kanevsky, in press).

Organizing and quantifying performance-based assessment data can be unwieldy. Two projects addressing that concern are the Texas Education Agency and Kent State University (Shaklee, 1992). The Texas project uses an Academic Portfolio, which is a collection of each student's work. Such student products are evaluated using an established criteria. The Kent State project, Early Assessment for Exceptional Potential in Young Minority and/or Economically Disadvantaged Students, employs a computer-assisted analysis of videotaped samples of student behavior. Specific student behaviors associated with using challenging instructional materials are identified and the frequency and duration of such behaviors are counted.

In summary, many student assessment activities and procedures are possible. Regardless of the combination of sources of information used, each should provide meaningful information and insights about the child.

> Criteria #2. Individually planned learning experiences are based on each child's abilities, interests, and needs. Such learning opportunities are child-centered, intellectually challenging, developmentally appropriate and reflect flexible scheduling.

Schools must be responsive to each young child's learning strengths, interests, and all areas of growth. Educators need to perceive the young gifted child as a total person within that environment. Using assessment data, other observational information and parent reports, the preschool teacher can develop an individualized educational plan reflecting the physical, social, psychological, and cognitive needs of the child. Concurrently, the child's readiness to learn or to participate in a new task is a determining factor in deciding the type of challenge to present. Simply because a child can perform complicated mathematical computations does not mean that he or she is ready to produce physical gyrations of a comparable level.

For example, Jonathan was an intense 5-year-old who loved solving problems, playing chess, and reading. Therefore, when the teacher introduced a mime game in which each child was to act out the role of an animal, Jonathan was quite clear in his thoughts about the suggestion that he play the part of a duck. He hedged from entering into the production and stated to his teacher, "people are not ducks." The teacher quickly responded by having Jonathan operate the tape recorder so the students could hear the music designed to accompany the activity.

Several basic considerations can be used to guide the systematic development of an appropriate learning environment for the preschool gifted child. Program goals are defined by the community values, the program's vision and mission, an early childhood and gifted educational philosophy, characteristics of young gifted children, and a definition of giftedness. Each student's program is defined by objectives and activities reflecting the results of ongoing assessment activities.

A quality program for young children who are gifted includes (Hanninen, 1979; Kitano, 1985, 1986):

1. A clear statement of vision and program goals
2. Flexibility in scheduling which responds to individual differences
3. A means for measuring program effectiveness and student objectives, activities, and outcomes
4. Documentation of the occurrence of higher levels of thinking, reflecting individual differences and abilities appropriate to mental age
5. Personnel who actively model desirable behaviors for children to learn (e.g., higher levels of thinking demonstrated by the use of open-ended questions), skillful use of deductive and creative thinking, use of appropriate advanced vocabulary
6. Opportunities for parents to be an integral part of the learning environment, serving as active classroom volunteers, mentors, career education resource people, and be involved in program planning

What constitutes "enriched and challenging learning experiences?" Such experiences are associated with learning models or strategies offering a framework for designing multilevel lessons.

Concepts are presented so that multiple dimensions of learning may occur; thus, each child is challenged at his or her level of readiness. Deciding what models are appropriate is not an easy task and may require the use of several different ones. Table 34.2 provides an outline of commonly used models in gifted and talented programs. The models are divided into three categories and using a combination of models from each of the categories can assure the completeness of a program's framework. "Process models" define complexity of thought. "Content models" use curriculum content as the basis for delivering instruction. "Delivery systems models" organize how services are provided. Therefore, a regular classroom based preschool program using multi-age grouping can use Bloom's Taxonomy with Whole Language Instruction as a program framework.

Table 34.2. Gifted and Talented Program Models.

PROCESS MODELS:
Bloom's Taxonomy: Cognitive Domain
Krathwohl's Taxonomy: Affective Domain
Talents Unlimited
Creative Problem Solving
Hilda Taba Teaching Strategies

CONTENT MODELS:	DELIVERY SYSTEM MODELS:
Junior Great Books	Multi-age grouping or cross-grading
Whole Language Instruction	Early admission
Math Their Way	Self-directed Learner Model
	Structure of Intellect (SOI)
	Ability grouping
	Renzulli's Schoolwide Enrichment

The vision for the Couer d'Alene Project was "to provide each gifted and talented 3-5-year-old youngster with the best services possible and challenge each child to his or her fullest potential." When observing how advanced Jeff was when entering the Project as a 3-year-old, systematically developing his learning plan required appropriately designing each of the six curriculum areas: communication skills, social skills, curiosity pursuits, problem-solving skills, self-awareness skills, and pre-academic skills. Because this preschool program included some young children who were twice exceptional, both gifted and disabled, providing for individual needs was most demanding. Each curricular area is described as follows:

1. *Communication skills* referred to the development of the various ways we communicate (e.g., language, music, drama, art, role playing, dance). Opportunity was provided for discussing current events, "show and tell," the weather and related calendar activities in addition to producing and appreciating music, drama, art, and dance.
2. *Social skills* referred to the development of the ways in which we get along with others. Specific skill development occurred during snack time, free play time, and cooperative learning activities.
3. *Curiosity pursuits* allowed each student to pursue topics of study that were of his or her interest. Such topics were gleaned through student conferences and learning center packets were developed for the various areas of interest even as they emerged during the school year. Such packets contained activities that incorporated Bloom's Taxonomy: Cognitive Domain. When volunteering in the classroom, a parent would use the learning center activities with a small group of children.
4. *Problem-solving skills* were developed by involving the young learners in a variety of strategy games (e.g., chess, checkers, Clue, "Lite Brite").
5. *Self-awareness skills* referred to the development of each child's self-concept by employing physical activities to learn about one's range of motion as well as a sense for one's feelings and emotions.
6. *Pre-academic skills* referred to the development of each student's ability to perform reading and mathematical processes. Such activities were based on each student's readiness and interest to pursue such tasks.

How can a learning plan be designed so that it assures accountability of each child's learning and allows for flexible pacing and challenging instruction? A criterion referenced Concept Assessment and Curriculum Plan (CACP) was devised to identify the skills and learning needs of each child in the Coeur d'Alene Project. As presented in Table 34.3, the assessment component of the instrument measured basic curriculum concepts for language, reading, mathematics, and fine motor skills in a scope and sequence format and using Bloom's Taxonomy, and provided for the application of higher level thinking processes when teaching each concept.

For curricular areas such as curiosity pursuits, problem solving and communication skills, a similar format was used. The activity entered for the respective concept was considered to be a good example of the behaviors implicit in the concept. Variations of the activities used for assessment or completely different activities were

Table 34.3. Excerpts from Shannon's Concept Assessment and Curriculum Plan (CACP).

Process Bloom's	Area	Concept	Activities	Assess	Start Teach.	Complete
	Math	Whole Numbers	1. Uses place	9/15 Mastered		
Application	Math	Whole Numbers	2. Orders >counts by 1's >counts by 10's	9/15	9/17	9/17
Application	Math	Measure- ment	1. Uses money >Selects coins to equal a given value	9/15	3/10	3/12
Application			>Makes change		3/27	4/10
Evaluation	Lang.- Express.	Describing	5. Give opposites	9/15	1/20	10/22

used to teach the concept and challenge the youngster to higher levels of thought. It was not necessary for the teachers to enter in each student's CACP each of the activities taught during the teachable moments. During the duration of the project, the teachers compiled a comprehensive curriculum guide for teaching preschool gifted children. The exciting features of the CACP were twofold: (a) it reflected the interests and learning needs of the students, and (b) it was flexible and constantly evolving while providing structure.

A working schedule was maintained for each student on a clipboard with his or her CACP. A typical schedule for a student would like that presented in Table 34.4.

The two classrooms in the Coeur d'Alene Project were arranged with learning centers and areas clearly designated so the students understood where they were to go during the different activities. An area was even designated for independent reading, exploration, or play if that was a student's choice. The teachers could also use the full 2 hours for a field trip, guest speaker, or high interest activity. The additional use of a teacher aid and parent volunteers allowed for flexibility in grouping and pacing of students, for a tremendous variation in activities with very diverse learners, and for accurate documentation of performance behavior.

Individually planned learning experiences based on each child's abilities, interests, and needs is an attainable goal of a preschool gifted program. This implies a systematic development of diverse learning opportunities that are child-centered, intellectually challenging, developmentally appropriate, and reflect flexible scheduling.

Table 34.4. Sample of a Classroom Individual Plan

TIME	Individual/Group Activity
9:15	Group—Current events discussion and calendar
9:30	Individual Plan—Continue work on writing and illustrating a story about stars
9:50	Individual Plan—Curiosity Pursuit—use interest packet on dinosaurs
10:20	Group—Self-awareness activity using Peabody Kit and focusing on how to receiving and giving compliments
10:45	Group Snack—Social Skills Development—using "thank you" when someone gives you a treat or passes you an item.
11:00	Individual Plan—Pre-academic—focus on math concept of money and the amounts of change that can equal a dollar.
11:20	Individual Plan—Problem Solving: Continue teaching chess piece moves
	CHILD'S NAME: Jeff _____

Criteria #3. Program effectiveness is defined in terms of program and student performance standards.

The essence of program effectiveness means answering the question "How do we know what we are getting is what we want?" Assessing the achievement of clearly stated program goals and objectives and the documentation of changes in each child's behavior determines program effectiveness.

The first standard to consider is that of identification of giftedness. The evaluation questions to be answered include:

1. Are the students selected by the assessment activities and instruments used successfully able to perform classroom activities in all or some of the curricular areas offered? What is the relationship of learner expectations to identification activities?

2. Are students able to respond to and extend open-ended activities with supervision and then without supervision? How does this correlate to assessment and observation data?

3. Are parents finding their child excited about participating in the preschool gifted program and is there carry-over of classroom activities into the home? What behaviors do parents perceive changing? How does that correlate to the initial observations made during the identification process?

The second standard reflects the quality of the program services provided:

1. Are the needs of each student planned for, provided for, and monitored?
2. In what ways do the activities challenge cognitive development, cultivate social/emotional growth, promote physical growth, and encourage use of the aesthetic and intuitive domain. How is the growth measured?
3. In what ways have parents continued to develop those abilities outside of the school setting? How are such efforts documented?

Sources of data are many. Standardized tests can be used for pre- and posttesting and subsequent statistical analysis. Such standardized measures also give credence to the effectiveness of the preschool program with the K-12 school system because such instruments use a common language system (e.g., reading achievement, mathematics grade equivalency scores). The CACP presented earlier provides a format for documenting the level of attainment achieved by each student for the respective concepts. Such a record is also helpful in alerting a first grade teacher as to the learning needs of the young gifted child. Parent feedback provides a valuable perspective (Mathews & Burns, 1992). If a behavior can be counted and illustrates that change has occurred, then the data can be quantified and analyzed.

In addition to determining the changes in student behavior, evaluation data should be used to determine which aspects of the program are working as expected and which ones are not. For example, with the Coeur d'Alene Project, a parent expressed a concern about the amount of time being spent in academics. A disproportionate amount of time would not have been consistent with the philosophy of the program. Therefore, the teachers calculated the amount of time each student spent in the curricular areas for one week. The outcome indicated the percentage of time spent was: communications—33%, social skills—24%, curiosity pursuits—7%, problem solving—11%, self-awareness skills—6%, and pre-academics—19%. This data provided the parent with accurate information and served as a baseline for program decisions.

Criteria #4. Parents are an integral part of the learning environment.

The important role of the parent in early childhood education cannot be underestimated and when coupled with a preschool program, can result in tremendous benefits to the child (Barbour, 1992; Bloom, 1964, 1981). Parent participation occurs best through parent education opportunities and involvement in the classroom.

Parents value learning ways to manage behavior and to stimulate growth in their children. Lists of resources, access to a parent
library, newsletters, copies of articles, and parent workshops are wel-
comed services. One of the best ways for parents to understand
behavior management strategies and techniques for challenging their
child is by working as a parent volunteer in the classroom. There are
many ways that parents can support the efforts of teachers.

> Criteria #5. Program has qualified personnel who understand
> giftedness, intellectual challenge, and social/emotional
> development.

Research on student perceptions supports the belief that the
most influential role in the school setting is played by the teacher
(Bloom, 1985; Cox, Daniel, & Boston, 1985; Goertzel & Goertzel, 1962).
The results of a parent evaluation conducted on preschool gifted programs in one state indicated that there was strong agreement with the
statement "certification for teachers of the academically gifted
improves instruction and should be enforced" (Mathews & Burns, 1992,
p. 71). The unique needs of preschool gifted youngsters warrants special
training for teachers. The decision to employ qualified and quality staff is
critical to the success of a program and to the experiences of children.
In a follow-up study of the Coeur d'Alene Project, students
recalled their teachers challenging them by using "big words," helping
them to develop an interest in books, increasing their perceptions of
youngsters with disabilities who were also gifted, and making learning
fun. The personal qualities these teachers possessed also supported the
students' remarks. Those qualities included: love of challenge, high
capability and creativity, diversity of interests, sensitivity toward the
needs of individuals, ability to response to diversity, and a commitment
to excellence.

REFERENCES

Barbour, N. B. (1992). Early childhood gifted education: A collaborative
     perspective. *Journal for the Education of the Gifted, 15*(2), 145-
     162.
Bloom, B. S. (1964). *Stability and change in human characteristics.* New
     York: Wiley.
Bloom, B. S. (1981). *All our children learning: A primer for parents, teach-
     ers, and other educators.* New York: McGraw-Hill.
Bloom, B. S. (Ed.). (1985). *Developing talent in young people.* New York:
     Ballantine.
Clark, B. (1986). Early development of cognitive abilities and giftedness.
     In J. R. Whitmore (Ed.), *Intellectual giftedness in young children*
     (pp. 5-15). Binghamton, NY: Haworth.

Cox, J., Daniel, N., & Boston, B. O. (1985). *Educating able learners: Programs and promising practices.* Austin: University of Texas Press.

Elkind, D. (1981). *The hurried child: Growing up too fast too soon.* Reading, MA: Addison-Wesley.

Ehrlich, V. Z. (1986). Recognizing superior cognitive abilities in disadvantaged, minority, and other diverse populations. In J. R. Whitmore (Ed.), *Intellectual giftedness in young children* (pp. 55-70). Binghamton, NY: Haworth.

Fetterman, D. M. (1988). *Excellence and equality.* Albany: State University of New York Press.

Gardner, H. (1983). *Frames of mind: The theory of multiple intelligences.* New York: Basic Books.

Gardner, J. W. (1961). *Excellence: Can we be equal and excellent too?* New York: Harper & Row.

Gesell, A., Halverson, H.M., Thompson, H., Ilg, F.M., Castner, B.M., Ames, L.B., & Amatruda C.S. (1940). *The first five years of life.* New York: Harper & Row.

Goertzel, V., & Goertzel, M. G. (1962). *Cradles of eminence.* Boston: Little, Brown.

Handler, E. (1972). Comparative effectiveness of four preschool programs: A sociological approach. *Child Welfare, 9,* 18-19, 21.

Hanninen, G. E. (1979, September/October). Developing a preschool gifted/talented program. *G/C/T, 9,* 18-21.

Hanninen, G. E. (1984). Effectiveness of a preschool program for the gifted and talented. *Journal for the Education of the Gifted, 7*(3), 192-204.

Hanninen, G. E. (1985). *The preschool gifted and talented child.* Reston, VA: ERIC Clearinghouse on Handicapped and Gifted Children, Council for Exceptional Children.

Johnson, L. (1983). Giftedness in preschool: A better time for development than identification. *Roeper Review, 5*(4), 13-15.

Kanevsky, L. (1992). The learning game. In P. S. Klein & A. J. Tannenbaum (Eds.), *To be young and gifted* (pp. 204-241). Norwood, NJ: Ablex.

Kanevsky, L. (in press). Dynamic or static assessment and gifted children: What was the question. *Exceptional Education Canada.* Burnaby, BC: Simon Fraser University.

Karnes, M. B. (Ed.). (1983). *The underserved: Our young gifted children.* Reston, VA: Council for Exceptional Children.

Kitano, M. K. (1985) Issues and problems in establishing preschool programs for the gifted. *Roeper Review, 7*(4), 212-213.

Kitano, M. K. (1986) Evaluating program options for young gifted children. In J. R. Whitmore (Ed.), *Intellectual giftedness in young children* (pp. 89-101). Binghamton, NY: Haworth.

Martinson, R. A. (1975). *The identification of the gifted and talented.* Reston, VA: Council for Exceptional Children.

Mathews, F. N., & Burns, J. M. (1992). A parent evaluation of a public preschool gifted program. *Roeper Review, 15*(2), 69-72.

Office of Superintendent of Public Instruction (OSPI). (1989). *Criteria for excellent programs for highly capable students: A highly capable students program guide.* Olympia, State of Washington.

Parke, B. (Ed.). (1989). *Program standards of the gifted and talented.* Reston, VA: The Association for the Gifted, A division of the Council for Exceptional Children.

Piers, M. W. (Ed.). (1972). *Play and development.* New York: Norton.

Pines, A. L. (1981). Learning theory and gifted education. *Roeper Review, 3*(3), 26-31.

Pulaski, M. A. S. (1971). *Understanding Piaget: An introduction to children's cognitive development.* New York: Harper & Row.

Robinson, N. M. (1992, January). *Gifted children and school readiness: Who makes ready for whom?* Presentation at Maternal and Children Health Issues Conference, Columbia, MD.

Robinson, N. M. (1993). Identifying and nurturing gifted, very young children. In K.A. Heller, F.J. Mönks, & A.H. Passow (Eds.), *International handbook of research and development of giftedness and talent* (pp. 507-524). Oxford, UK: Pergamon.

Robinson, N. M., & Robinson, H. B. (1992). The use of standardized tests with young gifted children. In P. S. Klein & A. J. Tannenbaum (Eds.), *To be young and gifted* (pp. 141-170). Norwood, NJ: Ablex.

Roedell, W. C. (1989). Early development of young children. In J.L. Van Tassel-Baska & P. Olszewski-Kubilius (Eds.), *Patterns of influence on gifted learners, the home, the self, and the school* (pp. 13-28). New York: Teachers College Press.

Roedell, W. C., Jackson, N. E., & Robinson, H. B. (1980). *Gifted young children.* New York: Teachers College Press.

Shaklee, B. D. (1992). Identification of young gifted students. *Journal for the Education of the Gifted, 15*(2), 134-144.

Silverman, L. K., & Kearney, K. (1992). The case for the Stanford-Binet L-M as a supplemental test. *Roeper Review, 15*(1), 34-37.

Slavin, R. E., Karweit, N. L., & Wasik, B.A. (1993). Preventing early school failure: What works? *Educational Leadership, 50*(4), 10-18.

Smutny, J. F., Veenker, K., & Veenker, S. (1991). *Your gifted child: How to recognize and develop the special talents in your child from birth to age seven.* New York: Ballantine.

Sternberg, R. J., & Davidson, J. E. (1986). *Conceptions of giftedness.* New York: Cambridge University Press.

U.S. Department of Education . (1993). *National excellence: A case for developing American's talent.* Washington, DC: Office of Educational Research and Improvement.

Vygotsky, L. S. (1978). *Mind in society.* Cambridge, MA: Harvard University Press.

Whitmore, J. R. (Ed.). (1986). *Intellectual giftedness in young children.* Binghamton, NY: Haworth.

35

Planning Curriculum for Young Gifted Children

Joan Vydra
Judy Leimbach

> The curriculum for gifted young children must play to the ages and stages of growth by always stretching just a bit beyond the normative expectations.
> —B. Clark (1983, p. 84)

The normative expectations mentioned by Barbara Clark have been tempered over time by the educational pendulums that swing to and fro, sometimes given extra impetus by research and public opinion. Our firm belief that young gifted children need a differentiated curriculum, different in content, process, and product, has remained constant over the last 10 years that we have worked, played, and learned together, first as teachers of gifted children and then later as teachers of the teachers of the gifted. The controversial curriculum storms brought on in the last 10 years by Hirsch, Ravitch, Finn, Resnick, and others have helped solidify our belief in the need for comprehensive and special curriculum programming for primary gifted children.

In *Cultural Literacy: What Every American Needs to Know*, E. D. Hirsch (1987) fired a cannon at public schools. In this bestseller, Hirsch contended that students have difficulty succeeding in schools because there is too much focus on process and not enough on content. Hirsch pushes for a curriculum that begins at the earliest levels to teach the information and ideas that are the foundation of American culture and he believed that too many educators focus on critical thinking to the neglect of factual information. Ravitch and Finn (1987) were even more critical than Hirsch in their condemnation of educators. Ravitch and Finn espoused the position that educators teach skills to the exclusion of content, and added heat to the fire with their contention that educators made the choice out of laziness.

Resnick (1987) brought some calm to the tempest. Resnick's research solidified the position that the achievement of literacy was not enough; that students must also become competent thinkers. Cognitive psychology defines curriculum in terms of thinking about knowledge. Children don't learn to think in a vacuum or become mere recorders of information. Curriculum for Resnick is that which treats children as the builders of knowledge structures.

Although the debate about appropriate curriculum continues to be a bit murky, the waters grow downright muddy when the focus changes to the curriculum needs of gifted students. VanTassel-Baska (1985) posed the questions succinctly:

> Should curriculum for the gifted be viewed as a separate area of endeavor, an adaptation of good general curriculum practices, or a division of special education practices? Are good teaching techniques and good teaching methodology all that gifted children need, indicating modification of the instructional pattern but not the curriculum? Should curriculum for the gifted be predetermined and stated on paper or be viewed as a set of experiences inherently to be organized by the child and brought out through interest assessments and appropriate teacher facilitation? Are individualized education programs (IEPs) the answer for gifted children? Or is there more to be considered in providing an appropriate curriculum for this group of children? (pp. 45-46)

We used VanTassel-Baska's final question as the writing prompt for this chapter. We do believe there is more to be considered in order to best meet the many and varied needs of young gifted children. In this chapter we present suggestions and ideas that have been successful for us as practitioners working with gifted children. The ideas presented are based on our own experiences and by no means should be considered as all-inclusive. Many of the materials that we use we developed ourselves when there wasn't much on the market for young gifted children. The publication of our books has given us the opportunity to share materials that we have used successfully with primary-aged children.

When planning the curriculum and the teaching strategies to meet the needs of young gifted children, we were guided in our work by these basic tenets. Young gifted children need to:

1. use, develop, and understand their higher mental processes
2. use, develop, and understand their own creativity
3. interact with and experience other gifted children
4. have more in-depth exposure in key areas of learning
5. have work that emphasizes exploration, manipulation, and play
6. have curriculum presented in an integrated manner to help them understand the interrelatedness of multiple subject areas
7. have instruction qualitatively different than that of nongifted children
8. have instruction that is developmentally appropriate
9. have a focus on content as well as on process
10. have direction in understanding and appreciating the diversity among individuals, in part to help them better understand themselves

Curriculum planning in any school district or program is the process that defines the current status of the educational program, deciding what the program should be, deciding what opportunities for children should be a part of that program, and then determining how to get there. We suggest that you define the current status of your educational program and hold it up to the guiding tenets of instructional practice listed previously. Determine if what you are doing is good for young gifted children, if your curriculum plan is in keeping with your district and school philosophy, and then make decisions for appropriate modifications.

CREATING THE APPROPRIATE LEARNING CLIMATE

One of the first and most important modifications necessary to meet the needs of young gifted children is to provide an appropriate climate for learning. It won't matter what is written within curriculum documents or lesson plans if the classroom climate does not foster learning and growth. When talking about young gifted children, it is not enough to talk about meeting academic needs. The appropriate learning climate will take into account the cognitive, social-emotional, and physical needs of each child. Each and every child will be recognized as an unique individual. It is not that difficult to do. Most young gifted learners are still in the "me first" stage and give off many signals about their needs and abilities. Teachers just need to be good observers and able to read their students.

Young gifted learners need opportunities to work together. Whether through cluster grouping or self-contained placements, students of like abilities and interests must have time to learn from and with each other (Allan, 1991; Fiedler, Lange, & Winebrenner, 1993). Children of comparable abilities are far more likely to challenge and motivate each other and far less likely to act elitist. As Winebrenner (1992) suggested, gifted students in a cluster group learn "that they are not the greatest thing since sliced bread" (p. 128). Finally, it is far easier for one teacher to modify and differentiate instruction than to expect all teachers at a grade level to do so.

Clark (1986) explained that the physical environment must be one that can provide exploration, stimulation, and challenge for students, while being a nurturing and exciting place for teachers. Young gifted students respond well to varied learning centers (reading, writing, science, math, communication, art, and building to name but a few), vivid wall displays, multimedia technology, animals, plants, common areas, and private spaces. These same students need hundreds of books in their classroom libraries and dozens of kinds of paper, pen, and pencils in their writing centers. Young gifted learners want to experiment with colors, textures, and tones.

Beyond the physical there is the cognitive environment, which includes the surroundings in which young gifted learners are accommodated and the growth opportunities these children are given. The classroom environment needs to sing with vitality. It should be filled with books, games, puzzles, bounty from nature, centers, writing materials, puppets, and displays. Children are stimulated by their environment and young gifted children especially so. Gifted students learn best when parents and teachers work together. Communication between home and school is critical to the success of young gifted students. Children thrive when the adults in their lives spend time discovering together what motivates and stimulates these young scholars to new learnings. To develop their cognitive and creative skills, students need to feel safe to take risks and to experiment. In fact, risk taking needs to become the norm rather than the exception in all classroom and home settings. Finally, a good learning environment is one that makes certain to include variety, challenge, change, bliss, and complexity in daily schooling experiences. The younger the student, the shorter the attention span. Work that is too easy is a turn-off to most of us, but especially to the young and very capable student. Young gifted students are easily hooked on learning when it is exciting and challenging.

Renzulli's study of gifted students who were forced to complete work that was already mastered led him to propose that we find ways to compact the curriculum (Starko, 1986). As outlined by Renzulli, curriculum compacting allows students to be tested out of areas of strength. In other words, a young gifted student faced with a traditional math curriculum might take a pretest on the first chapter of the book and then be exempted from that work if it is obvious that mastery has already been achieved. This strategy holds large appeal for our students who don't want to do work that is too easy. The student is then allowed to determine (with the teacher's assistance) what type of enrichment activities can be completed in math in lieu of the already mastered material. Math is a relatively easy area of the curriculum in which to experiment with compacting for primary-aged children. The wide variety of math manipulatives available for differentiated activities makes it easier for compacting to take place within the classroom setting. Winebrenner (1992) gave several examples of how to use curriculum compacting with gifted students in varied areas of the curriculum.

SUBJECT AREA—READING

Typically, young students spend a large amount of their school day in the core curriculum areas of language arts and math. Therefore, it is imperative that the special needs of gifted students be recognized in these areas, and that teachers make a strong effort to meet those needs. Many gifted students are already reading when they begin kindergarten. Others, who are just beginning to learn to read, will usually do so at a much faster pace than their age level peers. It would be totally inappropriate and unfair if those students were provided with only the same reading instruction and activities others in the class were receiving.

There are many benefits for all students in a whole language classroom, but educators must avoid the pitfalls that can occur for gifted readers. If everyone in the class is reading the same books at about the same level, and doing all the same activities, the gifted students are not being challenged. For example, some gifted first graders may enjoy reading *Frog and Toad* books and doing related activities with their classmates, whereas others may be completely bored. *Neither* group is having its instructional needs met. Every student has the right to learn, to grow, and to be challenged in school. If what the child is learning in reading class is to "go along with the group," rather than developing his reading skills, he is being cheated!

It is imperative that reading materials provided for gifted students be qualitatively different from those provided for less capable students. From the beginning, materials selected for them should be consistent with their reading levels. Activities should demand higher level thinking skills, including divergent thinking. If accelerated readers are only provided the same reading instruction as other students in a class, there is a tendency for their reading scores to regress toward the mean (Burns, Collins, & Paulsell, 1991). This same research report points out the need for young gifted students to not just be given advanced materials, but to also receive differentiated formal reading instruction at their own levels of performance. Working through a particular genre like Fairy Tales is one way for the teacher to provide instruction to a variety of ability levels within a classroom. Using *A Magic Carpet Ride* (Vydra, 1986), students can respond to questions and complete a variety of activities about fairy tales based on reading books and stories at their own reading levels. Many of our well-known fairy tales have been retold in a variety of cultural contexts and at a variety of reading levels.

Students who are already reading in kindergarten or at the beginning of first grade should be provided with a variety of independent reading experiences. *Primary Book Reporter* (Eckert & Leimbach, 1996b) guides young readers to explore and respond to various types of books by popular authors. Young gifted students who are fluent readers should be encouraged to go beyond the easy books in the primary section of the library and begin reading chapter books on their own. There are many wonderful books at their interest level that teachers may be using as read-aloud books, but that these young readers could read and enjoy themselves. Some gifted readers will already be doing this on their own outside of school, and others will still be reading only books they can read at one sitting and need to be led into chapter books. *Primarily Literature—(Study Guides for Children's Literature)* (Leimbach & Eckert, 1991) is one source for primary teachers who are introducing their advanced readers to chapter books. It provides complete literature units on five novels that appeal to young readers. Student activities go beyond literal meaning, requiring higher level responses and divergent thinking.

When teachers in whole language classrooms plan a topical unit, it is their responsibility to provide selections at varied levels appropriate for all their students. Young gifted readers may not always self-select the more challenging materials. Although the teacher should not restrict the gifted students' choices to only the more difficult books, the teacher may assign a particular book or require some of their selections to be made from the more challenging materials. For example, in a first or second grade classroom doing a unit on "Bears," the teacher will typically bring into the classroom a variety of fiction and nonfiction books on bears. The majority of these will usually be at a first- or second-grade level, but it is important to include a variety of above level books as well. For example, while all of the students may enjoy simplified stories about Paddington, the advanced reader could be reading the original version of *A Bear Called Paddington* by Michael Bond, or any of the many sequels.

Development of critical reading skills should begin at an early age. A first step would be distinguishing between fiction and nonfiction, then realistic fiction and fantasy. A next step might be distinguishing between fact and opinion. *Primarily Thinking* (Leimbach, 1991) provided lessons in understanding cause-effect relationships, differentiating between fact and opinion, comparing and contrasting, classification, and sequencing.

According to the late Paul Witty (1974), noted international authority in the area of reading, attention should also be given to the need for a "creative reading" approach. He described creative reading as:

> a thinking process in which new ideas are originated, evaluated, and applied. Divergent and varied responses, not right answers, are goals as thinking transpires and conclusions are reached. Finally, the pupil evaluates his conclusions and seeks to extend and use them. (p. 15)

Teachers using a creative reading approach will require responses that go beyond the literal meaning, with emphasis on higher level responses and thinking. Creative reading goes beyond facts and considers their meanings, implications, and usefulness. Students are never too young to begin thinking about what they read!

SUBJECT AREA—PROCESS WRITING

There are many opportunities to incorporate creative thinking into language arts. The current emphasis on a whole language approach encourages creative writing through a process approach at an early age. Young gifted students need not be frustrated because they lack the writing skills to put their ideas on paper. Preprimary and early primary students can dictate their stories to an adult or older student. Use of developmental spelling in the early years is appropriate as students begin to express their ideas in writing. The freedom to experiment with spelling (as with other aspects of writing) is important to the development of fluency and confidence. Our young students should be encouraged to express themselves freely without becoming self-conscious or inhibited. The mechanics of writing and correct spelling must be taught, but they should be an outgrowth of (rather than a roadblock to) the creative process. Some young gifted students have an almost compulsive need for correct mechanics and spelling. The skilled teacher will know how to negotiate the student's rational need for correctness with the right-brained need for creative thinking.

Every piece of writing need not be edited. The students should choose which stories they want to edit, rewrite, and illustrate for "publication." Making books out of the students' writing is well worth the time expended. Having your own book is a strong incentive for creative writing. Reading other students' books helps develop appreciation for others and their ideas. The books need not be elaborate, but adding little touches like a dedication or an "About the Author" paragraph can enhance their value in the eyes of our young authors.

To gain confidence in their creative writing abilities, young writers need to have their ideas appreciated for their originality, for the way they elaborated on a basic idea, for the way they described an event. Before young writers can be expected to write good original stories, they should have many opportunities to use descriptive language and to feel comfortable with divergency. *Primarily Creativity* (Leimbach & Vydra, 1988) provides young students with varied opportunities to come up with original thoughts, to elaborate on ideas, to demonstrate flexibility, and to generate fluent thoughts and concepts.

The writing curriculum for young gifted students should include activities like the following: describing memories, such as a time when you were really happy, or sad, or scared; writing sentences to describe a scene in a picture, by putting yourself in the picture and describing not only what you see, but what you hear or smell or feel; writing descriptive poems. *Primarily Poetry* (Steele, 1989) is a compilation of lessons from the California Poets in the Schools that develop language and creative skills which young students will use for poetry writing as well as other writing experiences.

SUBJECT AREA—MATH

In the area of mathematics young students should have opportunities to use manipulatives to explore and discover. Attribute block activities give young gifted students the opportunity to use manipulatives to discover and develop mathematical concepts including set theory (sets, subsets, negations, etc.) and geometry (basic shapes, transformations, etc.) *Attribute Games and Activities* (Marolda, 1976) and *Attribute Logic Block Activities* (Balka, 1985) are two excellent source books for the teacher. Activities provided include classification, negations, logical thinking, unions and intersections, intuitive geometry, symmetry, and transformations.

Tangram puzzles involve manipulating a square, a parallelogram, and five triangles into silhouette patterns. These puzzles can provide excellent problem-solving activities for an individualized learning center in the early childhood classroom. In addition, many aspects of these shapes lend themselves to the discovery or discussion of concepts such as size, shape, congruence, symmetry, and area.

The *Mathematics Their Way* (Baratta-Lorton, 1977) program uses manipulatives for concept development. Many activities in this program also incorporate creative thinking into the math curriculum. For example, students are asked to observe different characteristics in a group of objects and then to place the objects into categories. Creative thinking is encouraged when students are asked to think of many different ways to categorize the same group of objects. A box of buttons, for example, may be sorted in several ways: by color, by size, by composition (plastic, metal, etc.), by shape, by design, those with and those without shanks, and so on. This program also develops thinking through patterning. Young students discover a variety of patterns in and out of the classroom. Once students have demonstrated a basic understanding of the concept through observation in the real world, they can create a variety of patterns using manipulatives, and also apply the concept as a problem solving strategy.

The National Council of Teachers of Mathematics (1989) stressed the importance of problem solving and stated that learning to solve problems is the principal reason for studying mathematics. Of course, students need to learn basic number concepts and computation skills. However, gifted students usually master these at a much faster pace than their age level peers. This part of the math curriculum should certainly by compacted or accelerated for them. Enrichment activities that provide challenging, thought-provoking problems should be a part of their math curriculum. The units contained in *Enrichment Units in Math, Book 1* (Leimbach, 1995) and *Math Extension Units* (Eckert & Leimbach, 1996a) provide appropriate activities to help primary teachers enrich and extend the curriculum for their gifted math students. *Primarily Math* (Leimbach & Eckert, 1993) provides introductory and practice lessons teaching a variety of problem-solving strategies to young students, as well as pages of problems to solve by applying the strategies learned. These types of activities should be an important part of the math curriculum for young gifted students.

Logic is an area of the math curriculum frequently not taught until the intermediate grades. Too many curriculum developers, convinced that Piaget was right that students cannot handle logic until the age of 11 or 12, forget that gifted learners do not follow all of the traditional ages and stages of learning. Very young gifted students benefit from the logical thinking first introduced to them in *Lollipop Logic* (Risby & Risby, 1990). It has been our experience as teachers that most primary-aged gifted students thrive on logical thinking activities like those found in *Primarily Logic* (Leimbach, 1986a) and *Logic Problems for Primary People* (Stofac & Wesely, 1987) and especially enjoy solving easy grid logic problems in the introductory books of *Connections* (Risby, 1982) and *Logic Safari* (Risby, 1993).

SUBJECT AREAS—RESEARCH AND SCIENCE

Helping students take responsibility for their own learning is a goal that should be addressed early in the educational process. Involving young gifted students in research projects is one way of doing this. *Primarily Research* (Leimbach, 1986b) contains a series of eight study units that can be used for small group or individual research on a variety of interesting animals. In addition to fact-finding activities where students seek answers to specific questions, there are activities requiring critical and creative thinking as students apply information, analyze facts, make comparisons, and draw conclusions. Several suggestions for special projects are provided at the end of each unit.

Some young gifted students have special interests of their own that they would enjoy pursuing. The teacher need only provide the necessary help and encouragement for the child to do some independent study. Students should share their learning with their classmates in some form. Although this may sometimes be in the form of a written report, other options should be available and encouraged. For example, the child may build a model; present a puppet show; give an oral presentation using a model, diagrams, overheads; and so on.

If they are to become effective independent learners, young gifted students need instruction in the skills necessary to use reference materials and to locate information in the library. *Primarily Reference Skills* (Leimbach & Riggs, 1992) provides instruction and practice in alphabetical order; using the contents, index, and glossary pages in a book; using a dictionary; using encyclopedias; and finding books in a library.

Not all science is paper-and-pencil or reading research. Young gifted students especially enjoy learning about scientific problem solving through experimentation and hands-on research. *Minds on Science* (Davis & Dudley, 1989) provides many suggestions for science research geared to young learners and gives teachers several examples of ways to conduct and record experiments. *Activities to Integrate Math and Science* (AIMS)[1] materials do a wonderful job of bringing math and science together in ways that make sense for children. For example, in the early primary AIMS books, teachers are given examples of real graphs to use, such as people graphs, shoe graphs, and apple graphs. Although math activities like attributes, counting, comparing, estimating, measuring, predicting, recording data, sorting, and set manipulation are all a part of real graphs, so are many science skills and processes. In a real graph about apples, for instance, primary children learn to observe and classify, to measure, to estimate, to control variables, to record and interpret data, and to generalize conclusions.

---

[1]AIMS (Activities to Integrate Math and Science) is a continuing nonprofit project of Fresno Pacific College. AIMS Education Foundation, P.O. Box 7766, Fresno, Ca.

INTEGRATED CURRICULUM

Curriculum integration is important for all students, but perhaps is most necessary for young gifted learners who search for connections in order to understand the relevancy of learning to everyday life. Vars and Rakow (1993) asserted that integrated learning can replace the isolated subject area learning experiences that young gifted children often receive in accelerated classes and enrichment programs. Early materials available on education of the gifted (e.g., Kaplan, 1974) stressed the need for content to be developed around broad-based issues, problems, or themes. Using fairy tales as an example, young gifted children will read classic literature and enjoy discovering the six themes that are found throughout the genre of fairy tales. The multiple disciplines of art, music, history, drama, and math all come to life through fairy tales. Art prints featuring tales from the Brothers Grimm and Hans Christian Anderson can be enjoyed by even the youngest child. Music written for and about fairy tales can help those same tales come to life. Social studies is made meaningful as children learn about the evolution of the fairy tale in different countries and civilizations and learn about different lands and peoples by studying similar tales from diverse cultures. Creative dramatics is a natural outlet for the retelling of fairy tales or the dramatization of original fairy tales. Even math lessons can be derived from fairy tales as children write problems dealing with different numbered amounts, such as buying party supplies for the seven dwarfs, or figuring construction costs of houses for the three little pigs.

A differentiated curriculum encourages the mastery of abstract, higher level thinking skills. Instead of dealing with fairy tales at levels of knowledge and comprehension, questions can be asked that encourage young children to analyze, synthesize, and evaluate. Students can be asked to compare and contrast some of the magical characters for traits of good versus evil. Students can survey their classmates to discover fairy tale favorites and then learn how to chart those results. They can imagine what would happen in fairy tales if endings are changed or settings are different. They can develop games that build on fairy tale events and write poems that celebrate these same fairy tales. Young gifted children can design fairy tale castles and costumes. At the evaluation level, students can judge characters like Goldilocks or Jack (of Jack and the Beanstalk) and perhaps decide if either should be arrested for breaking and entering or for grand theft.

There are many prepackaged thematic units available on store shelves. Some are good for young gifted students and others are not. How do you decide? Beware of books filled with lots of cutesy activities with no clear goals or learning objectives. The best selections provide teachers with a wide variety of choices designed to promote both creative and critical thinking on the part of student learners. The best of these stretch young minds and provide relevant connections to prior learning. Integrated curriculum units, whether prepackaged or painstakingly prepared by individual teachers, must be meaningful with all activities planned to enhance learning.

CONCLUSION

Jefferson once said, "Nothing is so unequal as the equal treatment of unequal people." Just as all students in our classrooms, including the gifted, have the right to learn new things each day, all students also have the right to be challenged in their learning. If everything in school comes easy, as it often does for preprimary and primary gifted children, students do not learn the importance of perseverance, nor do they experience the joy of accomplishment felt at the completion of a challenging task.

Young students who always complete assignments quickly and easily, without errors, may come to place unreasonable expectations on themselves. They often confuse "smart" with "fast." When they do come up against a difficult problem or an assignment that they cannot complete quickly and easily, they may become quite frustrated and feel that they have failed. They need to learn that it's okay to make a mistake, that we can learn from our mistakes, and that they are not expected to be perfect. They need to learn to work through problems, to try different strategies, to persevere, and not expect to accomplish everything quickly.

Therefore, in planning curriculum for young gifted students, educators should consider compacting, pacing, acceleration, enrichment, independent projects, and inclusion of higher level cognitive and creative-thinking activities, all aimed at keeping the gifted child challenged and excited about learning. We cannot afford to waste bright young minds by doing any less!

REFERENCES

Allan, S. D. (1991). Ability grouping research reviews: What do they say about grouping and the gifted? *Educational Leadership, 48*(6), 60-65.

Balka, D. (1985). *Attribute logic block activities.* Oak Lawn, IL: Ideal School Supply Company.

Baratta-Lorton, M. (1977). *Mathematics their way.* Reading, MA: Addison-Wesley.

Burns, J., Collins, M., & Paulsell, J. (1991). A comparison of intellectually superior preschool accelerated readers and nonreaders: Four years later. *Gifted Child Quarterly, 35,* 118-124.

474   VYDRA AND LEIMBACH

Clark, B. (1983). *Growing up gifted.* Columbus, OH: Merrill.
Clark, B. (1986). *Optimizing learning: The integrative education model in the classroom.* Columbus, OH: Merrill.
Davis, H., & Dudley, A. (1989). *Minds on science, grade 1.* San Luis Obispo, CA: Dandy Lion Publications.
Eckert, S., & Leimbach, J. (1996a). *Math extension units.* San Luis Obispo, CA: Dandy Lion Publications.
Eckert, S., & Leimbach, J. (1996b). *Primary book reporter.* San Luis Obispo, CA: Dandy Lion Publications.
Fiedler, E., Lange, R., & Winebrenner, S. (1993). The concept of grouping in gifted education. *Roeper Review, 6*(1), 4-7.
Hirsch, E. D. (1987). *Cultural literacy: What every American needs to know.* Boston: Houghton Mifflin.
Kaplan, S. (1974). *Providing programs for the gifted and talented: A handbook.* Ventura, CA: Office of the Ventura County Superintendent of Schools.
Leimbach, J. (1986a). *Primarily logic.* San Luis Obispo, CA: Dandy Lion Publications.
Leimbach, J. (1986b). *Primarily research.* San Luis Obispo, CA: Dandy Lion Publications.
Leimbach, J. (1991). *Primarily thinking.* San Luis Obispo, CA: Dandy Lion Publications.
Leimbach, J. (1995). *Enrichment units in math, book 1.* San Luis Obispo, CA: Dandy Lion Publications.
Leimbach, J., & Eckert, S. (1991). *Primarily literature.* San Luis Obispo, CA: Dandy Lion Publications.
Leimbach, J., & Eckert, S. (1993). *Primarily math.* San Luis Obispo, CA: Dandy Lion Publications.
Leimbach, J., & Riggs. P. (1992). *Primarily reference skills.* San Luis Obispo, CA: Dandy Lion Publications.
Leimbach, J., & Vydra, J. (1988). *Primarily creativity.* San Luis Obispo, CA: Dandy Lion Publications.
Marolda, M. (1976). *Attribute games and activities.* Oak Lawn, IL: Creative Publications.
National Council of Teachers of Mathematics. (1989). *Curriculum and evaluation standards for school mathematics.* Reston, VA: Author.
Ravitch, D., & Finn, C. (1987). *What do our 17-year-olds know? A report of the first national assessment of history and literature.* New York: Harper & Row.
Resnick, L. (1987). *Education and learning to think.* Washington, DC: National Academy Press.
Risby, B. (1982). *Connections, introductory.* San Luis Obispo, CA: Dandy Lion Publications.
Risby, B. (1993). *Logic safari, book 1.* San Luis Obispo, CA: Dandy Lion Publications.

Risby, B., & Risby, R. (1990). *Lollipop logic.* San Luis Obispo, CA: Dandy Lion Publications.

Starko, A. (1986). *It's about time.* Mansfield Center, CT: Creative Learning Press.

Steele, L. (1989). *Primarily poetry.* San Luis Obispo, CA: Dandy Lion Publications.

Stofac, V., & Wesely, A. (1987). *Logic problems for primary people.* Oak Lawn, IL: Creative Publications.

VanTassel-Baska, J. (1985). Appropriate curriculum for the gifted. In J. Feldhusen (Ed.), *Toward excellence in gifted education* (pp. 45-67). Denver: Love.

Vars, G., & Rakow, S. (1993). Making connections: Integrative curriculum and the gifted student. *Roeper Review, 16*(1), 48-53.

Vydra, J. (1986). *A magic carpet ride.* San Luis Obispo, CA: Dandy Lion Publications.

Winebrenner, S. (1992). *Teaching gifted students in the regular classroom: Strategies and techniques every teacher can use to meet the academic needs of the gifted and talented.* Minneapolis: Free Spirit.

Witty, P. (1974). Rationale for fostering creative reading in the gifted and the creative. In M. Babuda (Ed.), *Creative reading for gifted learners: A design for excellence* (pp. 8-24). Newark, DE: International Reading Association.

36

Cultivating Creative Thinking Abilities in Young Children*

Bob Stanish

FROM WHENCE IT CAME

There are a variety of strategies and concepts that can cultivate the skills of creative productive thinking and extend individual creative potential. They come from a variety of experts, researchers, and others involved in developing rationales and ideational strategies for creative thinking and problem-solving purposes. The work of Torrance (1962, 1966, 1979), Guilford (1967, 1977), Gordon (1961, 1974), Eberle (1971) Eberle and Stanish 1981), Davis (1974, 1993), Parnes, Noller, and Biondi (1977), Biondi (1972), Noller (1977), Williams (1970), Taylor (1988), MacKinnon (1978), Isaksen and Treffinger (1985) Isaksen 1987), de Bono (1973), and Gowan (1972), among others, impacted on education in relationship to the acceptance and implementation of creative productive thinking in classrooms.

---

*"The Hippo in the Tub" was illustrated by Nancee Volpe. "Terrible Tommy Toefoot" was illustrated by June Weber. All other illustrations by Bob Stanish.

A PERSONAL PASSAGE

Having been involved in various capacities with the first state-legislated program for gifted and talented children, I worked with and trained teachers, administrators, parents, and others in making provisions for the development of a wide spectrum of intellectual talent in class-rooms. In addition to those experiences, I was involved in a variety of encounters such as participation in the annual Creative Problem Solving Institute in Buffalo, NY sponsored by the Creative Education Foundation. Having been a participant and later a staff member there, a number of human resources impacted on me personally. The beginnings of what was later referred to as the creative education movement originated from those annual summer institutes. The authorities mentioned in the first paragraph affected my philosophy in relationship to the development of the creative processes of thinking in classrooms. Another experience was my involvement in a nationally funded graduate fellowship program directed by Merrill Harmin at Southern Illinois University in Edwardsville. This had an impact on my thinking at a pivotal point in my life. Harmin, along with Sidney B. Simon and Louis E. Raths, had coauthored a book entitled *Values and Teaching* (1966). Raths had become one of the earliest pioneers in exhorting the merits of teaching thinking skills in classrooms with the publication of his book, *Teaching for Thinking* (1967).

Due to my interaction with many nationally known scholars over the years, I was able to put together ideas integrating a wide universe of concepts drawn from Gordon's synectics, the Parnes-Osborn model of creative problem solving, the Raths-Harmin-Simon model of values clarification, ideational fluency strategies drawn, in part, from the work of Torrance (1979) and Crawford (1954) and others. Building on these, I then began to format ways in which creative thinking could be presented and taught in classrooms. Of major importance was my association with Bob Eberle (1971), the author of *Scamper*. *Scamper* is an idea checklist strategy that simplified Alex Osborn's (1963) *73 idea-spurring questions* into a more manageable format. Osborn, the creator of group brainstorming, had impacted greatly on business and industry with the development of a method of problem solving called *creative problem solving*. Eberle and I devised a way to present creative problem-solving strategies to elementary-age children in a book entitled CPS for Kids (1981). This book, in addition to *Sunflowering* (Stanish, 1977), helped establish me as a developer of classroom strategies that fostered creative thinking and problem solving skills for classroom use.

Meanwhile, Eberle (1965) had launched a major research study with the assistance of state funding to prove the teachability of creative processes to early adolescent children. This research, among others, confirmed the postulate that it does not take a highly creative person to teach the skills of creative thinking. It is interesting to note that by using the instructional processes to teach creative thinking we, as teachers, become more creative. From that study, in association with other studies, it became very evident that almost everyone can be made more deliberately creative in their thinking.

Another important element in my thinking and work was J. Richard Suchman (1966) and his "Inquiry Development Program." Suchman used discrepant events to stimulate student inquiry into certain scientific principles within the physical sciences. In many of my teacher resource books I've used discrepant and fantasy events to stimulate or motivate divergent patterns of thinking with children.

It was obvious to me due to my early experiences as a teacher, administrator, and supervisor (and the aforementioned experiences), that creative thinking could be taught. It could be taught in association with subject matter content or it could be taught solely for the purposes of developing certain specific creative thinking skills and abilities. My mission in life has been that of raising consciousness levels about creativity, gaining acceptance for creativity in classrooms, and developing easy and practical strategies to assist teachers in developing creative thinking abilities among the children they teach.

What follows are, for the most part, strategies I've developed, field tested, used, and published to develop certain specific creative abilities among young children.

CULTIVATING FLUENCY, FLEXIBILITY, AND ORIGINALITY

Fluency refers to the fluent and uninterrupted production of ideas in quantity. The more responses to a given problem, task, or question, the greater the fluency proficiency. *Flexibility* deals with generating different categories of thought by viewing things in different perspectives or from different points of view. To establish a score for flexibility one simply counts the different topics or categories of thought associated with the responses given. *Originality* alludes to unique, novel, or unusual responses to a problem solution, task, or question. Within a classroom, originality would represent responses and insights not anticipated.

Here is an example taken from the book *I Believe in Unicorns* (Stanish, 1979), that has motivated young children to utilize their creative thinking abilities of fluency, flexibility, and originality.

List all the ways you can think of to get a hippopotamus out of a bathtub.[1]

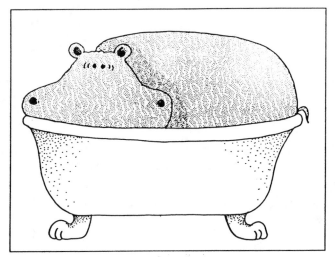

Some responses from a highly creative second-grade child on the hippopotamus problem:

1. Grease the hippo and then pull him out.
2. Promise him a big Mac.
3. Bring in a hippo of a different sex.
4. Use a crane.
5. Tickle him with an ostrich feather.
6. Pour in some hot water.
7. Scare him out with a bugle.
8. Throw some ice into the tub.
9. Bring in a mean lion.
10. Bring in a vet.
11. Give him some sleeping pills.
12. Bring in a hippo trainer.
13. Put wheels on the tub; roll him out side and dump him.
14. Use a pulley.
15. Call 911.

The motivating element in the hippopotamus strategy was the discrepant event of having a hippo in a bath tub. Young children, given a 7-minute time limit on the exercise, are anxious to provide a variety of clever ways to "untub" the hippo. In viewing the responses provided by the second grader, both fluency and flexibility of thinking scores were extremely high. Several of the responses, especially responses 3 and 5, demonstrated originality. When humor is used within classroom exercises there is a higher probability for originality. This is due to a distinct correlation between originality and humor.

---

[1]Permission to reprint granted by Good Apple.

It is extremely important, as teachers and parents, to accept all ideas and responses given by children to a given problem. One of the major blocks to creative thinking is that of squelching ideas with negative statements. Defer judgment until later or when an appropriate time as been set aside for evaluation. Never judge ideas during a period in which ideas are being generated. Always encourage quantity, for one great idea is usually the result of many ideas. An insightful resource on the mental blocks effecting creative thought and development is Roger Von Oech's book *A Whack on the Side of the Head* (1983).

CULTIVATING THE CREATIVE ABILITY OF ELABORATION— FIGURATIVELY AND SEMANTICALLY

The creative ability of elaboration is allied with the embellishment of an idea. It deals with details, descriptive elements, and additive components. The following example (Stanish, 1983) encourages figurative additions and details to a partially completed image.

Let your imagination go wild in finishing this drawing. Then tell us what it can do.[2]

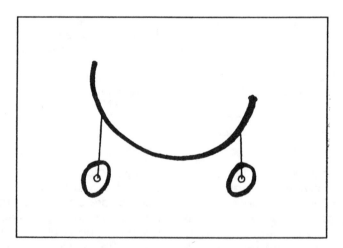

In viewing the ability of elaboration in this exercise, ask:

Were the additions numerous?
Where were the boundaries of the image extended?
Were the additions drawn representative of detail and embellishment?Did the completed image contain more than one function?

---

[2]Permission to reprint granted by Good Apple.

Was color, such as markers or crayons, used?
Was there a wide assortment of colors used?
Were background features added, such as landscapes or other characteristics?Was the verbal description elaborate and descriptive?
Was the verbal description richly or colorfully described?
Did the verbal description go beyond what was drawn?
Was imagery represented both in drawing and verbalization?

A response of "yes" to most of the previous stated questions would be an indicator of elaborative talent.

Torrance (1970) suggested using reading activities to strengthen and extend the skills of elaboration. One of the more effective ways to nurture elaboration is to provide limited information. By filling in the gaps of what is known to what would likely occur, forecasting opportunities are provided in which imaginative and descriptive embellishment occurs.

In working with very young children, I've found that a strategy known as *morphological synthesis* can extend and develop the skills of elaborative thinking through writing. Morphological synthesis is the selection of idea combinations from columns or within a matrix. By placing ideas in columns and interchanging components, it is possible to generate hundreds or thousands of idea possibilities from which to choose. For example, within the morphological columns below, there are 3,584 different story possibilities for creative writing purposes (8 x 8 x 8 x 7).

Morphological Columns for Story-Writing Purposes[3]

1. Select a hero:

   a. baby unicorn
   b. a good elf
   c. a beautiful princess
   d. a handsome prince
   e. a lost traveler
   f. a knight in armor
   g. the good magician
   h. someone else

2. Select a villain:

   a. a wicked witch
   b. to be fed to a dragon
   c. an evil wizard
   d. Wicked Willie
   e. a giant
   f. a gremlin
   g. a sorcerer
   h. a creature

3. Select a setting:

   a. a forest clearing
   b. a castle
   c. a mountain ledge
   d. a dungeon
   e. a cave
   f. a forsaken dwelling
   g. in a deep pit
   h. in a chamber

4. Select a problem:

   a. tied up with a rope
   b. an ogre
   c. being held for ransom
   d. given an evil spell
   e. about to be tortured
   f. about to be poisoned
   g. being held hostage
   h. about to be kidnapped

---

[3]Reprinted from Stanish (1992) with permission.

Children are asked to select idea combinations from the four columns. For example, a combination of b-e-c-g would be a story about a good elf on a mountain ledge in which the hero is being held hostage by a bad giant. After idea combinations are selected for story-writing purposes, children are encouraged to create conversations among the two characters, be descriptive in describing their characters, including behaviors and appearances, along with story scenes. Drawings are also encouraged along with dramatizations. In using this strategy with second and third graders, extraordinary elaborative stories occur. Developing elaborative thinking skills from limited information from a strategy such as morphological synthesis makes for marvelous learning in exploring possibilities and choices. Provisions can also be made with this strategy to randomly select idea combinations. By simply randomly selecting four letters between a and h, a story outline can be accomplished.

Morphological synthesis was named and used by Myron S. Allen (1966) as a means of improving communications within organizations and production plants. Some column headings used by Allen included areas of communications, functions of management, purposes of communication, interests inherent in communications, marks of effective communications, elements of an information system, and management-labor relations. An earlier type of format was similarly used by Fran Striker to generate radio and television episodes for his Lone Ranger series using column headings of characters, goals, obstacles, and outcomes (Shallcross, 1981).

CULTIVATING THE SKILLS OF MAKING TRANSFORMATIONS

Transformations is about making changes. It can be applied to both convergent thinking (intellectual processing requiring one answer or limited answers to a problem) or divergent thinking (intellectual processing requiring a multitude of answers to a problem). Transformations may deal with semantic, behavioral, visual, or symbolic alterations or modifications to things.

Troy Cole (1993) wrote a teacher resource book, *Figure 8 Animals*, for teachers of primary grade children. The book is based on making visual transformations with the figure 8.

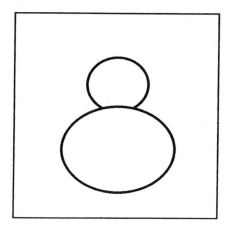

Figure 8 Animals[4]

1. Begin with a simple figure 8
2. Add two eyes
3. A nose
4. A mouth
5. Two ears
6. What do you have?

Cole's book encourages young children to draw, transform, and elaborate across a broad realm of academic areas. Most importantly, children have opportunities to transform the *what is* into *what it might become.* This, beyond anything else, builds and nurtures imagination and creative inventiveness.

Transformations, as a teachable component, can be advanced through the use of questioning techniques that stimulate creative ideas among young children. What follows are some open-ended questions that will cause transformations—be they written stories or projects.

Questioning That Promotes Transformations

How might we change it?	How could it serve a different purpose?
How might we alter it?	How could it serve a different meaning?
How might we reverse it?	How could it serve a different function?
What can be added?	What can be subtracted?
What can be combined?	What can be replaced?
What can be relocated?	What can be removed?
What can be redesigned?	What can be reshaped?
What can be made larger?	What can be made smaller?
What can be made thinner?	What can be made thicker?
What can be made stronger?	What can be made weaker?

[4]Permission to reprint granted by Good Apple.

What can be made wider? What can be made longer?
What can be made louder? What can be made softer?
What can be made simpler? What can be made complex?

In what ways might it be redone?
In what ways might it be resequenced?
In what ways might it be made more colorful?
In what ways might it be changed?
In what ways might it be tried?
In what ways might it be made more attractive?

These kinds of questions are often found in idea checklist strategies—such as Osborn's 73 *Idea-Spurring Questions* or Eberle's *Scamper*—that stimulate new or additional ideas to a given problem or task.

CULTIVATING THE SKILLS OF VISUALIZATION

Visualization is the ability to image ideas in colorful, graphic, and figural ways. By visualizing the "inside" of things, we can develop deeper insights and broaden our perspectives. For example, here is a "visualizing the inside" exercise that I've used frequently with young children:

1. Imagine what's on the inside.
2. Describe what you think is inside.
3. In your mind, cause it to work. What might be going in and coming out?
4. What kinds of purposes might the contraption serve?
5. What might cause it not to work?

There are many opportunities for encouraging young children to visualize the external elements of things or situations. When children are being read to or during the process of their own reading, ask open-ended questions or statements like:

1. What do you suppose this character looks like?
2. Please describe the . . .
3. What do you suppose will happen next?
4. Think of different ways this story might have ended.
5. What story events might make for good illustrations?
6. In what ways might you plan a story play or a movie about . . .?
7. Predict the outcome of . . .

Frederick Franck (1973) said, "The eye that sees is the 'I' experiencing itself in what it sees. It becomes self-aware, it realizes that it is an integral part of the great continuum of all that is. It sees things such as they are." It is more important to see rather than observe. Encouraging visualization from the perspective of seeing is extremely important with young children. Drawing, constructing, manipulating media, and expressing thoughts and feelings in graphic ways nurtures awareness and expands creative potential. Robert McKim (1980), Joe Khatena (1984), and Bob Eberle (1982), among others, have promoted the skills of visual thinking or visualization.

CULTIVATING THE SKILLS OF ANALOGICAL OR METAPHORICAL THINKING

William J. J. Gordon's (1961) experiences in working with groups involved in formulating creative solutions to selected problems enabled him to identify four analogical and metaphorical-based thinking strategies that creative people seemed to use intuitively. Gordon used the word *synectics* to describe the method. Synectics is the joining together of different and seemingly irrelevant elements. It is usually associated with the synectics problem-solving method and Synectics, Inc. There are over 200 patents issued to the Gordon-based organization.

The four synectics analogy strategies are *direct analogy, personal analogy, fantasy analogy,* and *symbolic analogy.* As a personal note, these strategies influenced my entrance into the field of developing teacher resource books for encouraging creative thinking among children. A direct analogy requires a comparison between associated facts in different disciplines. *Could we learn to build better shopping malls by studying anthills?* A personal analogy requires identifying oneself with a process or object. The losing of one's identity allows for imaginatively looking at things from differing points of view. *If I were a bottle cork, how would I react to the expansion of internal pressure?* A fantasy analogy requires making comparisons with the world as we know it and where anything is possible. *If we could use trained dolphins to monitor home swimming pools, what kinds of pool specifications would we need?* A symbolic analogy requires an image aesthetically satisfying as a means of looking at a problem—a bonding of metaphors. *Imagine a telephone that is like a pleasant secretary dealing with unpleasant business.* In many instances there is an oxymoron relationship with words within a symbolic analogy, such as "pleasantly unpleasant."

Analogies open windows of new understandings, glimpses of differing relationships, and the extensions of our creative beings. The important thing is not the answer given, but the explanation provided. For example, view the depths of thought required for these explanations:

Direct analogy.	Which has more bounce—a book or a tennis ball? Why?
Personal analogy.	How might I describe the sea if I were a sea shell?
Fantasy analogy.	How can we make homework recreational?
Symbolic analogy.	How might a book title like *Shyfully Popular* describe a character?

Here are a few responses from some second and third grade students from Kearney, MO on a personal analogy. No limitations were given as to the dimensions of the shoe. It could be of any size or proportion, be turned upside down or inside out. An additional addendum was to make the uses rhyme.

What could I do if I were an old shoe?[5]

I could make a summer home for the "Old Woman" in the shoe
Or I could be an experimental lab for studying the ocean blue.
I could be earmuffs for a bunny who has forgotten his hat
Or I could be used as a prop for a shoe acrobat.
I could be a weapon to shoot missiles down
Or I could be a mall for shopping in your town.
I could be a stage for a puppet play
Or I could be worn as a skin protector on a hot, summer day.
If the shoe were gigantic, I could be a slide
Or I could be attached to a horse for a dandy ride.
I could be a spaceship and to other planets sail
Or be a hammer to pound in a nail.
Add some handles to me and make a carrier for your cat
Or if placed on a table I could be a fish tank.
I could be a house in a tall, strong tree
Or be a place to keep your jewelry.
With some imagination, I could be a spy phone
Or be a cozy frog's home.

I could fill it with flowers and it could be a vase
Or . . . it's a rocket ship. Send it into space.
I could use it as a pot to cook a campfire stew
Or add some turbo springs for a pogo shoe.

---

[5]Student responses, which also included drawings, were provided by Jeanie Williams, a teacher at the Kearney Elementary School, Kearney, MO, to D.O.K. Publishers, publishers of *A Monster's Shoe* and the *Cat Kangaroo* by Bob Stanish. The responses were generated from the book and consequently sent to the author by the publisher.

I could fill it with water to make a puppy's dish
Or with its shoelace I could catch a wonderful fish.
I could use it as a boat with a white full sail
Or use it as a place to receive your U. S. Mail.
I could use it as a trap and catch an animal pest
Or give it to a mouse for a private nest.
I could fill it with rocks to make a stopper for a door
Or use it as a bank to collect money for the poor.

There is always an overlapping or interconnectiveness among the skills of creative thinking. For example, using the personal analogy as a device for viewing things from a different perspective; becoming the shoe, the creative skills of fluency and flexibility were cultivated. There are many possibilities for expanding thinking through the use of analogies.

CULTIVATING THE SKILLS OF PROBLEM SOLVING THROUGH THE CREATIVE PROCESS

Terrible Tommy Toefoot[6]

The skills of creative thinking have application and especially so within the domain of problem solving. In the early elementary grades, creative problem solving or modifications of it can be used very effectively. Here is an example of how a hypothetical problem can be presented for problem-solving purposes in which creative thinking skills can be applied:

[6]Adapted from Stanish and Eberle (1984) with permission.

The Problem: Terrible Tommy Toefoot, the biggest and strongest boy in class, will place his textbook beneath the chair in front of him. With his shoe and sock removed, he turns the pages with his remarkable toes. He does this every time there is a test. Everyone in class is afraid of Tommy and no one wants to tell the teacher.

Problem Statement: In what ways might we cause Tommy to stop cheating on tests?

1. Idea-Finding: list all the ideas you can think of that might solve the problem described in the problem statement.
2. Solution Finding: rate each of your ideas according to the following standards or criteria:
   [give 3 points for a yes response; 2 points for a maybe response, and 1 point for a no response.]
   a. Would it avoid a fight with Tommy?
   b. Would it be agreeable to Tommy?
   c. Would it be easy to do?
   d. Would it likely work?
   Which idea solutions have the most points? Select one solution from among the ideas with the high points.
3. Acceptance Finding: develop a plan for your best idea solution.

The idea-finding step of the problem-solving process will involve fluency, flexibility, and perhaps originality of thinking. Elaboration will be involved with the development of a plan to implement the solution in the acceptance-finding step of the process.

REFERENCES

Allen, M. S. (1966). *Psycho-dynamic synthesis*. West Nyack, NY: Parker.

Biondi, A. M. (Ed.). (1972). *The creative process*. Buffalo, NY: D.O.K.

Cole, T. W. (1993). *Figure 8 animals*. Carthage, IL: Good Apple.

Crawford, R. P. (1954). *The techniques of creative thinking*. Englewood Cliffs, NJ: Prentice-Hall.

Davis, G. A. (1974). Have an affair with your mind. In A. M. Biondi (Ed.), *Idea checklist for stimulating solutions* (pp. 9-18). Buffalo, NY: Bearly Limited

Davis, G. A. (1993). *Creativity is forever* (3rd ed.). Dubuque, IA: Kendall/Hunt.

de Bono, E. (1973). *Lateral thinking: Creativity step by step*. New York: Harper & Row.

Eberle, B. (1965). *Experimentation in the teaching of creative thinking skills*. Edwardsville, IL: Edwardsville Junior High School.

Eberle, B. (1971). *Scamper: Games for imagination development*. Buffalo, NY: D.O.K.

Eberle, B. (1982). *Visual thinking.* Buffalo, NY: D.O.K.

Eberle, B., & Stanish, B. (1981). *CPS for kids.* Buffalo, NY: D.O.K.

Franck, F. (1973). *The zen of seeing.* New York: Vintage.

Gordon, W. J. J. (1961). *Synectics.* New York: Harper & Row.

Gordon, W. J. J. (1974). *Making it strange* (Books 1-4). New York: Harper & Row.

Gowan, J. C. (1972). *Development of the creative individual.* San Diego: Knapp.

Guilford, J. P. (1967). *The nature of human intelligence.* New York: McGraw-Hill.

Guilford, J. P. (1977). *Way beyond the I.Q.* Buffalo, NY: Creative Education Foundation.

Harmin, M., Simon, S. B., & Raths, L. E. (1966). *Values and teaching.* Columbus, OH: Merrill.

Isaksen, S. G. (Ed.). (1987). *Frontiers of creativity research: Beyond the basics.* Buffalo, NY: Bearly Limited.

Isaksen, S. G., & Treffinger, D. J. (1985). *Creative problem solving: The basic course.* Buffalo, NY: Bearly Limited.

Khatena, J. (1984). *Imagery and creative imagination.* Buffalo, NY: Bearly Limited.

MacKinnon, D. W. (1978). *In search of human effectiveness.* Buffalo, NY: Creative Education Foundation.

McKim, R. H. (1980). *Thinking visually.* Belmont, CA: Wadsworth.

Noller, R. B. (1977). *Scratching the surface of creative problem solving: A bird's eye view of CPS.* Buffalo, NY: D.O.K.

Osborn, A. (1963). *Applied imagination.* New York: Scribner's.

Parnes, S. J., Noller, R. B., & Biondi, A. M. (1977). *Creative actionbook.* New York: Scribner's.

Raths, L. E. (1967). *Teaching for thinking.* Columbus, OH: Merrill.

Shallcross, D. J. (1981). *Teaching creative behavior.* Englewood Cliffs, NJ: Prentice-Hall.

Stanish, B. (1977). *Sunflowering.* Carthage, IL: Good Apple.

Stanish, B. (1979). *I believe in unicorns.* Carthage, IL: Good Apple.

Stanish, B. (1992, May/Summer). *Kids and creative writing.* Challenge, 10(5), 7-13.

Stanish, B. (1983). *Creativity for kids through writing.* Carthage, IL: Good Apple.

Suchman, J. R. (1966). *Inquiry development program in physical science.* Chicago: Science Research Associates.

Taylor, C. W. (1988). Various approaches to and definitions of creativity. In R.J. Sternberg (Ed.), *The nature of creativity* (pp. 99-121). New York: Cambridge University Press.

Torrance, E. P. (1962). *Guiding creative talent.* Englewood Cliffs, NJ: Prentice-Hall.

Torrance, E. P. (1966). *Torrance tests of creative thinking.* Bensenville, IL: Scholastic Testing Service.

CULTIVATING CREATIVE THINKING

491

Torrance, E. P. (1979). *The search for satori and creativity*. Buffalo, NY: Creative Education Foundation.

Von Oech, R. (1983). *A whack on the side of the head*. New York: Warner Communications.

Williams, F. (1970). *Classroom ideas for encouraging thinking and feeling*. Buffalo, NY: D.O.K..

37

Curriculum for the Young Gifted Child

Linda Meininger

There is an increasing emphasis on implementing programs based on an extensive body of research regarding how children learn and develop. These programs are based on what is referred to as *developmentally appropriate practices*. These practices are related to theories that intelligence develops in a series of stages which are age-related.

One comprehensive theory of intellectual development is that of Piaget (1952), who defined the stages as: sensorimotor, lasting from birth to approximately 2 years of age; preoperational, from 2 to 6 years of age; concrete operations, lasting from approximately 6 to 12 years of age; and formal operations, lasting from 12 years through adulthood. Within each stage there are certain types of thinking and learning activities that are appropriate for children within that stage.

Knowing what to expect from children and anticipating the learning experiences they will need based on which developmental stage they are in can be useful in planning school experiences; however, such decisions must be made based on signs of the child's development rather than age. This is critical for the gifted child who may think more like older children than age peers.

DEVELOPMENTAL LEVELS AND GIFTED CHILDREN

All young children show uneven patterns of development and will be quite adept at some tasks, although not yet ready to try other things. This uneven pattern is even more extreme for young gifted children. These children may be able to read about, and likely talk about, ideas that they do not completely understand. An adept child may be able to take a clock apart and put it back together, yet not know how to tell time. These uneven profiles may cause professionals (and sometimes parents) to question a child's abilities.

Educational experiences need to take into account this juxtaposition of developmental levels. These experiences should provide for children as children, as well as fostering their unique abilities. Appropriate curricula for young children with unique abilities should provide a balance in the following ways:

1. Meeting the needs that are common to all children. All children need to feel included with their age peers to provide psychological safety. They need opportunities to work and learn cooperatively, to play, and to communicate with other children and adults. The learning environment should respect children's unique cultural experiences and provide multicultural, nonsexist activities that foster an accepting, flexible attitude toward others. Young children tend to be curious and enthusiastic about the world around them; they should have opportunities to try things out, make choices and mistakes, and to learn from both their errors and successes. They should learn directly about the world, acquire skills and knowledge from the humanities, sciences, and fine arts, and participate in movement and play experiences that incorporate whole body activities. Children should have time and opportunity to create and express their thoughts and feelings through a variety of media and forms.

2. Meeting individual needs in a way that is appropriate for young children. Balance is not achieved by teaching more, sooner, by formal instruction in math and reading as if the child were 10 instead of 6. Elkind (1981) addressed this concern in his book, *The Hurried Child*. An early emphasis on academic subjects results in an overemphasis on narrow, specific skills rather than deepening children's interest and understanding. This doesn't mean avoiding teaching children

what they want to learn. Young gifted children expect to be challenged and to be actively involved in their own learning process. They need opportunities to select what they will learn about, how they will learn about it, and how they will show what they have learned. These children require concrete experiences that are appropriate to their developmental level as well as access to learning activities beyond that level. These learning activities should help children grow in their area of interest and strength. The curriculum should teach skills when a student is ready for them (rather than when set out by grade level or a skills sequence), in a form appropriate to both the child's understanding and age.

3. Meeting the needs of gifted children. Gifted children often work and play differently than their age peers. They explore ideas and issues earlier and tend to relate to older companions. They like games that involve individual skills or intellectual pursuits (Marland, 1972). When these children enter their first direct group experience on a regular basis, whether it is kindergarten or preschool, they can be in a situation that encourages them to act "like the other kids" (Malone & Moonan, 1975). Their differences and abilities need to be recognized, honored, and fostered. In addition to feeling accepted with their age peers, young gifted children need to feel that they belong with their group of intellectual peers. They need opportunities to play and learn with other children who think like they do and who are interested in learning the same things, or in the same way. This group of intellectual peers may include children of varying ages; however, such a group is developmentally appropriate for young gifted children and constitutes an essential part of respecting each child as a unique person, with an individual pattern and rate of learning and growth. Gifted children need opportunities to interact with and manipulate a variety of symbol systems, not only words, but sounds, music, graphics, measurements, and math symbols. The learning environment should provide many opportunities for children to stretch and reach for new ideas and understandings.

LEARNING MODIFICATIONS FOR GIFTED STUDENTS

The recommendations regarding learning modifications for gifted students should be incorporated into the curriculum plan for young children within a balanced program as described earlier. These recommendations are generally categorized as content, process, product, and learning-environment modifications.

CONTENT

Content is modified to allow children to learn in-depth and study "big ideas," broad-based themes and issues. The major focus is an ideas that have a wide range of application rather than on small pieces of information and factual data. Variety is a key component, with the ideas and content areas being extensions of what is in the regular curriculum, or sometimes in lieu of curriculum that students have already mastered. Content is organized around key ideas and generalizations, but also incorporates the study of productive individuals. Students should practice a variety of research methods to learn about their world and how to interpret and present what they discover. Even very young children can conduct interviews and chart (perhaps with assistance) the results of trying an experiment.

PROCESS

Process modifications are the teaching methods and the thinking skills developed in the students and include what is referred to as higher level thinking. Rather than simply memorizing facts and ideas, the focus is on having children put ideas together and make decisions about those ideas. Because gifted children rapidly acquire information (or may bring the information to the learning setting), they should be expected to apply their information in new situations, use it to develop new ideas and products, and evaluate its appropriateness. Questions and activities should be open-ended to encourage divergent thinking and student-student interaction, rather than soliciting a predetermined right answer. Students should be able to select topics and move rapidly through the material when appropriate. This provides challenge and maintains interest. A variety of activities should be available, and students should be led to express not only their conclusions, but also their reasoning. Students can give evidence of their reasoning by referring to something they have read, an example from their experience, something they heard or saw on television or at home. By explaining their reasoning to the teacher or to other students, children gain a deeper understanding of the subject as well as the ability to evaluate their own and other's thinking. Structured activities and simulation games should also be included to enable children to develop social and leadership skills.

PRODUCT

Product modifications encourage products that are novel and unique. These are then evaluated by both teacher and student, who analyze what was learned rather than assigning grades. The products should address problems that are real to the child and provide results that can be shared with a real or simulated audience. These products go beyond the traditional worksheet or test to determine knowledge, and instead allow young gifted children to explore meaningful topics of interest, conduct investigations, and share what they have learned.

LEARNING ENVIRONMENT

The learning-environment modifications are very similar to the ideas presented as needs common to all children. The key to creating a positive learning environment for gifted (and other) learners is the teacher. The teacher models the attitudes of acceptance, self-worth, risk taking, and self-evaluation. The teacher provides multiple opportunities to meet different learning needs and learner characteristics, and assists students in making selections among these opportunities. The teacher assesses student performance as the students interact with the learning process, and interacts with the students to foster understanding. The teacher accepts errors as representations of the child's knowledge, and discusses and questions to understand the meaning the child is creating.

APPROPRIATE CURRICULUM

There is no one right way to meet the needs of any group of learners, including the young gifted, or even to meet the needs of an individual. Classrooms may look very different and different curriculum models may be used, and all can be equally appropriate. There are, however, general expectations that represent what should be provided.

READING AND LANGUAGE ARTS

Reading is a valuable activity and a natural representation of language. Children's language is incorporated into the daily work of the class through charting, student dictation, student-authored books, and children talking about what they are doing. Many levels of written language are obvious, ranging from simple labels on objects to children's easy-to-read books to multiple sources on topics of interest. Children have opportunities to express their own ideas in writing and read books that they choose, which may, or may not, be those the entire group will read. A variety of writing and recording tools are available, including big paper, markers, paints, and tape recorders, as well as paper, pens, and pencils. There are quiet areas of the room that invite children to enjoy a book alone or with friends.

SCIENCE

Children should explore how things work and how they relate. This will vary by topic (or theme) and by the age of the children, but should include examples of how to measure and record weight, volume, and length; things to take apart and fit together; things to look at and handle; tools such as microscopes, hand lenses, scales, and balances; and activities that help children learn how ideas fit together, such as looking at a cocoon and butterfly as representations of growth.

MATHEMATICS

Learning activities should encourage an understanding of number systems and how they work. Base ten blocks, Unifix cubes, and Cuisenair rods are examples of manipulatives that encourage children to explore math concepts. Children should try out different ways of expressing calculations and solving problems that go beyond simple math facts and that encourage them to develop their own systems for finding out "what equals what." They should record their information in ways that provide meaningful representations as well as build to future knowledge, such as drawing pictures of addition problems and then labeling with numerals. In addition, children should use the language of math, that is, the appropriate, real terms for both its functions and tools.

SOCIAL SCIENCES

Multiple cultures should be represented, including those of the children in the class, which demonstrates that diverse perspectives are honored. Activities should encourage children to learn about the world around them and how people learn to live together. Students can explore ideas that represent the social systems (political, economic, geographic) we employ and how those systems work, through simulations and participating in the culture in the classroom. Historical events should be presented in a way that honors all participants and fosters an acceptance of different perspectives of events.

AESTHETIC AND ARTISTIC DEVELOPMENT

Space and materials are provided for children to "try on" different roles and personalities through dressing up, role playing, puppet play, and other dramatics. Children have opportunities to explore many mediums of art including clay, sculpture, paint, and crayons, building structures, and creating things that move. They also have opportunities to play with and learn about music and musical instruments.

PLAY

Children need opportunities to play: with ideas, with objects, with other children, with adults, and sometimes by themselves. Just as they try on clothes, they will try on ideas to see how these fit with what they already know. Making these connections, building on prior knowledge and experience, helps their understanding become more complex. They also need opportunities to play inside their own minds, to daydream and imagine. These flights of fantasy that take place in their minds become the creative, innovative ideas in their future.

TRADITIONAL CURRICULUM

The type of curriculum described here is considerably different than the traditional lock-step program that was present in some schools in the past (as when we were in school, perhaps). There used to be an attitude that kindergarten was the first time children came together as a group and the purpose of that year was to help these children learn to play together, to acquire social skills, and to begin to understand what school was all about. After kindergarten, children would be expected to settle in, settle down, and get busy working at learning. Providing for individual needs was usually done by adapting assignments and, for the gifted, by adding enrichment activities. The curriculum, the materials, and the expectations did not make it easy to provide for exceptional learners. Certainly there were wonderful teachers who created exciting classrooms that challenged all children to grow, provided a sense of success for most students, and taught many to love school and some to love learning.

What we want for our children today is to move beyond the very traditional to a more integrated, responsive learning environment that incorporates the various abilities and interests of students, honors diversity, promotes success for all children, addresses the needs of the whole child, and provides opportunities for children to learn at their highest level. In such an environment the gifted teacher can meet the needs of individual learners and create a true learning community (see Table 37.1).

Table 37.1. Summary Chart of Curriculum Perspectives.

Traditional Classroom Perspective	Developmental Perspective	Appropriate Modification for Gifted
Instruction is planned by the teacher and led by the teacher	Activities are child-initiated as well as adult-initiated	Active participation. Students can plan their own thinking activities and investigations.
Tasks are often narrow and discrete	Tasks focus on concept development	Can study in-depth on topic using a variety of skills
Students demonstrate understanding in objective formats at a pre-determined level of satisfactory performance	Authentic assessment using many examples. Emphasis on learning-rather than performance.- Student progress assessed primarily through observation	Student products can vary depending on pro-ject. Student is involved in the evaluation process.
A set order of skills is followed and specific content is designated by grade level	Decisions about knowledge and skills to be introduced based on knowledge of the children and typical patterns of learning. Broad range of content relevant, engaging, and meaningful to children.	Skills taught as students need them, or are inter-ested in learning them, even if usually taught at a higher grade. Variety and self-selection of topics
All or most children work on the same task at the same time, although the task may be modified for some.	Children work at different levels on different activ-ities. Flexible so teachers can adapt to individual children or groups.	Appropriate level and pace: Maximum level of achievement in basic skills and concepts. Rapid pacing when appropriate.
The goal is to get the right answer.	Values constructive errors; does not limit exploration for the sake of "right" answers.	Development of diver-gent as well as conver-gent thinking. Uses creative thinking and problem solving.

Table 37.1. Summary Chart of Curriculum Perspectives (con't).

Subjects are taught separately during specified blocks of time.	Integration across traditional subject matter division through focus on theme or topic.	Able to explore a topic in-depth. Exposure to a variety of fields of study and how they are related.
Students work individually	Students work cooperatively and alone. Interact and learn from peers	Interact intellectually, artistically, and affectively with other gifted, talented, and creative students.
Play is reserved to specific times or as a reward	Play is an integral part of the learning process	Through exploration and play develop mental imagery, imagination, and spatial abilities

The present trend of relying on developmentally appropriate practices to guide decision making in programs for young children results in environments that are much more supportive to gifted learners than many of the more traditional school settings. These practices also should encourage the types of modifications recommended for gifted children. This will occur if educators remember that "developmentally appropriate" is not synonymous with "age appropriate" and do not use the guidelines to put ceilings on children, but rather to build foundations for learning.

REFERENCES

Elkind, D. (1981). *The hurried child.* Reading, MA: Addison-Wesley.
Malone, C. E., & Moonan, W. I. (1975). Behavioral identification of gifted children. *Gifted Child Quarterly, 19,* 301-306.
Marland, S. (1972). *Education of the gifted and talented* (Report to the Congress of the University States, Commissioner of Education.) Washington, DC: U.S. Government Printing Office.
Piaget, J. (1952). *The origins of intelligence in children* (Margaret Cook, trans.). New York: International Universities Press.

38

From Theory to Practice: A Project for Young Creatively Gifted Children from Economically Disadvantaged Backgrounds*

Corliss J. McCallister
William R. Nash

> I don't think this kindergarten thing is going to work out. I don't have time for the really important things in my life. I've been there a whole week and we haven't danced once.
> —Grace, age 5

Grace was a child who appeared at preschool every morning with a bag full of costumes and dancing shoes. She was a joyful and tireless performer. During the course of the morning session she would change into different outfits, assemble a group of willing audience members, and perform improvisational works.

*The project described in this chapter was funded by the U.S. Department of Education/Jacob Javits Gifted and Talented Discretionary Grant Program ("Identifying Creatively Gifted Children from Economically Disadvantaged Backgrounds," Grant # R206A00585) from October 1991 to September 1993. Co-principal investigators were William R. Nash and Patricia A. Alexander of Texas A&M University. Subcontractors were Dorothy Sisk of Lamar University and Roberta Daniels of Arkansas State University

When observed in the first month of kindergarten, however, she had changed. Her eyes were glazed over in a look more appropriate for a bored third grader, her shoulders slumped, and her head hung over. Her mother reported that Grace had asked to drop out of kindergarten after the first week and became depressed when she was told she had 12 more years of school ahead. While her classmates were excused for gifted and talented class, Grace remained to do worksheets because her IQ and achievement scores were not acceptably high.

Fortunately, Grace was from a middle-class home where creativity and the arts were encouraged. Grace went to private dancing lessons and was encouraged by creative older sisters. Her mother, who didn't have to work, had considerable time to be Grace's audience and enough money to provide her with materials for her shows. Nevertheless, Grace found school irrelevant; the important events in her life occurred after 3 p.m.

Even in a progressive school system, the arts are not usually daily subjects and the young artists, like Grace, are not recognized for their precocious abilities. They have to wait far too long, sometimes with no emotional support, before their dreams can begin.

Robert, the storyteller, entertained his family with tall tales during their long trip across the desert from California. Once in school, however, Robert's stories and imagination were misunderstood and he was in trouble fairly often for "lying." Annie, the painter, had such precocious talent that she couldn't be ignored. However, her teacher's idea of dealing with Annie's abilities in the visual arts was to give her cans to decorate while Annie longed for canvases. Rajarshi, who thought he had invented multiplication as a kindergarten student and was upset to find out that it already existed, was taunted by the other students for his unusual ideas until his pediatrician insisted that the school protect him because he was getting ulcers.

Creatively gifted children, even in "good" school systems, are easy to overlook. They are misunderstood like Robert, or miseducated like Annie, or harassed, as was Rajarshi. Children with other types of gifts are easier to find. The children who excel in sports shine for their peers and teacher in Physical Education class. The young leaders make themselves seen and heard in almost any group situation.

How, then, does the exceptionally creative child show himself in the "regular" classroom? He can't get a score of 100 when the class gets out their workbooks in inventing. She doesn't achieve 98th percentile scores on standardized tests of visual arts. He won't find an A+ on his report card for music composition. Like Grace, she may never have an opportunity to perform for her class; her class may never know she has any talent at all.

The performers, artists, inventors, and writers wait for a teacher who recognizes their talents. Like all other exceptional children, the child who excels in creative endeavors has special educational needs.

The problems for exceptionally creative children from economically disadvantaged backgrounds are far more serious.

Economically disadvantaged children, in general, and minority children, in particular, are underrepresented in gifted programs (Baldwin, 1987; Bell & Bell, 1983; Torrance, 1980). Many experts, notably Torrance (1970) and Gallagher (1975), have advocated identifying creatively gifted individuals from these backgrounds. The need for early identification and intervention with such populations has been stressed repeatedly (Barbour, 1992; Karnes, 1980, 1983; Robinson, Roedell, & Jackson, 1979). Compelling arguments for creating these programs have been promulgated and the barriers to their success have been recognized (Karnes & Johnson, 1990). Despite these efforts, identification and assessment of young children remain problematic (McCallister, Nash, & Sandel, 1993; McCallister, Sandel, & Lockwood, 1984; Shaklee, 1992) and few programs exist (Gallagher, 1975; Karnes, 1980; Kitano, 1985; Maker, 1981; Rycraft, 1990).

The state of preschool education for creative children, especially those from economically disadvantaged backgrounds, has changed little in the past 25 years. Although Torrance (1970) documented his early efforts in the Creativity Workshop in Athens, GA, from 1967-1969, few programs have been established and even fewer have persisted. Isolated programs sporadically appear and disappear; however, the vast majority of children who will grow up to be creative and innovative adults receive little support in their developmental years.

In addition to the obvious funding problems, early identification of and intervention for young creatively gifted students has been hampered by practical problems such as the lack of widely accepted screening measures, the need for matrices based on theoretical models and experimental validation, and the dearth of effective teacher training programs. Without these necessary elements, which must be consistent with each other and with the programming options, school districts are unlikely to initiate programs for this subpopulation of gifted children. They are also far less likely to revise existing programs to meet the needs of economically disadvantaged children who might be served.

The Javits Grant proposal, "Identifying Creatively Gifted Children from Economically Disadvantaged Backgrounds," was submitted in 1991 by Texas A&M University's Institute for the Gifted and Talented in College Station and funded by the U.S. Office of Education. It outlined a 3-year project with research and service components that would design and field test programs for such students. The project contributed to a nationwide effort to identify and serve creatively gifted children from economically disadvantaged backgrounds by researching and developing the necessary elements for local education agencies to inaugurate special programs in their districts. A review of the literature on creativity was conducted and a new theory on creativity was developed. Grounded in theory and based on available research, the

project validated the practicality of assessment measures and classroom practices by field testing. The goal was to develop useful tools for
public education, not just for special programs at university campuses.
Two screening instruments were tested, an assessment matrix was
designed, and teacher and parent training materials were developed
and field tested. Approximately 200 economically disadvantaged
young children participated in three summer preschool programs at
Texas A&M, Lamar University in Beaumont, TX, and Arkansas State
University in Jonesboro, AR, to ensure that the project materials could be
used at different sites with varying populations. Although other programs
for preschoolers have been developed, this project is noteworthy primarily for its emphasis on the congruity between theory and practice.

The research efforts undertaken during this project built on previous studies by the authors and others in the field of gifted education,
especially Torrance (1977, 1979), Karnes, Schwedel, and Kemp (1985),
Karnes and Johnson (1987), Ehrlich (1978, 1980), and Roedell and
Robinson (1977). The first task of the project was to review existing theories of creativity to find the one best suited for this educational purpose.
As Gunsberg (1983) observed, "The classroom teacher who is interested
in promoting creative behavior in the classroom must first grapple with
questions of what creativity is and how it is made manifest, before considering ways to encourage it" (p. 144).

An exhaustive review of the literature on creativity numbering
over 500 entries was undertaken. However, finding no one theory that
seemed to encompass all the concerns of the project staff, and all the
needs of this population, the decision was made to develop a new
theory instead. Included in the project's final report (Nash, Alexander,
Parsons, Sisk, & Daniels, 1993) is a 70-page document entitled "Toward
a theory of creativity" (Alexander, Parsons, & Nash, 1993) containing
the four assumptions underlying the theory, a visual model of the factors impacting creative behaviors, and a new definition of creativity.

This theory contributes not only to the creativity literature, but
also to that literature on the education of creative individuals. It lists the
four components that impact creative development (biological, psychological, sociological, and knowledge) and, in so doing, targets
those areas for educational interventions. Although space does not permit a full explanation of the theory, its major assumptions are listed here.

Assumption One: Creativity is continuous, not dichotomous. All
people are creative; creativity is not a "special gift" bestowed on a
few, rare, human beings. However, while accepting creativity as a
basic human ability, the theory also acknowledges that, like other
human abilities, it may be possessed in various degrees or types, so that
some individuals excel in creative thought and performance. If children
are to retain and develop their creative qualities, they must accept this
creativity as part of a developing self-image and must feel valued for it.

Assumption Two: Creativity is a dynamic, interactive, and multi-dimensional process. Simply stated, creativity is dynamic because it changes. What is creative for a 3-year-old may be expected for a 5-year old. What is creative in 1994 may be completely standardized by 1996. Creativity is also dynamic because it links the past, present, and future. When a child comes to a classroom for the first time, he or she has already been learning outside school. Rather than leaving earlier lessons at the classroom door, the child must integrate into existing knowledge what the classroom teacher presents and models. Out of this learning comes the creative product that impacts the future. The creative process is interactive because it is the interplay of the genetic uniqueness of the individual with the unique life experiences of that individual. The mix of all the internal factors with all the external conditions of living create the combination that will result in a novel product or performance.

Assumption Three: Creativity may encompass intentionality, but requires awareness. This theory denies that creative acts are preconscious or unconscious. Given that creative behavior is conscious, therefore, the statement can be made that the mental processes involved in creative thinking can be learned, practiced, and changed by each individual. Thus, although children may "intuitively" or "naturally"choose creative behaviors, these can also be motivated and modified by the educational process.

Assumption Four: Creativity is higher order intellectual processing. According to Alexander et al. (1993), creativity is "neither a mystical experience nor a phenomenon without etiology" (p. 19). Like intelligence, creativity entails both convergent and divergent thinking processes. Like other intellectual processes, it requires the interactions of ideas and intentions and the recognition of both concrete and abstract interrelationships.

Together these four assumptions are the theoretical basis for all aspects of the project design. However, these assumptions are only the first part of the work and are supplemented by the model (see Figure 38.1), an even more important aspect of the theory for practical decisions about the operation of the preschool. The model illustrates what the theory states—that biological, psychological, sociological, and knowledge components must interact for a creative product or performance to occur. These components "function continuously and simultaneously" (Alexander et al., 1993, pp. 24-25). The boundaries around these components are flexible and permeable, changing with life experiences. The arrows indicate the many ways in which these components influence each other and the creative effort.

In addition to the assumptions and the model, a new definition of creativity was formulated. It reads:

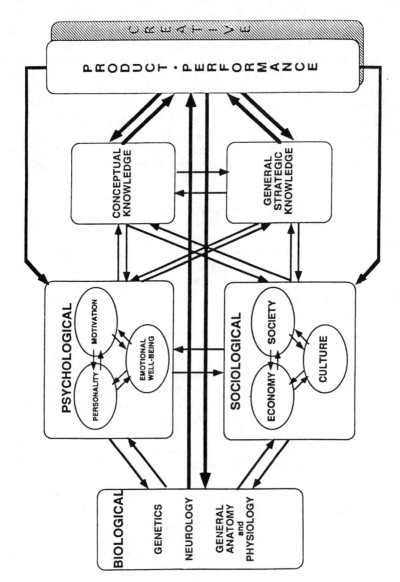

Figure 38.1. Multidimensional, interactive process model of human creativity

Creativity is a continuous, pervasive, interactive, and multidimensional process that gives rise to invention, transformation, generation, novelty, and originality. Creativity is an integral part of all human intellectual performance; a higher order of intellectual processing, influenced by biological, psychological, sociological, conceptual knowledge, and general problem-solving knowledge internal to the creator. (Alexander, 1993, p. 59)

The definition, model, and theoretical assumptions became the basis for all the other parts of the project. It provided consistency in planning and decision making. It was the basis for organizing the previously collected articles in the review of literature and also provided a framework for synthesizing previous research. It impacted the design of the screening instruments and the choice of instruments for the identification matrix. It is reflected in the objectives for teacher training, the curriculum design, the parent participation, and the student activities.

Two screening instruments were developed consistent with the creativity theory for use by teachers, aides, or parents. The Contrasting Behaviors Checklist (CBC) is a list of 33 paired adjectives, one representing a trait of creative children and the other, its opposite. Useful in a wide variety of settings and across diverse child activities, the CBC is both simple to administer and efficient with regard to time of administration and scoring. The second instrument is the Torrance List of Creative Positives (TCP) based on Torrance's (1973) Non-Test Indicators Checklist. Seventy items describe creative behaviors, and observers are asked to rate the strength of the child's behavior. The 70 items are arranged into 15 categories such as enjoyment of arts activities, responsiveness, and expressiveness.

The next major aspect of the project was the review of assessment instruments to determine which are appropriate for use with creatively gifted preschoolers. Included as an appendix to the project's Final Report, it describes and evaluates commonly available tests of creativity appropriate for preschool age children (Daniels, 1993). An example matrix of 10 measures is given. The project recommends that: (a) multiple assessment instruments be used, both subjective and objective; (b) that the instruments should be diagnostic/prescriptive in nature; (c) that they should include information from a variety of sources; and (d) that they should contain both qualitative and quantitative data. The identification process should stress not only the collection of assessment data, but also the intelligent interpretation of that data. Alexander et al., (1993) stressed that no one test score should be allowed to keep a child *out* of a program. The professional judgment of the psychologists, on consultation with parents and teachers, is considered sufficient to appeal the outcome if further testing or extenuating circumstances explain the child's "poor" performance on previous testing.

The design and implementation of the three summer preschools was consistent with previous successful interventions as summarized by Van Tassel-Baska (1991) because they were characterized by a small adult-child ratio, encouraged parent participation, provided mostly hands-on learning experiences, and offered extensive encouragement and recognition of student efforts.

Although the teaching staff realized that creative performances and products could not be guaranteed, they also realized that they had the responsibility for maximizing the four model components to increase the probability of creative behaviors by these children. As the project staff worked with the theory and applied the definition of creativity to a practical setting, it became translated from the phrases into lesson plans and materials lists. Every instructional design decision—the room layout, the questions asked, the schedule, the materials chosen—was expected to contribute to increasing creative behaviors. As the final report stated in 1993:

> As in every other phase of this project, the organizing principles of the themes, units and lessons conformed to the components of the general creativity theory. Each lesson was required to take into account children's physical, psychological, social and knowledge states, and to provide opportunities for expression. (Nash et al., 1993, p. 9)

The teachers were continually reminded of the many factors in the child's life impacting his or her creative production. The theory and the practice dictated that everyone, including teachers, parents, and the community, take responsibility for their impact on the young students' creative development.

Practical applications and suggestions for teachers were developed by Queen and McCallister (1991). The two words that emerged from the experience of the first preschool were "opportunity" and "affirmation." Students were to be given opportunities that they had previously been denied—opportunities to explore, to experience, to express. Affirmation, the behaviors that rewarded individuals for creative effort, was considered equally important. The adults and the students were expected to affirm everyone's right to be creative, to affirm their own efforts at creative behavior, and to affirm their creative products. Whether it was one teacher congratulating another on a particularly creative solution to a problem or one child hugging another after a song, the affirmations ensured that the opportunities and the creative behaviors would reappear.

Other important ideas on teaching this population that emerged were:

1. The theory identifies points of conflict important to the development of the creative child. For example, a conflict may occur when the expectations of creativity of the family conflict with the expectations of the school.

2. The theory specifies the areas in which children must develop as their creativity increases; it can be a basis for a taxonomy of creative development. For example, the theory could be used to describe the skills and attitudes to be included in the curriculum.

3. In laying out the influences on creative development, the model shows how to facilitate that development; it details the important issues and entities to be involved in program evaluation. For example, the model can be used to assess whether all components that impact the child's creativity are being maximized to support the child's creative efforts.

A curriculum document (Sisk, 1993) and a model thematic unit were prepared using 10 objectives taken from Karnes and Johnson (1987) and the eight guiding principles from Sisk's (1991) Project Step-Up. Preparing the teachers at each site was scheduled for 1 week, but as stated in the final recommendations, 2 weeks would have been preferable. Teacher education activities at all three sites were consistent with the Alexander/Parsons/Nash model and involved more than "training" teachers as stated in the final report: "It is the position of this project that teachers need to know not only what to do, but also—very importantly—they need to know why they do what they do" (Nash et al., 1993, p. 8).

Topics included assessment of creative behaviors, record keeping and lesson planning, special needs of economically disadvantaged children, parenting and advocacy issues, critical topics in preschool interventions, positive communication, and characteristics of creative children. Readings for teachers included Balkin (1990), Besemer (1984), Freeman (1985), Frey (1984), Harrington (1987), Heiss (1989), Isaacs (1987), Martin and Cramond (1984), and Moran, Sawyers, Fu, and Milgram (1988).

The parent participation and training aspect of the three preschools included both formal and informal activities. Training sessions were conducted to teach parents skills that would develop creative behaviors in their children after the summer preschool was over. Recipes and follow-up teaching ideas were sent home frequently along with bags of extra materials. Parents were invited to field trips to strengthen positive family experiences and interactions.

When viewed on the most basic level, this project was not only an important theoretical addition to the literature on creativity, it had very practical contributions about what did and didn't work in the field. First, it identified the singularly important problems connected with teacher recruitment, selection, and training. Project staff and teachers admitted that more in-depth training would have been beneficial because even for experienced classroom teachers, these children posed special challenges. Second, it recognized the problems with student attendance and transportation that are characteristic of economically disadvantaged populations. Although almost all students were eager to be at the preschool, life events for parents and economic circumstances for the family sometimes interfered. Additional efforts were required by teachers and administrators to motivate and assist parents. Phone calls, home visits, and mini-conferences at school were needed. Third, Daniels (personal communication, December 1994) reported that reaction to materials was different for these children and a developmental delay of 1 to 2 years was observed. Specifically, toys designed for toddlers were popular with 3- and 4-year-olds and offered both interest and challenge as they had never played with them before. Fourth, preferences were noted for modality even with this preschool population. Some students scored better on figural than on verbal responses; others responded best when action and movement were assessed. The resulting recommendation was, therefore, that the impact of personal preference, personality, and culture needs to be considered in choosing testing instruments and interpreting results even with young children.

Recommendations in the final report for future research projects concerned the problems and opportunities identified in the 3 years of the project. First, the theoretical framework initially developed for this project should be expanded and articulated with other educational frameworks. That is, the theory and model can and should be used in other settings and for other purposes. Second, long-term teacher training efforts are needed that are cooperative in nature and include parent training efforts. Universities involved in training pre-service or in-service preschool teachers should include information about this subpopulation in their curriculum. Third, transfer effects from model programs or short-term interventions should be monitored as preschoolers enter the educational mainstream; therefore, a longitudinal data base was recommended. Fourth, a national dissemination effort should be conducted to share both organizational and curricular models. Exemplary programs should be shared with education agencies serving similar populations on a regular basis as part of the Javits Program. Finally, the development of standards, tests, measures, and evaluation procedures should be a priority and these should be used in multiple settings for data-gathering purposes. Only with larger norming samples and longitudinal studies can the predictive validity of the instruments developed in this project be fully assessed.

In conclusion, the value of the products created during this project (the theory, screening measures, teacher and parent training materials) lies in four general areas. First, there are many general and specific uses of the theory and for the model for planning in all aspects of creativity training ranging from preschool use to corporate training. Second, there are implications for both curriculum and instruction of all kinds of gifted children; not just the creatively gifted, but any student from an economically disadvantaged background. Third, the specific suggestions on opportunity and affirmation can be used in any program for at risk children or arts education. Fourth, the products developed for these three sites can be used not only at other sites serving the creatively gifted young child, but adapted for other purposes within preschool education.

Viewing the project more broadly, five conclusions can be drawn from the theory that have tremendous implications for future projects serving creatively gifted students. First, programs that deal with only one component of the model will be less effective than program that encompass all the components of the model. Second, to effectively impact all components of the model, cooperative relationships must exist between schools, social service agencies, parent groups, and community institutions. A third implication is that differences in any of the internal or external components will impact the creative outcome and should be considered in designing and evaluating the program. Therefore, careful, complete, and ongoing assessments of the students and their environments are necessary. Fourth, programs that emphasize the creative process over, or to the exclusion of, the creative product (or vice-versa) will not be as effective as programs that take a balanced approach. Fifth, although the model represents an abstraction that is useful at any location, the local differences caused by biological, psychological, sociological, and knowledge factors dictate changes in the curriculum and instruction at different sites. To the extent that these changes in programming match the characteristics and needs of the population being served, the project will succeed.

Finally, at the most abstract level, the project's overarching goals represent four ideals for theories used in gifted education programs: congruity, completeness, coherence, and continuity. These ideals are, perhaps, the most important contribution to the literature. In this project, the congruity between theory and practice is an example that can make gifted programs not only effective, but also more defensible. The completeness of the theory lays out practical and systematic linkages between project activities—from screening through assessment to programming and evaluation—which strengthen this and any future project. The coherence of the theory, unifying previous efforts into a logical whole, provides a frame of reference for teachers and administrators that combines and validates the perspectives of many disciplines (the arts, psychology, education, and sociology) and their practitioners (artists, school psychologists and counselors, educators, and social workers). This coherence facilitates the establishment of a team approach for project personnel. Finally, the theory allows for a consistency of intervention. From preschool through adulthood the same model can be employed and because of the continuity allowed by the theory, subsequent efforts can be articulated with efficiency. Therefore, congruity, coherence, completeness, and continuity were goals for this project and will also be worthy goals for future endeavors.

In conclusion, this Javits Project offers both the theoretician and practitioner new directions to examine. Although there are many barriers to serving creatively gifted children from economically disadvantaged backgrounds, these barriers are not insurmountable, as demonstrated at the three summer preschools. Although both funding and motivation are currently lacking in most public school districts to attempt replications of this work, both initiating new programs and adapting existing programs could be realistically accomplished using the experience gained in this project. Additional research is needed to refine the products developed in this project; however they are an important first step toward enabling local education agencies to meet the needs of this population from theory to practice.

REFERENCES

Alexander, P.A., Parsons, J. L, & Nash, W. R. (1993). Toward a theory of creativity. In W. R. Nash, P. A. Alexander, J. L Parsons, D. Sisk, & R. Daniels (Eds.), *Identifying creatively gifted children from economically disadvantaged backgrounds. Final Report* (Appendix A). College Station: Institute for the Gifted & Talented, Texas A&M University.

Baldwin, A.Y. (1987). I'm black but look at me, I am also gifted. *Gifted Child Quarterly, 31*, 180-185.

Balkin, A. (1990). What is creativity? What is not? *Music Educators Journal, 76*(9), 29-32.

Barbour, N.B. (1992). Early childhood gifted education: A collaborative perspective. *Journal for the Education of the Gifted, 15*(2), 145-162.

Bell, M., & Bell, L. (1983, April). *Assessment procedures and enrollment patterns of Cuban-Americans, Mexican-Americans and Puerto Ricans in special education and gifted programs.* Paper presented at the annual meeting of the American Educational Research Association, Montreal, Canada.

Besemer, S.P. (1984). How do you know it's creative? *G/C/T, 32*, 30-35.

Daniels, R. (1993). Final report to Texas A&M University: Jacob Javits grant. In W.R. Nash, P.A. Alexander, J.L. Parsons, D. Sisk, & R. Daniels (Eds.), *Identifying creatively gifted children from economically disadvantaged backgrounds* (Appendix A). College Station: Institute for the Gifted & Talented, Texas A&M University.

Ehrlich, V.A. (1978). *The Astor program for gifted children: Pre-K through grade three.* New York: Teachers College, Columbia University.

Ehrlich, V.A. (1980). Identifying giftedness in the early years: From three to seven. In S. Kaplan (Ed.), *Educating the preschool/primary gifted and talented* (pp. 3-22). Ventura, CA: National State Leadership Training Institute.

Freeman, J. (1985). The early years: Preparation for creative thinking. *Gifted Education International, 3,* 100-104.

Frey, D. (1984, September/October). The use of metaphors with gifted children. *G/C/T,* 28-29.

Gallagher, J. J. (1975). The culturally different gifted. In J. J. Gallagher (Ed.), *Teaching the gifted child* (2nd ed., pp. 367-387). Boston: Allyn & Bacon.

Gunsberg, A. (1983). Creativity and play. In M.B. Karnes (Ed.), *The underserved: Our young gifted children* (pp. 144-157). Reston, VA: Council for Exceptional Children.

Harrington, R. G. (1987, October). Creativity is child's play: Verbal elaboration as a facilitator of creative play. *Techniques: A Journal for Remedial Education and Counseling, 3,* 312-319.

Heiss, G. (1989). Preschool teaching priorities: Reflections of a former home morning care provider. *Young Children, 44*(4), 31-36.

Isaacs, A.F. (1987). Identifying and parenting the gifted-talented creative (GTC) child beginning with preschool. *Creative Child and Adult Quarterly, 12*(1), 21-30.

Karnes, M. B. (1980). Elements of an exemplary preschool/primary program for gifted and talented. In S. Kaplan (Ed.), *Educating the preschool/primary gifted and talented* (pp. 103-140). Ventura, CA: National State Leadership Institute.

Karnes, M. B. (Ed.). (1983). *The underserved: Our young gifted children.* Reston, VA: Council for Exceptional Children.

Karnes, M. B., & Johnson, L. J. (1987). Bringing out Head Start talents: Findings from the field. *Gifted Child Quarterly, 31*(4), 174-179.

Karnes, M. B., & Johnson, L. J. (1990). A plea: Serving young gifted children. *Early Child Development and Care, 63,* 244-259.

Karnes, M.B., Shwedel, A.M., & Kemp, P.B. (1985). Maximizing the potential of the young gifted child. *Roeper Review, 7*(4), 204-208.

Kitano, M.K. (1985). Issues and problems in establishing preschool programs for the gifted. *Roeper Review, 7*(4), 212-213

Maker, C.J. (Spring, 1981). An experimental programme for young gifted children. *Journal of the World Education Fellowship in Australia, 65,* 14-19.

Martin, C.E., & Cramond, B. (1984, March/April). A checklist for assessing and developing creative reading. *G/C/T,* 22-24.

McCallister, C., Nash, W.R., & Sandel, A. (1993, December). Child search and screening activities for preschool gifted children. *Roeper Review, 16,* 98-102.

McCallister, C., Sandel, A., & Lockwood, B. (1984). *A preschool for developmentally advanced (gifted) children.* (ERIC Document Reproduction Service No. ED 249 745)

Moran, J.D., Sawyers, J.K., Fu, V.A., & Milgram, R.M. (1988). Measuring creativity in preschool children. *The Journal of Creative Behavior, 22*(4), 254-263.

Nash, W.R., Alexander, P.A., Parsons, J.L., Sisk, D., & Daniels, R. (1993). *Identifying creatively gifted children from economically disadvantaged backgrounds. Final report.* College Station: Institute for the Gifted and Talented, Texas A&M University.

Queen, K., & McCallister, C. (1991). *Theoretical perspectives on teaching the young creatively gifted or talented child.* Paper presented at the 9th World Conference on Gifted Children, The Hague, Netherlands. (ERIC Document Reproduction Service No. ED 354 693)

Robinson, H.B., Roedell, W.C., & Jackson, N.E. (1979). Early identification and intervention. In A.H. Passow (Ed.), *The gifted and talented: Their education and development* (pp. 138-154). Chicago: University of Chicago Press.

Roedell, W.C., & Robinson, H.B. (1977). *Programming for intellectually advanced preschool children: A program development guide.* Seattle: Child Development Research Group, University of Washington.

Rycraft, J.R. (1990). Behind the walls of poverty: Economically disadvantaged gifted and talented children. *Early Child Development and Care, 63,* 260-279.

Shaklee, B.D. (1992). Identification of young gifted students. *Journal for the Education of the Gifted, 15*(2), 134-144.

Sisk, D. (1991). *Project Step-up.* Javits Grant # R206A00520.

Sisk, D. (1993). Javits grant for creatively gifted preschoolers. In W. R. Nash, P. A. Alexander, J. L Parsons, D. Sisk, & R. Daniels (Eds.), *Identifying creatively gifted children from economically disadvantaged backgrounds* (Appendix B). College Station: Institute for the Gifted & Talented, Texas A&M University.

Torrance, E. P. (1970). *Encouraging creativity in the classroom.* Dubuque, IA: Brown.

Torrance, E. P. (1973, Spring). Non-test indicators of creative talent among disadvantaged children. *Gifted Child Quarterly,* 3-9.

Torrance, E. P. (1977). Creatively gifted and disadvantaged gifted students. In J. Stanley, W. George, & C. Solano (Eds.), *The gifted and the creative: A fifty-year perspective* (pp. 173-196). Baltimore: The Johns Hopkins University Press.

Torrance, E. P. (1979). *The search for satori and creativity.* Buffalo: Bearly Limited.

Torrance, E. P. (1980). Extending the identification of giftedness: Other talents, minority and handicapped groups. In *Educating the preschool/primary gifted and talented* (pp. 43-60). Ventura, CA; National State Leadership Training Institute.

Van Tassel-Baska, J. (1991, August). *Cultural diversity and disadvantaged issues in curriculum development for the gifted.* Presentation at the Symposium on Curriculum, World Conference on the Gifted, The Hague, Netherlands.

39

Developing Talent in Young Learners with Picture Books

Susan Baum

Youngsters with gifts and talents need a curriculum that offers sophisticated challenge in developmentally appropriate ways to nurture and develop their potential. Unfortunately, curriculum developed for the primary grades can be too basic in content, with an emphasis on practicing skills often mastered easily and quickly by high-ability youngsters. Today, early childhood educators are using more exciting curricular approaches like whole language, literature-based programs, and a problem-solving approach to mathematics. Without careful attention to individual differences among children, however, these strategies, like their predecessors, may underestimate the abilities of young gifted students and fail to nurture their talents (Baum, 1990).

To better serve youngsters in the primary grades, it is necessary to identify talents in students and provide opportunities for these youngsters to develop their talents and interests (Bruner, 1966; Erickson, 1959; Gardner, 1993; Katz, 1988; Renzulli, 1994). Through observing learning styles of young children (Cray-Andrews, in press) and the way they demonstrate above-average ability, creativity, and task commitment (Renzulli, 1978) we have developed an assessment tool, *The Teacher Searchlist* (Baum, in press) that helps to sensitize teachers to indicators of potential gifts and talents in young students. Teachers need to be sensitive to students' abilities and create curricular opportunities that nurture these youngsters' talents and skills in problem solving and critical thinking. This chapter explores an overview of talents found in young students and presents a strategy for developing an appropriate curriculum that will both enrich and accelerate the learning and intellectual development of young gifted students.

ESSENTIAL ELEMENTS OF AN APPROPRIATE CURRICULUM

How can curriculum incorporate talents and intellectually stimulate these bright young minds? First, gifted children require a curriculum that offers sophisticated challenge in developmentally appropriate ways. Several approaches to content have been found consistently to benefit bright youngsters—the use of authentic learning, based on addressing real-world problems, and constructing curriculum based on abstract themes or critical issues (Baum, 1990; Kaplan, 1986; Renzulli, 1994, Van Tassel-Baska, 1993). In either case, children should approach the content using inquiry, discovery, or other active learning processes that require critical and creative thinking.

Most important to the learning process is that students see the relevance or purpose in what they do (Bruner, 1966; Gardner, 1993; Renzulli, 1978, 1994). Using an approach that integrates basic skills into a meaningful project where students' ideas and learning are communicated to appropriate audiences motivates the youngsters to engage in the tasks of learning and to create high-level products.

As educators, we need to examine all the curriculum possibilities that can stimulate authentic learning experiences for students and carefully choose those that are sufficiently complex, meaningful to the students, and offer intriguing possibilities for investigation and learning.

A well-selected picture book provides an excellent opportunity around which to develop appropriate curriculum for talented young learners. The somewhat recent emergence of extraordinary picture books has allowed teachers to introduce young learners to advanced concepts, diverse topics, and challenging ideas in a developmentally appropriate fashion. Picture books are available that introduce students to the poetry of Emily Dickinson and Robert Frost, the history of England through the eyes of a castle, the intricate workings of a medieval feast, and the geographic features of the Mojave Dessert (a bibliography of select choices arranged by disciplines appears at the end of this chapter). Understanding new ideas and abstract concepts is made possible through excellent illustrations. By considering the themes and rich ideas contained within the pages of the book, teachers can create exciting learning experiences, introducing children to new areas of interest while developing their individual talents.

DESIGNING PICTURE BOOK EXPERIENCES: AN EXAMPLE

The first step in designing curriculum from a picture book is to select an appropriate volume. The following questions will facilitate this decision: What new content will the students gain from reading this book? Are there some abstract concepts to think about? Does the content lend itself to active inquiry and long term project ideas? Will new vocabulary be introduced? The second step requires brainstorming the variety of themes, concepts, and basic skills embedded within the context of the book. This is the idea bank from which you draw when beginning to conceptualize, synthesize, and organize curriculum units or projects. The final step is planning activities to develop the units that tap a variety of talents and interests of the learner. The activities must require the application of critical and creative thinking, as well as the integration of basic skills.

I have chosen the picture book *Thunder Cake* to illustrate the possibilities inherent in using literature to develop an enriched curriculum. Written and illustrated by Patricia Polacco, this book uses colorful folk art to acquaint students with Russian culture by using an experience shared by many children—the fear of a thunder storm. Using the oral history method of handing down stories to younger generations about situations occurring in the past, Polacco assures young learners that throughout the course of time approaching thunder storms have frightened people everywhere. In *Thunder Cake* a grandmother relates the story of how her grandmother helped her overcome her fear of thunderstorms by baking a special thunder cake before the storm arrived. The grandmother artfully describes the challenge of collecting the ingredients on the farm, while anticipating the closeness of the storm by counting the seconds between the flashes of lightning and the thunder claps that follow. The book even includes a recipe, which uses tomatoes as an ingredient for the chocolate thunder cake.

Thunder Cake's descriptive language and rich illustrations provide children with information and complex ideas. Truths like "Brave people can't be afraid of sounds" can lead to a lively discussion. Ways to overcome unfounded fears offer avenues for critical and creative thinking. Words like "Babushka," "samovar," "woodstove," "dry shed," and "trellis" build the vocabulary. Polacco's verbal descriptions of the sound of thunder introduce the idea of onomatopoeia. Polacco's artistry reveals intricate visual patterns from quilts on the chair to woven tablecloths.

Assuredly, this book offers sufficient complexity to use the story to initiate a number of learning excursions. Thunder Cake can be used to initiate any one of a wide variety of themes, such as patterns (quilting, thunder and lightning, design, stimulus, and response); children's feelings (fears, excitement, challenge); meteorology; chemical and physical changes (cooking, facial expression); oral history; the role of grandparents; cultural heritage; and life on a farm. The ideas must be evaluated: Which ones would excite the students? Which complement curriculum objectives? Which can be developed into interesting projects that apply basic skills? For the purpose of illustration I have chosen three ideas. Each project targets certain talents and skills that are summarized graphically at the end of each unit.

Example One—Exploring Fears: What Are You Afraid Of?

All children are afraid of the unknown. *Thunder Cake* offers an excellent opportunity to inform youngsters that they are not alone in their feelings. Through discussion they can discover ways to deal with fears and overcome them. Their inquiry can result in an in-depth project designed to help other children confront their fears. This long-term project will require the students to conduct research and compose an article to be submitted to *Creative Kids*, a journal by kids for kids.

Part One—Conduct a Survey
1. Brainstorm questions for your survey. What are children our age afraid of? What do they do when they are afraid? Have they ever been afraid of something and then stopped being afraid? What made them stop? Does age affect what you are afraid of?
2. Design the survey instrument and distribute it to students in grade 3 and kindergarten (or any age group you choose).
3. Collect and interpret data—classify fears, tabulate frequencies of the different responses to questions.
4. Graph results—Show students the interesting graphs found in *USA Today* or *Time* magazine to give them ideas for their own graph. Teach them how to make a bar graph, picture graph, or pie graph.
5. Write a summary of research—Include sample (who and how many), how data was analyzed, what the results were.

Part Two—Confront the Fear
1. Play "Whistle a Happy Tune" from *The King and I* (Rogers and Hammerstein musical).

2. Discuss with students what they do to chase away fears.
3. Invite a psychologist or social worker to discuss the topic of dealing with fears.
4. Choose stories for reading groups whose characters cope with fears.
5. Break into Fear Groups (each group discusses a particular fear. Make sure the group includes both students who have that fear and students who don't). Each group creates one or more strategies for coping or overcoming the particular fear.

Part Three—Write and Illustrate an Article
1. Have children generate an outline of the article.
2. Compose a rough draft. Show them articles from *Creative Kids* or other children's magazines to use as a model.
3. Revise and edit the draft. Include graphs and other illustrations.
4. Write a cover letter and mail the article to *Creative Kids*.[1]

Part Four—Extension ideas
Other related projects: (a) puppet show; (b) dance sequence personifying fear; (c) illustrated book "Fear is like . . . ;" (d) original songs or words to songs describing how to deal with fears; (e) panel of experts (kids describing their research and strategies from fear groups).

The activities comprising Part One of the unit on fear provide opportunities for students to apply or develop individual talents. The curious child, for example, is challenged by a mystery to solve. Leadership talent will also emerge as the youngsters assume or are given responsibility for different aspects of the project. Likewise, students who learn easily in math can be challenged to organize, tabulate, and interpret data collected from the survey.

The survey component of the unit also requires students to apply basic curricular skills. Specifically, tallying and graphing quantitative information are math skills taught in the primary grades. Developing questions for the survey, interviewing students, and writing a summary of the findings are important skills in language arts and communication.

In Part Two additional talents are acknowledged. For instance, students who enjoy music will appreciate hearing a selection from Rogers' and Hammerstein's *The King and I*. Writing and illustrating the article about ways to overcome fears integrates objectives in language arts, social studies, and art.

---

[1]P.O. Box 8813, Waco, Texas 76714- 8813.

Example Two—Oral History: A Memory Quilt

The story, *Thunder Cake*, can act as a springboard to a unit on oral history. Because the book's illustrations are rich in pattern imagery, a quilt would be an especially appropriate class project.

Quilts may be made from fabric or construction paper. Each square can have its own original pattern around the outside and a picture of the memory on the inside. One kindergarten teacher used a stiff black paper with holes punched around the edges so that the students could sew the squares together. Her students used pattern blocks to design their patterns and pasted pattern shapes corresponding to the pattern they invented around the border of their squares. They used a bright-colored wool to sew the squares together.

Ideas for the memory quilt are many. A youngster may choose to retrace the events of the school year, display his or her favorite memory, recall and document special birthday memories, or commemorate family traditions. For the purpose of this chapter, I have chosen to focus on the creation of a school memory quilt. This is an excellent project for the month of June.

Part One—Designing the Pattern
1. Visit a quilt exhibit or invite an expert to speak to the children about the history and purpose of quilts. Many families have quilts that have been handed down through the family or have acquired new quilts showing interesting patterns or symbols. Have some of these people bring in their quilts and discuss their history.
2. Read *Eight Hands Round* by Ann Whitford Paul. This outstanding picture alphabet book uses the names of early American patchwork patterns for its letters. It gives information about how and why a particular pattern got its name; this is a wonderful introduction to symbolism. Researching or guessing why certain patterns were used and what the patterns symbolized is exciting. For instance, the pineapple has traditionally represented hospitality, and hearts depicted love. Inspiration for the symbols came from many sources including the Bible, trades and occupations, nature, buildings, romance and marriage, literature, square dance calls, games, household items, politics and politicians, and wars and celebrations.
3. Explain the concept of patchwork patterns or the ways patterns repeat—these patterns may be one-patch, two-patch, three-patch, four-patch, or nine-patch. The students should experiment with patterns using pattern blocks, tangrams, and tesselations.

4. Read other quilt stories that represent the memory preservation aspect of a quilt. Three excellent choices are *The Quilt Story* by Tony Johnston and Tomie dePaola, *The Keeping Quilt* by Patricia Polacco and *My Grandmother's Patchwork Quilt* by Janet Bolton.

Part Two—Prepare the Quilt

1. Divide the class into five committees, keeping in mind the talents of the students in the areas of research, design, assembly, writing, and drawing. Each committee should have a committee chair to organize the steps and keep track of the group's progress.

   • *Research*—Take a survey of what events the class remembers about the school year. Have the group decide which are most important. The class may vote or set up criteria to use to select which events are indeed memorable. Choose 12 events.

   • *Design*—Design appropriate symbols to be used in the patchwork pattern to represent these events. Next, design the overall pattern for the quilt. Finally, create a border for the outside edges of the quilt.

   • *Drawing*—Illustrate selected events on 3" x 3" squares. Use magic markers or other mediums that will enhance the product.

   • *Writing*—Have this committee interview their classmates about what they remember about a particular event and have them incorporate facts from the interview into a paragraph about each event. These paragraphs should be written, printed, or typed neatly and mounted on 3" x 3" squares.

   • *Assembly*—Sequence events in the order of their occurrence within the school year. Sew all squares together.

Part Three—Exhibit the Quilt

Hold a reception during certain hours of certain days.

1. Design and send invitations.
2. Prepare and serve refreshments—may I suggest punch and Thunder Cake (prepared by the students, of course).
3. Select music to be played softly in the background. Students should choose a theme like "memories" and find songs that represent the theme. The music teacher, senior citizens, or parents should be happy to help put a tape together.
4. Have certain students act as guides and describe the purpose of quilts, and the symbolism.

Part Four—Extension ideas
1. Make quilts representing favorite stories.
2. Make a quilt come alive by acting out scenes from squares.
3. Design patterns for wrapping paper or fabric.

   This unit also provides many occasions for diverse talents to emerge. Spatial talents are needed to design patterns for the quilt. Curious youngsters will be motivated to explore symbols and their meanings as well as to discover which school memories are most popular. Avid readers are encouraged to explore stories and information about quilts, whereas students interested in the performing arts assume leadership roles in exhibiting the quilt. Skills in communication, math, and research are integrated into the steps of the quilt-making project.
   The development of a weather station is another project that naturally evolves from reading *Thunder Cake*. Students who are interested can become meteorologists, can make weather predictions and keep track of weather patterns during the year, and conduct experiments. Students who love to build can create weather instruments. Those who are articulate and enjoy public speaking can give a weather forecast over the school's intercom every morning. There are many resources available to help students build the instruments and conduct experiments. Often the weatherman from a local radio or television station will work with the students to help them become experts on weather.

CONCLUSION

The three ideas for learning explorations described here demonstrate how challenging curriculum can evolve from appropriate picture books. If a book is rich in complexity, it can stimulate an endless number of creative learning experiences for young able students. The following collection of books arranged by disciplines offers new ideas, a rich vocabulary, and masterful illustrations. Each selection can initiate a journey in talent development for students. By recognizing individual talents and designing activities based on these talents, teachers can provide appropriate challenges and exciting learning opportunities.

APPENDIX: PICTURE BOOK BIBLIOGRAPHY

Biology

Aragon, J. (1989). *Salt hands.* New York: Dutton.
Heller, R. (1981). *Chickens aren't the only ones.* New York: Putnam.

Heller, R. (1982). *Animals born alive and well*. New York: Grossett & Dunlap.
Heller, R. (1985). *How to hide a butterfly*. New York: Grossett & Dunlap.
Lear, E., with Nash, O. (1968). *Scroobious pip*. New York: Harper & Row Publishers.
Mazer, A. (1991). *The salamander room*. New York: Knopf.
Mc Cord, A. (1977). *Dinosaurs*. Tulsa, OK: EDC.
Pienkowski, J. (1980). *Dinner time*. Los Angeles: Price, Stern, & Sloan.
Ryder, J. (1989). *Where butterflies grow*. New York: Dutton.
Stout, W., Service, W., & Preiss, B. (1981). *The dinosaurs*. New York: Bantam.

Physics

Palin, M., Lee, A., & Seymour, R. (1986). *The mirrorstone*. New York: Knopf.

Ecology

Mc Clerran, A. (1985). *The mountain who loved a bird*. Natick, MA: Picture Book Studio USA.
Siebert, D. (1988). *Mojave*. New York: Crowell.

Geology

Butcher, J. (1984). *The sheep and the rowan tree*. New York: Holt, Rinehart & Winston.
Vita-Frenzi, C. (1989). *Planet Earth*. New York: Simon & Schuster.

Botany

Heller, R. (1983). *The reason for a flower*. New York: Grossett & Dunlap.

Mathematics

Anno, M. (1985). *Anno's hat trick*. New York: Philomel.
Anno, M. (1986). *Socrates and the three little pigs*. New York: Philomel.
Anno, M. (1986). *All in a day*. New York: Philomel.
Korab, B. (1985). *Archabet*. Washington, DC: The Preservation Press.
Merriam, E. (1993). *12 ways to get to 11*. New York: Simon & Schuster.
Schwartz, D. (1985). *How much is a million?* New York: Morrow.

Psychology (Social and Emotional Issues)

de Paola, T. (1983). *Sing Pierot sing.* New York: Harcourt Brace Jovanovich.

Greenfield, E. (1988). *Nathaniel talking.* New York: Black Butterfly Children's Books.

Espeland, P., & Waniak, M. (1980). *The cat walked through the casserole.* Minneapolis: Carolahoda.

Locker, T. (1985). *The mare on the hill.* New York: Dial.

Locker, T. (1986). *Sailing with the wind.* New York: Dial.

Martin, B., & Archambault, J. (1987). *Knots on a counting rope.* New York: Holt.

Pienkowski, J. (1983). *Small talk.* Los Angeles: Price, Stern, & Sloan.

Polacco, P. (1990). *Thunder cake.* New York: Philomel.

Steiner, T. (1976). *The warm fuzzy tale.* Sacramento, CA: Jalmar.

Tomkins, J. (1982). *Nimby.* New York: Green Tiger Press.

Literature/Writing

Browning, R., with Ianov, A. (1986). *The pied piper of Hamlin.* New York: Lothrip, Lee, & Shepard.

Cassedy, S. (1992). *Red dragonfly on my shoulder.* New York: HarperCollins.

Cummings, E.E. (1988). *Hist wist.* New York: Crown.

Dickinson, E. (1978). *I'm nobody! Who are you?* Owings Mills, MD: Stemmer House.

Dickinson, E., with Tudor, T. (1990). *A brighter garden.* New York: Philomel.

Eliot, T.S., with Le Cain, E. (1986). *Growltiger's last stand and other poems.* New York: Harcourt Brace Jovanovich.

Frost, R., with Jeffers, S. (1978). *Stopping by woods on a snowy evening.* New York: Dutton.

Heller, R. (1987). *A cache of jewels and other collective nouns.* New York: Grosset & Dunlap.

Longfellow, W., with Jeffers, S. (1983). *Hiawatha.* New York: Dial.

Melville, H., with Locker, T. (1991). *Catskill eagle.* New York: Philomel.

Stolz, M. (1993). *Say something.* New York: HarperCollins.

Thoreau, H., with Lowe, S. (1990). *Walden.* New York: Philomel.

Van Allsburg, C. (1984). *The mysteries of Harris Burdick.* Boston: Houghton Mifflin.

Wood, A. (1982). *Quick as a cricket.* Singapore: Child's Play International.

Anthropology

Aardema, V. (1981). *Bringing the rain to Kapiti.* New York: Dial.

Anno, M. (1981). *Anno's Britain.* New York: Philomel.
Baylor, B. (1978). *The way to start a day.* New York: Alladin.
Cox, D. (1983). *Ayu and the perfect moon.* Toronto: The Bodley Head.
de Paola, T. (1983). *The legend of the bluebonnet.* New York: Putnam.
Jeffers, S. (1991). *Brother eagle, sister sky.* New York: Dial.
Lim, J. (1981). *Merchants of the mysterious east.* Plattsburgh, NY: Tundra.
Musgrove, M. (1976). *Ashanti to Zulu.* New York: Dial.

Sociology

Buntins, E. (1988). *How many days to America?* New York: Clarion.
Provenson, A., & Provenson, M. (1987). *Shaker Lane.* New York: Viking.
Yolen, J. (1992). *Letting swift river go.* Boston: Little, Brown.

History

Aliki. (1983). *A medieval feast.* New York: Crowell.
Bedard, M. (1992). *Emily.* New York: Doubleday.
Blos, J. (1994). *The days before now.* New York: Simon & Schuster.
Buleigh, R. (1991). *Flight.* New York: Philomel.
Dragonwagon, C. (1990). *Home place.* New York: Macmillan.
Garland, S. (1993). *The lotus seed.* New York: Harcourt Brace Jovanovich.
Gerrard, R. (1988). *Sir Francis Drake: His daring deeds.* New York: Farrar, Straus, Giroux.
Goodall, J. (1986). *The story of a castle.* New York: Macmillan.
Goodall, J. (1987). *The story of a Main Street.* New York: Macmillan.
Hall, D. (1979). *The oxcart man.* New York: Viking.
Hartley, D. (1986). *Up north in winter.* New York: Dutton.
Hendershot, J. (1987). *In coal country.* New York: Knopf.
Johnston, T., & dePaola, T. (1990). *The quilt story.* New York: Putnam.
Knight, M. (1992). *Talking walls.* Gardiner, ME: Tilbury House.
Levinson, R. (1986). *Watch the stars come out.* New York: Dutton.
Lyon, G. (1992). *Who came down that road?* New York: Orchard.
Menton, T. (1977). *Victorian fashion paper dolls from Harper's Bazaar 1867-1898.* Mineola, NY: Dover.
Messenger, N. (1989). *Annabel's house.* New York: Orchard.
Muller, J. (1986). *The changing city.* New York: Antheneum.
Paul, A. (1991). *Eight hands round.* New York: HarperCollins.
Polacco, P. (1988). *The keeping quilt.* New York: Simon & Schuster.
Provenson, A., & Provenson, M. (1984). *Leonardo Da Vinci.* New York: Viking.
Rylant, C. (1982). *When I was young in the mountains.* New York: Dutton.
Seawall, M. (1986). *The Pilgrims of Plimoth.* New York: Atheneum.
Winter, J. (1988). *Follow the drinking gourd.* New York: Knopf.

Fine Arts or Aesthetics

Bell, A. (1986). *Swan lake*. Nadick, MA: Picture Book Studios.
Clement, C., & Clement, F. (1986). *The painter and the wild swans*. New York: Dial.
Clememt,C., & Clement, F. (1989). *The voice of the wood*. New York: Dial.
de Paola, T. (1989). *The art lesson*. New York: Putnam.
Fleischman, P. (1988). *Rondo in C*. New York: Harper & Row.
Locker, T. (1989). *The young artist*. New York: Dial.
Martin, B., & Archambault, J. (1988). *Listen to the rain*. New York: Holt.
Mayhew, J. (1989). *Katie's picture show*. New York: Orchard.
Raboff, E. (1979). *Paul Klee* (Art Start Books). New York: Doubleday.
Radin, R. (1989). *High in the mountains*. New York: Macmillan.
Rylant, C. (1988). *All I see*. New York: Orchard.
Venezia, M. (1988). *Van Gogh*. Chicago: Children's Press.

REFERENCES

Baum, S. (1990). The young gifted child: A dilemma in development. In C. Hedley (Ed.), *Cognition, curriculum and literacy* (pp. 137-147). Norwood, NJ: Ablex.

Baum, S. (in press). The role of teachers in identifying gifts in young children. In S Baum, S. Reis, & L. Maxfield (Eds.), *Nurturing gifts and talents of primary grade students*. Mansfield Center, CT: Creative Learning Press.

Bruner, J. (1966). *Toward a theory of instruction*. Cambridge, MA: Harvard University Press.

Cray-Andrews, M. (in press). Celebrating differences. In S. Baum, S. Reis, & L. Maxfield (Eds.), *Developing talent in young learners*. Mansfield Center, CT: Creative Learning Press.

Erickson, J. (1959). Identity and the life cycle. *Psychological Issues, 1*(1), 82-95.

Gardner, H. (1993). *Multiple intelligences: The theory in practice*. New York: Basic Books.

Kaplan, S. (1986) The Grid: A model to construct differentiated curriculum for the gifted. In J.S. Renzulli (Ed.), *Systems and models for developing programs for the gifted and talented* (pp 180-193). Mansfield Center, CT: Creative Learning Press.

Katz, L. (1988, January 18). Point of view. *New York Teacher, 4.*

Renzulli, J. (1978). What makes giftedness? Reexamining a definition. *Phi Delta Kappan, 60*, 180-184, 261.

Renzulli, J. (1994). *Schools for talent development: A practical plan for total school improvement*. Mansfield Center, CT: Creative Learning Press.

Van Tassel-Baska, J. (1993). *Comprehensive curriculum for gifted learners* (2nd ed.). Boston: Allyn & Bacon.

40

Appropriate Educational Programs for the Young Gifted Child: Curricular Concerns

Janice A. Jipson

It is a hot July afternoon. Erik gathers his *Jurassic Park* dinosaurs and his *Lion King* animals in a dirt pit in the backyard. He tells me that he will have to build movie sets because the creatures are not made in proper scale and did not even live at the same time or in the same place. He then forages through the lawn in search of appropriate vegetation and twigs to use in the scene and experiments with plastic, tin foil, and mud to attempt to create a pond that will hold water. As his frustration peaks, he storms to his room to play SIM LIFE on his computer, commenting that it is easier to be a "genetic engineer" and create sentient beings on computer.

Erik is 8. For the past several years, as the mother of a very bright little boy, I have struggled with the dilemma of providing "normal" childhood experiences for him and, at the same time, creating an environment that responds appropriately to his sometimes unusual interests and abilities. I ask myself, what is developmentally appropriate for a child like Erik?

THE ISSUE: APPROPRIATE EDUCATION FOR THE YOUNG GIFTED CHILD

During the past 20 years, educational institutions across the United States, as well as parents, have become increasingly aware of the important role of providing appropriate educational experiences for young talented and gifted children in their programs. Public schools have long debated the question of how best to improve the teaching of young gifted children in their kindergarten and primary classrooms. Day-care and preschool programs have also been confronted with the responsibility of providing experiences to meet the needs and interests of the unusually verbal, curious, creative, or active children entering their programs, children who seem bored with dolls and finger plays.

There are many questions regarding the implementation of curriculum for gifted children in early childhood classrooms (programs for children from age 3 through third grade). This chapter discusses current issues surrounding special provisions for students identified as being gifted and talented in early childhood and primary school programs and provides suggestions for integrating these provisions into the ongoing early childhood curriculum.

THE GIFTED CHILD AND DEVELOPMENTALLY APPROPRIATE PRACTICE

Questions about what constitutes developmentally and culturally appropriate early childhood education have been raised by many researchers (Bredekamp, 1987; Jipson, 1991; Lubeck, 1994). In June 1986, the National Association for the Education of Young Children (NAEYC) issued a position statement on developmentally appropriate practice in programs for young children. Based on research in developmental psychology, the NAEYC statement encompassed and extended the cognitive-developmental model and has become the dominant influence on early childhood education in the 1990s, thus providing the theoretical framework for contemporary curriculum development in early childhood education.

In their statement, the NAEYC emphasized that young children learn by participating in self-initiated, self-directed, and self-chosen activities (Lubeck, 1994) and that learning is a process resulting from the interaction of children's thinking with their experiences in the world. Through play, they asserted, children acquire knowledge about the physical and social worlds in which they live. The role of teachers is described as including the facilitation of children's learning through the preparation of the environment to provide a variety of stimulating and challenging materials and activities for the children. An analysis of some of the major components of the NAEYC statement in terms of young children with exceptional gifts and talents provides insight into the process of planning educational programs for these children.

CURRICULUM GOALS

The NAEYC statement described the goal of curriculum as developing children's knowledge and skills in all developmental areas: physical, social, and emotional, as well as intellectual. It also acknowledged the importance of developing the child's sense of self-esteem, sense of competence, and positive feelings toward learning. In its focus on the "whole" child, the NAEYC statement specifically broadened the scope of early childhood educational programs to include more than a focus on "cultural literacy," skills, and school-appropriate behavior.

In working with young gifted and talented children, one must recognize the importance of interconnections between all aspects of each child's development rather than focusing solely on a particular area of talent or accelerated intellectual achievement. Given the possibility of a widely varying range in cognitive, social, emotional, and physical abilities in young gifted children, it is critical to examine the complex possible interrelationships between different domains of abilities in considering what an appropriate educational experience might be. In other words, we must consider what is developmentally appropriate for a highly verbal, scientifically knowledgeable young boy who also has immature motor skills and age appropriate interests.

If, as the NAEYC statement advised, each child is viewed as developing at their own individual rate, and if, as they suggested, children are allowed to move at their own pace in acquiring important skills including those of writing, reading, spelling, math, and physical activity, the educational program for each child should emerge respecting and responding appropriately to each area of the child's development. Acceleration, tutoring, and supplemental pull-out programs and special classes must all be questioned as to their effectiveness in responding to the complex developmental needs of children in all domains.

The NAEYC statement also prescribed that curriculum should be integrated so that learning occurs primarily through play, projects, and learning centers reflecting the children's current interests and ideas. Teachers are to guide children's involvement in projects and enrich their learning experiences by extending children's ideas, responding to their questions, engaging them in conversation, and challenging their thinking. Central to this approach is the commitment to an emergent curriculum which responds to the changing interests of the children and the framing of that curriculum around questions which arise from each child's interactions with their environment. This expanded view of curriculum as potentially including everything that happens to the child again takes us beyond the focus on specific gifts and talents and redirects our attention to the possible connections between events in each child's life, experiences in school, and our interests as teachers.

THE TEACHING/LEARNING ENVIRONMENT

According to Williams and DeGaetano (1985), many early childhood teachers use the child-centered, developmentally based approach described earlier, acting as facilitators rather than as directors of children's learning. In these classrooms, teachers set up learning and activity centers based on their understanding of the children's interests, select experiences for individuals and groups of children, and interact with children in such a way as to introduce them to new ideas or to strengthen concepts already learned. The focus of these programs is on the child's processes of discovery and problem solving. Preparation of the environment to enhance such explorations becomes a central responsibility of the teacher along with the use of questions and dialog to further extend learning.

Children, in programs following the NAEYC practices, work and play cooperatively or independently in self-selected projects or activity centers. Much teacher planning effort goes into reflecting on the emerging interests of the children and preparing the environment and learning experiences to respond to these interests. The NAEYC guidelines suggested that materials and activities be concrete, real, and relevant to children's lives and include objects that can be manipulated and used in a variety of ways. Teacher encouragement of flexibility and reciprocity in the use of materials as well as regular and planned variations in the environment contribute to the effectiveness of this approach.

THE CURRICULUM IN USE

The continuing dilemma facing teachers, of course, is how to integrate the important and still-valued traditional goals of education into child-initiated activities in developmentally effective ways, while also responding appropriately to the often unanticipated needs of gifted and talented children in their classrooms. Current practice provides limited guidance for teachers faced with this challenge.

Numerous obstacles interfere with teachers' creation of developmentally appropriate curricula and instructional environments. From district- and building-level mandates on curriculum scope and sequence, to administrative and janitorial concerns about the physical appearance of the classroom, to parents' and other teachers' expectations, to resistance to implementing developmentally based curriculum, many external factors impinge on what children can experience in school.

Teachers may also lack available curricular materials to assist them in designing appropriate learning experiences that reflect the particular talents and abilities of the children in their classrooms. State-level curriculum frameworks and compendiums of essential learning skills still tend to focus on the cognitive domain. Teacher activity and thematic idea books do not respond appropriately to the breadth or intensity of children's multiple interests, nor are they usually sensitive to the potentially wide differences among various aspects of a child's development. Packaged curriculum, whether commercial or state mandated, frequently underserves all children in the classroom.

INCIDENTAL TEACHING

One effective strategy for planning and implementing developmentally appropriate early childhood curriculum to include the gifted and talented is the incidental teaching model (Allen & Ruggles, 1982). Used in conjunction with traditional practices of unit based curriculum, dramatic play centers, and story sharing, incidental teaching allows the teacher to integrate many aspects of the child's classroom experience with the child's unique developmental needs and abilities.

Incidental teaching is based on the belief that learning is an active process and should involve the whole child in developmentally appropriate experiences. Incidental teaching also seems consistent with Tharp and Gallimore's (1988) idea of assisted performance because it involves the teacher responding to child initiated activity in such a way as to extend the child's learning or to evoke another response from the child; that is, to assist the child's performance.

In the incidental teaching model, the child is the initiator of what happens to her in the classroom, often interacting with interesting activities and materials in the environment. The teacher is a facilitator, responding to the child so as to extend the learning of the moment, but also ensuring that the child continues uninterrupted in her exploration. Teaching occurs as the teacher asks for elaboration and tries to guide the child to the next step or idea or, conversely, stands aside and allows the exploration proceed without his or her interference.

Incidental teaching is especially important during child-initiated activity periods, when the child's interest level is presumably high. It is also an effective technique to use informally with children, individually and in small groups, as they bring to school their experiences, concerns, and interests. Rather than fragmenting children's experiences into separate subject-related areas, this approach permits teachers to integrate across all areas of the curriculum and emphasizes the interdependence of the personal and the formal, of experience and knowledge. Foremost, it allows the teacher to extend activities and experiences in the classroom to meet the individual needs of all children.

THEMATIC INSTRUCTION

An incidental teaching strategy lends itself well to thematic instruction. A thematic unit or project approach involves the integration of different subject areas around a common topical or conceptual theme. It provides a natural environment for the application of an incidental teaching model in that the thematic coherence across the day allows for multiple opportunities for curricular individualization. Unit or project themes revolving around topics such as jobs, houses, pets, or food let children discover and inquire about interesting puzzles in their personal environments, about differences between cultures in their classroom or communities, about similarities among people, and about problems that they have experienced. The curiosity and expressed interest of children can become the basis for these units of study (e.g., *The Lion King* leads to a unit on African animals), which can then provide multiple points of incidental entry at many levels of ability. From listening to stories about lions to writing stories, from identifying animals to classifying species, from constructing sandbox environments to creating clay models, the curriculum expands in response to each child.

Units based on conceptual themes have great potential for matching the needs and interests of the young gifted child because they open the curriculum to a richer variety of experiences. In conceptual units, concepts such as transformation, power, interdependence, or relationship can be explored across traditional subject and activity area domains. As children explore their environments, they can puzzle over what happens when they transform sand by adding water or shaving cream to it, what happens when they change the end of a story, what happens when they play a phonograph record at a faster speed, or what happens when there is not enough juice to go around at snack time. As they predict, experiment, and observe how the concept of transformation operates in their classroom, children bring their own level of understanding and interest to each activity.

Within both approaches to thematic-based units, children's literature, story sharing, and dramatic play permit the teacher to approach children's interests and concerns in a responsive and focused manner. The abundance and availability of high-quality, well-illustrated books for young children facilitates teacher selections. The typical early childhood classroom includes materials and props such as sand, paint, blocks, and paper, which can be used in multiple ways to encourage imagination and pretending. These materials along with found objects (such as junk, paper towel tubes, sticks, and shells) and familiar household items (such as measuring cups, shaving cream, buttons, and aluminum foil) provide an interesting and intriguing setting for the spontaneous discoveries of the child and for the reflective responses of the teacher.

CONCLUSION

As children are identified as having special gifts and talents, the focus becomes one of how they are different from their peers rather than on the perhaps larger similarities across children. Rather than providing experiences that enhance each child's personal and unique development, the tendency is to prescribe a qualitatively different curriculum, to provide alternative and sometimes separate educational experiences, or to accelerate the child within the standard curricular scope and sequence.

The goal, therefore, for those interested in educational provisions for gifted and talented primary and preprimary children should be the development, for all children, of student-centered curriculum. Critical is the creation of educational programs that are intellectually challenging and enriching and which also allow each child to explore and experiment in his or her own way, using his or her own skills and strengths. If curriculum is truly developmentally and culturally appropriate, then the needs of the gifted and talented child will be met.

REFERENCES

Allen, B., & Ruggles, C. (1982). Analysis of teacher-child interaction patterns in the preschool setting. In E. Edgar (Ed.), *Mentally handicapped children: Education and thinking* (pp. 151-168). Baltimore: University Park Press.

Bredekamp, S. (Ed.). (1987). *Developmentally appropriate practice in early childhood programs serving children from birth through age 8.* Washington, DC: National Association for the Education of Young Children.

Jipson, J. (1991). Developmentally appropriate practice: Culture, cur-
    riculum, connections. *Early Education and Development, 2*(2),
    137-152.
Lubeck, S. (1994). The politics of developmentally appropriate practice:
    Exploring issues of culture, class, and curriculum. In B. Mallory & R.
    New (Eds.), *Diversity and developmentally appropriate practices:
    Challenges for early childhood education* (pp. 17-43). New York:
    Teachers College Press.
National Association for the Education of Young Children (1986).
    Position statement on developmentally appropriate practice in
    programs for 4- and 5-year olds. *Young Children, 41,* 6.
Tharp, R., & Gallimore, R. (1988). *Rousing minds to life: Teaching, learn-
    ing, and schooling in social context.* Cambridge, England:
    Cambridge University Press.
Williams, L., & DeGaetano, Y. (1985). *Alerta: A multicultural, bilingual
    approach to teaching young children.* Menlo Park, CA: Addison-
    Wesley.

41

Technology-Based Instruction for Young Gifted Children*

Sandra L. Berger
Jay McIntire

EDUCATING CHILDREN FOR AN UNKNOWN FUTURE

By the time today's young gifted children become adults, the world will be very different. We have no idea what the future will look like, just that the children will mold it. In many ways, we are educating children for the unknown. The future will, in large part, be driven by new and emerging technologies, and young gifted children will be the engineers as well as the users.

Gifted learners, like all people, construct knowledge by modifying internal representations of the world in order to account for new experiences and ideas. Learning is an interactive process. Greater degrees of interaction with complex, but interesting, environments tend to result in more learning. The major goal of educators should be

---

*The ideas expressed in this chapter are the authors', and do not necessarily represent the views of The Council for Exceptional Children.

"expanding the quantity and quality of ways in which a learner is exposed to content and context" (Caine & Caine, 1991, p. 5). Recent advances in technology provide opportunities for learners, young and old, to do just that.

Technology, applied appropriately, shifts instruction from a teacher-as-expert model toward one of shared responsibility for learning (McClellan, 1985). "Chalk and talk" lessons can be supplemented by CD-ROMs, laser discs, interactive television, multimedia learning centers, computer simulations, and telecommunications technologies. Children become authors and creators of knowledge, rather than just receivers.

One of the most frequently used technologies is the Internet, a global, dynamic system of computer networks with millions of documents, resources, databases, and a variety of methods for communicating. Approximately 30 million people are currently linked to the Internet, and current estimates are that the Internet will have 100 million people online by 1998 (Ellsworth, 1994). The Internet has become a primary education resource, and many predict that it will become the technology of choice by the year 2000 because of the quantity, quality, and organization of available information. It can be used by young children as well as adults to communicate, retrieve information resources, and develop new products.

Recent statements by U.S. Government officials indicate a goal that most public schools will be connected to the Internet by the year 2000. Teachers who have not had direct contact with newer technologies will have difficulty making use of this tool. They need professional training, encouragement, and administrative support to ensure that they are teaching their students to live and work in a global community where information and technology go hand in hand. Because parents are a child's first teachers, they also should become at least familiar enough with educational technology to guide their children's explorations.

Technologies such as the Internet are not ends unto themselves, but can support achievement of valid instructional objectives and goals across the curriculum (McClellan, 1985). In part, this chapter offers information on some ways that technology is being used to accomplish important educational goals that might otherwise be difficult to achieve. Most of the examples used here are Internet-based because with a computer, a modem, appropriate software, and an Internet account, the resources are free, but reaching and using those resources can be a daunting task without some guidance.

Mann (1994), in one of the few articles written about gifted education and technology, indicated that the way students interact with technology supports their constructing knowledge:

[In constructivist-based classrooms] . . . students assume much of the responsibility for determining what to learn and how to learn it. Taskmasters in the form of teachers and technology assist by coaching and providing access to the information and skills needed by the learner. . . . To learn, the student must venture from what is known and construct a new reality. Through this process, the student learns how to learn. (p. 173)

TECHNOLOGICAL CONTRIBUTIONS TO EDUCATION

Morgan (1993) described three categories of ways in which technology can contribute to education: (a) increasing productivity; (b) exposing students to new technology; and (c) enhancing the instructional environment. Here we discuss how each of these relate to young gifted children, then offer some ways in which technology can contribute to differentiating instruction specifically for young gifted learners.

Increasing Productivity

Individuals who have written and revised papers by using pencils, pens, typewriters, and reams of paper and who now use word processors are aware that technology allows us to produce more than we ever could before. Writing still involves selecting a topic, generating ideas, writing, and revising, but we are freed from the task of constant rewriting each time we want to explore an option. Cutting and pasting of paragraphs has been replaced with moving text within a document. Time and energy can now be directed toward manipulating and interacting with ideas—the very process of constructing knowledge.

For young children, manipulating a keyboard or a mouse is developmentally possible, whereas manipulating a pencil is possible for only brief periods of time. Feldman (1986), in his book on child prodigies, described Randy, a boy who spontaneously began writing at age 3 and wrote poems, essays, stories, and plays amounting to thousands of pages by the time he was 8. It seems unlikely that Randy would have developed his prodigious skill were it not for his discovery of the typewriter. Feldman wrote: "The importance of the technology of the typewriter to Randy's writing should also not be underestimated. . . . He simply could not manipulate paper and pencil well enough to express himself adequately with these tools" (p. 53). Randy's gift might have gone undetected and unnurtured without technological assistance. The young potential computer geniuses of today benefit from early exposure. For these children and others, not only does technology offer increased productivity; it opens up vast content and domain options.

Exposing Students To Emerging Technologies

Randy was fortunate to have extraordinary writing ability at a young age and also was fortunate to live in a family where he saw both of his parents typing. Randy taught himself to type while watching his father spend hours at the typewriter writing a novel. Although the typewriter was hardly "emerging" in the 1980s, one would assume that Randy took to computer keyboarding more easily than did his age peers.

To the extent children are familiar with today's cutting-edge technology, tomorrow's unknowns will seem a logical progression and nonthreatening. Among the leaders in society today is a sizable subgroup who rely on their junior partners, assistants, secretaries, graduate students, or their own children to produce technological solutions to problems that could not be solved without those technologies:

> At the rate computer technology changes, attitudes towards the technology may be as important as skills with a specific machine. Individuals who are not anxious, but rather view computers positively and are confident about their ability to use computers, will be more likely to learn whatever skills are required by future developments in hardware and software. (Sutton, 1991, p. 487)

Enhancing the Instructional Environment

For children, every setting is a learning environment and a potential instructional environment. Children who experience a wider variety of instructional environments or more complex environments are more likely to discover domains that match their interests, skills, and learning styles. Radio and television have expanded the horizons of children by providing opportunities to see and hear places and things they could not have experienced otherwise. These media, at their best, have provided a world of information for children to absorb. Unfortunately, the public has demanded radio and television programming with simple, rather than complex, ideas. Caine and Caine (1991) wrote:

> Children growing up with "electronic miracles" are different. They live in a world of vast media and technological input that entertains and influences them in both conscious and unconscious ways. . . . Unfortunately, television, audio tapes, and CD players do not allow students to raise searching questions, enter into debate, formulate their own ideas, develop a moral philosophy, engage in problem solving or critical thinking, or test their view of reality. (p. 17)

More recent innovations, such as computers, CD ROM, the Internet, and image processing allow students to actively engage information, solve problems, and construct more complex understandings of the world. These technologies, like television and radio before them, are likely to provide some great learning options while offering even more simple or inane ones. It will fall on parents, teachers, and other adults to assist children in selecting among the plethora of choices. Some technologies, such as virtual reality, actually allow children to construct their own realities.

DIFFERENTIATION FOR GIFTED CHILDREN

Maker (1982) suggested that differentiation of instruction for gifted learners can take place in four dimensions: (a) content; (b) process; (c) product; and (d) learning environment. Technologies are underutilized in each of these areas. Goldberg (1994) pointed out, "The typical check-out counter has a higher level of technology than the typical classroom."

Content

The study of technology itself is one which interests many curious gifted children. Feldman (1986), in discussing domains in which prodigiousness is likely to occur, suggested that such domains have highly organized knowledge bases and complex symbol systems. He stated that computer programming is "a domain that fairly screams its availability for prodigies" (p. 89).

Technology offers access to more information, a wider variety of content, and more complex and abstract content for highly able learners. A wide range of lesson plans can be found on the Internet. Twenty-five years ago, when one of the authors wanted to respond to her daughter's barrage of questions about dinosaurs, *Dinosaurs and Other Prehistoric Animals* (Geis, 1959) was an extremely rich resource. Now, by connecting to the AskERIC Virtual Library (ericir.syr.edu), one can access lessons on making a dinosaur fossil, brainstorming exercises, suggested readings about dinosaurs and the work of paleontologists, and directions for building replicas of different types of dinosaurs (see the Appendix for information on specific Internet sites). No longer is a creative teacher limited to the books in the school library when searching out advanced content that is directly or thematically related to the educational content being studied by other children. Teachers can search lesson plans in places such as the AskERIC Virtual Library (ericir.syr.edu) or BigSky Internet site (bigsky.bigsky.dillon.mt.us), facilitating curriculum differentiation.

Technological resources are appropriate in a wide variety of settings, whether you are home schooling, providing summer enrichment, or extending the curriculum in specific subject areas. Educational opportunities are available via the Internet, interactive television, computer telephony, and other media. New books emerge regularly that describe specific details regarding the use of these media (e.g., Ellsworth, 1994).

Process

Many applications of technology require higher level thinking processes. Gifted children can interact with information through technology and can organize, analyze, and synthesize information. For example, in teaching about space science education, teachers can obtain resources and lesson plans from the NASA Spacelink Internet site (spacelink.msfc.nasa.gov). Students can use the Argonne National Laboratory online bulletin board service and "Ask a Scientist" (newton.dep.anl.gov), as well as "Ask Mr. Science" (apscichs@ pen.k12.va.us), an Internet-based, student-run question-answering service. Teachers can construct projects around a question such as "If an extraterrestrial came to your town, what would you show it, where would you take it and why, what food would you share with it?"

Technology can be used to allow highly gifted children who do not have access to achievement level peers in their grade or neighborhood to interact with others like themselves. Gifted children who learn how to communicate via e-mail can share and gather information from distant places and from people with different experiences than can be found locally. For example, using KIDLINK (ftp: VM1.NoDak.EDU; telnet: 134.129.111.1), an Internet network of students, one classroom spent a week charting weather in different parts of the world. They had agreed to exchange weather-related information with classrooms around the world, and received daily weather information from students in distant geographic locations.

Because the purpose of much of the educational technology is information finding, gathering, and organizing, young children are likely to discover new areas of interest in their explorations of the media. The open-endedness of communication systems allow children to have choices and greatly diminish the likelihood that a child will already know all of the information available.

Some software makes it very easy for children to explore different ways that information can be organized or symbolized. Children have very clear ideas about whether a set of data looks best as a line graph, a pie chart, or some other graphic form. Because they can easily convert data from one graphic representation to another, they incidentally learn a great deal about how numbers can be shown and how to understand tables and graphs.

Product

Young children can learn to search a CD-ROM for examples of a concept and easily create complex demonstrations showing the full range of their knowledge and organizational and communication skills. Multimedia products are no longer limited to boardrooms; they can be found in classrooms—but only in classrooms of teachers who allow and encourage students to actively explore and create the newest media in order to construct their own knowledge and their own ways of communicating knowledge.

Recently, a 5-year-old student demonstrated to the authors an automated Lego structure that retrieved bricks from one location and placed them in a different location. During this project, a group of young students collaborated to learn how to program a computer to send commands to the Lego structure, and built the structure to carry out the computer's commands. "This is a computer!" a kindergarten child excitedly explained. Pointing to a "Hot Button" icon on the screen, he said, "Press this button and I'll show you something." A hand-held robotic control then sent the command to the computer and the Lego structure. The children who demonstrated the project provided a detailed description of how they learned to program the computer. They were very proud of the results.

By freeing young children from the developmental barriers of producing traditional products, (which often require fine motor skills beyond their years), we allow them the opportunity to communicate a greater extent of their knowledge. Too often the gifted children who have a two-page essay in mind tire out after writing a paragraph, or else they get so frustrated at the illegibility of their own printing that their products are more a measure of their frustration level than their ability to manipulate content and organize information.

Learning Environment

Through the use of technology, students can interact with high-level, complex, open-ended content in nearly any environment. Not only can they work independently, they can be grouped for learning with children or adults who are hundreds of miles away. Because of the complexity and nonlinearity of the experiences available via technology, children share the organization of learning with teachers. Teachers in highly technological learning environments become information resources and specialists in helping children organize and direct their own learning.

Concerns have been raised (Webb & Shavelson, 1985) that students working on computers are so independent that they lose out on interactions with classmates. Hawkins, Sheingold, Gearhart, and Berger (cited in Sutton, 1991) found that more social interactions take place between students when they are working on computers than take place when they work without them. Although computers and other technologies provide advantages for individualized instruction, they also have applications for group and collaborative work. Groups of students throughout the nation have collaborated in a wide variety of activities. One interesting ongoing project, The Earth Day Treasure Hunt (Douglas & Levin, 1992), is a networking project that involves students in history, math, map reading, geography, and writing. Participating classrooms were asked to submit clues by e-mail describing a geographical place. All clues from across the country were compiled and sent back to participating teams prior to Earth Day. Students were asked to conduct the hunt on Earth Day if possible.

Stephanie Tolan (1985), herself a mother of a highly gifted child, noted that "Exceptionally gifted children typically learn by total immersion" (p. 24). Not all learning environments have enough content in which to immerse oneself, and often children are not given large blocks of time in which to process complex situations via immersion. It has been noted that the simulated environments found in complex video games have exactly the qualities that lead to immersion (Feldman, 1986). Although most commercially available video products have little directly to do with educational concepts, some software is available that seeks to take educational advantage of the medium. Pattridge (1994) suggested that some of the following criteria be considered in selecting educational software:

- The level is sufficiently wide ranging to maintain interest
- Teaches educational curriculum
- Develops higher level thinking skills
- Requires outside research/decision making
- Provides extensive feedback

These suggestions correspond well to those made by proponents of both constructivist learning (Strommen & Lincoln, 1992), and "brain-based learning" (Caine & Caine, 1991).

ENVISIONING THE FUTURE

A federal report (U.S. Department of Education, 1994) on the use of time in American classrooms stated:

> Technology is a great unrealized hope in education reform. It can transform learning by improving both the effectiveness of existing time and making more time available through self-guided instruction, both in school and out. Technology has already changed much of

the rest of American society—profit and nonprofit, private sector and government alike—because it makes it possible to produce more with less. A similar revolution is possible in education. (p. 37)

REFERENCES

Caine, R. N., & Caine, G. (1991). *Making connections: Teaching and the human brain*. Alexandria, VA: Association for Supervision and Curriculum Development.

Douglas, C., & Levin, S. (1992). *The Earth Day treasure hunt*. A project designed at the University of Illinois Department of Curriculum and Instruction. (Internet address: gopher.cic.net; cicnet-gophers/K12-gopher/classroom/earth-day)

Ellsworth, J. (1994). *Education on the Internet*. Indianapolis, IN: Sams.

Feldman, D. H. (1986). *Nature's gambit*. New York: Basic Books.

Geis, D. (1959). *Dinosaurs and other prehistoric animals*. New York: Grosset & Dunlap.

Goldberg, M. (1994, December 9). *National Commission on Time and Learning*. Unpublished speech presented at the meeting of the Javits Gifted and Talented Students Education Program, Washington, DC.

Maker, C. J. (1982). *Curriculum development for the gifted*. Austin, TX: Pro-ed.

Mann, C. (1994). New technologies and gifted education. *Roeper Review, 16*, 172-177.

McClellan, E. (1985). *Technology for the gifted and talented*. (ERIC digest ED262514)

Morgan, T. D. (1993). Technology: An essential tool for gifted & talented education. *Journal for the Education of the Gifted, 16*, 358-371.

Pattridge, G. (1994). Software challenges for the gifted. *Understanding Our Gifted, 7*(2), 1, 10-12.

Strommen, E. F., & Lincoln, B. (1992). Constructivism, technology, and the future of classroom learning. *Education and Urban Society, 24*(4), 466-476.

Sutton, R. E. (1991). Equity and computers in the schools: A decade of research. *Review of Educational Research, 61*, 475-503.

Tolan, S. S. (1985 November/December). Stuck in another dimension: The exceptionally gifted child in school. *G/C/T, 41*, 22-26.

U.S. Department of Education. (1994). *Prisoners of time. Report of the National Education Commission on Time and Learning*. Washington, DC: Author.

Webb, N. M., & Shavelson, R. J. (1985). Computers, education, and educational psychologists. *Educational Psychologist, 20*(4), 163-165.

APPENDIX: MAJOR INTERNET LINKS AND SOURCES OF INFORMATION

This section provides some Internet address for the resources mentioned throughout this chapter. The authors assume that readers who pursue the information have access to a reference book that provides basic information on connecting to the Internet and reaching particular sites.

SITE NAME:
AskERIC (ERIC Clearinghouse on Information and Technology): askeric@ericir.syr.edu
Internet Address: ftp, telnet, or gopher: ericir.syr.edu
URL: http.eric.syr.edu
Description: AskERIC and the AskERIC Virtual Library provide a host of online services, including searchable K-12 lesson plans in each academic discipline. Many Internet site menus include pointers to the Internet-based AskERIC question-answering service (askeric@ericir.syr.edu).
Login Sequence: Telnet to <ericir.syr.edu> and type "gopher" at the login prompt.

SITE NAME:
Big Sky Telegraph
Internet Addresses: bigsky.bigsky.dillon.mt.us;
  telnet: 192.231.192.1
Description: Big Sky Telegraph is a user-friendly network that offers resources for any level telecommunicator and a multitude of ideas for use in classrooms. From lesson plans to science labs, there is something for any teacher of students K-12. Library resources, bulletin boards, and community networks are available.
Login Sequence:
1. At Telnet prompt type open bigsky.bigsky.dillon.mt.us
2. When asked to login, as a visitor, type bbs
3. You will be asked the following information before you reach the main bulletin board:
a. Your name, first and last
b. Your city and state
c. Your password—invent something simple, it must be a four number password
Remember, out of courtesy, to limit your visits as a guest to 20-minute periods!
Exit Sequence:
1. From (F)iles, ^K exits the listings.
2. When back at Main Menu, G is for Goodbye.
3. From telnet prompt, type bye

SITE NAME: NASA SpaceLINK
Internet Addresses: spacelink.msfc.nasa.gov
telnet: 128.158.13.250
URL: http://spacelink.msfc.nasa.gov/
Description: This database is arranged to provide access to current and historical information on NASA aeronautics and space research. Also included are suggested classroom activities that incorporate information on NASA projects to teach a number of scientific principles.
Login Sequence:
First time only: user-id: newuser
password: newuser
Exit Sequence:
Go to the main menu by typing "1" at any submenu. At the main menu type 1 to log off NASA Spacelink.

SITE NAME:
Newton
Internet Addresses: newton.dep.anl.gov
telnet: 130.202.92.50
Description: Newton is an educational Bulletin Board Service (BBS) sponsored by the Argonne National Laboratory Division of Educational Programs. The purpose of this BBS is to promote the networking of teachers and students and the exchange of ideas. This site is primarily aimed at teachers in the science and math fields. Any novice should be able to navigate this BBS.
Services: It has most the features of any BBS. The group menu selection and teaching topics menu will be of interest to all teachers. In particular, the discussion submenu choice from the group menu has many interesting choices, such as "Ask A Scientist," "Teacher talk on Science, Math, and Engineering," etc.
Login Sequence:
Login as cocotext.
At the Menu select item 1 (specify your signon name).
First time users will need to signup for using the BBS by typing new at the signon prompt.
Exit Sequence:
Return to the main menu and select 5 (signoff).

SITE NAME: KIDLINK
Internet Address: ftp: VM1.NoDak.EDU or telnet: 134.129.111.1
LISTSERV@vm1.nodak.edu or LISTSERV@NDSUVM1.BITNET
Description: A huge global pen pals network for kids, with many parts and projects. KIDLINK's purpose is the dialog itself.

There are no political objectives. All children in all countries between the age of 10 and15 are invited. Many thousands of kids are currently involved. Includes and art gallery of digitized artwork from children around the world. For more information send the message GET KIDS-93 GENERAL to LISTSERV@vm1.nodak.edu.

Biographical Information

Susan Baum is past President of the Association of the Education of Gifted Underachieving Students (AEGUS), and Associate Professor at the College of New Rochelle. In addition to teaching, her professional activities include consulting, writing, and researching in the areas of gifted learning disabled, primary, underachieving, and economically disadvantaged students.

Susan F. Belgrad is Assistant Professor of Education at Roosevelt University, Program Director of Early Childhood Studies and Coordinator of the Master of Arts in Teacher Leadership. She is the author of *The Portfolio Connection* and has written many articles on early childhood with a focus on developmentally appropriate practices.

Sandra L. Berger is Information Specialist, Gifted Education, for the ERIC Clearinghouse on Disabilities and Gifted Education, The Council for Exceptional Children, Reston, VA. She has spoken throughout the country and is author of *College Planning for Gifted Students*. She is currently focusing on the integration of technology into classroom practices.

Patricia Reid Brooks is Principal of Heather Hills Elementary School, a talented and gifted magnet school in Bowie, MD. She has been a TAG (Talented and Gifted) specialist in Prince George's County School District in Maryland and was a classroom teacher for 23 years.

Barbara Clark is Professor in the Division of Special Education at California State University, Los Angeles, where she is Coordinator for graduate programs in the area of gifted education. Past President of the National Association for Gifted Children and current President of the World Council for Gifted and Talented Children, she is author of the internationally used text, *Growing Up Gifted*, now in its fifth edition.

Starr Cline is Adjunct Instructor in the graduate division at Adelphi University in Garden City, NY, as well as Coordinator of the gifted elementary school program in the Herricks School District. Author of several books, she has lectured extensively, and conducted seminars on independent study and creativity in the U.S. and abroad.

LeoNora M. Cohen is Associate Professor of Education at Oregon State University at Corvallis and has focused her research and writing on gifted young children. She is author of the book, *Coping for Capable Kids*, of the monograph, *Teaching Young Gifted Children*, and *Great Expectations*, a professional development package introducing educators to gifted education.

Carolyn Cummings has been a classroom teacher, a consultant for early childhood education, and a university lecturer for over 30-years. Most recently she helped write *Early Childhood Standards of Quality for Prekindergarten Through Second Grade* for the Michigan Department of Education.

Hazel J. Feldhusen is a teacher at Cumberland Elementary School in Indiana and a recent winner of the Golden Apple Award from the Chicago Foundation for Excellence in Teaching. Through extensive writings and workshops throughout the U.S. and abroad, she demonstrates the positive effects of utilizing gifted research as it applies both to the young and to the gifted.

John F. Feldhusen is Robert B. Kane Distinguished Professor of Education at Purdue University in Indiana. Director of the Purdue Gifted Education Resource Institute, Editor of the *Gifted Child Quarterly*, and Distinguished Scholar in the National Association for Gifted Children, he is the author of over 300 articles, books, and reports, and has consulted and made presentations in 12 countries.

Maurice D. Fisher established the Gifted Education Press, located in Manassas, VA, in 1981—a company that distributes its books to many school districts, parents, and libraries across the nation—and publishes the *Gifted Education Press Quarterly*. He is currently working for the Fairfax County of Virginia Public Schools in program evaluation, research, statistics, and computer applications. He has lectured throughout the country.

Judith A. Gelbrich was a special education and elementary school teacher for 14 years. She currently works as an educational consultant for a major computer company and on special projects for the University of Oregon Department of Special Education.

Judith Wynn Halsted is an educational consultant for gifted children and their families in northern Michigan. An author of several books, she has also taught classed for parents and teachers on emotional and enrichment needs of the gifted, and directed a gifted program for preprimary and primary students in an independent school.

Gail E. Hanninen is Senior Faculty/Director of Department of Special Education of City University in Renton, WA. She has been Washington State Supervisor of Gifted Education and Dropout Prevention Programs, and has published her work with preschool and highly gifted students in rural areas and, more recently, with gifted students at risk of dropping out.

Pamela Hildebrand is an Australian educator who pioneered the development of a private learning center in Melbourne, specializing in teaching exceptional (learning disabled and gifted) children and adults to read and write. Her book, The *Reading Connection*, is currently used in primary schools and adult education centers throughout Australia.

Patricia Duggins Hoelscher is Curriculum Enrichment Specialist for the Clayton School District in St. Louis, MO. She served as Supervisor of Gifted Education for the Missouri Department of Education, has taught preschool through graduate school, and has published widely in the areas of gifted education, curriculum development, and early childhood.

Patricia L. Hollingsworth is Director for The University of Tulsa School for Gifted Children, the editor of the *Network News Quarterly*, and now serves on the Board of Directors of the National Association for Gifted Children. She is a writer, consultant, and speaker in gifted education.

Janice A. Jipson is Associate Professor of Education at Sonoma State University in California. In addition to many years of teaching college, her professional experience includes nursery school director, Head Start Coordinator, school psychologist, and learning disabilities teacher.

Margie K. Kitano is Associate Dean for Faculty Development and Research for the College of Education at San Diego State University, and previously established and directed the New Mexico State University Preschool for the Gifted. She is a licensed psychologist in New Mexico and California, and has written extensively on identification and programming for young gifted children.

Bertie Kingore is Shelton Professor of Education and Chairperson, Elementary-Secondary Education at Hardin-Simmons University in Texas. Texas Gifted Educator of the Year in 1992 and a keynote speaker at numerous conferences, she has recently written several books, including The *Kingore Observation Inventory*.

Dorothy Knopper, owner of Open Space Communications, is Editor/Publisher of the journal *Understanding Our Gifted*. She has been Colorado State Consultant for Gifted/Talented education, an instructor of teacher education at the University of Colorado, and Consultant for Gifted/Talented Education at Wayne County Intermediate School District in Michigan.

Judy Leimbach taught gifted elementary students in Glen Ellyn, IL for 14 years. She teaches graduate courses and leads workshops in gifted education and has developed and co-authored a range of challenging curriculum materials for primary grade students, including *Primarily Thinking*, *Math Extension Units*, and *Primary Book Reporter*.

Elaine S. LeVine is a professor of Social Work at New Mexico State University, where she teaches courses in family theory and family systems intervention. She maintains a full-time private practice in child and family psychotherapy through her clinic, The Center through the Looking Glass, in Las Cruces, NM.

Corliss J. McCallister is an educational psychologist who has been involved in gifted preschool education since 1983 as a parent, teacher, curriculum-writer, consultant, and researcher. She also serves as an adjunct faculty member at Southeast Missouri State University in Cape Girardeau, MO.

Jay McIntire is Policy Specialist for Governmental Regulations of the Council for Exceptional Children, Reston, VA. Former director of gifted education programs and author of many publications, he has focused his writing on the general field of gifted education and on educational policy that impacts gifted students and children with disabilities.

Elizabeth A. Meckstroth is a licensed professional counselor and is currently Director of the Center for Gifted Resources in Evanston, IL. She is co-author of *Guiding the Gifted Child: A Practical Source for Parents and Teachers*, which received the American Psychological Association's 1983 award for "Best Book." and also a co-author of *Teaching Young Gifted Children in the Regular Classroom*.

Linda Meininger is consulting teacher for gifted programs in the Lincoln Public Schools, Lincoln, Nebraska. She has served the National Association for Gifted Children as Chairman of the Division of Early Childhood, has given numerous presentations, and has written articles on the young gifted child. She is a trainer for Nebraska's Starry Night, a Behavioral Observation Protocol for Early Identification.

William Nash is Professor of Educational Psychology and Director of the Institute for the Gifted and Talented at Texas A&M University in College Station, TX. Past President of the National Association for Gifted Children, he was recently co-principal investigator for a U.S. Department of Education Jacob Javits Grant on gifted children from economically disadvantaged backgrounds.

Rosa Isela Perez is Curriculum Resource Teacher for the San Diego City Schools, Gifted and Talented Program. She has spoken widely and written many articles on multicultural primary gifted children and has served as Project Manager for two federal projects—the Javits and Title VII.

Philip A. Perrone is Professor of Counseling Psychology at the University of Wisconsin at Madison. For 10 years he directed the Guidance Institute for Talented Students—a research through service program—and has written three books, 12 monographs, and over 80 research studies.

Phyllis J. Perry has been active in public education for almost 30 years, including 8 years as Director of Talented and Gifted Education for the Boulder Valley Public Schools, CO. She currently writes for teachers, parents, and children and consults as Project Director for Boulder Valley 2000, working on the national Goals 2000 effort.

Jane Piirto, formerly Principal of Hunter College Elementary School in New York City, is currently Professor of Education at Ashland University in Ohio. She has written a number of articles and books focusing on creativity including, *Understanding Those Who Create* and *Talented Children and Adults: Their Development and Education*.

Tom Potter is founder and Executive Director of the Parent Education Program, Inc., in New York. He has founded the Cattaraugus-Allegany Association for the Education of Young Children and is the current President of Prosperous Mentors' Association, a national counseling organization.

Gina Ginsberg Riggs is Executive Director of the Gifted Child Society in Glen Rock, NJ, where she has served 45,000 students over a 40-year period. She has written many articles and two books—*How to Help Your Gifted Child* and *Parentspeak*. She has spoken, lectured, and led workshops in all states in the U.S. except three, and has served on the board of the National Association for Gifted Children.

Sylvia B. Rimm is a psychologist and Director of the Family Achievement Clinic at MetroHealth Medical Center in Cleveland, OH, as well as a member of the Board of Directors of the National Association for Gifted Children. An international speaker and consultant, she has authored many books and articles on gifted children. She is a clinical professor of Psychiatry and Pediatrics at Case Western Reserve University School of Medicine and is a contributing correspondent for *The Today Show*.

Jessie Hugh Butler Sanders is a teacher, guidance counselor, director of gifted programs, and special education coordinator at elementary and secondary schools, colleges, and universities. Her publications include local and regional articles on gifted education, especially in the areas of preprimary and primary.

Beverly D. Shaklee is Professor in Special Education-Gifted at Kent State University in Ohio. Through the Jacob Javits grant, she has coordinated a three-year research project, Early Assessment for Exceptional Potential. She also directs the Academically Talented Teacher Education Program (ATTEP), recognized in 1990 as a Distinguished Program in Teacher Education by the Association of Teacher Educators.

Dorothy A. Sisk, the Dorothy Anne and C. W. Conn Professor in Gifted Education, is the founding Director of the Gifted Child Center, Director of the Center for Creativity, Innovation and Leadership at Lamar University in Beaumont, TX, and Editor of *Gifted International*. Former Director of the Office of Gifted and Talented in Washington, DC., she has written many volumes and articles on gifted education and leadership, including a recent book with E. Paul Torrance on the gifted child in the regular classroom.

Joan Franklin Smutny is Founder and Director of the Center for Gifted at National-Louis University in Evanston, IL and the 1996 recipient of the National Association for Gifted Children's Distinguished Service Award. An active teacher (preprimary to graduate level), lecturer, and co-author of four books, she most recently co-wrote *Teaching Young Gifted Children in the Regular Classroom*.

W. Thomas Southern is Assistant Professor in Special Education and Coordinator of gifted programs at Bowling Green State University in Ohio. His research has focused on the problems of identification among preschool children, as well as economically disadvantaged, geographically isolated, and culturally diverse populations.

Howard H. Spicker is Professor of Special Education and Director of the Gifted and Talented Program at Indiana University in Bloomington, where he has developed a summer residential gifted program. He was also instrumental in establishing an early childhood division within the Council for Exceptional Children and has served as president of that division.

Bob Stanish is a nationally known full-time writer and consultant, and has taught a variety of subjects at nearly all levels from primary to college. He has written and published 18 teacher resource books on creativity and creative problem solving; many gifted educators have applied his teaching style, methods, and curricula.

Stephanie S. Tolan, a co-author of the best-selling book, *Guiding the Gifted Child*, is well known as an advocate of highly gifted bright children and as a consultant to their parents. An award-winner, she is widely recognized as the author of many novels for children and young adults, including *A Good Courage, Plague Year, The Witch of Maple Park, Save Halloween!*, and *Welcome to the Ark*.

E. Paul Torrance is Alumni Foundation Distinguished Professor Emeritus at the University of Georgia in Athens and the author of over 1,500 books, articles, and monographs. Extraordinary pioneer and researcher in creativity, he developed the *Torrance Tests of Creative Thinking* and, for preschool children, the *Mother Goose Problems Test* and *Thinking Creatively with Action and Movement*.

Stephen and Kathleen Veenker are the parents of five gifted children and serve as consultants to gifted educators. Their interviews with hundreds of parents of gifted children in the Chicago area led them to co-author, with Joan Franklin Smutny, a book for parents—*Your Gifted Child*—on how to recognize and develop special talents in their young children.

Joan Vydra is Principal of Hawthorne Elementary School in Wheaton, IL. She has taught primary gifted children in a variety of settings, graduate courses in gifted education, and served as an educational consultant for state and local agencies. She has written extensively, most recently co-authoring a book on preprimary and primary curriculum materials for the gifted.

Sally Walker is a consultant in gifted education and author of *The Survival Guide for Parents of Gifted Kids*. She co-wrote *Teaching Young Gifted Children in the Regular Classroom* and is author of *Making Memories Apparent Portfolio*. She has consulted and lectured throughout the U.S. and is especially focused on differentiating for children's needs.

Nancy Wingenbach is Director of Curriculum and Instruction for Independence Public School in Ohio, where she coordinated gifted programs for students in grades 2 through 12. As lecturer, writer, and teacher at the graduate and undergraduate levels, she has focused on the gifted reader and the gifted learning disabled child.

Author Index

Subject Index